THE BIBLE'S
GREATEST PROPHECIES
UNLOCKED!

A Voice Cries Out

by David C. Pack

The Bible's Greatest Prophecies Unlocked!
A Voice Cries Out
Copyright © 2010 by The Restored Church of God

Scriptures quoted are from the King James (or Authorized) Version of the Bible unless otherwise noted. (Archaic words have been modernized in most cases. Emphasis added is author's own.) The use of selected references from various versions of the Bible in this publication does not necessarily imply publisher endorsement of the versions in their entirety.

Library of Congress Control Number: 2010942932

ISBN: 978-0-9831815-2-1 (Paperback)
ISBN: 978-0-9831815-1-4 (Hardback)
ISBN: 978-0-9831815-0-7 (E-Book)

Published by Park One Publishing, LLC.
www.parkonepublishing.com

The Bible's very *greatest prophecies* are on the threshold of fulfillment, with some already underway. They will soon explode with a force far beyond what *anyone* anticipates, including religious leaders, theologians, prophecy watchers and "experts" who think themselves in the know!

The time for understanding COLOSSAL PROPHECIES—history written in advance—has come! You *can* comprehend all that lies ahead. After reading this book, you *will*.

Described in Scripture as "*closed up* and *sealed* till the time of the end," knowledge of AWESOME FUTURE EVENTS has been opened, revealed and explained.

Incredible prophecies now thunder a POWERFUL WARNING to all who will hear and heed!

TABLE OF CONTENTS

Introduction

There is gnawing concern on the minds of millions about the course of human events. As world trends and conditions grow worse, and ever more confusing and complex, uncertainty is *increasing*—and worry is *deepening*—about what lies ahead for all mankind.

Towering questions loom over every nation!

Everyone wants to know what the future holds. So many are confused, not knowing where to turn for *answers* to the GREAT QUESTIONS about the future!

Suppose you could know the direction and *conclusion* of world events—*world history*—in advance of the outcome. What if you could know the courses of nations *before* they happen? What if the future of great nations—indeed the *greatest* nations—could be known? Imagine knowing tomorrow's biggest headlines before they come to pass, and how events will affect *you*, and every human being, *personally*.

Approximately one-third of the Bible is prophecy—history written in advance. Over four-fifths of this *future history* is yet to be fulfilled. Tragically, most Bible readers are completely unaware of awesome, impending world events, soon to involve all nations. Vast sections of Scripture are hidden, and remain outside their understanding—completely lost to them. The result is that most simply have no idea what the future holds.

Many have opinions, but few recognize how to find the answers. Others think they already understand the prophecies of the Bible. The result? They remain ignorant of fascinating, incredible—vital!—knowledge, *life-changing* knowledge.

No book you have read, or ever will, on prophecy is like this one. Different from all others on the subject, it is destined to be read by vast numbers—and probably soon.

Ominous Signs Abound

Turmoil, fear and confusion now grip all nations of the world. Terrorism, economic upheaval and resultant widespread uncertainty are everywhere. Many sense that the differences between and within nations are intensifying and are threatening to spin out of control. New and different power blocs are forming, with traditional alliances wavering, waning or disappearing.

Ominous signs of grave difficulty in resolving humanity's most fundamental problems abound. Many sense that the world is hurtling toward trouble, even possibly terrible calamity. Disease, famine and war sweep the planet as never before. New diseases are continually emerging and old ones are re-emerging worse than ever. Famine now decimates entire segments of local populations. Weapons of mass destruction, so incomprehensibly lethal and devastating that they boggle the mind, now threaten humanity—also as never before. Many nations are learning to live "on alert" to terrorist cells, which can strike anywhere without notice.

World conditions, events and trends speak daily in frightening terms about how things could *quickly* turn in the wrong direction. The future of nations, including the greatest nations, hangs in the balance. History shows that *all* the great civilizations eventually crashed, having become decadent, awash in material prosperity and greed—and educated in wrong knowledge. This can happen again!

Now think of poverty, illiteracy, disasters of every kind, violence, religious division and confusion, governments collapsing or under siege, increasing riots and protests, shortages of food and drinking water, shallow, pleasure-driven, immoral entertainment, breakdown of family values—and of virtually all *other* values held sacred for generations—that fill the headlines of newspapers and newscasts.

Then there are the stunning events and conditions throughout the financial world that are affecting every nation. One development after another—virtually all of them bad!—are impacting both Wall Street and Main Street. The effects are seen in tight credit, global stock markets, banks and other lending institutions, rising unemployment, rising inflation, rising fuel prices, declining retirement and pension funds, fallen home values, frozen business and home equity lines, corporate bankruptcies and bailouts—as well as the projected budget deficits of city, state and federal governments, in America and many other countries. These also have a rippling effect through all levels of politics in every democratic or Western nation. The entire global economy is being regularly revisited, reviewed and revised, with many acknowledging they simply do not know what to do next.

Where is it all going?

No Solutions

The question of what lies ahead for the whole world has become the very greatest question today. *Millions* are searching—wondering about the course of events. More and more world leaders are also expressing pessimism about the rise of troubles, evils, ills and woes also both within and between nations, including those that are the most powerful. So are educators, military planners, sociologists and scientists.

With all nations of Earth increasingly overwhelmed by a complicated and worsening array of difficulties confronting and challenging them, the greatest thinkers are being employed to find answers—SOLUTIONS! The problem? There are *no* solutions to any of the world's *biggest problems* anywhere on the horizon, but rather only new ideas that never seem to work!

Of course, many are unmoved—not concerned—about the tumultuous events surrounding them, trusting that things will work out in the end "because they always do." Also believing things will eventually "turn out all right," others close their eyes, choosing to pursue pleasure and the accumulation of material goods at an even more frantic pace. But for the short term, things will *not* turn out all right. World conditions are and will become far more serious than any imagine.

Almighty God will soon have to intervene and save humanity from itself. But before this occurs, world trouble will greatly increase—intensifying to staggering proportions. This will be followed by unexpected and cataclysmic events that will shake the whole world, affecting the life of *every* human being on Earth! Events are building to a final *culmination*—a tremendous CLIMAX! Nothing that has occurred over the past 6,000 years even remotely compares to what is yet to come upon this world! Civilization, as we know it, will change forever.

Countless Ideas—One Authority!

Knowing something is terribly wrong, many sense the world has reached what the Bible calls the "last days." This has caused a mushrooming of interest in prophecy.

A growing percentage of thinking people are now asking whether the answers lie in the realm of *biblical* prophecy. We hear from them every day, and from all over the world. In effect, a market has developed for information. With opinions everywhere, books about prophecy now abound. Just count the number of volumes about this subject within the expanding "Christianity" sections of major bookstores. Again, there has been an explosion of books presenting popular scenarios, ideas, theories, suppositions and interpretations of "how it will all play out."

Millions of people now routinely discuss terms such as "Antichrist," "Great Tribulation," "Millennium," "Armageddon," "Beast," "Mark of the Beast," "666," "False Prophet," "God's Wrath," "Abomination of Desolation," "Babylon the Great" and others, without proper context, meaning or comprehension. Again, they simply do not know *where* or *how* to look within God's Word to get correct understanding of what these and other terms mean, and how they will play out, sequentially, within God's Master Plan for the end of the age. Like a kind of "Rubik's Cube," the many critical elements of prophecy never line up—never come together—for millions wanting to know. This is because, instead of examining for themselves the hundreds of clear scriptures on these and other aspects of prophecy—for *proof*—many seem content to trust in "experts."

These supposed experts have set themselves up as authorities on Bible prophecy. There are fiction writers, history-based writers, technical commentators, "mathematicians" and "code experts," as well as a nearly endless stream of outright false prophets, phony prognosticators, crystal ball gazers and self-proclaimed seers and psychics spewing little more than ignorant confusion on unwitting, but willing, listeners and readers.

When understood, all popular *human* interpretations of Bible prophecy are ridiculous—a complete jumble of ideas where a little truth is mixed with much error. They are almost painful to read—yet large numbers now subscribe to dangerous, counterfeit scenarios. Those sincerely interested in learning the TRUTH remain tangled in a Gordian knot of disjointed, confusing, competing—and PLAIN WRONG!—popular ideas and opinions.

This is because none knows *how* to understand—either how to use, or even that there are, KEYS to unlocking climactic Bible prophecies.

But who *is* an AUTHORITY? Who really *knows?*—who really *understands* what the future holds as outlined in the Bible? While religion should hold the answers, it has not even figured out most of the *questions*—and, when understood, is seen to be the biggest part of the problem. However sincere at least some preachers and religionists may be, all of their publications merely *add* to the confusion offered to those desperately seeking answers in all the wrong places.

What is the *truth* about prophecy? What does the Bible *really* say about events preceding Christ's Return? Sobering world conditions make this question larger than ever.

The Keys to Understanding

Most who write about the Bible do not realize that this Book interprets itself, that if a symbol is mentioned within a prophecy—*any* prophecy!—and virtually every prophecy involves symbols—the Author of this greatest of books would not leave the most crucial questions, those involving all humanity, subject to human interpretation. He would provide *clues*—necessary VITAL KEYS!—to understanding the large portions of His Word devoted to future events. He would also make known that He *is* the Author of the Bible. And He would make absolutely clear that the Bible is a book backed by *His* authority—that it is His divinely revealed INSTRUCTION BOOK—and that this need not merely be "accepted on faith."

God would provide PROOF of all the things He says!

The Bible commands its readers: "*Prove* all things; hold fast that which is good" (I Thes. 5:21). This certainly applies to prophecy. You will find that what the chapters ahead explain can be PROVEN—that it is not just opinion from one more ill-informed, self-appointed "expert."

Tragically, most who read the Bible *remain* in near total ignorance of its meaning, including being completely unable to recognize the *speed*, *sequence* and *seriousness*—and the AWESOME MAGNITUDE!—of certain onrushing prophecies. And again this is *on top* of not truly comprehending what any of them actually MEANS!

So many just cannot untangle the maze of *what* happens *when*, as well as *where* and *to whom*—and *why*.

The Questions

In pursuit of the truth, some people never seem able to correctly identify the questions that must be answered to get to it. They cannot create a road map to their destination. They stumble around "ever learning" but "never able to come to the knowledge of the truth" (II Tim. 3:7) of a matter. If we are to answer the great questions about Bible prophecy, we must first correctly identify them—carefully spell them out. Then we must understand *why* they are important, and be unwilling to accept any but *proven facts*, whether from God's Word or history.

All that is written in the coming chapters is the truth about the greatest prophecies of the Bible. This book presents numerous *facts*, much *evidence* and *real proof* in answering the many questions that one might have—that one *should* have.

Realize that every explanation of a biblical teaching has a reasonable and natural limit, or it could almost go on without end. This is true of prophecy. But this subject also cannot be shortchanged. Its explanation must be conclusive. Therefore, this book has been written in thorough fashion. The reader will be left with inescapable conclusions—ANSWERS!—to all the crucial questions regarding Bible prophecy.

Many Bible Prophecies

Here are but a few examples of questions (a great many others appear as the book develops): Many wonder if the world has entered what is called the "end time." How can you *know* if this time has come, and if it has, what does this mean?—for you and the rest of the world?

Then there is the Middle East, the region prophesied thousands of years ago to lie at the center of the very biggest—the most planet-rattling—and *shattering*!—events ever to occur on Earth! While some Bible students seem to sense at least this much, they do not know in any detail *what* these events are, or *why* they will come. Others seem to know the Middle East should be avoided at some point, but assume the rest of the world will be largely "okay."

Of course, the book of Revelation evokes an endless stream of questions about its meaning and purpose. The last book of the Bible stands shrouded in mystery to almost all who read it. Seen as filled with terms—metaphors, symbols and descriptive language—that seem impossible to decipher, many lose hope that they will ever understand even its most basic messages.

Within Revelation is the often talked about, but almost universally misunderstood, mysterious "beast." Who or what is this multi-headed, strange and fierce-looking beast?—and who (or what) is the "woman" that rides it? Then, what is the dreaded "*mark* of the beast"? The Beast of Revelation is the topic of countless speculative books promoting popular theories—but they are all terribly, even disastrously, WRONG!

What about the meaning and timing of the infamous battle of Armageddon—and the lead-up of events surrounding it—as well as the abomination of desolation, the four horsemen, the seven seals, the antichrist, the great tribulation, the day of the Lord, the 144,000 and the great multitude...and so many other topics mentioned either in Revelation or by various prophets of the Old Testament?

These are just some of the greatest questions.

The Last Days—and a Way of Escape

Jesus Christ foretold that immediately preceding His Return these and other prophecies would slam into a completely unsuspecting, unprepared world. Here is what He told His disciples: "And take heed... lest...that day come upon you unawares. For as a *snare* shall it come on *all* them that dwell on the face of the *whole earth*" (Luke 21:34-35).

These are truly stunning words. Yet, most do not concern themselves with conditions and events that Jesus plainly states will affect *everyone* on the entirety of the planet—"*all* them that dwell on the face of the *whole* earth"—and that these things are to occur without notice or warning, as with a snare.

Jesus continued in Luke with this all-important instruction—for those who are listening (heeding): "*Watch* you therefore, and *pray* always, that you may be accounted worthy to ESCAPE all these things that *shall come to pass*, and to stand before the Son of man" (vs. 36).

Are you *concerned* about a prophecy of such magnitude?—one with so much at stake for every man, woman and child alive today? You can escape what lies ahead. You need not fear—*if* you do exactly what God instructs.

The Sign of Christ's Coming

In the Matthew 24 parallel of Luke 21, Jesus went on to spend this chapter, and all of chapter 25, explaining exactly what would occur— what the careful Bible student should be looking for and *expect*— before His Coming.

So then, naturally following this is the most central, all-important question that should be on the minds of all who care about these prophecies—"Can I *escape* what is coming, and, if so, *how*?" In the chapters ahead, you will find the answers to these and many related questions—straight from the pages of your Bible.

There is a related group in all of this who, not knowing God's *supreme purpose*—His MASTER PLAN—believe that the meaning of gigantic prophecies is *permanently sealed*. These seem to think that God would inspire a host of very specific prophecies, large and small, and have them recorded—but never intend anyone actually know their *meaning*. Isaiah 29, verses 11-12, is its own prophecy of—first—how some would say all prophecy is "sealed," and—second—how others would openly profess themselves "unlearned"—ignorant!—and thus unable to know God's intended meaning. Take time to read this passage.

However ridiculous, these are positions held by many millions who describe themselves as Christians! Obviously, these would be little concerned with escaping that which they neither know nor understand—nor think can be understood.

You *can* know the PLAIN TRUTH ANSWERS to all crucial questions about the future—in fact, you *should*! And they are all laid out right there on the pages of your Bible! Like so many pieces of a large puzzle that only make sense when fully assembled, each of these questions and others represent a part of a bigger picture, one that is shocking far beyond the imagination of those who think they know the meaning of Bible prophecy.

However, you must come to recognize that this picture not only speaks to the *bad news* of the near future, but also to the marvelous GOOD NEWS just beyond in store for a world desperately in *need* of this news. It is the awe-inspiring *hidden knowledge* presented within the *true* gospel—the *real* Message that Jesus Christ the Messenger brought! This understanding overarches everything you can learn about the Bible.

The Greatest Prophecies

The Bible's very biggest prophecies are on the threshold of fulfillment, with the early effects of some *already underway*. They will soon crash and explode with a force completely beyond what *anyone* anticipates, including "prophecy watchers" who think themselves in the know and on God's inside track!

The time for understanding these colossal prophecies *has come*! You CAN comprehend the message they bring. And after reading this book, you *will*—I repeat, *if* you are resolved to do what God requires.

In a few pages—and this will be hard to believe—you have already learned more about the truth of Bible prophecy—just in correct terms alone—than most will ever know. But this is only the barest *introduction* to the subject. Again, one full third of the Bible, prophecy is a topic that requires all the many chapters comprising this book.

When a large subject is being covered in detail, sometimes a reference of varying size to a connected or related subject *must* be made. The book does this often. (It also repeats certain crucial scriptures in different contexts.) This could happen more than once—or even many times—with a topic until that topic is eventually covered somewhere in its own greater detail. The Table of Contents will let the reader know when this is scheduled to occur. Do not let these references pull you prematurely to later chapters. The correct view of any prophetic topic involves much setup—and context—to be *properly* understood.

If you are serious about understanding the future, the book should be read twice. The first time is for flow of events and overall understanding. The second should be done more slowly and for more careful examination of facts and verses cited.

The book builds in layers, and the reader does himself a disservice by hopping around. Chapters *must* be read in order! This book builds toward TREMENDOUS UNDERSTANDING—and at many points as it develops. In fact, no other book on prophecy even comes close to the impact of this one.

I repeat: You are holding one of the most important volumes you could read. It is written with a tone of urgency and pulls *no* punches. After a point in your reading, you will be unable to put the book down. (Chapters Thirteen through Eighteen alone will prove this.) What it reveals is so compelling, so powerful, so clear—and so *provable!*—you will fight anger over the MASS DECEPTION that has been perpetrated on you—and is still being foisted on millions around you.

You are about to see prophecy made clear—the very biggest and most crucial elements of it—*all* of them—made easy to understand through use of plain language. You will be intrigued—truly fascinated—by what can be known about the future, and will close this book with a firm grasp of *everything* that is about to happen on planet Earth. Necessarily covered from every conceivable angle, these prophecies will be obvious in meaning to all who sincerely seek to understand—and ACT UPON—what is learned. In the chapters ahead, you will see *the Bible's greatest prophecies unlocked!*

Crucial foundation must first be put in place—layer by layer...

Why Prophecy!

Any study of prophecy begins with the simple definition of what prophecy *is*. Most lack an understanding of even this most basic knowledge. Bible prophecy is "the inspired, divine revelation or foretelling of historical events, written *in advance* of those events, pertaining to the unfolding of God's Plan for mankind." A shorter definition is simply "foretelling the future."

Prophecy is factual history recorded *in advance*! God foretells major events *before* they happen. He wants His servants to *know* what the future holds—what lies ahead for the world. The Bible is approximately 750,000 words. This means that 250,000 words are devoted to prophecy. Over 80 percent is yet to be fulfilled. Therefore, *many* major events must yet come to pass.

Before examining in detail the array of events foretold to occur, we must ask: What possible PURPOSE would God have for devoting a full third of His divine Word to a subject—*any* subject—and then leave mankind in the dark about it?

Prophecy Only Understood by Christ's Servants

Many have been taught or believe that it has always been God's intention to leave all prophecy *sealed*, closed from understanding.

However, the very introduction to the book of Revelation shows God's intent is to *reveal* to "His servants" what lies ahead for all nations. The apostle John begins recording Christ's words with, "The Revelation [a *revealing*] of Jesus Christ [not John]...to show unto *His servants* things which must shortly come to pass...signified...unto His servant John: who bare record of the word of God, and of the testimony of Jesus Christ...Blessed is he that *reads*, and they that *hear* the words of this prophecy, and *keep* those things which are written therein: *for the time is at hand*" (Rev. 1:1-3).

At the end of Revelation it states this for emphasis: "*Seal not* the sayings of the prophecy of this book: for the *time is at hand*" (22:10).

How many have noticed this? Then, even more important, is how many have concerned themselves with whether or not they truly *are* God's servants? Do not be so sure you know who is and is not.

Obviously, none can "keep" the prophecies of Revelation, or any others, unless they *understand* them. God must provide the necessary *clues* to understanding all that lies ahead. We will examine these.

Matthew 24, Luke 21 and Mark 13 are all parallel accounts of what is called the Olivet Prophecy. This all-important prophecy works in combination with the books of Revelation and Daniel. It puts in sequence events that span the entire period from Christ's First Coming until His Return, almost 2,000 years later.

Most have not understood the events of this long prophecy because they do not understand how *keys* unlock it—and they do not understand that Jesus spoke it "privately" to only *His disciples*—"His servants" (Rev. 1:1). This *must* be understood because it identifies who are and are *not* able to really comprehend what lies ahead for the world!

Matthew 24 uses the most detail, so we look there, where the prophecy starts in verse 3. (Because of its central importance, note that this chapter will be referenced as much as any other in the Bible.) Now notice: "As He sat upon the Mount of Olives, the disciples came unto Him *privately*, saying, Tell us, when shall these things be? And what shall be the *sign* of Your coming, and of the end of the world [age]?"

In verse 4, "Jesus answered and said unto them, *Take heed* that no man *deceive* you." Jesus goes straight to the problem that would exist at the end—there are many deceivers at work today. How many people are doing what He said, and *taking heed*? How many are carefully doing their homework regarding men claiming to represent God?

There are an ever-increasing number of "prophets" arising, exactly as Christ warned *three times* (just in Matthew 24) would occur at the end of the age. Also, just as He warned, "many will be [and are being] deceived." Most are not aware of this phenomenon—and its impact in all corners of Christianity.

Next consider verse 15, which concludes referring to "Daniel the prophet" and the admonition "whoso reads, *let him understand.*" Most today do not—and *will not*—understand the events soon to smash into civilization. Here is one big reason. God's servants obey Him (Acts 5:32). Understanding flows directly from obedience to God: "The fear of the LORD is the beginning of wisdom: a *good understanding* have all they that *do His commandments*" (Psa. 111:10).

Grasp this. All real understanding of God's Plan and spiritual truth comes from God. It is only the action of His Spirit that opens one's eyes. Notice: "That the God of our Lord Jesus Christ, the Father of glory, may give unto you the *spirit of wisdom* and *revelation* in the *knowledge* of Him: the *eyes of your understanding being enlightened*" (Eph. 1:17-18).

All who yield themselves in obedience to God, wishing to be His disciples—His servants—*will be able to understand all the great prophecies to be fulfilled in the last days!* Professing Christianity refuses to obey God, rejects His authority over them—and remains blind as a result. No amount of trying to understand will unlock God's purpose to those who ignore His commands.

This is the great *first* KEY to grasping the meaning of major biblical prophecies. They are intended for, and will only be understood by, *God's people.* All others will remain in confusion, mangling and misunderstanding the horrific, world-shattering events that will soon directly impact every person on the planet!

All Prophecy Sealed Until "the End"

There is a crucial *second* KEY that must be identified, and understood, by all seeking to grasp God's end-time purpose. Without it, nations have remained in *total blindness* regarding even the question of human survival. Scales cover their eyes. Of course, unable to understand, cynics and skeptics have dismissed all the prophecies of the Old Testament as dusty, antiquated, "old Hebrew literature and poetry, of no use to us today."

They will soon learn how terribly wrong they have been!

Now note this second *key* well, for almost none have understood it. All the major prophecies of the Bible have been *sealed* by God until the "time of the end"—the "last days." This key hearkens to the group that says prophecy is sealed. Accidentally *close* to the truth, they have missed a central point. All the great prophecies are *no longer sealed!*

You do not need to take my word for it. The prophet Daniel, under the direct inspiration of God, makes this point plain—for all who will believe it. Recognize that *God* is speaking through Daniel, rather than Daniel giving some personal opinion about future events.

The book of Daniel spans a period of over 2,500 years, detailing the fulfillment of events then all yet to occur. Generations of Bible students, unwilling to believe God, have attempted to interpret Daniel's prophecy. All have failed, resulting in endless disagreement and confusion.

Here is what an angel instructed Daniel at the end of his prophecy: "But you, O Daniel, *shut up* the words, and *seal the book*, even to the *time of the end*: many shall run to and fro, and knowledge shall be increased" (12:4). (Seven times, in just this one chapter, it speaks of the "end," "time of the end," or when all things would be "finished.")

Unsatisfied, and not grasping what was being told him, Daniel once again sought to understand. Notice: "I heard, but I understood not: then said I, O my Lord, what shall be the *end of these things*?" (vs. 8).

The angel repeated himself: "Go your way, Daniel: for the words are *closed up* and *sealed till the time of the end*. Many shall be purified, and made white, and tried; but the wicked shall do wickedly: and none of the wicked shall understand; *but the wise shall understand*" (vs. 9-10). Jesus later cited Daniel when He repeated that "the wise shall understand" events described to occur at the end of the age. Let me reiterate that God says *obedience* brings understanding. No wonder Daniel adds, "none of the *wicked* shall understand." Any who rebel against God's Law, regardless of how they see themselves, fall into this category.

Daniel foretells a time—now here—when "knowledge shall increase" and reveals the compelling, even electrifying, story of what God plans to do in our time. Daniel's message had no application for his own time!

God's promise was always to *unseal* the prophecy when the end time arrived!

So, the second vital *key* to properly understanding Bible prophecy is that all previous generations—of even God's true servants—had *no chance* to comprehend events described in Daniel's book, or in other biblical passages related to it.

Beginning in the twentieth century, having been *revealed* and *explained*, the Bible's greatest prophecies now thunder a POWERFUL WARNING to all who will hear—and heed!

A "Sure Word"

The apostle Peter wrote this about how God intends that prophecy illuminate the understanding of those who study it: "We have also a more *sure word of prophecy*; whereunto you *do well* that you *take heed*, as unto a light that shines in a dark place..." (II Pet. 1:19). This verse reveals God's purpose—His *"sure* word of prophecy," bringing "light" to "dark places"—so people will "take heed." *You* must be willing to heed what is written.

Now continue: "Knowing this first, that no prophecy of the scripture is of any private interpretation" (vs. 20). This is most crucial to understand. No single verse—or even any two or three passages—is sufficient to bring full, correct prophetic understanding on big events.

Grasp this. *All* of the verses on every aspect of prophecy must be carefully *assembled* first. Second, building the truth begins with the most clear and obvious passages. These are two of the greatest rules of Bible study when exploring *any* of this Book's topics. Sadly, these rules, and the rest of the twelve rules of Bible study, are not followed by, or even known to, almost any who read God's Word. Prophecy "experts" are no exception.

Continue again in II Peter 1: "For the prophecy came not in old time by the will of man: but holy men of God spoke as they were moved by the Holy Spirit" (vs. 21). In short, prophecy comes from *God*, through His servants, as He inspires them to record *His* words.

Many of the Bible's greatest servants were prophets. These men held high office. In fact, most whom God worked through in the Old Testament held this office. Their names jump from Scripture.

Acts 3:19-21 reveals that prophets can announce the kingdom of God. With one exception (Jonah), every prophetic book of the Old Testament records something about God's coming kingdom. Others delivered powerful messages—usually *warnings*.

Proof of God's Existence—and Power

Prophecy can be summarized as having *four distinct purposes*. All four must be understood. But before this comes some necessary setup.

In ever-increasing numbers, people are seeking psychics, channelers, tarot card and palm readers, fortune tellers, astrologers, crystal ball gazers and every other medium to tell them what is going to happen.

But no human being operating on his own power can foresee the future. Historians can only record what has already happened. Meteorologists, with the aid of modern technology, can forecast the weather with reasonable accuracy. But even these predictions become unreliable when they model patterns more than perhaps a week ahead.

Psychics and seers can sometimes see elements of the future, because they are connected to the wrong side of the spirit realm. However, these visions invariably have errors alongside any correct elements. (For example, mediums or false religious leaders have on a number of occasions predicted that an earthquake would occur on a certain day and at a particular place, and a quake *did* strike—but a day earlier or later than predicted, or on the right day but in a different place.)

Few go to the one infallible source, which foretells all the important events that will soon come upon the entire world. This can be done—and with astounding, absolute accuracy!

So plain is the proof, you can easily learn it for yourself! And afterward, you can rest assured that what you have learned will occur—that it is no less certain than tomorrow's sunrise. When you have completed reading the balance of this book, you need never again doubt the authority of *anything* found in the Bible—including all matters discussed in its remaining two-thirds, the *other* 500,000 words it contains about other subjects. In fact, just Chapter Four makes this the case.

So then, the FIRST PURPOSE is that, when proven to have been fulfilled, prophecy becomes undeniable evidence of the *existence* and *power* of God. God alone can fulfill prophecy. No human being has even the *knowledge* of what are world-shattering future events, let alone the power to bring them to pass centuries or even millennia beyond his lifetime. For this reason, it has been said that prophecy is the challenge the skeptics dare not accept!

How true!

God openly taunts all such skeptics in Isaiah 41. We read from the Moffatt translation: "Now, the Eternal cries, bring your case forward, now, Jacob's King [God] cries, state your proofs. Let us hear what happened in the past, that we may ponder it, or show Me *what is yet to be*, that we may *watch how it turns out*; yes, let us hear *what is coming*, that we may be sure you are gods; come, do something or other that we may marvel at the sight!—why, you are things of naught, you can do nothing at all!" (vs. 21-24).

This passage becomes God's challenge to disbelievers.

Another bold statement, also in Isaiah: "Behold, the former things are come to pass, and *new things* do I declare: *before they spring forth I tell you of them*" (42:9).

God is careful to ensure that the credit for foretelling events goes to *Him alone*, rather than any false prophet or false god. Again from Isaiah: "I have declared the former things from the beginning; and they went forth out of My mouth, and I showed them; I did them suddenly, *and they came to pass*. Because I knew that you are obstinate, and your neck is an iron sinew, and your brow brass; I have even from the beginning declared it to you; *before it came to pass I showed it you*: lest you should say, My idol has done them, and my graven image, and my molten image, has commanded them" (48:3-5).

God does not guess at what will occur. He is not merely the best *forecaster* or *prognosticator*. Acting deliberately, He brings to pass what He says *will happen*. If He tells us something—anything—is to occur, it *will occur*! Moffatt renders verse 3, "What has occurred *I foretold long ago*; it fell from My lips, I predicted it, then suddenly *I acted—it was done*."

Here is yet another scripture from Isaiah: "Remember the former things of old: for I am God, and there is none else; I am God, and there is none like Me. *Declaring the end from the beginning*, and from ancient times the *things that are not yet done*, saying, My counsel shall stand, and *I will do* all My pleasure" (46:9-10).

Prophecy is simply God telling human beings what He WILL do!

Understand that God has a steady hand in the affairs of men—that He is capable of thwarting and overthrowing the stated purposes of governments and nations. Notice this from Moffatt: "The Eternal wrecks the purposes of pagans, He brings to nothing what the nations plan; but the Eternal's purpose stands forever, and what He plans will last from age to age...The Eternal looks from heaven, beholding all mankind; from where He sits, He scans all who inhabit the world; He who alone made their minds, He notes all they do" (Psa. 33:10-15).

Yes, men may have their plans about how to solve the big, complex problems facing civilization, but God "wrecks"—smashes—them, "bringing them to nothing." And God has plainly told us *how* He plans to do this at the conclusion of 6,000 years of human affairs.

A Means of Encouragement

A SECOND PURPOSE for prophecy is to *encourage* Christ's true followers. Jesus understood that the Christian way involves trials and difficulties throughout life. This is an inescapable fact for those in whom God is working. These are essential to the character-building process.

One of these trials is *persecution*. Just before His crucifixion, Jesus warned, "Remember the word that I said unto you [He must have taught this previously], The servant is not greater than his lord. If they have persecuted Me, they will also persecute you" (John 15:20). In the preceding verse, He had reminded His disciples that "I have chosen you out of the world, therefore the world *hates you*" (vs. 19). Of course, Jesus was persecuted to the point of horrible torture and crucifixion.

The apostle Paul recorded, "All that will live godly in Christ Jesus shall suffer persecution" (II Tim. 3:12). The word "all" means what it says! Jesus said His servants would be HATED! In light of this often difficult path, He reassured His disciples, "I am with you always, even unto the end of the world" (Matt. 28:20).

Another element of encouragement flows from prophecy itself.

Some may assume that all biblical prophecy is "gloom and doom" and "fire and brimstone." This is not true! In fact, far from it. The ultimate message of prophecy is the most *positive* news in all history. Hundreds of verses give a preview of a time of peace, prosperity and happiness—drawing closer daily—that all human beings will ultimately have an opportunity to experience.

Those who choose to yield to God and learn His way of life *look forward* in a special way, and draw encouragement from these prophecies.

To Warn and Call to Repentance

A careful study of the Bible demonstrates that God always *warns* before punishment—whether it be the destruction of cities such as Nineveh, or Sodom and Gomorrah—or of individuals such as wayward kings of Israel and Judah—or of the whole inhabited world in the Flood. God gives us this certain promise of what will happen in advance of events He intends to fulfill: "Surely the Lord GOD will do nothing, but He *reveals His secret* unto His servants the prophets" (Amos 3:7). God keeps His promises. He always reveals MAJOR EVENTS *before* they happen.

So then a THIRD PURPOSE of prophecy is that a loving God gives human beings—free moral agents who must choose between right and wrong—space to repent.

Ancient Israel has been the main recipient of such admonitions: "If My people…shall humble themselves, and pray, and seek My face, and turn from their wicked ways; then will I hear from heaven, and will forgive their sin, and will heal their land" (II Chron. 7:14).

When giving the prophet Ezekiel his commission, God stressed what His servants were to do: "O son of man, I have set you a WATCHMAN unto the house of Israel; therefore you shall hear the word at My mouth, and *warn them* FROM ME. When I say unto the wicked, O wicked man, you shall surely die; if you do not speak to warn the wicked from his way, that wicked man shall die in his iniquity; but his blood will I require at your hand. Nevertheless, if you warn the wicked of his way to turn from it; if he do not turn from his way, he shall die in his iniquity; but you have delivered your soul" (33:7-9).

It has been my long and sad experience that most people simply will not truly listen to what God says. They cannot seem to make themselves take *seriously* His commands, instructions and warnings.

However, with each warning through the ages, some few do heed and repent. And those who do not—having been WARNED!—bear responsibility for their choices and actions.

Powerful Motivator

A FOURTH PURPOSE of prophecy is to *motivate* those who wish to seek God and claim His promise of protection. Knowledge of what is ahead—of both the terrible and wonderful elements—motivates true Christians to serve God more fully.

We saw that the most serious events just before Christ's Return will descend like a snare on an unsuspecting world—except for those who "watch," "pray" and "escape" (Luke 21:36). So then a group is promised to be protected during the times just ahead.

The apostle Paul wrote this sobering warning: "But of the *times and the seasons*, brethren, you have no need that I write unto you. For yourselves know perfectly that the day of the Lord so comes as a thief in the night. For when they shall say, Peace and safety; then *sudden destruction comes* upon them, as travail upon a woman with child; and *they shall not escape*. But you, brethren, are not in darkness, that that day should overtake you as a thief. You are all the children of light, and the children of the day: we are not of the night, nor of darkness. Therefore let us not sleep, *as do others*; but let us WATCH and BE SOBER" (I Thes. 5:1-6).

Those who take the Bible seriously know what is coming, and live their lives accordingly.

Isaiah explained that God's Word is written, "...*precept upon precept*, precept upon precept; *line upon line*, line upon line; *here a little*, and *there a little*..." (28:13). Nowhere is this Bible pattern more true than of prophecy. But the passage continues with God explaining WHY His Word is written this way: "...that they might go, and fall backward, and be broken, and snared, and taken."

Recall that Revelation is written to God's servants—to "show" *them*, not others, what must "shortly come to pass." Isaiah underscores that prophecy cannot be understood by those who do not seek to serve and obey God. God has scattered bits and pieces of information on prophecy (and all other subjects) throughout His Word in a way that will cause the mere casual reader to *"fall* backward, and be *broken*, and *snared*, and *taken"*—by FALSE UNDERSTANDING.

They will not comprehend.

This ought sober the reader, who should now be asking, "How serious am *I* about understanding—and *acting on*—all that follows in this volume?" Now is the time to consider this question.

With God's purposes for biblical prophecy established, we now examine "prophecies" of a *different* kind...

Is 2012 the End?

We saw *why* God records prophecy. Before examining the prophecies of the Bible, a distinction must be made between *true* and *false* prophecy—that which is inspired of God, and what is not. This chapter examines one of the most popular modern "prophecies."

Irrational Fears

The 2012 phenomenon has reached fever pitch. Alarm has spread like wildfire. Uncertainty, anxiety—and FEAR—have gripped many people. Literally, *millions* are panicking, wondering whether 2012 will be their last year. The end date is supposedly either December 21 *or* 23, 2012. Doomsday authors point to December 21, the winter solstice. But the Mayan calendar, on which the end-of-days theory is based, ends December 23.

Like the Y2K panic of 1999 regarding the arrival of the year 2000, 2012 hysteria is all over the Internet—in endless books—and in a $200 million movie, filled with the usual sensational Hollywood graphics. And so-called prophecy experts are weighing in on the subject.

People of all ages are asking if cataclysmic events will occur in late 2012 and bring the end of the world. Some are deeply concerned—truly frightened!—that they will not live into their teen years or enter adulthood. They desperately want lives beyond 2012—but fear this will not happen.

Incredibly, some teenagers, and even younger children, have asked if they should *end their own lives*—and some mothers have expressed thoughts of killing their children—and then themselves—rather than enduring "Earth ending" events!

No one predicts exactly what will happen in 2012, but according to some, it will be *"Big!"*—*"Earth shattering!"*—and *"Civilization ending"*! There are concerns that the entire earth will be flooded, or burned up by solar flares. The North and South Poles may suddenly reverse, wreaking untold havoc on electrical systems. Catastrophic earthquakes may rock the planet, destroying all buildings and opening huge holes in the earth's crust. Chaos will reign. Mankind will come to the *brink* of annihilation...and on and on go the theories.

Source of Belief

The Mayan "Long Count" calendar tracks "Great Cycles" of time, and is one of at least three calendars that the ancient Mayans used. It is important to note that one particular calendar indicates that December 23, 2012, is the end of the current *cycle of time*—which began August 13, 3114 BC on the Gregorian calendar. The Mayan calendar itself states *nothing* of the world coming to an end, or of *any* cataclysmic events occurring. It states only that the current *time cycle* will end.

Many of the fantastic stories and much of the hype come from various *archaeological* and *astronomical* speculation, as well as mythology and numerological interpretation. Predictions of impending doom and destruction are *nowhere* to be found in Mayan accounts or in the Long Count calendar itself. To the modern Mayans, including those who study the ancient calendar, 2012 is actually inconsequential.

If you were to travel to any of the many present day Mayan communities and ask about 2012, and the end of civilization, you would see looks of *bewilderment*. Modern Mayan sources explain that this calendar was *never* intended to suggest the world would end in 2012, or at any other time. They will also tell you that professing Christians have deliberately twisted their calendar to suit their own prophetic theories and timelines. Yet millions, with little or no understanding of the Mayan culture, attach civilization-ending significance to 2012. All but two ancient Mayan inscriptions are strictly historical. They make no prophetic declarations whatsoever. The two that supposedly do are unclear at best, and open to a wide array of speculation and interpretation.

Regardless of what the ancient Mayans *actually* predicted (the mere end of a time cycle!)—wild ideas about 2012 abound. The frenzy is worldwide and picking up steam, with no slowdown in sight. 2012 has also become big business, and many are cashing in on the uncertainty!

Will either the planet or civilization come to a *violent end* on December 21, 2012, as so many believe? Could the speculation still somehow be *true*? What does the Bible say? Does it in any way validate 2012 as the "end of all things"?

You will soon have no doubt of the correct answers. It is time to *prove* whether late December 2012 is the end.

Endless Speculation

The idea of the end of the world has been a subject of great speculation, ridicule, general discussion, fascination and fancy for 2,000 years—ever since Jesus Christ announced He would return to Earth. I repeat: With opinions everywhere, there has been an *explosion* of literature presenting popular scenarios, ideas, theories, suppositions and interpretations of what will occur just before Christ's Return.

For Christians, the 2012 question begins with what Jesus said about His Return: "Watch therefore, for you know neither the day nor the hour wherein the Son of man comes" (Matt. 25:13).

If people were reading even such basic verses, they would *never* worry about December 21 or 23, 2012 because no man knows the day of Christ's Return. What a tragic commentary on the state of people who profess to be Christians—but cannot logically compute such rudimentary understanding. But then, most who profess to follow Christ study little or nothing of what He said.

Get this! Just this passage, and other similar ones, rule out this date— or *any* specific date—that might be suggested for Christ's Return, or even for the end of all things.

Next read again Jesus' Olivet prophecy: "The disciples came unto Him privately, saying, Tell us, when shall these things be? And what shall be the sign of Your coming, and of the *end of the world* [age]?" (Matt. 24:3). We saw His long answer began with: "Take heed that no man deceive you" (vs. 4).

Jesus goes straight to the biggest problem that would exist at the end. There is an unending and growing number of deceivers at work today. Are their followers taking heed? Ask again: How many are doing their own research regarding men postulating prophetic scenarios, such as 2012? This is only one. There are many others, and more appearing all the time.

The 2012 Impossibility

Now let's examine whether it is even *possible*—prophetically—for 2012 to be the end. Follow carefully. We have to establish the *timing* of certain events.

Many are familiar with the term "Tribulation" or "Great Tribulation." The Bible speaks of this event as one of terrible trouble and indescribable horror. Jesus referred to this time as unparalleled in history: "For then shall be *great tribulation*, such as was not since the beginning of the world to this time, no, nor ever shall be" (Matt. 24:21). The prophet Daniel also speaks of this period in chapter 12, verse 1. Jeremiah references it in a similar way in chapter 30, verse 7.

The Bible reveals that a certain very specific amount of time must elapse between the start of the Great Tribulation and the Return of Jesus Christ—or "the end of the age." So understand. If it can be proven that there are not enough years in God's plainly revealed timeline for 2012 to be the end, then all the hysteria is for nothing!

Numerous passages explain that the Tribulation lasts 2½ years, followed by the year-long Day of the Lord. Together, these events last 3½ years, fulfilling 1,260 days before Christ's Return.

Let's understand the implications! If the Great Tribulation were to begin today there is not enough time for December 21, 2012 to be the end. But it is also important to realize that certain *biblically described pre-conditions* that must lead up to the Tribulation are not, however close they now are, yet here. (The book explains them all.)

So then, just the 1,260 days—again, were it to begin today—would greatly overshoot December 21, 2012. It is therefore ABSOLUTELY IMPOSSIBLE for this date to be the end of the world! All fear of it can disappear! None need be afraid of this fictional doomsday!

It *is* possible, however, that something of significance could happen in late 2012 because the demon world has a general idea of prophecy, and these fallen spirits do everything in their power to thwart God's Master Purpose for mankind. They could pull some trick or stunt to confuse the gullible.

Will the World End?

But what about the Return of Christ? Will this usher in the end of planet Earth sometime *after* 2012? In other words, will *all people* alive today die in the fulfillment of end-time prophecies—as so many seem to almost assume? The answer is a resounding NO! And here is proof.

When Jesus described world conditions leading to His Return, He stated, "Except those days should be shortened [cut short], there should no flesh be saved" (Matt. 24:22).

Some religionists believe the phrase "no flesh be saved" refers to *spiritual salvation*. But that is *not* what Jesus is talking about. Rather, that unless God cuts the Tribulation short, no human beings—"no *flesh*"—would survive. The human race would become extinct *if* Christ did not return. The implication is that He will return *before* this happens. For those who believe God, this is further proof that 2012 could not possibly end human existence.

Other prophecy writers speak of the "end of the world"—that the earth itself will supposedly be destroyed. This could not be further from the truth. This idea often stems from a misunderstanding of Christ's disciples asking Him for a sign of the "end of the world." The Greek word (*aion*) translated *world* means "age." The disciples were asking when the period of *man's rule* would end—and the kingdom of God would be established. They well understood the many Old Testament prophecies that speak of the Messiah setting up the kingdom of God on Earth.

But again, beyond all the bad news is the very greatest possible *good news*! Yet few speak of this! Most talk only about disaster, calamity and the possible annihilation of all people. This is because they are largely unaware of the most positive elements of prophecy—and of the *true* gospel!

Unraveling the Myth

God's servants understand the basic framework of His overall prophetic timetable and plan. They are not confused about "what happens next," once certain prophecies begin to take place. Many prophecies involve a tremendous amount of understanding that God makes available, and with all necessary details. They understand exactly what lies ahead for all mankind, and for themselves—if they are faithful. Those of Christ's one Church—the one He promised to build (Matt. 16:18) almost 2,000 years ago—have heeded the Bible's many warnings about what lies ahead.

December 21, 2012, is NOT the end! Do not fear this date! Human beings will never be wiped out. All the hysteria is for NOTHING! In fact, at a certain point this book will be available—at least for a short period—*after*

2012 has come and gone! Understand that—while this chapter will still be written as though 2012 is yet future—the *strength* of everything that the book discusses *increases* with its passing!—and this date WILL PASS!

Countless verses could have been cited to disprove the 2012 deception. As the prophetic picture gradually becomes clear, you will not only understand the ridiculousness of such false prophecies, but more importantly the TRUTH behind what is soon to play out before the world.

Scripture makes plain that 2012 does *not* mark the "end of the world," and that such ideas are preposterous to the point of almost humorous—were it not for the fear and confusion they spawn. But whether we are in the last days *is* a big question. Before we can answer it, and delve into proof, many other "end of days" scenarios—and a famous seer and author—must be examined...

Did God Send Nostradamus?

Nostradamus has captured the world's attention since the sixteenth century. His mysterious, cryptic writings have been the subject of endless debate. Hailed by millions, and known the world over, this man is among the most famous people in history.

Many believe Nostradamus' writings hold the key to understanding the future's greatest events. To followers, he accurately predicted the French Revolution—the rise of Napoleon—and then Adolf Hitler—the assassination of United States President John F. Kennedy—and the bombing of the World Trade Center—among others.

Nostradamus is revered as a prophet. But was he a *true* prophet—one sent by God—or a fraud—a *false* prophet?

Nostradamus has been the subject of many books and films, including popular television programs. According to one scholar, "...Nostradamus is probably the only author who could claim that his work has never been out of print for over 400 years, apart from the Bible. The interest he generates is extraordinary" (Erika Cheetham, *The Prophecies of Nostradamus*).

In recent years, as millions of people seek to understand end-time prophecy, this interest has increased. Believing him inspired by God, some think his prophecies are on par with those in the Bible.

In light of the interest surrounding this man, we must ask: "Did God send Nostradamus?"

You can know—and by the end of this chapter you will.

God does not want His servants in doubt about those He sends. They should *know* whether Nostradamus—or any *other* man—was sent by God. Let's learn what most will never know, nor even seek to know.

From Doctor to Seer

Michel de Notredame—or Nostredame—was born in southern France in 1503 to Jewish parents, who later converted to Catholicism. Europe had been undergoing the Renaissance. This was the time that produced Galileo, Copernicus, Michelangelo, Christopher Columbus and Leonardo da Vinci.

Son of a merchant and grandson of scholars, Nostradamus grew up in an environment of learning. As a young boy, he studied classical languages, astrology—and possibly the occult! At 14, he left home to study in Avignon, an ecclesiastical and academic center in southern France. Later, he studied medicine at the prestigious University of Montpellier.

Nostradamus became a physician. Early on, he traveled throughout France, caring for victims of the infamous bubonic plague, and gained a reputation as one who healed patients by innovative, but simple, methods. Gravely ill people recovered, and then so did entire towns and villages. He became a celebrated figure in southern France.

In time, Nostradamus returned to Montpellier for further study, eventually obtaining a medical doctorate. He married into a wealthy family and settled into the comfortable life of a doctor.

Soon after, the plague hit, killing his wife and two children. Unable to save his own family, his credibility was questioned. Compounding his troubles, a simple remark about a statue led to charges of heresy against the Catholic church. Summoned to stand trial, Nostradamus chose to flee instead—and spent the next several years traveling in southern Europe. He eventually returned to France in 1544, re-established his practice, re-married and had six more children.

A practicing Catholic, Nostradamus became heavily involved in astrology and the occult. He would sit for hours, deep into the night, meditating in a trance before a bowl of water.

Here is his description of this strange ritual: "Sitting alone at night in secret study; it [the bowl of water] is placed on the brass tripod. A slight flame comes out of the emptiness...The wand in the hand is placed in the middle of the tripod's legs. With water he sprinkles both the hem of his garment and his foot [in all of this he is speaking of himself]. A voice, fear; he trembles in his robes. Divine splendor; *the god sits nearby*" (*The Prophecies of Nostradamus*, book I, verses 1-2, emphasis mine).

During these sessions, Nostradamus would have visions. After returning to his senses, he would record them. He began including them in what were called *Almanacs*. The first was published in 1550. These contained predictions for every month of the year. His *Almanacs* were so popular he produced them annually for the rest of his life.

Nostradamus' fame grew. His services were now sought by the wealthy and powerful. In 1555, he began publishing a monumental project, a 10-part series of predictions called *The True Centuries*. Each consisted of 100 quatrains (four lines of rhyming verse) written in Latin, French, Greek, Italian and other languages—but in riddles difficult to understand so as to protect himself from accusations of witchcraft.

Nostradamus eventually attracted the attention of Catherine de Médicis, the French queen. She was so impressed she had him produce horoscopes for the royal family's children. Later, he was appointed royal court physician.

Nostradamus died in 1566, allegedly stating the day before his death that he would live just one more day.

The Legend Grows

After Nostradamus' death, the legend grew. Followers claimed he had predicted the death of King Henry II of France—and he was said to have predicted that a young monk, Felice Peretti, would go on to become pope by addressing him as "Your Holiness." Peretti did become Pope Sixtus V.

So great was Nostradamus' influence that in the period following the bombing of the World Trade Center, his name was one of the top Google search terms.

People have always wanted to know what the future holds. And they have also always consulted with soothsayers, fortune-tellers, clairvoyants and so-called prophecy experts—alongside the Bible—to learn it. Books on prophecy are often instant bestsellers. Remember, Nostradamus is regarded by many as a prophet.

But again, did *God send him*?

Let's ask: How does God describe those who are *not* sent by Him? Notice: "And when they shall say unto you, Seek unto them that have familiar spirits, and unto wizards that peep, and that mutter: should not a people seek unto their God? For the living to the dead? To the *law* and to the *testimony*: if they *speak not* according to *this word*, it is because there is *no light in them*" (Isa. 8:19-20).

There is no evidence whatsoever that Nostradamus ever based his prophecies on the Bible. They came solely from *visions*. He neither spoke, nor attempted to speak, according to God's Word—or *Law*. Therefore, GOD says—not I—there is *"no light in him."* Think of it this way. The man was *not* enlightened—nor can he *shed light* on the future. We will, however, later learn why some of his predictions *did* come true.

It is widely acknowledged that many of Nostradamus' prophecies failed. One author outlined five that were false:

(1) Venice would have great power and world influence by 1792.

(2) The Catholic clergy would fall in 1609.

(3) Persecution would arise against the Catholic church, also in 1792.

(4) Astrologers would be persecuted in 1607.

(5) China would subdue the northern part of the world by 1700.

But *other* predictions never came true, and most were grand failures:

(1) The Bourbon line of kings would be restored to the French throne. It never was.

(2) French king Charles IX would live to 90. He died at 24.

(3) A dramatic reduction in world population in the eighteenth century would occur due to famine and disease. Instead, the population *exploded* during the eighteenth-century Industrial Revolution.

These events clearly did not happen. Based on number and size of failures, Nostradamus is a particularly poor prophet. Among false prophets, he could be classified as *extra* false!

A related question—and it is enormous: Could the God of the Bible inspire prophecies that did *not* come to pass? What about *even one*?

The answer is obvious—No! If this were possible, God becomes a liar. Recall from Chapter One: "...I am God, and there is *none like Me*, declaring the end from the beginning, and from ancient times the things that are *not yet done*, saying, *My counsel shall stand*, and I *will do* all My pleasure" (Isa. 46:9-10).

Only God can declare the future! Hebrews 6:18 says it is *impossible* for God to lie—His Word is certain. What He foretells—remember God does not *predict*—WILL come to pass! Thus, even a single failed prophecy means one was *not sent by God*.

Signs of a False Prophet

Nostradamus was known to be involved in the occult, having a large occult library. In a book dedicated to his son, who carried on after him, he wrote this strange and revealing description: "Dreading what might happen in the future, after reading them [his occult books], I presented them to Vulcan [the pagan Roman god of fire], and as the fire kindled them, the flame...shot forth an unaccustomed brightness, clearer than the light is of natural flame, resembling more the explosion of powder, casting a subtle illumination over the house..." (Nostradamus, *Preface a Mon Fils*). By any standard, this description, and Nostradamus' conduct, is strange.

God utterly condemns the occult. Let's read: "There shall not be found among you any one...that uses *divination*, or an observer of times, or an enchanter, or witch, or charmer, or consulter with familiar spirits, or wizard, or a necromancer [one who supposedly can reach the dead]. For all that do these things are an *abomination* unto the LORD..." (Deut. 18:10-12).

How many know that this early psychic consulted the dead? Ask: Would God send someone who is involved in practices He explicitly *condemns*? Of course not.

One either believes such verses or he does not.

Plain Warnings

False prophets prey on people's natural fascination with the future. The apostle John warned of them: "Believe not every spirit, but try [test] the spirits *whether they are of God*: because *many false prophets* are gone out into the world" (I John 4:1). Jesus added this warning: "And *many false prophets* shall rise, and shall *deceive many*" (Matt. 24:11). Now ask: How many worry about being deceived? Most ignore these passages. But this comes with a price.

Understand. God calls such possessors of "enlightened" knowledge "angels of light" (II Cor. 11:13-14). Such "angels" are only too willing to share their "knowledge."

Jesus also warned, "Beware of *false prophets*, which come to you in sheep's clothing, but inwardly they are ravening wolves" (Matt. 7:15).

It is not always easy to detect these deceivers. None of them wear signs exposing who they are. They are smooth operators, but their teachings tear people's understanding as wolves rip prey.

How can you tell a false prophet? Let Jesus answer: "You shall KNOW them by their *fruits*..." (Matt. 7:16). And four verses later, "By their *fruits* you shall KNOW them" (vs. 20). One key to knowing whether a prophet is true or false is by fruits—good or bad. Nostradamus did very strange things—followed practices God *condemns*—and did not otherwise practice obedience to God's laws. While possibly sincere, he was deceived and false!

Remember, most of Nostradamus' prophecies failed. And again, this could not occur with a prophet of God. Recall: "We have also a more *sure word* of prophecy..." (II Pet. 1:19). God's prophecies are *sure*. They *never* miss. Not one!

Here is God's command regarding prophets: "And if you [ask] in your heart, How shall we *know* the word which the LORD has *not* spoken?" (Deut. 18:21). God's answer is, "When a prophet speaks in the name of the LORD, if the thing *follow not, nor come to pass*, that is the thing which the LORD has *not* spoken, but the prophet has spoken it *presumptuously*: *you shall not be afraid of him*" (vs. 22).

This passage reveals that men can *presume* to speak for God. This is very serious to the God of the Bible. It should also be serious to you. You must KNOW if God sent a man—or if the man sent himself.

The *true* prophet Ezekiel recorded, "Son of man [Ezekiel], prophesy against the prophets of Israel...and say you unto them that prophesy out of *their own hearts*, Hear you the word of the LORD; thus says the Lord GOD; woe unto the *foolish prophets*, that follow their *own spirit*, and have seen *nothing*" (13:2-3).

Think of the worldwide fear that Nostradamus' presumptuous prophecies have engendered. But God declares, "you shall *not* be afraid of him" (Deut. 18:22). What was the Old Testament punishment for false prophets? "But the prophet, which shall presume to speak a word in My name [meaning, by God's authority], which I have not commanded him to speak...*even that prophet* SHALL DIE" (Deut. 18:20).

Again, this is SERIOUS to God—and it should be to *you*!

But what if a prophecy is correct? Some of Nostradamus' at least *seemed* to be. Notice what God also says in Deuteronomy: "If there arise among you a prophet, or a dreamer of dreams [one who sees visions, like Nostradamus], and gives you a sign or a wonder, and the sign or the wonder come to pass...you shall not hearken unto the words of that prophet, or that dreamer of dreams: for the LORD your God proves you, to *know* whether you love the LORD your God with all your heart... You shall walk after...and fear HIM [God only], and keep HIS commandments, and obey HIS voice [How many preachers teach that all 10 of God's Commandments must be kept? Few!], and you shall serve HIM, and cleave unto HIM. *And that prophet, or that dreamer of dreams, shall be* PUT TO DEATH...So shall you put the evil away from the midst of you" (13:1-5).

Of course, such executions cannot be carried out today. The point becomes: get away from the evil—put it away from you.

All Bad News

Another point bears consideration. Nostradamus' prophecies arc interpreted *after* events pass, not before. What is the value of this? Nothing! One author admitted, "As far as is known, Nostradamus did not leave a 'key' to his predictions...If he did, it has certainly been lost in the dust of the centuries. The need of having to interpret his predictions without the help of such an aid has led to some curious and widely varied versions of his quatrains" (Rene Noorbergen, *Nostradamus Predicts the End of the World*).

True prophecies—and *true prophets*—present events *before* they occur, *never afterward*. That is the job of *historians*.

Nostradamus was also an astrologer. In short, stemming from the natural tendency toward superstition within human nature, this is one who seeks guidance from the stars. God also condemns *this* practice: "Thus says the LORD, Learn not the way of the heathen [pagans and unbelievers], and be not dismayed at the signs of heaven; for the heathen are dismayed at them" (Jer. 10:2).

Get this. Nostradamus not only read, but literally *produced* horoscopes—practices that God outright condemns! So tragically, in total disobedience to God's command, millions today are also fascinated with their daily horoscopes.

In addition, Nostradamus never recorded *good* news. All of his writings involve bad news—assassination, war, famine, dictators, disasters—never anything good. However, the Bible is a Book filled with *good* news about the future.

Nostradamus' Prophecies—Not of God

Make yourself confront the *source* of Nostradamus' prophecies—where they actually came from. Notice: "Whether the majority of his visions came...from a psychic inspiration, necromancy, tarot cards or a refined form of witchcraft, we will probably never learn. We might conclude, however, that his hidden source of knowledge knew much of the course history would take, and possibly had the power to control or at least influence some of the major future historical developments" (ibid.).

What could be this "hidden source"? The Bible describes the existence of a spirit world. On one side are God, Christ and righteous angels. In opposition are Satan and fallen angels. Earlier we saw Nostradamus spoke of a "god that sits nearby." Who is this god?

The Bible describes Satan as the "god of this world" (II Cor. 4:4). The devil and his demons are the true authors of Nostradamus' visions and writings—not the man himself, and certainly not the true God. Remember from earlier that demons have a certain partial, but always twisted, knowledge of how God's Master Plan will play out. This allows them therefore to partially predict the future through humans. I have seen this many times.

The Bible records a story of the apostle Paul encountering a demon-possessed girl: "And it came to pass, as we went to prayer, a certain damsel possessed with a spirit of divination met us, which brought her masters much gain by soothsaying [fortune-telling]: the same followed Paul and us, and cried, saying, These men are the servants of the most high God [yes, demons will sometimes acknowledge God if it benefits them], which show unto us the way of salvation. And this did she many days. But Paul, being grieved, turned and said to the spirit [not the girl], I command you in the name of Jesus Christ to come out of her. And he came out the same hour" (Acts 16:16-18).

How many search God's Word for instruction about astrologers, palm readers and psychics? Most do not care what God says, and besides, it is too much work. They enjoy the fascination, but ignore the danger, of toying with powerful, destructive spirits who want people looking to *them*, not God.

Now this: "Regard not them that have *familiar spirits*, neither seek after wizards, to be defiled by them..." (Lev. 19:31).

Understand. Satan and his demons want to *destroy* mankind, and will stop at nothing to achieve their goal! This includes using phony visions to confuse man's understanding of God's plan of salvation and the many prophecies that relate to it. Nostradamus was simply a tool of Satan, the father of murder and lies. Read John 8:44. Nostradamus was almost certainly demon-possessed.

The apostle Peter compared false prophets in the Old Testament to false teachers in the New. Notice: "But there were *false prophets* also among the people [in ancient Israel], even as there shall be *false teachers* among you..." (II Pet. 2:1).

False ministers come in many shapes and sizes. Some specialize, particularly today, in confusing, incomplete, deceitful theories of how the future will play out. You are beginning to see that the utter nonsense of these conflicting scenarios is almost without end.

No "Private Interpretation"

While the most famous, Nostradamus is but one of many who have sought to interpret the future. Other well-known deceivers include Edgar Cayce and Jeanne Dixon. Again, all such astrologers, psychics, wizards, seers, fortune-tellers and channelers have exploded in number all over the world in recent years, alongside "experts" on end-time Bible prophecy.

All of these bring their *own* interpretations—virtually NONE of them correct even on the details. We saw the Bible warns that "*no* prophecy of the scripture is of any *private* interpretation" (II Pet. 1:20). God works through His chosen servants—and no one else. Ephesians 4:11 and I Cor-inthians 12:28 show that He does occasionally send a prophet, but also that this would only be within His *one* Church.

Understand. God does not—and would *never*—send *different* people to say *different* things—private interpretations—about the SAME events. In fact, this is one of the greatest ways you know that the many disagree-ing prophecy writers so popular today cannot be of God.

God's servants always speak with *one unified voice* (I Cor. 1:10)!

Nostradamus was a false prophet. Give him not another second of your time. NEVER fear this world's seers—including all the phony proph-ecy writers and supposed prophecy scholars. They do not know what they are talking about. God *did not send them*! They do not speak according to His Law—or almost any other of the plain truths of His Word. They are FALSE! Reject them! They will only confuse you.

Confusion—or Clarity

Most are not interested in anything that God may require them to DO—or not do. They want to be titillated by special prophetic knowledge more than to obey their Creator. Other books on prophecy will not tell you this. Instead of addressing *spiritual* causes behind man's unending ills, they focus on political, social, judicial or economic causes.

Because all of modern Christendom ignores even God's most basic biblical commands, preferring to hold to cherished traditions (Mark 7:7, 9), it does not—and will never—correctly understand true prophecy.

Understanding true *conversion* and *obedience to God* opens the door to understanding *prophecy*. Acts 2:38 explains that repentance and water baptism precede receiving God's Spirit. Also reread Acts 5:32. Without God's Spirit, one cannot understand the Bible, which means he will never correctly understand—beyond misapplied bits and fragments—what the future holds.

The all-importance of obedience to God, and to all of His truth—on prophecy and everything else—will loom ever larger through the book!

Behind the scenes, enormous events are taking shape. Prophecy will soon culminate in events terrifying beyond description. These will shake every nation on Earth. Vast numbers will perish. Stay focused as you read.

In this and the previous chapter, we have addressed the beliefs and fears of millions—all founded on EASILY DISPROVABLE FALSE PROPHECIES perpetrated by deceivers. So says the Bible! In the pages ahead, we will see the clarity and logic that GOD brings to explaining what will *actually* happen. Remember to *prove* what is written here. Compare it with your Bible!

Now for the single, longest unbroken prophecy in the Bible...

The Middle East in Prophecy

The Middle East lies in constant turmoil. Disagreement, violence and confusion have defined this region for millennia, making this geographic area a bubbling caldron of unrest, contention, terrorism and failed attempts at peace. Humanly devised solutions never work.

Few understand the historic *roots* of the Middle East. There, nations, cultures, religions, history and politics collide—*with prophecy*! How will it be resolved? What does the Bible say? Events in the Middle East carry far greater significance than most even begin to understand!

It has been said that every eight years the Middle East suffers another war. Recent history bears the truth of this statement. Its problems defy a simple solution—but this chapter will prove that God has been carefully guiding events there much longer than any can imagine.

The whole world is tied to the Middle East in a remarkable way. The problems there will *not* go away, nor can the world pretend they will by simply looking the other way!

The Middle East is at the center of a powerful and vitally important prophecy of which the world is ignorant. But God's Plan *can* be known.

Daniel's Amazing Prophecy

God is working out a Supreme Purpose on Earth. Most people are completely unaware that there *is* a purpose for mankind—let alone *what* it is! The present and *future* of the Middle East play a large role in God's Master Plan for humanity, and this region is at the center of an astounding prophecy that will affect the lives of all people on Earth before this age is finished.

Only God can solve the "Middle East problem."

Over 2,500 years ago, God inspired Daniel to record a long and detailed prophecy involving many fascinating twists and turns through history. This prophecy will culminate with tremendous events that will occur in *our time*! These events will impact *all nations*—and yet they have been sealed, closed until this age!

Some Bible prophecies are general. Others are specific, or even highly specific. Some involve single events that occur at specific moments in time. Others are fulfilled slowly over many years—or even over many centuries or millennia—and involve many events. You will learn that Daniel's prophecy involves many smaller prophecies that we will examine one by one, until we arrive at the modern age.

We are about to examine one long chapter in the Bible. It will become clear that there is only one way to explain each of the 45 separate verses in this chapter. The fulfillment of each verse is not subject to human reasoning, opinion or interpretation.

Many of these very intricate separate prophecies have already been fulfilled exactly as God foretold, and have taken their place in history. They are now facts that can be examined—and are *powerful proofs that a Supreme Being foretold them* and then BROUGHT THEM TO PASS! As you read, recognize that the evidence presented serves to make PLAIN the CERTAINTY of Bible prophecy—leaving those who disregard all yet-to-be-fulfilled prophecies without excuse!

The authority of the Bible stands at stake in this series of prophecies. If they stand true—PROVEN by the facts of history!—then a Divine Author recorded them, and all other prophecies to be discussed carry the same authority. If the prophecy failed, then the Bible is a book of men and can be thrown away as not worth the paper it is written on.

This extensive prophecy is found in Daniel 11. In chapter 10, Daniel is left astonished—completely shocked and overwhelmed by what God revealed would happen "at the end," or in the *last days*. Chapter 12 plays a part in concluding the lengthy prophecy of chapter 11.

Consider opening your Bible to read each verse beside the text of this chapter. No other approach will have the same impact. Also, bear in mind that men inserted all chapter and verse divisions of the Bible. While these are often helpful to Bible students, they can also inadvertently break up longer stories, thoughts or, as in this case, prophecies. The true meaning and scope of the subject matter can be obscured or completely lost from view due to these divisions.

In this case, the entire chapter builds to an unexpected conclusion, yet to be fulfilled. Let's examine.

Two Prophesied Great Kings

God gave Daniel this prophecy during the third year of the reign of Cyrus, the king of the Persian Empire.

Notice chapter 10, **verse 1**: "In the third year of Cyrus king of Persia a thing was revealed unto Daniel, whose name was called Belteshazzar; and the thing was TRUE, but the time appointed *was long*: and he understood the thing, and had understanding of the vision."

Daniel recorded that two powerful kings (actually competing kingdoms we will see to be tied directionally to "north" and "south") would play an overarching role in Middle Eastern events, until the time of the end. These kings set the stage for the unfolding of vitally important future events, which culminate before Christ returns!

Two key verses set the stage. In Daniel 10:21, the archangel Gabriel speaks to Daniel: "But I will show you that which is noted in the *scripture of truth*." Chapter 11 introduces the time setting. **Verse 2** continues, "And now will I show you the TRUTH." When God foretells events, He speaks the *truth*! They are *certain*! They *will happen*! Since no scripture can be broken (John 10:35), neither can any verse of this prophecy! Each must stand the test of close scrutiny. (Verses are in bold for the reader to more easily follow.)

Now consider the following from Daniel 11: "Behold, there shall stand up yet *three kings* in Persia; and *the fourth* shall be far richer than they all: and by his strength through his riches he shall *stir up* all against the realm of Grecia. And *a mighty king* shall stand up, that shall rule with great dominion, and do according to his will" (**verses 2-3**).

Who are these four kings—where the last is greater than the first three? And who is the "mighty king"? Daniel was speaking of kings Cambyses, Smerdis and Darius of Persia as the first three, with Xerxes being historically the greatest and richest of the four. It was Xerxes who "stirred up" war with Greece.

We must now briefly understand verses in Daniel 8. Alexander the Great's father, King Philip of Macedonia, created a master plan to conquer and defeat the Persian Empire with a Greek army. But Philip died before he could execute his plan. His son invaded Persia in his stead, and Alexander the Great's army fought the Persian army at the famous Battle of Issus in 333 BC (Daniel 8:2, 5-6).

Two years later, in 331 BC, in a second battle at Arbella, Alexander completely defeated the Persian Empire. Having already conquered Egypt shortly before this, he followed this battle with the destruction of everything from the Middle East to India. This happened precisely as prophesied!

Verse 4 says this of Alexander: "And when he shall stand up, his kingdom shall be broken, and shall be divided toward the *four winds* of heaven; and not to his posterity, nor according to his dominion which he ruled: for his kingdom shall be plucked up, even for others beside those."

Numerous historical authorities acknowledge that Alexander died suddenly, at age 32, when "Cut off unexpectedly in the vigour of early manhood, he left no inheritor, either of his power or of his projects" (Rawlinson's *A Manual of Ancient History*, p. 208). Alexander's kingdom *did* break into four separate kingdoms, because he had no son to take his place. Prophecy *was* fulfilled just as God foretold.

The following four of Alexander's generals represent the "four winds of heaven"—or directions to which his kingdom was divided: (1) *Lysimachus* ruled Asia Minor, (2) *Cassander* ruled Greece and Macedonia, (3) *Seleucus* ruled Syria, Babylonia and all regions east to India and (4) *Ptolemy* ruled Egypt, Judea and part of Syria.

From this point, the prophecy tracks two of these four kings or divisions of territory. The Syrian kingdom represents the "king of the north." The Egyptian kingdom represents (vs. 5) the "king of the south," because Egypt is generally south of Jerusalem. (Jerusalem is the central focus of all prophecy and, therefore, directions are always established by identifying locations in relation to this city.) These two kingdoms often fought back and forth across Palestine—the Holy Land and Jerusalem—with possession of this area constantly shifting, depending on the outcome of the last battle.

Ptolemy I, named Soter, established *Egypt* as a far greater, more dominant power than when Alexander was alive. Seleucus also became very strong. By 312 BC, he had established an equally powerful kingdom in *Syria*. These two kingdoms became and represent, respectively, the "king of the south" and the "king of the north," mentioned throughout this prophecy. **Daniel 11:5** states, "And the *king of the south* shall be strong, and one of his princes; and he shall be strong above him, and have dominion; his dominion shall be a great dominion."

Amazing Fulfillment of Verse Six

Verse 6 is a very specific and truly remarkable prophecy. Let's carefully examine various phrases within it: "And in the end of years they shall join themselves together; for the king's daughter of the south shall come to the king of the north to make an agreement [note the term used in the margin, "rights," meaning *marriage union* or *rights*, in this case]: but she shall not retain the *power of the arm*; neither shall he *stand*, nor his arm: but she shall be given up, and they that brought her, and *he that begat her*, and he that strengthened her in these times."

What could all of this refer to?

Fifty years later, Antiochus II (called Theos) was the king of the north, ruling at Syria. His wife, Laodicé, carried great influence in the kingdom. But Theos divorced her and married Bernicé, the daughter of the king of the south. Bernicé was to lose the "power of her arm." Her husband, the king of the north, was prophesied to not "stand," and she and her father ("he that begat her") were both prophesied to be "given up." These three did come to a bad end.

An amazingly detailed, precisely fulfilled prophecy ensues from verse 6. Rawlinson states that "Her [Laodicé's] influence...engage[d] him in a war with Ptolemy Philadelphus [king of the south], BC 260, which is terminated, BC 252, by a marriage between Antiochus and Bernicé, Ptolemy's daughter...On the death of Philadelphus ["he that begat her"], BC 247, Antiochus repudiates Bernicé, and takes back his former wife, Laodicé, who...doubtful of his constancy, murdered him to secure the throne for her son Seleucus [II] BC 246...Bernicé...had been put to death by Laodicé" (p. 222).

Control of the Holy Land Shifts Repeatedly

Now **verse 7**: "But out of a branch of *her roots* [Bernicé's parents] shall one [this is her brother who would take the throne in his father's stead as the king of the south] stand up in his estate ["in his office," margin reference], which shall come with an army, and shall enter into the fortress of the king of the north, and shall deal against them, and shall prevail."

Rawlinson states, "Ptolemy Euergetes [the III, eldest son of Philadelphus, and therefore Bernicé's brother, a branch of her roots] invades Syria, BC 245, to avenge the murder of his sister Bernicé...In the war which follows, he carries everything before him" (p. 222).

Verse 8 speaks of the king of the south carrying silver and gold vessels, with captives, back to Egypt (**verse 9**) after a successful invasion of the north. In fact, Ptolemy III did conquer Syria, the Port of Antioch (capital of the kingdom) and Seleucia. He took a vast amount of spoils, including the return of 2,500 idolatrous vessels and molten images that, in 526 BC, the northern king, Cambyses, had taken from Egypt.

The passage also states that King Ptolemy III would rule longer ("more years") than the king of the north, Seleucus II. Seleucus died in 226 BC, and Ptolemy III reigned *four years longer*, until 222 BC.

At the death of Seleucus II, his kingdom was ruled successively by his two sons. Seleucus III reigned just three years (226-223 BC), while his brother, Antiochus III, also called "the Great," reigned for 36 years (223-187 BC). Each established great armies to fight Egypt, recover their port city of Seleucia and avenge the defeat of their father.

It took 27 years for Antiochus to recapture Seleucia and conquer Syria and the area from Judea to Gaza. **Verses 10** and **11** state, "But his sons shall be stirred up, and shall *assemble* a multitude of *great forces*: and one shall certainly come, and overflow, and pass through: then shall he return and be stirred up ["be stirred up again," margin reference], even to his fortress. And the king of the south shall be moved with choler [anger], and shall come forth and fight with him, even with the king of the north: and he shall set forth a great multitude; but the multitude shall be given into his hand."

Ptolemy IV fulfilled verse 11 exactly. After gathering an army of 20,000, he did "move with [anger]" against Antiochus the Great. He fulfilled **verse 12** because he did "cast down [kill] many ten thousands." However, he retreated too soon to Egypt, having made too hasty a peace with Antiochus, and wasted the substance he had gained, hence the phrase, "but he shall not be strengthened by it" (i.e., his victory over Antiochus in 217 BC).

Twelve years later (205 BC), Ptolemy Philopator, king of Egypt, died. His baby son, Ptolemy Epiphanes, was given the throne. Thus, Egypt became vulnerable to attack. Antiochus took advantage of this vulnerability "after certain years" by defeating Egypt. **Verse 13** explains, "For the king of the north shall return, and shall set forth a multitude greater than the former, and shall certainly come after certain years with a great army and with much riches."

Soon thereafter, Antiochus formed an alliance with Philip of Macedonia to attack Egypt and retrieve Phoenicia and Southern Syria from Egypt. The famous Jewish historian, Josephus, states that a large number of Jews joined Antiochus in this campaign. **Verse 14** describes this.

(Again, you should try to carefully read each verse from your Bible as these events in history are outlined before you.)

Next, Antiochus laid siege all the way from Egypt to Sidon, eventually seizing control of Judea in 198 BC, at the Battle of Mount Panium. Notice the reference to the Holy Land (Judea) as "the glorious land" (**verses 15-16**).

At this time (198 BC), Antiochus arranged to have his daughter, Cleopatra, and the now little boy king, Ptolemy Epiphanes, marry. But this plan to control and possess Egypt, through deceit, failed, because Cleopatra deceived her father, Antiochus, and did *not* help him take control of Egypt (**verse 17**). (This was not the same Cleopatra as the famous Egyptian queen of 31 BC.)

This caused Antiochus to focus on defeating and taking control of the coasts of Asia Minor, including the islands around it (197-196 BC). However, in the Battle of Magnesia (190 BC), Lucius Cornelius Scipio Asiaticus, the Roman general, defeated him and destroyed his army (**verse 18**).

Daniel records what came next: "Then he shall turn his face toward the *fort* [fortresses] of his own land: but he shall stumble and fall, and not be found." Antiochus, after redirecting his concerns toward his own fortresses, was killed in 187 BC while seeking to consolidate his assets by plundering the Oriental Temple of Belus in Elymais (**verse 19**).

Heliodorus, the "raiser of taxes," was sent by Seleucus IV Philopator to raise money throughout Judea. However, Heliodorus poisoned Seleucus IV, who consequently reigned only eleven years—187-176 BC (**verse 20**).

Seleucus IV had no heir, so his younger brother (Epiphanes or Antiochus IV) won control of the kingdom by flattery ("flatteries") and deceit. The next verse states: "And in his estate shall stand up a vile person, to whom they shall not give the honor of the kingdom: but he shall come in peaceably, and obtain the kingdom by flatteries" (**verse 21**). This man *was* an extremely "vile," contemptible person and his aid, Eumenes, *did* come to assist him. Rawlinson states that "Antiochus [Epiphanes], assisted by Eumenes, drives out Heliodorus, and obtains the throne, BC 176. He astonishes his subjects by an affectation of Roman manners...His good-natured profuseness [flatteries]" (p. 225).

The Role of Antiochus IV (Epiphanes)

Verse 22 pictures an effort by Antiochus Epiphanes to remove the Jewish High Priest ("prince of the covenant"). Antiochus' purpose was to install someone who would be loyal to him. Some misunderstand the term "prince of the covenant" to be a reference to Jesus Christ. However, it is not.

The next three verses are an insight into Antiochus' character and manner. He started with a small group of supporters, yet through flattery and deceit he slipped into greater power and secured larger numbers of followers. Although his ancestors granted *favor* to the Jews, he swept into Lower Egypt and Galilee, thereby alienating the Jews. Rawlinson states that the Jews "were driven to desperation by the mad project of this self-willed monarch" and "Threatened with war by the ministers of Ptolemy Philometor [the then king of the south], who claim Coelé-Syria and Palestine as the dowry of Cleopatra, the late queen-mother, Antiochus marches against Egypt" (p. 225).

This occurred in 171 BC. It was then that his nephew (Ptolemy Philometor) attacked him with a "great army." However, Ptolemy's officers betrayed him to Antiochus and he lost the battle (**verses 23-25**).

In 174 BC, Antiochus had joined his young nephew Ptolemy at a feast. Antiochus feigned support for Ptolemy against his brother, Euergetes II, in a case of mutual deceit (**verses 26-27**).

The Abomination of Desolation

Next, Antiochus decided to attack and slaughter as many Jews as possible. Upon returning from Egypt in 168 BC, with "great riches," he sacked the Temple at Jerusalem and took from it the golden vessels—all as part of his planned genocide of the Jews. He turned back toward Egypt, this time without similar success, because Ptolemy Philometor had secured assistance from Rome (**verse 28-29**).

The Roman commander, Popillius, brought his fleet of ships to attack Antiochus. Popillius secured surrender on his own terms, which included leaving Egypt after returning the island of Cyprus to Egypt. This caused Antiochus, once again, to vent his anger against Judea (the Jews) as he was returning to Antioch. This "indignation against the holy covenant" offered favor to any Jews who would *renounce* their beliefs and practices (**verse 30**).

Antiochus dispatched troops to Palestine one year later, in 167 BC, with terrible results for all who fell in his path. He destroyed the Temple and its sanctuary—doing away with the daily sacrifice (described in Daniel 8:11, 24), while setting up an image, the *abomination of desolation*, directly on the altar of the Temple—thus defiling it, or making it *deso-*

late! (There are those who attempt to portray this verse as having been fulfilled at the time the Dome of the Rock was built on the Temple site, over eight centuries later, in the seventh century AD. For this to be true, *all* of the verses that have been explained to this point would require some *other* equally plausible explanation to "work" with the precision we have seen every step of the way thus far. This would also apply to all the verses that follow verse 31.) Antiochus Epiphanes placed the "abomination that makes desolate" in the Temple in 167 BC (**verse 31**).

But understand. Antiochus' prophetic fulfillment of this verse is a crucial TYPE of a *latter day* fulfillment to occur in *our time*. Luke 21:20 reveals that Jerusalem will be left in "desolation" by "armies" that will "surround" and destroy it. The gravity of this prophecy will be briefly further addressed at the end of the chapter and covered in full detail in a coming chapter.

It is important here for the reader to recognize that God often uses *duality* to show the world, through prior similar events—as TYPES—exactly what He intends to do again—to *repeat*—usually in a far *greater way* in the *future*!

This is an absolutely VITAL KEY to understanding the meaning of *all Bible prophecy*!

Christ and the Apostles Enter the Prophecy

The first part of **verse 32** describes Antiochus' attempt to destroy the Jewish religion. He outlawed both the daily sacrifice and the daily ministration of the Temple through a system of flattering (with favors) any Jews who would renounce their beliefs.

It is critical to understand that, from the middle of verse 32, the prophecy *shifts forward* to the time of the New Testament Church. We have watched each step of this prophecy unfold through two centuries of time. The time setting now fast-forwards approximately 200 more years to depict true Christians, "even to the *time of the end*: because it is yet for *a time appointed*" (vs. 35). Notice that verse 32 speaks of "people that do *know their God* shall be *strong* and do *exploits* [great works]." **Verse 33** continues, "they that *understand* among the people shall *instruct many*."

At this point, many theologians and commentaries note that the highly detailed, precisely fulfilled, verse-by-verse story appears to come to an *abrupt end*. But this is not true!

These two portions of verses picture two entirely different time settings—the first being a *type* of the latter. Certainly Antiochus did "corrupt by flatteries" a great many Jews. The latter part of verse 32 speaks of the time of the Maccabees, who resisted Antiochus' pattern of corruption and slaughter. They represented a *type* of what Christ and the apostles would begin to do when Christ built His Church (Matt. 16:18).

Christians are supposed to be "strong" and should always be prepared to "instruct *many*"—because they "understand" what God is doing in His Plan on Earth! Of course, Jesus Christ and the apostles certainly fulfilled these verses toward "many."

We saw Daniel specifically records that at the time of the end (12:10), "none of the wicked shall understand; *but the wise shall understand.*" The entirety of Daniel 12 is a continuation of this end-time setting—established from here forward.

The latter part of verse 33 is a picture of the martyrdom of Christ and all of the apostles except John. For true Christians, persecution and martyrdom continued into the Middle Ages. (For even those *true* Christians who have grown lukewarm, this will occur again before Jesus returns.)

Verses 34-35 are a clear, powerful description of the path of God's true people from the time the New Testament Church was founded all the way to the present. Notice: "Now when they shall fall, they shall be [helped] with a little help: but many shall cleave to them with *flatteries*. And some of them of understanding shall fall, to *try* them, and to *purge*, and to *make* them *white*, even to the time of the end: because it is yet for a time appointed." (For the moment, these verses are in part better understood by comparing them with Revelation 12:6, 11, 13-17.)

Verse 36 describes the king of the north just before and during the early centuries of the New Testament Church. From 65 BC forward, the Roman emperor (king of the north) controlled the Holy Land (Judea). Each Roman emperor certainly did "exalt himself, and magnify himself above every god," by requiring all his subjects to worship him—and he even required sacrifices to be offered to him, like he was a god! Roman emperors *did* act as though they were gods. They *did* speak against the true God, and persecuted His true servants—Christians—for many hundreds of years.

Verse 37 shows how Roman kings, prior to AD 476, had worshipped idols. History records that these Roman emperors did "magnify [themselves] above all"!

Verse 38 describes how the entire Roman Empire *did* "honor the god of forces [margin, "munitions"]." The Roman army *did* develop into the most powerful war machine in history to that time, and the empire *did* amass gold, silver, jewelry, etc. From Justinian's reign, in AD 554, when the "deadly wound" of Revelation 13 "was healed" (after a 78-year period from AD 476, when three northern barbarian tribes had swept into and temporarily controlled Rome), the civil emperors in Rome *did* begin to honor (with power, gold and silver) a god that had been unknown to their ancestors or "fathers." (More about this "wound" is covered several chapters ahead.)

This "god" held a *high religious office* and received great deference from Roman emperors.

Through these emperors, this high religious office controlled or "ruled over many" and had great power and wealth given to it. Carefully compare this portion of the prophecy with Revelation 17:4-5 and 18:3 and 16, where this religious power is described as "babylon" and "the mother of harlots" who "fornicates" with the "kings" and "merchants of the earth" (**verses 38-39**)! (This and related prophecies are also explained in much detail later.)

The Time of the End

Verse 40 plainly uses the term "at the time of the end." It then makes reference to "the king of the south shall *push* at him," while it states that "the king of the north shall come against him like a *whirlwind*..." What does this mean? Who are these two kings? Who in particular is this end-time king of the south?

Anciently, this was Egypt. Rome seized Egypt and made it a province. Today, Egypt does not have a king and is a modern republic. During the intervening centuries, there has been no *great* king of the south. However, recall that Ptolemy III Euergetes did seize part of Ethiopia, as the king of the south in Egypt, in 247-222 BC.

Both Rawlinson and the *Encyclopaedia Britannica* (11th edition) explain that Egypt and Ethiopia were governed together several different times. Ethiopia was the *only part* of the territory controlled by the king of the south that remained independent until the twentieth century.

The King of the South

Once again, *only* Ethiopia continued and remained independent in East Africa from the time of the Roman Empire. Therefore, no other country or government could fit as the king of the south—i.e., by having been a part of the ancient land controlled by the "king of the south." Remember, verse 40 explains that the setting is the time of the end. The king of the south "push[es]" toward the north—or Rome. This occurred in 1895. At that time, about 10,000 men, under the Ethiopian King Menelik, came against the Italian army led by General Baratieri. It should be noted that Eritrea (north of Ethiopia) belonged to Italy, while southeast of Ethiopia was Italian Somaliland.

One year later, in 1896, the Italian General Baratieri attempted to defend Eritrea against the Ethiopian attack. Over 11,000 people were either killed or taken prisoner. The greatly outnumbered and inexperienced Italian army was almost completely destroyed in a battle fought over rugged, mountainous terrain.

Italy never forgot this defeat and vowed revenge. It took almost 40 years, but the opportunity finally came.

In 1927, Mussolini determined that he would attack Ethiopia in eight years (1935), at a point 39 years after the defeat. He followed through, and this did occur in 1935! Again, notice verse 40, in its reference to Mussolini's attack: "...and the king of the north shall come against him like a *whirlwind*, with *chariots*, and with *horsemen*, and with *many ships*; and he shall enter into the countries, and shall overflow and *pass over*."

A whirlwind is the equivalent of a tornado, which is a powerful storm that drops out of the sky. Mussolini did, in fact, bring a large air force to attack Ethiopia. Of course, his "chariots" were modern tanks and other armaments. The "many ships" were part of an armada carrying over 100,000 soldiers to the battle. Verse 40 ends with an amazing statement—it describes this large force as "pass[ing] over."

Just as God foretold, Mussolini withdrew and did not completely finish his attack. This is because God has reserved one final influential and very powerful leader who will arise in Europe and complete this prophecy! We have now arrived at our point in time—today—when the verses that follow verse 40 are those that are *yet to be fulfilled*—while all verses preceding and through verse 40 are *already fulfilled*, and have become established facts of history!

May all who read the next five verses come to understand their message for our time! They become a kind of overview for many things that follow in the book.

Final Coming Revival of the Roman Empire

Many Bible prophecies (we will learn them) reveal that there is yet coming one *final* resurrection of the Holy Roman Empire—when a *final* king of the north will seize the world stage for a short period prior to the Return of Christ. While this understanding will be covered in much greater detail later, for our purpose here understand that the world is now moving toward this final terrible period of trouble. This dictator will gather 10 other kings (Rev. 17:12-13), who will give their power and allegiance to him, in this last revival of the Holy Roman Empire.

Verse 41 says of this king, "he shall enter also into the *glorious land.*" This entrance into the glorious land, or Holy Land, has not yet happened! The prophecy continues, "And *many* countries shall be overthrown: but these shall escape out of his hand, even Edom, and Moab, and the chief of the children of Ammon." (Incidentally, Moab and Ammon comprise the modern Middle Eastern nation of Jordan—Ammon the northern half and Moab the southern half. Many prophecies indicate God will likely spare this region for a reason yet to be covered.)

Since verse 42 declares "Egypt shall not escape" this time, Egypt could *not* be the king of the south. Then, verse 43 says, "the Libyans and the Ethiopians shall be at his steps." The king of the north will, once again, control these two countries, which Italy lost control over at the end of World War II. After the invasion by Mussolini, Ethiopia is no longer referenced.

Verse 44 makes reference to "*tidings* [news] out of the *east* and out of the *north* shall trouble him." Russia and the Orient lie north and east, respectively, from where the final resurrection of the Holy Roman Empire will be established in the Middle East.

Remember that, prophetically, God uses Jerusalem as the geographic point from which to reference any direction. The king of the north will hear some troubling news and Russia, coupled with many nations from the east, will join the war, centered in the Middle East.

Verse 45 summarizes the end of this now seen-to-be longest of all Bible prophecies. The king of the north (the final civil ruler over the last revival of the Holy Roman Empire) will sweep into the modern land of Israel, "the holy mountain," to establish his religious headquarters. Another prophecy, in Zechariah 14:2, declares that "the city [Jerusalem] shall be taken." The rest of this verse must be read to fully understand the horror that occurs when Jerusalem is taken and conquered.

Take a moment to read Luke 21:20, where Jerusalem's future destruction comes from *armies* that for a time merely surround it. Zechariah 14:3 continues, explaining what ultimately happens: "Then shall the LORD go forth, and *fight against those nations*, as when He fought in the day of battle. And His feet shall stand *in that day* upon the Mount of

Olives which is before *Jerusalem* on the east" (also vs. 4). In the end, the all-powerful, returning Jesus Christ destroys the armies that destroyed Jerusalem! Much more detail of this will follow at the right juncture.

When speaking of the final Beast and False Prophet, Daniel 11:45 concludes, "Yet he [the Beast] shall come to his end, and none shall help him." Zechariah 14:3 explains that Christ will deal with him—as well as with the False Prophet. Revelation 19:19-20 and Zechariah 14:12 give more explanation to the terrible end that will come to these two infamous figures!

Undeniable Proof

You have seen but one, albeit a very big one, of the many undeniable PROOFS of the Bible's authority, as understood through fulfilled prophecy. We saw Daniel 10:1 declare, "The thing [this prophecy] was TRUE," and verse 21 ties this long prophecy to "the scripture of TRUTH." Foretold by God, specific event after specific event *has* come to pass—and exactly as prophesied! God's Word has been shown to be true.

What will you do about it?

The future—*your* future—turns on the understanding and application of the prophecies detailed through the chapters ahead. You can be certain that the final events (the last five verses) of the Daniel 11 prophecy *will* come to pass—and SOON.

And God will use certain "triggering" events...

The Coming Global Financial Collapse!

The global economy is in the worst crisis since the Great Depression of the 1930s! In 2008 alone, a staggering $50 trillion in wealth was erased around the world.

Despite unparalleled affluence in the Western world, personal and corporate bankruptcies are soaring. So is use of credit by consumers. Millions are losing jobs. More millions their homes. The U.S. national debt is measured in *trillions* of dollars! Headlines of credit fraud, identity theft, graft and corruption fill the news. Thinking people know events are spinning out of control.

Sobering Statistics

The sobering statistics that follow are but a snapshot in time and grow worse by the day. As you read, factor in an increased amount to each statistic and trend.

The world's largest economy, the United States, the place to begin review, is now more than *$13.7 trillion* in debt—and this debt is growing by over three billion dollars daily! This amounts to an over $44,000 bill for every U.S. citizen—or over $124,000 per taxpayer. Some expect the debt to be above *$14.5* trillion after the next fiscal year—which means a growth of additional billions *each day* next year! (In reality, these numbers will almost certainly be higher.) Such debt can *never* be repaid! In fact, most nations of the West are also now being crushed by *impossible* debt. Catastrophe now looms—and, in the case of America, here is why.

The United States received about $2.1 trillion in tax *revenue* in 2009—a number much lower than what the government originally projected. *Spending* was over $3.5 trillion for 2009.

Now suppose that these numbers represented the income and spending pattern of an American family of *median* income. Such a family would take in just over $50,000 (2008 estimate), but be planning to spend over $83,000—while already carrying more than $326,000 in debt! Individual families would *never* do this—or if they tried, would go bankrupt before it could happen.

But governments can print money.

Exploding Deficits

The national debt is projected to approach $20 trillion in 2014!—and hit $26 trillion in 2019!—almost double the present. Such deficit spending is unsustainable.

Money is borrowed at existing rates of interest. Understand that just a very small 1 percent rate increase on the debt will raise the interest payment of $200 billion by several hundred billion each year. But this is only true if the deficit *did not rise*! Many think *all* these projections to be *very* conservative. They will likely be *much* worse.

No thinking person believes such overspending can continue without end. Further, the addition of expensive new government programs and exotic new kinds of taxes will only *greatly* exacerbate the downturn. America will not stop spending because it is conditioned to believe it can have anything it wants. It need never deny itself. A country this big, this great, and one with such a rich history, cannot fail.

This thinking is tragically *wrong*. What world empire—with *half* America's problems—survived?

The economies of America and other nations of the West will in time collapse into full-blown bankruptcy. This *will* happen, although things could temporarily get a little better. Various individual states will in fact likely precede the federal government and country into bankruptcy, and thus, hasten the overall collapse. Of course, nature abhors a vacuum, and a European-based world government will step in to fill America's abdication as global leader. This cannot now be far away.

The world as you know it—including *your life*—will change beyond your wildest imagination.

Private Debt

So far, we have only discussed government debt. Private debt—from loans and credit cards—amounts to an *additional* $52,000 for every American, compared to an average savings of only $3,120.

In 2008, $6.9 trillion was lost in the U.S. stock market and $3.3 trillion in its housing market. These are devastating losses to peoples' investments, including stocks, bonds, retirement plans, employee stock ownership and home values. Lifelong hopes and dreams crash daily!

Employment is now shrinking at the fastest rate since the Great Depression. Unemployment lingers around 10 percent in the United States. And this does not include the (many millions of) discouraged workers who have given up looking. Many other countries are *much* worse!

The combination of exploding debt and unemployment is hitting home! In 2009 alone, well over one million Americans declared bankruptcy, with more and more families also winding up jobless and in despair—facing *abject poverty*. This problem is worldwide. Many well-educated middle class people now live on unemployment, or welfare and food stamps—having never thought this could happen to them. Tent cities are springing up across America. Thousands are living in cars, and a small but growing number now live in *sewer systems.*

The Federal Reserve reported that the total American household worth dropped 2.7 percent in the second quarter alone (April to June) in 2010—or $1.5 trillion—to $53.5 trillion. This is *18.7 percent* below its pre-recession peak of $65.8 trillion. Worse, this sudden unexpected decline comes after slight improvement over the previous four quarters.

The combined budget deficit and weakening dollar threaten to introduce hyperinflation, ruin the finances of its citizens, and *totally* destroy America's economy. China, Japan, Germany and other creditor nations are deeply concerned about investing more money in an essentially bankrupt country. If they either pull out of American investments or call in their loans, the consequences will be disastrous. One of the world's richest men, Warren Buffett, declared *early* in the crisis that the U.S. economy has "fallen off a cliff." But things have worsened.

Banking System Gone Wrong

Most troubling for this superpower—long the engine of the world's economy—are the ongoing woes in its banking system. In 2008, 25 banks collapsed. In 2009, the number was about *six times* worse, and in 2010 the rate has accelerated, with a much higher toll expected for the year.

What started with subprime mortgage losses has now grown into a full-blown financial crisis. U.S. banks have lost many, many billions of dollars, and this will grow *much* higher. No one knows how much—and thus where it ends.

America's economic problems have ignited a global firestorm! Several European and Asian countries are also in recession. The Japanese Nikkei index trading on the Tokyo Stock Exchange—the world's second largest market—continues its long fall. Markets in Russia and throughout the European Union are also suffering. Many countries face shrinking economies, big deficits, mounting debt, unstable currencies and rising unemployment. Financial markets are unraveling with a speed not seen since the Crash of 1929.

To compound matters, increasing economic, health and hunger crises in Third World nations are adding to the *First* World economic burden. As leaders scramble for solutions, deep fear pervades the world's corridors of power!

All of this threatens to destroy the global economy. Attempting to solve the crisis, leaders are calling more often for a unified economic system. More now suggest *one* currency, *one* economy and *one world government*!

Understand. The world economic outlook is grim and growing darker daily. It is important to first understand the origins—the *causes*—of today's economic distress.

The crisis began with the so-called "credit crunch"—the reduction in the availability of loans. Banks became reluctant to lend—whether to individuals, businesses or other lenders.

Banks traditionally operated by taking deposits from customers and lending to those seeking loans. The difference between the interest rate paid on deposits and the *higher* one charged on loans—the "spread"—was profit. If customers defaulted, banks were liable to depositors for payment. They held the risk "on the books"—it was *their* responsibility.

What Changed

It was therefore in a bank's interest to carefully screen customers before lending. The customer needed a good job and sizeable down payment. This conservative approach enabled banks to be sound—and highly profitable—for decades.

In the 1990s, banks changed their way of operating. Seeking ever-higher profits to satisfy shareholders, and to secure executive bonuses, they decided they could make even higher profits if they loaned more. Careful screening of applicants stopped.

Customers who previously never qualified under standard lending procedures—"subprime" customers—were aggressively targeted as a lucrative source of income. Loans were provided to people with *no* income, *no* job and *no* assets—so-called NINJA loans.

Other "sweeteners" were provided, such as no down payment and interest-only payments. Those who *approved* these loans were no longer attached to the *risk of default*—and were handsomely paid for their efforts. The subprime mortgage market became a ticking bomb, waiting to explode.

Look at how this has come home to roost. In 1980, only one in every 400 mortgages had a down payment of 3 percent or less. By 1990, it was one in every 200 mortgages. In 2003, it had become one in every *seven*—and by 2007, it had fallen to one in every *three*! As the housing bubble grew, banks lowered standards to get as large a slice of the real estate market "pie" as they could. In less than three decades, they grew 133 times more eager to approve loans with tiny down payments.

In the process banks in effect *invited* large numbers of homebuyers to default. The inevitable crash in home values came to pass, devaluing the average home by far more than 3 percent! (Some counties in Florida have seen home prices drop by over *50 percent* from their 2006 peak.)

With the steep and steady decrease in home values, resale rates are also plummeting. At the time of this writing, the National Association of Realtors (NAR) reported a decrease of *over 27 percent* in month-over-month U.S. home resales from June to July 2010—the steepest drop ever recorded (*The Associated Press*). Annual resale estimates were scaled back to 3.8 million—also the lowest number the NAR has ever recorded (*The Wall Street Journal*).

Such decreases can be largely attributed to the unwillingness of sellers and buyers to budge: "Potential buyers are hesitating because they think home prices still have further to fall. Potential sellers—those with the stomach to put their homes on the market at all, anyway—are reluctant to lower their prices" (*The Associated Press*). This self-perpetuating cycle is almost certainly destined to continue!

The result? Every day, due to inability to reverse or control their losses through sale of their home, growing numbers of Americans are simply mailing their house keys to mortgage lenders and walking away from houses. And many of these homes are insured by the government. The number of families in danger of home foreclosure is said to be 10 times greater than its pre-recession rate of just two years ago! This is resulting in billions of dollars' worth of homes sitting empty, with banks left holding the bag. Despite all this, some banks *still* offer jumbo loans with little or nothing down for "qualified buyers"!

Economic upheaval in the United States will yield untold troubles there. Weak defense. More enemies. *Emboldened* enemies. Less aid to other nations. Collapsing infrastructure. Wide-ranging political repercussions. Civil unrest and violence. A loss of prestige and influence. A spiral toward second- and eventually third-world status!

Two Critical Factors

Two more developments have played a significant role in the onset of the current crisis. The first was deregulation of the U.S. financial services industry with the 1999 repeal of the Glass-Steagall Act. Carefully crafted during the Great Depression to control stock market speculation, Glass-Steagall prevented retail and investment banks, and insurance companies, from owning each other.

With the repeal, huge financial services conglomerates rapidly formed, combining these types of financial institutions. Industry behemoths such as Citigroup and JP Morgan were born. This meant that retail banks seeking ever-higher profits could dive into high-risk speculative ventures through ownership *of*—or being owned *by*—investment banks. This brought disaster in 1929.

The second change was the low interest rate policy pursued by the Federal Reserve. These rates encouraged banks to target subprime customers with *variable rate* mortgages. They offered initially low "teaser" rates that would reset upward in two or three years. With home prices rising, customers took the bait, believing that when the reset arrived they could refinance at affordable rates.

Many mortgage brokers misrepresented terms and conditions to eager customers who were *themselves* providing fraudulent information. Many banks did not bother to check the information. Predatory *lending* invited predatory *borrowing*!

Banks then sold risky bonds as safe investments to unsuspecting investors. Rating agencies, paid by the banks, rated these bonds (those with subprime components) as being safe—even giving some the highest rating.

The Big Picture

With big, steady, annual increases in real estate prices, builders nationwide went on a building spree. This created a sense of "easy money"— "something for nothing." In their *greed*, many scammed the system. This does not count the many others who were *outright corrupt*—and scammed people in the usual ways. And of course predatory lawyers are now enjoying a field day at every turn!

The crisis began slowly in the middle of 2007. Due to a glut of homes for sale, housing prices fell moderately. But the scales were tipped— as the first round of rate resets was coming due. Faced with exploding payments, falling prices, and inability to refinance mortgages, millions defaulted. Confronted with higher payments, and on mortgages now *greater* than the home's value, owners began abandoning their mortgages—again, many simply turning in keys.

Rising numbers feel *no moral obligation* to fulfill what they promised to repay, believing it better to just walk away. This is in stark contrast to years ago when borrowers felt an obligation—a moral and ethical *duty!*—to pay off loans. With moral values long disintegrating nationwide—and throughout the West—many lack the fiscal responsibility— the character!—of previous generations.

As the crisis intensifies, mortgage defaults are multiplying. And *everyone* is on the hook. "Monoline" insurance companies have suddenly become liable for vast *billions* in debt. Investors have been left holding bonds that will *never* be repaid. Banks are finding it difficult to sell additional bonds as investors have backed out of the market, leery of poor investments. The banks' fee income has dried up—leaving them with massive capital deficiencies.

Thus, banks have sharply reduced lending to each other, and to the public, fearful that loans will go unrepaid.

Evidence is clear that shockwaves from the crisis are being felt in other sectors of the economy. *Liquidity* is drying up and less money is available to finance *commercial* loans.

The credit crunch has pushed beyond retail banking, and now affects major business deals and commercial real estate. Municipal bonds (that fund cities, colleges and hospitals)—once considered safe investments— can no longer easily find buyers.

As more loans reach interest rate resets, more defaults will occur. The crisis will deepen.

This will not be helped by the fact that many economists have formally declared that the world has become "unstable." The International Monetary Fund announced in October 2010 that "Southern Europe" is condemned "to death by slow suffocation" and "that fiscal tightening will trap North Europe, Britain and America in slump for a long time" (*Telegraph*).

A more accurate statement is that a fast-moving financial tsunami now approaches the shores of the world economy! While governments will enact an array of gimmicks attempting to turn it back, and will almost certainly bring an *appearance* of improvement—or even of permanent solution!—the levees they build will this time not hold. These barriers will be breached, and blown out. All temporary economic "upticks" will be washed away with them.

The discerning realize this!

The Role of Greed

The main motivating factors behind the crisis were *greed* and *covetousness*. Human nature has been accurately described as vanity, jealousy, lust and greed. Understand. Banks were greedy for ever-higher profits. So were investors who took foolish risks for higher return on investment. And greedy individuals sought loans they could not repay to purchase material goods they coveted, but did not need—and could not afford!

Simple lack of self-control drives many into bankruptcy. Impulse buying has turned the loan industry into a thriving business. Credit is now used for *luxuries*, leaving little to show for it except the monthly bill.

Obsession with material goods is fueling—in fact, *supercharging*—the mounting debt crisis. People now *routinely* spend more than they make. They want the *best* clothes, *newest* gadgets and *fanciest* cars. "Keeping up with the Joneses" and "Everyone else is doing it!" drives millions of consumers.

Jesus warned, "Beware of *covetousness*: for a man's life consists *not* in the abundance of the things which he possesses" (Luke 12:15).

Do *any* still believe this?

Governments, financial institutions and millions of citizens are *all* sliding toward bankruptcy.

The present generation is very different from those of the past. Most now live solely for pleasure, ease, comfort, gain and entertainment. Thoughts of personal responsibility and character-building have almost disappeared. Tens of millions today reflect—"I want"—"I want a lot"—and "I want it *now!*"

Foretold Long Ago

The apostle Paul foretold all that is happening: "This know also, that in the last days *perilous* [dangerous] *times* shall come. For men shall be lovers of their own selves, covetous...unthankful...lovers of pleasures more than lovers of God..." (II Tim. 3:1-2, 4).

Make no mistake. As trends and conditions degenerate, violence will ensue—and in a big way. Uprisings, riots and tumults will increase in number and severity—so will violent crime, as the increasing number of desperate people take desperate action in an attempt to save themselves—at all costs. With this, the confusion of people asking, "What do we *do?*"—"Where do we *go?*"—"Who do we *listen to?*"—will grow beyond anything ever before seen.

The cacophony of fearful uncertainty will be DEAFENING!

Back to the subject of finances. Differing opinions on *why* the personal debt crisis—and how to take control of your finances—fill newspapers, magazines, books and radio talk shows. But financial counselors offer advice that misses the crux of the problem.

With so many "experts" presenting theories (so often contrary to what *other* "experts" say), whose advice should be followed? Where can people find *real* solutions to *real* problems?

The answer to the above questions is *the Bible—God's Instruction Manual* for mankind! Just as manuals exist for how to operate complex machines, the Creator God included a Manual for the most complex creation ever made—human beings.

Cause and Effect

Only by carefully following the guidelines—the immutable LAWS—in this Manual, can humanity achieve success.

Think of the following. God has created laws to govern every aspect of His Creation. Just as the laws of *gravity* and *inertia* govern portions of it, God has ordained laws that govern all aspects of money matters. By following them, people can ensure financial security.

Most just do not understand that laws govern *every* action in life. The law of CAUSE and EFFECT—where actions *always* bring *re*actions—applies to everything.

For example, everyone understands the law of gravity. If one accidentally drops a brick on his foot, the result could be broken bones. If a skydiver jumps from an airplane, and the parachute fails to open, the result is certain death. This is easy to understand.

Here are examples of the law of *cause* and *effect* that are just as real. If a person is constantly sick, it is obvious laws of health (proper diet, enough exercise, sufficient sleep, etc.) are being broken. The *effect* of bad health has one or more *causes*. If a marriage ends in divorce, it can be attributed to one or more causes: poor communication, financial woes, death of a child, sexual problems, drug use, etc. If someone is arrested for drunk driving, it is not hard to see the *cause* of the arrest.

Most never identify "cause and effect" as a universal law governing almost every action in life. They are unaware that this is a general principle at work in the world.

Yet *every* effect can be traced to one or more causes. Unwanted or illegitimate pregnancies, crime, drug addiction, bankruptcy, and a thousand other effects, can all be linked to specific causes.

The Bible teaches, "…the curse *causeless* shall not come" (Prov. 26:2). Another translation is, "…the *baseless* curse never goes home" (Moffatt). This scripture is saying that every difficulty carries a reason—there is a cause for every effect! Most people ignore right causes—and, as a result, reap a host of bad effects.

Why can man not see this law at work when looking either at the world as a whole or at lives individually? Why has religion also ignored this important relationship between cause and effect?

There is *a hidden cause* for the conditions of the world and its inhabitants!

Choice Before You

Jesus explains what most never notice because they never pick up the Bible: "I am come that they might have *life*, and that they might have it more *abundantly*" (John 10:10).

Before entering this path, a choice must be made. Almighty God revealed this choice to ancient Israel: "I call heaven and earth to record this day against you, that I have set before you life and death, blessing and cursing: therefore CHOOSE life, that both you and your seed may live" (Deut. 30:19).

God will not force anyone to follow His ways. The choice is simple: Obeying Him leads to blessings and happiness—disobedience leads to misery and unhappiness. Like the Israelites, many refuse God's warnings. They ignore the fact that by not following His laws, bad effects *will come*. Through man's rebellion, unhappy lives result, with none having any idea *why*.

Many workers now face the fearful reality of losing their jobs. The majority of these *still* do not budget and save. As spending and standards of living have *risen*, family saving has dropped—*drastically*! The result? Millions of people are on the brink of financial disaster, only a couple paychecks from the street.

Impulsive spending is the product of a generation lacking in *strength* and CHARACTER, and is the *accelerant* bringing the mountain of debt now burying so many! Successful countries run on budgets. So do successful businesses—and successful *households*!

While consumer, corporate and national debt are now monumental, another *far greater* debt has been ignored! This one is toward God. Mankind has been stealing from Him for 6,000 years.

God declares, "The silver is Mine, and the gold is Mine" (Haggai 2:8), and "The earth is the Lord's, and the fullness thereof" (Psa. 24:1). God owns everything—so says your Bible! He designed, created and maintains all things. This sets the stage for vitally important knowledge.

Can Steal from God

Everything people take for granted as theirs really belongs to God! But He has permitted man to use *His* planet and *His* resources. He allows us to be His stewards. All will one day *give account* of how they managed what was *never* theirs. God commands that we not steal from Him.

Yet most do.

How? Notice: "Will a man rob God? Yet you have *robbed* Me. But *you* say, Wherein have we robbed You? [God's answer is] In *tithes* and *offerings*. You are cursed...for you have robbed Me, even this WHOLE NATION [the nation of Israel, referenced hundreds of times in the Bible, here referring to the modern nations descended from ancient Israel]. Bring you all the *tithes* into the storehouse...and *prove* Me now...if I will not open you the windows of heaven, and pour you out a blessing, that there shall not be room enough to receive it" (Mal. 3:8-10).

God only asks for a tithe—10 percent!—of what one makes (plus "offerings")—and lets you keep the remaining 90 percent, although that still belongs to Him! He challenges skeptics to "prove" His promise of blessing the tithepayer.

There is a Church that knows and *obeys* God's tithing laws—but also all the *other* laws and many TRUTHS in His Word. Part of the final Work of this Church is putting this book in your hands!

Again, most Western nations are staggering under *impossible* debt. There is a reason. So are millions of people. There is a *reason*. Terrible, national punishment now lies just ahead for the world's greatest nations, in part because hundreds of millions of *individuals* in them have stolen from God—every day. This is just one of a long list of these nations' sins. (I cover all of this, plus much more, in detail in my book *America and Britain in Prophecy*. It is one of the most important books you could ever read.)

The Normal Approach

God's servants do not *ever* take political positions. We saw they are called "out of the world" (John 15:19). They "do not *entangle* themselves in the affairs of *this* life" (II Tim. 2:4)—and this includes involvement in the ineffective governments of men.

Voting for *better politicians* is not going to solve what are *insoluble* problems. The national and individual financial troubles catalogued here are consequences of nations and peoples disobeying God, not of merely bad politicians or wrong government policies. Most blame government policy instead of their own human nature.

Activists' marches on the Capitol or letters to congressional representatives about today's mushrooming political, social and economic problems will be in vain. None of these efforts will stop the fulfillment of horrific prophecies. Financial collapse will come!

Naturally then, comes the question…

Are These the Last Days?

With world trends and conditions growing more frightening by the day, millions are searching—wondering about the course of events, and whether the world is on the brink of destruction.

Jesus' disciples wondered the same thing almost 2,000 years ago, and asked Him about the "end of the age" (Matt. 24:3). We saw the prophet Daniel spoke of "the time of the end" (Dan. 11:40; 12:9). The apostle Peter foretold, "There shall come in the *last days* SCOFFERS" (II Pet. 3:3). And we saw Paul warned, "In the *last days* PERILOUS TIMES shall come" (II Tim. 3:1). The last verse makes the subject more serious.

Has this final interval in world history arrived? Can you be sure? You CAN—in fact, God expects you to KNOW!

Many sense or even firmly *believe* that we are in the last days. We hear from them daily. But these have rarely sought to *prove* this. They can—and should—know whether we are. So must you.

Let's pull back and look at the big picture. It has become painfully obvious that this world is in terrible trouble. Mankind is overwhelmed with every kind of trouble, evil and ill—war, terrorism, violence of every kind, famine, disease, pollution, overpopulation, political upheaval, religious confusion and tremendous economic turmoil and decline, which we saw is threatening to make the Great Depression look like child's play. Then there are the hundreds of millions who live in abject poverty, ignorance and oppression. Now add rampant and worsening immorality and perversion in every Western nation—and growing hatred, unrest and the already-discussed never-ending cycle of war in the Middle East—and deteriorating conditions throughout Africa—and earthquakes, volcanoes and frightening weather patterns across much of the world—and devastating fires, tornadoes, hurricanes, drought and floods occurring with greater frequency and intensity—and headlines screaming of murder, rape, robbery and crimes of every kind.

These mushrooming problems now threaten all nations.

Is all of this really only a little temporary worsening of what is otherwise "business as usual" for planet Earth? Many *more*—and much *louder*!—are the voices that say no, and that time is running out to solve the really big problems facing the world. More world leaders are expressing concern about the rise of division within and between nations. So are other voices of authority in education, the military, science and sociology. Yet, because this is also an age of religious sundowners and doomsayers, most will not pay real—serious!—attention.

But some will.

Big Questions

How long until Jesus Christ returns? For those who believe He will, no question is bigger. But there are other questions, some big, that must be answered first. This chapter looks primarily at perhaps the *second* biggest question, with *later* chapters addressing more of when Christ returns and events surrounding it.

The Bible speaks of the period preceding Christ's Return as "the last days"—"the time of the end"—"the end of the age"—"the end of these things"—"the end of the days"—and of a time when the course of human history as we know it, Daniel wrote, "shall be finished" (12:7).

Of course, many professing Christians do not believe in a literal return to Earth by Jesus Christ. Of those who do, most think it could be decades away, with sometime just before 2050 having become a popular date. Others think it could be hundreds of years away. Some even believe it could be "a thousand years away." Others feel time may be short, but see no way to know.

The Apostles Misunderstood

The original apostles thought for a time that Jesus would return in their lifetimes. Paul spoke of the Resurrection of the dead at Christ's Second Coming, and (twice) used the words "*we* which are alive and remain unto the coming of the Lord" (I Thes. 4:15, 17), because he expected to still be alive when it happened. Paul later came to realize he had misunderstood the timing of specific events that must precede Christ's Return. In fact, he had to warn of those who would deceive others about when this would occur. He wrote about "the coming of our Lord Jesus Christ" and that brethren should be careful to "Let no man deceive you *by any means...*" (II Thes. 2:1, 3).

Could you be deceived?

So then, have we entered the last days? Do you and I live at the time of the end? If so, how can we be certain?

Jesus told His disciples, "I will come again" (John 14:3). Forty days later, as He was ascending to heaven, two angels underscored His words, "This same Jesus, which is taken up from you into heaven, shall so come in like manner as you have seen Him go into heaven" (Acts 1:11). Matthew 24 records more of Christ's words: "For as the lightning comes...so shall also the coming of the Son of man be" (vs. 27). Seven times just in this chapter (vs. 27, 30, 37, 39, 42, 44, 46), Jesus spoke of His Coming again, and the need to *watch* for key events, trends and conditions preceding it.

Make no mistake! The Bible is plain about the Return of Jesus Christ. Many verses speak of His Second Coming to Earth. It will happen—and it does not hinge on the opinions of men. However, in the period leading to this climactic event, many other things are foretold to happen—some, in fact many of them, catastrophic!

The idea of the end of the world has been a subject of speculation, discussion, ridicule, fascination and fancy for almost 2,000 years. Of course, most do not realize how much the Bible shows can be known about this time.

Is the world nearing Christ's Return—are these the end times? Again, can we know?

In Matthew 24, when the disciples asked Christ to tell them "when shall these things be? And what shall be the SIGN of Your coming?" (vs. 3), we saw He answered, "But of that day and hour knows no man, no, not the angels of heaven but My Father only" (vs. 36).

Does this mean we cannot know the *general time* of Jesus' Second Coming?—and then also about the last days before it? Many think this—and therefore shrug off any need to be concerned with either.

Then what do verses 50-51 mean? "The lord of that servant shall come in a day when he *looks not for him*, and in an hour that he is not aware of, and shall cut him asunder, and appoint him his portion with the hypocrites." Most will simply not be looking for Jesus' Return at the right time. Worse, many will not be looking at all. But His indictment shows they will have no excuse.

Why will so many be unable to recognize the onset of such an awesome, whole-world-altering event?

In verses 32-33, Jesus gave a parable: "Now learn a parable of the fig tree; when his branch is yet tender, and puts forth leaves, you know that summer is near: so likewise you, when you shall see all these things, *know* that [He] is near, even *at the doors.*" Since this could only apply to those alive at the end, Jesus is stating that *we*—"YOU"—can *know* the "season" of His Return, or when He is "at the doors."

Do not be willing to settle for less than what the Bible reveals!

"Signs of the Times"

Years ago, a catchy tune called "A Sign of the Times" became popular. You may remember it. The title actually came from another verse here in Matthew. Religious leaders had confronted Jesus, desiring a "sign." He called them hypocrites, adding, "You can discern the face of the sky; but can you not discern the signs of the times?" (16:3).

While the intent of their question was to get a sign that Jesus was the Messiah (read Matthew 12:38-40), His point was that they were unable to discern events they were witnessing all around them—or the "signs of the times"—and in their case, the signs of *their* times regarding Jesus' *First* Coming!

Will you discern the signs of *our* times?

Jesus told His disciples, "And when *these things* begin to come to pass [He had just carefully listed them], then look up, and lift up your heads; for your redemption draws *near*" (Luke 21:28). The "these things" He referred to include a whole series of events prophesied to occur for the first time in history! What He spoke of is happening—and intensifying—*now*!

A closer look helps to see the "signs of the times."

First remember this. The apostle John recorded the words of Christ that open the book of Revelation (remember also that this book is *Christ's revealing* of things to come, not John's): "The Revelation of Jesus Christ...to *show* unto His servants things which must *shortly* come to pass...blessed is he that reads [you have to pick up your Bible to do this], and they that hear the words of this prophecy, and keep those things which are written therein: *for the time is at hand*" (1:1-3). At its end, the book repeats *"for the time is at hand"* (22:10).

Two thousand years later, how much more—today!—has the time for understanding colossal prophecies come! You CAN comprehend the message they bring.

But time is short.

God has allotted man 6,000 years to try his own governments, philosophies, religions, attempts at world peace, values and forms of education. But humanly devised ideas do not and can never solve the world's truly big problems. They always fail in the end. And, in the last 200 years or so, the world has changed dramatically—and rapidly. Events are speeding up in a way that has never been seen before! The 6,000 years are almost up.

The Twenty-first Century World

Everyone is familiar with sign-carrying kooks on street corners saying, "Repent! The end is near!" Hollywood has depicted many. For the most part, such people are not taken seriously. But times have changed, and, I repeat, now many are the voices of reason who report, for those who will listen, that something is terribly wrong! And again, this has caused the idea of *one world government*, designed to save the planet and mankind from itself, to be heard more often. I recently read an article calling for this. However, no one seems to know how to create such a government and then acquire the cooperation of everyone necessary to make it succeed!

Look all around. What do you see?

As a whole, the world was a much more stable place until the early nineteenth century. At that time, the Industrial Revolution gave birth to the Modern Age. It was not until about a century ago that men began to drive cars and fly, and civilization went from the Modern Age to the "Nuclear Age" on to the "Space Age" and then to the "Information Age" in just a little more than a half century.

The arrival of new inventions, at the fastest rate in history, is changing life daily. Just think of the impact of the printing press and you can appreciate how dramatically a single invention can change the world. Computers have done the same—and there is no turning back from the huge impact, good and bad, of just this one invention. Remember, jet travel only arrived in the last half century.

Although estimates vary, it is believed that mankind's total fund of knowledge is doubling every few years. Some think this could soon accelerate to every six months!

In the early 1970s, a book appeared titled *Future Shock*. Written by Alvin Toffler, it described a certain psychological stunning or shock effect on minds due to the high speed of changes in society. The author demonstrated that these changes began in the 1970s at such a rate that people could no longer properly process them. Society as a whole began to go into what was described as mental overload—or "shock"—explained as the "future" slamming into the present so fast that people were "short-circuiting" in a way never seen before. Some time after, a sequel described the advancement of this condition.

The picture presented was not good, and has only gotten worse!

Yet, with all man's supposed "advancement," his problems have never seemed greater or more insoluble!

The projections of the HIV/AIDS epidemic are constantly being revised to reflect an outlook far more alarming than previously thought. Entire sections of Africa's population are forecast to be wiped out in a few years by this single, awful disease.

Earth's population of almost 7 billion people is rising consistently at 1.2 percent each year. This means it would reach over 11 billion by 2050—if time were to permit, and it will not come close! This rise is despite the fact that disease and starvation are worst in the fastest growing parts of the world! High fertility rates in these less-developed countries have been bringing these increases right on schedule.

End-time Prophecies

Let's look at some passages that describe crucial, end-time prophecies!

We explained that the apostle Paul came to realize he did not live in the age when Christ would return. However, God did use him to record what conditions would be like when that time finally came. Consider this now expanded excerpt detailing the widespread degeneration of attitudes and character, just before Christ's Return: "This know also [many more *are* coming to know this], that in the *last days* PERILOUS TIMES shall come. For men shall be lovers of their own selves, covetous, boasters, proud, blasphemers, disobedient to parents, unthankful, unholy, without natural affection [just ponder fast-changing marital laws], trucebreakers, false accusers, incontinent, fierce, despisers of those that are good, traitors, heady, highminded, lovers of pleasures more than lovers of God"—so true, but strangely at the same time—"having a form of godliness but denying the power thereof: from such turn away" (II Tim. 3:1-6).

This is a graphic picture. It describes a *complete* breakdown of character in "the last days." This time has come!—and these conditions are rapidly growing worse! Again, look around. People's conduct is changing—seemingly always for the worse. More authority figures are sounding the alarm that human nature is running wild—and conditions are exploding out of control!

No thinking person could any longer disagree.

The degeneration of people's attitudes and behavior is stark when compared to only a generation ago. There have always been acts of violence, but now they occur more often, and are more depraved. There have always been liars, but now deceit is more pervasive. There has always been adultery, but the percentage of people who commit it is now epidemic, and close to pandemic. There has always been divorce, but today it is much more common. There have always been disrespectful young people, but soon an entire generation will have forgotten the Fifth Commandment, "Honor your father and mother." There have always been thievery and fraud, but statistics show these have never been worse—even in the most affluent countries, where people have a lot, but want more.

Much more could be said of each term used in Paul's prophecy. And we have not discussed pornography, child abuse, crime and trends in perverted sex, drug abuse, hatred, war and others! All these conditions have combined to create an age correctly described as "perilous"—or dangerous!

They become another powerful indicator that these *are* the last days!

Christ's Greatest Prophecy

Christ's disciples originally believed that His Return would occur in their lifetime. This is because they misunderstood Him and tied it to the destruction of the Temple in Jerusalem. While the Temple was destroyed by the Romans in AD 69-70, Jesus knew that His Second Coming would be almost 20 centuries later.

Jesus foretold certain other, much later events would precede it. He also described the breakdown of character. He warned that conditions would mirror "the days of Noah," which Genesis 6 describes this way: "The earth also was *corrupt* before God, and the earth was *filled with violence*. And God looked upon the earth, and, behold, it was *corrupt*; for *all* flesh had *corrupted* his way upon the earth" (vs. 11-12).

Corruption is mentioned three times in this one short passage. But this description is at the same time highly specific and speaks of men as having *individually* and *collectively* degenerated into absolute corruption—with civilization "filled with violence." God uses both the collective "all" and the singular "his" to drive this point home!

Again, the long age of man's rule is nearing an end. The total collapse of principles, values, morals, character, ethics, integrity and respect for all law and authority will soon come together and strike the entire world in a terrible and final way!

Consider how often acts of mass violence now occur in schools, campuses, restaurants, malls and workplaces in ways unheard of until recently! The terms "serial snipers" and "suicide bombers" were unknown 15 years ago. And the relatively new phenomenon of terrorism has become global in nature.

Sodom and Gomorrah

Jesus also compared conditions before His Return to those in Sodom and Gomorrah. He leads in with Noah's time again: "...As it was in the days of Noah, so shall it be also in the days of the Son of man. They did eat, they drank, they married wives, they were given in marriage [society looked like it would continue on], until the day that Noah entered into the ark, and the flood came, and *destroyed them all*. Likewise also as it was in the days of Lot; they did eat, they drank, they bought, they sold, they planted, they builded [again, society looked as if it would continue right along]; but the same day that Lot went out of Sodom it rained fire and brimstone from heaven, and *destroyed them all*" (Luke 17:26-29).

Genesis 18 and 19 show that these two cities were so rotten—so evil—that, just before God incinerated them, only four people were deemed worthy to escape: Lot, his two daughters and wife, who looked back and turned to salt. Only eight people were allowed to enter the Ark before God flooded the world.

Ask: How much longer before conditions cannot grow worse?

An aside at this point that has much to do with whether you will believe Christ: Many have been told that the early chapters of Genesis do not describe real people and real events. This is to accommodate the nonsensical fiction of evolution in place of a literal Adam and Eve. But had you realized Jesus said that Noah, the ark and The Flood existed?—and that so did Sodom and Gomorrah, including their destruction?

Those who dismiss these and related Genesis accounts seem unaware that *Jesus Christ* validated this first book of the Bible. They also forget—or willingly ignore—Jesus' (and also the apostle Paul's) references to

Adam, and how this validates the Creation account. (Most simply do not know that, while *man* has been here for only 6,000 years, the earth has existed for many billions of years—and the key to this is understanding what happened between Genesis 1:1 and the very next verse 2. But this lies outside prophecy, the subject of this book.)

We are left to ask: How many will believe and act on Christ's warning about oncoming events—when He compared these future events to Bible parallels that most do not accept as true—as having ever happened?

Scoffers at the End

This chapter opened with a reference to "scoffers" in the last days. Let's now read the whole passage containing it before continuing to read through a warning for us today. Notice: "Knowing this first, that there shall come in the last days *scoffers*, walking after *their own lusts*" (II Pet. 3:3)—people choosing and following the course of human nature, as in Sodom and Gomorrah, and Noah's time.

Now verse 4, "And saying, Where is the promise of His coming? [This is not saying they do not know which book it is—the Bible—that talks about Christ's Return. Rather, they are thinking "it will never happen" because they do not yet see it being fulfilled.] For since the fathers [Abraham, Isaac and Jacob] fell asleep, all things *continue as they were* from the beginning of the creation." This describes people who are unwilling to believe that serious times—the last days!—could actually come, never mind in their own lifetime. They choose to dismiss obviously worsening conditions and trends, declaring that these things "continue as they were from the beginning."

God declares in verse 5, "For this they *willingly* are *ignorant...*"—this speaks for itself!

And verse 6: "Whereby the world that then was, being overflowed with water, perished." Remember, Jesus supported the Noachian account and signified its warning for us.

So did Peter.

Now see this in verse 9: "The Lord is not slack concerning His promise...but is longsuffering to us-ward [patiently waiting, because He is] not willing that any should perish, but that ALL should come to repentance."

Sadly, of course, most will not do this.

Next comes a stark warning to those who are *not* looking at what is happening all around them: "But the day of the Lord [the time of His

wrath upon a sin-sick world] will come as a thief in the night..." followed
by "Seeing then...what manner of persons ought you to be in all holy
[conduct] and godliness," and "Looking for and hasting unto the coming
of the day of God," and also "...Seeing that you *look for* such things, be
diligent that you may be found of Him [God] in peace, without spot, and
blameless" (vs. 10-12, 14).

Finally, the very personal verse 17: "*You* therefore...seeing *you* KNOW
these things before[hand], beware lest *you* also, being led away with the
error of the wicked [scoffers and ungodly people walking in their lusts all
around you], fall from *your own* steadfastness."

Now a caution: be careful you are neither among the pooh-pooh-
ing, unbelieving scoffers—nor of those who will not seek and obey God
while there is still time.

The Bible promises that those who are faithful and obedient will be
protected through the worst calamities that could fall upon an unsuspecting world. While the last days certainly are perilous—*dangerous*—this
is just the run-up period prior to the *infinitely worse* final three and a half
years to follow before the good news of the gospel is fulfilled in Christ's
Coming.

But there is more to know about whether we have reached this time.
This chapter's title question now comes into sharper focus...

Is the End Near?

The question of whether we are in the last days has within it a related, but somewhat different, question—and it towers over that of *when* the Bible's greatest prophecies will be fulfilled. It is summarized in the chapter's title—have we possibly even reached the period near the *close* of the last days—is *the end* of the last days near? In other words, is there now almost no time left in the 6,000 years allotted to mankind to rule its own affairs?

We have already discussed character breakdown, the warnings of Christ and other "signs of the times." We also briefly examined the last 200 years and how a series of societal changes, generally thought to be advancements, bringing civilization to the Industrial Revolution, and subsequently the Modern Age, the Space Age, and lastly the Information Age—culminated in the FINAL AGE—the perilous LAST DAYS before the glorious Return of Jesus Christ.

This rapid progression of a changing civilization laid the foundation for the time of the end. Remember, the disciples' question to Christ was about what would *precede* His Return and the end of the age.

Religious Deception

Now we ask: What about religious confusion at the end? Jesus warned more than once about future great deception: "Take heed that no man deceive you. For many shall come in My name, saying, I [Jesus] am

Christ; and shall deceive many" (Matt. 24:4-5). In other words, many would claim to represent Jesus, and would acknowledge that He was indeed the Christ, but bring a message that deceives their listeners. The confused, competing, disagreeing and multiplying groups within professing Christianity today confirm Jesus' words.

Jesus' warning is critical. Modern preachers all stress the *Person* of Jesus Christ, instead of His Message! They focus on the Messenger not His Message! Saying Christ was, in fact, the Christ—the Messiah—is a true statement! The deception starts when His message of a coming world-ruling kingdom—with all that this means—is ignored, and even suppressed.

Herein lies the greatest deception! Understand this!

False Gospel Proclaimed

Jesus proclaimed the gospel of the kingdom of God. Here are His first recorded words: "Jesus came into Galilee, preaching the gospel of the *kingdom of God*, and saying...the kingdom of God *is at hand* [Christ was there representing it]: repent you, and believe the gospel" (Mark 1:14-15). Many verses show Jesus consistently preached this message.

Within 30 years of Jesus' crucifixion, Paul warned of those who were already perverting Christ's gospel with a counterfeit message. This understanding was so central that he pronounced a double curse on any who did this (Gal. 1:6-9). He also warned, "But I fear, lest by any means, as the serpent beguiled Eve through his subtlety, so your minds should be corrupted from the simplicity that is in Christ. For if he that comes preaches another Jesus, whom we have not preached, or if you receive another spirit, which you have not received, or another gospel, which you have not accepted, you might well bear with him" (II Cor. 11:3-4).

Preachers misrepresent Christ by bringing what is "another Jesus," "another spirit" and "another gospel," other than the kingdom of God.

The power of deception is very real. This includes those who specialize today in confusing, incomplete hodgepodges of prophetic theories about how the last days will play out. We saw the utter nonsense of these conflicting "experts" and prognosticators, like Nostradamus and other supposed prophets and prophecy fiction writers, is without end.

In Matthew 24:14, Christ foretold, "This gospel of the kingdom"—the TRUE gospel!—"shall be preached in all the world for a witness unto all nations [this describes a huge, worldwide effort, and just before the end]; and then shall the end come."

Christ's prophecy is still true! Its fulfillment having begun in 1934, The Restored Church of God continues this commission for a few more years. (More on this later.)

Wars, Famines, Pestilences and Earthquakes

The previous two subheads and this one involve five subjects (four of which are the horsemen of Revelation) that are so large and important that each commands its own later extensive chapter. But it is necessary to very briefly cover them here in the context of whether the *end* of the last days is near.

The most *cursory* look—our purpose at this point—reveals that this world is not led by God. Just the world's biggest problems prove this. After Christ warned of the danger of false Christianity, His warning continued, "And you shall hear of *wars* and rumors of wars...and there shall be *famines*, and *pestilences* and *earthquakes*, in divers [various] places," but then explaining that "all these are [just] the *beginning* of sorrows" (Matt. 24:6-8).

Who can doubt these things have come to pass in a greater way? For instance, how often do we now hear of devastating earthquakes? A well-known television commentator stated that "for some reason" there are now more earthquakes occurring every day. Seismologists record 12,000 separate, measurable earthquakes annually. 88,000 died in them just in 2009.

New, serious outbreaks of old diseases—some now antibiotic-resistant—are reported more frequently. These include the HIV epidemic, cholera, typhoid, dengue fever, flesh-eating bacteria, Legionnaire's disease, the Ebola and West Nile viruses, malaria, the return of stronger, more resistant strains of tuberculosis and diphtheria, and an explosion of sexually transmitted diseases. Whooping cough is again on the rise. These are but a small part of an immense, constantly emerging picture of frightening new diseases—and old ones returning with a vengeance!

Consider one illustration. Over 10,000 die from lung disease every year just in Hong Kong—just due to pollution. But *1.28 million* die in China—one country!—each year!—just due to *lung-related* diseases.

About 24,000 people on Earth now starve to death every day—with this number steadily rising! Think. I live in a city of just about 24,000. This means a medium-sized city disappears from the face of the earth every 24 hours!

Wars, and what the gospel writer Luke called "commotions," including acts of terror and protracted riots in more places, fill headlines—

bringing more suffering and death. Greater disease and starvation are merely natural byproducts of the population displacement and confusion that always follow in the wake of armed conflict.

In recent years, scientists have warned of climate change. Few any longer doubt that more extreme weather has arrived on the front edge of a worldwide phenomenon, whatever the cause. Storms are more severe, and more often. Abnormal flooding and devastation of the land are contributing to famines and disease epidemics in unheard of proportions. Weather catastrophes, earthquakes, wars and resulting disease and hopelessness tend to exacerbate what is already an epidemic of suffering.

The Bible also foretells more volcanic activity—and this is happening!

God Must Intervene

The world needs God's Law, which, if kept by all nations, would bring universal peace, happiness, abundance and prosperity!

Cities *could* become beautiful. Disease, famine and war *could* disappear, as *could* racism, ignorance, poverty and all false religion. Yet, no man, no government, nor all the governments of men put together can bring these things!

Only God's kingdom can, led by Christ and the saints who have qualified to join Him. The world must learn about the laws of God. Both Isaiah 2:2-4 and Micah 4:1-4 also speak of the "last days," when this will happen. God's Law universally obeyed and His love are prophesied to replace the lawlessness and hate between people and nations today!

God has to intervene! You saw Christ explain, "Except those days should be shortened [cut short], there should no flesh be saved [alive]: but for the elect's sake those days shall be shortened" (Matt. 24:22)!

Think! When has mankind held the capability to destroy all human beings? Only with the advent of nuclear, chemical, biological and now "radiological" weapons could this be possible. We live when all of these are available—and nuclear weapons alone possess the capability, with the stockpiles that currently exist, to wipe out all mankind many times over! As one leader said, "Once would be quite enough."

Some assert that these weapons are too terrible to ever be used—that they exist only as a "deterrent" against their use.

Do not be fooled! They *will* be used. Many prophecies make this clear. Remember, the moment these weapons became available, and the United States felt it in its interest to use them, President Truman ordered bombs be dropped in August 1945—and without hesitation! Yet, the two bombs that landed on Japan were little more than "firecrackers" compared to what exists today.

It is no coincidence that the true gospel began being preached around the world at the time weapons of mass destruction became available— proving correct the timing of Christ's prophecy about danger to the survival of all humanity!

All of what you have seen shows that we are *now* in the very last of the last days—the end of man's rule *is* near.

Daniel Revisited

There is an element of Daniel's long prophecy that must be brought out here—and it is absolutely crucial. The first reference in Daniel's book to "the time of the end" is in chapter 8, verse 17. Later, in chapter 11, verse 40, and six times in chapter 12 alone, the word "end" is used.

Now get this! Daniel was not permitted by God to understand what he recorded. Recall God told him that his prophecy was *sealed* until the end of the age—and it would only then be *unsealed*. This has happened— and Daniel's prophecy has now been opened to understanding.

Next, in 12:10 it states, "the *wise* shall understand," but "none of the *wicked* shall understand." This means some—a relative few—will comprehend events around them—step by step by step! They WILL be able to understand *what* happens *when*, as well as *where* and to *whom*. And they will understand *why*.

Daniel 12:4 gives two more vital clues to knowing when the end time has arrived: "the time of the end: many shall *run to and fro*, and *knowledge shall be increased*."

We have already discussed the astonishing knowledge explosion brought about just by the arrival of computers (and cellphones) in scores of millions of homes. Great numbers now have access to vast amounts of knowledge—instantaneously! What can be quickly known by anyone seeking information is staggering! Surely we have arrived at the time when "knowledge shall be increased"—along with its easy access!

What about "many shall run to and fro"? The arrival of railroads in the middle of the nineteenth century—then great ships driven by powerful engines to move them ever faster across oceans—followed by automobiles—and finally, passenger jets, made our planet universally accessible, and quickly. Jets turned the Atlantic Ocean into little more than a large lake.

Earth seemingly grew much smaller because of its inhabitants' ability to "run to and fro" almost anywhere at any time!

Four Prophesied Kingdoms

Daniel addresses other great prophecies. The second chapter contains another unusually long prophecy spanning over 2,500 years, concluding with Christ's Second Coming. It pictures a giant man consisting of four metals (gold, silver, brass, and iron mixed with clay), which represent four succeeding world-ruling kingdoms that began in Daniel's time and culminate with a final revival of the Holy Roman Empire.

This will be the final Beast of Revelation 17 that will come upon an unsuspecting world with stunning speed and force. With the collapse of the Iron Curtain and the reunification of Germany, the last resurrection, consisting of countries and kingdoms throughout Eastern and Western Europe, will be a kind of United States of Europe.

This chapter has brought light on subjects you have almost certainly not even heard referenced, never mind explained.

Fifty Bibles are sold every minute worldwide. This translates to over 26 million each year. How many believe and act on its contents? All *convicted* Bible readers should by now be sobered and motivated to want to carefully study all the events we have discussed—and we are only beginning. All others, including less convicted Bible students, will soon wish they had brought a more serious approach to the greatest events in all human history.

How Scoffers Think

Today's world is truly filled with "scoffers." They do not believe God will intervene—or that this is even necessary! Most believe man is capable at the last minute of "snatching victory from the jaws of defeat," and will save himself by solving his own problems! They think "everything will turn out all right—somehow!" And "Everything may look bad now, but it will get better because it always does."

Though wrong in the short term, this is ultimately *correct*—but by means they have not anticipated!

Scoffing at the thought that Jesus Christ is returning, people choose to live rotten, sinful lives, following "their own lusts." But dismissing them as irrelevant will not change the truth of God's prophecies! Men must learn bitter lessons—that they have utterly failed to bring the conditions everyone longs for—that peace, happiness, prosperity and abundance will remain elusive despite humanity's best efforts to find them.

Armies "trying to make the world safe for democracy," humanitarian efforts, missionaries, "think tanks," new scientific laborsaving devices, computers, cellphones, better school systems, fundraising efforts to eradicate deadly diseases, etc., will all fail—because humanity will not humble itself and seek the God who *does* have solutions—all of them!—to man's greatest troubles!

But, when it is almost too late, the living Christ will intervene in power and glory to save man from himself!

What About You?

Daniel also foretold: "At that time...there shall be a time of *trouble*, such as never was since there was a nation..." (Dan. 12:1). Paralleling Christ's own words in Matthew 24, this is serious. In fact, one could scarcely imagine a passage in the Bible that could be more serious!

Admit now that you are the "captain of your own ship"—the "master of your own destiny." It is YOUR CHOICE to reject God's warning or to yield yourself to Him and ask Him to prepare you for rulership in His kingdom!

More than reading a book, you are being WARNED. You now know the last days *are here*. Will you prepare yourself for what lies ahead?

If you do not intend to *act* on what you are learning, put the book down now, for it contains a great deal more knowledge for which you will be held accountable. You are better off to join the "willingly ignorant" scoffers in the "bliss" of not knowing the shocking details of the long, violent storm just ahead.

A formal inset statement is vital here. Many write or call our World Headquarters to thank us for what they call the "service" we are performing—for "boldly" or "courageously," they often add, "educating" or "informing" the public about matters others will not address. Of course, we appreciate such gratitude. But *The Real Truth* magazine, *The World to Come* broadcast and our vast library of literature, including this volume, are *infinitely more* than a mere "service" or attempt to "inform."

Just knowing about the last days means nothing. There is a warning attached to this subject. Here is what God said in Ezekiel (twice) to one who would be alive at the end of the age: "I have made *you* a WATCHMAN unto the house of Israel [again, my book *America and Britain in Prophecy* explains in detail who is the house of Israel]: therefore hear the word at My mouth, and give them WARNING FROM ME" (3:17; 33:7)—meaning, this is from *God*, not any human.

The meaning of the Hebrew word translated "watchman" is instructive. It is *tsaphah*, and means "to lean forward," "to peer into the distance; by implication to *observe*, await: - behold, espy, look up (well), wait for, (keep the) watch (-man)." It is of interest that *espy* means "to catch sight of (something distant, partially hidden, or obscure); glimpse."

This definition describes a responsibility that involves scrutiny—the term "to lean forward" paints a picture of one taking a very serious look at what lies ahead "in the distance." He is one intently interested in "catching sight of" what is apparently obscured to the view of most or all others.

Just before His crucifixion, Jesus told His disciples, "Verily, verily, I say unto you, He that receives whomsoever *I send* receives Me; and he that receives Me receives Him [the Father] that sent Me" (John 13:20).

Another verse amplifies this point, making absolutely crystal clear just how important this principle is to God. It is found in Matthew 10: "He that receives you [God's representatives] receives Me, and he that receives Me receives Him that sent Me" (vs. 40). This is almost identical to John 13:20.

To receive those whom God sends is to receive both Christ and the Father. Conversely—and obviously—to *reject* or *ignore* those Christ has sent is to reject or ignore Christ and the Father!

God would not send someone without ensuring we could *know* that he came from God. If God sends a man, He would obviously want it *known*. He would make it PLAIN!

Understand. Someone, somewhere—yes, *someone, somewhere!*—had to be raised up to fulfill Ezekiel 33. God does not speak audibly from the heavens, but rather through His human servants. But make no mistake. The warning is not from the servant, it is from GOD!

No one else is saying these things.

Similarly, Jesus Christ—not the apostle John, who merely recorded His words—*revealed* to His servants an entire book of prophecy...

Revelation Unveiled!

Monumental events will soon shock the entire world! Great prophecies in the book of Revelation—in fact, the greatest in all the Bible—show *how* and *when* these catastrophic events will occur.

In this chapter comes understanding that will completely change
your outlook on the *near* future. But you must have the KEYS that *unlock*
it! And you must examine every scripture quoted—along with the *entirety* of Revelation. This stunning book of prophecy is opened, revealed
and explained—*at last*!

Many think they understand prophecy—and this is possibly most true
of at least some parts of the book of Revelation. Yet the most common
human interpretations of this book, at best, border on ludicrous. Usually,
a very little truth is mixed with much error! They are almost unbearable
to read—yet major magazines report that great numbers do believe these
dangerous, counterfeit scenarios.

World trouble will soon greatly increase—intensifying to staggering
proportions. This will be followed by unexpected and cataclysmic events
that will *shake* the WHOLE WORLD!

But God has not left mankind without a SOURCE of answers that reveals in detail what lies ahead. Tragically, believing things will eventually "work themselves out," many take the ostrich approach and bury
their heads in the sand, choosing to pursue pleasure and the accumulation
of material goods. But world conditions will become much more serious
than most realize.

God understands human nature and where it always leads when left to its own devices. This allows Him to know, and to *guide*, the awesome future events that will occur from now on!

We saw it has become God's time to REVEAL what lies ahead. The stage is set and He has lifted the curtain on the future. Revelation describes terrible plagues and truly earth-shattering events!

Mystery Book

Signs, seals, symbols, Satan, vials, visions, images, trumpets, thrones, plagues, angels, demons, destruction, beasts, heads, horns, women, witnesses, woes, wars, judgment, numbers, multitudes, messages and *mystery*! Revelation contains all of these terms. But what do they *mean*?

As we discussed from Isaiah in Chapter One, most believe the book of Revelation is sealed, *closed* from understanding. It is called a MYSTERY BOOK *without meaning*. Yet it is an entire book of important—vital—MEANING. It is filled with answers. The above terms *can* be unlocked! They *can* be understood—and the next two eye-opening chapters contain the necessary KEYS!

You will be fascinated by the clarity of what can be *known* from Revelation. You can *know* that events are building to an unanticipated EXPLOSION!

Almost half the books of the Old Testament are included in the so-called "major" prophets (Isaiah, Jeremiah, Ezekiel) or "minor" prophets (Hosea, Joel, Amos, Jonah, Micah, etc.).

Paul explained that the New Testament Church was "...built on the foundation of the apostles *and prophets*" (Eph. 2:20). Recognize that, since the Church *stands* on the words of the prophets, Christians are expected to understand prophecy. Because God *commands* men to "live by EVERY WORD of God" (Matt. 4:4; Luke 4:4; Deut. 8:3), He would not *exclude* the full third that is prophecy!

We read that Daniel spoke of a time and of events "*the wise shall understand*" (12:10). Jesus directly paraphrased Daniel in the Olivet prophecy, where He answered the disciples' question about the sequence of events to occur at "the end of the age." He reinforced Daniel's statements about those events by saying, "Whoso reads, let him UNDERSTAND" (Matt. 24:15).

What are the wise to understand? Important KEYS exist, which OPEN UP Bible prophecies, but the world knows nothing of them! No wonder so many claim that the meaning of Revelation cannot be explained. How *could* they understand without the KEYS?

Imagine. Forty-two percent of Americans actually believe that they can consult *the dead* about matters involving the future. But mankind refuses to seek and consult *GOD*! Only *He* can reveal the future. Men cannot, through intelligence, human reasoning or scientific discovery, know or discern events to come. And many "religious" people believe the book of Revelation offers no help anyway, because it cannot be understood.

Revelation Means a Revealing

God reveals a basic *framework* for understanding future events. This framework is primarily laid out in Daniel and Revelation. Daniel, recorded over 600 years earlier, sets the stage for the larger and more detailed book of Revelation, which describes events found nowhere else in the Bible.

The Greek word *apocalypse* is translated "revelation." A fuller look at this English word starts with to *reveal*—not *conceal, hide, veil* or *close up*. The actual definition of *revelation* is: "The act of revealing or disclosing; something revealed, especially a dramatic disclosure of something not previously known or realized" (*American Heritage Dictionary*).

We saw that Revelation closes with, "*Seal not* the sayings of the prophecy of this book: for the *time is at hand*" (22:10). Comprehend John's words. The time for understanding Revelation IS now at hand!

We will see that this awesome revelation of future events was sealed with seven separate seals. It is crucial to understand another KEY point: *The seven seals in God's hand essentially span all but the last two chapters of the book!* The seven seals are opened one by one, in sequence. Each reveals future events before they happen. Only Christ is qualified to remove the seven seals and *open* the book to understanding.

Revelation outlines a long *series* of events that relate to one another in a continuous *flow*—comprising an entire *story*. These occur in order of time sequence. (This chapter contains two overview graphs—an *outline* and a *story flow*—to which the reader may occasionally refer.) Also, Christ periodically insets certain events into the course of the Revelation. You now understand the first KEY to unlock the book!

Grasp this central, all-important point. While there are *keys* to understanding Revelation, the book itself is the single greatest key to understanding almost all *other* prophecies in the Bible!

An important point must be made. Many subjects in the book of Revelation that will be covered only briefly in the next two chapters command their own full chapter. Remember that the Table of Contents tells the reader which of these subjects reappear in greater detail.

The Signs of Christ's Coming Parallel the Seven Seals

The basic rule of Bible study, that the Bible always interprets itself, is probably never truer than in the book of Revelation. This will be done as we progress through the opening of the seven seals.

Since John sees many *symbols*, we need to be able to understand the *actual events* that they *represent*. Otherwise, we will not know what is being described. How do we do this?

Mark 4:10-12 and Matthew 13:10-15 hold another KEY to understanding *how* Jesus teaches. In both places, He explained that He spoke in parables so that His servants *would* understand Him—*but all others would not*! Carefully read this: "And when He was *alone*, they that were about Him with the twelve asked of Him the parable [Jesus had just told the parable of the sower]. And He said unto them, Unto YOU it is given to know the mystery of the kingdom of God: but unto them that are without, all these things are done in parables: that seeing they may see, and *not perceive*; and hearing they may hear, and *not understand*; lest at any time they should be converted, and their sins should be forgiven them" (Mark 4:10-12).

Note exactly what Jesus said! *Only* His servants can understand His real meaning. Others might *think* they do—but they cannot!

Jesus never leaves His servants in the dark about matters He wants them to understand. But He does record them in ways that keep them hidden from the view of all others. This will help you see why so *few* understand a book that has been read by so *many*. Others may—and many do—sincerely seek to understand the many truths of Bible prophecy, but they are wasting their time. So says Christ.

Jesus explained, in *plain, clear language*, the key events of the last days preceding and leading to the time of His Second Coming. Central to your thinking and understanding is Jesus answering the disciples' question, "...*when* shall these things be? And *what* shall be the *sign* of Your coming, and of the *end* of the [age]?" (Matt. 24:3; Luke 21:7).

We must briefly examine the critical Matthew 24 for vital CLUES, which explain the *symbols* that we will study in Revelation. Jesus gave a list of six different events that are to happen before His Second Coming. They precisely *parallel* what we will read beginning in Revelation 6.

First—false prophets and false christs (vs. 5). *Second*—wars (vs. 6) throughout the age, culminating in the end time with *world war* (vs. 7). *Third*—famines (vs. 7). *Fourth*—pestilences (vs. 7). It is at this point that Christ inserted a reference to the destruction of Jerusalem, in AD 70, because this was a forerunner, or TYPE, of the yet future siege of Jerusalem and final "battle of Armageddon" (review Matthew 24:17-28 with Luke 17:30-37). Therefore, Matthew 24:9-28 (also Luke 21:12-24) applies to the period of AD 70—*but only as a forerunning type of the final time of the end* to which His warning refers LITERALLY!

Fifth, in Matthew 24:21-22, Jesus explains that the Great Tribulation occurs. *Sixth* are the heavenly signs (vs. 29)—when the stars fall and the sun and moon are darkened. The *sign* of Christ's coming (vs. 30) occurs at this same time. His *actual* coming is right on the heels of it.

We will now examine Revelation, chapter by chapter.

Chapter 1: Christ the Revelator and the Book's Theme

Understanding who is the true *author* of the Revelation—as well as the critically important *theme*, the centerpiece of the book—is vital. Without these two keys, many have bogged down either into arguments about whether "the Lord's Day" (vs. 10) is a reference to Sunday—or whether John, instead of Christ, authored the book.

Why does almost everyone refer to this book as "The Revelation of St. John the Divine"? Nowhere does it refer to John as either divine or the Revelator.

Notice again: "*The Revelation of Jesus Christ*, which GOD GAVE unto HIM…and He sent and signified it by His angel unto His servant John: *who bare record* of the word of God, and *of the testimony of Jesus Christ*, and of all things that he saw" (vs. 1-2).

The book of Revelation contains *Jesus Christ's* words, as the Revelator, not *John's*. John was merely a scribe—a secretary taking dictation. Sadly, modern commentators love to picture John as a deranged old man in exile on an island where he dreamed up lunatic visions that cannot be understood. These accusers do not realize that they are actually attacking *Jesus Christ!*—the book's true Author.

Anyone who will even quickly examine the above passage will plainly see that the Revelation originated with God (the Father), who gave it to Christ. Christ sent and signified the Revelation by His angel, who then gave it to John, "Who bare record of the word of God, and of the testimony of Jesus Christ, and of all things that he saw" (vs. 2). John merely *recorded* these events, preserving them for the servants of Jesus Christ—His end-time Church.

As soon as the book was copied and canonized (circa AD 100), the founders of the developing universal church at Rome denied its origin. The highly authoritative and famous 11th edition of *Encyclopaedia Britannica* states, "Instead of this [Rev. 1:1] the Church substituted the name of the disciple through whom the message was delivered for that of his Master, and designated our Apocalypse 'The Apocalypse of John.' This title was familiar before the end of the 2nd century" (vol. 23, p. 212).

If the world's best minds cannot even discern the book's correct *title*—and *Author*—how could they possibly discern its MESSAGE?

Jesus Christ used John to "bare record of" (vs. 2)—write down—what He was revealing. In short, John wrote three things: (1) The word of God, (2) the direct testimony (words) of Christ, and (3) what he saw in vision.

With this background, you now understand the introduction to the book.

The Theme

Most *reputable* scholars generally agree, and admit, that the term "the Lord's Day" is, in fact, a reference to God's coming day of reckoning, or judgment upon the world—THE DAY OF THE LORD!

Yet almost no one else understands this. Without this central point correct in one's thinking, the entire book will make no sense. Reading Revelation becomes a fruitless exercise.

Now notice verse 10. It actually reveals the central focus or theme of the whole book. Understand that John lived 1,900 years ago—long before the events of this book were to be fulfilled. He wrote, "I was in the Spirit on the *Lord's day*, and heard behind me a great voice, as of a trumpet." Both the Rotherham translation and the Concordant version render this verse, "I came to be, in Spirit, in the Lord's Day."

Centuries of controversy have sprung from this reference, because people argue about to which day of the week John is referring. The presumption is that he is talking about Sunday, though the prophecy says nothing of the kind. This verse has nothing to do with Sunday—and is not a reference to any day of the week! The day of the week on which John may have received this prophecy is irrelevant.

The "Lord's Day" is speaking of the time of God's wrath. Over 30 different Old Testament prophecies refer to "the great and terrible *day of the LORD*."

The prophet Joel speaks of it in detail. And he is graphic. Here is a small portion of how he describes the day: "Blow you the *trumpet* in Zion, and sound an alarm in My holy mountain: let all the inhabitants of the land tremble: for the *day of the LORD* comes, for it is near at hand; *a day* of darkness and of gloominess, *a day* of clouds and of thick darkness, as the morning spread upon the mountains: a great people and a strong; *there has not been ever the like* [again, this is shown to be part of the worst time ever], neither shall be any more after it, even to the years of many generations. A fire devours before them; and behind them a flame burns: the land is as the garden of Eden before them, and behind them a desolate wilderness; yes, and nothing shall escape them" (2:1-3).

The prophet Zephaniah is even more graphic: "Hold your peace at the presence of the Lord GOD: for the *day of the LORD* is at hand: for the LORD has prepared a sacrifice, He has bid His guests. And it shall come to pass *in the day of the LORD'S sacrifice*, that I will punish the princes and the kings' children, and all such as are clothed with strange apparel. In *the same day* also will I punish all those that leap on the threshold, which fill their masters' houses with violence and deceit. And it shall come to pass *in that day...*" (1:7-10).

A few verses later, Zephaniah gives more insight into just how terrible this time will be. Consider this sobering picture: "The *great day of the LORD* is near, it is near, and hastes greatly, even the voice of the *day of the LORD*: the mighty man shall cry there bitterly. That day is a day of wrath, a day of trouble and distress, a day of wasteness and desolation, a day of darkness and gloominess, a day of clouds and thick darkness, a day of the trumpet and alarm...And I will bring distress upon men, that they shall walk like blind men, BECAUSE THEY HAVE SINNED AGAINST THE LORD: and their blood shall be poured out as dust, and their flesh as the dung" (vs. 14-17).

This presents a horrible picture. Verse 18 refers to this time as "the day of the LORD'S WRATH." Verse 17 identifies the *cause* of God's wrath: "because they [all mankind] have SINNED against the LORD."

Events depicted here are almost more awful and terrifying than words can describe. This day literally belongs to God—it is the "LORD'S Day." Man's conduct has made God *angry*. And He will soon intervene in the affairs of this world and send horrific *plagues* on a sinning mankind.

The Day of the Lord is the truly terrible time of God's punishments, plagues and judgments at the culmination of mankind's *practice* of sin for six millennia. Jesus Christ, through John, is revealing *to His servants* what occurs prior to—and through—His Return!

Ezekiel 8:3 gives some insight into *how* John could be transported 1,900 years into the future. Notice: "The spirit lifted me up between the earth and the heaven, and brought me *in the visions of God* to Jerusalem." Like the prophet Ezekiel, John was *in vision*—"in the spirit"—from the Isle of Patmos, where he recorded the Revelation. God projected His servants (through visions) into important future events so that they could record them.

The book of Revelation does not speak to unknown events in the distant past in the Roman Empire, as many assert. It warns of colossal events that spring from world troubles affecting the masses of humanity alive *now*. Grasp that the Day of the Lord is the towering centerpiece of the entire book. Thus, it requires more explanation to understand what we will read in the balance of this and the following chapter.

In Revelation 1:3, God states, "…he that *reads*, and they that *hear* the words of this prophecy, and *keep* [obey] those things which are written" are "blessed." What would be the point of this verse if God did *not* want the reader—the "hearer"—the "keeper" (obeyer)—to understand the book's message? This is an important statement to all who read the book.

It means you!

Verses 14-16 are a direct description of Christ, as He now exists in full glory. This is an awe-inspiring picture. Take a moment to meditate on it—and how it is a far cry from the common image of the popular long-haired, sallow-complexioned, sad-faced, effeminate-looking, weakling false "Christ" of this world: "His head and His hairs were white like wool, as white as snow; and His eyes were as a *flame of fire*; and His feet like unto *fine brass*, as if they burned in a furnace; and His voice as the sound of many waters. And He had in His right hand seven stars: and out of His mouth went a sharp two-edged sword: and His countenance was *as the sun shines in his strength*."

There are two symbols used in the first chapter of Revelation. One is mentioned in verse 12, where John saw "seven golden candlesticks." Also, in verse 16, he saw "seven stars" in Christ's hand.

Their meaning is explained by simply continuing to read the context: "The mystery of the seven stars which you saw in My right hand, and the seven golden candlesticks. The seven stars are the angels [messengers] of the seven churches: and the seven candlesticks which you saw are the seven churches" (vs. 20).

The Bible just interpreted itself! And we have now introduced the subject of chapters 2 and 3.

Chapters 2 and 3: The Seven Church Messages

Chapters 2 and 3 contain Christ's messages to seven congregations—"churches"—in Asia Minor—today's western Turkey. Together, these messages represent the first overall message of God's book. They are directed to the seven successive eras, or stages, of the Church, and span the entire New Testament period—from the time Jesus *built* His Church (Matt. 16:18) in AD 31, until His Second Coming! God has chosen to work with His Church through sequential eras.

Each message contains Christ's brief *description* of the spiritual condition of these seven consecutive Church *eras*.

These messages are not spoken to the many well-known, respected denominations of this world's professing Christianity. They are directed to God's *one true Church*. Men have never understood the messages because they have never recognized how to identify *God's* Church.

All eras are described as having their own unique set of doctrinal and spiritual problems (Smyrna and Philadelphia are exceptions) that eventually lead to Christ raising up a new leader to establish the next era. The eras are *Ephesus* (2:1), *Smyrna* (2:8), *Pergamos* (2:12), *Thyatira* (2:18), *Sardis* (3:1), *Philadelphia* (3:7) and *Laodicea* (3:14).

These locations were actually seven cities lying close together (in this order) on a mail route. God knew that each city would reflect a corresponding attitude existing in the era it represents. Christ was able to use them to show a *pattern* that would span the 2,000-year history of His Church.

History demonstrates that most in each of these eras did not heed the warnings spoken to them by Christ. This is never truer than at the end of the age. While the Church has now progressed into the deplorable seventh (or last) era, known as Laodicea, the most faithful brethren in the Church of God today are a remnant of the sixth, the Philadelphian era. Doctrinally sound and more zealous in spiritual condition, they remain separate from the "lukewarm" condition of the seventh era. (The serious reader will want to study my book *Where Is the True Church? – and Its Incredible History!*)

Chapter 4: Before God's Throne and the Twenty-four Elders

Chapters 4 and 5 represent the setting for the central part of the Revelation, which is to follow. They set the stage for unveiling the great prophecies explaining the theme of the book.

In verse 1, John describes a door opening in heaven and an invitation from a great voice to "come up" to be shown things "which must be hereafter." Keep in mind that John was actually on a small island (Patmos) in the Mediterranean Sea and all of what he saw was occurring in vision. He was not literally in heaven.

In verse 2, John saw the Father on His throne. The verse introduces God and presents a magnificent picture of the setting in which He exists.

Surrounding Him are 24 additional "seats" (lesser thrones), occupied by "twenty-four elders."

It is important to study chapter 4 with chapter 5, because together they present a descriptive picture of four "beasts" (living creatures), as well as the twenty-four elders—and Jesus Christ, as the Lamb of God (5:6), standing before God's throne.

This awe-inspiring setting pictures the environment—the magnificent beauty—of and around God's throne. The description is simply stunning!

Chapter 5: Christ Unseals the Prophecy

Verse 1 pictures the Father holding the entire book of Revelation (with seven seals upon it) in His right hand. At this point, the book (actually a scroll or parchment) is still unopened—sealed—LOCKED! Now notice: "And I saw in the right hand of Him that sat on the throne a book written within and on the backside, *sealed with seven seals*."

Seven is God's number of completeness—and, of course, the book was also completely sealed. This means that the explanation of the prophecy would remain *hidden* from view—*unavailable* to mankind until God's appointed time! It has not even been possible to read it correctly in proper sequence, let alone understand it.

Here is the description: "And I saw a strong angel proclaiming with a loud voice, Who is worthy to open the book, and to loose the seals thereof? And *no man* in heaven, nor in earth, neither under the earth, was able to open the book, neither to look thereon. And I wept much, because *no man* was found worthy to open and to read the book, neither to look thereon" (vs. 2-4).

The account reveals that no *man* is qualified to open the book. If only people would simply believe God, there would not have been so many *men*, over the centuries, giving *their* interpretations of a prophecy that cannot possibly be understood. Like Daniel, who recorded a prophecy he did not understand, John was also unable to comprehend this prophecy. He actually cried because he did not see any way to open the book (vs. 4).

It is at this point that Christ, and Christ alone (not any *human being*), is deemed "worthy" to UNSEAL THE BOOK!

Understand this! The interpretation of the book of Revelation is not that of The Restored Church of God, or any person within it, including me. No *man* is capable of opening a single prophecy in this book.

The book of Revelation has been available in English since the King James Version was translated from the original Greek in 1611. So, on the surface, this is a difficult point to understand because, of course, many *have* opened the Bible to this book and read all of its 22 chapters. But they have not *correctly* understood it. This is because they have not believed chapter 5—that Jesus Christ has sole authority to unseal the book. Endless differing, competing, humanly devised "interpretations," creating much confusion, have floated around for almost 2,000 years. Popular modern novelists have only made this worse.

Do not be confused about who alone can open this book to correct understanding. And remember, Daniel's book is a companion to all the main prophecies of Revelation, and his book was "SEALED till the *time of the end*" (12:9).

But Christ reveals the meaning of these prophecies: "And He came and took the book out of the right hand of Him that sat upon the throne" (Rev. 5:7).

The Twenty-four Elders Explained

Let's notice something else about the twenty-four elders—and clear up a misunderstanding that has existed about who and what they are.

First read an additional reference to them in chapter 5: "And when He had taken the book, the four beasts and *four and twenty elders* fell down before the Lamb, having every one of them harps, and golden vials full of odors, which are the prayers of the saints. And they sung a new song, saying, You are worthy to take the book, and to open the seals thereof: for You were slain, and have redeemed *us* [them] to God by the blood out of every kindred, and tongue, and people, and nation; and have made *us* [them] unto our God kings and priests: and *we* [they] shall reign *on the earth*" (vs. 8-10).

Some claim the twenty-four elders are taken from saved human beings. This idea comes from a mistranslation of the italicized words "us" and "we." They should be replaced by the words in brackets. See the Revised Standard Version, and also the margin of the New King James Version. Both render them correctly.

These elders are spirit beings created by God to be His counselors. They were probably created before the physical creation, along with the cherubim (Michael, Gabriel and Lucifer—who became Satan), the seraphim, the four living creatures and the billions of other angels (vs. 11) that serve God.

It is impossible for the twenty-four elders to be resurrected saints. Jesus said, "And *no man* has ascended up to heaven, but He that came down from heaven, even the Son of man which is in heaven" (John 3:13). Only when Jesus returns to Earth will Christians be given immortality (I Cor. 15:23)!

The twenty-four elders rule with God *in heaven*, having an obvious advisory role to Him. The resurrected saints will rule *on Earth* (Rev. 20:4; Matt. 5:5; Dan. 7:27). Though the vision that John saw is unsealed in heaven, it reflects events that will occur "on the earth."

Chapter 6: The Seals Are Opened

We now come to the critically important chapter 6—and the beginning of Christ's one-by-one removal of each of the SEVEN SEALS. Watch end-time events unfold in sequence.

First, again understand that, beginning with chapter 6, unsealing the seven seals spans the next 15 chapters of the book. But since chapter 6 explains six of the seven seals, obviously they do not individually receive a large amount of space. The seventh seal is *so* important—and *so* multi-faceted—that God devotes much space to its complete explanation. *Most of the remainder of Revelation is devoted to just the* SEVENTH SEAL!

This is another KEY to understanding the whole book.

The world sees the *Apocalypse* as a mystic, cryptic message of DOOM! The first four seals are represented by four riders, on four different-colored horses. Of course, much has been said and written about them. But the "Four Horsemen of the Apocalypse," as they are commonly referred to, are still viewed as mysterious, *unexplained* horrors to be unleashed upon the world without warning. Again, only briefly explained now for context, each horse and rider receives its own chapter later in the book. But it is still important that we lay enough foundation here regarding the meaning of these horses and riders that you comprehend what is happening as the unveiling of Revelation progresses.

To clearly understand the *first seal* of Revelation 6:2, we must accept a basic fact. Recall, the Greek term *apocalypse* simply means "revelation." So let's now *explain* what is to be revealed—THE SEVEN SEALS.

We will read the description of each seal before discussing it. Remember, God wants His servants—"the wise"—to understand!

The First Seal—FALSE CHRISTIANITY

Let's now examine the *first seal*: "And I saw when the Lamb opened *one of the seals*, and I heard, as it were the noise of thunder, one of the four beasts saying, Come and see. And I saw, and behold a *white horse*: and he that sat on him had a *bow*; and a crown was given unto him: and he went forth *conquering*, and to *conquer*" (vs. 1-2).

What John records is written in SYMBOLS. He does not speak in plain language. It is impossible to understand these symbols by merely rereading Revelation 6 over and over until their correct *meaning* sort of "pops into your head."

It is also absolutely critical to recognize that a list of *human* interpretations is available for what this horse and its rider, and the others, represent. But, once again, the Bible interprets the Bible. *We must permit Christ to explain what He is unsealing!* No one else has authority to speak for what God gave to *Christ*—and authorized only *Him* to reveal!

Christ Interprets

Jesus reveals the meaning of the *white horse*. Recall that His disciples asked Him, "...when shall these things [the destruction of the Temple] be? and what shall be the sign of Your coming, and of the end of the world?"

Understand that Christ is speaking in *both* Matthew 24 and Revelation 6. He is addressing the very *same questions* in both chapters. He answers His disciples by listing, *in time sequence and order*, the events and trends that precede the end of the age—and thus His Coming.

Now notice the exact parallel between Revelation 6:1-2 and Matthew 24:4-5: "And Jesus answered and said unto them, Take heed that no man deceive you. For many shall come in My Name, saying, I am Christ [that Christ *is* Christ]; and shall deceive *many*." That's right! Christ warned that the *many* will be deceived by those who claim to represent Him—not the *few*.

The *white horse* that John described represents *false* "christs." Here is proof. The one sitting on this horse is actually a *counterfeit* of the true Christ and a *counterfeit* of His Second Coming, described in Revelation 19:11-16. There, the *real* Christ wields a sharp two-edged SWORD, while the *false* christ is represented as carrying a BOW. Do not overlook this critical difference!

Here is a partial description of the *true* Jesus Christ returning in great power and glory. While it does show Him riding a white horse, the rest of the description is very different from Revelation 6: "And I saw heaven opened, and behold a *white horse*; and He that sat upon him was called Faithful and True, and in righteousness *He does judge and make war*... And out of His mouth goes A SHARP SWORD, that with it He should smite the nations: and He shall RULE THEM with a rod of iron: and He treads the winepress of the fierceness and wrath of Almighty God" (19:11, 15).

Consider for a moment. Most who study Revelation believe that the white horse of the first seal pictures the *true* Christ coming *before* war, famine and disease strike the earth. How ridiculous! Such ignorance and misunderstanding has clouded the timing of the glorious Return of Jesus Christ described in Revelation 19:11-16. This is but one more way Satan's ministers have deceived false Christianity—the *other* white horse.

Parallel Chapters

Before proceeding, let's read more of Christ's answer to His disciples in Matthew 24. It will prepare us to see further the precise parallel between it and Revelation 6.

Carefully notice the rest of Jesus' answer: "And you shall hear of *wars* and *rumors of wars*: see that you be not troubled: for all these things must come to pass, but the end is not yet. For nation shall rise against nation, and kingdom against kingdom: and there shall be *famines*, and *pestilences*, and *earthquakes*, in various places. All these are the *beginning* of sorrows" (vs. 6-8).

Christ gives a direct answer to a direct question. The events He describes require no interpretation. In fact, they are CHRIST'S INTERPRETATION of Revelation 6. By having them in mind as we read the opening of the remaining seals, we have Christ telling us in advance what we are viewing—and what the symbols *mean*. All mystery is stripped away. This is most crucial to see!

The *same* Christ would not give two *different* versions of what happens immediately prior to His Return. He would not tell one thing to His disciples of the *first century*, and give an entirely different explanation to His servants of the *twenty-first century*! This should be obvious.

But, it is important to understand that only relatively recently, after almost 2,000 years, has the book of Revelation been opened up to plain understanding for all those who will heed. The words have always been there, but, as with Daniel's prophecy, their meaning has been "sealed till the time of the end."

Grasp what you have just read! In effect, Jesus has given an advance newscast—newspaper *headlines*—of events now lying just ahead, and increasingly already around us today. Jesus' greatest single prophecy, the entirety of Matthew 24, Mark 13 and Luke 21 contain much *more information* than just Matthew 24:3-8. But we are not yet ready to discuss it.

In John 1, Jesus Christ is referred to as "the Word." Compare verse 1 and verse 14. "The Word" is translated from the Greek word *logos*, meaning "Spokesman." Actually, Jesus not only inspired Matthew 24 and Revelation 6, but also the entire Bible! (I Cor. 10:4, among other places, reveals that Jesus Christ is in fact the God of the Old Testament. However shocking this is to most, it is true and easily provable!)

For those with "eyes to see and ears to hear," in Matthew 24, Jesus is revealing in *plain language* the true meaning of the SYMBOLS recorded in Revelation 6.

Understanding the last sentence is the single biggest KEY to understanding the entire book of Revelation!

Parables are much like *symbols*. Both are different from the actual things or figures being described. As explained, while most believe that Jesus spoke in parables to *illustrate* His meaning, He said otherwise in Mark 4 and Matthew 13, when discussing the parable of the Sower and the Seed. The real reason Jesus spoke in parables was to HIDE His meaning. The same is true of symbols! It is the use of these symbols in Revelation 6 that kept the prophecy locked—sealed!

If you read the account in Mark, you will find that Jesus explains the Parable of the Sower, but only *privately* to His disciples. This is exactly what He did in Matthew 24. He explained *privately* to His disciples then— "and His disciples came to Him *privately*"—and for His disciples of the end time, the meaning of the Revelation 6 symbols.

When the disciples wanted to understand the events that would precede Christ's Return, they asked HIM, not some uninformed churchman or theologian who could have no idea what he was talking about.

You can do the same. Christ is "the same yesterday, today and forever" (Heb. 13:8). What He revealed to the disciples long ago is just as true for us today! And the events are foretold to occur in *our* time. So, if the first-century disciples desired to know the answer to their question of Matthew 24:3, how much *more* should today's disciples want to plainly understand what will directly affect *their lives*?

Understand one final point about Christ's explanation of the opening of the seals. Each represents a prophetic trend that begins *and remains continuous* from the moment it is opened, all the way to His Second Coming.

In II Corinthians 11:13-15, Paul recorded how false ministers (or false christs) do their work—deluding, deceiving and causing vast numbers of people to accept counterfeit christs (vs. 4). While this has been happening for 2,000 years, all but the few—to whom Christ is revealing His precious truth—are completely oblivious! This includes deceitful misrepresentation of the entire book of Revelation. You will later learn this in stunning detail.

False ministers and deceivers were prophesied to delude the "many"—not the few.

Almost immediately after Jesus' death and Resurrection, false ministers and deceivers entered His true flock. This is the very reason He warned His Church, in each of its seven eras of chapters 2 and 3, with separate messages.

The Second Seal—WAR

When the *second seal* opens, a *red horse* appears: "When He had opened the SECOND SEAL, I heard the second beast say, Come and see. And there went out another *horse that was red*: and power was given to him that sat thereon to *take peace from the earth*, and that they should *kill* one another: and there was given unto him a *great sword*" (Rev. 6:3-4). As with Christ in Revelation 19, the sword is here shown as an instrument of war and killing.

This horse and rider "take peace from the earth." The opposite of peace is war. When peace is removed, war is what remains. This pictures the "wars and rumors of wars" that Christ referenced in Matthew 24:6.

Wars have continued and grown steadily worse since the time of Christ's prophecy. But this part of John's astounding vision has the gravest implications for all alive on Earth today.

This horseman represents the dreadful destruction of world war. In the Matthew 24 parallel prophecy, *war* immediately follows *false Christianity*. By the end of the age, the potential for devastation in war has become so great that it holds the power to take peace not just from two or more nations, but now "from the earth."

Only in the modern age have such terrible weapons of mass destruction been available. The twentieth century saw the two most devastating wars in history, with World War II far more destructive than World War I.

We are now in the last recess—intermission—preceding the time of the truly greatest war, prophesied to exceed anything in the last century. A sinning, rebellious humanity will soon reach the end of its rope. We have reached a time when war's potential cannot grow worse, because it can now erase *all* life from Earth in one final blast of complete destruction—if Christ did not intervene and cut events "short" (vs. 22). You will also later learn much more about this.

But the pattern of history is that *famine* always follows war. This is why famine (the third seal) follows on the heels of war (the second seal).

The Third Seal—FAMINE

The *third seal* opens and a *black horse*, a symbol of famine, appears: "And when He had opened the THIRD SEAL, I heard the third beast say, Come and see. And I beheld, and lo a *black horse*; and he that sat on him had a pair of balances in his hand. And I heard a voice in the midst of the four beasts say, A measure of wheat for a penny, and three measures of barley for a penny; and see you hurt not the oil and the wine" (Rev. 6:5-6).

This pictures extreme worldwide famine—a widespread lack of food beyond anything civilization has *ever* seen—and any student of history knows that it has seen a great deal. This devouring condition is seen to be seizing the entire world in an extraordinary way. Famine is *now* far worse than most imagine. Again, much more will follow later in a separate chapter.

The Fourth Seal—DISEASE

The opening of the *fourth seal* reveals a *pale horse*, which represents pestilence or disease: "And when He had opened the FOURTH SEAL, I heard the voice of the fourth beast say, Come and see. And I looked, and behold a *pale horse*: and his name that sat on him was Death, and Hell followed with him. And power was given unto them over *the fourth part of the earth*, to kill with sword, and with hunger, and with death, and with the beasts of the earth" (vs. 7-8).

This horse is depicted as *pale* because it is *sickly*. It obviously represents disease—*pestilence*! Invariably, war leads to famine—and resulting malnutrition invites a host of diseases. New diseases, or old ones grown worse, seem to be appearing almost daily. The death toll from disease around the world is staggering—now over 82,000 die *every day*!

Disease is a subject tremendous in size, and the topic of an endless number of entire books. As with the fulfillment of the other seals, far more information is available about it than could begin to fit in this short section. Yet again you are left to prepare for a fuller picture later.

The Fifth Seal—THE GREAT TRIBULATION

The opening of the *fifth seal* does not reveal a horse. Instead, it introduces and briefly overviews the soon-to-come worst time of world trouble in history (Matt. 24:21; Jer. 30:7; Dan. 12:1)—the Great Tribulation!

Again, many prophecies in both the Old and New Testaments explain and describe this period. This world-changing event will be truly colossal in nature—and thoroughly explaining all elements of it involves far more than the space available in this chapter.

Of course, the most terrible wars, famines and diseases still lie ahead. And these will greatly intensify *before* the Great Tribulation begins. Even so, remember that, after Jesus had described the first four seals, *plus earthquakes*, He concluded, "All these are the BEGINNING of sorrows [travail or tribulation]" (Matt. 24:8). They are far from the *end* of matters.

The first thing to follow these *beginning* events and conditions is the Tribulation. We will shortly prove this.

But first we need to explain another important aspect of what the Tribulation means.

Here is what Jesus told His disciples would occur next: "Then shall *they* deliver YOU up to be afflicted, and shall kill YOU: and YOU shall be hated of all nations for My Name's sake" (vs. 9).

Now understand something. Two different pronouns appear in this passage—"they" and "you." Jesus did this for a very specific reason. Whenever Jesus was describing true Christians, He spoke of "you." Those who were deceivers and not of the truth—the many who are falsely converted—are generally referred to in Scripture as "they" or other similar pronouns.

Sometimes the term "you" can also refer to *national* Israel or *national* Judah, or to these *and* to true Christians. Whenever the passage is speaking nationally, it is either referring to Israel or Judah, or both. When coupled with Mark 13 and Luke 21, it is obvious that Jesus is referring to both in Matthew 24.

Final Martyrdom of Saints

Before continuing with more of Christ's explanation in Matthew 24 about the Tribulation, we need to read John's description of the *fifth seal*: "And when He had opened the FIFTH SEAL, I saw under the altar *the souls of them that were slain for the word of God*, and for the testimony which they held: and they cried with a loud voice, saying, How long, O Lord, holy and true, do You not judge and *avenge* our blood on them that dwell on the earth? And white robes were given unto every one of them; and it was said unto them, that they should rest yet for a little season, until *their fellow servants* also and their *brethren*, that should be killed as they were, should be fulfilled" (Rev. 6:9-11).

The fifth seal portrays the martyrdom of true saints (along with vast numbers from national Israel and Judah). This occurs during the Tribulation. Verse 11 is a symbolic instruction to the martyrs of the Middle Ages to await this *latter* martyrdom of the end time.

The context develops with the souls asking God a question.

Some cite these verses to validate both the immortal soul doctrine and that the saved go to heaven—and thereby miss the whole point of what Christ is revealing. They obviously also do not put this verse with Christ's Matthew 24:9 explanation, which again is seen to be His *interpretation* of its meaning.

This description is not literal, but rather is *symbolic*, as is much of Revelation. No one believes that the four horses, or their riders, are literal. It is obvious that they are symbolic and part of a *vision*. A consistent standard must be used, without randomly picking and choosing which passages are literal and which are part of the vision.

In *vision*, John was shown a preview of a future event ("hereafter," 4:1). Since John was "in the spirit" as the seals were opened (vs. 2), the events he witnessed were not actually occurring when he saw them. They were *heavenly previews* of things that would happen later *on Earth*.

Upon the opening of the fifth seal (Rev. 6:9), John "saw under [at the base of] the altar the souls of them that were slain."

Remember, in the vision, John was shown the future. A long period of martyrdom had taken place (up to and through the Middle Ages). A later one (the Great Tribulation) is yet to happen in our time. The souls who were already "slain" were martyred Christians throughout the ages. These earlier martyrs were told to "rest yet for a little season, until their *fellow servants* also and their *brethren*, that *should be killed* as they were, should be fulfilled" (vs. 11).

Many of God's people in the end time have partially drifted away from being as close to Him, or as on fire for His truth and His Work as they should. They have not been praying, studying, fasting, meditating and seeking Him on a daily basis as they should. This has allowed many to be deceived, and to fall into various false doctrines. Only the Tribulation will awaken these brethren—and even then only about half (Matt. 25:1-12)!

During the Tribulation, there will be a great religious persecution. Jesus was very specific about this in Matthew 24: "And then shall many be offended, and shall betray one another, and shall hate one another. And many *false prophets* shall rise, and shall *deceive many*. And because iniquity [lawlessness, occurring worldwide] shall abound, the love [Rom. 13:10; I John 5:3] of many shall *wax cold*. But he that *shall endure unto the end*, the same shall be *saved*...For then shall be GREAT TRIBULATION, such as was not since the beginning of the world to this time, no, nor ever shall be... For there shall arise *false Christs*, and *false prophets*, and shall show great signs and wonders; insomuch that, if it were possible, they shall *deceive* the very elect" (vs. 10-13, 21, 24).

The elect must remain on guard!

This is a very specific prophecy about tremendous deception that seduces "many." The "souls under the altar" await God's punishment of the great governmental power that persecuted them, when God "avenges [their] blood."

All true but lukewarm Christians will have to suffer this final martyr-dom (Rev. 3:14-22). Those faithful Christians who were previously killed must continue to "rest" (remain "asleep" in their graves—Eph. 5:14; I Cor. 11:30) until others join them through martyrdom.

The "souls" (dead saints) crying "avenge our blood" (Rev. 6:10) is akin to Abel's blood (his *life*—note Leviticus 17:14) crying to God from the earth (Gen. 4:10) after Cain's murder of his brother. Since neither blood nor the dead talk (Psa. 115:17; Ecc. 9:5, 10), the meaning is symbolic, not literal.

So then, in Matthew 24:9-10 Jesus was actually describing a final mar-tyrdom yet to occur among His people. Therefore, the "souls under the altar" represent those awaiting a future martyrdom of lukewarm saints— "their brethren." These are of the seventh and last era, Laodicea, described in Revelation 3:14-22.

Invasion and Captivity

The Tribulation will also include the invasion and captivity of the "ten lost tribes" of the modern-day descendants of Israel, *and* Judah (the modern nation of Israel).

Recognize that God often works prophetically through the principle of DUALITY. Many prophecies work in this way. For instance, I Corinthians 15:21-22 shows that Adam was a type of Christ, and vice versa (a problem for those who believe there was no literal Adam and Eve).

As alluded to previously, most Bible students are unaware that some prophecies have first a *former*, then a *typical* and, lastly, a *final* great fulfill-ment. This causes big problems for those trying to understand and explain such prophecies. The results are always mixed up and confused.

In Matthew 24:2, Jesus prophesied that the Temple would be com-pletely destroyed, with not "one stone" remaining. So would Jerusalem be destroyed. This occurred in AD 69-70 to the nation of Judah, as an early TYPE of a final, infinitely greater fulfillment at the end of the age.

Here is how Christ described this final fulfillment of national invasion, war and captivity: "But woe unto them that are with child, and to them that give suck, in those days! For there shall be *great distress* in the land, and wrath upon this people. And they shall fall by the edge of the *sword*, and shall be led away *captive* into all nations: and *Jerusalem shall be trodden down* of the Gentiles, until the times of the Gentiles be fulfilled" (Luke 21:23-24).

This describes a time of truly great fear and real horror for the modern peoples and nations descended from Israel. (*America and Britain in Prophecy* covers in detail where these peoples are *now*, and *why* they are foretold to go through such national punishment.)

We must now examine an inset of the prophecy that precedes and leads up to the Great Tribulation. We briefly covered it earlier: "And this gospel of the KINGDOM shall be preached in *all the world* for a witness unto *all nations*; and then shall the END come" (Matt. 24:14).

Remember, the true gospel is about the kingdom of God. Men have devised many false gospels, but Christ preached a message about a divine, world-ruling SUPERGOVERNMENT to be established at His Return. God's Church is preaching this marvelous truth, and about how His perfect spiritual Law will soon be established in all nations. This is the wonderful good news referenced earlier—the word "gospel" means good news. When our task is complete, "then shall the end come"! (Look forward to the full chapter on this subject, which makes plain the gospel truth in its component parts!)

Though there is still time for announcing God's kingdom, it will soon run out. Some few will yet turn to God as a result of this Work. May you "hear and understand" while there is yet time!

The Sixth Seal—HEAVENLY SIGNS

Next comes the *sixth seal*—the HEAVENLY, or astronomical, SIGNS: "I beheld when He had opened the SIXTH SEAL, and, lo, there was a great earthquake; and the *sun* became black as sackcloth of hair, and the *moon* became as blood; and the *stars of heaven fell* unto the earth, even as a fig tree casts her untimely figs, when she is shaken of a mighty wind" (Rev. 6:12-13).

How do we know that the heavenly signs come directly on the heels of the Great Tribulation? Here are Christ's words: "*Immediately after* the tribulation of those days shall the *sun* be darkened, and the *moon* shall not give her light, and the *stars shall fall from heaven*, and the powers of the heavens shall be shaken" (Matt. 24:29).

This is an almost verbatim, phrase-by-phrase description of Revelation 6:12-13. The parallel is unmistakable. *Jesus* has again interpreted the sixth seal, and its timing, for us. The phrase "immediately *after* the tribulation" removes all doubt about *when* the heavenly signs occur.

The arrival of the heavenly signs heralds a tremendous overall change in the direction—and speed!—of events. This is understood by continuing in Revelation 6, a few verses later. Let's read: "For the *great day of His wrath is come*; and who shall be able to stand?" (vs. 17).

There it is in plain English. The Day of the Lord, or Day of God's Wrath, follows the sixth seal. Heaven and Earth are shaken! This time reveals God's AWESOME POWER! It is comparable to nothing that has ever happened before, or ever will again.

The prophet Joel was speaking of this time when God's tremendous power and great wrath will be displayed when he said, "The sun shall be turned into darkness, and the moon into blood, BEFORE the great and dreadful Day of the LORD come" (2:31).

Some have claimed that these signs have *already* occurred. This is *impossible*! Matthew 24 makes plain that they all *follow*—not *precede*—the Tribulation. In addition, when they occur, they are either *immediately* followed by or accompany the *sign* of Christ's Coming (vs. 29-30).

The terrible period of God's wrath is foretold to last an ENTIRE YEAR—after the initial two and a half years of the Tribulation. Here is how Isaiah described it: "For it is the *day* of the LORD's vengeance, and the YEAR of recompenses for the controversy of Zion" (34:8). Jeremiah refers to this period as "the YEAR of...visitation" (11:23; 23:12—also see Ezek. 4:6 and Num. 14:34).

A Great Earthquake

Notice verse 12 of Revelation 6 speaks of a "great earthquake." This earthquake occurs after the fifth seal, upon the opening of the sixth seal. The terrible time of the fifth seal involves the military invasion and the captivity of the peoples of the modern nations (which are merely ancient tribes grown larger) of Israel. This includes the two and a half years of unparalleled suffering and tribulation—unrivaled in history. It is coming on THIS GENERATION—soon!

By its very timing and context, this earthquake proclaims the *end of the Tribulation* and the *beginning of signs that appear in the heavens*.

Revelation 6:12 states, "And I beheld when He had opened the sixth seal, and, lo, there was *a great earthquake*; and the sun became black as sackcloth of hair, and the moon became as blood."

This event was also covered in Matthew 24:29. Reread it: "Immediately after the tribulation of those days shall the sun be darkened, and the moon shall not give her light, and the stars shall fall from heaven, and the powers of the heavens shall be *shaken*."

Luke 21:25-26 describes this same event, adding more: "And there shall be signs in the sun, and in the moon, and in the stars; and upon the earth distress of nations, with perplexity; the *sea and the waves roaring* [tsunamis]; *men's hearts failing them for fear*, and for looking after those things which are coming on the earth: for the powers of heaven shall be *shaken*."

This earthquake will be of such awesome magnitude that "*every mountain*" and "*every island*" will be shaken out of position (Rev. 6:14).

Remember, this is the time of God's GREAT WRATH! This earthquake will be worldwide in scope. But all the earth's topography will not necessarily be changed by one final earthquake. This process appears to take place in stages. God will bring it about in such a way as to preserve life on the earth, with each of *five* final earthquakes contributing to some aspect of the transformation.

If only one cataclysmic earthquake did this, it could threaten all life on Earth. Still, only a fraction of humanity will survive into the Millennium. Again, this earthquake announces the SIXTH SEAL—*the heavenly signs*.

Notice Isaiah's description of this time: "In that day a man shall cast his idols of silver, and his idols of gold, which they made each one for himself to worship, to the moles and to the bats; to go into the clefts of the rocks, and into the tops of the ragged rocks, for fear of the LORD, and for the glory of His majesty, *when He arises to shake terribly the earth*" (2:20-21). This compares with Revelation 6:15-16.

All of Revelation 6:14-17 shows that this sign is the *heavens rolling together like a scroll*. This time will be so awful that John records people, in sheer terror, hiding themselves in caves and rocks and crying out to die. Verse 17 asks, "...and who shall be able to stand?" The masses fear facing the full wrath of the One they have disobeyed!

Three World Events

Understand! The Tribulation and the Day of the Lord are *not synonymous*! These are completely separate, *different* events. The heavenly signs come *between* the Tribulation, which *precedes* them, and the Day of the Lord, which *follows* them. (Although only Matthew 24:21, 29 and Revelation 7:14 use the term *"Great* Tribulation," at least 30 scriptures speak of it.)

The religious leaders of this world are in almost complete ignorance of how these three earth-shattering events come—in what *order* they appear. Most believe them to be *synonymous.* They are not!

The Tribulation comes first. "Immediately after the tribulation" (Jesus recorded) come the heavenly signs. These introduce the Day of the Lord (God's wrath), which is a separate period of events. We have seen how Joel, Zephaniah and Matthew have explained what Jesus revealed in vision to John in the Revelation. By now, these great events should be clear.

Jesus also taught His disciples, "...in *vain* do they worship Me, teaching for doctrines the *commandments of men.* For laying aside the commandment of God, you hold the *tradition of men...*" (Mark 7:7-8). There are many "traditional," but incorrect, views of prophecy.

More and more people are writing of prophecies they know nothing about. They ignore what God says, in order to promote time-honored, empty theories—or even newer, more far-fetched ideas. I have just reviewed an article in a national magazine about much of what has been covered so far in this and the two previous chapters. It demonstrates appalling ignorance of even the most *basic* facts of scriptures pertaining to end-time prophecies. Yet the article shows that almost three out of five Americans (scores of millions) believe that the mixed-up jumble of ideas it references about Revelation will soon come true, but only in some inexplicable, *mysterious* way. Millions of other professing Christians, no doubt because they either do not care or are confused, reject *anything* to do with prophecy! Either way, people remain ignorant.

I repeat: The great majority of people believe the Tribulation, heavenly signs and Day of the Lord are *identical*—one and the same. Anyone who cannot distinguish between these obviously separate events has no hope of understanding what God has prophesied.

Here is an important distinction: The Day of the Lord reflects the wrath of *God.* The Tribulation is actually the wrath of *Satan* the devil. It is a sobering thought to realize that this time sees the unleashed wrath of the second most powerful force in the universe. This fallen angel is well aware that he has but a short time to remain the god of this world (II Cor. 4:4), deceiving the nations (Rev. 12:9). His time is almost up (vs. 12).

The Tribulation is also Satan's final persecution and martyrdom of many of God's true servants in a lukewarm condition. *If* they return to and remain close to God, Satan cannot deceive them—so he is furious.

Chapter outline
of the book of Revelation

Chapter	Story flow
1	Introduction
2-3	Message to the Seven Church Eras
4-5	Prelude—Setting
6	First Six Seals
7	The Two Companies
8-10	The Trumpets
11	The Two Witnesses
12	The True Church
13	The Two Beasts
14	The Three Messages
15-16	The Seven Last Plagues
17-18	The Great False Church
19	The Return of Jesus Christ
20	The Millennium
21-22	New Heaven and New Earth

Inset chapters

Story flow
of the book of Revelation

THE SEVEN SEALS	PROPHETIC EVENTS	
FIRST	False prophets	
SECOND	War	
THIRD	Famine	
FOURTH	Pestilence	
FIFTH	Tribulation	
SIXTH	Heavenly signs	
SEVENTH	Seven Trumpets	
	1st	Trees injured
	2nd	Sea injured
	3rd	Rivers injured
	4th	Heavenly catastrophes
	5th	First Woe
	6th	Second Woe
	7th	Third Woe (or The Seven Last Plagues)
	The Return of Jesus Christ	

If you seek God, you need not worry about events soon to strike all nations. Take a moment to review Luke 21:36. It is a reassuring promise from Christ that requires you to "WATCH...and PRAY...that you may be *accounted worthy* to ESCAPE all these things...and to stand before the Son of man." Then remember Christ's sobering description in the preceding verses in Luke of how these events will strike a completely unsuspecting world—billions of people—"like a snare."

The goal of a Christian is to stand before Jesus Christ at His Return, and rule with Him when the kingdom of God is established!

Chapter 7: Why God's Wrath Temporarily Held Back

Right before the Day of the Lord, an angel temporarily holds back *the four winds*, which Revelation 8:7-12 explains are the first *four trumpet plagues* of the seventh seal. Now notice: "And after these things I saw FOUR ANGELS standing on the four corners of the earth, holding the FOUR WINDS of the earth, that the wind should not blow on the *earth*, nor on the *sea*, nor on any *tree*. And I saw another angel ascending from the east, having the *seal* of the living God: and he cried with a loud voice to the four angels, to whom it was given to hurt the earth and the sea, Saying, Hurt not the earth, neither the sea, nor the trees, till we have *sealed* the servants of our God *in their foreheads*. And I heard the number of them which were sealed: and there were sealed an *hundred and forty and four thousand* of all the tribes of the children of Israel" (7:1-4).

This is a dramatic scene. Four winds are about to "hurt the earth"— devastate its landscape! (Though symbolic in language, the plagues they bring will be most *real* to all who suffer them.) God's wrath, which is the beginning of His direct intervention in world affairs, is poised to appear. But it is temporarily restrained. Something must happen first before this can occur.

These winds are held back so that the well-known (but little understood) 144,000 can be sealed—and the great (innumerable) multitude— each the subject of later chapters—stand before the throne of Christ wearing white robes.

First, most briefly, the 144,000 are sealed (7:4-8) with the Father's Name (14:1)—and represent 12,000 from each of the twelve tribes of Israel. Revelation 14 adds more about this group (vs. 1-5). These are obviously converted people. They are sealed with the Father's Name (and the Holy Spirit "in their foreheads") because this is how Christ prayed, in John 17:11, that the Father would "keep" His servants. This world's churches are named after men, doctrines, locations, etc. God's Church (in 12 places in the New Testament) is always named after Himself—Church of God!

The *innumerable multitude* is comprised of those who are drifting along, not heeding God's instruction now, though some may know His commands. These "came out of the great tribulation" (7:14).

John records the following: "After this I beheld, and lo, *a great multitude*, which no man could number, of all nations, and kindreds, and people, and tongues, stood before the throne, and before the Lamb, clothed with white robes, and palms in their hands...And one of the elders answered, saying unto me, What are these which are arrayed in white robes? And whence came they? And I said unto him, Sir you know. And he said to me, These are they *which came out of great tribulation*, and have *washed their robes*, and *made them white in the blood of the Lamb*" (vs. 9, 13-14).

Many know the truth today but are either not acting on it, or are only responding to it in a limited way. Hundreds of millions heard the voice of Herbert W. Armstrong during his 52-year ministry. He boldly proclaimed the true gospel of the kingdom of God, and restored many true doctrines to the sixth era (Philadelphia) of God's Church. The vast majority did not heed. They were "choked by the cares of the world."

Some *will* finally wake up during or after the Tribulation, after experiencing the terror of the heavenly signs—and after much suffering. These stupendous events will sober and awaken many before it is too late. In complete submission, they will repent and turn to God.

Why God Sends Plagues

A loving God never punishes people before He warns them. Proverbs 3:11-12 states, "...despise not the chastening of the LORD; neither be weary of His correction: for whom the LORD loves He corrects; even as a father the son in whom he delights." (A later chapter describes in graphic detail *why* God plans such severe correction and chastening.)

These are the plain words of God about how He works with people. Theologians and ministers focus almost solely on God's love. They ignore such verses as Proverbs 3:11-12, or others like "Behold...the goodness *and severity* of God" (Rom. 11:22), among *many* others.

We are about to read of terrible plagues to be poured out on a God-hating, truth-rejecting, self-willed, rebellious world. This punishment is coming for a reason. Six thousand years of ignoring God have come to the FULL—and God is filled with WRATH...

The Seventh Seal— The Day of the Lord!

The emphasis God places on the final and complex SEVENTH SEAL re-quires its own chapter. Remember, nothing in this last book of God's Word receives close to as much attention! Also remember that the seven seals represent the entire book of Revelation. But exactly what is the *seventh* seal?

We pick up in Revelation 8, which depicts the opening of this seventh seal. As it is opened, seven angels stand before God and receive the seven trumpets. A different angel took a censer "...and filled it with fire of the altar, and cast it into the earth: and there were voices, and thunderings, and lightnings, *and an earthquake*" (vs. 5).

This earthquake represents the *beginning* of the seven trumpet plagues, which begin the seventh seal's fulfillment—and the Day of the Lord.

Revelation 8:1-2 shows that the *seventh seal* is the same as the *seven trumpets*: "And when He had opened the SEVENTH SEAL, there was silence in heaven about the space of half an hour. And I saw the *seven angels* which stood before God; and to them *were given* SEVEN TRUMPETS."

Now understand! This verse proves that all seven seals are *not* the same as, or equal to, all seven trumpets. This is critical to recognize—and is another big KEY to understanding Revelation. Make this important distinction now: (1) The seventh seal *is* all seven trumpets and (2) the seventh trumpet *is* all seven *last plagues* or *vials*. This is confusing to almost everyone, because most believe that the seven trumpets and the seven last plagues are synonymous. Also, the seven trumpets do not *follow* the seventh seal—they *are* the seventh seal. Simply reading more carefully eliminates this error.

The seven trumpets represent seven stages—Revelation 9:20 calls them "PLAGUES," but again they are not the seven *last* plagues, or vials, as we shall see.

Recall that the four winds comprise the first four trumpet plagues. Revelation 8:3-12 reveals that they blow on the (1) *trees*, (2) *seas*, (3) *rivers*, and (4) a third part of the sun, moon and stars are smitten and darkened. Space prohibits explaining in detail the fuller meaning of the incredible effect of these great winds.

Various places in the Old Testament show that, anciently, a trumpet was always blown as an alarm of war (Num. 10:9; Jer. 4:19; Ezek. 33:2-6; etc.). When heard, it signaled approaching armies and the onset of battle. Israel and Judah always went to war with the sound of a trumpet.

The fifth and sixth trumpets clearly depict war—*in two stages*. (But this is not to be confused with any part of the second seal, or red horse. This is a later and completely separate element of war.) Make note of another important point. The last three trumpets, the fifth, sixth and seventh, are *synonymous* with the THREE WOES (Rev. 8:13). The chart in the previous chapter helps make this plain.

The world loves war—and has practiced it since Creation! And man has always pursued war on his *own* terms. When God goes to war with the world, He is choosing to speak in a language men understand—and this time HE controls the terms! However, this is also His way of *pleading* with all humanity to "WAKE UP!"

These seven trumpet plagues are a truly frightening and horrific punishment from God on those remaining unresponsive in their disobedience: "And the rest of the men which were not killed by THESE PLAGUES [the seven trumpets] yet *repented not* of the works of their hands, that they should *not worship devils, and idols* of gold, and silver, and brass, and stone, and of wood: which neither can see, nor hear, nor walk" (Rev. 9:20). Obviously, many continue unrepentant after these plagues, and continue to serve the myriad of false gods worshipped around the world.

Chapter 9: The Three Woes

Chapter 9 pertains entirely to the first two of the THREE WOES—the fifth and sixth trumpets.

In verses 1-11, the fifth trumpet, or FIRST WOE, is described as a great power that comes out of what the Bible calls the "bottomless pit." This, of course, is a symbol and not an actual pit somewhere on the earth. Revelation 17:8-14 interprets it. The old Roman Empire (with its *seven* separate *resurrections* or *heads*) emerges from this "pit" *one last time.* The sixth head, Mussolini's revival of this *Roman system,* was small and relatively insignificant. The soon-coming last revival will be much greater!

In 9:11, John calls Satan "a destroyer," referring to him as a "king over *them*"—a *system* of people led by a final, world-ruling, counterfeit figure soon to appear, just prior to the Return of Christ. The Hebrew word *Abaddon* means *"destroying angel,"* and the Greek word *Apollyon,* also used there, means *"a destroyer"* or simply *"Satan."* Understanding Satan as a *destroyer* sets the stage for the next scripture.

Verses 13-21 describe the SECOND WOE. Open your Bible and read these verses. An army of 200 million "horsemen" attacks and temporarily repels the European system led by the final super-dictator known as the "Beast." These eastern hordes (Ezek. 25:4, 10), probably led by Russia or China, and allied with India and Japan, compose the 200-million-man army of verse 16.

The prophet Ezekiel describes the same events of Revelation 9:13-21, revealing more: "And I will turn you back, and put hooks into your jaws, and I will bring you forth, and all your army, horses and *horsemen,* all of them clothed with all sorts of armor, even *a great company* with bucklers and shields, all of them handling swords...and you shall come from your place out of the NORTH parts, you, and many people with you, all of them riding upon horses, a great company, and *a mighty army*" (38:4, 15; also see Joel 2:4). The reference to horses and horsemen is obviously a representation of an immense *army.* 200 million is certainly "a mighty army." This is almost certainly an attack by the Russian and Northern Asian hordes (armies) against what is called the *Beast* and *Babylon* (Rev. 17 and 18). Jeremiah 50 and 51, as well as Isaiah 13 and 14, and 47 and 48, describe this coming system and its destruction.

Forces on Earth are forming even *now,* so they can come into play at the right moment within God's Plan!

Chapter 10: The Little Book

Chapter 10 is almost entirely about a "little book" held in the hand of a "mighty angel." This little book is "sweet as honey" in John's mouth, but "bitter" in his belly. This is a reference to the book of Ezekiel and its long warning (see Ezekiel 3:1-3, 14) to Israel today, but perhaps also working in conjunction with the book of Revelation itself.

The most important part is verse 7, which explains that the seventh angel (that sounds in the end of chapter 11) brings an end to the mystery of God's Plan as declared by all of His prophets.

Verse 11 reveals that the message of the little book, and the book of Revelation, was to be taken by one (not the apostle John because he never did this) to "peoples, and nations, and tongues, and kings." Also, for this to happen "*again*," as it says, it must previously happen in a first fulfillment. This occurred in the twentieth century for the first time, and is now happening "again."

Chapter 11: The Two Witnesses

The first 13 verses contain the description of the previously mentioned final end-time servants known as the *Two Witnesses*. Ridiculous interpretations, and at least one Hollywood movie, have brought much confusion as to who these men are.

These two "prophets" (vs. 10) witness for three and a half years before being killed by the Beast (vs. 7) of Revelation 13 and 17, and Daniel 2 and 7. The identity of these two individuals is yet unknown. However, when they do come on the scene, it will be clear that Christ's Return is imminent.

A later chapter brings detail regarding their unique roles, and where they will come from.

Another Earthquake

After the Two Witnesses are resurrected following three and a half days of lying in the streets of Jerusalem, another great earthquake occurs. The timing of *this* earthquake is *prior* to the time of the seventh trumpet, the Return of Christ and the First Resurrection (I Cor. 15:51; I Thes. 4:16).

Notice Revelation 11:12-13: "And they heard a great voice from heaven saying unto them [the Two Witnesses], Come up here. And they ascended up to heaven in *a cloud* [the first heaven—Revelation 19:17— where birds fly—where the clouds are]; and their enemies beheld them. And the same hour was there a *great earthquake*, and the tenth part of the city [Jerusalem] fell, and in the earthquake *were slain of men seven thousand*: and the remnant were affrighted, and gave glory to the God of heaven [the third heaven—II Corinthians 12:2—of God's throne]."

This particular earthquake precedes and announces the most pivotal event in mankind's history—Jesus Christ's Return!

No doubt, this earthquake is God punctuating the world's failure to permanently destroy these two extraordinary servants. It also appears to be centered mainly in the area of Jerusalem, but could still be worldwide in scope.

It cannot be the same one described in Zechariah 14:4, because all nations will not yet have gathered (the sixth vial) for what is called the Battle of the Great Day of God Almighty (the time of the last plague, or seventh vial—Revelation 16:17-21).

The Seventh Trumpet or Third Woe

Remember, the *seventh trumpet* equals the *third woe*. But these are also synonymous with the SEVEN LAST PLAGUES! Chapter 11, verses 15-19, describe them, and, coupled with 15:1, prove the last statement.

Now notice verse 15: "And the SEVENTH ANGEL SOUNDED; and there were great voices in heaven, saying, The *kingdoms of this world* are become the *kingdoms of our Lord*, and of His Christ; and He shall *reign* forever and ever."

Both I Corinthians 15:52 and I Thessalonians 4:16 speak of this moment. In these verses, Paul states that Christ comes at the "trump of God" and at the "last trump." Matthew 24:31 speaks of the same event using "a great sound of a trumpet." These are all references to the *seventh trumpet.*

With this event, the greatest moment in all history has arrived. At His glorious Return, Christ replaces all human powers and laws with His own. *All* the governments of men—including that of every great and small country on Earth today—are smashed and replaced by God's government. Fairness, justice and peace finally come to a sick and broken planet!

Of course, the seventh trumpet brings the *forced* establishment of Christ's GOVERNMENT, based on God's LAWS, over the nations. But they are not happy to see *this* Christ—they are "*angry*" (vs. 18)! They will have come to believe and trust in a counterfeit system, and many will have expected to be "raptured away" to safety by what is actually a *false* christ, not the Christ of the Bible.

Even professing Christianity, while pretending that God governs "in the hearts of men," has not *truly* wanted to be GOVERNED by Him. Neither has the world, which hates His Law (Rom. 8:7). Mankind has rejected the only way to peace, happiness, abundance and universal prosperity. In a final and terrible way, the seven last plagues get the world's attention. They signal that Jesus Christ is KING of kings—and He is now in CHARGE!

Christ wants the world to know that He is about to save humanity from itself.

Still Another Earthquake

This earthquake occurs *after* the seventh trumpet has sounded (Rev. 11:15). This is the time of Christ's Second Coming: "...and there were great voices in heaven, saying, The kingdoms of this world are become the kingdoms of our Lord, and of His Christ; and *He shall reign forever and ever.*"

Verse 19 states, "And the temple of God was opened in heaven, and there was seen in His temple the ark of His testament: and there were light-nings, and voices, and thunderings, *and an earthquake*, and great hail." This earthquake occurs immediately *after* Christ's Return and the First Resurrection, and punctuates the fulfillment of these events.

Christ's Return makes possible the fulfillment of all the wonderful prophecies of the Bible foretold to come to pass on Earth. This pivotal event is the most crucial in all history! Earthquakes, before and after it, underscore its momentous importance in God's Plan. No other event bears such distinction.

This earthquake also results from Christ's actual *presence*, now ruling in glory. The earth literally quakes with gladness, along with the whole Creation: "Let the sea roar, and the fullness thereof; the world, and they that dwell therein. Let the floods clap their hands: let the hills be joyful together before the LORD; for He comes to judge the earth: with righteous-ness shall He judge the world, and the people with equity" (Psa. 98:7-8).

As with the seventh seal, the seventh trumpet is divided into *seven parts*. These are called the SEVEN LAST PLAGUES, and they "fill up" (Rev. 15:1)—*complete*—the wrath of God! Revelation 14:10 reveals that the last plagues are "poured out...in the presence of the holy *angels*, and in the presence of the LAMB." Of course, Jesus Christ is the Lamb of God (John 1:29, 36).

Before we examine these plagues, beginning in chapter 15, several inset chapters appear in Revelation.

Chapter 12: The Woman—Christ's Church

Chapters 12, 13 and 14 represent an interruption—an inset—in the overall flow of Revelation. This is because God wants readers to be aware of what *His* Church—*His* people—will be doing for the nearly 2,000 years from John's vision until the Return of Christ. God has always had His true Church—the *persecuted* (John 15:20; II Tim. 3:12), *few* (Matt. 7:14; 20:16; 22:14), *little flock* (Luke 12:32) that will rule with Christ (Rev. 2:26; 3:21)!

We have seen that Christ will be established as King of kings and Lord of lords. But the saints will be resurrected and join Him. Chapter 12 introduces more directly the Church through which Jesus has been preparing these others to rule with Him.

John describes God's Church from before Christ's birth (vs. 4), through His life, Resurrection and ascension (vs. 5). He then describes the 1,260 years of persecution this Church endured and how it had to flee to remote areas to avoid the government powers that sought to destroy it. But Christ promised that the true Church—His "flock"—would always exist (Matt. 16:18)—and it has!

This is also an important chapter in that it shows (Rev. 12:14) that God will *protect* His Church—described as a woman here—from the horrible time of intense trial soon to befall this world! All of Revelation 12 describes her, and the devil's attacks against her. Soon, an angry Satan will lash out at Christ's Church one last time, forcing her need for protection: "And when the *dragon* saw that he was cast unto the earth, he *persecuted the woman* which brought forth the man *child*. And to the woman were given two wings of a great eagle, that she might fly into the wilderness, into HER PLACE, where she is nourished for a time, and times, and half a time, from the face of the serpent" (vs. 13-14). Those of the condition of the faithful sixth era of the Church escape!

The "time, and times, and half a time" are the three and a half years of the Tribulation and wrath of God. Verse 17 shows how the devil turns his attention to the "remnant"—the lukewarm era, previously explained.

Understand. This is *not* the "woman" pictured in chapter 17—she is depicted as a *great whore* (vs. 1)! *That* woman is the great *false* church, representing the *false* Christianity of this world. The woman of chapter 17 actually *persecutes* the chapter 12 *different woman* that is God's true Church. Chapter 12, verse 17, describes it as those who "keep the commandments of God." Recognizing the difference between these two women is another vital KEY to understanding the book of Revelation!

Chapter 13: Two "Beasts"

The 13th chapter describes a symbolic "Beast" *and* a second beast with "two horns" (vs. 11). The first Beast is a description of the

Roman Empire—a *political* kingdom. The second two-horned beast represents the *headquarters* of the large, organized false *church* that controls the first Beast. (Much proof follows later.)

Only by comparing Revelation 13 and 17 and Daniel 7, with Daniel 2, can you fully understand the scope and magnitude of the beasts, and the system they represent. Numerous Old Testament scriptures refer to them, but these chapters most describe them. (A fuller explanation of these beasts comes in the next chapter.)

Chapter 14: The 144,000

Chapter 7 introduced the 144,000, and the 14th chapter gives more details about their identity. Verses 1-5 give a nine-point description of them standing before God's throne as "the firstfruits" (vs. 4) of God's kingdom.

As when He protected Israel from the plagues of Egypt, God often protects His servants. We will see in the next chapters of Revelation that the seven last plagues will soon be poured out on the earth. The 144,000, carefully covered in a later chapter, are plainly the number of saints in the First Resurrection, are with Christ in His kingdom, and are therefore protected from these terrifying last plagues.

The Three Angelic Messages

Chapter 14 also pictures *three angels* bearing *three messages* (vs. 6-11). Examine these angelic messages, which include a warning not to receive the "*mark of the beast*." Other prophecies show that *most* will *ignore* this all-important warning!

Those of the final great Babylonish system will be deceived into receiving the much talked about, but little understood, MARK OF THE BEAST. These messages announce the fall of Babylon through the seven last plagues and warn against receiving the *mark*.

The final destruction of this system is an incredible event. Like so much of Revelation, many take phrases out of context in order to support the false ideas and doctrines of men. Verse 11 states, "And the smoke of their torment ascends up forever and ever." Many dismiss this as merely a reference to souls burning forever in hell, and misunderstand the point of the context.

The timeframe of this event is yet to come. It refers to "Babylon" (vs. 8), "that great city, because she made all nations drink of...

her fornication." This is the religious/political/military/economic final revival of the Holy Roman Empire, also described in Daniel 2:42-43 as the "toes" and in Daniel 7:7 and 24 as the 10th horn. Revelation 13 describes it as the seventh and last horn. Revelation 17:12 describes it as the seventh head (which has not yet appeared), and having 10 horns.

Revelation 14:9-10 states, "If any man WORSHIP THE BEAST [this final end-time revival and its leader] and his IMAGE, and receive his MARK...he shall be tormented with fire and brimstone...in the presence of the Lamb." As long as those participating in this "beast" system continue to rebel against God, they will receive "no rest day nor night" (vs. 11). This does not say that they will be burning in hell for eternity. What it does say is that once their bodies are burned up, the *smoke* ascends forever. The fire extinguishes itself, but the gases from the *smoke* will continue to circulate in the atmosphere.

The fire that is talked about is here on Earth, not in an "ever-burning hell." Malachi plainly states, "And you shall tread down the wicked; *for they shall be ashes under the soles of your feet* in the day that I shall do this, says the LORD of hosts" (4:3).

Revelation 14:12 contains a description of God's servants, who will *not* take the mark of the Beast. These are only a relative few commandment-keepers in a sinning world that has followed a system that has rebelled against God. This verse explains that only the "faith *of* Jesus" (not merely belief IN Jesus) gives them the strength to resist receiving the mark. Typical human faith will be of no value!

Chapter 15: The Seven Last Plagues Introduced

We have now reached the *last part* of the *seventh seal*—which is the *seventh trumpet*, the *third woe*, or the *seven last plagues* (vs. 1). All four of these terms represent the exact same thing—they are synonymous! Let's now examine what they *mean*.

Recall from chapter 11 (vs. 15-19) that the blowing of the *seventh trumpet* represents the moment when Christ returns to set up His kingdom. The time setting is that God's WRATH has come!

Here is what John wrote: "And the nations were *angry*, and YOUR WRATH is come, and the time of the dead, that they should be judged, and that You should *give reward* unto Your servants the prophets, and to the saints, and them that fear Your Name, small and great [the First Resurrection]; and should *destroy them which destroy the earth*" (vs. 18).

John records that the nations "were angry." But so is God! Notice it said, "*Your* wrath is come." Keep this straight! The last part of the seventh seal, the seventh trumpet, the third woe, the *seven last plagues*—and the *vials*—are all one and the same event—GOD'S WRATH! It is *this time* that will have finally come to all surviving inhabitants on Earth!

Notice: "And I saw another sign in heaven, great and marvelous, seven angels having the seven last plagues; for in them is *filled up* the WRATH OF GOD" (15:1).

Before this occurs, verses 2 and 3 show that the resurrected saints sing praise to God. God's anger is about to be *complete*. If something is "filled up," there is room for no more. This represents the final *sum* of God's punishment.

Chapter 16: The Seven Last Plagues (Vials) Are Poured Out

Chapter 16 describes these plagues (called vials here—vs. 2-4, 8, 10, 12, 17). They reflect God's final judgment against the false system, called "Babylon the Great" (17:5; 18:2, 8, 10)!

The first vial is poured out upon the earth, "…and there fell a noisome and *grievous sore* upon the men which had the *mark of the beast*, and upon them who worshipped his image" (Rev. 16:2). These individuals belong to the false church-state system.

The second plague is similar to that suffered by the Egyptians just prior to the Exodus (Ex. 7:14-25). "And the second angel poured out *his vial upon the sea*; and it became as the blood of a dead man: and every living soul died in the sea" (Rev. 16:3).

Read for yourself the next three plagues. The rivers and fountains will turn to blood. The sun will become so hot that it will scorch men with fire. Darkness and pain will become unbearable. Now look at verse 11. After all these plagues from God, men continued to "blaspheme the God of heaven because of their pains and their sores, and *repented not* of their deeds."

One look around thunders that this rotten, awful, degenerate, disobedient age has *almost* come to the full! But this last generation is so vile, corrupt and contemptuous that God will subject them to the worst punishment possible—and they *still* will not understand—or repent!

How did we previously see God viewed such a time? "And God saw that the wickedness of man was great in the earth, and that every imagination of the thoughts of his heart was only evil continually" (Gen. 6:5). A similar time is upon us!

The Sixth Plague

The sixth of these last plagues sets the stage for the final battle to resist Christ at His Return. Forces of spiritual wickedness are released to bring destruction and devastation on the inhabitants of the earth. Covered in more detail in an important later chapter, a short summary is helpful here.

Verse 12 describes how God uses an angel to dry up the Euphrates River so that armies coming from the east can gather with the largest army in history (the one of 200 million men). This is just a prelude to even more significant events to come.

Verse 13 continues by addressing the role of demons sent by the devil into the Beast (a civil ruler) and the False Prophet (the religious leader associated with him). The next verse says, "For they are the spirits of devils [demons], working miracles, which go forth unto the kings of the earth and of the whole world, to *gather* them to *the battle of that great day of God Almighty*" (vs. 14). These "spirits of devils" are simply demons—fallen angels who followed Satan.

Notice! This leader will be accompanied by a charismatic religious leader, who will perform miracles with the power of the devil (Rev. 19:20; 13:11-14). When the peoples of the earth witness these miracles, they will be deceived into thinking that this false system is of God, and that they are able to successfully fight what they will perceive as outer space invaders! These two men will no doubt be possessed by demons (16:13), or even the devil himself, driving this religious-political-military system toward the final battle.

Battle of the Great Day of God Almighty

The final, seductive False Prophet (II Thes. 2:3) will lead the world to worship the Beast (Rev. 13:4, 16:2 and 19:20)! This deception will be so great, so widespread, that they will even deceive mankind into fighting Jesus Christ at His Second Coming (Rev. 16:9, 13-16; 17:13-14).

The seventh plague (vial) is commonly referred to as the Battle of Armageddon. This is a misnomer. Revelation 16:16 records that they *gather* at "a place *called*" Armageddon. At this time, the Beast and False Prophet are feverishly working their final miracles to delude the masses (16:13).

Verse 14 reveals that the proper name of this battle is "The battle of the great day of God Almighty"—not Armageddon! This is GOD'S battle. It is not like so many famous battles today that are named after a *location*—such as Gettysburg, Waterloo, Verdun or Stalingrad. The battle takes place 60 miles away (from Megiddo), outside Jerusalem. The location is not important—but God's purpose IS!

Two major forces (the Beast and the men of the East) will see Jesus Christ coming out of the clouds (Acts 1:11-12). Considering Him their greater threat, they will unite, forming an alliance to fight what they perceive to be their common enemy. These men will be angry. They will not submit to God's government. They will think the true Christ is actually the "Antichrist" and will "make war with the Lamb" (Rev. 17:14).

There is no battle prophesied to occur *between human armies*! This last decisive battle will be fought by armies outside Jerusalem (those who *gathered at* Armageddon) *against Christ and His saints*! A subject of near-endless speculation, you will later learn the truth of "Armageddon" is more horrific than the imagined scenarios of men.

One Final Greatest Earthquake

There is one final earthquake that signals that God is going forward to battle! This earthquake will be the most powerful of all time. Revelation 16:17-18 states, "And the *seventh angel* poured out his vial into the air; and there came a great voice out of the temple of heaven, from the throne, saying, It is done. And there were voices, and thunders, and lightnings; and there was A GREAT EARTHQUAKE, *such as was not since men were upon the earth*, so mighty an earthquake, and so great."

This earthquake changes the entire topography of the earth. Notice verse 20: "And every island *fled away*, and the mountains *were not found*." It appears to complete the process begun by the earthquake of Revelation 6:12-14, in which "every mountain and island were *moved* out of their places." It is mentioned in Zechariah 14.

Verse 4 states, "And His feet shall stand in that day upon the *mount of Olives*, which is before Jerusalem on the east, and the *mount of Olives shall cleave in the midst* thereof toward the east and toward the west, and there shall be a very great valley; and *half of the mountain shall remove* toward the *north, and* half of it toward the *south*." There, verse 9 states, "And the LORD shall be King over all the earth…"

At least three of the five earthquakes of Revelation are accompanied by *voices, lightning*, and *thunder*. These occur at the time of Revelation

8:5 (at the beginning of the Day of the Lord), Revelation 11:19 (after the Return of Christ), and the *final* earthquake of Revelation 16:18 (at the end of the seven last plagues). (Revelation 6:12 and 11:13 describe the other two earthquakes, totaling five.)

For voices to be heard in the midst of an earthquake, especially when accompanied by lightning and thunder, they would have to be those of mighty angels.

Chapter 17: The Woman of Babylon the Great

Chapters 17 and 18 are another inset describing the influential Roman religious system that is destroyed at the end of chapter 16. These chapters give a somewhat more detailed picture of the large *universal* church. The picture includes her *harlot "daughters"* (17:5), which have helped to deceive all nations (17:1-2; 18:3).

Many end-time prophecies use terms like *heads, horns, toes, kings*, etc. Several whole chapters must be studied to make their meaning clear. They clarify the different revivals of the same Roman system. A complex subject needing many pages to explain, the prophecies of chapter 17 are covered separately in the extensive next chapter.

Chapter 18: Babylon's Judgment

This chapter describes the final judgment and actual destruction of Babylon. Verse 17 shows that her collapse comes quickly. The merchants of the world are aghast at how this powerful economic system could so suddenly come to such complete ruin.

The nations of the West are deceived and have become part of this Babylonish system! (Jeremiah 50:4-8, 13-15; 51:6-9 and Isaiah 47:1, 5, 7-9, 11; 48:1, 12, 17-20 describe it.) Ancient Israel was in Egypt when God poured out His plagues. Like Israel, God calls His people *out* of this world's "Egypt."

Understand this basic instruction about the Christian calling. God's people are not of this world or its systems (John 17:14-16). Regarding the religious and political systems of this Babylon, God instructs, *"Come out of her, MY PEOPLE, that you be not partakers of her sins"* (Rev. 18:4). Babylon means *confusion*. The true servants of God have come out of this world, its governments and its confusion (I Cor. 14:33). Because they are separate from it, they shall also be separated and spared from its plagues.

Chapter 19: The Wedding Supper—and "Another" Supper

The setting of chapter 19 is in heaven. Many angels surround God's throne (vs. 1-2), describing His "righteous...judgments" on the great whore.

Now that she is gone, and Christ has returned, what happens next? "I heard...the voice of a great multitude...saying, Alleluia: for the Lord God omnipotent reigns. Let us be glad and rejoice, and give honor to Him: for the MARRIAGE of the Lamb is come, and His WIFE has *made herself ready.* And to her was granted that she should be *arrayed in fine linen,* clean and white: for the fine linen is the *righteousness of saints.* And He said... Write, Blessed are they which are called unto the MARRIAGE SUPPER of the Lamb..." (vs. 6-9).

The New Testament identifies the Church Jesus built as His BRIDE. Several passages reveal this (Matt. 25:1-10; Eph. 5:23). At His Return, in one of the most awesome events in all history—the Wedding Supper—Jesus Christ will marry His Church!

Revelation 19:11-13 describes Christ, and verse 14 describes "armies" of angels joining Him from heaven. Verses 17-18 show that a vast flock of birds of prey eat the flesh of the dead armies, slain in chapter 16. This other "supper" is referred to as the "supper of the great God."

The chapter concludes with a description of the execution of the Beast and False Prophet in a localized lake of fire.

Chapter 20: The Three Resurrections

Chapter 20 introduces Christ's 1,000-year reign on Earth. At this time, the world will truly be "paradise," since Satan will have been bound and cast into the bottomless pit (vs. 1-3). This chapter also explains the three separate resurrections that are central to God's Plan.

Verses 4-6 describe the FIRST RESURRECTION and the reign of the saints with Christ for 1,000 years, which you now know occurs when the seventh trumpet is blown and Christ returns to Earth.

In Matthew 25, which is actually a continuation of the Olivet Prophecy of chapter 24, Jesus speaks of this momentous event. The angels come from heaven with Him when He establishes His kingdom.

Notice the picture once Christ is established on His throne: "When the Son of man shall come in His glory, and *all the holy angels with Him,* then shall He sit upon the *throne of His glory:* and before Him shall be gathered all nations: and He shall separate them one from another, as a shepherd divides His sheep from the goats: and He shall set the sheep on His right hand, but the goats on the left. Then shall the King say unto them on His right hand, COME, you blessed of My Father, *inherit the kingdom* prepared for you from the foundation of the world" (Matt. 25:31-34).

This is a truly awesome scene. Just before His crucifixion and ascension to heaven, we read where Jesus said, "If I go...I will COME AGAIN" (John 14:3). Here, Christ gives the reward to each of His saints. They "inherit the kingdom" with Him and rule for 1,000 years.

But we must ask a larger question, beyond the immediate events prophesied through the first 19 chapters of the book of Revelation: What will take place *after* Christ's 1,000-year reign on Earth?

The description of other events is found starting in Revelation 20:7 and continues through the end of the book. Verses 7-9 actually describe a prophecy pertaining to the end of the Millennium, when Satan is briefly loosed from his prison and seeks to reverse the 1,000 years of peace. Verse 10 describes his fate.

Starting with verse 11, the next five verses describe the *Second* and *Third resurrections*, of which most have little or no knowledge. Let's read first: "And I saw a great white throne, and Him that sat on it, from whose face the earth and the heaven fled away; and there was found no place for them. And I saw the dead, small and great, stand before God; and *the books* [the 66 books of the Bible] were opened: and another book was opened, which is the book of life: and the dead were judged out of those things which were written in the books, according to their works" (vs. 11-12).

This has been referred to as the White Throne Judgment, in which *all* human beings who have *ever lived* will receive an opportunity for eternal life. This is when all mankind, since Adam, will be resurrected to physical life for 100 years. (Read Isaiah 65:17-25.) All these masses will be "judged" from God's Word—"the books" of the Bible. This judgment is nothing like the supposed "judgment" that most envision, where people are thought to at some point in God's Plan "line up in heaven" before Him for "sentencing." The *period of time* described here is a judgment that lasts 100 years (Isa. 65:20), and people are given a full opportunity to respond to, or reject, God's Way—and eternal salvation!

Then verse 13 continues with, "And the sea gave up the dead which were in it; and *death and hell* [the grave] delivered up the dead which were in them: and they were *judged* every man according to their works." The first part of the verse probably still refers mostly to the *Second Res-*

urrection, but the latter part directly refers to the Third Resurrection, with verse 14 adding, "And *death and hell* were cast into the *lake of fire*. This is the SECOND DEATH."

When it speaks *again*, a second time, of men being judged according to their works, this is certainly referencing the *Third Resurrection* (vs. 14) because the context pertains to *hell* (gehenna) and *death* (the entire idea and reality of physical and eternal death—Revelation 21:4) being destroyed in the lake of fire. Notice: "And whoever was not found written in the *book of life* was cast into the *lake of fire*" (20:15).

This last fulfillment—the *Third Resurrection*—occurs at the very end of God's Plan, the time *after* He will have given every person who has ever lived a full opportunity to qualify to enter His kingdom.

There will be no escaping the final result of unrepentant sin—the "second death" in the "lake of fire."

Jesus stated, "Then shall He say also unto them on the left hand, Depart from Me, *you cursed*, into everlasting fire, prepared for the devil and his angels" (Matt. 25:41). He explained that everlasting fire—the lake of fire—was prepared for the "devil and his angels [demons]." In verse 46, Jesus continued, "And these [disobedient people] shall go away into everlasting punishment [not punish*ing*]: but *the righteous into life eternal*." Those judged unfit—disqualified—for eternal life will be thrown into the lake of fire!

When cast into the lake of fire, these people will go through what God defines as "the second death," from which there is no resurrection: "But the *fearful*, and *unbelieving*, and *abominable*, and *murderers*, and *whoremongers*, and *sorcerers*, and *idolaters*, and all *liars*, shall have their part in the lake which burns with fire and brimstone: which is the SECOND DEATH" (Rev. 21:8). Those cast into this lake of fire *after the Millennium* will be burned up forever.

May all fear such a fate!

When chapter 20, verse 10 refers to the Beast and False Prophet being cast into "a" lake of fire (19:20), this is a TYPE of the second death. This evil duo will likely be raised in the Great White Throne Judgment (Rev. 20:11-13) to receive what is their first opportunity for salvation.

Chapter 21: New Heavens, Earth and Jerusalem

Finally, the closing chapters 21 and 22 of Revelation picture the last phase of God's Plan with the establishment of the *new heaven*, the *new earth* and the *new Jerusalem*!

Eventually, at the end of His Plan, God will dwell on Earth instead of in heaven. John records the time when the new Jerusalem will come *here* from heaven.

Chapter 21 reveals more about the completion of God's plan of salvation, and the purging of the earth by fire (II Pet. 3:10-12). Verses 1-3 state: "And I saw a NEW HEAVEN and a NEW EARTH: for the first heaven and the first earth were passed away; and there was no more sea. And I John saw the holy city, NEW JERUSALEM, coming down from God out of heaven, prepared as a bride adorned for her husband. And I heard a great voice out of heaven saying, Behold, the tabernacle [dwelling] of God is with men, and He will dwell with them, and they shall be His people, and God Himself shall be with them, and be their God."

At this time, the earth will become the headquarters of God's government. This government will continue to grow, literally, without end. Take time to read Isaiah 9:7 and Luke 1:33.

God's MASTER PLAN encompasses eternity. Those entering His kingdom will not be idle. They will be active and productive—and will continue to fulfill His purpose! Hebrews 2:6-8 explains that God will ultimately place man in authority over "all things"—the entire universe.

It is difficult to grasp the glory and magnitude of what we will be doing for eternity. But Revelation 21:5 gives a hint: "Behold, I make all things new."

Chapter 22: Promises and Warnings

In verse 7, Christ says, "Behold, I COME quickly: *blessed is he that keeps the sayings of the prophecy of this book.*" Reread this *promise* until it sinks in!

Now read verses 18-19, which give a dire warning to any who would add to or take away from this book, or Scripture in general. Then reread this *warning* until it sinks in!

Verse 15 describes those who, unwilling to repent of their degenerate lifestyles, will never be in the kingdom of God: "For without are *dogs* [false ministers], and *sorcerers*, and *whoremongers*, and *murderers*, and *idolaters*, and whosoever loves and makes a *lie.*" Also see Galatians 5:19-21.

There is urgency in Christ's words throughout Revelation 22. For a second time, He states He will come again, but this time reveals what He brings with Him: "And, behold, I [Christ] *come* quickly; and MY REWARD IS WITH ME, to give every man according as his work shall be" (vs. 12;

also see I Corinthians 15:50-54). Christ is coming to Earth, bringing re-wards for each saint with Him—not the other way around. The saved do not go to heaven!

Jesus Christ's very last words in Revelation are: "He which testifies these things says, Surely I will come quickly. Amen! Even so, come, Lord Jesus!" (vs. 20).

God help *you* to heed the warning of Revelation—and this book—and to receive *reward* from Christ when He returns—SOON!

But the most wonderful good news possible is preceded by the *worst* possible bad news…

The Beast of Revelation

The book of Revelation speaks of a terrifying "Beast" to appear at the end of the age. Theories abound surrounding this mysterious entity's identity, yet the pages of your Bible plainly reveal its identity—and what this means for you!

The subject of the Beast now receives in-depth examination in its own chapter. Earlier referenced scriptures will sometimes be repeated for impact and clarity in this fuller context.

The world is drifting along—sleepy, drunken and oblivious to what lies ahead. The average person has no idea what the future holds—and, again, many do not care. Few are concerned beyond "tomorrow"—and fewer still remotely suspect what is coming in our time.

When God's Plan—His great overarching PURPOSE—is understood, confusion, mystery and misunderstanding disappear. Events become clear!

Historians can only record what has already happened. They cannot see into the future—prophecy—I repeat: *history written in advance*! God foretells major events *before* they happen. Over 80 percent of Bible prophecy remains unfulfilled. Many major events must yet come to pass.

Behind the Scenes—Now

Conditions in Europe and around the world will soon dictate that a single great authority must be given power for a short time. Much is written of the

Beast, and events surrounding its appearance, but little is understood of what the Bible *actually* reveals about this powerful, dominant governing system, eventually united under two men.

World history is the study of the rise and fall of empires. But few know *why* dominant civilizations ebb and flow—*why* governments rise and fall—*why* events move as they do. Most see these things as products of the normal cycle of economics, war, disease and natural calamities.

This thinking is about to change—in a BIG WAY! This chapter explains how—and *why*.

Christ's Grave Warning

Recall yet again that Matthew 24 (including chapter 25), Mark 13 and Luke 21 are parallel accounts of Christ's greatest prophecy. Each of these chapters adds additional details, *together* forming the picture of what will happen from here on.

Luke's account contains a *strong warning* to all who live at the end of the age. Jesus explains that those who serve God must be careful not to be swept away by conditions that give a false impression of what is happening—or coming. Here is how He began: "And *take heed* [be careful!] to yourselves, lest at any time your hearts be overcharged with *surfeiting* [indulgence], and *drunkenness*, and *cares of this life*, and so THAT DAY [terrible, world-shaking events] come upon you *unawares*" (21:34).

This passage pictures the values and lifestyle of most people. Almost no one is "taking heed," and "that day" *will* come on them "unawares." Here again is how Jesus describes the sudden arrival of worldwide cataclysms: "For as a *snare* shall it come on ALL them that dwell on the face of the WHOLE EARTH" (vs. 35).

Jesus carefully chose this analogy. *Snares* catch unsuspecting victims, who carelessly step into them—and find themselves suddenly trapped, often hanging upside-down, completely disoriented. This is a graphic picture of what will soon strike "the whole earth"! And these are the words of Christ, not some "doomsday prophet" speaking without facts or authority.

But this snare need not catch YOU—or anyone who heeds Christ's words. Calamity will not come without notice to those who are vigilant. Here is what Christ said to do: "*Watch* you therefore…" (vs. 36).

The snare that Christ spoke of will entrap the *entire world*. Despite His warning, almost no one is preparing for what lies ahead.

Stark Reality

To "watch," you must know WHAT to watch for. Otherwise, such watching is useless—it has no value. Many will be deceived—fooled—because they will be watching in the wrong places for the wrong things, or expecting events to occur in a wrong sequence or timeframe.

The Bible is: (1) A *history* book, (2) a *prophecy* book and (3) a book about essential, *revealed* knowledge that man could not otherwise discover for himself. If *world history* is the study of the rise and fall of *past* empires, then *prophecy* is primarily the study of the rise and fall of world empires *before* they appear.

Men cannot discover what the future holds without God REVEALING it!

Early world history records little about nations, kingdoms and empires that may have existed prior to the great Flood of Noah's time. However, the Bible *does* discuss the empires of Egypt, Assyria, Babylon and various other nations as they came into contact with God's people, the nation of Israel, after the Flood.

The first great empire that God focuses on, both through history and Bible prophecy, is Babylon. It was founded by Nebuchadnezzar in the 600s BC, and consisted of multiple nations and regions unified under his leadership. King Nebuchadnezzar was perhaps the first great *Gentile* leader—and Scripture focuses on this man and *his system* all the way to the Return of Christ!

Paralleling this foretelling of the rise and fall of great Gentile empires are prophecies describing the nation of Israel—both ancient Israel and the modern-day nations populated by its descendants.

The role of the symbolic Beast of Revelation has everything to do with WORLD EMPIRES. Many know that it represents *"Babylon the Great"* (Rev. 17:5) in some way, but are unsure how. And the nature and identity of this "wild beast" remains shrouded in mystery, even for those who profess to and think that they understand who or what it is. Yet, the REAL TRUTH of how the Beast will eventually affect and change the earth will shock you beyond belief!

Terrible plagues will strike the disbelieving and unprepared. Notice this most blunt WARNING to all: "If any man *worship* the *beast* and his *image*, and receive his *mark* in his forehead, or in his hand, the same shall drink of the wine of the WRATH OF GOD, which is poured out *without mixture* [Greek: undiluted]" (Rev. 14:9-10).

This is serious! God is not a "respecter of persons," playing favorites. He says, "If ANY man worship..." Woe to ALL who remain ignorant of the facts surrounding this awesome prophecy. They will suffer horribly in ways God describes most graphically. There is no room for misunderstanding on this most sober of Bible warnings.

So then, the following questions must be answered:

• Who or what is the Beast of Revelation 13 and 17? Is it a man?—a church?—a government?—an empire?

• Who is the "WOMAN" of Revelation 17 who rides it?

• What is the "MARK of the Beast"?

• What is the "IMAGE of the Beast"?

• Who is the "FALSE PROPHET" often spoken of in conjunction with the Beast?

• When will these things occur—*how long* must we wait to see these figures appear?

• How will world trends, conditions and events spawn the Beast's *arrival*?

• Why is it so important to correctly identify the Beast, with all related prophecies?

• How will it affect YOU?

The world does not know God. It is unaware of the Plan and Purpose that He is working out "here below." While worldwide disobedience to His laws, and rejection of His truths, will cause plagues to be poured out on a God-hating humanity, the God of the Bible is a loving God. Before punishment takes place, He always makes certain His "watchman" (Ezek. 33:7) sounds the alarm to those in harm's way. He wants no one to have an excuse, saying, "I didn't know" or "Why didn't you tell me?"

There is a responsibility to caution—to WARN—all who will yet take heed of the seriousness and *meaning* behind world-shaking events and calamities, lying just over the horizon. –

The Bible speaks of several *different* beasts. To understand them all, each must be explained separately. Revelation 13 speaks of a Beast in its first 7 verses. Another Beast, ridden by a woman, is described in Revelation 17. Daniel 7 speaks of four separate beasts, with a reference to a "little horn" that appears during the time of the fourth beast. Revelation 13 describes a second "two-horned beast," beginning in verse 11. Daniel 2 describes a giant image of a man composed of four separate metals. Relative to most of these descriptions, a specific number of "heads," "horns" and "toes" are mentioned.

No wonder this subject is so confusing. It *does* require thorough explanation, and God must supply the CLUES—the critical knowledge to *unlocking* all of the above terms.

God says, "My people are destroyed for lack of *knowledge*" (Hos. 4:6). This chapter will strip away the confusion, misunderstanding, wrong knowledge and outright deceit that is now deluding so many who do not *know* the PLAIN TRUTH of this prophecy. Every day, end-time conditions grow more ominous—and YOU MUST UNDERSTAND!

The Beast, Its Mark and Plagues

In the last chapter, we learned the Bible foretells a series of catastrophic events, which involve seven trumpets, to occur immediately prior to Christ's Return. The seventh trumpet "fills up" what the Bible calls "the wrath of God." This last trumpet is comprised of the seven last *plagues* (also called *bowls*, or *vials*), which punish a rebellious, sinning mankind. Seven angels "pour out the vials of the wrath of God upon the earth" (Rev. 16:1). We saw the Bible depiction of how this occurs is very graphic.

When the first vial is poured out upon the earth, the Bible states, "there fell a noisome and grievous sore upon the men which had the *mark* of the *beast*, and upon them which *worshipped* his *image*" (Rev. 16:2). All those who receive this plague belong to a false church-state system. Of course, we saw this is but the first plague.

I have heard endless theories about what the Beast's mark may be. It is a subject of almost unending opinion, and has generated a veritable "cottage industry" of speculation, debate and disagreement. For almost every person who reads of the mark, another idea is born. But all attempts to explain the mark, the image of the Beast and who will receive the plagues are fruitless unless one first establishes who or what the Beast *is*!

We must start with the Bible description of the Beast.

Revelation 13 and Two Beasts

As we read, comparing Revelation 13, 17 and Daniel 7, with Daniel 2, brings full understanding of the scope and magnitude of the beasts, and the SYSTEM they represent. Numerous Old Testament scriptures also refer to them, but these chapters are the most critical to understand. Combined, they explain a staggering—and profoundly sobering!—prophecy about latter-day events that—I continue to emphasize—will affect *all humanity in your lifetime*!

Revelation 17:8-9 describes a "beast" that ascends out of a "bottomless pit" and is ridden by a "woman." Verse 12 shows that this Beast involves 10 kings who shall receive power and unite to bequeath it to a leader who will take the role of the final Beast.

This again will be the seventh, and last, short-lived resurrection of the Holy Roman Empire—arising *now* in the heart of Europe! A United States of Europe is coming—and now lies just ahead. When it appears, the entire world will stand in shocked amazement. Let's establish, and then PROVE, these stunning prophecies. It is *vital* that you grasp what they mean!

In Revelation 13, the apostle John describes a Beast with seven heads, 10 horns and 10 crowns.

Revelation 13 contains a symbolic description of the "Beast"—*and* a description of a second beast with "two horns" (vs. 11). The first Beast represents the Roman Empire—a *political* kingdom. The two-horned beast represents the *headquarters* of an influential, false prophetic "woman" that controls the first Beast. This chapter also describes both the "image" and the "mark" of the Beast.

The apostle John wrote what he saw in vision, offering significant detail in his description of the Beast: "And I stood upon the sand of the sea, and saw a BEAST rise up out of the sea, having SEVEN HEADS and TEN HORNS, and upon his horns TEN CROWNS, and upon his heads the name of blasphemy. And the beast which I saw was *like unto a leopard*, and his feet were as the *feet of a bear*, and his mouth as the *mouth of a lion*" (13:1-2).

These first one and a half verses of chapter 13 contain a physical description of what the Beast looks like. This will be important to remember. But the next three and a half verses tell more about the *nature*—the source of power, size, scope and conduct or behavior—of the Beast. The following verses give important *clues* for later examination. These clues go far in telling us exactly who or what the Beast is.

Now read: "And the DRAGON gave him his *power*, and his *seat*, and *great authority*. And I saw one of his heads as it were *wounded* to death; and his deadly *wound was healed*: and all the world wondered after the beast. And they worshiped the DRAGON which gave power unto the beast: and they *worshiped* the beast, saying, Who is like unto the beast? Who is able to *make war with him*? And there was given unto him a *mouth speaking great things and blasphemies*; and power was given unto him to continue *forty and two months*" (vs. 2-5).

Many mistakenly equate this last description of the Beast with the papacy. They fail to recognize that history is filled with accounts of its citizenry worshipping the *Roman Empire* and its *emperors*. Here is what one source states: "The worship of the emperor...In a word, the Roman government was not only wonderfully organized...Every one was required to join in the worship of the emperor because he stood for the majesty and glory of the Roman dominion...all were obliged, as good citizens, to join in the official sacrifices to the head of the State, as if he were a god" (*Medieval and Modern Times*, Robinson, p. 7).

Notice that the question was asked, "*Who* is able to make war with him?" It would not be difficult to make war with the papacy, because they only have a tiny group of guards around the Vatican. But making war with the Roman Empire was always most difficult. Also, the papacy, as an institution, has lasted much longer than 42 months, or the prophetic fulfillment of this period—1,260 years (Ezek. 4:4-6; Num. 14:34). So this is *not* a picture of the papacy, or Vatican. We shall soon see more proof of this.

John's description of the Beast's appearance leaves many questions. Perhaps the three biggest are: (1) Is John's description that of a *literal creature*? (2) Does it represent a *single individual*—a kind of anti-Christ, superman, world dictator? (3) Or does it picture *something else*?

These all require answers.

First, there is no living creature on Earth that this could be describing literally. If there is, who has ever seen it? Where does it live? How did it come to be alive? How could three known creatures (a leopard, a bear and a lion) come together in the worship of a *dragon*, when there are no real dragons? This passage does not remotely describe any known animal on Earth. Obviously, it must represent something other than a literal creature.

Second, regarding whether it is some kind of human being—superman or otherwise—similar questions arise. What kind of person looks like this? What man looks like a leopard, has feet like a bear and the mouth of a lion?—and has seven heads, 10 horns and 10 crowns on the horns?—*and* comes out of the ocean? Again, the obvious answer is no one. This depiction then cannot possibly refer to either a literal man or creature.

This leaves the third possibility.

How Bible Symbols Are Understood

There is only one other possible explanation for the Beast. It must be *symbolic*. Many recognize this, so it has produced an endless stream of *human* interpretations for what the Beast, and other descriptions in Revelation, represent. But it is useless to try to assign an arbitrary meaning to such graphic symbolism.

If the Bible does not explain who or what the Beast is, then its identity is subject to every possible human interpretation. No one would have a right to claim to be more correct than anyone else. Many others attempt to understand the Beast, only to give up in hopeless frustration, thinking that no proper explanation and meaning of this, or of the other two beasts, is possible!

In other words, if God does not reveal the meaning and identity of the beast(s)—then either *anything goes*, or one can rightly conclude that there is no correct explanation and this prophecy *cannot be understood*!

So then, unless one is to give up or choose to rely on human interpretation, we must accept a basic principle:

What John records in Revelation is written in SYMBOL. As established earlier, while he speaks in plain language, it *is* impossible to understand his symbols by merely rereading various passages again and again until their *meaning* suddenly "comes clear." Since John uses *many* symbols, we need to be able to understand the many *actual events* that these symbols *represent*. Otherwise, we will not know what is being described. Therefore, John's description must contain sufficient clues that can be deciphered by examining other verses in the Bible. Only *God* can interpret what He inspired. This is most true of the book of Revelation. Since God inspired Scripture, *He* must *always* interpret its meaning.

So let's understand!

Beginning to Understand

Through a series of dreams and visions, God used the prophet Daniel to reveal enormous prophetic understanding about how and when His kingdom would come to Earth (Dan. 1:17). Understanding Revelation is inseparable from, and impossible without, understanding Daniel—and vice versa—hence we revisit certain passages while examining new ones.

Daniel reported *tremendous* news that will affect you in your lifetime! We saw his entire message is for us today!

One of the most important visions that Daniel recorded is in chapter 7, where, inspired by God, he clearly explains and *interprets* the symbolism of the Beast. This is actually where proper understanding of Revelation 13 begins.

Verse 3 speaks of *"four* great beasts that came up *from the sea."*

Verse 4 describes the first beast as "like a *lion*." The verse contains other important descriptive phrases.

Verse 5 describes the second beast as "like to a *bear*." The rest of this verse also contains additional descriptive information.

Verse 6 describes the third beast as "like a *leopard*." While this verse gives more description, make note that this beast had "four heads."

Verse 7 describes the fourth beast as unlike any creature or animal on Earth. It states that this beast is "dreadful and terrible, and strong exceedingly; and it had *great iron teeth*." It is important to note that this fourth beast had "ten horns."

Remember, God interprets His own word. He needs no help from men. What has He told us?

Daniel's beasts, like the Beast of Revelation 13, come "from the sea." This is our first clue that what we are reading in Daniel 7 is a *parallel* to the Beast.

Other obvious parallels exist between the description of the Revelation 13 Beast and those that Daniel pictures. Daniel's four beasts have a total of *seven heads* (the leopard had four), as does the Revelation 13 Beast. The Revelation 13 Beast had 10 horns, and so does Daniel's fourth beast.

The most important parallel is that John and Daniel both describe beasts that involve a leopard, a bear and a lion. This cannot possibly be a coincidence. Both obviously describe related beasts! We will later see that the unmistakable parallels continue.

But what exactly are the *four beasts*? In verse 16, we see that the "interpretation of the things" can be known. God's immediate answer to Daniel's question (vs. 17) is, "These great beasts, which are four, are four *kings*, which shall arise out of the earth." The term "kings" is often synonymous with *kingdoms*, which, of course, kings represent (vs. 18, 22, 24, 27).

From verse 19 forward, Daniel focuses particularly on the fourth beast. Carefully read his description, noticing verse 23: "The fourth beast shall be the FOURTH KINGDOM UPON EARTH, which shall be *diverse from all kingdoms*, and shall *devour the whole earth*, and shall tread it down, and break it in pieces."

And what are the "ten horns"? Verse 24 interprets them: "And the *ten horns* out of this kingdom are *ten kings* [or kingdoms] that shall arise." The 10 kings represent 10 separate kingdoms, nations or governments.

It is now clear that this beast cannot be a human being or a church. Remember, the kings all come out of a *kingdom*. The obvious meaning of the 10 horns is that they are also 10 separate and sequential *kingdoms* because they all come from the fourth kingdom, which is described as ruling "the earth."

This is a basic scriptural explanation of terms, requiring no human interpretation to understand.

Christ and Saints Replace Fourth Beast

The four beasts of Daniel 7 span over 2,500 years, from Nebuchadnezzar's reign to the Return of Christ. Here is how we know this. Recall that the fourth beast is described from verses 19 through 26. Prior to verse 19, in the introduction of more detail about the fourth beast, it states in verse 18, "But the saints of the Most High shall take the kingdom, and possess the kingdom forever, even forever and ever."

Many other prophecies in the Bible explain that the saints rule with Christ. But there are two other verses here in Daniel 7, which prove most emphatically that this is true. Notice verse 22: "Until the Ancient of Days came, and judgment was given to the saints of the Most High; and the time came that the saints possessed the kingdom."

Verse 26 concludes by summarizing what happens to the fourth beast after it "shall wear out the saints of the Most High" (vs. 25), when it says that the saints then "shall sit, and they shall take away his dominion, to consume and to destroy it unto the end." Now verse 27, again speaking of the saints: "And the kingdom and dominion, and the greatness of the kingdom under the whole heaven, shall be given to the people of the saints of the Most High, whose kingdom is an everlasting kingdom, and all dominions shall serve and obey Him" (vs. 27).

We have established that the four beasts continue until Christ's Return brings the last beast to an end. But who are the four beasts—the four *kingdoms*?

What Are the Four Kingdoms?

Now we must turn our attention to Daniel 2. It also contains a parallel prophecy spanning the same 2,500-plus years concluding, as we will see, with Christ's Second Coming. This prophecy pictures a giant man consisting of four metals (gold, silver, brass, and iron mixed with clay), which represent four very large and powerful kingdoms, with the first starting in Daniel's time.

So then, the "great image" of Daniel 2 symbolizes four world-ruling *governments*.

For several verses, Daniel discussed with the Chaldean (Babylonian) King Nebuchadnezzar certain matters that had come to the king in a dream. Nebuchadnezzar was king of an empire that he had established approximately 600 years prior to Christ's time.

The king's court magicians were not able to interpret what only God could explain. God's purpose was to reveal, through Daniel, that there is an Almighty living God who *rules the entire universe*—and holds sovereignty over all *kings, governments* and *nations* on Earth. The humanly wise King Nebuchadnezzar had no knowledge beyond the existence of other human kings and their many false gods. But it was God's purpose to reveal to this human king the existence of His government and that it rules the universe. He also intended to make plain His great *purpose* in bringing that government to the earth "in the latter days" (vs. 28).

Several verses introduce and describe the image (statue) of a giant man. Let's read: "This image's head was of fine *gold*, his breast and his arms of *silver*, his belly and his thighs of *brass*, his legs of iron, his feet *part of iron and part of clay*" (vs. 32-33). This is clearly an image of a man, but one that is constructed of four distinct parts.

Then, verses 34-35 describe a great supernatural "*stone* that smote the image [and] became a great mountain, and filled the whole earth." Note that verse 34 states that the stone "was cut out *without hands*." This is because God, not men, had formed it. We will discuss this momentarily.

Since the "stone" shatters the image and replaces it, eventually encompassing the entire earth, this can only be the *Government of God* coming to Earth. Notice: "*Jesus Christ* of Nazareth, whom you crucified, whom God raised from the dead...*This* is the *stone* which was set at nought of you builders, which is become the Head of the corner" (Acts 4:10-11).

This verse identifies *Christ* as the stone of Daniel 2. When God's kingdom is established, we have already seen that the saints "possess the kingdom" (of God). Again, many verses show that they rule with the returning Christ. Christ's identity is proven and clarified in verses 44 and 45, which describe "the God of heaven set[ting] up a kingdom, which shall never be destroyed...it shall break in pieces and consume all these kingdoms, and it shall stand forever." The end of verse 45 adds, "and the dream is *certain*, and the *interpretation* thereof *sure*." Notice that God does His own interpreting, requiring no help from me or anyone else.

God leaves no doubt as to whether these prophecies will be fulfilled. He has spoken them—and they will happen! This is why it is so important for you to comprehend—really *grasp*—the identity and the meaning of the Beast and the events preceding Christ's Coming. He will destroy the final kingdom and set up God's all-powerful world-ruling government—supplanting all humanly devised governments! Daniel 2:34 and 44 *prove* that these 10 toes (10 *final* kings—and kingdoms—united under one leader) exist at the time of Christ's Coming, because the stone replaces them!

The Four Metals Explained

Now, what do the four metals of the image represent? We will see they are four Gentile kingdoms. But you do not need anyone, including me, to interpret them for you. Allow God to interpret the giant image—and the meaning of the four elements of which it is composed.

Verse 37 states, "*You*, O king [Nebuchadnezzar], are a king of kings: for the God of heaven has given you a kingdom, power, and strength, and glory." Verse 38 adds, "*You* are this head of gold." The Bible has just interpreted itself. Nebuchadnezzar and Babylon represent the first kingdom. Verses 39-40 go on to describe *three successive kingdoms* that would follow the kingdom of Nebuchadnezzar and Babylon. Here is how they are described: "And *after* you [Nebuchadnezzar] shall arise *another kingdom* [of silver] inferior to you, and another *third kingdom* of brass, which shall bear rule over all the earth. And the *fourth kingdom* shall be strong as iron: forasmuch as iron breaks in pieces and subdues all things: and as iron that breaks all these, shall it break in pieces and bruise."

These verses show a succession of WORLD EMPIRES depicted by different metals composing the giant image. These were literal kingdoms. What you have just learned is vital knowledge that very few understand today. God expressly reveals to us *now* that He is the One who establishes and removes—and establishes and removes again—earthly kingdoms. This has much to do with the identity of the Beast.

The first kingdom, which was the head made of gold, represented Nebuchadnezzar's Babylonian or Chaldean Empire (625-539 BC). In 539, the Medes and Persians defeated the Babylonians. The silver breast and arms represent this second empire. The duration of the Medo-Persian kingdom was 558-330 BC. The belly and thighs of brass represented the third kingdom, the Grecian (333-31 BC) or Greco-Macedonian Empire.

The Greco-Macedonian Empire was led by Alexander the Great. After just a one-year reign, Alexander died and his generals (recall Lysimachus, Cassander, Ptolemy and Seleucus) divided his enormous empire into *four* regions: (1) Egypt, (2) Macedonia and Greece, (3) Thrace and Western Asia, and (4) Syria and all territory east to the Indus River. These are obviously the four heads of Alexander's "leopard" kingdom.

Finally, the fourth kingdom is depicted by lower legs of iron, with feet and toes of iron mixed with clay. This represents the greatest of the four kingdoms—the Roman Empire, which defeated and succeeded the Greco-Macedonian Empire.

These are well-known facts of world history. Few dispute the basic historical accuracy of the timing, scope, strength and greatness of these four kingdoms.

However, we must understand *why* God focuses on *these* Gentile kingdoms.

In the greatest sense, the Bible is almost entirely a book about how God worked with the nation of ancient Israel. He chose, revealed Himself to, and gave His Law to govern this nation. God had warned Israel that if they disobeyed him, they would be punished (Lev. 26; Deut. 28). After a long series of ups and downs, Israel rejected God, His leaders and His Law for the last time. After sending most of the tribes of Israel into captivity in Assyria about 125 years earlier, God sent the last tribe, Judah, into captivity in Babylon under Nebuchadnezzar. (Daniel himself was a young Jewish slave.)

From the time of Judah's captivity forward, starting with Babylon, God raised up successive Gentile world empires that He foretold would continue for the remaining over 25 centuries before He established His kingdom.

The Fourth Beast Explained

The Roman Empire, which began in 31 BC, has existed and waned through a succession of historic resurrections. Starting from Rome, the empire slowly expanded until it had absorbed the four pieces of Alexander's kingdom. In time, it became the largest and most powerful empire the world had ever seen. Eventually, it encompassed all of the regions of the three empires that preceded it, and more. (Thus, the characteristics of Babylon, Medo-Persia and the four Greco-Macedonian divisions of Alexander's empire are reflected in an upcoming artist's rendering *within* the composite Beast of Revelation 13—the Roman Empire. The nondescript other six heads of this Beast carry no special meaning, individually.)

Rome slowly took on the qualities of the kingdoms it replaced. It had the lightning-speed, cruelty and striking-power of Alexander's small leopard-like army, which typically attacked like a World War II German blitzkrieg. But it also possessed the massive power of the Medo-Persian armies, which at a point boasted a standing army of over one million men. This is why God depicted the Medo-Persian Empire as having the tremendous power of a bear, and as the chest and arms of a man.

The city of Rome in particular, and the entire empire in general, also reflected and held much of the splendor that Babylon reflected, as the head of gold.

Rome embodied all the qualities of the bear, the lion and the leopard, yet was different in that it was unlike any other animal because it had "great iron teeth." All of this is why John saw one beast, not four, in Revelation 13. The four beasts of Daniel 7 had a total of seven heads. This is why John's one Beast also had seven heads.

The duration of the Roman Empire nearly covered the period of world dominance of the three kingdoms it succeeded put together!

The first period of the Roman Empire lasted from 31 BC to AD 476, when it collapsed after having been overrun by barbarians from the north.

If we are to be honest, and reject the nearly endless stream of human opinions and theories about the fourth beast being a church, a country, the pope or some mysterious final superman, then we are left to simply believe the Bible and the facts of history.

The fourth beast represents the Roman Empire from 31 BC to the present. All other theories collapse under the weight of Bible clues and facts, presented by God as proof to all minds that are truly open.

What Is the "Deadly Wound"?

Recall that John, in Revelation 13, said the Beast would receive a "deadly wound," which would eventually be "healed." After this healing, the Beast was prophesied "to continue forty and two months." What did John mean? What was he speaking of? The answer lies in understanding what happened to the Roman Empire in AD 476.

John wrote that "one of his heads" was "wounded to death" (vs. 3). This has to be referring to the *last* of the seven heads of John's Beast, which is the Roman Empire, because John was living in the time of the seventh head, when the Roman Empire ruled. Since the other three beasts had passed into history, there would have been no point in addressing them in a book intended to reveal the *future*. Recall that Daniel explained that the "ten horns" were 10 successive governments, which arose out of the Roman Empire and continue until the Second Coming of Christ. Daniel 7:24 stated, "And the *ten horns* out of this kingdom *are ten kings* [governments] that shall arise."

Who are these 10 kings (governments)? And how do they fit with the wound that was healed? Start by recognizing that the kings must be *successive*, not contemporaneous, for how can they rule at the same time if they span a period from AD 476 until the time of Christ's Return? Obviously, no single human being can live this long and neither has any *single* government, empowered by Rome, done this.

Let's examine the first three (Daniel 7) horns of the Roman Empire, for they represent the period that encompasses the wound. The deadly wound was brought on the Roman Empire by barbaric tribes from the north. Three Germanic kingdoms from Northern Europe, called the *Vandals*, the *Heruli* and the *Ostrogoths*, conquered Rome in succession.

Some brief explanation of these tribes and their timing is helpful. In 455, the Vandals swept through Northern Africa, and eventually attacked and defeated the city of Rome itself. (This tribe was so barbaric and destructive that the modern term "vandalize" is derived from its name.) Twenty-one years later, in AD 476, the Heruli, under Odoacer, established an occupying government at Rome. Historians universally accept 476 as the official date of the fall of the Roman Empire.

The kingdom of the Ostrogoths, which lasted from AD 493 to AD 554, in turn, replaced the Heruli. Like the Vandals and Heruli, the Ostrogoths were eventually driven from Rome, and together they represented what has often been called the "transition age" of the Roman Empire. But it is important to understand that these three brief successions of Northern Tribes were not actually Roman governments, but were governments *in* Rome. Yet they were still part of the "ten horns."

Recall that Daniel 7:8 said that these "three horns" were "plucked up *by the roots*." In fact, these three tribes did completely disappear from history. However, seven more horns were prophesied to rule this empire after them, until Christ returned.

Beginning in AD 554, the Roman Empire became known as the *Holy* Roman Empire. Historians almost universally acknowledge that the pope's crowning of *Justinian*, after he had defeated the Ostrogoths, signaled this change. Events in Europe, surrounding the Holy Roman Empire, rose and fell for many centuries. Periodically, new rulers appeared—*Charlemagne* (the Frankish head in AD 800)—*Otto the Great* (the German head crowned in AD 962)—followed by the Hapsburg Dynasty of *Charles V* (the Austrian head crowned in AD 1520)—which, in turn, was followed by *Napoleon's* reign (the French head crowned in AD 1805)—with the sixth head being that of Garibaldi's united Italian head from AD 1870-1945! This sixth resurrection of the Holy Roman Empire culminated in the defeat of Adolf Hitler and Benito Mussolini. Mussolini, after signing a secret agreement (Concordat) with the Vatican in 1929, united Ethiopia, Eritrea and Italian Somaliland back to Italy in 1935. He declared this union to be the Roman Empire re-established!

A regathering of power under one man is foretold to happen one more time!

Understand! The Roman Empire had two capitals—in Rome and Constantinople. The *10 toes* on the *two feet* of Daniel 2 represent 10 different nations or kingdoms in Eastern and Western Europe. This religious, political combine of nations (also the 10 horns of Rev. 17) will unite under one final powerful leader. Again, this united system is now quietly forming behind the world stage. Much more on this later.

Only the 10th horn of Daniel 7:7 (the same as all 10 toes of Daniel 2) is yet to appear. *This* will be the final great *Beast* of Revelation 17 that will explode upon an unsuspecting world with stunning speed and force (Rev. 17:12). With the 1989 collapse of the Iron Curtain and the reuniting of Germany, the final resurrection, consisting of countries and kingdoms throughout Central Europe, will soon appear, as a super-power United States of Europe. But we have already read how Christ will smash this union of kingdoms at His Coming!

The Wound Healed

Recall that John said, "the dragon gave him [the Beast] his power, and his seat, and great authority." Revelation 20:2 shows who the dragon is: "And he laid hold on the dragon, that old serpent, which is the Devil, and Satan." Revelation 12:9, 12-13 adds, "The great dragon...that old serpent, called the Devil, and Satan...was cast out into the earth... having great wrath...and when the dragon saw that he was cast onto the earth..."

These verses leave no doubt as to the identity of the dragon and that the devil empowers the system of government that culminates in the final Beast power that Christ smashes.

The wound was prophesied to be healed, and, speaking of the Beast, "power was given unto him to continue forty and two months."

This requires explanation. The healing occurred in AD 554, when the Emperor of the East at Constantinople, Justinian, re-established the Roman Empire at Ravenna, Italy. History records this as the "Imperial Restoration" of the Roman Empire.

The history of the Roman Empire changes entirely from AD 554. The seven successive revivals all had something in common never seen in the previous period of governments ruling from Rome.

We may now read Daniel 7:8: "I considered the horns, and, behold, there came up among them another *little horn*, before whom there were three of the first horns *plucked up by the roots*: and, behold, in this horn were eyes like the eyes of man, and a mouth speaking great things." Verse 20 adds of this "little horn" that it "came up, and before whom *three* fell" and it had a look "more stout than his fellows." Clearly, this is a distinct and *different* horn from the remaining seven of the horns that appear *after* the first three Germanic heads (horns) of the empire.

Let's understand! It is the appearance of this little horn in AD 554— this timeframe is established by Daniel's two verses—that redefines the kingdom and allows it to continue for another "forty-two months."

Here is what happened: The *pope* crowned Justinian in this year!

What is the meaning of the forty-two months? Ezekiel 4:4-6 and Numbers 14:34 show that, in prophetic fulfillment, each *day* counts for a *year*. This is critical to understand in regard to many other prophecies. Without recognizing this principle, all of these Bible prophecies have remained closed—sealed—to those who sought to understand them. How does "a day for a year" apply here?

Forty-two months is three and a half years. God's sacred years contain 360 days. 360 days times 3½ equals 1,260 days—or 1,260 *years* in prophecy. This defines the *duration* of the healing of the "deadly wound."

Counting 1,260 years from AD 554 takes us to 1814. Why is 1814 significant? This is when Napoleon abdicated, before his 1815 Waterloo defeat. As one historian put it, "So closed a government that dated from Augustus Caesar"—from 31 BC (*Modern History*, West, p. 377). The 1,260 years of the "healed beast" had ended. The Beast disappeared into the abyss of history—the "bottomless pit" of Revelation 17:8—from this moment forward, until it suddenly reappears.

With eight horns of the fourth beast (five heads of Revelation 17 Beast) gone, it was not until 1870 that Garibaldi began to unite the many fractured little kingdoms of Italy under one authority—thus beginning the revival of the ninth horn (sixth head of Revelation 17 Beast) that climaxed in Mussolini's fascist government.

The end of Revelation 17:8 also describes this Beast as "the beast that was, and is not, *and yet is.*" This sixth resurrection (1870-1945) was so weak in power, when compared to previous resurrections such as Charlemagne and Napoleon, as a revival of the generally much more powerful Roman Empire, that it is described as "was, and *is not*, and *yet is*" (at least in *name*).

The Little Horn and the Saints

We have discussed the little horn as it relates to the coronation of Justinian. Each of the additional five revivals of the Holy Roman Empire (Frankish, Germanic, Austrian Hapsburg, Napoleonic and Italian Garibaldi to Mussolini kingdoms) were recognized, endorsed and, to varying degrees, directly guided and steered by the Vatican.

There is another important aspect of the little horn to be explained here. Daniel 7:20-21 states, "even of that horn that had eyes, and a mouth that spoke very great things, whose look was more stout than his fellows. I beheld, and the same horn *made war with the saints, and prevailed against them.*"

Finally, verse 25 adds this, "And he shall speak *great* words against the Most High, and shall *wear out the saints* of the Most High, and think to change times and laws: and they shall be given into his hand until a time and times and the dividing of time."

From AD 554, when the "deadly wound" of Revelation 13 "was healed," the civil emperors in Rome began to honor (with power, gold and silver) a god that had been unknown to their ancestors or "fathers." This "strange god" held a *high religious office* and received great deference from Roman emperors (Dan. 11:37-39). From the time of Justinian, this church/state system functioned *together* for 1,260 years, with the "little horn" using and guiding the civil authorities to do its bidding.

This system "made war with the saints [of God's true Church]," "prevailed against them," "spoke great words against the Most High," and did "wear out the saints of the Most High." This "little horn" is precisely the same large universal counterfeit movement whose rise to power has been documented from Church history. As we proceed, it will become evident how deadly this "little horn speaking great things" would become in regard to the true Church—and to all civilization. (My book *Where Is the True Church? – and Its Incredible History!* documents this. This book and a later chapter here will open your understanding to both the history

of God's Church and the work of the counterfeit church that has relent-
lessly sought to destroy it.)

The Revelation 13 "Two-horned Beast"

The 13th chapter describes a second beast, this one having "two horns"
(Rev. 13:11). We have seen that the first Beast is a description of the
Roman Empire—a *political* kingdom. What is this "two-horned beast"?

Recall that Revelation 12:9 said, "Satan...deceives *the whole world.*"
Revelation 20:3 states that he "deceive[s] the nations." Also recall that
Satan ("the dragon") gives power to the first Beast of chapter 13. The
devil has a civil government headquarters on Earth to which he gives "his
power, and his seat [a city], and great authority."

Satan does not usually speak directly to human beings. He works
through his servants—his ministers. The Bible teaches that Satan has
"*his* ministers." These ministers pretend to be ministers of Christ, but
Paul calls them "false apostles" and "deceitful workers," who appear to
be "angels of light" and "ministers of righteousness" (II Cor. 11:13-15).
The vast majority of those who claim to be true ministers of God are not.
Jesus said that His Church would be little, and its faithful ministers *few*.

The Bible Explains It

There are many theories about the "two-horned beast." Some have
thought it is a grouping of Protestant churches, and others think that it is
the papacy linked to the United States. Most, however, claim not to know
what it is, and speak little of it. Therefore, we must let the Bible explain
its true meaning.

Now let's examine the passage that describes this other Revelation
13 Beast: "And I beheld *another beast* coming up out of the earth; and he
had *two horns* like a LAMB, and he spoke as a DRAGON. And he exercises
all the power of the first beast before him, and causes the earth and them
which dwell therein to worship the first beast, whose deadly wound was
healed. And he *does great wonders,* so that he makes fire come down
from heaven on the earth in the sight of men, and *deceives them that
dwell on the earth by the means of those miracles* which he had power
to do in the sight of the beast; saying to them that dwell on the earth,
that they should make an *image* to the beast...and *cause* that as many as
would not worship the *image* of the beast should be *killed*" (vs. 11-15).

Some important points emerge.

This two-horned beast gives "power" to the first Beast of verses 1-5. Daniel 7:17, 23 revealed that "beast" is a term for a civil government or kingdom, or the leader of the kingdom. Therefore, our first important conclusion is that this beast *must* be a government or kingdom. Second is that it gives power to the Roman Empire system.

It also appears like a "lamb," but speaks like a "dragon." This is critical to understand. Here is why. Christ is depicted in the Bible, in several places, as a lamb (John 1:29; Rev. 17:14). We have seen that the dragon is Satan. So this beast, then, *appears* to be Christian, but is really of the devil. In other words, this is a *satanic* kingdom that appears on the surface to be the kingdom of God, and of Christ. Many scriptures reveal that Christ did not establish His kingdom at His first Coming. He carefully explained this to His disciples in Acts 1:6, John 14:1-3 and Luke 19:11-27. We have already seen verses in Daniel 7 describing when Christ and the saints smash the fourth beast as they are given rulership over Earth.

When Revelation 13:12 states that "he exercises all the power of the first beast before him, and causes the earth and them which dwell therein to worship the first beast, whose deadly wound was healed," it was the Roman Empire to whom he was giving power. This occurred from the time of the Beast's healing in AD 554.

For the full 1,260 years that the wound was healed, Roman emperors acknowledged the supreme authority of religion throughout the empire. This is one way it portrays itself as the kingdom of God on Earth. Many encyclopedias state that the Holy Roman Empire was declared to be the "kingdom of God on Earth." In fact, in 554, many felt that the kingdom of God had officially arrived.

The second Revelation 13 beast, however, has *two* horns. This is because it represents a two-fold combination of church and government. But since it is an actual kingdom, it does, in fact, have to be its own independent, sovereign state. Remember also, this two-horned beast possesses such awesome power that it inspires the world to worship the Beast, whose deadly wound was healed. The power to bring fire down from heaven and to perform miracles will win vast numbers of people as worshippers of the Beast.

Verse 14 explains this: "And deceives them that dwell on the earth by the means of those miracles which he had power to do in the sight of the beast," with verse 13 stating, "he does great wonders."

Recognize these facts: The second beast is able to perform miracles. He does this "in the sight of" the first Beast—the Holy Roman Empire. These miracles are so extraordinary—so mesmerizing—that they allow him to *deceive the whole earth*! And the Beast is worshipped as a result.

This future religious leader will lead the final resurrection of the Holy Roman Empire alongside a great civil leader. In II Thessalonians 2:3, this same religious leader is called the "man of sin." Revelation 19:20 refers to him as a "false prophet." This False Prophet embodies all that counterfeit Christianity has represented through the centuries. In the near future, when the modern-day descendants of Israel are taken into captivity, many will see the bitter reality of its killing machine firsthand.

This has been typical of this Babylonish church throughout the course of history. Millions have been put to death for not worshipping according to its false beliefs and practices.

Plainly, the "two-horned beast" is the *headquarters* of the great false *church* that controls the first Beast. The description we have just read is an unmistakable parallel with the "little horn" of Daniel 7:8, 20-21, 24-25.

We must know what is coming and be able to recognize it when it emerges in full power.

The Revelation 17 Beast and Woman Riding It

We saw Revelation 12 describes a "woman," which is to marry Christ (Rev. 19:7; Matt. 25:1-10; Eph. 5:23) at His Return. These verses, and others, show that the word "woman" is a symbol for a church. The entire chapter 12 is devoted to God's Church and how she has been persecuted by a false "Christian" church system throughout most of her 2,000 years. Many earmarks of *this* woman of chapter 12 demonstrate and prove that she is God's Church—the true Church.

Revelation 17 introduces a seven-headed Beast, different from any mentioned previously, but it also described a very *different* woman riding it. Let's examine this woman and the Beast she rides. It is vital to understand her critical connection to seven revivals (resurrections) of the Roman system. She never rode the first three heads of the Roman system. Rather, she only rode it after the Beast was "healed" in AD 554. The now *healed Beast* is the Beast of Revelation 17.

Recall chapters 17 and 18 are an inset to the book of Revelation, and describe the great Roman system that is destroyed at the end of chapter 16. These chapters give a somewhat more detailed picture of the great, false *universal* church. The picture includes the woman's "*harlot*" *daughters* (17:5), which have helped her to deceive all nations (17:1-2; 18:3).

The Revelation 17 woman is "arrayed in purple and scarlet" and rides a seven-headed, 10-horned Beast.

We have discussed the seven revivals of the Holy Roman Empire. Six have come and gone—and the last 10-horn revival, consisting of 10 kings (of 10 governments), is now forming! The 17th chapter of Revelation describes the final revival of this religious-political system. This revival (or resurrection) will last at least three and a half years, coinciding with first the Tribulation (Matt. 24:21-22) and then the time of God's wrath. It is prophesied to come "out of the bottomless pit, and go into perdition" (Rev. 17:8). The Holy Roman Empire has been in the abyss of history, or the bottomless pit, since Napoleon's 1814 abdication prior to Waterloo.

Chapter 17, verse 10, speaking of the heads, states, "five are fallen, and one is, and the other is not yet come." The five "fallen" heads are those the woman rode during the 1,260 years from 554 to 1814. The "one *is*" head was the *sixth* head, now past, which began with Garibaldi and culminated in Mussolini. The "is" has become "was."

Now understand. This verse is written from the time perspective of *when* God revealed the meaning of this prophecy, and many others, to the leader of His Church, in the late 1930s. This is the only time that this *present tense* representation of the sixth head could be accurate. (We would today say "six have fallen.") It also reveals when God wanted Daniel's closed and sealed prophecy opened and taken to the world as a warning!

Understand another important connection to these resurrections of the Roman system. Revelation 17 describes each as having "a *woman* sit[ting] upon a scarlet colored *beast*, full of names of blasphemy, having *seven heads* and *ten horns*" (vs. 3). The seven heads are seven separate revivals, with a *10-horn* (composed of 10 kings) *final revival*. It is *this* woman who spreads the "mystery of iniquity" spoken of by Paul in II Thessalonians 2:7.

Of this woman, Revelation 17:5-6 state, "And upon her forehead was a name written, MYSTERY, BABYLON THE GREAT, THE MOTHER OF HARLOTS AND ABOMINATIONS OF THE EARTH. And I saw the woman *drunken with the blood of the saints*, and with the blood of the *martyrs* of Jesus."

Verse 1 calls her a "great whore that sits upon *many waters*."

Let's pause and ask: What are the "many waters"?

This is a classic example of allowing the Bible to interpret the Bible. Fourteen verses later, the term is explained: "And he said unto me, The *waters* which you saw, where the whore sits, are *peoples*, and *multitudes*, and *nations*, and *tongues*" (vs. 15). This shows that the influence of the whore and her harlot daughters encompasses the earth. This reflects truly enormous power!

In this case, the term "many waters" was not *immediately* explained, but simply continuing to read revealed what it means. The Bible interpreted itself!

Verses 5-6 are a graphic description of an immense *Gentile church* that is a modern-day descendant of Babylon. She is a "mother" of many "harlot" daughters, who came out of her in protest because they disagreed with a *few* of her abominations. This is not a small church, but rather a "great" church ("great whore") ruling *many* peoples. Verse 2 speaks of her "fornication" with the "kings of the earth." And verse 18 speaks of the woman as "that *great city*, which reigns over the kings of the earth." So then, this is a very large church that has sought to influence kings, nations and world events. Only one city and one church fit this description.

Once again, this is seen to be a very *different* woman than that of Revelation 12.

This large Gentile *false* church has long persecuted God's true Church (17:6). God will destroy this whore and her harlot daughters by turning the Beast she rides against her (vs. 16). But first she must "ride" the final revival of the Holy Roman Empire—with her Babylonian system!

Daniel 7:19-20 sheds light on what happens when the saints return with Christ. Their first job is to replace the "fourth beast" (the final world-ruling empire), which rules with the assistance of the "little horn" whose "look was more stout than his fellows." This *little horn* is a *religious* kingdom, and is the same as the woman who rides the Beast of Revelation 17. Again, this religious "woman" kingdom has ruled over all of the previous resurrections of the *Holy* Roman Empire.

The saints will have endured tremendous persecution at the hands of this "little horn"—"woman" church. But eventually the faithful saints will be rewarded in an incredible way. Now more from Daniel: "I beheld, and *the same horn* [the Babylonish system of Revelation 17:5-6] *made war with the saints*, and prevailed against them; until the Ancient of Days came, and *judgment was given to the saints* of the Most High; and the time came that *the saints possessed the kingdom*" (vs. 21-22).

A final explanation should be made. The beginning of Revelation 17:8 described this different Beast as "the beast that was, and is not," with verse 11 similarly beginning with, "And the beast that was, and is not, even he is the *eighth* and is of the seven, and goes into perdition." This healed Beast, now the *Holy* Roman Empire (the resurrections ridden by the "woman" since AD 554), is both different—like an "eighth" system—and yet is "of the seven" heads of the Revelation 13 Beast and the Daniel 7 fourth beast, last seven of 10 horns of each.

Important Clarification

It is necessary and helpful to summarize what we have learned so far. Some believe the Revelation 13 Beast is the woman who rode the Revelation 17 Beast. This cannot be because the woman is a church and the beast is the government. Others believe Napoleon's abuse of the pope in 1798 was the "deadly wound." While this is on the surface ridiculous, it is also impossible that the Roman church would last another 1,260 years until AD 3058.

Now review and understand these points. The accompanying graphics and charts complement and expand them:

• The Beast of Revelation 13 equals the fourth beast of Daniel 7 and is the Roman Empire.

• The (healed) Beast of Revelation 17 is the *Holy* Roman Empire, from 554 to 1814, and continues to Christ's Return.

• The *woman* of Revelation 17, which rides the *Holy* Roman Empire, equals the *little horn* of Daniel 7 and the *two-horned beast* of Revelation 13—the great false *Christian church* and her little *kingdom.*

• The last seven horns of the Daniel 7 fourth beast equal the last seven horns of the Revelation 13 Beast's seventh head, ridden by the woman.

• These seven *horns* equal the seven *heads* of the Revelation 17 Beast ridden by the woman. (This "horns equals heads" is where many go astray.)

• The 10 *horns* of the seventh head of the Revelation 17 Beast equal the 10 *kings* or *governments* united in the final future revival under the woman of the Holy Roman Empire, which Christ destroys at His Coming.

• The 10 *toes* of the Daniel 2 giant image equal the same 10 *kings* or *governments* (10 horns) of the seventh head of Revelation 17, and are on the "feet" that Christ (as the Daniel 2:34, 44-45 "stone") "breaks to pieces" at His Return. (The graphic just ahead harmonizes these statements.)

Identifying the Beast's Number—666

There are endless opinions and theories about the number 666 and how it relates to the Beast. Seemingly, new ones arrive every day. But, like other aspects of the beasts, we must let God reveal the answer to this mystery.

First read the only five references to the "number" and then we shall discuss them. They are all in just two passages.

In Revelation 13, the apostle John describes a beast with seven heads, 10 horns and 10 crowns.

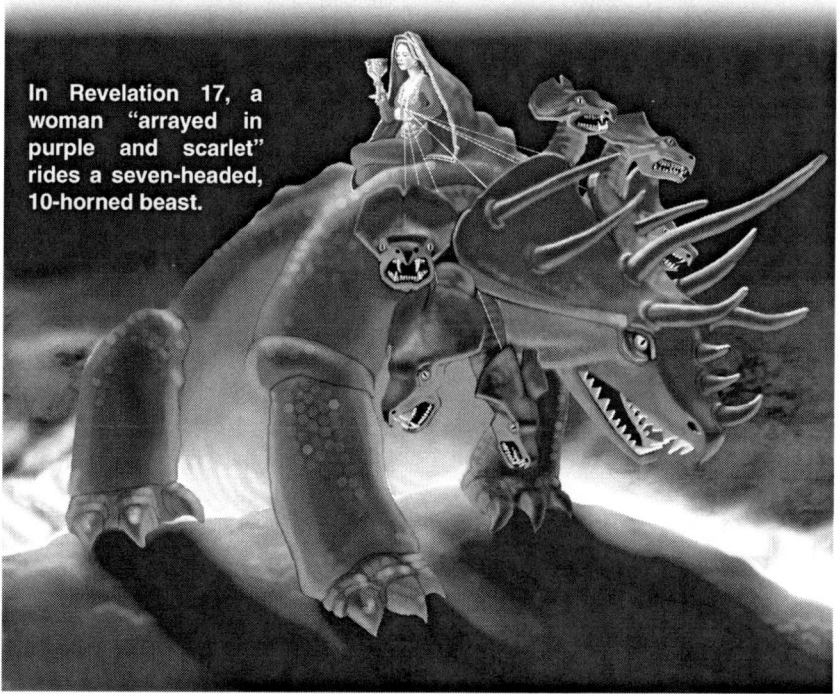

In Revelation 17, a woman "arrayed in purple and scarlet" rides a seven-headed, 10-horned beast.

PROPHECY UNFOLDS:
THE REIGN OF GENTILE KINGDOMS

THE IMAGE Daniel 2	THE FOUR BEASTS Daniel 7 (State) (Church)	THE RAM AND THE GOAT Daniel 8	THE BEAST AND THE IMAGE Revelation 13 (State) (Church)	BABYLON AND THE BEAST Revelation 17	MEANING OF THE SYMBOLS	FULFILLMENT IN HISTORY
Head of **Gold** vs. 32, 38	1st beast (like **Lion**) vs. 4				**1st Head** of prophetic Babylon	**Chaldean Empire** (Babylon) 625-539 BC
Chest and arms of **Silver** vs. 32, 39	2nd beast (**Bear**) vs. 5	**Ram** with 2 horns vs. 3-4, 20			**2nd Head** of prophetic Babylon	**Persian Empire** (Medo-Persia) 558-330 BC
Belly and thighs of **Brass** vs. 32, 39	3rd beast (**Leopard**) 4 heads vs. 6	**He-goat** with great Horn and 4 notable horns vs. 5-8, 21-22			**3rd, 4th, 5th and 6th heads** of prophetic Babylon	**Greece**, led by Alexander the Great and 4 divisions 333-31 BC
Legs as **Iron** vs. 33, 40-43	4th beast (strong like **Iron**) with **10 horns** vs. 7, 23-24		The **beast** with **7 heads** and **10 horns** vs. 1-2		**7th Head** of prophetic Babylon, with **10 horns**	**Roman Empire** 31 BC-AD 476 In 2 divisions, "Christianity" becomes official religion, AD 324
			Deadly Wound vs. 3			**Rome falls** AD 476
	1st Horn (plucked by roots)		**1st Horn**		**3 horns destroyed** on the authority of the pope; this period is later called the "Transition Age"	**The Vandals** AD 429-533
	2nd Horn (rooted up)		**2nd Horn**			**The Heruli,** Odoacer's govt. AD 476-493
	3rd Horn (rooted up)		**3rd Horn**			**The Ostrogoths** AD 493-554

among 10 horns vs. 8, 20-22, 24-27	("1st of last 7 horns")	"Lamb Dragon" and "image" vs. 11-18	Woman riding the beast vs. 1-2	Christianity rules the beast —"Babylon the Great"	...and church government, or "image" of Roman Empire government
4th Horn	1st of last 7 horns—**Deadly Wound healed** (to continue 1,260 years) vs. 5	← AD 554 to 1814 = **1,260 years** beast continued →	**1st Head of beast** (healed) ridden by scarlet-clothed woman	The "Great Whore" did not ride any of the 7 heads of the first 4 beasts. But she did ride the last 7 horns of Daniel's 4th beast. Thus, **the last 7 horns of Daniel 7 and Revelation 13 are the 7 heads of Revelation 17**	**"Imperial Restoration"** of empire by Justinian, AD 554; he recognized supremacy of this world's Christianity
5th Horn	2nd of last 7 horns		**2nd Head** ridden by woman		**Frankish Kingdom;** began AD 774; Charlemagne crowned AD 800
6th Horn	3rd of last 7 horns		**3rd Head** ridden by woman		**Holy Roman Empire** (German head); Otto the Great crowned AD 962
7th Horn	4th of last 7 horns		**4th Head** ridden by woman		**Hapsburg Dynasty** (Austrian head); Charles V crowned AD 1530
8th Horn	5th of last 7 horns		**5th Head** ridden by woman	("five have fallen" at Napoleon's defeat)	**Napoleon's Kingdom** (French head); crowned AD 1804

In AD 1814—1,260 years after the "deadly wound" was healed in AD 554—the "Holy Roman Empire" ended with Napoleon's defeat.

among 10 horns	last 7 horns	"Lamb Dragon" and "image"	Woman riding the beast	Christianity rules the beast	"image" of Roman Empire government
9th Horn	6th of last 7 horns		**6th Head** ridden by woman	"One IS" Rev. 17:10 (revealed in the 1930s)	**Italy,** united by Garibaldi, AD 1870, culminating with Mussolini, 1945
10th and final Horn	7th and last Horn	Beast ascends out of the pit	**7th Head and 10 horns**	One "NOT YET COME" Rev. 17:10	**Revived Roman Empire,** led by 10 rulers under one leader

10 toes on 2 feet of **iron mixed with clay**

In Daniel 2, the "great image" symbolizes four world-ruling governments.

Head of fine gold: The Chaldean (Babylonian) Empire

Breast and arms of silver: The Medo-Persian Empire

Belly and thighs of brass: The Greco-Macedonian Empire

Legs of iron; feet partly iron, partly clay: The Roman Empire

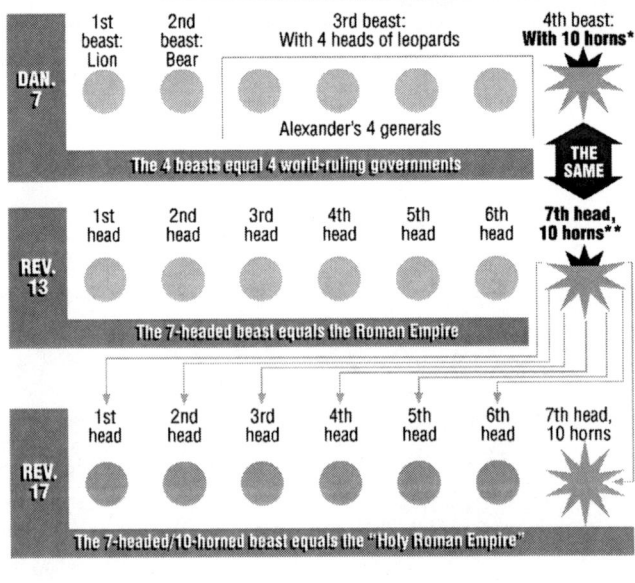

DAN. 7

1st beast: Lion — 2nd beast: Bear — 3rd beast: With 4 heads of leopards — Alexander's 4 generals — 4th beast: **With 10 horns***

The 4 beasts equal 4 world-ruling governments

THE SAME

*The last **7 horns** of Dan. 7 and Rev. 13 **equal the 7 heads** of Rev. 17

The **10 horns** of Dan. 7 and Rev. 13 are **successive**

REV. 13

1st head — 2nd head — 3rd head — 4th head — 5th head — 6th head — **7th head, 10 horns****

The 7-headed beast equals the Roman Empire

The last **7 horns of Rev. 13 **equal the 7 heads** of Rev. 17

The woman rides (controls) everything red

REV. 17

1st head — 2nd head — 3rd head — 4th head — 5th head — 6th head — 7th head, 10 horns

The 7-headed/10-horned beast equals the "Holy Roman Empire"

The **10 horns** of Rev. 17 are **simultaneous** and **equal the 10 toes** of the "great image" of Dan. 2

Revelation 13:17-18: "And that no man might buy or sell, save he that had the *mark*, or the name of the beast, or the NUMBER of his name. Here is wisdom. Let him that has understanding *count* the NUMBER of the beast: for it is the NUMBER of a man; and his NUMBER is *six hundred threescore and six*." Now Revelation 15:2: "And I saw as it were a sea of glass mingled with fire: and them that had gotten the victory over the beast, and over his image, and over his *mark*, and over the NUMBER of his name, stand on the sea of glass, having the harps of God."

These basic points emerge: (1) All who will are told to "count [add up] the number," (2) the number is 666, (3) the Beast has this number and this is what identifies it, if we exercise "wisdom" in properly counting it, (4) 666 is the number of a kingdom, government or empire, or of the king who establishes or leads it (Dan. 7:18, 22-24, 27), and (5) the terms—"the name of the *beast*"—"or the number of his *name*"—"it is the number of a *man*"—directly identify the number as both the name of the kingdom, government or empire *and* the king or ruler that leads it.

If God says to count the number, He obviously intends that we know how to do this!

Counting Names

There are a number of important and famous names that are linked to the Roman Empire, and Rome itself.

The name *Rome*, and thus the Roman Empire, is derived from its legendary first king and founder—Romulus. Quite literally, this name is stamped on every man, woman and child within the kingdom, as well as on all of its kings and the kingdom itself.

Many have recognized this much but have failed to recognize that they should not count the number in Latin, but rather in Greek—the language in which God inspired the New Testament to be written. Remember, John wrote Revelation in Greek.

Ignoring this point has caused many to apply 666 to the pope, by claiming that the phrase "Vicarius Filii Dei" is written on the pope's triple crown. First, while the pope has such a crown, these words are not on it. Besides, these are Latin words, which do not apply to a kingdom or empire, but would only apply to a man—the pope. Also, these words are a title, not a name!

In the second century AD, it was recognized that Romulus' name was originally spelled *Lateinos*, meaning "the name of Latium" or "Latin man." The Romans took their language and origin from this region.

Like the value of Roman numerals, the Greeks assigned values to letters. In the Greek, L counts for 30, A is 1, T is 300, E is 5, I is 10, N is 50, O is 70, S is 200—totaling precisely 666! It is not then strange, or incorrect, to conclude that every citizen, king and the kingdom itself, adds up to or "counts" to 666.

Now consider Benito Mussolini. He called himself "Il Duce," which means the leader or the chief. Everywhere he went, people proclaimed, "Viva Il Duce," meaning *long live the chief.* The Italians abbreviated this on signs throughout Italy as "vv il duce."

This time, let's count the name in Latin, recognizing that the letter U was commonly replaced with a V: V is 5 (twice), I is 1, L is 50, D is 500, V is 5, C is 100, E has no number. The total—precisely 666!

The Beast and Roman Empire—and a system—have been identified!

Mass Worldwide Deception

Remember that the Revelation 17 woman is a false church that rides the Beast with seven heads and 10 horns. We have established that the Beast she is riding is a powerful world empire that exists until Christ returns. Like one who rides a horse, camel or elephant, the woman directs, controls and guides the animal to go where she wants it to go and to do what she wants it to do.

Two individuals, "the Beast and the False Prophet," will lead this religious-governmental system. Revelation 16:13-14 describes demons as having the power to "work miracles" through their system.

The embodiment of the final Beast will be a charismatic figure who arrives on the world scene shortly before Christ's Return.

Also, the final, world-charming False Prophet will lead the world to worship the Beast (Rev. 16:2; 19:20)! This deception will be so profound (18:3)—and so widespread—that we saw these men will actually deceive all mankind into fighting Christ at His Second Coming (16:9, 13-16; 17:13-14). Ponder the power of deception!

Now notice II Thessalonians 2:3-4 and 8. Verse 3 refers to one called *"the man of sin"* and *"the son of perdition;* who opposes and exalts himself above all that is called God, or that is worshipped; so that he *as God* sits in the temple of God, showing himself that he *is God."* Recognize that the False Prophet *professes* that he is God.

Compare this with Ezekiel 28:2 and the reference to the "prince of Tyrus"—a man. Ezekiel wrote that this "prince" says, "I am a God, I sit in the seat of God." II Thessalonians 2:8 describes this "man of sin" as the "wicked [one]" who would "be revealed" for what he is when Christ returns and destroys him with the Beast in a lake of fire (Rev. 19:20). Isaiah 14:4 refers to the False Prophet as the "*king* of Babylon." This is the same man as the "*prince* of Tyrus."

Continuing in II Thessalonians 2, verse 9 makes a startling statement about the False Prophet. It says that his "coming is after the working of *Satan* with all *power* and *signs* and *lying wonders.*" Verse 10 shows that he is able to deceive everyone who does not "*love the truth.*" Verse 11 reveals that God shall send "strong delusion" to all who willingly believe his lies.

We saw that the leaders of this dominating false system will be possessed by a demon, or the devil himself! This will give the False Prophet *tremendous power* to deceive and perform miracles. Satan, having always wanted to replace God with himself, will be able to speak through this human religious leader and declare to the whole world that he is, in fact, GOD!

This Bible warning is unmistakable. Also unmistakable, the miracles he performs *will* deceive the vast majority!

The work of the False Prophet will continue all the way to Armageddon. Now read Revelation 16:13: "And I saw three unclean spirits like frogs come out of the mouth of the dragon [Satan], and out of the mouth of the beast [civil end-time ruler], and out of the mouth of the false prophet [religious leader guiding the Beast]."

Verse 14 states, "For they are the spirits of devils [demons], working miracles, which go forth unto the kings of the earth and of the whole world, to *gather* them to *the battle of that great day of God Almighty.*" These "spirits of devils" are the fallen angels who followed Lucifer (now Satan) in his insurrection against the Creator (Rev. 12:4).

Here is how the Bible describes the Beast (the civil Roman ruler) and False Prophet working together: "And I saw the *beast*, and the kings of the earth, and their armies, gathered together to make war against Him [Christ] that sat on the horse, and against His army. And the *beast* was taken, and with him the *false prophet* that wrought miracles before him, with which he deceived them that had received the MARK of the beast, and them that worshiped his IMAGE. These both were cast alive into a lake of fire burning with brimstone" (Rev. 19:19-20).

Now let's read the full description of how the False Prophet works. Let's see the reach of his power, influence and ability, through miracles and lying wonders, to bring the whole world to worship the Beast—the final civil Roman ruler.

This following passage, some repeated from before, removes all doubt that the two-horned beast is the woman of Revelation 17, and that the final False Prophet represents it, working in concert with the Beast:

"And I beheld another beast [second beast] coming up out of the earth; and he had *two horns like a lamb*, and he spoke *as a dragon*. And he exercises all the power of the first beast before him, and causes the earth and them which dwell therein to worship the first beast, whose deadly wound was healed. And he does great wonders, so that he *makes fire come down from heaven* on the earth in the sight of men, And *deceives them that dwell on the earth* by the means of those miracles which he had power to do in the sight of the beast; saying to them that dwell on the earth, that they should make an IMAGE *to the beast* [the first Beast], which had the wound by a sword, and did live. And he had power to give life unto the IMAGE *of the beast* [first Beast], that the IMAGE *of the beast* should both speak, and cause that as many as would not worship the IMAGE *of the beast* should be killed. And he *causes* all, both small and great, rich and poor, free and bond, to receive a MARK in their right hand, or in their foreheads: and that no man might buy or sell, save he that had the MARK, or the name of the beast, or the NUMBER of his name" (Rev. 13:11-17).

These verses speak four times of the *image of the Beast*, which requires explanation, and of the all-important *mark of the Beast*, which does as well.

The Beast's Image Revealed

The Bible is a book about government—how God governs His Church and His Work—the gospel of the kingdom of God—and how He will govern the entire world upon Christ's Return—among other points. The world also has its own many forms of government. This includes churches, which are governed in various ways, none of them after the fashion of God's government. The counterfeit universal false church system—which counterfeits everything of God—has also fashioned its government after a certain model. This knowledge has everything to do with the *image* of the Beast. Let's understand by looking at the two-horned beast.

This second beast of Revelation 13, besides causing people to receive the Beast's mark, was also responsible for creating an "image" that led to the martyrdom of true saints. Yet it was not this church that killed them for not worshipping the image—but rather it *caused* them to be PUT TO DEATH. History reveals the saints were killed and persecuted by civil government, under direction of the false church who had labeled them "heretics" and "anathema from Christ."

Now let's compare the woman of Revelation 17 with the two-horned beast of Revelation 13 who causes the Beast to kill those who refuse the mark: "And I saw the woman drunken with the blood of the saints, and with the blood of the martyrs of Jesus" (Rev. 17:6). There can be no doubt that these two are the same.

Now *how* were the people deceived into worshipping the image of the Beast? Let's see: "And [the False Prophet] deceives them that dwell on the earth *by the means of those miracles* which he had power to do in the sight of the beast [the civil leader]; saying to them that dwell on the earth, that they should make an image to the beast..." (13:14).

What is the Beast's image? First, what is the dictionary definition of "image"? *The Second Edition of the Webster's New International Dictionary* defines it as a "representation...modeled figure...likeness; semblance...a copy or counterpart."

Now notice this statement from the *Cyclopaedia of Biblical, Theological, and Ecclesiastical Literature*: "The first pope, in the real sense of the word, was Leo I ([AD] 440-461). Being endowed by nature with the old Roman spirit of dominion, and being looked upon [by] his contemporaries, in consequence both of his character and his position, as the most eminent man of the age, he developed in his mind the ideal of an ecclesiastical monarchy, with the pope at the head..."

Pope Leo admired the Roman Empire for the government structure it had, and copied its principles in creating the papacy of the Roman Catholic Church. It is this form of church government that is the image (representation or semblance) of the Beast!

This false church models its ecclesiastical church government after—in structure and organization—the ancient Roman civil government. God's government is not a humanly devised structure based on pagan ideas or manmade laws. It is based solely on *God's* Law and will be led by Jesus Christ and the resurrected, spirit-born saints. It is this divine form of government that exists in the true Church today.

Further, Philip Van Ness Myers, in his work *Ancient History*, confirms this: "[During the reign of Leo I, the Church set] up within the Roman Empire an ecclesiastical state [government], which in its constitution and its administrative system was shaping itself upon the imperial model." This author could plainly see that church government was indeed modeled after the Roman Empire's system of governance. He even called it an ecclesiastical world empire!

So then, people were deceived into worshipping the church, which was organized in the likeness of a manmade form of government—the ancient Roman imperial model! Therefore, all such worshippers commit idolatry!

Also notice this verse in Revelation 17: "Upon her forehead was a name written, MYSTERY, BABYLON THE GREAT, THE MOTHER OF HARLOTS" (vs. 5). This false church is called a mother of harlots. Her daughters protested against her. Collectively, the mother church and her harlot daughters are called "BABYLON." These churches all have a form of worldly government, and are based on pagan customs and false doctrines, yet claim to be Christian.

Do you now see how Satan has so cleverly counterfeited God's government?—and why God tells His people to "Come out of her, My people, that you be not partakers of her sins" (18:4)?

Related to the Beast and its image is the intriguing, mysterious, much talked about MARK OF THE BEAST...

The Mark of the Beast

Few prophecies in the Bible are as fascinating—and as frightening—to its readers as the subject of the *mark of the Beast.* As with other aspects of prophecies already described, theories attempting to explain this mark abound.

This intriguing, mysterious mark is much talked about, but almost universally misunderstood. Some believe it is a computer chip implanted in people's foreheads or right hands. Others have thought it was Hitler's swastika and still others have thought it has been this or that government program. Despite endless sermons preached and articles written about its possible meaning, millions remain baffled by it.

We saw previously that Revelation 14 pictures *three angels* bearing *three messages* (vs. 6-11). These messages announce the fall of Babylon through the seven last plagues and warn against receiving the "*mark of the beast.*" Many prophecies show that most people—*all* who belong to the powerful false church-state system—will *ignore* the warning, and will be deceived into receiving it!

The prophecies that describe the mark are stark—and horrible! Sadly, most all preachers focus on just one passage to the exclusion of the many others on the subject. Let's read it: "And he causes all, both small and great, rich and poor, free and bond, to receive a MARK in their *right hand,* or in their *foreheads*: and that no man might buy or sell, save he that had the MARK, or the name of the beast, or the NUMBER of his name" (Rev. 13:16-17).

This is a critical statement, for it speaks of some kind of a universal mark backed by authority in a way that controls people's ability to conduct normal matters of commerce ("buying and selling"). Those who do *not* have the mark are isolated from the most routine matters of purchasing food, goods and services.

Being able to buy and sell goods is certainly essential—something that everyone needs to be able to do. But understand. This is not speaking of whether stores and retail establishments will be *willing* to sell goods to people without the mark, but rather whether people can earn a living—meaning a wage and a salary—in order to have *income*. The implication of the Greek is that one will not be *able* to buy or sell—will not have money in hand to do so—because he is *unemployed*!

So then, the "mark of the beast" involves ability to obtain and hold a job in order to make a living.

Obviously then, many millions will have it—and it will have to be considered *desirable* and *attractive*, or else the masses would not seek or accept it.

But the mark will be a trap to those who are charmed by the surface of its attraction. Recall from earlier what will happen to all those who receive it: "And I saw another sign in heaven, great and marvelous, seven angels having the *seven last plagues*; for in them is filled up the WRATH OF GOD…And the seven angels came out of the temple, having the seven *plagues* [vials], clothed in pure and white linen, and having their breasts girded with golden girdles…And I heard a great voice out of the temple saying to the seven angels, Go your ways, and pour out the *vials* [plagues] of the WRATH OF GOD upon the earth. And the first went, and poured out his vial upon the earth; and there fell a noisome and grievous sore upon the men which had the MARK *of the beast*, and upon them who *worshipped his* IMAGE" (Rev. 15:1, 6; 16:1-2).

This is serious! Unprecedented, terrible punishment will fall on all who have taken this mark. However unwittingly they did this—however sincere they saw themselves to be—the result will be the same: horrible plagues on all, including you or me, if we have this mark!

God Must Explain the Mark

To get a complete picture of the mark of the Beast, we must study all of the verses that pertain to it. There are many, and studying just a few will not reveal the full truth. Using imagination and human reasoning to invent various silly—and some are truly ludicrous—conclusions about what the mark of the Beast may be only serves to further deceive and confuse those with interest in the subject.

First ask: Would God foretell plagues on all who receive the mark and then leave mankind in the dark about what it is? Would He say, in effect, "I am going to pour out terrifying, horrible PLAGUES—causing the death of millions—on those who receive the mark of the Beast, but I will not tell you what it is or how to avoid it—so that you can *escape*"?

Of course not.

Comprehend this vital point. Men cannot reveal the meaning of or explain the mark—only God can. Plain reality is that He *must* do this—and He does tell us *most plainly* exactly what it is!

The Beast's Mark

Now understand this basic point. The mark is plainly identified as one pertaining to the Beast. It is the "mark *of the Beast*." We have identified the Beast as the Roman Empire. But the Revelation 17 Beast exists at and just before Christ's Return. We have seen that this is the Holy Roman Empire. Therefore, the mark of the Beast is the mark of the seventh and last head of the (Holy) Roman Empire.

The mark of the Beast is not the mark of the Roman Catholic Church. This is because the woman is the large church that *rides* the (Holy) Roman Empire. The Bible does not speak of the "mark *of the woman*," but rather again of the "mark of the Beast" the woman rides. Get this clear!

Certainly the woman is also a small organized civil kingdom, or government, as well as being a church—and she does guide, direct and lead the far greater kingdom that she rides. But, while the Beast has much greater *power* than she has, like any large animal would always have greater power than its rider, the rider—in this case, the "woman"—steers the animal to do its bidding.

Keep firmly in mind what we read, now with more context: "And he had power to give life unto the image of the beast, that the image of the beast should both speak, and CAUSE that as many as would not worship the image of the beast should be killed. And he CAUSES all, both small and great, rich and poor, free and bond, to receive a MARK in their right hand, or in their foreheads" (Rev. 13:15-16).

We can summarize in this way: This great false church steers, guides and directs—"causes"—others to receive the mark. She does not directly administer it herself, but rather *causes* all in the empire to accept—"receive"—the mark. She is the same woman that caused the martyrdom of saints throughout the ages. The mark is received in the right hand and the forehead—and it is a kind of brand of the (Holy) Roman Empire, not of the church. This mark will be brought—imposed—upon the entire civilized Western world!

Martyrdoms—Past and Future!

We revisit Matthew 24 where Christ, in answer to a question by His disciples about when He would return, spoke of and clarified events that would precede "the great tribulation" (vs. 21-22). We saw this, followed by the wrath of God, comprises the three and a half years preceding His Second Coming.

A few verses before explaining the Tribulation, we also saw Christ explained that a final martyrdom lay ahead for true Christians at the end of the age: "*Then* shall they deliver you up to be *afflicted*, and shall *kill* you: and you shall be *hated of all nations* for My name's sake" (Matt. 24:9). It is obvious that Christians will be doing something that identifies them as different from all those around them. Some will be hated with such intensity that they will be tortured ("afflicted") and martyred in great numbers ("killed").

It is critical at this point that we review elements of what was learned concerning Revelation 6—the precise parallel of Matthew 24.

In Revelation, John, in vision, was shown a preview of future events ("hereafter," 4:1). Since John was "in the spirit" as the seals were opened (vs. 2), the events he witnessed were not actually occurring when he saw them. They were *heavenly previews* of things that would happen *later on Earth*.

Revelation 6:9-11 contains a description of the *fifth seal*, which we now understand to be the Great Tribulation and future martyrdom of saints. Upon the opening of the fifth seal (vs. 9), John "saw under [at the base of] the altar the souls of them that were slain."

Here again was John's full description of the fifth seal: "And when he had opened the FIFTH SEAL, I saw under the altar *the souls of them that were slain for the word of God,* and for the testimony which they held: and they cried with a loud voice, saying, How long, O Lord, holy and true, do You not judge and AVENGE our blood on them that dwell on the earth? And white robes were given unto every one of them; and it was said unto them, that they should *rest* yet for a little season, *until their fellow servants* also and their *brethren*, that should be *killed* as they were, should be fulfilled" (vs. 9-11).

We saw that some cite these verses to validate both the pagan immortal soul doctrine and the belief that the saved go to heaven (which is not true)—and thereby miss the whole point of what Christ is revealing. And we saw this description is not literal, but rather *symbolic*.

More basic review is now essential.

The fifth seal portrays the martyrdom of true saints (along with vast numbers from national Israel and Judah). This occurs during the Tribulation. The context develops with the already-martyred souls asking God a question: "How long, O Lord..." (vs. 10). Verse 11 is a symbolic instruction to these martyrs of the Middle Ages to await this *latter* martyrdom of the end time.

Remember, in the vision, John was shown the *future*. A long period of martyrdom, at the hands of the "woman," who was "drunken with the blood of the saints, and with the blood of the martyrs of Jesus" (17:6), will have already taken place. And recall that Revelation 12 describes the true Church. There, this period is described as "a thousand two hundred and three score (1,260) days"—or 1,260 *years*, from 325 to 1585. (This does not parallel the 1,260 years of the healed Beast.)

Revelation 12:6 describes how the Church had to flee "into the wilderness" to escape. Accounts from history indicate that more than *50 million* human beings were killed during this time because of their unwillingness to compromise beliefs that were contrary to the Roman church! (Most of these were not true Christians striving to hold to all of God's doctrines, but were "protestors" holding to some few areas where they disagreed with Rome.)

Again, a later martyrdom (the Great Tribulation) is yet to happen in *our* time. The "souls" who were *already* "slain" were *previously* martyred Christians from past ages. These earlier martyrs were told to "rest yet for a little season, until their *fellow servants* also and their *brethren*, that should be *killed* as they were, *should be fulfilled*" (6:11).

I repeat for emphasis: The Tribulation is not *God's* wrath. God's wrath is the seven trumpet plagues. The Tribulation is *Satan's* wrath on God's true servants—and on the modern descendants of ancient Israel and Judah. This wrath will be perpetrated by the final empire of 10 kings in Europe, united under one powerful leader—and done at the behest of Satan's universal church system. Matthew 24:22 shows that God will have to cut "short" this persecution "for the elects' sake."

The "souls under the altar" are now awaiting God's punishment of—His "vengeance" on—the great governmental power that persecuted them. God said that He would "AVENGE [their] blood" through the seven last plagues on those who carry the mark of the Beast. God will pour His vengeance on this false Babylonish murderous woman and her daughter churches. But this cannot take place until the second great and final martyrdom is past.

Elect Must Remain Fervent, Vigilant

Also repeated here for emphasis, many of God's people in the end time have partially drifted away from God. They have not remained as close to Him as they should be. They have not zealously sought and obeyed God on a daily basis. This has allowed many to be deceived, and to fall into false doctrines and practices—the sad pattern of history when false ministers capture the leadership of the flock. Only with the arrival of the Tribulation will about half of these brethren awaken (Matt. 25:1-12)!

These "lukewarm" true followers of God will have to endure this final martyrdom (Rev. 3:14-22). The earlier true Christians previously killed must continue to "rest" (remain "asleep" in Christ) until joined by these later martyrs.

During the Tribulation, there will be extraordinary deception, unlike any time in world history. As we have seen, Christ was very specific about this in Matthew 24: "And then shall many be *offended*, and shall *betray* one another, and shall *hate* one another. And many *false prophets* shall rise, and shall *deceive many*. And because iniquity shall abound [worldwide lawlessness toward both human laws and God's Law], the love of many [obedience to God—Rom. 13:10; I John 5:3] shall *wax cold*. But he that *shall endure unto the end*, the same shall be *saved*...For then shall be GREAT TRIBULATION, such as was not since the beginning of the world to this time, no, nor ever shall be...For there shall arise *false christs*, and *false prophets*, and shall *show great signs and wonders* [we have seen that the False Prophet—of the woman who rides the two-horned beast—will lead in this]; insomuch that, if it were possible, they shall *deceive* the very elect" (vs. 10-13, 21, 24).

This is a very direct prophecy about tremendous deception that seduces "many" at the end of the age, before Christ's Coming.

At His Return, Christ will bring with Him the individual rewards of all His servants. They will have qualified for great glory: "For the Son of Man shall come in the glory of His Father with His angels; and then He shall *reward* every man according to his *works*" (Matt. 16:27).

Your *works* in this life, your obedience to God's plain commands, have a direct bearing on your *reward* in the next life!

Satan's Wrath on Modern Israelite Descendants

Let's now take a moment to compare two critically important scriptures that shed much light on the Tribulation. Doing this will give us a precise picture of who else receives the brunt of Satan's wrath during this time. We have seen that lukewarm Christians will be martyred—but many more than these will be forced to endure this terrible time of trial.

First reread Matthew 24:21: "For then shall be great tribulation, such as *was not* since the beginning of the world to this time, no, *nor ever shall be*." This verse plainly establishes the Tribulation as the single worst time in all world history. Take this verse for exactly what it says.

Now let's examine a second scripture that relates to this one. It is longer and more extensive, and is found in Jeremiah 30. The last phrase of this chapter is "in the latter days you shall *consider* it." Now what does this chapter contain that we must "consider" in these final days?

Verse 2 was instruction to Jeremiah to record in a book all that God had told him. Verse 3 establishes to whom God is speaking—Israel and Judah. Now notice: "And these are the words that the LORD spoke concerning Israel and concerning Judah. For thus says the LORD; We have heard a voice of trembling, of fear, and not of peace. Ask you now, and see whether a man does travail with child? Wherefore do I see every man with his hands on his loins, as a woman in travail, and all faces are turned into paleness? Alas! For that day is great, so that *none is like it*: it is even the time of Jacob's trouble; but he shall be saved out of it" (vs. 4-7).

This is a shocking description of punishment prophesied to come on Israel and Judah. Unmeasured fear and horror accompany this national chastisement.

–- But focus for a moment on two phrases in verse 7 describing this time. The first is "that day is great, so that *none* is like it." This is almost identical to Matthew 24:21. They cannot be speaking of two separate times, because it is impossible to have two periods in history that are *both* described as the *worst of all time*. These two scriptures have to be speaking of the same time. And remember, these verses both depict events in the "end of the age" and the "latter days."

Now notice the second phrase: "it is even the time of *Jacob's trouble*." This phrase unlocks vital meaning and explains who else suffers Satan's wrath in this time of terrible anguish and misery.

Understand that the Old Testament patriarch Israel was originally named Jacob (Gen. 32:28). Prophecies referencing either name describe the same peoples today who came from this man.

Many Old Testament prophecies describe the scope and severity of national punishment that God plans for the peoples descended from Jacob. Their modern lands will be destroyed by the Beast, and many millions will be taken into captivity at his hands.

The Great Tribulation will be a time of terrible suffering for both *physical* Israel and the less vigilant, lukewarm "remnant" of *spiritual* Israel, the Church. But numerous verses in Revelation show that it will be a time of general *prosperity* for many *non-Israelitish* nations—when the Beast's "merchants" bring much "buying and selling." *These* nations will be punished during the time of God's wrath.

The Mark—Past and Future!

Let's return to the subject of the true Christian's initial reward. It involves rulership, lasting 1,000 years. But the test has been the same for those of previous ages. Those who hold fast their convictions, in the face of impending martyrdom, when this test comes again, will be victorious even in death—but they will truly be "gold tried in the fire" (Rev. 3:18).

Here is what God says awaits those who have been faithful unto death. Read each word carefully: "And I saw thrones, and they sat upon them, and judgment was given unto them: and I saw the *souls* of them that were *beheaded for the witness of Jesus, and for the word of God*, and which had not worshipped the beast, neither his image, *neither had received his mark* upon their foreheads, or in their hands; and they *lived and reigned with Christ a thousand years*" (Rev. 20:4).

This is an astonishing verse. Did you notice that *all* those killed in past ages for holding to the truth of God also refused to receive the MARK? In other words, those of *previous* eras were required to withstand the enforcement of the mark as well. But, because they would not yield to pagan beliefs, festivals, customs, rank idolatry and worship of the Holy Roman Empire—and the "woman" church—they were killed. The mark of the Beast was *first* enforced well over 1,000 years ago. And, though it is not *yet* being enforced, for the plagues to fall on those who have it, and for those who refuse it to be forced into martyrdom— IT MUST BE ENFORCED ONCE AGAIN!

Christians of previous times were killed because they refused the mark of the Beast and the worship of its image. They "obeyed God rather than man" (Acts 5:29)—they obeyed the government of God rather than the Roman government guided by the woman riding it. They did not resist punishment, but willingly yielded to their punishment—torture and death! These future rulers proved themselves faithful to God and have qualified to reign with Jesus Christ when He comes, bringing "His reward with Him."

Some more review for context. Also in Matthew 24, Christ foretold that the "gospel of the kingdom" would be preached to all nations "and then shall the *end come*" (vs. 14). In John 9:4, He warned His disciples that "the *night comes*, when no man can work."

Soon, deep spiritual darkness will descend on the whole world. The time for announcing the coming of the kingdom of God will come to an end. Final opportunity to seek God and *escape* what lies ahead will be gone. There is the responsibility to preach—and WARN—before it is too late. Notice a second parallel passage in Ezekiel: "When I say unto the wicked, You shall surely die; and you [God's designated watchman] give him not warning, nor speak to warn the wicked from his wicked way, to save his life; the same wicked man shall die in his iniquity; but his blood will I require at your hand" (3:18).

God, through this end-time Work, is warning all who will listen now. Soon, you will have to choose who and what you will obey. Will you obey God or will you obey the final revival of the Holy Roman Empire, governed by the great false "woman" church leading recognized, traditional "Christianity"?

But the Bible reveals that there will be three final warnings to the rebellious nations under the woman and Beast's deception. This will occur through three separate angelic messengers, referenced earlier. Again, these are found in Revelation 14.

The third message states, "If any man *worship the beast* [this final end-time revival] and his *image*, and receive his *mark*...the same shall drink of the wine of the WRATH OF GOD...He shall be tormented with fire and brimstone...in the presence of the Lamb" (vs. 9-10).

True Christians "Marked" by Obedience

We have not yet identified the exact *nature* of the mark. But we will see that it has something to do with obedience—whether we will obey "God or man" (Acts 5:29).

As we have seen, two churches are described in the New Testament. The true Church that Jesus built (Matt. 16:18) is the bride of

Christ, forsaking involvement with this world and its customs in order to be pure when He comes to marry her.

Throughout the New Testament are warnings that false teachers would creep in (Jude 3-4; II Thes. 2:3-11; II Cor. 11:13-14) and gain control of the church organization, forcing faithful Christians to flee from their original congregations to continue to obey God. Remember, the true people of God were foretold to remain a "little flock" (Luke 12:32), often scattered, never having political power in this world.

Despite continual persecution—even during periods of great martyrdom—by the large popular churches that have continually sought to destroy it, a determined remnant has always remained throughout the last nearly 2,000 years.

The world has kept little track of this small, scattered Church, but Jesus promised that He would never leave or forsake it, and that "the gates of hell [the grave] shall not prevail against it" (Matt. 16:18). Though it has periodically been forced to flee for its life (Acts 8:1; Dan. 12:7), Jesus has faithfully kept His promise to remain with it, empowering and strengthening it through His Spirit. *His* Church is loyal and obedient to *His* government structure, above all others!

Immediately after the third angel's warning in Revelation 14:9-10, verse 12 contains a description of God's servants who will *not* take the mark. Remember, there are only two categories of people—those who take the mark and those who do not.

God declares, "Here is the patience of the saints: here are they that keep the *commandments of God*, and the *faith of Jesus*" (vs. 12).

In a disobedient world that has followed a system in rebellion against God, there are relatively few commandment-keepers. God's little Church has always been willing—and determined—to obey Him.

This verse explains that only the "faith *of* Jesus" (not merely faith *in* Jesus) gives them the strength to resist receiving the mark. Shallow human faith will be of no value in avoiding the mark!

When Jesus was approached by a young man seeking salvation, He was asked, "What good thing shall I do, that I may have eternal life?" (Matt. 19:16). Jesus answered, "If you will enter into life, keep the commandments" (vs. 17).

It has always been this plain for all who would serve God! The commandments of God must be kept.

Regarding obedience to His Law, God has always had but one standard: "For whosoever shall keep the whole law, and yet offend in one point, he is guilty of all. For He that said, Do not commit adultery, said also, Do not kill. Now if you commit no adultery, yet if you kill, you are become a transgressor of the law" (Jms. 2:10-11).

Christians keep *all* the laws of God. They make *no* exceptions!

Disobedience Is the Mark

The above scriptures reveal that God's people refuse the mark, keep His commandments and obey His government. Those of the world receive the mark, obey *something else*, and thereby disobey God and reject His rule over them.

Now here is the description read in the last chapter of those who have triumphed over Satan's mark, expanded for context: "And I saw as it were a sea of glass mingled with fire: and them that had gotten the victory *over the* BEAST, and *over his* IMAGE, and *over his* MARK, and over the number of his name, stand on the sea of glass, having the harps of God. And they sing the *song of Moses* the servant of God, and the song of the Lamb, saying, Great and marvelous are Your works, Lord God Almighty; just and true are Your ways, You King of saints" (Rev. 15:2-3).

God likens those who have achieved victory to those who escaped Egypt and Pharaoh's rule. Under Moses' leadership, Israel escaped the plagues that fell on Egypt, which were a forerunner and type of the plagues to fall on those who have received the mark. Paul spoke of how Old Testament examples "are written for our admonition, upon whom the *ends of the world* are come" (I Cor. 10:11).

God's saints are shown to "sing the song of Moses" standing on a sea of glass (before God), just as Israel stood on the shore of the Red Sea having been delivered from oppression in Egypt. They sing Moses' song because Moses reflects God's commandments. They sing the song of the Lamb (Christ) because, through faith ("of Christ"), they have conquered sin, and received salvation.

Now back to Revelation 12 and key events happening to the Church at the very end.

Remember, Satan is angry, and directs his wrath against God's people. This is contrasted to great joy in heaven because of God's final victory through His servants. Notice: "Therefore rejoice, you heavens, and you that dwell in them. Woe to the inhabitants of the earth and of the sea! for *the devil* is come down unto you, having GREAT WRATH, *because he knows that he has but a short time*" (vs. 12). The last phrase reveals *why* the devil is angry.

Verses 13-16 explain that a very select few of God's completely faithful servants will be protected in the Church's "place" for three and a half years (also see Revelation 3:10-11). But those who are less vigilant, less convicted and lukewarm, and who have accepted certain doctrines of the Revelation 17 "woman," while remaining generally faithful in keeping the commandments, will *not* be protected.

Here is what Satan does to this lukewarm group next. Read it carefully, for it is further proof that God's people keep the commandments, and is proof that they suffer Satan's wrath as a result.

Continue with the final verse of the chapter: "And the dragon was wroth with the woman [God's true Church], and went to make war with the remnant of her seed, which keep the *commandments of God*, and have the *testimony of Jesus Christ*" (vs. 17).

Christians are commandment-keepers, and the testimony of Jesus Christ is God's Word—the Bible. The "testimony of Jesus Christ" is also referred to as the "spirit of prophecy" (Rev. 19:10). God's servants understand the basic framework of His overall prophetic timetable and plan. They are not confused about "what happens next," once certain prophecies begin to take place.

However, just as God knows His servants, and they are marked by obedience to Him, so Satan knows *his* servants, and marks them as his own, so that they may be protected from his wrath—the Tribulation!

Understand this in the following way: Satan marks his servants and protects them from his wrath, while persecuting and martyring those who will *not* take his mark. On the other hand, God protects His most faithful servants (Rev. 3:10-11; 12:13-16), because they will *not* take the mark, or in any manner compromise His way, but pours *His* wrath on those who *do* take Satan's mark. (But even those who are lukewarm can in the Tribulation, through death, triumph over the mark and receive salvation.)

Get this picture absolutely clear in your mind!

Those Who Receive Plagues Made Plain!

There are plain New Testament scriptures that tell us exactly *why* God pours His wrath on certain people. We will momentarily briefly examine one before a more in-depth look later.

We must first examine what God says sin is, for His plagues will be poured out on a sinning humanity. Once we understand how God defines sin, we can better understand how Satan marks all those who are his servants.

Here is sin, defined by God: "Whosoever commits sin transgresses also the law: for sin is the transgression of the law" (I John 3:4).

In plain words, just as the faithful are commandment-*keepers*, those who sin are commandment-*breakers*.

Now let's examine for specific understanding what *exactly* brings the wrath of God. Here is what Paul wrote: "Mortify therefore your members which are upon the earth; fornication, uncleanness, inordinate affection, evil concupiscence, and covetousness, which is idolatry: for which things' sake the WRATH OF GOD comes on the *children of disobedience*" (Col. 3:5-6).

There it is! God pours out His wrath on those who DISOBEY Him! There is no misunderstanding the meaning of this verse. Again, this will be made clearer, with more plain verses, in its own later chapter.

Let's now summarize what we have read.

The mark of the Beast is commandment-breaking, and he that breaks one breaks them all. The mark is that of the Roman Empire—the Beast—not the woman who rides it. The false woman church "caused" the masses to receive the mark through deception. The human government through which Satan deceives the world, the Roman Empire, receives its power, its seat and authority from him. Holding a job and engaging in commerce—buying or selling—is impossible for those without the mark. Martyrdoms, past and future, occur because some refuse the mark, and keep the commandments of God instead. So, the mark is something the apostate church enforces, which is directly contrary to God's Law, and has a direct relationship to earning a living—holding a job.

What Would Satan Choose?

Since Satan has "deceived the whole world" (Rev. 12:9; 20:3), we must ask how has he accomplished this? On what point has he seized, which he can most naturally replace with a counterfeit? What command would Satan most easily change, and then expect carnal human reasoning to conclude is merely an innocent *adjustment*?

Now understand. The carnal mind is "enmity against God: for it is not subject to the law of God, neither indeed can be" (Rom. 8:7). Human beings are most agreeable to sin in *all* of its forms. People are perfectly willing to break *every one* of God's commandments. Whether idolatry, stealing, adultery, murder, dishonoring of parents, coveting or lying, people willingly—and eagerly—do these things. And, of course, Satan has certainly led people into all of these practices.

But none of these represent, in any particular way, a *test* that direct-ly connects to how one might earn a living or hold a job—to whether or how one could or could not "buy and sell." And Satan must select a commandment that affects *this* ability of those who will not compro-mise God's Law.

There is only one commandment that Satan would see as a candi-date for such a test. It is a commandment that God has always said is a *sign* between Him and His people. We will soon learn it.

But first we should ask, "What is a mark, brand or sign?" What do these terms signify—what do they *mean*?

In practical application, ranchers brand their cattle to signify own-ership. In many cases, retailers hang up a sign above their establish-ment to show whose hardware store, restaurant or shop it is. In Genesis 4:15, after he killed Abel, Cain received a "mark," signifying that he had sinned. This was also a kind of brand or sign telling those who met Cain who and what he was. The famous novel *The Scarlet Letter* is the story of a woman who committed adultery and had to wear a large "A" on the front of her clothing to signify what she had done.

It is no different with a church. God does not force anyone to obey Him. But Satan, through *his* church, *does* force his brand on *his* people in the same way that ranchers force their brand on cattle.

Now what is the sign that God says identifies *His* people? What point of obedience tells Him who are His people?

What Is God's Sign?

In Genesis 2, immediately after God had made man, He finished the week with one final creation: "Thus the heavens and the earth were finished, and all the host of them. And on the *seventh day* God ended His work which He had made; and He *rested* on the *seventh day* from all His work which He had made. And God *blessed* the *seventh day*, and *sanctified* IT [none other]: because that in IT [none other] He had *rested* from all His work which God created and made" (vs. 1-3).

From Creation, God established, "blessed" and "sanctified" (set apart) the seventh day of the week as a day of rest. He never established any other day—and confirmed that this was His Law "forever." He told ancient Israel to "Remember the sabbath day, to keep it holy…the SEV-ENTH DAY is the sabbath of the LORD your God" (Ex. 20:8, 10).

After a few generations in Egypt, God's people, the ancient Israel-ites, lost all knowledge of His Law. God had to teach it to them again.

After freeing them from slavery, the first great law that He gave them was the command to keep the Sabbath (Ex. 16).

The Sabbath originated before the Old Covenant was established. The Ten Commandments were not given as part of the Old Covenant. They had been in force since Creation. (You may read my book *The Ten Commandments – "Nailed to the Cross" or Required for Salvation?*)

In Exodus 31:12-17, God made a special covenant with Israel regarding His Sabbath: "And the LORD spoke unto Moses, saying...Verily My sabbaths you shall keep: for it is a SIGN between Me and you *throughout your generations*; that you may know that I am the LORD that does *sanctify* [set apart] *you*. You shall keep the sabbath...the seventh [day] is the sabbath of rest, *holy* to the LORD...Wherefore the children of Israel shall keep the sabbath...for a *perpetual covenant*. It is a SIGN between Me and the children of Israel *forever*: for in six days the LORD made heaven and earth, and on the seventh day He rested..."

This last phrase proves that the Sabbath was established from the Creation week, over 2,000 years prior to Exodus 31.

The Sabbath "sanctifies" those who keep it. They are set apart as belonging to—as being *owned* by—God. Christians are told that "you are *bought* with a price; be not you the servants of men" (I Cor. 7:23) and "you are *bought* with a price: therefore glorify God..." (I Cor. 6:20).

Those who observe the Sabbath are signified as *God's* people—and that He owns them. They are also publicly identified as people who keep the commandments. Civil laws require people to obey several of the *other* commandments (against stealing, murder, lying [perjury], etc.), so obedience to most or all of the *other* commandments, which the world at least generally acknowledges in one form or another, does not identify one as a commandment-keeper!

The Sabbath does! It is a sign that people are of God, since no one would ever think or choose to keep this law without it having been revealed by God.

Notice that God established the Sabbath as a "perpetual covenant" to be kept "throughout your generations"—and "forever." This is iron-clad. God's command is for all time. The Sabbath was to be kept *forever*! Doing this kept people in touch with the true God. It was the way God intended that people never lose sight of who He was (their God)—and who they were (His people)! If all peoples and nations kept the Sabbath, as Israel was commanded to do, no one would have ever fallen into idolatry and the worship of other gods—which has happened to all nations who have not kept it.

Now we must ask: Which commandment would Satan choose to overthrow? Which commandment would he most hate—and why? Which commandment signifies that those who obey it do not belong to him?

The only commandment *signifying* (is a *sign*) that one belongs to God—and the only commandment that directly points to the true God of Creation, thus displacing Satan—is the SABBATH!

Satan most hates the *Fourth* Commandment! There is no way to get around whether one does or does not literally observe the seventh day of the week as the Sabbath. You either do or you don't! God and Satan are not confused on this point. They know what is at stake. And the world can readily see whether one keeps the Sabbath—or does not.

Israel and Judah Failed the Test

Israel would not keep God's Sabbath for any length of time. From time to time, they would temporarily observe it, but they always fell back into the practices of the nations around them. The following summarizes how God says Sabbath-breaking brought His WRATH on disobedient Israel:

"In the day when I chose Israel...saying, I am the LORD your God...I gave them *My sabbaths*, to be a SIGN between Me and them, that they might know that I am the LORD that *sanctify them*. But...Israel REBELLED against Me...*My sabbaths they greatly polluted*: then I said, I would pour out My *fury* [God's wrath] upon them in the wilderness, to consume them...Nevertheless Mine eye spared them from destroying... But I said unto their children...hallow *My sabbaths*; and they shall be a SIGN between Me and you...Notwithstanding the children REBELLED against Me...they *polluted My sabbaths*: then I said, I would pour out My *fury* [His wrath] upon them, to accomplish My *anger* [His wrath]" (Ezek. 20:5, 12-13, 17-21).

Because of their repeated disobedience and rebellion against His government, God eventually did send Israel into captivity (by Assyria) and the Jews into captivity (by Nebuchadnezzar into Babylon).

And lest any say, "Well, the Sabbath was only made for the Jews and Israel," Christ answers, "The Sabbath was made for MAN...therefore the Son of man is Lord also of the Sabbath" (Mark 2:27-28).

Yes, Christ is Lord of the Sabbath, *not* the Lord of Sunday! The Sabbath was *not* made for the Jews or Israel *only*, it was made for MAN. It was made for *all* humanity—but humanity has rejected it!

Where Did "Sunday Keeping" Come From?

Since God commanded that the Sabbath be kept forever, how did Sunday keeping originate? It certainly did not come from God or His Church.

Remember, Sunday is commonly referred to as "the Lord's Day." While the true Lord's Day of the Bible is actually the *Day of the Lord*—the *Day of His Wrath* (Joel 2:1-11; Rev. 1:10; 15:1, 7), the term "the Lord's Day" has come to be synonymous with Sunday.

But why?

The reason is simple. Many have assumed to be true the unscriptural tradition that Jesus was resurrected from the tomb on Sunday. If Sunday can be established as the day that Jesus was resurrected, it can be a means of artificially validating and "authorizing" the keeping of Sunday by the churches of the world—in place of God's true Sabbath. Then, the pagan Easter festival and celebration, with its Sunday sunrise services, also becomes much easier to establish.

Many pagan festivals, including Christmas (the Saturnalia), Easter (the festival of Ishtar) and worship on the day of the Sun, were observed throughout the Roman Empire long before Christ. The apostate church (the "woman") simply adopted them into practice, and enforced them on all citizens in the empire through the civil government. Actually, the first one to enforce Sunday worship was not a pope or a church, but was Constantine, the emperor.

Here is what happened. At the Council of Laodicea, in AD 363, the following decree was passed: "Christians must not Judaize by resting on the Sabbath, but must work on that day, resting rather on Sunday. But, if any be found to be Judaizing, let them be declared anathema from Christ."

Understand what this decree meant. When one was branded "anathema" (accursed or heretic) by the church, he was arrested by the state, tortured and, unless he recanted, this continued until death. This was enforced so strictly that people were *required* to rest on Sunday, and work on Saturday, in order to engage in business or hold a job. This enforcement governed their "buying and selling."

Now briefly back to the beast and "little horn" of Daniel 7. Verse 25 sheds important light on what happened in the Roman Empire. Daniel wrote, "And he [the little horn] shall speak great words against the Most High, and shall wear out the saints of the Most High"—now get this next point and do not misunderstand—"and think to change *times* and *laws*."

This is a remarkable statement about how the false "woman" church sought to alter God's LAW as it had to do with TIME. The single most obvious way has been to change the *time* of God's Sabbath to the pagan SUN'S DAY (the day long set apart by men for worship of the sun), thus altering the fourth great *law* of God! (More and more people today speak of Sunday as their "sabbath.")

HOW PLAIN has been the work of this church in its efforts to "wear out the saints"!—and to speak against "the Most High"!

Is it any wonder that God will pour out His wrath without mercy on any who would dare to do these things to His Word and to His people?

God has never authorized His Church or mankind to keep the pagan Sun's day. Nor did He ever command or allow His people to keep numerous other pagan festivals and days of worship—He has always explicitly commanded *against* them!

When people celebrate Sunday as the "Lord's Day," they unwittingly celebrate the very wrath that God will pour on them for keeping this pagan custom in place of His Sabbath! Astonishing, but true.

Exodus 20:8-11 showed that Sabbath-keeping is the Fourth *Commandment*! The Sabbath has always been the seventh day of the week, and God never authorized Sunday, the first day of the week. God hallowed the Sabbath at Creation. Jesus kept it (Luke 4:16). So did Paul (Acts 13:42, 44; 17:2; 18:4). And so did the New Testament Church.

God has always said, "Remember the Sabbath day, to keep *it* holy" (Ex. 20:8). He has *never* said, "Remember *Sunday* to keep it holy—and just call it the Lord's day!"

Most do not realize how open are the admissions of how Sunday observance came to be. Here is a short, very simple statement from (Archbishop) James Cardinal Gibbons speaking in 1893 in *The Catholic Mirror*: "The Catholic Church...by virtue of her divine mission, changed the day from Saturday to Sunday." Here is one more candid admission from a signed letter by the same Cardinal: "Is Saturday the seventh day according to the Bible and the Ten Commandments? I answer yes. Is Sunday the first day of the week and did the Church change the seventh day—Saturday—for Sunday, the first day? I answer yes. Did Christ change the day? I answer no!"

Keeping the Sabbath as God's command for true Christians is a big subject requiring its own large volume to explain. (My book *Saturday or Sunday – Which Is the Sabbath?* brings extensive and absolute proof of which day is the Christian Sabbath. It includes many more equally frank admissions by Protestant and Catholic leaders about the only day

God ever sanctified in His Word. You may also read my booklet *God's Holy Days or Pagan Holidays?* to learn more about God's seven *annual* Sabbaths and how the false church has substituted these days with abominable, pagan, counterfeit "Christianized" festivals.)

What You Obey

Paul, in his letter to the Romans, explained that people are the servants of whatever and whomever they obey: "Know you not, that to *whom* you yield yourselves servants to obey, *his servants you are* to whom you obey; whether of sin unto death, or of obedience unto righteousness?" (6:16).

Human beings either serve and obey God, and are given eternal *life*—or they serve and obey sin and the "god of this world" (II Cor. 4:4), Satan, and earn eternal *death* (Rom. 6:23)!

In the Old Testament, Sabbath-breaking was punishable by death (Ex. 31:14 *and* 15). II Corinthians 3:7-8 describes the Old Testament administration of a civil death penalty, which is no longer applicable, because God is now building the nation of *spiritual* Israel (Rom. 2:28-29; 8:9; 11:24-26; Gal. 3:29; Eph. 2:11-13, 19; I Pet. 2:5, 9).

The Sabbath was to be kept perpetually, throughout the generations of Israel. There are still generations of Israel today—and there is *spiritual* Israel, which keeps the commandments of God and the faith of Jesus, and the testimony of Jesus Christ. Israel is not synonymous with Jewish. The Jews, who came from Judah, represent but one of twelve tribes of Israel that descended from the patriarch Jacob. Recall that the Tribulation is "Jacob's trouble," not merely "Judah's." (*America and Britain in Prophecy* makes all of this abundantly clear.)

Take heed whether and how you will obey God. For "He that despised Moses' law died without mercy under two or three witnesses: of how much sorer punishment, suppose you, shall he be thought worthy, who has trodden under foot the Son of God, and has counted the blood of the covenant, wherewith he was sanctified, an unholy thing, and has done despite unto the Spirit of grace?" (Heb. 10:28-29).

This is most serious!

How the Mark Is Made

During the Middle Ages, the Holy Roman Empire caused people to receive a "mark." What was this *mark*? Those who had it lived—those who did not, died. This mark *protected* all who received it.

The Roman system "set" this mark on all who obeyed and submitted to its pagan religious practices. These included observance of Sunday as the day of worship (instead of the true Sabbath), along with other pagan holidays (Christmas, Easter, New Year's and others). We saw history records that tens of millions were *killed* for not obeying the Roman Empire in regard to Sunday observance.

Notice this revealing verse in Daniel 7: "I beheld, and the same [little] horn made *war* with the saints..." (vs. 21). This "war" is referring to the period that the Roman Empire, under the false church's direction, put to death all those who would not worship on Sunday! Let me repeat: The universal church in Rome, working with the civil government, caused everyone under the Roman system to receive this mark. Sunday became the official day of worship for all—throughout the empire. Sabbath observance was outlawed, and anyone observing it was *killed*! *Millions* lost their lives in this persecution, and God's Word tells us that it will HAPPEN AGAIN!

We have already seen that the book of Revelation is largely one of visions and symbols. We read that the beast "causes all, both small and great, rich and poor, free and bond, to receive a mark in their *right hand*, or in their *foreheads*..." (Rev. 13:16).

What does this mean?

Let's understand. What do people do with their hands? They *work*! So the "right hand" referenced in Revelation is a symbol for *working*—making a living. What about the forehead? The forehead is a symbol for what people *believe*. This is referring to one's intellect or mind—specifically, what one obeys.

Again, God also has a "mark," or a sign, He puts on those who follow His laws. In Exodus 13:9, God is explaining one of His annual Sabbaths to the nation of Israel. Notice this: "It shall be for a *sign* unto you upon your *hand* [they could not work on the Sabbath], and for a memorial between your *eyes*, that the LORD'S LAW may be in your mouth."

This could not be more plain! Let's examine two more passages: "Now these are the commandments...and these words, which I command you this day, shall be in your heart...and you shall bind them for a SIGN *upon your* HAND, and they shall be as frontlets *between your eyes*" (Deut. 6:1, 6, 8), and "Therefore shall you lay up these My words in your heart and in your soul, and bind them for a *sign* upon your *hand*, that they may be as frontlets *between your eyes*" (Deut. 11:18).

The Fourth Commandment, of God's Sabbath, is the one command that professing Christianity outright *rejects*! This commandment separates those who have the mark of the Beast and those who carry God's sign of Sabbath-keeping. It is the TEST *command* of one's obedience to the true God.

God's Law is not negotiable. If one breaks any of His laws, that person is guilty of sin. We saw that "sin is the transgression of the law" (I John 3:4). If you break it, you earn a penalty—death (Rom. 6:23). So both God, with His sign, *and* the Beast, with his mark, identify their followers. And both bring death—if disobeyed!

You must CHOOSE which mark to take. Choose correctly. Your future depends on it!

Now notice again Exodus 31:13: "...Verily My Sabbaths you *shall keep*: for it is a *sign* between Me and you throughout your generations; that you may know that I am the LORD that does sanctify you."

So then, in plain terms, the mark of the Beast is SUNDAY-KEEPING and THE KEEPING OF PAGAN FESTIVALS—in place of God's weekly and annual Sabbaths! The mark is *disobedience* to God's Way!

Not Yet Enforced...

Today, there is no governmental power to enforce this mark. However, the final revival of the Holy Roman Empire soon will rise, and again have POWER to force this mark on an unsuspecting world. The enormous false church—the *great whore*—will again ride this Beast. Together they will cause all mankind to carry this mark in their forehead (obedience or submission), and without it, people will not be able to work (the right hand) and ultimately feed themselves.

The Bible reveals that the whole world today is deceived (Rev. 12:9). All nations, in one form or another, practice paganism. The physical descendants of Israel (the United States, Britain, Canada, Australia, New Zealand, South Africa, the Israelis and others) are unwittingly already following these false ways of "Babylon"—a system of religious confusion. In Revelation 18:4, God warns all who will listen: "Come out of her, My people, that you be not partakers of her *sins*, and that you receive not of her *plagues*"!

If you take heed to what you have learned, you can receive DIVINE PROTECTION from the living God. Obey God, and be "accounted worthy to escape"! This also means great reward: "And I saw *thrones*, and they [the faithful] sat upon them, and judgment was given unto them: and I saw the souls of them that were beheaded for the witness of Jesus, and for the word of God, and which had not worshipped the beast, neither his image, neither had received his mark upon their foreheads, or in

their hands; and *they lived and reigned with Christ a thousand years*"
(Rev. 20:4).

The identity of the Beast of Revelation and all the biggest questions
connected to it, are now known to you. Now you must decide what you
will do with the knowledge you have received. Take responsibility for
where you are.

I cannot, nor can any man, *make* you act on the understanding you
have received, or *make* you obey God. I can only jostle you—shake
you. You must rouse *yourself* from the comfort zone of your life. Wake
up! Throw cold water on your face! Clear your vision! Don't waste
time! Get going! Start down the road, one step at a time, to where you
should be! Determine to keep your eyes on the truth of events!

A transcendent WORLD TEST *is coming*, and this will crash into an
almost entirely *unprepared* and *unsuspecting* world.

Some are looking for the Beast, but most think in other terms...

The Antichrist—
Who, What, When!

The Bible teaches that a powerful antichrist will arise to rule the world just before Jesus Christ returns. But what does the word "antichrist" *mean*? Is this just one person? And what is the biblically referenced "*spirit* of antichrist?" Most are confused. Yet, the Bible plainly answers all of the most important questions about the antichrist!

A final, great antichrist IS coming. You must understand what this means—and how the Bible makes plain that the *last* antichrist is far from the *only* one to avoid.

Prophecy watchers, popular preachers and authors, and other supposed experts also butcher the truth about the coming antichrist. Some *reduce* this prophecy, others badly *twist* it, still others declare it *already fulfilled*, and another group *dismisses* it entirely. On top of this, many so-called Bible authorities speak with competing, disagreeing voices about the subject, and thus—consistent with what they do to all other points of prophecy—add to the confusion.

The appalling IGNORANCE of these voices—ALL of them—is painful to hear.

Wrong Understanding

Satan counterfeits every doctrine of the Bible. The antichrist would hardly be an exception. While generally understood to be a figure of horrific evil and a threat to all mankind, the antichrist is today seen by most to be largely focused against the *Jewish people*. Based on a completely wrong understanding of Daniel 9:27, tens of millions generally believe that this world-deceiver will make a "seven-year covenant" with the modern country of Israel, before breaking the agreement halfway through, thus introducing the Great Tribulation for the last 3½ years of his "reign." It is commonly believed that *at this point* he will throw off his cloak and reveal his true colors.

This entire belief is *wrong*! We will later learn *how*. Daniel 9:27 simply *does not say this*. But this thinking is having an effect on great numbers of people who have come, largely over the last 150 years, to believe this idea.

Here is the great irony. Due to misunderstanding, one school of rapturists is even *eagerly awaiting* the antichrist's arrival—practically salivating over it in anticipation because of what they have been told it means for *them*. Tragically, these are completely unprepared for his coming—in fact, for *their* coming, because technically, in effect, there will be *two* FINAL antichrists. We have been discussing them, but using their more proper names—the Beast and the False Prophet. One, the *religious* arch-deceiver will point to and underscore the Beast's authority with powerful, spellbinding miracles. In almost all of the modern scenarios, however, an antichrist—the Beast—is confused with verses talking about another antichrist—the False Prophet—such as II Thessalonians 2:9 and Daniel 7:8.

Understand. Most who write about the Bible do not know, let alone comprehend, almost any of what you have read in the book's first 11 chapters. Attempting on their own authority to "interpret" the Bible without guidance, they ignore its Author—GOD!—and seem unable to grasp that He would never—I repeat—leave the most crucial questions, those involving all humanity, open to interpretation. Some preachers *do* get an occasional stray fact right, but none are able to put *all* the facts—*all* the scriptures on a subject—together.

Misconceptions About the Antichrist

In regard to the Beast and False Prophet, almost all have no idea where to look—for what *system*—in fact, the *only* system—that could spawn these final deceivers. They are busy trusting in a RAPTURE. They expect to be snatched away—so there is "no need to worry." Many others *unnecessarily* fear that they will be "left behind," as one popular fiction writer likes to term it, after the expected rapture.

Hollywood has added to the interest in prophecy and the rapture fantasy through imaginative special effects, coupled with actors depicting popular ideas. Silly artwork and bad actors have only hindered correct understanding.

The most basic prophetic understanding reveals that the final two antichrists must be alive today—simply because of the obvious shortness of remaining time in this age. This monstrous final deceiver (the Beast) is not a single historical figure, such as Nero, Saladin, George III, Napoleon, Saddam Hussein or Hitler—who, it could be said, *was* certainly a TYPE of the antichrist. Neither is he Putin, Ahmadinejad or any of several American presidents who have been suggested.

In all of this, *everyone* is looking in ALL THE WRONG PLACES!

If you cannot understand what *is* an antichrist—what they *are*, and what they *do*—and that, according to the Bible, *many* of them are all around you *now!*—you will *never* recognize the *final* antichrist. You must know what to look for—and avoid. You must be able to understand the setting—and gravity—of what is now being spawned in Europe.

You will soon come to understand both the terms "antichrist" and "*final* antichrist." You will have also learned all of the most essential knowledge about this subject—and *much* more.

Simple Definition

What comes to mind when you hear the word "antichrist"? *Webster's New World College Dictionary* defines "antichrist" as "the great antagonist of Christ, expected to spread universal evil before the end of the world, but finally to be conquered at Christ's second coming."

Hollywood has produced countless films, most of them ridiculous, promoting this thinking. The entertainment industry consistently ignores, blurs—and even knowingly erases—the line between truth and fiction. When it comes to the Bible, filmmakers and others distort and reshape the facts of history to promote preconceived ideas—and their own agendas.

Most people assume that the entire Bible teaching about antichrist is summarized in the belief that an end-time *Hitler-like* super dictator—"*the* antichrist"—in league with the devil, will arise to rule the world. While *Webster's* definition is *partly* correct, nowhere does the Bible actually refer to "THE antichrist." Most do not know this—including professing Christians! Ministers and theologians are little better.

Basic Background

The subject of the antichrist cannot be understood until first recognizing the clear difference between the Beast and the False Prophet. Again, the Beast is often confused (as is sometimes the final False Prophet) with *the* antichrist. This man will certainly be *an* antichrist, but not *the* antichrist. The misunderstanding that the Beast is *synonymous* with a sole human antichrist partly comes from the knowledge that the Beast is also the number of a *man* (Rev. 13:17-18).

Although the Beast of Revelation 13 is seen to obviously not be a human being, the one who leads the final resurrection of the Holy Roman Empire—the coming union of church and state centered in Europe, and described in Revelation 17—will plainly *represent* the *system* that is the Beast. The *embodiment*—the *representative*—of the Revelation 13 Beast *will* be a single charismatic figure who arrives on the world scene shortly before Christ's Return. This *will* of course be a HUMAN BEING!

The reader must understand. Any chapter solely about "a" final antichrist would be absolutely identical to the previous chapter identifying the Beast of Revelation. There would be quite literally *no differences* whatsoever as per the Beast being synonymous with "a" *final* antichrist. Therefore, this chapter discusses the subject of antichrist from a much broader and historically longer perspective. But it must be seen as a vitally necessary companion to the previous chapter, truly making the subject complete. This explanation will shortly be understood—and seen to carry supreme importance!

We now look more deeply into fascinating knowledge about *different forms* of antichrist. You will learn that the Bible defines *several* different *ways* that antichrists or the *spirit* of antichrist are manifested.

Now is the time to stop assuming about the antichrist—and to PROVE (I Thes. 5:21) the truth of the subject. Open your Bible. Come to know what *God* says about antichrist—and, as usual, permit the Bible to interpret itself!

Bible Definition of Antichrist

The word "antichrist" is found only five times in the Bible, and in only four passages, all written by the apostle John. Originally written in Greek as *antichristos*, the word means "an adversary or opponent of the Messiah"—in other words, *against Christ*.

Remember this!

In the first passage, notice how the apostle John warned: "It is the [a] last time: and as you have heard that ANTICHRIST shall come, even *now* [in the first century] are there *many* ANTICHRISTS..." (I John 2:18).

It says, *"many* antichrists"—plural, more than one. So then—and this is central in importance—the term is not limited to *one person.* You have probably never heard this before.

John continues by explaining in the next verse that antichrists can come from within God's Church: "They went out *from* us, but they were not *of* us; for if they had been *of* us, they would no doubt have continued *with* us: but they went out, that they might be made manifest [obvious] *that they were not all of us"* (vs. 19).

Here is the point not to miss. Sooner or later, antichrists always become obvious to God's people. They eventually leave the Church for reasons of doctrine or conduct.

Some history. John recorded these verses near the close of the first century and the end of his 65-plus-year ministry. Of Jesus' apostles, he lived the longest by far after Jesus' crucifixion, and was the only one still living at the end of the first century. John had witnessed the birth of the true Church on Pentecost, AD 31. He saw it grow like the proverbial mustard seed as it spread across the Roman Empire—and he saw it come under vicious attacks, as well as suffer religious deception. The apostle John was very familiar with antichrists.

According to *Halley's Bible Handbook,* the antichrist "...is commonly identified with the Man of Sin (of II Thessalonians 2), and the Beast of Revelation 13. But the Bible itself does not make the identification. The language implies that John's readers had been taught to expect an Anti-Christ in connection with the closing days of the Christian era. However, John applies the word, not to One Person, but to the whole *group* of Anti-Christian Teachers. The New Testament idea seems to be that the Spirit of Antichrist would arise in Christendom, manifesting itself in many ways, both Within the Church and Without, finally culminating in One Person, or an Institution, or Both."

Make no mistake. Antichrists *have* continued throughout the 2,000-year history of God's Church—and into *our time.* In fact, the greatest number of them—and the worst ones—are at work today. And these deceivers operate in and around *all* of the groups and organizations of professing Christianity. The next chapter, about the Revelation 6 white horse of false Christianity, is devoted entirely to this subject, and is brought from the historical perspective.

Antichrists Are Deceivers

Here is John's second reference: "For *many deceivers* are entered *into the world*, who confess not that Jesus Christ is come in the flesh. *This is a deceiver and an* ANTICHRIST" (II John 7). So antichrists are deceivers, plain and simple.

The apostle Paul warned of "false apostles" and "deceitful workers," disguised as "ministers of righteousness" (II Cor. 11:13-15), who went about seducing and deceiving even some *true* Christians into believing "another gospel"—following "another Jesus"—and bringing "another spirit"—*not* the Spirit of God (vs. 3-4).

False *ministers* and *teachers*, and false *brethren*, are the "tares" among the "wheat" that Jesus referred to in His Matthew 13 parable. All of these function in a sense to some degree as antichrists. They sound sincere—*seem* godly—but are far from real Christianity. On the surface, these tares (false ministers and false Christians) are often hard to discern from the wheat (those who obey God and are led by His Spirit of truth). The confusion of distinguishing tares from wheat (Matt. 13:24-30) made it easy for false Christians to rise into leadership positions and then infect the Church with false doctrines—thus deceiving the many.

Among the worst deceivers in the late first century were the Gnostics, who claimed to possess "special knowledge," which they considered higher than Scripture. (Gnosticism derives from the Greek word meaning "knowledge.") They used this inside "knowledge"—that transgressing God's Law carried no consequences—to lead many brethren back into sin, meaning disobedience to God's Law (I John 3:4).

According to *The MacArthur Study Bible*, "...Gnosticism was the most dangerous heresy that threatened the early church during the first 3 centuries." This is who—and what—John was dealing with.

Again, antichrists are DECEIVERS. They deceive by *denying Christ*—and in a variety of ways. What are these?

"Denying Christ"

Now John's third reference: "Who is a liar but he that *denies* that Jesus is the Christ? He is ANTICHRIST, that *denies* the Father *and the Son*" (I John 2:22). Obviously, antichrists in John's time would not have openly declared, "I deny Christ," or they could not have blended among God's people.

So then, what *did* John mean by "deny Christ?" Vital explanation is required. Follow carefully. Fascinating, powerful and *deeply sobering* points appear from now on. We will learn *four* distinct teachings of antichrist.

Think. The problem of denying Christ *must* be other than the obvious—which is merely stating, "I deny Christ." Notice *how*—in what way—Jesus had long before warned His disciples, including John, as we revisit Christ's bedrock statement: "Take heed that no man deceive you [true Christians]. For *many* shall come *in My name*, saying, I AM Christ [certainly no denial here] and [still] shall deceive many" (Matt. 24:4-5). This deceit would have to do then with *other truths* in God's Word—obviously including how God defines antichrist. The devil—who we have seen to be the "god of this world" (II Cor. 4:4)—does not want civilization, including you, to prepare for what is coming. He wants the truth about antichrist suppressed.

So then, again, *how does* one deny Christ?

The Gnostics taught that flesh is entirely evil and that spirit is entirely good. Except for demons, this is *true.* But the famous Gnostic leader Cerinthus, who lived in Ephesus (modern southwest Turkey), denied that God, who is Spirit, *could* become flesh. He taught that this was impossible. Thus, some believed that when Jesus walked the earth, He did not have a real body—it only *seemed* real. He was a kind of phantom.

Others believed that a *divine* Christ (who is *spirit*) joined with the *human* Jesus (who was *flesh*) at baptism, but left Him just before He died. Since the divine Christ did not die, they next reasoned that He did not need to be resurrected from the dead.

Both ideas are false. They deny that Jesus was once a flesh-and-blood human being—that He was tempted like all men, and capable of sinning, but did not. This belief centers around the idea, therefore, that His death was not *actual.* However, were this true, mankind would have no Savior. This certainly *denies Christ*—and is thus ANTIchrist.

The false doctrines of Cerinthus and the Gnostics are based on human reasoning (Prov. 14:12; 16:25). They reject the clear, simple truth of Scripture—the greatest problem with so many today.

Did Christ Overcome Temptation?

But this goes further—in fact, much further: If Jesus was not flesh, then He was not *tempted* to sin. If He was never *tempted*, He was not *capable* of sinning. If He was *incapable* of sinning, then He did not *overcome* sin—and therefore could not set a perfect example *for us to follow*.

But the apostle John also recorded that Jesus Christ *did* become flesh: "In the beginning was the Word, and the Word was *with* God, and the Word *was* God. The same was in the beginning *with* God...and the Word was *made flesh*, and dwelt among us" (John 1:1-2, 14). That's plain! Jesus Christ *was* God and came to Earth in the flesh.

Matthew 4 describes Jesus' 40-day temptation in the wilderness by Satan: "Then was Jesus led up of the Spirit into the wilderness to be *tempted* of the devil" (vs. 1). Again, if Jesus was not flesh, temptation was no worry. Also consider. There would have been no need for Jesus to *fast* during the 40 days to remain spiritually strong so He could *resist* what would not have been, in fact, temptation. False teaching is always illogical in the end.

Let's understand. James 1:13 states, "God [as a spirit—John 4:24] *cannot be tempted* with evil." This is also plain. But Hebrews 4:15 states, "But [Jesus] *was* in all points TEMPTED *like as we are*..." And this is just as plain.

The point is that ALL flesh is subject to *temptation*.

Jesus declared plainly, "I have *overcome* the world" (John 16:33). And, "To him that *overcomes* will I grant to sit with Me in My throne, *even as I also overcame*..." (Rev. 3:21). How was overcoming possible if Jesus was never tempted and therefore never capable of sinning? Again, this means Jesus did not *overcome sin*, as He said, and He could not have set an example for Christians to do the same, as the apostle Peter wrote. Notice: "For even hereunto were you called: because Christ also suffered for us [via crucifixion, but also in overcoming and defeating sin. How do we know this?], *leaving us an example*, that you should *follow His steps*: *Who did no sin*..." (I Pet. 2:21-22).

So then—and let's continue to be *plain*—teaching that Christians do not have to OVERCOME SIN in their own personal lives—the breaking of God's Ten Commandments (I John 3:4)—and we must add for emphasis, this includes the fourth one about the seventh-day Sabbath that almost all reject—*is the doctrine of* ANTICHRIST.

You must comprehend this entire statement. Read and reread it until it thunders at you!

Jesus Christ Still "Coming in the Flesh"

Let's make this even stronger. Let's directly connect antichrists to *evil works*. So many do not understand John's warnings—actually God's through him—against those who "confess not that Jesus Christ is come in the flesh" (I John 4:3; II John 7). The Williams translation (among others) renders "is come" more clearly as *"continues* to come," meaning Christ "is *still* coming" in flesh today.

Although Jesus came in the flesh 2,000 years ago, He is also *coming* in the flesh *right now*—in the lives of true Christians! He is actively *working* in them, living His perfect, sin-free life through them daily (Gal. 2:20). He is guiding them to become perfect (Matt. 5:48)—spiritually mature—just like He is (I John 3:1-3). You must *grasp* this.

Acts 5:32 revealed that God only gives His Spirit to those who *obey* Him—who *keep* His commandments. This permits Christ to live His perfect life *through* them. Notice this: "And whatsoever we ask, we receive of Him, *because we keep His commandments*, and *do those things that are pleasing in His sight*" (I John 3:22). Followed by, "He that *keeps* His commandments dwells in Him [Jesus], and He [again, Jesus] *in him* [the individual]. And hereby we know that He abides in us, by the Spirit which He has given us" (vs. 24).

Antichrists deny Christ by their evil works. These popular preachers claim (and the masses tragically believe them) that Jesus "kept the law *for* Christians." Therefore, one need not obey those "harsh commandments"—they were "nailed to the cross."

This thinking is ANTICHRIST! And you should now see *why.* So many forget (or never knew, because preachers never speak about it) that Paul wrote how God's "Law is holy, and the commandment holy, and just, and good" and "spiritual" (Rom. 7:12, 14).

The Bible states, "They profess that they know God [and millions do]; but *in works* they deny Him [see *how* people deny Christ], being abominable, and *disobedient* [this can *only* refer to *God's Law*], and unto every *good work* reprobate [Greek: unapproved]" (Titus 1:16).

So then, antichrists are *against* God's laws, and they are against the idea of any kind of *qualifying* for (not earning) eternal life through good works. In *this way* they deny the POWER of Christ at work in His servants.

Many technical attempts are made to explain away this truth. I have read them—and the ignorance and confusion they reflect are almost breathtaking. But these efforts should be transparent to you.

Understand. Jesus came in the flesh! And, since His Resurrection, He is sending His Spirit into Christians, to relive His *righteous life* through them. Properly understanding these things is vital to discerning any spirit *not* of God!

My book *The Ten Commandments – "Nailed to the Cross" or Required for Salvation?* covers everything discussed here in detail.

The Trinity Doctrine in Its True Light

Now for a second way to deny Christ—and it will absolutely SHOCK you! Again, read carefully—and without bias. What follows is *very serious*—and to YOU! The popular trinity doctrine, taught to and believed by billions for centuries, promotes that God is "one Being, in three Persons, with one Nature," and that Jesus is "one Person, with two Natures." As referenced earlier, supposedly one "nature" of Jesus came to Earth and died at the crucifixion, while the *other* remained alive, still in heaven.

Let's stop and consider—let's "reason together" (Isa. 1:18), using the central question: How can one *half* of one *third* of one *Being* die? Are you confused? You should be! This IS doctrinal confusion—and "God is not the author of confusion" (I Cor. 14:33).

Here is what the *New Catholic Encyclopedia* openly admits about the trinity. Read slowly: "...one should not speak of Trinitarianism in the New Testament without serious qualification...when one does speak of an unqualified Trinitarianism, one has moved from the period of Christian origins to, say, the last quadrant of the 4th century. It was only then that what might be called the definitive Trinitarian dogma 'one God in three Persons' became thoroughly assimilated into Christian life and thought.

"Herein lies the difficulty. On the one hand, it was the dogmatic formula 'one God in three Persons' that would henceforth for more than 15 centuries structure and guide the Trinitarian essence of the Christian message...On the other hand, the formula itself does not reflect the immediate consciousness of the period of origins; it was the product of three centuries of doctrinal development."

In other words, the idea of "three persons in one God" did not originate in the Bible—the New Testament (the "period of origins"). Neither Christ nor the original apostles taught it. Nor did Paul. Instead, the trinity doctrine simmered in the minds of false Christians for over three centuries. It originated with Roman Catholic theologians, and by the late fourth century became the official doctrine of this universal church.

It was *never* the teaching of *God's* Church. This "god" is manmade—a human invention.

Grasp this. The trinity *denies* and *limits* the nature of God. It falsely teaches that God is Father, Son and Holy Spirit, which denies that God is a *Family*, and that He is *reproducing* Himself, expanding His Family with *many* sons (Rom. 8:29; Heb. 2:10). These sons are Holy Spirit-*begotten*, which empowers them to develop righteous godly character. At Christ's Return, they will be changed from mortal to immortal, from physical to spirit, from the human kind to the God kind. The trinity doctrine both limits God and denies His Master Plan of Salvation for mankind.

Plainly then, and for many reasons, the doctrine of the trinity is AN-TICHRIST!

To understand *much* more about this false view of God, and why—how—it completely overthrows the entire Purpose of the *true* God, read my thorough book *The Trinity – Is God Three-In-One?* To learn how God's Master Plan involves *you*, read *The Awesome Potential of Man*.

Chapter Thirty-two here addresses the true God of the Bible.

God as One Person?

A third, and somewhat related, doctrine of antichrist is the idea that God is just *one* Person. This derives from a misunderstanding, in fact, mistranslation, of the Old Testament passage, "Hear, O Israel: the LORD our God is one LORD" (Deut. 6:4). Referred to by Jews as the "Shema," the proper rendering of the Hebrew into English yields a completely different meaning. It is "Hear, O Israel: the LORD our God, *and Him only*." Merely recognizing that Israel had a long history of turning to other gods makes God's intent even plainer. He wanted Israel worshipping and listening to Him only. Of course, she never did.

Here is the problem. The false view of this verse *forces* the belief that Jesus appearing in the New Testament is *not* God, but merely His *Son*, meaning He holds a lesser status than actual *God*.

This ignores Jesus' own plain words: "I and My Father are ONE" (John 10:30)—*two* beings in *one* Godhead. When confronted on this occasion by the Jews, Jesus also stated this: "Many good works have I shown you from My Father; for which of those works do you stone Me? The Jews answered Him, saying, For a good work we stone You not; but for blasphemy; and because that You, being a man, *make Yourself God*" (vs. 32-33).

Read the entire chapter. Jesus did not say, "You misunderstood Me" or "You did not listen carefully" or "I make no such claim." This is because He knew that He *is* God, just like the Father *IS* God.

Recall that John recorded how Christ was God from the very beginning. All contrary teaching then is ANTICHRIST!

"Against Christ"

Now for the fourth way of being antichrist. Remember, the word means "an adversary or opponent of Christ," or *against* Christ. Interestingly, Jesus Himself adds more than anyone else in Scripture to simple comprehension of who and what is antichrist. Let's read what He said to the accusative Pharisees near the end of an important exchange with them. It was regarding the difference between Satan's spirit (and his kingdom) and the Spirit of God—and the danger of committing the unpardonable sin: "He that is not *with* Me is *against* Me; and he that *gathers* not *with* Me *scatters* abroad" (Matt. 12:30).

This next statement is absolutely crucial to grasp, and it explains why John and Paul warned of *many* antichrists in the first century who infiltrated and harassed the true Church. Get this.

Remember that Jesus Christ built a Church—*His* Church—the TRUE Church. *His* people are part of that one, undivided Church—and none other. Anyone working AGAINST *that Church*—who is not *with* it, and therefore not "*with*" Christ—or is in any way attempting to "scatter" Christ's flock, rather than "gather" it to where He is leading—is obviously AGAINST Christ.

All such then would be ANTIChrist! Is that clear? If not, reread the last paragraph until it is.

"The Spirit of Antichrist"

The fourth and final passage containing "antichrist" warns, "Believe not every spirit, but TRY the spirits *whether they are of God*: because many *false prophets* are gone out into the world. Hereby know you the Spirit of God: every spirit that confesses that Jesus Christ is come in the flesh is of God: and every spirit that confesses *not* that Jesus Christ is come in the flesh is *not* of God: *and this is that* SPIRIT *of antichrist*, whereof you have heard IT should come; and even now already is IT in the world" (I John 4:1-3).

This passage is of giant importance. False prophets—and these are all throughout the world today—are tied in this passage to the *spirit of antichrist*. This would certainly include those who teach falsely regarding the very truth about antichrists. It also includes those who teach falsely about all other aspects of prophecy—as well as the many additional plain truths of God's Word.

This passage makes these modern thought-to-be prophecy experts *antichrists themselves!*

Believe God on this. Stop listening to preachers who are *not* teaching you to obey God's Law—including the Fourth Commandment—and to overcome sin, but who *do* talk a lot about prophecy—even though they have no idea what they are talking about. You must disregard *who* they are—how *well-known* they are—how *popular* they are—how *charismatic* they are—how many people *read their books*—or *watch their programs*. Stop listening to them! They may be sincere, but they are sincerely WRONG. They will only confuse you.

They are AGAINST CHRIST!

Also notice that I John 4:3 uses the word "it"—not *he*—"should come," and that "it"—not he—"is already in the world." An antichrist is more than just a *person* or *group* of people. It is an *attitude*, an *idea*, a teaching—a SPIRIT!—and these all flow from a spirit that is alien to God.

The next three verses in the context of John's warning (vs. 4-6) are absolutely crucial to understand. They become vital instruction for you: "You are of God, little children [true Christians], and have *overcome* them [all false prophets and false ministers]: because greater is He that is in you, than he that is in the world. They [the antichrists] are of the world: therefore speak they of the world, and *the world hears them* [yes, but not true Christians]. We are of God: he that knows God hears us [God's faithful ministers]; he that is not of God hears not us. Hereby know we the *Spirit of truth*, and the *spirit of error*."

Let's continue being plain: God's people *overcome* the spirit of antichrist—the "spirit of error." They listen only to God's ministers. This spirit applies to people, authorities, attitudes and actions. And it permeates all cultures of the world because *this* world is led and deceived by the devil (II Cor. 4:4; Eph. 2:2; Rev. 12:9).

Can you now see more fully how the mixed-up "Jesus" of the trinity is truly *another* Jesus, brought by another *spirit* (II Cor. 11:4)—that of *antichrist?*

The Antichrist's Supposed Seven-year Reign

With the Bible teaching about antichrist made clear, let's return to the idea that the phrase "one week" in Daniel 9:27 refers to the final seven *years*, or supposed seven "prophetic days," before Christ returns. The prophetic understanding of rapture theorists is false! Let's first examine the verse: "And he shall confirm the covenant with many for *one week*: and in the *midst of the week* he shall cause the sacrifice and the oblation to cease, and for the overspreading of *abominations* he shall make it *desolate...*"

This verse *actually* refers to the "abomination of desolation" (Dan. 12:11), when occupying armies end the Jews' daily sacrifice at the Temple. (This is covered later. The prophesied coming abomination of desolation is *much* bigger—and *much* more crucial to understand—than you think.) This passage also addresses the *final week* of the 70 weeks prophecy and shows Jesus Christ would be cut off in the middle of the "week," after the 3½ "days"—actually 3½ *years*—of His earthly ministry and mission. The antichrist—and therefore any supposed 7-year reign by him 2,000 years later—is not the subject of this verse! There is simply no prophesied "7-year reign" of the antichrist that supposedly begins when he signs a "treaty" with the Middle-Eastern nation of Israel. The Beast (a final antichrist) will not suddenly throw off his cloak to reveal his true colors *halfway through* his "reign," thus ushering in the 3½ year Great Tribulation and Day of the Lord (which indeed *are* biblical periods totaling 3½ years, as we have seen and will later conclusively prove in a crucial, fuller context).

Consider. It should not be surprising that those who teach the *doctrines* of *anti*christ cannot even correctly discern when *Jesus* Christ is the subject of a passage!

Daniel's amazing prophecy in chapter 9 in fact reveals the exact year that the Messiah would begin His ministry, and how long it would last. It points to one major event that He would fulfill—His sacrifice!—as the beginning step in God's Plan of Salvation. It further shows that the final segment of this prophecy is yet to be fulfilled! While somewhat technical, this *series of events*, when studied carefully, can be understood for the inspiring—and truly fascinating—fulfillment of prophecy that it is! But this is not our subject here.

The "Rapture"—Antichrist Connection

While the "rapture" falsehood is systematically disproven in its own later chapter, it is necessary here to examine its connection to the doctrine of antichrist. This false teaching purports that only those who are "saved," "born again," and have "accepted Jesus in their hearts" will be secretly whisked away without warning—regardless of where they are or what they are doing—to the safety of heaven. This supposed event, signaled by the sudden vanishing of millions "whooshed off to heaven," it is said, will "shock the world."

All "unbelievers" remain to suffer the Great Tribulation. The antichrist will rule those who are "left behind," who missed out on their
chance to be "vacuumed" into heaven at Christ's so-called *secret* second
coming. All believers are thought to *escape* the antichrist by going to
heaven. The rapture theory also states that the antichrist will allow the
Jews to build a temple in Jerusalem, which, 3½ years into this tragically
mistimed "tribulation," he will turn on and destroy.

At the end of this period of turmoil, Christ will return—*supposedly*
in effect now His *third* coming—but this "third" time He will bring final
defeat to the antichrist and his forces.

Why is this teaching so dangerous?

When you come later to understand the rapture "theology," you will
realize that those who believe in a secret rapture will escape *nothing* because God *nowhere* promises this kind of protection! Put another way,
the very means by which millions hope to escape the coming final antichrist *does not exist*—leaving them among the most obvious candidates
for deception!

Ripe for Deception

Understand. The spirit of antichrist already blankets the world as mankind
continues to *rely on itself* to bring world peace, justice and prosperity—
while at the same time *denying* the power of Christ and *rejecting* His help
and rule in their lives.

As the end of Satan's reign draws near, the *power* of HIS spirit will
culminate in the rise of two men—the Beast and False Prophet. Neither
will be *the* antichrist, but both will *embody* and *represent* the ultimate
spirit or attitude of antichrist!

More religious deceivers will arrive throughout Christendom.
Some will perform miracles. One, the final mesmerizing False Prophet,
will use *great* miracles (Rev. 13:13-14) to lead the world to worship
the Beast (recall Revelation 16:13; 19:20)! We saw their deception will
be so seductive, so persuasive, so widespread, and so great, that this
evil tandem will even deceive mankind into fighting Jesus Christ at His
Second Coming. (So say Revelation 13:4; 16:9, 13-16 and 17:13-14.)

When the Beast and the eastern hordes *gather* at Armageddon, the
False Prophet will feverishly work his final miracles to delude the masses. The "battle" will be one-sided. Christ and the resurrected, spirit-born
saints will destroy this army right where it stands, before it can even think
about fighting. Read Zechariah 14:1-3.

The WHOLE WORLD is foretold in Revelation 16:14 to sell out to these antichrists, and only Christ's "little flock"—His true Church—the one you have come in contact with—will *not* be deceived, and will be protected.

Like players on a stage, personalities are quietly moving into position. The seeds of events that will stagger all nations have been planted—they will soon sprout!

Therefore, the first big order of concern is…

The White Horse
—False Christianity

Everyone hates having been deceived—lied to—especially by those they have known and trusted. The reader has probably experienced this. In every case, it is painful and disillusioning. The shock of betrayal can shake one to the core of his being.

For a moment, in your mind's eye, try to place yourself in this situation. Now imagine that those who have done this to you are widely considered to be men of truth. And then next imagine that what you trusted them with were the *most important things in life*.

We have just framed the level of deceit that counterfeit Christianity represents, where presumably all people understand that *eternal life* is at stake. This introduces the much-talked-about, but little-understood, subject of the "Four Horsemen of the Apocalypse."

The book now takes another serious turn.

But before continuing, something else must be grasped in order to set up the subject.

Horses with Riders

Sometimes God chooses to use common experiences or activities as symbols or analogies in His Word. This is done to help human minds comprehend what is being described. God's selection of analogy makes the next four chapters of this book easier to understand—especially for those who have ridden horses.

I have done this many times, in many situations, and ridden at virtually every speed. I have sat on horses at a standstill. I have ridden them at a walk, a trot and a canter, as well as at a gallop, and even at the exhilarating clip of a full run, flat-out, across a level field with my head down beside the horse's mane.

As we turn to the subject of the Revelation 6 horses (with horsemen), fix in your mind this animal's physical prowess. Bear in mind that for much of history, including the age of the writing of the New Testament, horses were man's preferred means of transportation—for rapid travel, communication and, in the case of armies, invasion and conquest. The horse and rider are virtually inseparable from a place within every picture of history.

God knows this. Hence His choice of analogy.

For the past 2,000 years, millions have sought to understand the so-called "Four Horsemen of the Apocalypse" described in Revelation 6. Much written about, and seen in Hollywood films, none grasp their true significance. Religionists have crafted their own explanations, but have all ignored important CLUES in properly understanding what these symbolize. As with so much of Bible prophecy, this is also because they have not understood the KEYS to God's Word.

In Revelation 6:2-8, we saw a series of mysterious horses are described—white, red, black and pale—each with its own rider, and coming in sequence. We also saw that none seem to recognize that Christ, the Revelator, had already shown to His disciples the prophetic *meaning* of these horses. With so much at stake, because of the unparalleled destruction these first four opened seals are foretold to bring, we must understand in fuller context their *true*—and truly *horrific*—meaning.

In the next six chapters there is a second purpose—and question. This question is big. We are also examining whether Jesus' prophecies have been *accurate*. Did He speak the *truth* to His disciples about events preceding His Return—or are His words a jumbled hodgepodge of human imagination, perhaps put on His lips by others—or even by the apostle John? If so, we must again admit that at least some of the Bible is not worth the paper it is written on. And *all* of Jesus' words stand in doubt.

This chapter describes the real meaning of the FIRST SEAL of Revelation 6:1-2. But at this point, another question arises—and it is also BIG! As you read the chapters about the horsemen, and the two chapters that follow them, this towering question presents itself: Are the first four seals of Revelation still closed, or has Christ unsealed them? In other words, are they in effect today? Stay focused on this question as you read.

We now bear down. The next six chapters are not pleasant to read!

RCG ILLUSTRATION/PAULA RONDEAU

The Identity of the Rider of Revelation 6:2

John described what he saw as Christ began to remove the seals. Let's read it again: "And I saw when the Lamb opened one of the seals, and I heard, as it were the noise of thunder, one of the four beasts saying, Come and see. And I saw, and behold a WHITE HORSE: and he that sat on him had a *bow*; and a *crown* was given unto him: and he went forth *conquering*, and *to conquer*" (Rev. 6:1-2).

You learned that the first horseman's identity has been almost universally misunderstood. You *must* understand this! The rider of the white horse is *not* who most think he is. Religionists and so-called prophecy experts have invented numerous theories about what the rider of Revelation 6:2 pictures. Some think he pictures Christ's servants announcing His Second Coming. Others believe the white horse represents "the Church." This could not be the case since *God's* Church never went forth to conquer and subdue nations. Rather, the true Church is represented by a woman (Rev. 12:1) who *nurtures* those whom God calls. These and all other human interpretations are wrong.

Many Bible commentaries, referring to Revelation 19, which portrays Jesus Christ returning on a white horse, hastily conclude that the Revelation 6 rider *also* must be Christ. Let's examine more closely whether these riders are the same.

Subtle, and not so subtle but overlooked, differences will be seen to be *very* important.

Notice Revelation 19 once again: "And I saw heaven opened, and behold a *white horse*; and He that sat upon him was called Faithful and True, and in *righteousness* He does judge and make war. His eyes were as a flame of fire, and on His head were *many crowns*; and He had a name written, that no man knew, but He Himself. And He was clothed with a vesture dipped in blood: and His name is called The Word of God…And out of His mouth goes a sharp *sword*, that with it He should smite the nations: and He shall rule them with a rod of iron: and He treads the winepress of the fierceness and wrath of Almighty God" (vs. 11-13, 15).

Clearly *this* is the true Jesus Christ. *No one* doubts this much.

Of course, there are similarities between the descriptions. Both riders are astride a white horse. Both are wearing a crown or many crowns, and they both conquer and rule. But, again, there are subtle *differences*. For instance, the Revelation 6 horseman wears "*a crown*," whereas Jesus Christ wears "*many crowns*."

"Sword" and "Bow"

Notice again another crucial difference. The Christ in Revelation 19 brandishes a *sword* (also see Revelation 1:16) out of His *mouth*, not a *bow* in His *hand*, as in Revelation 6. The sword, symbolically, is His Word, the Bible (Heb. 4:12; Eph. 6:17). Christ comes reproving nations with His Word, while the horseman of Revelation 6 comes with another source of power, represented by a bow. Even if we did not know the meaning of the bow, it could clearly *not* be the Word of God—a "two-edged sword"—or it would not be identified differently. And nowhere in the Bible is God's Word referred to as a bow.

The presence of a bow connects the rider of this horse to the ancient patriarch of false religion, Nimrod—described as a "mighty hunter" in Genesis 10. Nimrod, whose name means "rebellion," founded the city of Babylon (meaning "confusion"). This city eventually grew into the capital of the Babylonian Empire and seat of the Babylonian Mystery religion, referenced a number of times in Scripture.

Notice this powerful, identifying quote from Alexander Hislop's *The Two Babylons*: "But we have seen that Kronos was the first King of Babylon, or Nimrod; consequently, the first Centaur was the same. Now, the way in which the Centaur was represented on the Babylonian coins, and in the Zodiac, viewed in this light, is very striking. The Centaur was the same as the sign Sagittarius, or 'The Archer.' If the founder of Babylon's glory was 'The mighty Hunter,' whose name, even in the days of Moses, was a proverb—(Gen 10:9, "Wherefore, *it is said*, Even as Nimrod, the mighty hunter before the Lord")—when we find the 'Archer' with his bow and arrow, in the symbol of the supreme Babylonian divinity, and the 'Archer,' among the signs of the Zodiac that originated in Babylon, I think we may safely conclude that this Man-horse or Horse-man Archer primarily referred to *him*, and was intended to perpetuate the memory at once of his fame as a huntsman and his skill as a horse-breaker" (p. 42).

How revealing!

The *sequence of events* in both accounts is also revealing. As the first seal is opened, the Revelation 6 white horse is unleashed at the beginning of a series of end-time events. It is followed by the remaining seals leading up to the Great Tribulation. Then, as the seventh seal is nearly completed, the *second* white horse and its rider (Jesus Christ) appear. This is at the sound of the last trumpet of the seven trumpet plagues. This is the Return of Christ and His victory over those who attempt to oppose His triumphal Return. The horsemen of Revelation 6 and 19 represent opposite ends of this spectrum of time. These could not possibly describe the same event. The riders plainly arrive years apart.

So then, these are *different riders* on *different horses* at *different points in time*!

A Specific Counterfeit

A vital distinction must be made at this point. The rider of the Revelation 6 white horse does not represent *all* false religion. This first seal does not encompass belief systems such as Buddhism, Hinduism, Islam and others. What the rider *does* represent is a counterfeit *Christianity*—a *counterfeit* CHRIST. This is so obviously then *"another* Jesus"—and the one that the apostle Paul warned about (II Cor. 11:4).

Anything that passes as a counterfeit must *seem* authentic. Counterfeit money is designed to closely resemble real bills and coins. Any differences are very subtle, else the user is not fooled.

In the same way, the counterfeit of the true Church has to seem real. It *appears* "spiritual" and thoroughly organized. It *appears* to be well-established, with centuries-old "roots" reaching back to the original apostles. To the undiscerning, this "Jesus" and his teachings look, sound, feel and *seem* like the genuine article. But they are not the Christianity of the Bible—the one taught by the *true* Jesus Christ.

We will see that this false religious system is a counterfeit of God's true Church!

Almost immediately after Jesus founded His Church, Satan devised a counterfeit to keep the masses unaware of the message the true Church was proclaiming after Jesus' death. Read again: "The god of this world [the devil] has *blinded* the minds of them which believe not, lest the light of the glorious gospel of Christ, who is the image of God, should shine unto them" (II Cor. 4:4).

Satan's purpose has been to deceive mankind about God's truth, and he has done this through his counterfeit religious system, masquerading as genuine Christianity.

Matthew 24 Reveals More

Recall that Jesus foretold the confusion and misunderstanding that would surround this rider's identity! He disclosed events that would occur prior to His Second Coming. You will remember that the first event was synonymous with the white horse. Answering His disciples' question pertaining to the sign of His coming and of the end of the age, Jesus first warned of religious deception in the sequence of what would occur.

Let's review this all-important element of Jesus' Olivet Prophecy to now set a larger stage: "Take heed that no man deceive you. For *many shall come in My name*, saying, I am Christ; and shall *deceive many*" (Matt. 24:4-5). Only *after this* did He proceed to mention war, famine and pestilence. The "many" are the vast majority of thought-to-be Christian ministers who say that Jesus Christ *is* Christ (the Messiah), but who do not believe or teach what Christ taught, nor do they come with *His* authority.

Later in the same chapter, Jesus expanded upon these verses: "And *many* false prophets shall rise, and shall *deceive many*" (vs. 11). According to this and related prophecies outlined throughout this book, not only would false prophets arise to deceive the great majority, but they would also infiltrate the true Church, causing many of God's servants to fall away.

Toward the end of the last days, and especially during the time of the prophesied false religious leader of Revelation 13, false prophets were foretold to increase in number and means of deception. Here is Christ's chilling warning: "For there shall arise false christs, and false prophets, and shall show great signs and wonders; insomuch that if it were possible, they shall *deceive* the very elect. Behold, I have told you before. Wherefore if they shall say unto you, Behold, He is in the desert; go not forth: behold, He is in the secret chambers; believe it not" (Matt. 24:24-26).

Here Jesus shows that false prophets will work miracles. Human beings are always impressed by such "signs and wonders," regardless of their source, and will only too happily attribute the power of the performer to God.

Matthew 24 also mirrors the time sequence of the two riders of the white horses. The real Christ does not return (as shown in Revelation 19) until the time of the seventh and last trumpet (Matt. 24:27-31).

Beginning in the first century, false Christianity almost immediately arose, while war, famine and pestilence—depicted by the other three horses—continued more or less as they had always been. The counterfeit system became more firmly entrenched in the *third* and *fourth* centuries, but this was only a *precursor*—a tiny TYPE—of what would follow at the end of the age.

Since false teachers and ministers have been plying their trade for centuries, Jesus' warning for the end of the age must involve a *big increase* in the power, prevalence and influence of false Christianity. Think of it this way: at the very end, the white horse suddenly accelerates from a relative standstill to a full run!

False Christianity, war, famine and pestilence have continued off and on for the last two millennia. But this does *not* mean that the first four seals of Revelation 6 were opened almost 2,000 years ago, and have been slowly accelerating to an all-out sprint just before Christ's Return. (Realize that John did not record the Revelation until about 65 years after Jesus spoke to the apostles in Matthew 24. He would certainly not introduce things SEALED that had already been *unsealed* long before!) So then, the absolute *explosion* of these things—these conditions—in the last days is such that Jesus is telling us (in Revelation 6 and Matthew 24) that the *tremendous increase* of these things *is* the opening of the seals!

This and the next five chapters will bring a chilling picture of how this is happening, and will continue to happen.

Warnings from the Apostles

Before examining some history of this counterfeit Christian system, let's review a number of scriptures that warn of a movement that attempts to pass itself off as the standard-bearer of truth, but that is shrouded in mystery and deceit. Despite these inspired warnings from Peter, Paul, John and others, most have been ensnared by this clever fraud:

"Beloved, believe not every spirit, but try [test] the spirits whether they are of God: because *many false prophets* are gone out into the world" (I John 4:1).

"Beloved, when I gave all diligence to write unto you of the common salvation, it was needful for me to write unto you, and exhort you that you should earnestly contend for the faith which was once delivered unto the saints. For there are certain men *crept in unawares*, who were before of old ordained to this condemnation, *ungodly men*, turning the grace of our God into lasciviousness [license], and denying the...Lord Jesus Christ" (Jude 3-4).

"For the *mystery* of iniquity [lawlessness] does already work..." (II Thes. 2:7). (Again, false teachers always deny the necessity of keeping God's Law.)

Briefly referenced earlier, the apostle Paul's admonition to the Corinthians defines how effectively these early false teachers misled the unsuspecting: "But I fear, lest by any means, as the serpent beguiled Eve through his *subtlety*, so your minds should be corrupted from the simplicity that is in Christ. For if he that comes preaches *another Jesus*, whom we have not preached, or if you receive *another spirit*, which you have not received, or *another gospel*, which you have not accepted, you might well bear with *him* [or 'put up with it']" (II Cor. 11:3-4).

In verses 13-15, we saw Paul singles out *ministers* who appear to represent the truth and the true Christ, but are actually led by "another" spirit: "For such are *false apostles*, deceitful workers, transforming themselves into the apostles of Christ. And no marvel; for Satan himself is transformed into an angel of light. Therefore it is no great thing if his ministers also be transformed as the ministers of righteousness; whose end shall be according to their works."

Can you comprehend the gravity of this passage, viewed in an end-time context? Most do not recognize false ministers because they *appear* to be ministers of *light*—just as the "god of this world" *appears* to be the true God. The devil is an effective COUNTERFEITER! He *counterfeits* true ministers with false, true doctrines with false and the true God with the false god—himself!

Peter added to Paul's warning with a similar one: "There shall be *false teachers among you*, who privily [craftily, secretly] shall bring in damnable heresies...And *many* shall follow their pernicious ways" (II Pet. 2:1-2).

Paul also warned that this condition will worsen at the end of the age: "This know also, that in the *last days* perilous times shall come... evil men and seducers shall *wax worse and worse, deceiving*, and *being deceived*" (II Tim. 3:1, 13).

Deceit is not new to planet Earth. But Paul warns of deceivers— "seducers"—growing worse "in the last days"!

With this foundation laid, we are now ready to examine how this counterfeit system began. As this is done, bear in mind that it is not my purpose to attack or slander churches or individuals. But the Bible and history clearly identify a large and powerful false system, with its offshoots (or "daughters"), and there is simply no escaping directly identifying this system.

Growth of Counterfeit Movement
Parallels True Church

Not long after the establishment of the New Testament Church at Jerusalem in AD 31, men motivated by a different spirit than that given to the disciples on Pentecost began to infiltrate and influence the Church. The result is well known to honest historians.

The German historian Johann Lorenz von Mosheim wrote of the early Church: "Christian churches had scarcely been gathered and organized, when here and there men rose up, who, not being contented with the simplicity and purity of that religion which the apostles taught, sought out new inventions, and fashioned religion according to their own liking" (*Institutes of Ecclesiastical History, Ancient and Modern*, Vol. 1).

Author Jesse Hurlbut called this period after the time covered by the book of Acts "The Age of Shadows." He wrote, "...of all periods in the [Church's] history, it is the one about which we know the least...For fifty years after St. Paul's life a curtain hangs over the church, through which we strive vainly to look; and when at last it rises, about 120 AD with the writings of the earliest church fathers, we find a church in many aspects very different from that in the days of St. Peter and St. Paul" (*The Story of the Christian Church*, p. 33).

A study of first-century history confirms that a corrupted form of Christianity appeared on the scene shortly after the start of the New Testament Church on Pentecost AD 31, brought by agents such as Simon Magus (the word *magus* means "magician" or "sorcerer")—then the leader of the Babylonian Mystery religion in Samaria.

Simon Magus can be considered the *founder* of the heretical movement in the New Testament age. Ironically, many who rejected this *man* unwittingly followed his *practices*. Among them were Justin Martyr, Jerome and other writers of the second and following centuries.

Simon's first contact with God's Church is found in Acts 8: "But there was a certain man, called Simon, which beforetime in the same city used *sorcery*, and bewitched the people of Samaria, giving out that himself was some great one: to whom they all gave heed, from the least to the greatest, saying, this man is the great power of God. And to him they had regard, because that of long time he had *bewitched them with sorceries*. But when they believed Philip preaching the things concerning the kingdom of God, and the name of Jesus Christ, they were baptized, both men and women. Then Simon himself believed also: and when he was baptized, he continued with Philip, and wondered, beholding the miracles and signs which were done..." (vs. 9-13).

After Simon was baptized, he witnessed the Holy Spirit being given with the laying on of the apostles' hands. Showing his true motivation, Simon offered money for this power (vs. 18-19).

Starting with other Samaritans, Simon Magus later managed to attract a large following in Rome. Many there considered him a god, erecting a statue to him on the Tiber River. Much of his success could be attributed to his magic demonstrations, such as demon-assisted levitation (*Ecclesiastical History*). These supernatural parlor tricks later earned him several audiences with Nero (*Encyclopaedia Britannica*, 11th edition, vol. 25, p. 129).

Two Simons

It is the confusion of *two different "Simons"* that has given rise to one of the very greatest frauds of all history. Catholics have always claimed the apostle Peter (Simon Peter) was the first Roman bishop, and was martyred and buried in Rome. But Peter's commission was to serve those called to God's Church among the tribes of Israel that had been scattered after being taken into captivity—those of the "circumcision" (Gal. 2:7-8). In neither his nor Paul's letters is there *any* indication that Peter was *ever* in Rome.

Even if he were brought there for execution, the fact remains that he *never* served there. (There are at least 10 solid biblical PROOFS of this, and they are carefully listed in my book *Where Is the True Church? – and Its Incredible History!*) *Halley's Bible Handbook* labels the claim that Simon Peter was the first pope "Fiction pure and simple" (p. 768).

Now notice these facts from history in Alexander Hislop's *The Two Babylons* (emphasis mine): "The keys that the Pope bore were the keys of a 'Peter' well known to the Pagans initiated in the Chaldean Mysteries. That Peter the apostle was ever Bishop of Rome has been proved again and again to be an arrant *fable*. That he ever even set foot in Rome is at the best highly doubtful. His visit to that city rests on no better authority than that of a writer at the end of the second century or beginning of the third…it can be shown to be by no means doubtful that before the Christian era, and downwards, there *was* a 'Peter' at Rome, who occupied the highest place in the *Pagan* priesthood. The priest who explained the Mysteries to the initiated was sometimes called by a Greek term, the Hierophant; but in primitive Chaldee, the real language of the Mysteries, his title, as pronounced without the points, was 'Peter'—i.e., 'the interpreter'" (p. 208).

One such person of great "distinction" who bore the title of "Peter" at Rome was, in fact, Simon Magus! The title of "Peter" or "Pater" or "Patre" was one of religious primacy. Thus, Simon Magus carried the title Simon "Peter." "Papa," "Father" and "Pope" are derived from the word *Pater*, from which come our words *paternal* and *patriarch*. (Notice Jesus' command in Matthew 23:9 pertaining to such titles: "And call no man your father upon the earth: for One is your Father, which is in heaven." This verse *forbids* "Father" as a religious title, as was practiced in the Babylonian Mystery religion. We might add, never mind the blasphemous "*Holy* Father," which is solely the role of *God* the Father.)

It should be said that crediting Simon Magus as the founder of today's universal church system would not be fully accurate. He died around AD 68. It took nearly three centuries for that system to amass power and evolve, through all the stages of modifying and counterfeiting doctrine, into the form recognized today. Simon Magus' successors were equally zealous in sowing the seeds of heresy to counter the true apostles' work. His followers included Menander, Nicholas, Cerinthus and Marcion. (To learn much more, again, I urge you to read *Where Is the True Church? – and Its Incredible History!*)

By the beginning of the second century, churches advocating a hybrid Christianity—mixing the name and some few teachings of Christ with rank Babylonish paganism—were gaining strength. Although it would take another two centuries before they would be given substantial authority, their mission accelerated during the 100s AD.

The emerging counterfeit church substituted the true doctrines taught by Jesus and the apostles with false teachings from the Babylon Mystery religion. Alexander Hislop also wrote that there are very few of the current practices of this counterfeit church system that cannot be directly traced to the pagan mystery rituals of Babylon. The doctrines of God's Sabbath and Holy Days were dismissed as "Judaizing." The popular pagan ideas of the immortal soul, "going to heaven," and "burning in hell" were adopted. The doctrine of the millennial rule of the kingdom of God was gradually phased out. The unbiblical trinity concept was gradually accepted. Idolatry (including image and Mary worship) became acceptable, and the Second Commandment was effectively rejected.

Notice again in Matthew 24 that the *many* are deceived, not the *few*: "For *many* shall come in My name, saying, I am Christ; and shall deceive *many*" (vs. 5). Both the "manys" here—ministers and lay members—represent the *overwhelming majority*, as demonstrated by history. By the middle of the second century, the true followers of Christ were a small minority! The counterfeit movement openly denounced those who remained loyal to the teachings of the original apostles. Leaders such as John's successor, Polycarp, and Polycarp's disciple, Polycrates, were among the very few holding to the full truth in the Greco-Roman world.

The Time of Constantine

In the early 300s, during the time of the most severe persecution against all professing Christians, the Roman armies declared their favorite general, Constantine, to be Caesar. He had claimed victory after subduing the opposition in the Battle of Milvian Bridge outside Rome.

Prior to that battle, he was said to have had a vision of the first two letters of the name of Christ—*chi* (X) and *rho* (P) in Greek—and to have heard a voice say, "By this sign you will conquer." Constantine believed that the meaning of the letters was symbolic of Christ and therefore felt indebted to Christianity for his victory, despite being a devout sun-worshipper.

One of Constantine's first acts as emperor was to issue the Edict of Toleration in AD 311. It legalized Christianity in the empire, ending 10 years of severe persecution against the true Church. However, the edict sped up *false* Christianity's rise to prominence.

The Roman leader saw this new religion as a potential means of unifying the empire. Yet its practice in the Western empire was quite different from that in the east and from other sects in North Africa. So Constantine took measures to standardize his newfound ally—counterfeit Christianity.

Constantine convened the ecumenical Council of Nicea in AD 325 to resolve doctrinal differences between various Christian divisions. Before this, again, as a former sun-worshipper, he had naturally already decreed that Sunday—the day of the sun—would be kept throughout the empire. The Council of Nicea went further, in effect outlawing the practice of *true* Christianity. But the unscriptural teachings of the emerging counterfeit church were now decreed as part of the new state religion. As its protector, Constantine forced everyone, pagan or Christian, into either conformity or exile.

Prior to Constantine, the professing Christian church—founded by Simon Magus—had suffered persecution by the state, alongside the small true Church. But now in their elevated position of power, the "persecuted" became the "persecutors." This counterfeit false church's goal had now been achieved, and it now vengefully pursued the true people of God.

Persecution Foretold

Jesus' admonition of "then shall they deliver you up to be afflicted [tortured], and shall kill you" (Matt. 24:9) began very early (in *type*), with 11 of the 12 original apostles being martyred. But the book of Acts reports many others were included.

Daniel 7 gave a prophetic picture of one of the horns (the false church) of what you will recall is "the fourth beast" (the Roman Empire). We saw that this system "made war with the saints," "prevailed against them," "spoke great words against the Most High," and was to "wear out the saints of the Most High." This "little horn" is the same counterfeit movement whose rise to power we earlier summarized from Church history. As we proceed, it will become evident how *deadly* this "little horn speaking great things" would become regarding the true Church, and for the whole world.

A Killing Machine!

We saw Jesus declared, "I am come that they might have *life*, and that they might have it more *abundantly*" (John 10:10). But when the universal church system—the Revelation 6 white horse and rider—asserts power, it has brought *destruction* and *death*!

Most have assumed that the counterfeit church, having developed into a large and powerful organization, has brought a stabilizing influence to the world. They have believed that this church has injected a sense of morality and responsibility into mankind's collective consciousness.

But the rider of *this* white horse has called down numerous wars in the name of religion. History reveals that this church has been the *chief cause* of war within its jurisdiction, either indirectly or *directly*. It *has* inspired "conquering, and to conquer" (Rev. 6:2).

Let's read a more extensive quote from history: "Now, this Ninus, or 'Son,' borne in the arms of the Babylonian Madonna, is so described as very clearly to identify him with Nimrod. 'Ninus, king of the Assyrians,' says Trogus Pompeius, epitomised by Justin, 'first of all changed the contented moderation of the ancient manners, incited by a new passion, the desire of conquest. He was the *first who carried on war against his neighbours*, and he conquered all nations from Assyria to Lybia, as they were yet unacquainted with the arts of war.' This account points directly to Nimrod, and can apply to no other" (Alexander Hislop, *The Two Babylons*, p. 23).

And also, "...'Ninus, the most ancient of the Assyrian kings mentioned in history, performed great actions. Being naturally of a warlike disposition, and ambitious of glory that results from valour, he armed a considerable number of young men that were brave and vigorous like himself, trained them up a long time in laborious exercises and hardships, and by that means accustomed them to bear the fatigues of war, and to face dangers with intrepidity'" (ibid.). How obvious the connection of an ancient system and its first leader to its modern descendant.

Consider a few more examples of the merciless approach this horrific system has taken through the centuries, beginning with God's Church. Not content with merely driving God's servants into the wilderness, armies controlled by the counterfeit church pursued them, intending to wipe them out completely.

Accounts speak of how in AD 1290, in the town of Beziers, Crusaders entered churches and butchered refugees hiding inside. The bodies of slaughtered thousands—men, women and children, including babies— were stacked like cordwood. (I have personally read such accounts.) Now another. Nearby, in Montsegur, 200 accused "heretics" were seized, pulled outside the city and thrown onto a giant funeral pyre where they were incinerated alive.

Here is an account of what happened next: "This done…the Bishop, together with the monks and their attendants, returned to the refectory and, after giving thanks to God and St. Dominic, fell cheerfully upon the food set before them" (*Massacre at Montsegur*, p. 291).

Now consider this chilling description as witnesses saw the flames: "The people shout their approval; the inquisitors sit, hands folded, deeply shocked by all the wickedness in the world, serene in their own virtue, in bringing about justice, so clever that—although they have brought those groaning, fainting men and women to this horror—because they abandoned them in time to the secular arm [the civil government], there is no blood on their hands…" (Jean Plaidy, *The Rise of the Spanish Inquisition*, p. 158). The same author adds, "The long ceremony, the chanting of monks, the tolling of bells, the smell of incense, the holiness of the proceedings has a comforting effect. All has been sanctified by these things."

Could anything be more abominable than such *officially sanctioned* evil?

The leadership of this church believed it held limitless power over human lives, and much more. The next quote by Dr. Henry Halley shows how particular popes literally elevated their position above that of God Himself. It may be the single most revealing quote about the nature of the thinking at the top of this system (capitalization for emphasis is always Halley's):

"Innocent III (1198-1216). Most Powerful of all the Popes. Claimed to be 'Vicar of Christ,' 'Vicar of God,' 'Supreme Sovereign over the Church and the World.' Claimed the right to Depose Kings and Princes; and that 'All things on earth and in heaven and in hell are subject to the Vicar of Christ.'

"He brought the Church into Supreme Control of the State. The Kings of Germany, France, England, and practically all the Monarchs of Europe obeyed his will. He even brought the Byzantine Empire under his control. Never in history has any one man exerted more power" (*Halley's Bible Handbook*, pp. 776-777).

In light of the title taken by Innocent III, consider all the titles held by the pope today before continuing with Dr. Halley's quote: "[*His Holiness Pope* (name)], *Bishop of Rome, Vicar of Jesus Christ, Successor of the Prince of the Apostles, Supreme Pontiff of the Universal Church, Patriarch of the West, Primate of Italy, Metropolitan Archbishop of the Province of Rome, Sovereign of the State of Vatican City, Servant of the Servants of God*" (*Encyclopaedia Britannica*). The title of "*Patriarch of the West*" has been dropped by the current pope.

It should go without saying that *none* of these titles—or anything like them—are found anywhere in God's Word!

Now continuing Dr. Halley's quote about popes attached to the Inquisition: "The Inquisition, called the 'Holy Office,' was instituted by Pope Innocent III, and perfected under the second following Pope, Gregory IX. It was the Church Court for Detection and Punishment of Heretics. Under it everyone was required to inform against Heretics. Anyone suspected was liable to Torture, without knowing the name of his accuser. The proceedings were secret. The Inquisitor pronounced sentence, and the victim was turned over to Civil Authorities to be Imprisoned for Life, or to be Burned. The victim's property was confiscated, and divided between the Church and the State" (ibid.).

Finally, Halley summarizes the dark time of the Inquisition: "In the period immediately following Pope Innocent III the Inquisition did its most deadly work against the Albigenses [a name given to the true Church in northern Italy and southern France]...but also claimed vast multitudes of victims in Spain, Italy, Germany and the Netherlands.

"Later on the Inquisition was the main agency in the Papacy's effort to Crush the Reformation. It is stated that in [just] the 30 years between 1540 and 1570 no fewer than 900,000...were put to death in the Pope's war..."

"Think of Monks and Priests, in holy garments, directing, with Heartless Cruelty and Inhuman Brutality, the work of Torturing and Burning alive Innocent Men and Women, and doing it in the Name of Christ, by the direct order of the 'Vicar of Christ.'

"The Inquisition was the Most Infamous and Devilish Thing in Human History. It was devised by Popes, and used by them for 500 years, to Maintain their Power" (ibid., p. 777).

Can you imagine a church, professing to represent Jesus Christ and His government on Earth, maintaining control through this kind of *reign of terror*? Such is the counterfeit rider of the white horse, with his hunting bow of slaughter in hand!

Seeds of the Protestant Reformation

By the early 1500s, after decades of blood-stained Inquisition history, it was clear to many the Roman Church was corrupt and scandalous at every level. (But this does not even speak to its scores of deceptive, false teachings.)

In addition to church-sanctioned *violent persecution* and *mass murder*, the practices of *simony* (offices and positions for sale) and *indulgences* (remission of sin—past, present and future—for a price) proved too much for some of its followers. Many European monarchies had already been drifting away from quiet submission to papal authority. In Germany, anti-Catholic and anti-papal sentiment was growing.

It was at this time that Martin Luther entered the scene. According to most sources, while studying law at the University of Erfurt, Luther was marooned in a severe thunderstorm. Terrified, he vowed to become a monk, and joined the Augustine order of friars. In 1507, he became a priest, and in due time became a doctor of theology. He was then given a professorship at the University of Wittenberg.

Some of Luther's own theology had developed before any open confrontation with the church. What initially began with rejecting the Catholic definition of "works" (keeping the "sacraments") eventually led to rejecting the concept of *any* works (including obedience to God's Law). He concluded that faith *alone* was required for salvation, openly dismissing the book of James as an "epistle of straw" because it teaches works alongside faith—"faith without works is dead" (Jms. 2:20, 26).

In 1517, incensed by a Dominican friar selling indulgences near Wittenberg, Luther began protesting. This was in written form through his "95 Theses," nailed to the door of the Castle Church in Wittenberg. Although he did not intend to cause a revolt, these points of contention appealed to German anti-papal attitudes. Convicted on the matter, Luther was unyielding.

Opposing Forces

But the church confronting him was just as stubborn. Three years of bitter disagreement and confrontation led Luther to condemn the pope, the clergy and the sacraments. Pope Leo X declared him a heretic. Luther countered by torching Catholic documents, including the Canon Law.

In 1521, Luther was put on trial at Worms. His judge was a young Charles V of Hapsburg, along with a gathering of ambassadors, princes and bishops. Luther took the position of elevating, in certain limited areas, the authority of the Bible above papal and church authority. He adamantly held his ground.

Luther was escorted to Wartburg by imperial forces. Most of his countrymen now held him in high esteem. Various princes of adjoining territories promised allegiance to Luther and left the Roman church to follow him, marking the birth of the Lutheran church.

One reason Luther was permitted to question and resist the dictates of Rome was that German emperor Charles V was entangled in a series of conflicts with France. Without the emperor's participation, the clergy was powerless to enforce its decrees on Luther, now protected by an increasing number of northern German princes.

A series of events bought time for the Protestants. Charles abdicated in favor of his younger brother, and died two years later at a secluded monastery in Spain. The next two emperors supported the Protestants.

Other schools of Protestant thought flourished in Europe and eventually the New World—Calvinism, Methodism, Anglicanism and others. There would be no reconciliation with Rome. There are now thousands of Protestant denominations, with new brands arising daily.

In Rome's eyes, this affront to its authority must end.

Mother Rome

We have seen that the Bible portrays this end-time church system as a woman (Rev. 17:4-6). The scriptural pattern is that churches are personified as females, while civil governments are characterized in the male gender. The counterfeit church of course is called a "woman," but also a "whore," a "mother" and a "queen." (And she has "daughters.")

Recall that the extent of her domain and rulership is given in 17:1: "And there came one of the seven angels which had the seven vials, and talked with me, saying unto me, Come here; I will show unto you the judgment of the great whore that sits upon many waters." Recall we saw the symbol "many waters" is defined in Revelation 17:15: "And he said unto me, The waters which you saw, where the whore sits, are peoples, and multitudes, and nations, and tongues."

History shows that no *other* single church has reigned over so many "peoples, multitudes, nations and tongues." Neither has any *other* large church system been "drunken with the blood of the saints, and with the blood of the martyrs of Jesus" (vs. 6).

Verse 2 continued describing this "whore": "With whom the kings [world leaders] of the earth have committed fornication, and the *inhabitants* of the earth have been *made drunk* with the wine of her fornication." What *other* large church receives and calls upon heads of state, and has done so for centuries?

Revelation 18:7 shows she considers herself a "queen." (These sleep with kings.) Chapter 2, verses 20-23 personify the universal system as the Gentile Queen Jezebel, wicked wife of King Ahab (I Kings 16-22). Jezebel "stirred up" her husband to adopt evil practices, martyred many faithful prophets, and attempted to kill the prophet Elijah (19:2-3). The parallel with a church that persecutes the saints through the ages is striking.

Revelation 12 depicts God's Church as a woman of very *different* character. There are numerous examples in Scripture of *righteous* women whose faithful, upright character reflected that of the true Church: Sarah, Ruth, Esther, Hannah and Mary (Jesus' mother).

In the case of Mary, the counterfeit church has deified her as equal or superior to Christ, whom they always portray as either a baby or hanging helplessly on a cross. Millions of Catholics, members and clergy, have signed a petition to declare Mary the co-redemptrix (meaning she works beside Jesus in redeeming humanity).

The adoration of Mary—really Mary worship—originated with Semiramis, the mother-wife of Nimrod. This symbolism was then passed down through the Babylon Mystery religion, and was later adapted into the counterfeit church. Simon Magus applied parts of this symbolism to himself and his mistress, Helen the prostitute.

The rejection by Protestants of such "Mariolatry" has long been among the sharpest distinctions between Catholics and Protestants. But times are changing.

Today's Ecumenical Movement

Revelation 17:5 described the universal church as the "mother of harlots." Children generally retain some or many of the characteristics of their mother. Likewise, Protestant churches retained more than 90 percent of the same false, idolatrous observances their mother taught them, such as Sunday, Christmas and Easter observance, rejection of God's Law as done away and trinitarianism.

Rome's protesting daughters have now been gone for over four centuries. Today an ecumenical movement is paving the way for reunion. The term "ecumenical" derives from the Greek word *oikoumene*, meaning "the inhabited world." How telling of its goal.

The current movement rose to prominence in the 1960s, originating in the Protestant Pentecostal and Charismatic movements. The Catholics accepted their overtures toward closer ties, because these groups emphasized emotional religious experience rather than doctrine, on which Rome rarely budges. This "truce" was called the Catholic Charismatic Renewal movement and resulted in warmer relations with many Evangelical groups. This led to the Second Vatican Council (Vatican II) in 1965. During this time, the Catholics made a few concessions toward the Protestants. For example, instead of "heretics," they were now officially deemed "separated brethren."

But if Vatican II slightly softened the Catholic view of Protestants, its conclusions were still uncompromising: "This Sacred Council exhorts the faithful...[that their] ecumenical action must be fully and sincerely Catholic...faithful to the truth which we [they claim] have received from the apostles and Fathers of the Church, in harmony with the faith which the Catholic Church has always professed" (*Unitatis Redintegratio*).

The Ecumenical movement has gained momentum. More prominent and larger Protestant groups, such as the Anglican Church and its American Episcopal branch, have caught on to this spirit. A much closer association with the Eastern Orthodox Churches, whose main difference is submission to the pope at Rome, has been reached.

Since the Reformation, Rome has added additional dogma that would *seem* to make reconciliation *less* likely. These include: Papal Infallibility (1870), the Immaculate Conception (1854) and the Assumption into heaven of Mary, Mother of God (1950).

Yet the daughters are still coming home! Alarms sounded in Protestant circles have less and less impact.

A 2005 *Time* magazine story shows that adoration of Mary is making inroads in the Protestant world: "A man stands at the lectern at the El Amor de Dios church on Chicago's South Side reading in Spanish, tears streaming down his cheeks. His text is a treatment of the Virgin Mary from one of the Bible's apocryphal books. Another congregant follows, reciting his own verses to the Virgin...Flanking the altar are two Mary statues...hanging from the hands of the baby Jesus is a Rosary. The altar cover presents the church's most stunning image: Mary again, this time totally surrounded by a multicolored halo, in the traditional iconography of the Our Lady of Guadalupe.

"The church is Methodist."

Relations with the Orthodox churches are progressing the fastest. Vatican II declared, "These Churches, although separated from us, yet possess true sacraments and above all, by apostolic succession, the priesthood and the Eucharist, whereby they are linked to us in closest intimacy" (*Unitatis Redintegratio*).

The last Roman leader's memorial service in 2005 was the first papal funeral in centuries attended by the Patriarch of Constantinople, the leader of the Eastern Orthodox Church.

May 2010 saw Vatican City celebrate the "Days of Russian Culture and Spirituality in the Vatican." Consider its purpose: "The event, which is sponsored by the Moscow Patriarchate, the Pontifical Council for Promoting Christian Unity and the Pontifical Council for Culture, includes a photographic exhibition, a symposium and a concert in honor of [the pope]" (*Zenit*).

The event included a symposium titled "Orthodox and Catholics in Europe Today: The Christian Roots and the Common Cultural Heritage of East and West."

In July 2010, "Patriarch Kirill of Moscow and All Russia...said that he sees eye-to-eye with [the] Pope...on many pressing moral issues" (*Interfax*).

The Patriarch stated, "'I must say that the stance of [the] incumbent Pope...gives rise to optimism...on many public and moral issues his approach fully coincides with the approach of the Russian Orthodox Church. This gives us an opportunity to advocate Christian values together with the Catholic Church, in particular at international organizations and on the international arena'" (ibid.).

Luther's own church is drifting with the current. In a bid to promote unity, the pope visited an evangelical Lutheran Church in Rome on Laetare Sunday, the fourth Sunday during Lent in 2010. According to *Zenit*, the Catholic leader warned against being content "with the successes of the ecumenism of recent years," regretting that Protestants and Catholics still "cannot drink of the same chalice and we cannot be together around the altar...This should make us sad because it is a sinful situation..."

During the German-language service, the President of the Lutheran Community of Rome remarked, "May you feel at home here, Your Holiness" (ibid.).

This pope, when still a Cardinal, supported the joint declaration by the Vatican and the Lutheran World Federation on spiritual justification signed on October 31, 1999, and has continued to stress unity between the two churches since assuming the papal role.

Is it coincidental that the Greek word *oikoumene*, mentioned earlier, was often used to refer to the *Roman Empire*? This is what the Vatican has in mind—all ecumenical roads lead to Rome!

Tradition vs. Scriptural Authority

Alongside Mary worship, Sunday and Easter observances constitute centerpieces of the counterfeit church. To highlight their continuing importance, the previous pope, John Paul II, in his "Sunday Letter" (July 5, 1998), made the Catholic position clear:

"Therefore, in commemorating the day of Christ's Resurrection not just once a year but every Sunday, the Church seeks to indicate to every generation the true fulcrum of history, to which the mystery of the world's origin and its final destiny leads.

"It is right, therefore, to claim, in the words of a fourth century homily [not the Bible], that 'the Lord's Day' is 'the lord of days'...Those who have received the grace of faith in the Risen Lord cannot fail to grasp the significance of this day of the week with the same deep emotion which led Saint Jerome to say: 'Sunday is the day of the Resurrection, it is the day of Christians, it is our day'...For Christians, Sunday is 'the fundamental feastday,' established not only to mark the succession of time but to reveal time's deeper meaning.

"...The fundamental importance of Sunday has been recognized through two thousand years of history and was emphatically restated by the Second Vatican Council: 'Every seven days, the Church celebrates the Easter mystery'...The coming of the Third Millennium, which calls believers to reflect upon the course of history in the light of Christ, also invites them to rediscover with new intensity the meaning of Sunday: its 'mystery,' its celebration, its significance..."

Apart from the fact that Jesus Christ was *not* resurrected on Sunday—and was *not* crucified on a Friday—the Fourth Commandment requires the observance of the seventh day—*not*—and *never*—the first day!

The Origin of Sunday Worship

Let's now examine some of how Sunday worship—through its connection to Easter—originated. About AD 154, a meeting occurred between Polycarp, leader of the true Church, and the Bishop of Rome, regarding the Roman church's changing Passover observance to Sunday.

The following account reveals the tactics used to establish precedent. An unusual letter appeared after Polycarp had left. Most historians consider it a deliberate forgery. Consider these two sources.

First, "Pope Pius, who lived about the year 147, had made a decree, That the annual solemnity of the Pasch [this Greek word is derived from the Hebrew word *pesach*, meaning Passover] should be kept only on the Lord's day [Sunday]; and in confirmation of this he pretended, that Hermes his brother, who was then an eminent teacher among them, had received instruction from an angel, who commanded that all men should keep the *Pasch* on the Lord's day" (*Origines Ecclesiasticae: Antiquities of the Christian Church*, Joseph Bingham, pp. 1148-1149).

And, "...one of the letters forged in the name of Pius, where one [Hermes] is mentioned as the author; and it is stated that in his book a commandment was given through an angel to observe the Passover on a Sunday" (*The Apostolical Fathers: A Critical Account of Their Genuine Writings and of Their Doctrines*, James Donaldson, p. 324).

If Hermes *did* receive instructions from an "angel," would they outweigh *God's* instructions through His apostles and prophets? (Read Ephesians 2:20.) Paul wrote in Galatians 1:8: "But though we, or an *angel from heaven*, preach any other gospel unto you than that which we have preached unto you, let him be accursed."

Plainly, man nor angel holds authority to override God's Word. But the counterfeit church appropriated to itself the power to supersede and change the "times and laws" of God (Dan. 7:25).

They have done this—and continue to—under the pretext of *tradition*. Here is the theologian Tertullian's classic statement from about AD 200: "...If, for these and other such rules [for Sunday observance], you insist upon having positive Scripture injunction, you will find none. Tradition will be held forth to you as the originator of them, custom as their strengthener, and faith as their observer. That reason will support tradition, and custom, and faith, you will either yourself perceive, or learn from some one who has" (*The Writings of Quintus Sept. Flor. Tertullianus*, Volume 1, p. 337).

A more recent quote echoes the same approach. Read and reread this one until you cannot forget it: "A rule of faith, or a competent guide to heaven, must be able to instruct all the truths necessary for salvation. Now the Scriptures alone do not contain all the truths which a Christian is bound to believe, nor do they explicitly enjoin all the duties which he is obliged to practise. Not to mention other examples, is not every Christian obliged to sanctify Sunday and to abstain on that day from unnecessary servile work? Is not the observance of this law among the most prominent of our sacred duties? But you may read the Bible from Genesis to Revelation, and you will not find a single line authorizing the sanctification of Sunday. The Scriptures enforce the religious observance of Saturday, a day which we never sanctify" (*The Faith of Our Fathers*, James Cardinal Gibbons, pp. 111-112, 1905 edition).

A stunning admission!

The leadership of the universal church openly asserts that human tradition outweighs God's inspired Word, all while claiming to be led by the "Word" made flesh—Jesus Christ (John 1:14). Yet Protestants, who profess the doctrine of *Sola Scriptura* ("by Scripture alone"), are still being drawn back to Rome. Having never left Sunday observance, the return journey is much easier—and shorter.

The False Church's Final Resurgence

This powerful church has grand designs of dominating all nations. Again, it is not my purpose to attack or slander churches or individuals. The Bible *and history* directly identify this system and its offshoots. But believers within traditional Christianity are spiritually blind. They may be sincere, like those of all religions, but they are sincerely *wrong*. The *real* architect of this system is Satan, not people.

The *human* architects of all these things are deceived. They are not, certainly for the most part, *consciously plotting* evil. While they are deceivers, they are also themselves deceived. They are playing a role on a stage within a great Purpose that God is working out.

I take no joy in reporting these truths. Truly I do not. In fact, I wish the responsibility to warn were someone else's. But it is not. And all those who *care* about taking action must have the *opportunity* to do it.

In the darkest periods of Catholic domination, its influence was largely limited to Europe. The first seal—white horse and rider—is now open, preparing to ride at all-out speed across the entire world!

Deception achieved by the counterfeit church in its teachings could hardly be more complete today. Virtually every truth of Scripture has been denied, overturned or discarded by Rome, in favor of tradition or papal "revelation." Therefore, the opening of the first seal must mean that this deception will eventually become *much* more widespread!

Yes, millions today, while they would scoff at this notion, who consider themselves staunch Protestants, or non-religious, or even agnostic or atheist, will come to *follow* the Babylonian system!

The current pope does not expect that unity of all professing Christians will be accomplished through human effort: "[He] has also emphasized that the way toward unity is not a matter of our programs and schedules but of faithful waiting upon a new initiative of the Holy Spirit which we can neither control nor anticipate" (*Zenit*).

A "new initiative," led by a very real "spirit," is coming! History shows that decisive action taken by large numbers of people is usually sparked by a crisis, and facilitated by a strong central figure or figures—leaders who can offer the masses what they long for, whether it is prosperity and prestige, freedom from oppression, deliverance from suffering or a bolstering of pride and resolve.

How will this happen? We have seen that the fragile global economy is providing the crisis. And the central figures? Recall Revelation 13:

"And he [the final False Prophet] does *great wonders*, so that he makes *fire come down from heaven* on the earth in the sight of men [think of this as a "new initiative of the spirit"], and DECEIVES them that dwell on the earth by the means of those miracles which he had power to do" (vs. 13-14).

When the False Prophet calls fire from heaven—probably witnessed by *billions* through television and the Internet—skeptics and scoffers will become "believers." Miracles will support his endorsement of a civil partner: "I beheld another beast [the false church] coming up out of the earth; and he had two horns like a lamb [purporting to represent Jesus Christ], and he spoke as a dragon [Satan]…and causes the earth and them which dwell therein to worship the first beast" (Rev. 13:11-12).

Who Is Searching?

A closer but brief look at the work of doctrinal and religious deception on matters of Bible truth is important in understanding how hundreds of millions of people—indeed billions over centuries—can come to believe doctrines that are untrue.

It starts this way. Most never reflect on *why* they believe what they believe or do what they do. In a world filled with customs, traditions and beliefs, few seek to understand—to research—the *origin* of things. The great majority happily accept what is presented to them without question. Most people basically do what everyone else does—following the crowd because it is easy! They simply adopt common practices because they are well-recognized—the norm—fashionable. Most follow along as they have been taught, assuming what they believe and do is right. They take their beliefs for granted.

One must be willing to ask: Where did popular beliefs *come from*? What are their *roots*?

To find the *truth* of a biblical matter—*any* biblical matter—one must be willing to open his Bible and honestly accept what it says. The majority of people stoutly defend what they have merely *assumed* is right or biblical. And they read with prejudice anything that contradicts cherished beliefs.

Now recall Jesus' statement, "*In vain* they do worship Me, teaching for doctrines the commandments of men" (Matt. 15:9). In Mark's parallel account, He continued, "Full well you reject the commandment of God, that you may keep your own *tradition*" (7:9).

Why are not millions combing the Bible for such passages in order to escape religious deception? Why are they not discovering additional statements from Christ such as "Why call you Me, Lord, Lord, and DO NOT the things which I say?" (Luke 6:46), as well as Paul's plain words, "Not the *hearers* of the law shall be justified before God, but the DOERS of the law shall be justified" (Rom. 2:13), among so many other basic passages? The obvious answer is that most do not care what God says. They are only too willing to be deceived by their ministers.

These are summarized by a passage describing worshippers today: "This is a rebellious people, lying children, children that will NOT HEAR the law of the LORD: which say to the seers, See *not*; and to the prophets, Prophesy *not* unto us *right* things, speak unto us *smooth* things, prophesy *deceits*: get you out of the way [forget the right thing], turn aside out of the path [teach what we want to hear], cause the Holy One of Israel to *cease from before us*" (Isa. 30:9-11). Countless thousands of ministers have been perfectly willing to fulfill the people's demands.

The tragic result is that most who "profess Christ" never connect the Bible to anything they should be *doing* in their lives!

How So Many Are Deceived!

Another factor comes into play for those who may wish to see at least a little biblical backing from their minister or their church for beliefs. And it is critical.

First understand this. Modern Christendom misunderstands, twists, perverts and ignores *all* the plain truths of the Bible. Over the centuries, it has counterfeited *every one* of its true doctrines and replaced it with a cheap substitute. This has been possible because certain less easy to understand passages of Scripture can be easily misrepresented—made to say something that they do not. It is these verses that invariably become the vehicle through which a false doctrine can be introduced—with almost no one able to recognize that it all may have begun with a single wrong scriptural premise. From this can flow an entire doctrine that is nothing more than a house of cards.

Unaware of the most important rule of Bible study, most students of Scripture do not build their doctrinal understanding by beginning with the clearest verses on any subject. Rather, they enter God's Word with preconceived ideas and go in search of passages that *appear* to support what they have *assumed* it teaches. This makes them candidates for confusion and deception.

The apostle Peter stated that the apostle "Paul [wrote]...some things hard to be understood, which they that are unlearned and unstable wrest, as they do also the other scriptures, unto their own destruction" (II Pet. 3:15-16). Understanding how most people think, and probably completely unaware of *any* of the rules of Bible study, teachers and "scholars" can then much more easily take advantage of the way certain parts of God's Word have been written. This applies to areas of Scripture beyond what Paul wrote.

The theological institutes and seminaries of this world have developed a systematic way—done consciously or unconsciously (Rom. 8:7; Jer. 17:9)—of spinning, twisting or dismissing God's PLAIN WORDS and PLAIN MEANING in favor of making passages seem to say what they *need* them to say. These theologians and religionists portray—and sell!—Satan's doctrines through use of *specific verses*, wrongly understood, that supposedly teach their ideas. This permits them to come from a basis—a premise—of Bible AUTHORITY for their beliefs. This, in turn, helps them to much more easily snare the unwitting and unwary.

Paul warned of "dishonest" people who "handle the word of God *deceitfully*" (II Cor. 4:2), because they, like their students who are willing to believe them, "received not the *love* of the TRUTH" (II Thes. 2:10).

God's servants—*true* ministers—never, under *any* circumstances, follow these practices!

In most cases, if one is properly trained and sufficiently grounded in the truth of the Bible, it is easy to see through and expose the deceptive logic misapplied to a verse, and to correctly explain it.

One Horse Leads to the Next

The devil has always sought to position himself in place of the true God. Through his universal system, he blinds and enslaves humanity. Billions are deceived. Previous billions have been. Many more will be. Even you have been lied to. A complete seduction has taken place, and the false church has played the central role in it. The most important knowledge has been kept from you by those you most trusted!

No matter its length, no one chapter could possibly cover everything about the reach and effects of the counterfeit universal system that has ravaged the world of Christendom. For instance, so much more could be explained about the almost unending number of individual false doctrines that this system has devised about salvation and the afterlife, heaven and hell, law and grace, baptism and conversion, judgment, the true Church, among many others. In addition would be the origin of the many different pagan holidays that have been imported into professing

Christianity, as well as the stories of how those bringing them have gotten away with it usually by merely pasting Christian-sounding names over them. (There are certain other counterfeits of individual Bible truths that will be covered in later chapters.)

However, for those willing to accept the plain words of the Bible and history—and just the volume of facts, evidence, proof, fruit and scriptures presented here—the white horse and rider are plainly identified as false, counterfeit Christianity!

This horse and rider—armed with a very real bow—are almost done with attempts to gain converts through missionary work and dialogue. The European political, legal and military machine will soon be used by the final Beast to *enforce* the practice of Roman state religion—again! Powerful "*arrows*" will target all resistors, unleashing the most horrific global war and religious persecution the world has ever seen!

The historical pattern re-emerges: *Religious* authority harnesses the power of *civil* authority to impose its will. False Christianity begets unthinkable destruction. Hence, the second horseman...

The Red Horse—War

The horror of war has swept the world since Cain killed Abel. It has been the result of man's unrelenting murderous rage toward his fellow man. Its fruits are terror, destruction, economic upheaval, orphaned children, population displacement, widespread devastation of the land, rape, hunger, disease, untold suffering, misery, despair, maiming and crippling, atrocities, death and even genocide. All of this yields *greater* hatred and revenge, endless retaliation and more war, because nothing is ever permanently resolved through military conflict. No matter the diligence or sincerity of their efforts, men and nations CANNOT find a way to peace!

Setting the Stage

Let's revisit Revelation 6:4: "And there went out ANOTHER HORSE that was RED: and power was given to him that sat thereon to *take peace from the earth*, and that they should *kill* one another: and there was given unto him a *great sword.*" John's vision has grave implications for all people today.

Compare once again the parallel passage in Matthew 24:6-7 to better understand the meaning of this symbolic horseman: "And you shall hear of wars and rumors of wars: see that you be not troubled: for all these things must come to pass, but the end is not yet. For nation shall rise against nation, and kingdom against kingdom…"

We find that the rider of the red horse has the power to "take peace from the earth"—which of course means that *war* replaces it! He represents the dreadful devastation of armed conflict between and within nations.

The phrase "wars and rumors of wars" refers to a *general condition* of warfare that would be amplified just before Christ's Return. The next statement—"For nation shall rise against nation, and *kingdom* against *kingdom*"—indicates a *further intensified state* of war to emerge ("kingdom against kingdom"), at this point near the very end—total world war.

Luke 21:9 adds a broader understanding of these events: "But when you shall hear of wars and *commotions*, be not terrified: for these things must first come to pass; but the end is not by and by." The Greek word for "commotions" means "disorder," "confusion" and "tumult." An expanded definition could include acts and effects of terrorism, such as bombings. Could any thinking person doubt this condition has arrived in full force?

But war has existed from the beginning of mankind. How then could Jesus use "wars and rumors of wars" as a special sign announcing the arrival of "the last days"?

The answer: The ever-present grim specter of war has reintroduced itself, having morphed into something with potential for destruction *far beyond* what has EVER been seen before. In fact, this has already begun. Now time is running out.

A Bloody Track Record

It has been observed that human history has primarily been a chronicle of war. What began as family or tribal conflicts later developed into ones between nations. Some international conflicts begin with one-sided action, others with mutual aggression. Additionally, long-standing ethnic, tribal and religious differences, coupled with boundary disputes and outright intent to seize the land or property of others, have always served to fuel the *next* war fought between the same peoples or nations.

War has affected all nations in every period of history. In fact many nations have made war their primary means of livelihood—not just a means of defense, as so many claim. Those that chose not to actively pursue war were still forced to expend much time, money and effort to protect themselves—sometimes having to "buy" peace by paying tribute to powers that could have dominated or destroyed them.

In the mid-1960s, a Norwegian statistician programmed a computer to count all of the wars through the 6,000 years of mankind's history. It concluded that 14,531 wars had been fought. But this was merely the number that were *known* and *recorded*. How many more were not? And consider that this was several decades ago. Countless more have been fought since then. Of course, this does not count the endless stream of individual terrorist acts, such as suicide bombings and other assaults, which occur in undeclared wars.

My Family History

I grew up in a family filled with Army and Navy officers—some of them senior career officers. Even both of my female cousins married Naval officers. A step-cousin was an army officer. His younger brother attended Annapolis, and I was also appointed to Annapolis, though I declined because God was calling me into His truth at that time.

My father was an Army officer and pilot in WWII, and his older brother, also a pilot (who later rose to the rank of Captain in the Navy—equal to a full Colonel in the Army), was present at Pearl Harbor during the attack. Their father (my grandfather) fought in WWI. I was born on December 7, 1948, and my mother referred to me as her "Pearl Harbor baby." My uncle (on my mother's side) studied the Civil War most of his life. Much of his enormous Civil War library (with other sections about General Grant, Custer and Napoleon) was passed to me. He was also a signal corpsman in WWII.

I have visited Pearl Harbor, West Point and Annapolis, Arlington National Cemetery and other military cemeteries, endless forts, and many Civil War, as well as Revolutionary War, battlefields. I have also been to the site of the Battle of Little Big Horn, among so many other sites, including Jerusalem, the Masada, Jericho and many battlefields in Israel. Then there are all the books I have read about war beginning as a child.

I am a classic example of how some grow up hearing and learning much about war. Stories from military history were a large part of my childhood. So was learning about (many) ancestors who always seemed to have fought in wars, where some of them died. I understand Isaiah 2:4 and Micah 4:3, which speak of those who "learn war."

Truly, speaking personally, war is the worst of "man's inhumanity to man."

Assyria

Of the nations familiar from biblical history and prophecy, Egypt was among the first to develop the art of war as an organized endeavor.

Yet it was the Assyrians who developed and perfected many military techniques. In fact, the sword—the weapon held by the red horse's rider—is said to have been introduced into war by the Assyrians.

Assyrian military advances far surpassed all other powers, due to their ability to borrow effective techniques pioneered by others alongside their own inventions. Illustrating their success, the following quotes come from *The Harper Encyclopedia of Military History*:

"The Egyptian chariot was a mobile firing platform for well-trained archers...The Assyrians developed chariot warfare to its greatest sophistication in Western Asia, with light chariots for archers and heavier chariots carrying as many as four spearmen."

"After 1000 B.C., more order was introduced into warfare by the Egyptians, who certainly understood and employed maneuver by well-organized and disciplined units. Soon afterward the Assyrians contributed even more order, organization, and discipline into military affairs, both on and off the battlefield."

The book continues: "No effort was spared that would contribute to the efficiency of the army or assure continued Assyrian supremacy over all possible foes...[King] Tiglath-Pileser I saw to it that this technical superiority was maintained by constant and systematic improvement of weapons, and by the careful training of the soldiers in the use of their arms."

"...it was the skill and organization of employment which brought success to Assyrian siegecraft...Terror was another factor contributing greatly to Assyrian success. Their exceptional cruelty and ferocity were possibly reflections of callousness developed over centuries...But theirs was also a calculated policy of terror—possibly the earliest example of organized psychological warfare. It was not unusual for them to kill every man, woman, and child in captured cities. Sometimes they would carry away entire populations into captivity."

God has often used the Assyrians to punish the nation of Israel as His "rod of correction" (Isa. 10:5-6). But there were times that He suppressed the Assyrians' power so that they would be out of the picture for a while. One example was the deliverance of Judah's King Hezekiah and Jerusalem from Sennacherib and his army of 185,000 elite soldiers that besieged the city: "Then the angel of the LORD went forth, and smote in the camp of the Assyrians" (Isa. 37:36).

God took away Assyria's pride overnight. This greatly weakened the proud nation and removed them from the picture for a time, in order for the Babylonian Empire to emerge—serving the next step in God's Purpose.

After the Babylonian Empire came the Medo-Persian Empire, which defeated Babylon in 539 BC. During the height of this empire, the advancement of the Persians was effectively halted in the Eastern Mediterranean by formidable warriors, including the Spartans. Later, Alexander the Great led the Greek Empire to victory over the Persians in 331 BC. For a period of time, we saw the Greco-Macedonian Empire reigned supreme.

The Romans

The Roman Empire, which emerged about 31 BC to supplant Greece, was described as "dreadful and terrible, and strong exceedingly" (Dan. 7:7).

Records of the Jewish War of AD 69-70 illustrate the Roman Empire's brutality. While Jerusalem was under siege, and in dire need of food and water, many Jews were captured trying to escape or bring in desperately needed supplies.

This account by Josephus illustrates in graphic detail the utterly unmerciful bloodlust of Roman legions and soldiers:

"So, now Titus's banks [mounds of earth used to breach the walls of Jerusalem] were advanced a great way, notwithstanding his soldiers had been very much distressed from the wall. He then sent a party of horsemen, and ordered they should lay ambushes for those that went out into the valleys to gather food...and when they were going to be taken, they were forced to defend themselves, for fear of being punished; as, after they had fought, they thought it too late to make any supplications for mercy; so they were first whipped, and then tormented with all sorts of tortures before they died, and were then crucified before the wall of the city. This miserable procedure made Titus greatly to pity them, while they caught every day five hundred Jews; nay, some days they caught more...The main reason why he did not forbid that cruelty was this, that he hoped the Jews might perhaps yield at that sight, out of fear lest they might themselves afterwards be liable to the same cruel treatment. So the soldiers, out of the wrath and hatred they bore the Jews, nailed those they caught, one after one way, and another after another, to the crosses, by way of jest; when their multitude was so great, that room was wanting for the crosses..." (*Wars of the Jews*, bk. V, ch. XI, sec. 1).

During the period of the Holy Roman Empire, the same merciless brutality abounded. As the last chapter established, the decisions were not made by military generals but by a church! The most merciless of all wars was the campaign instigated by the Roman church to murder, by the thousands, citizens of entire towns and villages in Europe (later in the area of Jerusalem and Palestine). This came to be known as the Crusades. The victims were mostly civilians.

Continental Europe would continue to be torn by war through the centuries, usually triggered by animosity between the Universal Church and other religious belief systems, primarily Protestantism or Islam.

World War Arrives

It was also on European soil, but many centuries later, that the horror of war was redefined. Conflict on an unprecedented scale ushered in a new phenomenon: *world* war.

The infamous battle of Verdun (France), fought during World War I, was one of the most costly battles ever, in terms of human lives. Fought from February 1916 until November 1918—two years and nine months— it was also one of the longest single battles in history. It captured the very essence of a "war of attrition." Nearly one million soldiers died!

Visitors to the battle area (over 250 square kilometers) are cautioned not to stray from designated walkways. The danger of the multiple thousands of unexploded shells, which still occasionally kill or maim, awaits any who dare to wander onto the battlefield. Imagine the state of the land after artillery had hit every square meter *many times*.

Today, just scraping the surface with a shoe reveals rusted belt and canteen strap buckles, rifle shell casings and similar items. It would take many pages to adequately describe the scope of just this one battle. The constant artillery, as well as chlorine, mustard and nerve gases used, stand as further stark testimony to man's inhumanity to man.

Here is a summary of just the *first two days* of battle:

"On February 21st 1916, at 7:15 a.m., the enemy opened fire on the two banks of the Meuse [River], over a front of 40 kilometers. Simultaneously Verdun was systematically bombarded, the last residents being evacuated by the military authority at midday on the 25th.

"For ten hours, all the enemy guns and trench mortars kept up a running fire without intermission. In all the woods adjoining the front it was a regular firework display. A feature of this overwhelming bombardment was the enormous proportion of heavy caliber shells, 150's and 210's coming over like hailstones.

"Under this deluge of projectiles all trenches were levelled, the woods became a twisted mass of trunks and branches, and villages collapsed and were blotted out.

"The infantry attack was launched at 5.15 p.m...."

"Three [German] army corps...advanced. They thought that they had only to march, with their rifles slung, over ground like a ploughed field.

"The [French] 51st...and 72nd Divisions...sustained the first shock and...covered the arrival of French re-enforcements.

"A heroic combat followed the most formidable artillery preparation hitherto known. The chasseurs [light cavalry troops] of Colonel Driant resisted the attack, inch by inch, in the wood of Caures. By nightfall the advance of the enemy was insignificant compared with their losses...

"[The next morning], with snow falling, the bombardment was resumed with, if possible, greater intensity. Colonel Driant in the wood of Caures was outflanked on both sides and died fighting, after first evacuating his chasseurs to Beaumont" (*Verdun, an Illustrated Historical Guide*).

This long battle was waged back and forth over a single piece of ground! Today the battlefields are quiet, reminiscent of when the German soldiers famously reported to their superiors in Erich Maria Remarque's novel, "All quiet on the western front," because things were temporarily static on the French front lines.

The Era of Total War

Some of the most telling effects of war are seen through statistics. These paint a clear picture in terms of casualties and financial burdens, proving that the severity of wars *has* intensified, beginning primarily with WWI.

During this war, the total *mobilized* military force of the Allied nations (France, the British Empire, Russia, Italy, the U.S., and six other smaller countries) was more than 42 million. Of this number, about 5 million were killed in action, with over 3 million civilian casualties. The cost incurred by the Allies was approximately $194 billion. The total mobilized military force of the Central powers (Germany, Austria-Hungary, Turkey and Bulgaria) was about 23 million, of which over 3 million were killed in action. Their cost was something over $86 billion. (It took until September 2010 for Germany's *WWI* debt to finally be paid off.)

World War I was the first war in which aircraft were more widely used—primarily for reconnaissance purposes. Also, the internal combustion engine allowed for much better logistical support (mobility of troops and munitions). Not-seen-before poison gas delivered by artillery was another "innovation."

Another telling statistic of WWI is the percentage of mobilized forces lost in battle. The following is a sampling of some of the major participants: Germany, 16.4 percent—France, 16.1 percent—the British Empire, 10.2 percent. The U.S. lost only about 1.2 percent, partly due to the relatively short time that it was involved in the conflict before the Armistice (*The Harper Encyclopedia of Military History*).

Some statistics from World War II, which reflected a war with far more sophisticated weaponry, demonstrate heavier losses. Aircraft had evolved into fighters, dive-bombers, heavy bombers, heavy transports, troop carriers for paratroopers and other specialized aerial-combat machines. Bazookas, rocket launchers, and a host of other "advancements" were used on the battlefields. Tank divisions were also a force to be reckoned with. Artillery had far greater ranges than previously achieved.

As a child, my father told me stories of his harrowing time as a reconnaissance pilot near Remagen, Germany, in the wake of the Battle of the Bulge, while another Lieutenant beside him in the cockpit of his tiny Piper Cub directed American artillery in its effort to destroy German artillery, which was trying to destroy the Bridge at Remagen, and thus halt the Allied advance into Germany toward Berlin as the war was coming to an end.

Here are some of the statistics pertaining to the combined figures for both the Allies and Axis powers: 105 million total mobilized forces, of which 15 million were killed in action, with up to 34 million civilians killed. The total cost this time was $1.6 *trillion*!

The world learned that "total war" casualties draw no boundary between military and civilian. Never before were so many civilians in harm's way. The percentage of mobilized forces lost in WWII: Germany, 22.8 percent—France, 3.5 percent—the United Kingdom, 6.4 percent—Soviet Union, 30 percent—Japan, 20.4 percent. The U.S. was just under 2 percent. One factor that accounted for the lower numbers of France and Britain was that they had not recovered from their staggering battlefield losses of WWI and were not in a position to field nearly as many troops as they needed. Also, France was overrun and defeated in 1940 and thereafter only fielded smaller resistance forces.

Although the U.S. entered the conflict in December 1941 in the Pacific, and only a little later in the European theater, it is miraculous their percentage of military losses was so low. Part of the explanation is that no air attacks were launched on the homeland other than Pearl Harbor. There was also God's hand then still at work on America's behalf.

The Holocaust

No discussion of horror related to WWII would be complete without mention of the Holocaust. This was Adolf Hitler's "final solution" to the "Jewish question"—and, for those with eyes to see, a foretaste of what will happen again.

The Wannsee Conference of January 1942 was convened for the purpose of formalizing a plan to exterminate all Jews within the confines of nations to the east, which were later occupied by Germany. For the next three and a half years, until the defeat of Germany in mid-1945, this "final solution" was implemented: "There were more than nine thousand camps scattered throughout German-occupied Europe. They included transit camps, prisoner-of-war camps, private industrial camps, work-education camps, foreign labor camps, police detention camps, even camps for children whose parents had been sent to slave-labor camps. More than three hundred camps were for women only.

"By mid-1942, within a few months of the Wannsee Conference, six camps served as killing centers where the victims were gassed: Treblinka, Sobibór, Belzec, Chelmno, Auschwitz / Birkenau, and Majdanek. The last two also doubled as slave-labor and penal camps" (*The World Must Know: The History of the Holocaust as Told in the United States Holocaust Memorial Museum*, Berenbaum, p. 116).

These six killing centers were located in Poland. Multiple railroad lines facilitated a constant flow of trainloads of victims. At Treblinka, some 750,000 or more Jews were murdered by a staff of approximately 150. Fewer than 100 known survivors of Treblinka were found.

At Sobibór, up to 250,000 Jews were murdered in carbon monoxide gas chambers. A revolt was staged there by 300 prisoners in the camp. While attempting to escape, many were killed. By the end of the war, there were only 50 known survivors of Sobibór.

At Belzec, up to 600,000 Jews and a few thousand Gypsies were murdered, and at Chelmno, up to 360,000 Jews were killed. Here, thousands of Gypsies, Poles and Soviet prisoners of war were also exterminated.

Birkenau (Auschwitz II) was the largest and deadliest of all the Nazi death camps. Here were the biggest, newest and most efficient gas chambers, which used the vapors from "Zyklon B" pellets to kill Jews, Poles, Gypsies and Soviet prisoners of war. Many more Jews (1.1 million) were killed here than the other groups represented.

244 The Bible's Greatest Prophecies Unlocked!

At Majdanek, nearly 500,000, from 28 different countries, were murdered. According to Polish sources, about 360,000—more than 70 percent, many of which were Poles—died there from starvation, exhaustion, disease and beatings. Seven gas chambers were employed (using "Zyklon B" pellets), as were the camp's two wooden gallows (ibid., pp. 123-124).

Many contemporary historians and scholars view the Holocaust as an anomaly—a freak occurrence, impossible to happen again. They believe that man has now developed to a higher order, more "considerate" and "tolerant" than the ancients.

The memory of the Holocaust should obliterate modern man's idealistic reasoning. All "baser instincts" are still with us. This action by the Germans was in the tradition of their forefathers, the ancient Assyrians. These also believed themselves a master race, and carried out organized deportation and genocide whenever they saw fit.

In a 1995 television interview, British Prime Minister Margaret Thatcher stated of Germany, "I, to this day, cannot understand why so many Germans, who are so highly intellectual…let Hitler do the things he did…There is something in the character of the German people which led to things which should never have happened…Some people say, 'You have got to anchor Germany into Europe, to stop these features ever coming out again.' You have not anchored Germany to Europe. You have anchored Europe to a newly dominant, large Germany…In the end, my friends, it will not work" (*Houston PBS*).

New Destructive Capability

Beginning with the conclusion of World War I—originally called the Great War or "The War to End All Wars"—the world slowly began to ratchet up toward the next great world conflict, only 20 years later. Near the end of World War II, the world entered a new and yet more frightening era.

On August 6, 1945, man's destructive capabilities greatly intensified, and the scope of warfare would never be the same. Mankind had come to a turning point—when ALL LIFE on Earth could now be erased in a single brief orgy of war!

Fast-forward to the present: weapon proliferation is today escalating at an alarming rate, with a number of volatile, aggressive nations seeking to join the nuclear club. The power that once destroyed a city—the atomic bomb—now serves as a mere "trigger" for the *hydrogen* bomb!

Weapons of mass destruction, so incomprehensibly destructive that they boggle the mind, now threaten humanity as never before.

Recall Christ's words: "Except those days should be shortened, there should *no flesh* be saved: but for the elect's sake those days shall be shortened" (Matt. 24:22). At the end of 6,000 years of man going his own way, he is approaching the brink of extinction on a number of fronts.

The awesome evil of nuclear weapons, unleashed on Hiroshima and Nagasaki by the United States, sobered prominent leaders and thinkers. They realized that survival of the human race was now at stake. Consider their words:

• "...no physical peril greater than atomic war has confronted mortal man since the Flood." – Adlai Stevenson

• "Never since human beings first existed have they been faced with so great a danger as that which they have brought upon themselves by a combination of unrivaled skill and unrivaled folly." – Bertrand Russell

• "Rifle bullets kill men, but atomic bombs kill cities. A tank is a defense against a bullet, but there is no defense in science against a weapon which can destroy civilization." – Albert Einstein

• "To destroy these weapons by common consent, to enter the commitment not to manufacture any others, to open up all territories to reciprocal supervision, there is no other hope for the future of our species." – French President Charles de Gaulle

With the dropping of the first atomic bomb, war forever changed. No longer were large standing armies the sign of a nation's strength. According to an article in the *Encyclopaedia Britannica* on the advent of the nuclear age, "These revolutionary characteristics of nuclear weapons have given rise to a phenomenon that is entirely new: there is no longer any relation between power and numbers."

Suddenly, political influence and the balance of world power could shift instantly.

Recall that the Bible summarizes the decadent condition of human character in the last days. Let's read again: "This know also, that in the last days *perilous times* shall come. For men shall be lovers of their own selves, covetous, boasters, proud, blasphemers, disobedient to parents, unthankful, unholy, without natural affection, trucebreakers, false accusers, incontinent, fierce, despisers of those that are good, traitors, heady, highminded, lovers of pleasures more than lovers of God; having a form of godliness, but denying the power thereof..." (II Tim. 3:1-5).

Brutal dictators and despots, who would do anything to stay in power, have always existed. Now, in this age, we are witnessing individuals of the worst CHARACTER *ever* having access to the worst WEAPONS *ever*! In our time exists the ultimate nightmare!

The world entered what authorities called the Age of Conflict, and set the stage for what the Bible terms the red horse and rider—wars and rumors of wars, nation against nation and kingdom against kingdom—in the years following World War II. But were governments sufficiently horrified by the mushroom clouds over Japan to say, "This must never happen again"?

The thundering answer is NO, they were *not*!

In fact, the occurrence of war has increased nearly four times since 1946, unleashing an incredible arms race. Dr. Herbert F. York, an American nuclear physicist who helped unleash the devastating power of nuclear weapons as a member of the Manhattan Project, and Jerome B. Weisner, a science advisor to President John F. Kennedy, warned, "...the arms race is a steady downward spiral to oblivion."

Little Time Remains!

Consider: From 1900 to 1946 the world experienced more than 120 armed conflicts—over two per year. Between 1946 and 2001 there were 225 wars—over four per year.

In his book *Out of Control: Global Turmoil on the Eve of the Twenty-first Century*, former national security adviser Zbigniew Brzezinski estimated that 87.5 million people lost their lives from war between 1900 and 1999. (This included about 33.5 million military deaths and 54 million civilian deaths.) But there are higher estimates.

Above those directly killed in warfare, Brzezinski estimates no fewer than 167 million *more* people died as a result of war-related oppression in just the twentieth century. Together, these numbers are "the approximate equivalent of the total population of France, Italy, and Great Britain; or over two-thirds of the total current population of the United States...This is more than the total killed in all previous wars, civil conflicts, and religious persecutions throughout human history."

Consider a few of the many wars, conflicts, revolutions, civil wars and coups that occurred just between 1967 and 1987: The Six-Day War (Israel vs. Egypt, Syria, Jordan); India vs. Pakistan; the Vietnam War; Iran vs. Iraq; Afghanistan vs. USSR; civil wars in Angola, El Salvador, Nicaragua and South Africa; the Falkland Islands (Great Britain vs. Argentina); Grenada; France vs. Libya and Chad—the list goes on.

Dozens of countries today, such as Somalia, Sudan and Afghanistan, have armed guerilla groups seeking the overthrow of their governments.

What is taking place in the world today far outpaces anything seen by Alexander the Great or even George Patton, the renowned WWII general.

Also, considered only a footnote by most, there is the problem of landmines. Around the world, huge numbers of unexploded mines—in 1996 the UN estimated 110 million—have never been retrieved. These cause adults, and often little children, to lose limbs and sometimes their lives. Easy to lay down, they are difficult to recover.

Deadly Technology

Incredible new weapons technology has permanently altered the face of war. "Smart" bombs, which are laser-guided to bring precision and efficiency to the art of killing, have replaced many types of "dumb" bombs. Military scientists have now developed cluster bombs, called "daisy cutters." Named after their pattern of explosion, these cut down large numbers of human beings like a lawnmower cuts grass. Also, there are "bunker-buster" bombs that before detonating can penetrate deep into the earth in pursuit of enemies hiding in caves.

More and better precision-guided missiles are also continually appearing. But these are nothing compared to the defensive missiles, called "kill vehicles," that are now reported to be "loitering" in outer space awaiting a signal to seek and destroy, regarding any nuclear launch that needs to be quickly knocked out after offensive missiles containing warheads have become airborne.

Various highly sophisticated and incredibly lethal attack aircraft now exist—helicopters, jets, bombers, gunships and drones—that have brought conventional warfare to a pinnacle of destructive capability never before known. Large, precision, satellite-guided bombs have gigantic "kill zones" of more than a thousand yards. Then there is the so-called "MOAB," or Massive Ordnance Air Blast bomb (also known in the military as the "Mother of All Bombs"), which is a conventional bomb that creates almost the same blast effect as a small nuclear weapon.

Of course, all of these kill and maim indiscriminately. So this can sometimes involve "friendly fire" casualties, in which one's own troops or civilians are hit. This is generally considered to be "acceptable and necessary collateral damage."

Modern military thinkers and strategists now speak in terms of protection from, or delivery of, "weapons of mass destruction." The killing capability of nuclear, chemical and biological weapons and, now, radiological or "dirty bombs," is indescribably horrible. Yet these weapons are now apparently in the hands of unstable countries and regimes, which may not be capable of controlling their use or safeguarding their inventory.

This is why the famous American General Douglas MacArthur, while attending the signing of Imperial Japan's surrender on September 2, 1945, said, "Men since the beginning of time have sought peace... Military Alliances, Balances of Power, Leagues of Nations, all in turn failed leaving the only path to be by way of the crucible of war. The utter destructiveness of war now blots out this alternative. We have had our last chance.

"If we will not devise some greater and more equitable system Armageddon will be at our door. The problem basically is theological and involves a spiritual recrudescence and improvement of human character that will synchronize with our almost matchless advances in science, art, literature, and all material and cultural developments of the past two thousand years. It must be of the spirit if we are to save the flesh..." (*The Reports of General MacArthur*).

Bear in mind that MacArthur spoke 60 years ago! Since then, it seems the whole world has become a "killing field."

Newer Threat

The twenty-first century has seen the rise of a new kind of warfare. This form transcends all national borders. Its battlefields are moveable and know no limits. Its combatants often look just like ordinary citizens, wearing no uniform and carrying no visible weapons. And it has no qualms about civilian casualties—in fact, they are usually the intended targets.

This describes the scourge of *terrorism*.

The events of September 11, 2001, changed forever the thinking of all Americans. Prior to this attack, it was common thought that the mainland of the United States was secure. America's strong military and missile defense system was felt to be adequate protection against invasion—war had always been thought of as something that happened somewhere else—to someone else. It stunned the nation to realize what just a *handful* of terrorists could do. In a moment, Americans in New York City, Washington, D.C., and rural Pennsylvania faced the horror that has been experienced daily by citizens in the Middle East and elsewhere.

A new term was introduced to the American mindset—"Homeland Security," with budget-busting new safety measures introduced across the country. For the first time since the Civil War, the front lines were in every state in America, not just faraway locales.

In the wake of this whole-world-changing trend, other attacks, smaller in scale but still devastating in effect, hit Spain, the United Kingdom and other countries.

Many nations are learning to live "on alert" to terrorist "cells," which can strike anywhere without notice. Enemies once kept outside a nation's borders are now living among the populace. Citizens who sympathize with the cause of extremists can evolve into homegrown terrorists. Often, they train themselves via the Internet, but many sympathizers also train abroad with groups such as the Taliban or al-Qaeda. It has become impossible to keep track of these groups as they form independent covert cells both in cities and rural areas.

The lengths to which terrorists will go are limitless. British intelligence has reported that terrorists have now devised explosive breast implants designed to bypass airport scanners! The new modern world!

The *EUobserver* reported that the number of arrests connected to terrorism doubled in the European Union in 2007. The EU Anti-terrorism chief Gilles de Kerchove said, "Al-Qaida is still and will continue to dominate international terrorism for years to come." The news site further stated, "Out of the total 1044 arrested last year, the vast majority was EU citizens suspected of membership in a militant organization. In cases of Islamic extremism, the would-be attackers appear to increasingly have been born in the union's territory and having EU citizenship."

Speaking about the failed attack on a Detroit-bound plane in December 2009, Andrew Thomas, aviation expert at the University of Akron in Ohio, told *The Christian Science Monitor*, "The terrorists are constantly developing more sophisticated attacks. They are hyper-motivated, they're not going to stop." The paper continued, "Meanwhile, the range of explosive devices that terrorists are developing is outstripping the ability of screening systems to catch them. Last August, an alleged suicide bomber who had explosives implanted in his body injured Saudi Prince Mohammed bin Nayef. Even controversial full body scans don't pick up such hidden devices."

Recognize that terrorism is also *financial* and *psychological* warfare. On September 11, with 19 people, a terror network in a single attack took *$1 trillion* out of the American economy, and for weeks after the attack, Manhattan offices were frequently evacuated and society brought to a standstill as a result of false alarms.

Drug cartels in Mexico have introduced the concept of "narco-terror." What is happening in Mexico and on America's southern border is a form of war—and one in which the stated goal of the narco-terrorist combatants is to bring chaos through the slaughter of Mexican officials and civilians.

In the coming years, terrorism on a much larger and horrific scale will be experienced by Westerners. Leviticus 26:14-16 states, "But if you [the nations of modern Israel in context] will not hearken unto Me, and will not do all these commandments; and if you shall despise My statutes, or if your soul abhor My judgments, so that you will not do all My commandments, but that you break My covenant: I [God] also will do this unto you; I [God] will even *appoint* over you *terror…*"

Why War?

We can now ask: What does God's Word say about the reasons that nations continually go to war? You will be shocked at its simplicity! But will you accept it?

First, recognize that no war can be fought unless there is an aggressor! Someone has to initiate or begin it. Like a football game, one team has to be on offense while the other plays defense. Yet, almost all nations speak in terms of their "Department of Defense" or of their "Defense Budget." Theoretically, if all nations merely defended themselves, there would be no wars because there would be no aggressors. While someone must "start it," combatants invariably see themselves as defending their interests, territory or rights.

Speaking from the human, worldly approach, military preparation is an absolute prerequisite for existence in a hostile world. The citizens of all nations pay a huge price to maintain their national sovereignty. Without a ready military, there is the constant threat from a plundering, destructive invading force, seeking to secure land, wealth or power.

The Bible reveals the *true* cause of war: "From where come wars and fightings among you? Come they not hence, even of your lusts…You lust, and have not: you kill, and desire to have, and cannot obtain: you fight and war, yet you have not, because you ask not. You ask, and receive not, because you ask amiss, that you may consume it upon your lusts" (Jms. 4:1-3). God says war comes when people lust for what belongs to others. When all else fails, men scheme to obtain what they want by brute force.

After a life of revolutionizing both science and war, Albert Einstein wrote, "…it is a problem not of physics but of ethics…it is easier to denature plutonium than it is to denature the evil spirit of man…the real problem is in the minds and hearts of men" (*The New York Times*).

Abraham Lincoln saw it this way: "Human action can be modified to some extent, but human nature cannot be changed" (*The Lincoln Encyclopedia*).

After examining Vietnam-era U.S. Secretary of State Robert McNamara's life lessons in the documentary *Fog of War*, filmmaker Errol Morris concluded: "You can't change human nature. It tells you that all of the other lessons are valueless, that the human situation is indeed hopeless."

Long ago the Bible outlined man's true nature: "The WAY OF PEACE they know *not*; and there is *no judgment* in their goings: they have made them *crooked paths*: whosoever goes there shall *not know peace*" (Isa. 59:8).

Exercise in Futility

Despite this, man continues to profess a yearning for peace in the era of world war. Two international organizations have been inaugurated to help promote peace and settle disputes. They represent man's best attempt to bring world peace—and the extent to which he has miserably failed to reach this goal.

After the Armistice of 1918, the League of Nations was instituted in an international effort to prevent, through arbitration, the outbreak of war in the future. The establishment of this organization became part of the treaty that ended WWI. One of its weaknesses from the outset was the refusal of the U.S. and various other key nations to join the league. The League of Nations was able to head off only a tiny few of the dozens of outbreaks of smaller wars between WWI and the outset of WWII. It was *completely unable* to defuse the inevitable developments that later resulted in the next round of total war! The League collapsed.

The end of WWII brought another attempt by mankind to establish "peace on Earth." The United Nations was formed to be a more perfect instrument to ensure such peace. Hundreds of smaller wars, fought around the world since the UN's inception, testify to its utter failure as a "guardian of peace." It is essentially a toothless bureaucracy, issuing condemnations that are ignored and sanctions that are rarely enforced.

Peace Will Remain Elusive

Today the world is fast approaching 7 billion people. Though global leaders strive to find "peace" through international conferences and meetings, war and its aftermath continue to be felt the world over.

Man, in his rebellion against God, likes to present his own versions of civilization in the best possible light, often ignoring harsh reality. In like manner, the false prophets of Israel, as Jeremiah foretold of our time, will soon declare, "Peace, peace; when there is no peace" (6:14).

God shows that peace will be elusive to those who forsake His ways. Ezekiel 7:23-25 foretells the coming tumult to engulf Israel: "The land is full of bloody crimes, and the city is full of violence. Wherefore I will bring the worst of the heathen, and they shall possess their houses: I will also make the pomp of the strong to cease; and their holy places shall be defiled. Destruction comes; and they shall *seek peace*, and there shall be NONE."

This cycle of war is destined to grow *much* worse!

"Wars and Rumors of Wars"

The Real Truth magazine, of which I am editor-in-chief, reports on global conditions as nations on every continent edge toward all-out war. Here are but a few snapshots from our regular "World News Desk" feature:

China Upgrades Nuclear Arsenal: After marked increases in military spending, China announced that it must possess second-strike capability—which would enable it to defend itself against a nuclear attack—and said it is in the process of upgrading and expanding its nuclear forces with increasingly sophisticated weaponry.

"Like all the nuclear weapons states, China is secretive about its arsenal, developed from a first atomic test explosion in 1964. The Stockholm International Peace Research Institute has estimated that by 2009 China possessed 186 deployed strategic nuclear warheads" (*Reuters*).

As major world powers collectively attempt to contain nuclear proliferation, China is moving away from easily monitored, silo-based, liquid-fueled rockets and opting for highly mobile, solid-fuel-powered rockets that are easier to launch and difficult to track. Among its upgrades are anti-satellite and nuclear-tipped cruise missiles that arm the nation's new generation Jin-class nuclear ballistic submarines.

A retired Chinese general stated the upgraded missile system "is able, should a foe launch an initial nuclear strike, to really possess, and to convince the other side that it faces, an intolerable second-strike nuclear capability, thereby deterring an enemy from using nuclear weapons against us.

"It must make them grasp, without the least ambiguity, that we possess a deterrent" (ibid).

Germany Calls for an EU Army: Germany has expressed a desire for the European Union to create an army under the political control of the EU, according to the nation's Foreign Minister.

"The long-term goal is the establishment of a European army under full parliamentary control. The European Union must live up to its political role as a global player. It must be able to manage crises independently. It must be able to respond quickly, flexibly and to take a united stand," he said (*AFP*).

At the Munich Security Conference, held earlier this year (2010), he stated that the door for a European army was opened by the passing of the Lisbon Treaty, a revised version of an EU constitution draft, and that this army would be a cohesive factor in creating a *European defense policy*.

Iran Declares Itself a Nuclear State: In early 2010, Iran's president declared that Iran was now a nuclear state: "I want to announce with a loud voice here that the first consignment of 20 percent enriched uranium was produced and was put at the disposal of the scientists," he said to a gathering of thousands waving flags and banners to demonstrate their support.

While Iran maintains its nuclear work is for generating electricity and producing radioactive isotopes to be used for therapy in hospitals, world powers, particularly Western nations, are not convinced.

The German newspaper *Der Spiegel* claimed to have access to an intelligence dossier showing the existence of a secret military branch of Iran's nuclear research program, whose aim of producing a bomb has reached an advanced stage. According to the paper, "Experts believe that Iran's scientists could produce a primitive, truck-sized version of the bomb this year, but that it would have to be compressed to a size that would fit into a nuclear warhead to yield the strategic threat potential that has Israel and the West so alarmed—and that they could reach that stage by sometime between 2012 and 2014."

South America Increases Military Spending As Poverty Grows: Leaders of South American nations have embarked on record military spending, while their citizens face the worst level of poverty in years!

Tension between neighboring countries and the Colombian government's decision to forge closer ties with the United States in its fight against drugs have fueled what some are calling an arms race.

Massive arms spending includes an air defense system, combat aircraft and tanks for Venezuela, as well as military aircraft for Chile and Ecuador. Other countries in the region have also increased their military budget. (Venezuela, an ally of Iran, is the most recent nation to openly tell the world that it too will now develop nuclear weapons.)

"In 2008 the 12 South American countries together channeled more than $50 billion into military expenditures, about 30 percent more than in 2007. Most prominent among countries where arms buying went up are Argentina, Bolivia, Brazil, Chile, Colombia, Ecuador, Paraguay, Peru, Uruguay and Venezuela" (*UPI*). This is virtually every country.

North Korea – Demanding World Attention: A statement from North Korea's Central News Agency read, "If the U.S. imperialists start another war, the army and people of Korea will...wipe out the aggressors on the globe once and for all."

This bellicose assertion came just days after Japanese intelligence sources reported that North Korea would fire a missile toward Hawaii, possibly on America's Independence Day.

The next day, marking the 59th anniversary of the outbreak of hostilities in the Korean War, Pyongyang's rhetoric continued. This time, the nation threatened a "fire shower of nuclear retaliation" for any attack. State news sources were filled—more than usual—with venom against the U.S. for its military action in 1950, and with charges that Washington is seeking another opportunity to show aggression toward North Korea.

October 2006 saw the nation provoke worldwide outrage with its first nuclear test, which violated the Nuclear Nonproliferation Treaty it had signed years before. A second underground test took place on May 25, 2009 (America's Memorial Day), followed by a number of offshore missile tests. Two days later, the Central News Agency reiterated that it was not bound by the 1953 armistice that set its southern boundary.

The Human Toll

Other news sources also demonstrate the never-ending, awful toll that the many forms of war take on human lives:

The Associated Press: "Southern parts of this impoverished Central Asian nation [Kyrgyzstan] were thrown into chaos by five days of ethnic violence, mostly Kyrgyz attacks on ethnic Uzbek neighborhoods. The violence followed a bloody uprising in April that toppled President Kurmanbek Bakiyev."

The Guardian (of London): "Mobs of Kyrgyz men rampaged through southern Kyrgyzstan today, slaughtering ethnic Uzbeks and burning down houses in a third day of ethnic bloodshed...The country's interim government granted its security forces shoot-to-kill powers and promised to send a volunteer force to the region—but the violence continued to rage, taking the death toll...to more than 100. At least 1,100 have been wounded in what are the country's worst ethnic clashes in 20 years."

The Los Angeles Times: "At least 50 people were killed...in attacks west of Baghdad, including a double suicide bombing against Sunni Arab paramilitary members waiting to receive their paychecks outside a military base."

The Washington Post: "Peshawar, Pakistan – The death toll in a massive suicide bombing climbed to more than 100 victims…115 [more were] wounded, making it Pakistan's deadliest attack of the year…The bombing targeted government offices and a prison in Pakistan's volatile tribal borderlands. The blast tore through a large crowd, including disabled people who were at the government center in the Mohmand Agency to collect wheelchairs, Pakistani officials said."

The Christian Science Monitor: "In the…Congo, sexual violence has become so common that the eastern provinces are sometimes called 'the ground zero of rape.' Tens of thousands of women here have been raped by armed combatants seeking to destroy communities by assaulting the women, who are often shunned and sometimes abandoned after sexual assaults. In Congo, it has become common to say rape is a weapon of war."

The New York Times: "I've never reported on a war more barbaric than Congo's, and it haunts me. In Congo, I've seen women who have been mutilated, children who have been forced to eat their parents' flesh, girls who have been subjected to rapes that destroyed their insides."

Sadly, almost before these stories are even printed, they are out of date—overtaken by another round of atrocities.

The "Just War" Concept

Nations have sought to justify this state of affairs through rationalizing and moralizing about the "inevitability" and "necessity" of going to war, and with the concept of the "just war." Understand. It is at *this point* that the *white* horse and rider are directly connected to war in a central way!

First we must ask: Is it possible for human beings to come together to fight and kill each other and be even a little bit noble, just or righteous—or even godly—in their cause? A greater question: Are human beings *inherently capable* of making correct judgments about war—or for that matter about other fundamental issues in life? The answer to these questions has much to do with *why* the world is filled with turmoil, strife and war.

Let's look at what God says regarding human nature and judgment. This is vital to understand.

Wise King Solomon recorded several Proverbs that, when placed together, present a sobering picture. He wrote that "All the ways of a man are CLEAN *in his own eyes*; but the LORD weighs the spirits" (16:2) and that "Every way of a man is RIGHT *in his own eyes*: but the LORD ponders the hearts" (21:2). Together, these similar passages make a profound statement. Anyone who has ever tried to correct someone who was wrong will have no difficulty believing their message.

However, another Proverb reveals that this natural tendency of human beings—to believe that all that they do is clean and right—carries an even greater implication: "The way of a FOOL is *right in his own eyes*" (12:15).

When combined, these three verses reveal that all people are born naturally foolish! If *all men* and *all fools* see themselves as right—clean—then they are naturally one and the same.

Stop and ponder the impact of these verses—and then notice another twice-recorded Proverb: "There is a way that *seems right* unto a man, but the end thereof are the ways of DEATH" (14:12; 16:25).

War may *seem* right to puny, foolish men who do not consider they have chosen a "crooked" path that leads to *death*—both now, and eternally, if they do not repent of it. The carnal human mind always deceives itself—Jeremiah 17:9!—into thinking that its ways are clean and right. People do not naturally feel a need to seek God's view on matters. They believe that they are inherently qualified to correctly make their own judgments. But Jeremiah also wrote, "The way of man is *not in himself*: it is not in man that walks to *direct his steps*" (10:23).

In the end, God is not *truly* consulted or included in men's thoughts or plans, even on the most complicated social issues. The human reasoning of "experts" guides policy on abortion, the cloning of human beings, pornography, the definition of immorality, the definition of a family, the acceptability of "alternative lifestyles," "mercy killing," political correctness and many other issues.

Men devise ways to justify *whatever* they do. *War*, the greatest of all social problems, is no exception! And man's pattern of not asking God what He thinks is also no exception. When nations have *already decided* it is in their best interest to go to war, all that remains is the task of spelling out the human rationale to justify what they have *pre-determined to do*! Enter the moralists, ethicists, philosophers, politicians and religionists for support.

Here is an example. Some time ago, when several soldiers were killed in a U.S. war by "friendly fire," it was said that they died "for a noble and just cause." This was said to soften the grief of the families they had left behind. But who decided that their deaths were "noble and just"? Certainly not God!

In the same conflict, a very high government official offered his assessment of why the war in question was being fought in the way that it was. He spoke of the "infinite judgment of the *world community*" that stood behind the war. He stated that *"thoughtful people believe…"* such and such. He made other similar references to what world leaders, the United Nations, moralists and military strategists thought or felt.

But he neglected entirely to reference any opinion or instruction that *God* might hold in the matter!

During every war, endless television talk shows parade politicians, generals, colonels, war heroes and other "analysts" before the cameras. They offer nonstop "insight" into what it all means, what must be done and why. For instance, they speak of being "bold" and "innovative" in the world's war on terror because it is a "new kind of war." Each "expert" seems to have a different opinion on what will, or will not, work. Where God is absent, disagreement abounds!

Again, not once have I heard a single one of these leaders, generals, war heroes or military planners ask what *GOD* thinks about war!

I have certainly heard many ministers, evangelists, religionists and theologians—usually representing well-known church denominations, ministries or organizations—express their own *personal* view about particular wars. But their views are nothing more than what *they* think or feel! Almost without exception, such "religious" thinkers believe that war can be "just and noble" in purpose. Also, virtually without exception, these same churchmen were part of the country that was attacked. Is it surprising that they agreed with the opinion of the overwhelming majority surrounding them, which was already driving the course of the country?

Modern religious leaders lack the moral and spiritual strength to reflect what *God* commands, so they cave to national peer pressure.

However, I *have* heard nearly all of these same churchmen beseech God—*after the fact*—to BLESS what men had already decided to do through means of war. In their weakness, they have the gall to ask God to bless their sin—war!

In reference to a particular U.S. war, a large conference of religious leaders said that it was "regrettable but necessary," and that they felt military action was "appropriate" as long as "the principles of morality and human dignity" were followed. Another group of leaders stated the hope that a "wise, just and effective" response could occur. All of these statements flow from *human reasoning*. None are based on the Bible—and none of these groups or individuals made a pretense that they were.

Asking God to bless the horrific nature of war is like asking Him to work through a Frankenstein monster! (My booklet *War, Killing and the Military* tells the truth of what God's Word really teaches on this subject.)

In Their Own Words

Let's now hear from religious leaders in their own words. First comes Rome. Authors Gordon Thomas and Max Morgan-Witts, in a book about papal diplomacy, wrote this in the 1980s about influential Philadelphia archbishop John Krol's views, which "are in keeping with the church's position, itself based upon St. Augustine's original 'just war' theory, which had been refined and developed by Thomas Aquinas and other theologians. The theory...is that a war can be 'just' when it is declared by a legitimate authority, when it is conducted for a 'righteous cause,' when it is launched with 'good intentions,' when it is a 'last resort'..." (*Averting Armageddon*).

The authors added, "Nine years after Hiroshima, he [Pope Pius XII] had approved the use of atomic, bacteriological, and chemical weapons only if 'they did not totally escape from the control of man' or produce 'annihilation of all human life within the radius of action,'" and further added that, in an address to the United Nations in June 1982, John Paul II said that nuclear "deterrence" was "morally acceptable" (ibid.).

Rome's daughters agree—and have from the beginning. Martin Luther, the father of the Reformation, said, "He who starts a war is wrong and that it is just for him who draws the sword first to be defeated or at least to be punished in the end" (*What Luther Says*, vol. 3, Ewald Martin Plass).

Before the first Gulf War, America's most famous televangelist stated, "There is an ethical responsibility that goes with power, and sometimes it becomes necessary to fight the strong in order to protect the weak...There come times when we have to fight for peace" (Billy Graham, quoted in the *Los Angeles Times*).

Another famous minister asserted, "If one depends on the Bible as a guidepost for living, it is readily apparent that war is sometimes a necessary option" ("God is pro-war," Jerry Falwell, *WorldNetDaily*).

A Southern Baptist Convention official wrote, "Conducting war in a just manner is an act of Christian love that seeks to accomplish the divinely ordained duty of the state: to punish and restrain evil and to protect and reward good. The Bush administration's policy vis-à-vis Saddam Hussein fits well within the framework of Just War theory" ("The Time Has Arrived," Richard Land).

Before World War I, the American Federal Council of Churches declared, "As American citizens, members of Christian churches...we

are here to pledge both support and allegiance in unstinted measure...
the hour lays upon us special duties...to keep ever before the eyes of our
allies and ourselves the ends for which we fight..." (*The Churches of
Christ in Time of War*, Charles S. MacFarland, pp. 129, 131).

It is religious leaders, throughout professing Christianity, who have
validated—and even suggested and promoted—such thinking about war.
Yet ask: How could they *endorse* and empower such AWESOME EVIL
in Christ's name?

The answer? Ignoring God's instructions has never been a problem
for a universal religious system long unconcerned with what GOD says!
Lost are such simple statements as this from Jesus about war: "My
kingdom is not of this world: if My kingdom were of this world, then
[and not otherwise] would My servants fight" (John 18:36).

One Honest Man

Some have been willing to tell the truth. Dr. Harry Emerson Fosdick, a
famous Baptist minister, told the League of Nations in 1925 (emphasis
mine):

"We cannot reconcile Jesus Christ and war—that is the essence of
the matter. That is the challenge which today should stir the conscience
of Christendom. War is the most colossal and ruinous social *sin* that
afflicts mankind; it is utterly and irremediably *unchristian*; in its total
method and effect it means everything that Jesus did not mean and it
means nothing that He did mean; it is a more blatant denial of *every*
Christian doctrine about God and man than all the theoretical atheists
on earth ever could devise. It would be worthwhile, would it not, to see
the Christian Church claim as her own this greatest moral issue of our
time, to see her lift once more, as in our fathers' days, a clear standard
against the *paganism of this present world* and, refusing to hold her
conscience at the beck and call of belligerent states, put the Kingdom of
God above nationalism and call the world to peace? That would not be
the denial of patriotism but its apotheosis" (*Best Sermons 1926*, Joseph
Fort Newton).

Never believe that, given opportunity, the system which "fornicates
with the kings of the earth" will even *hesitate* to empower generals
looking for moral and religious authority to butcher vast millions with
weapons of mass destruction. It becomes clear *why* God will *use war*—
from HIM!—to destroy the whole war-making universal system, with her
daughters.

Nowhere to Hide

Horrific events will unfold in affluent First World nations. While the inhabitants of the West bask in hedonism, and live the "good life" on borrowed funds, horses' hooves can be heard in the distance. The sword in the hand of the red horse rider will first slash across all primarily non-Israelite nations of the world. It will then move to the comfortable suburbs and idyllic countryside of the United States, United Kingdom, Canada, Australia, New Zealand, South Africa, France, Scandinavia, and certain other countries—before returning to again assault the entire inhabited world in the greatest way ever.

But even those who are not near the battlefields will feel the effects of the red horse's ride. Those who are not wounded or killed in current and future battles will soon be profoundly affected—by the hundreds of millions. The pattern of history is that always following in the wake of war is a second and different, much slower and *darker* face of death…

The Black Horse—Famine

This chapter will be one of the most distressing things you will ever read. But it is necessary.

Most people, including almost all in the Western world, have never been hungry. They have never experienced and have no real knowledge or comprehension of the lives of those who awaken every day to hunger pangs they took to bed with them the night before—and that are still present when they go back to bed the next night. Millions of human beings across the world spend their every waking hour trying to find more food. This could be for either themselves or their children. A lucky few eventually solve the problem permanently—but the majority never do, and in time pay the final price: starvation.

Famine—severe shortage of food—has stalked the planet for 6,000 years. Countless millions have died, their names lost to history.

To most in the Western world, *famine* is just a word. The same is true for *hunger* and *starvation*. If these terms are used at all, it is generally in glib phrases such as "I'm starving!" or "I'm famished!"—when the reality is that a full meal had been eaten only hours before.

Each day, many millions of shoppers across the United States casually walk into supercenter grocery stores. One section holds lush produce from around the world: lettuce from California, oranges from South Africa, avocados from Mexico, kiwis from New Zealand. In another section, there are perhaps 60 varieties of sliced bread, next to hot dog buns, bagels, breakfast biscuits and French baguettes. Down another aisle sit

17 brands of canned soup and a dozen kinds of olives in glass jars. The meat section stretches along a wall of the store, with many options such as ground beef and steaks, cuts of lamb, chicken and pork, as well as seafood. People browse comfortably, checking, weighing, picking and choosing among endless choices—what they expect will always be available to them.

These citizens do not think twice about the abundance and blessings contained in just *one* such store—and they are everywhere. They wander the aisles, make selections, routinely pay the bill and go home. After all, this is everyday life!

Bigger Picture

For most of the world, however, such a grocery store is a faraway dream. They live an entirely different reality. According to the United Nations World Food Programme (WFP):

• "1.02 billion people do not have enough to eat—more than the populations of USA, Canada and the European Union."

• "907 million people in developing countries alone are hungry."

• "Asia and the Pacific region is home to over half the world's population and nearly two thirds of the world's hungry people."

• More than 60 percent of chronically hungry people are women.

• "65 percent of the world's hungry live in only seven countries: India, China, the Democratic Republic of Congo, Bangladesh, Indonesia, Pakistan and Ethiopia."

Those in industrialized countries are shielded from the harsh reality of life in these impoverished areas. But this chapter is not about starvation in distant, remote places. It is not the written equivalent of a heartrending documentary about drought in Africa or pictures of starving babies in a news magazine. It is about who will die from hunger among those you know and love. Your neighbors—spouses—*children*!

Recall again Christ's list of end-time trends in Matthew 24: "Nation shall rise against nation, and kingdom against kingdom: and there shall be *famines*..." (vs. 7).

We have seen that the famines mentioned here are connected to the black horse of Revelation. Let's reread the passage for context: "And I beheld, and lo a BLACK HORSE; and he that sat on him had a pair of balances in his hand. And I heard a voice...say, A measure of wheat for a penny, and three measures of barley for a penny; and see you hurt not the oil and the wine" (6:5-6).

We also saw that false Christianity leads to war. In turn, armed conflict invariably brings famine, which begets disease.

But, again, to those in well-off nations, these words seem implausible—IMPOSSIBLE. They believe life will go on happily forever. Yet famines *are* on the increase now, and the world is poised for a never-before-seen global food crisis. The scene in Revelation 6 will *soon* come to pass!

A Familiar Cycle

The order in which Christ presented conditions before His Return reflects a *cycle* of events that has always accompanied mankind's civilizations: "Kingdom against kingdom"—WAR—with famine and pestilence on its heels.

According to the U.S. Agency of International Development (USAID), the horrors of armed conflict often give way to famine: "Wars triggered most of the great famines of the late twentieth century. War not only contributes to the creation of famine, but also poses huge challenges to famine relief operations."

The organization explains that war "drives farmers from their land, disrupts markets, destroys stores of harvested foods, creates food shortages that drive prices above levels that low income families can pay, and disrupts the agricultural cycle."

As Jesus foretold, the black horseman of famine always rides in the wake of the red horseman of war—and the world knows this!

Famine means starvation, which quickly wears out the human body. With a sustained low-calorie diet, physical effects begin to show first: Fat deposits begin to shrink, as do organs such as the heart, lungs, liver and kidneys. Malnourishment damages the walls of the intestines, making absorption of nutrients more difficult and causing chronic diarrhea. More obvious outward signs also appear: The body begins to retain fluid and the stomach becomes distended, hair loses its luster, eyes sink, and skin becomes paper-like, dull and inelastic.

In the final stages of starvation, the body's immune system fails, opening the door to disease, or the third condition mentioned in Matthew 24:7: *pestilences.*

These are the same conditions that Jesus said signal the end of this age. Yet how can one know these three disasters mean mankind has entered the last days? Have they not persistently plagued mankind throughout history?

Again, famine has *always* stalked the planet. And again, when stating, "there shall be famines," Jesus could only have meant that they will grow worse in *number, scope, duration* and *intensity* throughout the world. They will also appear in regions that have never before seen famine, or at least not on any similar scale. Even First World nations are scheduled to be affected.

But how can you be certain?

What the Black Horse Means

One of the basic principles of Bible study is to read slowly, and carefully examine the key words of a passage. Seek to absorb what you are reading. And remember that the New Testament, originally written in Greek, was only later translated to other languages. Therefore, to more clearly understand the picture of the black horse and rider, we must examine the passage, word by word, occasionally examining the Greek. By doing so, the conditions of an impending global food crisis become clear.

Now read Revelation 6:5-6 again: "I beheld, and lo a black horse; and he that sat on him had a pair of balances in his hand. And I heard a voice…say, A measure of wheat for a penny, and three measures of barley for a penny."

Verse 8 explains the meaning of the "black horse" and "rider." They bring famine or "hunger." In the rider's hand is a "pair of balances" to weigh out the meager rations—or "measures"—of food described in verse 6.

Each time the words "measure" and "measures" are used, it is the Greek word *choinix*. According to *Vine's Expository Dictionary of New Testament Words*, the term means "a dry 'measure' of rather less than a quart, about 'as much as would support a person of moderate appetite for a day…'"

In short, the black horse and rider bring conditions that result in daily ration lines!

But how much will the food cost?

The Greek word for "penny" is *denarius*. A denarius was about a day's wage for a worker in Palestine 2,000 years ago. So the implication is that *one* day's pay—all of it!—is required to buy just *one* day's food.

Think of all your monthly expenses: rent or mortgage payment, car payment, utilities, phone bill, cable and Internet access, clothing, gas for your car, and others. Now consider—a whole day's pay just for that day's food! If this were the price of food, how would you pay for your other *necessities*?

Chapters Five and Six showed that we are in the last days, and this can be proven even more conclusively. World conditions make clear that the black horse is about to accelerate toward the worst famines of all time!

Permanent Famine

Ethiopia's severe drought in 1984 affected 8 million people, with approximately one million dead. Only after Western nations learned the extent of the crisis did they donate enough grain to end the famine by 1985.

After that time, aid organizations and wealthier nations made a general push to eradicate hunger everywhere. According to the International Food Policy Research Institute's "2009 Global Hunger Index" (GHI), "Progress was made in reducing chronic hunger in the 1980s and the first half of the 1990s."

However, this effort to erase famine faltered. The report continues, "For the past decade hunger has been on the rise."

In Ethiopia today, WFP estimates that 46 percent of the population is undernourished. And the GHI warning level is "extremely alarming."

What began in the 1980s for Ethiopia was something new: pockets of permanent famine. Despite years of foreign assistance, hunger still grips that land. Today, 39 percent of Ethiopians live on less than $1.25 per day. In the last 30 years, farm production has fallen despite the population doubling. Even worse, continual crop failure has meant the nation must rely largely on aid groups for survival.

But Ethiopia is far from alone in suffering continuous drought and famine. Other nations received ratings of "alarming," "extremely alarming," and "serious" on the GHI, including Sierra Leone, Chad and the Democratic Republic of Congo. Zimbabwe—once considered a breadbasket of southern Africa—is in the "alarming" category. Citizens in these nations remain under threat of famine due to inconsistent rains, civil unrest, military conflict and infertile land. Ever-worsening famine in these areas cannot be solved!

The country of Niger's government report to the World Health Organization (WHO) "showed that rates of acute malnutrition among children under five had risen to 17 percent from 12.3 percent in 2009." The WHO considers figures above 15 percent an emergency. It stated, "A severe form of hunger that can leave children permanently underdeveloped, acute malnutrition affects as many as one in five children in the hardest hit regions of Niger..." Niger's rise of almost five percent occurred in just one year.

The WFP reported that in Chad, "Poor harvests, erratic rainfall and high food prices have hit countries throughout the Eastern Sahel [belt]... The number of people categorised as 'food insecure' in the Sahelian belt of Chad increased from 41 percent of the population in May 2009 to 61 percent in March 2010—just ten months time. WFP is responding with general food distributions to some 850,000 vulnerable people and assistance to pregnant women, nursing mothers and moderately malnourished children in supplementary feeding centres. The number of centres open went up from 36 in March to 52 in June and this figure is expected to increase to around 140 in the coming weeks."

As devastating as recent African drought has been, history says it can get much worse. A news release from The University of Texas at Austin revealed, "Droughts far worse than the infamous Sahel drought of the 1970s and 1980s are...normal...for sub-Saharan West Africa, according to new research...These decades-long droughts were dwarfed by much more severe droughts lasting three to four times as long, scientists report..."

"According to a 2002 report by the United Nations Environment Program, the most recent Sahel drought killed more than 100,000 people and displaced many more."

In Bangladesh, the WFP reports that 60 million people do not have sufficient food to eat. Nearly 8 million of its children under five years old are underweight. Make yourself ponder such huge numbers.

In Pakistan, an estimated 1.55 million people have fled their homes due to conflict, especially near the war-torn Afghanistan border. They rely on humanitarian aid for assistance. The World Food Programme reports that 24 percent of its population is undernourished.

The list of nations requiring assistance could go on and on. Since the 1980s, aid agencies and rich nations have used money to stave off hunger in the developing world. But this support system has begun to collapse.

A July 2010 article, "Is the Next Global Food Crisis Now in the Making?", provided a sobering reality check: "Recent weeks have produced a series of grim and related headlines: Russia has declared a state of emergency because of drought in 12 regions, while in major wheat exporter Ukraine, severe flooding may depress crop yields. Dry conditions threaten Vietnamese rice production. The USDA has projected a disappointingly low Midwest harvest, and China has raised questions on the demand side by doubling its imports from Canada.

"Fortunately, this run of unfavorable farming news follows strong harvests that for now should keep grain prices in check, according to the U.N. Food and Agriculture Organization. But to see the effects of a bad year for food—and what the world could be in for if the present trend persists—one only has to look to 2008…[when] a confluence of environmental causes compounded by rising fuel costs and a global credit crunch caused food prices to skyrocket an average of 43 percent worldwide, leading to starvation and riots from Mexico to Bangladesh.

"Some are worried that was just a warning" (*AOL News*).

Drought—Lethal Accelerant

Among the causes of famine is drought. Perhaps none is larger. Without water, crops languish and food production grinds to a halt.

While the nations of the West have not experienced the plague of drought in life-threatening levels in recent years, this longstanding accelerant to famine will re-emerge. Extreme—devastating!—drought is long overdue. More than just a fact of science, God actually *promises* such drought among His many forms of punishment. Let's read: "I will break the pride of your power; and I will make your heaven as *iron*, and your earth as *brass*" (Lev. 26:19).

Understand. "Iron" heavens produce no rain, and "brass" earth is the result. I know. I have dug many postholes in severely drought-hardened ground where even a power auger would not penetrate the earth with my full weight on it—and I am a big man.

Amos 4:9 adds this: "I [God] have smitten you with *blasting* and *mildew*: [and also] when your gardens and your vineyards and your fig trees and your olive trees increased, the palmerworm *devoured them*: yet have you not returned unto Me, says the LORD." Notice that blasting (hot, dry winds) and mildew (too much rain) are both mentioned. These opposite extremes produce the same thing—low crop yield and famine. So do worms eating plants.

The impact of drought in just the twentieth century—only part of the run-up to *awful* droughts soon to canvas the earth—is important to contemplate. 1930s America saw a near 10-year drought with effects reaching across a staggering 65 percent of the United States. During this same time, drought in China claimed 5 million people—just in 1936!

Consider a single day during this decade-long period: On April 14, 1935, referred to as "Black Sunday," a massive dust storm more than 8,000 feet high engulfed the entire lower Midwestern United States—from Kansas to Texas—with winds exceeding 70 mph.

Such storms accompanying drought can produce mile-high "black blizzards," which are truly terrifying to behold. The debris and silica particles in the air stirred up by these storms—invariably inhaled by human beings—can cause several serious lung diseases.

Pollution, overwatering, misuse of the land and SIN will give rise to catastrophe of epic proportion. Drought—paling America's "Dust Bowl" years into near insignificance—lies just over the horizon!

God says this, not I.

Global Water Shortage

Everything in this chapter so far has spoken to lack of food. But water shortages of colossal proportion are also on the way. Crumbling water systems in Western nations, coupled with global pollution and increasing drought, will lead to widespread *thirst* alongside hunger.

Understand that just *2.5 percent* of the earth's water is fresh. Only 20 percent of *this* (or 0.5 percent!) is accessible ground or surface water. Current population needs consume over half of this available water. By 2025, water use is expected to rise by 50 percent in developing countries, and 18 percent in other areas. As the earth grows by 77 million people per year, an additional amount of water equivalent to the mighty Rhine River is required *each year*.

Also, developing countries dump up to 90-95 percent of their sewage, untreated, and 70 percent of all industrial waste into surface waters. Population growth guarantees this problem will *only grow worse*. In addition, chemical runoff from fertilizers, pesticides, and acid rain sufficiently ruin water quality to make it unusable. Some experts predict the world will also *completely* run out of usable drinking water by 2050.

Trends indicate that most of the world will soon be thirsty. Water wars have already long been the subject of various legal fights between states and countries. This will grow *much* worse!

Growing Global Crisis

Famine has been steadily spreading and worsening for years. Recently, the worst contributing factor has been the continued international financial

First World Food Supplies

To increase profit margins, industrialized nations have made food delivery into a science. Grocery stores and many restaurants rely on "just in time" delivery, meaning they keep a low stock on hand and rely on regular shipments of products. If these shipments are delayed—even by just a few days—the shelves empty out. In turn, the customer must go without.

This principle was seen in living color when ash from an Icelandic volcano hung over Europe, causing a continent-wide flight ban in April 2010. On top of air travelers being stranded, there was another troubling problem.

During that time, the *Guardian* reported, "Britain's supermarkets could soon run short of perishable goods including exotic fruits and Kenyan roses as the ongoing ban on UK air travel brought Britain's largest perishable air freight handling centre to a standstill..."

Realize that this airline disruption lasted just under a week. What if it continued?

Many First World nations are consistently producing and exporting less grains and vegetables, while they are increasing imports of such products. This leaves them wide open to massive food shortage if their suppliers fail to deliver.

For example, the United Kingdom imports about *90 percent* of its fruit and *60 percent* of its vegetables. Their fresh produce comes from all across the globe: broccoli and strawberries from Spain, apples from the United States, grapes from Egypt, carrots from South Africa, tomatoes from Saudi Arabia, asparagus from Peru, bananas from India, but also meat such as lamb from New Zealand.

For potatoes, England mostly looks to Israel. The British Potato Council reports that the UK imports over 385,000 tons of potatoes per year (*Guardian*).

Where would Britain be without regular shipments of fresh food? And this is just *one* wealthy nation—there are many others in the same position, some much larger.

Famine in just one part of the world, whether the Middle East, Africa, South America or elsewhere, can automatically mean shortages in many First World nations. The increasingly interconnected global economy means an increasingly *fragile* food supply. This fragility will become more obvious with each passing "incident."

downturn. Wealthy nations are no longer able to support impoverished peoples financially.

After the 2008 Cyclone Nargis disaster in Myanmar, the Director of U.S. Foreign Assistance and USAID Administrator at the time, Henrietta Holsman Fore, said, "We are in the midst of a global food crisis unlike other food crises we have faced, one not caused simply by natural disasters, conflict or any single event such as drought. It is not localized—but pervasive and widespread, affecting the poor in developing nations around the world."

Understand. The *financial* crisis has brought us to the brink of pervasive, widespread *famine*!

The World Food Programme, also in 2008, said global increases in food prices were creating "the biggest challenge" it has faced in the organization's 45-year history—what the organization termed "a silent tsunami threatening to plunge more than 100 million people on every continent into hunger."

Ms. Fore pointed out that the international food price index rose 43 percent in 2007, immediately affecting the world's poor. "For the poorest one billion, living on just a dollar per day, very high food prices mean stark choices between taking a sick child to the clinic, paying school fees, or putting food on the table."

USAID estimates that of the world population one billion people subsist on less than a dollar per day. Of these, 162 million live on less than a tiny 50 cents per day. These households are generally spending 50 to 60 percent of their income on food, compared to less than one-fifth in nations such as the United States.

Remember what is coming: "A measure of wheat for a penny, and three measures of barley for a penny" (Rev. 6:6).

Meeting with the British government in April 2008, WFP Executive Director Josette Sheeran described the millions now priced out of the food market as "the new face of hunger." Price increases from the global economic collapse have left millions in urban areas around the world hungry, unable to afford the rising cost of groceries.

As the economic crisis worsened, the World Food Programme announced a $500 million deficit in its budget in February 2008, and urged wealthy nations to increase contributions. Two months later, Ms. Sheeran announced that the gap had risen to $755 million. At that time, she said the WFP was "putting out an urgent appeal for the world to help us meet not only our base budget to meet the accessed needs of people from Darfur to Uganda to Haiti and beyond, but also to meet this gap."

In July of 2009, the situation grew even more dire. Ms. Sheeran said that the WFP's "assessed approved needs" were $6.7 billion for the year. After discussions with governments, the agency received only $3.7 billion in donations—a $3 billion budget deficit!

Clearly, this *is* a "crisis unlike other food crises." Something on this scale *has* never been seen before. This is the makings of *global* famine!

For now, though, it seems there is only one solution—throw money at the problem. Yet this is money that governments—ever more frequently—*no longer have.*

Depleted Grain Supplies

Another factor holds the potential to invite sudden widespread famine. Recent years have seen record increases in grain prices, with supplies reaching record lows as expanding nations such as China bring ever-growing demand.

In 2007 and 2008, a global food crisis was marked by dangerously low grain reserves. There were only "64 days of carryover stock [harvested grain stored in stockpiles and silos] in 2007" (*Earth Policy Institute*). Wheat reserves then plummeted to a 60-year low, and the price per bushel of Chicago wheat futures surged to more than $11.00 for the first time.

As of this writing, the planet is *again* threatened with a major food supply crisis. Carryover stock in September 2010 hovered around 72 days, dangerously close to the levels that ignited the crisis three years before.

This has in part been caused by a chain reaction: Heat waves, the drought and wildfires in Central Europe and Russia—leading to a 32 percent grain output decrease in Kazakhstan, a 19 percent decline in the Ukraine, and a 27 percent *decrease* in Russian wheat production over the previous year—which in turn led to a government-imposed wheat export ban.

The *International Business Times* brought grim news from Russia: "July was the hottest month in Russia—the world's third-largest wheat exporter—since record-keeping commenced over 130 years ago, with deadly forest fires causing more than 30 deaths. Moreover, large parts of the wheat harvest are being destroyed. The expected amount available for export by Russia has been nearly halved, and could fall further if the drought continues."

Russian Prime minister Vladimir Putin stated, "I think it would be expedient to introduce a temporary ban on export grains and other agricultural goods...We cannot allow an increase in domestic prices and we need to maintain the number of cattle."

This problem could worsen dramatically if drought deprives the region of the water needed for the 2010-11 winter wheat crop. Given that Russia and its neighbors account for one quarter of *all wheat exports worldwide*, prices for this staple crop have again spiked sharply. Now 40 percent of the crop could be lost.

But the Black Sea region is not the only part of the globe where wheat supplies are dwindling. Canada—afflicted with the opposite crop-destroying condition of *too much* rain—is lagging in production and accompanying exports. Germany and Poland are also suffering.

Consider. The United States Department of Agriculture *continues* to *slash* world wheat crop-yield estimates for the fourth straight month (as of September, 2010). Wheat prices worldwide during this time period exploded, punctuated by "a record surge of 38 percent in July" (ibid.).

Corn supplies are also lagging, with similar price-inflating results. In late 2010, corn stockpiles were projected to fall to the lowest levels in seven years. The reduced corn crop has the added effect of making livestock feed, often corn-based, much more expensive. This price increase is then passed on to consumers of beef, pork and poultry products.

This snapshot summarizes the worsening scenario: "Corn prices surged once again—this time on worries that the U.S. harvest will come in well below initial estimates. As yield statistics flow in from farms in the Midwest, many farmers are reporting that the corn haul is lower than last year. The U.S. Department of Agriculture recently cut its official projection for the 2010 harvest, and many analysts expect that farms across the country will produce [only] an average of 160 bushels of corn per acre—or perhaps even lower" (*ETF Database*).

"Although a loss of five bushels an acre may seem small, it makes a big difference to supplies when multiplied across the 87.9 million acres planted, and would likely push U.S. supplies in storage next year below one billion bushels, a psychologically significant threshold. Avoiding that scenario will require higher prices" (*The Wall Street Journal*).

Consumers are beginning to see this firsthand. The U.S. Agriculture Department projects a jump in retail prices for a wide variety of foods in late 2010 and 2011—beef and other meats, cereal and breads, dairy products, coffee and more.

This is an ominous trend. Do not expect it to go away more than temporarily—if at all! It is only the beginning.

U.S. Wheat Reserves

Since the 1980s, the U.S. strategic wheat reserves, as well as another grain stockpile called the Bill Emerson Humanitarian Trust, have been sold for cash—reducing stockpiles to near zero. In fact, by 2000, all government-owned stocks of wheat were sold out.

The only remaining reserves in the country were those privately held by Farmer Owned Reserves (FOR) and commercial grain buyers. These stockpiles have been *severely* depleted as well, with no government plans to replenish the reserves.

Here is what Larry Matlack, President of the American Agricultural Movement (AAM), explained (emphasis mine): "Our concern is not that we are using the remainder of our strategic grain reserves for humanitarian relief. AAM fully supports the action and all humanitarian food relief. Our concern is that the U.S. has *nothing else in our emergency food pantry*. There is no cheese, no butter, no dry milk powder, no grains or anything else left in reserve" (*Tri-State Observer*).

This same official went on to state that the entire USDA Commodity Credit Corporation (CCC) inventory would be reduced to 2.7 million bushels of wheat—roughly enough to make only *one-half loaf of bread for each person in the United States*!

Pause to reflect on what has happened to what has been called the world's breadbasket. How have the mighty fallen!

Reserves of other agricultural commodities such as sorghum, rice and corn have also come to be virtually non-existent. Income generated by the sale of U.S. grain is being held (rather than the grain itself) as a surplus by the CCC in a "trust for food," to be spent by the government in the event of a domestic or global crisis. The rationale is that food could then be purchased with grain sale profits rather than burdening taxpayers with the cost of maintaining large stores of grain. Such foolish, shortsighted and dangerous thinking!

The only arena left that could maintain stockpiles of wheat without returning to government-sponsored storage is the FOR and commercial buyers, which collectively hold approximately *one bushel* of wheat per person in the U.S., the lowest in 60 years.

Add to these crises the growing trend of farmers devoting more acreage to other crops such as soybeans and corn, motivated by higher profit margins made possible by government-subsidized bio-fuel programs.

These statistics are all early "handwriting on the wall"!

Competitors for Food

But livestock bred for human consumption are not the only animals affected by food shortage. With naturally-growing food supplies reduced by drought, urban sprawl and other factors, wild animals are looking to suburbs and even cities for sustenance.

Notice this: "Huckleberries, nuts and pine cones are in short supply this year because of poor growing conditions, so bears have taken to breaking into cars, nosing around backyards and raiding orchards...when bears roam into towns, they end up trapped or dead. In New Mexico, 83 bears have been killed so far this year, more than three times as many as last year...'They're going to be searching for food,' said Rich Beausoleil, bear and cougar specialist at the Washington Department of Fish and Wildlife" (*The Associated Press*).

The same pattern is being found in a number of species looking for food where people live. Newly very aggressive wild turkeys are returning to suburban and urban areas where they had long ago been eliminated by hunting. They are now feeding at backyard bird feeders and municipal trash cans.

Urban deer hunts are becoming increasingly common, as overpopulated does and bucks graze in backyard gardens—eating food that would have gone to people!

Elsewhere, alligators are ranging far beyond their normal habitats near the Gulf of Mexico. In the space of two days, these dangerous reptiles have been found in New York, Massachusetts and Illinois. Animal control officials captured an 18-inch-long baby alligator on the streets of Queens, New York. On the same day, in a Boston suburb, a three-foot gator was caught, and the next day, another of roughly the same size was reportedly seen in the Chicago River. Experts say that unknown numbers of alligators and snakes now reside in the sewer systems of America's great cities, having been flushed down the toilet when they grew too big.

Next is a look at the insect kingdom: "Some ants find urban life so accommodating that their populations explode and they form supercolonies in cities.

"Grzegorz Buczkowski, a Purdue University research assistant professor of entomology, found that odorous house ant colonies become larger and more complex as they move from forest to city and act somewhat like an invasive species...The ants live about 50 to a colony with one queen in forest settings but explode into supercolonies with more than 6 million workers and 50,000 queens in urban areas...

"'Native ants are not supposed to become invasive. We don't know of any other native ants that are outcompeting other species of native ants like these...It's possible that as the ants get closer to urban areas they have easier access to food, shelter and other resources,' he said" (*National Geographic*).

This little understood—and little thought about—side effect of food shortage will bring additional strain on urban existence, forcing city dwellers to spend energy and resources trying to defend their homes and food supplies from invading animals!

Coming Locust Plagues

But these local invasions are barely more than anecdotal sidenotes compared to how God declares that He will use *locusts*. He warned Israel, beginning long ago, of this instrument of punishment.

First notice this passage from Deuteronomy: "You shall carry much seed out into the field, and shall gather but *little in*; for the *locust* shall consume it...*All* your trees and fruit of your land shall the locust consume" (28:38, 42).

The book of Joel in chapter 2 calls hordes of locusts a "great army" sent by God (vs. 25). The previous chapter describes *successive waves* of crop destruction wrought by this "army": "That which the *palmerworm* has left has the *locust* eaten; and that which the locust has left has the *cankerworm* eaten; and that which the cankerworm has left has the *caterpiller* eaten" (1:4).

The original words for the insects referenced in this passage present a truly sobering picture. They speak to the sense in Hebrew of "devouring," "chewing" and "cutting down" plants. They also involve "swarming," "ravaging," "lapping up," "licking" and finally the "finishing" of crops and other green plants.

Next look at the connection of these insects to famine, along with disease: "*If* there be in the land famine, *if* there be pestilence, blasting, mildew, locust, or *if* there be caterpiller [Hebrew: ravager]; *if* their enemy besiege them in the land of their cities; whatsoever plague, whatsoever sickness there be..." (I Kings 8:37).

This passage is part of a longer prophecy that describes how "if" a series of certain punishments are sent, God will pull back the punishment "if" the nation comes to repentance. While prophecy indicates that the nations today, or even one nation, will almost certainly not repent, *individuals* can.

Some nations are already seeing the front edge of these verses coming to pass. In 2010, the possible largest ever recorded locust infestation is threatening to sweep across Australia's croplands like a hailstorm. It is projected to devastate tens of thousands of acres and cost farmers millions of dollars. The quick-breeding locusts, which multiply after periods of severe drought followed by intense rains, have stripped clean crops, pastures, orchards, gardens and sports fields from Queensland (northeast Australia) to Melbourne (the far south) and Adelaide (in the center).

"You've got to see it to believe it," an owner of one of Australia's largest carrot producers told *The Age*. "One centre pivot [plantation] got destroyed completely. We had about 25 million carrots in there. That gives you an idea of how many locusts there are."

Some single swarms cover areas as much as 186 square miles. These highly mobile insects can travel over 300 miles in one day in search of food. According to the Australian Plague Locust Commission (APLC), a *small* swarm of just 0.4 square miles can contain over 50 million locusts with the ability to devour 11 tons of forage in a 24-hour period.

The Independent reported, "A one-kilometre wide swarm of locusts can chomp through 10 tons of crops—a third of their combined body weight—in a day. The New South Wales Farmers Association said an area the size of Spain was affected and the Government of Victoria alone forecasts [$1.95 billion] of damage.

"Though locusts move slowly when the sun's up, at night they can fly high and fast, sometimes travelling hundreds of kilometres." One professor said this: "'A farmer can go to bed at night not having seen a grasshopper all year and wake up in the morning to find his fields full of them.'"

"The warm, wet weather that prevailed last summer meant that *three generations* of locusts were born, each one up to *150 times larger* than the previous generation" (emphasis mine).

This is one of many points in the book when the serious reader must make himself *stop* in order to ponder the sheer power of such statements!

Loss of Pollinating Insects

While an explosion of locusts has terrible implications for crop yields, elsewhere, ironically, a *shortage* of insects will lead to similar results.

A September 2010 *BBC News* article explained another very ominous trend. Here is a series of quotes from the article: "A decline in pollinating insects in India [1.1 billion people] is resulting in reduced vegetable yields and could limit people's access to a nutritional diet, a study warns...Each year, India produces about 7.5 million tonnes of vegetables. This accounts for about 14% of the global total, making the nation second only to China in the world's vegetable production league table."

"The UN Food and Agriculture Organization (FAO) estimates that of the slightly more than 100 crop species that provide 90% of food supplies for 146 countries, 71 are bee-pollinated, primarily by wild bees, and a number of others are pollinated by other insects."

"In a 2007 assessment of the scientific data on the issue, the UN Environment Programme observed: 'Any loss in biodiversity is a matter of public concern, but losses of pollinating insects may be particularly troublesome because of the potential effects on plant reproduction and hence on food supply security.'"

"In 2007, about one third of the US domesticated bee population was wiped out as a result of a phenomenon known as Colony Collapse Disorder (CCD), with some commercial hive owners losing up to 90% of their bees."

Other population drops among the natural predators of *bad* insects are also disrupting the fragile balance necessary for crop production. The *Associated Press* reported, "A fungus has killed off about 90 percent of [New Jersey's] bat population, according to scientists who recently conducted a count of hibernating bats...[It is] linked to the deaths of more than a million bats in 11 states...and has also spread to Ontario, Canada."

"Experts warn that the widespread loss of bats has potential ramifications for humans, since bats consume huge quantities of bugs, including insects that damage crops or carry West Nile and other potentially fatal diseases."

Some kinds of bats also play a role in *pollination* similar to that of bees. If the fungus spreads, crop losses increase.

Hunger's Psychological Effects

Again, realize that famine is coming regardless of where you live! And starvation always brings with it the darkest, most unthinkable conduct known to man. This is the true face of hunger.

History has repeatedly demonstrated a change in society when famine takes hold. As you read, do not let these words be distant. Make each one real in your mind!

Before the Irish Potato Famine, Ireland was pressing for greater self-rule, with half of its people living in poverty, surviving solely on the yearly potato crop. Then in 1845, a disease that thrived in Ireland's wet climate destroyed that year's harvest. Half of the population hovered on the brink of starvation. The blight continued for two more years. In the end, *one million* died from lack of food or ensuing disease.

Upon hearing reports, some of the British believed the Irish were exaggerating the dire conditions and refused to send sufficient aid. As the famine worsened, another million Irish fled, migrating to North America. Many, weakened by hunger, died en route.

In six years, the population dropped by two million. The number of Irish, prior to the famine, was about 8 million, compared to approximately 15 million on the British mainland. Ireland has *never recovered.* The current population of the north and south combined is still *less than* 8 million—compared to about 60 million on the British mainland, a 300 percent increase.

But the potato famine also exemplifies hunger's *psychological* effects. When a brain is deprived of nutrients, coupled with the mental and emotional stresses of famine, a change comes over the individual's personality.

In her book *Famine: The Irish Experience*, E. Margaret Crawford describes what characteristics first present themselves: "apathy, depression, and mental restlessness." In addition, "food becomes an obsession."

The book quotes Dr. Daniel Donovan, who worked with 1845 Irish Potato Famine victims: "I have seen mothers snatch food from the hands of their starving children; known a son to engage in a fatal struggle with his father for a potato; and have seen parents look on the putrid bodies of their offspring without evincing a symptom of sorrow."

Severe hunger quickly leads to the unthinkable. During famine, victims often eat human waste out of desperation. (Ezekiel 4:12-13 declares this will again happen!)

Severe famine leads to even more horrific conditions. God foretells through Ezekiel in the bluntest of terms: "The fathers *shall eat the sons* in the midst of you, and the sons *shall eat their fathers*" (5:10). Hunger quickly turns to violence—and cannibalism!

Though it seems unbelievable, the record of history proves that when hungry enough, people will eat the dead. The book *Flesh and Blood: A History of the Cannibal Complex* details an AD 1200 famine in Egypt: "'There was no longer any hope that the Nile would rise; and as a result the cost of provisions had already gone up...A vast multitude sought refuge in Misr and Cairo, where they were to meet with frightful famine and appalling mortality…and pestilence and a deadly contagion began to take their toll, and the poor, under the pressure of ever-growing want, ate carrion, corpses, dogs, excrement, and animal dung. They went further, and reached the stage of eating little children…roasted or boiled.'"

Notice again what God explains is the end result of famine, always brought on by disobedience to His Law: "And when I have broken the staff of your bread, ten women shall bake your bread in one oven, and they shall deliver you your bread again *by weight*: and you shall eat, and not be satisfied…you *shall eat the flesh of your sons*, and the flesh of *your daughters shall you eat*" (Lev. 26:26, 29).

Those who are convinced that people could never sink to such depths will find their thinking changes—and in chilling fashion. What comes next is even worse, and it is what *God* says will happen: "And you shall eat the fruit of your own body, the flesh of your sons and of your daughters... The *tender* and *delicate* woman among you [the refined and sophisticated woman], which would not adventure to set the sole of her foot upon the ground for delicateness and tenderness, her eye shall be evil toward the husband of her bosom, and toward her son, and toward her daughter, and toward her young one that comes out from between her feet, and toward her children which she shall bear: for she shall eat them for want [lack] of all things..." (Deut. 28:53, 56-57).

God brings more graphic detail of the desperation—and ensuing action—brought by extreme hunger in the book of Lamentations, recorded by Jeremiah. Having recorded what is to come in multiple passages and in multiple books of the Bible, God wants these prophecies *understood*, leaving those who have been warned *without excuse*.

God first indicts cold-blooded parents for *withholding* food from their starving children. Notice: "Even the sea monsters draw out the breast, they give suck to their young ones: the daughter of My people is become cruel, like the ostriches in the wilderness. The tongue of the sucking child cleaves to the roof of his mouth for thirst: the young children ask bread, and no man breaks it unto them" (Lam. 4:3-4).

The prophecy continues, now including young, middle-aged and old alike: "They that did feed delicately are desolate in the streets: they that were brought up in scarlet [think the privileged nations of the West] embrace *dunghills*. For the punishment of the iniquity of the daughter of My people is greater than the punishment of the sin of Sodom, that was overthrown as in a moment, and no hands stayed on her" (vs. 5-6).

Understand! This punishment is *far worse* than the hail of fire that quickly destroyed the city of Sodom—"that was overthrown as in a moment." This death is slow and painful—allowing victims to contemplate their horrible state of affairs.

Verses 7-9 drive this home, speaking of those who were once "purer than snow...whiter than milk...more ruddy in body than rubies, their polishing was of sapphire," but whose appearance transforms to an awful condition en route to agonizing death by famine: "Their visage is blacker than a coal; they are not known in the streets: their skin cleaves to their bones; it is withered, it is become like a stick. They that be slain with the sword are better than they that be slain with hunger: for these pine away, stricken through [this death is *slow*—prolonged] for want of the fruits of the field."

The account ends with the same cannibalism described elsewhere: "The hands of the pitiful women have sodden their own children: they were their meat in the destruction of the daughter of My people" (vs. 10).

Do not easily dismiss such prophecies as describing things that cannot happen, or at least not today, in our modern civilization. In times of war and famine, people *invariably* return to the horror of cannibalism. Trapped without food for an extended period, almost *everyone* will resort to such behavior given the opportunity. Many will even kill *living* people to defeat hunger.

I have talked to American prisoners of war from World War II—who were interned in both Europe and Asia. They reported to me that *without hesitation* Allied prisoners would eat their fellow soldiers the moment they died. Their descriptions were too graphic for this book.

What Will Come!

Additional historical examples create a fuller picture of what is to come—bringing to life Bible passages that warn of looming mass starvation:

Germany: During the Thirty Years' War in central Europe, famine struck. "By 1630, western and eastern Germany and nearby lands had been embroiled in 10 years' fighting...Famine and pestilence had cut [Germany's] population from some 70000 to only 16000. People had survived by eating rats and chewing hides; in one reported case a woman dined upon a soldier who had perished in her home" (*Catastrophe and Crisis*, Jeremy Kingston and David Lambert).

The Soviet Union: The following quote, describing Ukranian children in the early 1930s, helps present the horrible picture of starvation: "And the peasant children! Have you ever seen the newspaper photographs of the children in the German camps? They were just like that: their heads like heavy balls on thin little necks...one could see each bone of their arms and legs protruding from beneath the skin, how bones joined, and the entire skeleton was stretched over with skin that was like yellow gauze...the children's faces were aged, tormented, just as if they were seventy years old" (*Forever Flowing*, Vasily Grossman, pp. 156-157).

Also, after the German army invaded the USSR during World War II, it quickly encircled Leningrad, beginning a 900-day siege of the city. In the end, about one million died. The conditions of the city during the blockade show how quickly human conduct can shift during famine.

In his book *The 900 Days: The Siege of Leningrad*, Harrison Salisbury pieced together the accounts of those who lived during the Nazi siege. He states: "More and more, Leningrad seemed to its residents to have become the city of the white apocalypse where humans fed on humans and the very water which they drank carried the sweet stench of human corpses." Because of all the bodies being dumped into the rivers and canals, the water tasted "faintly sweet, faintly moldy, tainted with the presence of death."

Ancient Israel: Flavius Josephus describes an account of Jerusalem when it was under siege by the Romans in the first century. From Josephus' *The Wars of the Jews* comes this: "Now, of those that perished by famine in the city, the number was prodigious; and the miseries they underwent were unspeakable..." The account describes the dearest friends fighting over scraps of food. Even while people lay dying of starvation, thieves would search them to be sure they were not feigning death, hiding food in their clothing.

Josephus describes, "These robbers...gaped for want, and ran about stumbling and staggering along like mad dogs, and reeling against the doors of the houses like drunken men; they would also, in the great distress they were in, rush into the very same houses two or three times in one and the same day. Moreover, their hunger was so intolerable, that it obliged them to chew every thing, while they gathered such things as the most sordid animals would not touch, and endured to eat them; nor did they at length abstain from girdles and shoes, and the very leather which belonged to their shields they pulled off and gnawed: the very wisps of old hay became food to some..."

Worse, he describes, "a certain woman that dwelt beyond Jordan; her name was Mary" who was trapped in the city. After it was "impossible for her any way to find any more food" and "famine pierced through her very bowels and marrow...She then attempted a most unnatural thing, and, snatching up her son, who was a child sucking at her breast, she said, 'O thou miserable infant. For whom shall I preserve thee in this war, this famine, and this sedition? As to the war with the Romans, if they preserve our lives, we must be slaves. This famine also will destroy us even before that slavery comes upon us…Come on; be thou my food, and be thou a fury to these seditious varlets, and a byword to the world, which is all that is now wanting to complete the calamities of us Jews.'

"As soon as she had said this, she slew her son, and then roasted him, and ate the one half of him, and kept the other half by her concealed."

These horrific events are in the past, but they are at the same time a sobering glimpse of things to happen again. God paints a powerful picture of the coming famine—and of which nations will suffer the most.

Famine Like No Other

God declares that He "will make you [the American and British peoples] *waste*, and a *reproach* among the nations that are round about you, in the sight of all that pass by" (Ezek. 5:14). What should this startling punishment mean to the rest of the world?

First let's read more: "When I shall send upon them the evil arrows of *famine*, which shall be for their destruction, and which I will send to destroy you: and I will increase the famine upon you, and will break your staff of bread: so will I send upon you *famine*…I the LORD have spoken it" (vs. 16-17).

Make yourself understand that these are things God says HE will do. Notice how many times God uses the word "I" to declare what HE will bring to pass. This is another moment in the book where the reader is left to decide whether he believes God.

As the black horse and rider of famine intensifies, drastic changes will come to an interconnected modern world. No more will there be vast exports to other nations. No more will supermarket shelves brim with abundance. No more will wealthy nations be able to assist countries stricken with drought and famine.

These will all be replaced by daily ration lines, starving men, women and children scouring garbage heaps for meager scraps of food, while infants die from malnourishment.

Worse, it will pit parents against children for food, with hunger also driving people to eat the unthinkable. It means repeating horrors from history a *final* time—for the *worst* time ever.

This is not my opinion—it is straight from your Bible!

The white horse of false Christianity gives rise to war, which invites famine. When starvation ravages millions of human bodies, the result is always the same…

The Pale Horse—Pestilence

Disease, in all its forms, is loathsome to every human being. It has brought untold suffering for millennia to billions of people—many of whom never saw it coming.

Disease epidemics—rapid, widespread outbreaks among many thousands or millions of people—often strike suddenly. Before authorities can react, the damage has been done. Such has been the case all through history.

Of the 59 million people who die each year, approximately half—nearly 30 million—perish from sickness. The world loses the rough equivalent of one nation of Canada every year to disease.

And it is about to get MUCH worse!

Disease will soon alter the course of history in a profound way. The coming disease *pandemics* will dwarf all that have previously occurred. Hundreds of millions will perish—and this will not only happen in poor, underdeveloped countries. Horrific epidemics, the likes of which have never been seen, will strike the world's wealthiest nations—which will collapse from the impact. The ensuing chaos will affect you, and all of your loved ones. *Everything* around you will change for the worse. *Your* life will be at risk.

The Last Horseman

The fourth and last horse and rider now enter the picture—PESTILENCE! The final horseman carries a different, broader description, and summarizes the horses riding together: "I looked, and behold A PALE HORSE: and his name that sat on him was Death, and Hell followed with him. And power was given unto them over the fourth part of the earth, to kill with sword, and with hunger, and with death, and with the beasts of the earth" (Rev. 6:8).

The word "pale" comes from the Greek word *chloros*, which indicates the sickly, pale yellow-green color of disease—from which derives the name of yellow chlorine gas.

Coming on the heels of the first three horsemen, the pale horseman's arrival portends that more hundreds of millions will perish through terrifying disease epidemics. The reference to "Death"—the end result of disease—and "Hell"—*hades*, meaning the grave—make this clear.

This prospect may seem impossible to believe in this sophisticated modern age—where air travel has allowed man to run "to and fro" across the earth without boundaries (Dan. 12:4)—where the tallest building is nearly half a mile high—and where the Internet has created a global village, connecting every corner of the earth.

This is, however, also a time in which men's bodies have degenerated through thousands of years of abuse—where "super-diseases" now resist even the strongest antibiotics—and where doctors and scientists no longer speak of *if* a pandemic is coming, but *when*.

Growing Threats

As modern medicine seeks to conquer disease, civilization is falling further and further behind. Man and his governments have lost control.

Understand. As new diseases emerge and older ones suddenly mutate, modern medicine has fallen far behind in the effort to eradicate them. Today, diseases thought long ago conquered are back with a vengeance. Tuberculosis, cholera and other deadly scourges from the past have reemerged—this time much more resistant to standard treatments. This, coupled with poor sanitation, war, overcrowding and poverty, is creating environments ripe for the *massive* spread of sickness.

At the same time, the world has become more interconnected than at any other time in history. The advent of relatively cheap and fast air travel means that more people now travel abroad. More now also travel for vacations and business—increasing their chances of being infected by foreign viruses, or carrying one with them to others. According to noted Swedish pathologist Folke Henschen, "Infectious diseases...have probably been the most dangerous enemies of mankind, much more so than war." The global threat posed by infectious diseases has never been greater.

Despite man's best efforts, old scourges such as tuberculosis, cholera, dysentery, typhoid, anthrax and malaria are still very much alive. Add to this the more recent arrivals of Ebola, hantavirus, E. coli, salmonella (currently spreading very quickly), HIV, West Nile and swine flu. Understand that these are just a few of the possible disease epidemics— or pandemics—on the horizon.

To appreciate the potential impact of any one of these, consider HIV. Over 30 million people in the world are HIV positive—and millions more contract the virus every year. To date, more than 25 million have died from AIDS—which originates from HIV—with the prospect of millions more a virtual certainty. Not surprisingly, AIDS has been called "a viral nightmare that ravages all nations and threatens the very existence of our species" (*Killer Germs: Microbes and Diseases that Threaten Humanity*, Barry E. Zimmerman and David J. Zimmerman).

Now add the threats of biological warfare and bio-terrorism. The prospect of these occurring is simply too horrifying to contemplate. Yet it is very real. Recall that in 2001, multiple cases of anthrax broke out in the U.S. when letters laced with anthrax were sent to news media outlets and congressional offices. The event, widely thought to be an attack by a foreign terrorist, created havoc nationwide.

With all of the biological agents, biological weapons, and terrorists, with their networks in circulation today, the danger of an intentional biological attack is a very real threat. Here, the red and pale horses ride together.

On top of ever-worsening disease epidemics, the world's resources—including clean air, water and food—are also being stretched to the limit. Wars between desperate countries competing for scarce resources are increasing, both in scope and intensity. War leads to famine, which ultimately results in disease.

Worse Than Ever?

This begs the question: Has it *always* been this way—or has there been an escalation in the number of disease outbreaks now widespread across the globe?

Health authorities acknowledge that an acceleration is underway—especially within the last 50 years.

According to a study published in the *Journal of the American Medical Association*, death rates from infectious diseases are rising. The U.S. Centers for Disease Control and Prevention (CDC) recognizes the threat, stating that "we continue to confront new and potentially devastating infectious disease threats." It has also noted that the threat of an influenza pandemic is "as high as before." The European Society of Clinical Microbiology and Infectious Diseases has also affirmed that infectious diseases are an increasing threat to public health.

Indeed, in the United States, infectious diseases rose by nearly 60 percent from 1980 to 1992 and continue to be one of the leading causes of death in this country. According to leading microbiologist Alexander Tomasz, the onset of an era in which antibiotics are useless would be "nothing short of a medical disaster."

There are further ominous signs of the peril to come. One-third of the world's population is currently infected by the germs (bacilli) that cause tuberculosis, and new infections are occurring at the rate of one per second! AIDS is devastating entire regions in sub-Saharan Africa and is spreading rapidly around the world. And AIDS and tuberculosis have linked up, becoming tandem infections, with greater devastating effect.

Scientists estimate that around two billion people, 30 percent of the world's population, have a form of Staphylococcus aureus. And up to 53 million worldwide are thought to be carrying the deadly superbug methicillin-resistant Staphylococcus aureus (MRSA – pronounced "Mersa"). They say these strains could "potentially become explosive" in hospitals.

In the United States, outbreaks of waterborne diseases are increasing. Globally, rates of diseases like dengue fever are growing. Outbreaks of insect-transmitted diseases like Chikungunya fever are occurring in unexpected locations and are now a threat to even the U.S.

Diseases long thought conquered are proving more difficult to treat. This is true of a new more lethal form of C. difficile, which is more resistant to drug treatments and can cause a potentially fatal strain of diarrhea. This is but the briefest of glances at the growing predicament facing the world.

How Did We Get Here?

Man has battled disease for as long as there has been civilization. Soon after Creation, human beings encountered microbes that infected their drinking water, food and environment.

As men built cities and began to live in more confined spaces, the risk of outbreaks increased. One of the earliest-known diseases was tuberculosis. Spread from person to person through the air, tuberculosis was even found in ancient Egypt.

As trade between nations increased, diseases often proliferated along commercial routes. The impact on those who had not previously known such diseases was disastrous. Illnesses such as influenza and the bubonic plague, which spread from Asia to Europe, were two such examples, as was cholera, an intestinal disease believed to have originated in India. After cholera's inception, millions died, and the disease went on to spread across the Middle East, Europe, China, North Africa and Japan. Eventually, it even reached as far as England and the United States.

During the Age of Exploration in the fifteenth, sixteenth and seventeenth centuries, advances in shipbuilding and navigation made it possible for explorers to visit foreign lands and develop new territories. This also contributed to the spread of various diseases. One of the most deadly of these was smallpox, which killed perhaps as many as 5 million people worldwide from AD 165 to 180 in the Antonine Plague, with as many as 5,000 per day purportedly dying in Rome alone.

When Europeans arrived in the New World in the fifteenth century, they unwittingly brought smallpox with them. This and other diseases wiped out up to 90 to 95 percent of the indigenous native population.

Despite the development of vaccines, smallpox killed between 300 and 500 million people during the twentieth century alone. Consider. Far more were killed by just this disease than by the gun!

Another of the oldest-known diseases still taking a tremendous toll today is malaria. Carried by mosquitoes, malaria was mentioned in ancient Chinese and Egyptian writings as far back as 4,000 years ago, with the Greeks also describing its devastating effects. Malaria is also thought to have been a factor in the fall of the Roman Empire.

But God never intended for man to live this way, stating in III John 2, "I wish above all things that you may prosper and be in health, even as your soul prospers." Recall that, after creating Adam and Eve, He said that all of His Creation was "very good" (Gen. 1:31). This leaves no room for God having placed hidden, inactive viruses and bacteria within their bodies, waiting for the right moment to afflict them with horrible sickness and disease of every kind. Man did this to himself—inviting disease as the natural consequence of broken laws.

All man's efforts to cure diabetes, arthritis, cancer, heart disease, blindness, deafness, Alzheimer's (and other diseases of the mind), strokes, AIDS, and a host of infant and childhood diseases have failed. Add to this the ongoing quest for new wonder drugs, treatments, specialized diagnoses, surgeries and procedures, breakthroughs in technology—and every other

kind of medical advancement thus far. Again, all efforts have ultimately
failed!

A Present Crisis

Hardly a week goes by without reports of another disease outbreak
somewhere in the world. News headlines such as the following are
commonplace: "Rift Valley Fever Hits South Africa," "New Strains of
Lyme Disease Bacteria Identified, Study Claims," "AIDS Remains the
World's Worst Epidemic," "Dengue Fever Surges in the Americas."

Officials worldwide are now reporting the resurgence of dengue fever. Once a rare disease, it is spreading around the world at an alarming
rate. So much so that it has become a major international public health
concern. In fact, dengue is a leading cause of hospitalization and death of
children in many countries.

The potential for disaster is immense, with *2.5 billion people* living
in areas where this virus has been transmitted. In fact, an additional 50
to 100 million are already known to be infected by dengue every year.
Although it is not yet the fatal hemorrhagic strain, once the disease enters
the pandemic level—and there is every indication this could happen—
there is greatly increased potential for it to mutate in this direction.

It is now even affecting the U.S., which has never seen such a surge.
In the past, dengue had always remained outside American borders. But
in the last few years, it has slowly been migrating north, and is now found
across Central America and some American border states. According to
health authorities, dengue cases in the Americas have increased almost
fivefold over the past 30 years, skyrocketing from 2.7 million cases in the
1990s to 4.8 million between the years 2000 and 2007.

This has alarmed authorities on the Texas border, who have also seen
a higher number of cases, as has Florida. Puerto Rico also has been suffering, and has now declared a dengue fever epidemic.

Dengue fever is just one of dozens of diseases that health authorities
report are increasing! These and other rapidly spreading illnesses paint
a grisly picture! Even more dangerous diseases lurk in the shadows. Yet,
with dwindling numbers of doctors and nurses entering the medical pro-
fession, there is even greater heightened alarm about the nation's ability
to combat them.

The Wall Street Journal reported, "Experts warn there won't be
enough doctors to treat the millions of people newly insured under the
[universal healthcare] law. At current graduation and training rates, the

[U.S.] could face a shortage of as many as 150,000 doctors in the next 15 years, according to the Association of American Medical Colleges."

Compounding the problem, widespread wars have resulted in influxes of thousands into refugees camps, most of which feature conditions that can only be described as absolute squalor—fertile breeding grounds for disease.

Then there are the polluted overcrowded cities, which often result in contaminated water—which is drunk by most residents. The United Nations estimates that more than half of all hospitalizations are as a result of people not having access to clean water.

Children are among those most affected. According to the United Nations Children's Fund, of the estimated 6.8 billion people on Earth, 2.6 billion—almost 40 percent—"live without access to even a toilet at home and thus are vulnerable to a range of health risks." This lack of access to proper sanitation, including clean water, "is a major cause of diarrhoea, the second biggest killer of children in developing countries, and leads to other major diseases such as cholera, schistosomiasis, and trachoma."

Add to this rampant immorality, which has caused an explosion of sexually transmitted diseases, with a host of devastating effects.

As an example of an unprecedented catastrophe still unfolding as of this writing, monsoon rains left 20 percent of Pakistan underwater in the summer of 2010—an area larger than the entire nation of England. Some areas by then had already received *180 percent* of the normal precipitation for the whole season. Twenty million Pakistanis have lost their homes, with 3.5 million children at severe risk of infection by cholera and other rapidly spreading diseases. Millions face starvation.

Aside from the flooding, the situation is worsened by a slow dispatch of international aid, due to the global economic downturn and the way the crisis has intensified gradually, rather than arriving in a single dramatic event such as an earthquake or a tsunami. Add to this an already fragile government being further destabilized, with opportunistic terrorist groups, as well as the Pakistani military, taking advantage of the situation and compounding the mayhem.

How Soon?

So obviously this world is in serious trouble. Mankind is teetering on the edge of global disease catastrophe!

Although skeptics say that great global pandemics could not happen again because of improved hygiene and sterilization, this is wishful thinking. Some bacteria have become resistant to antibacterial soaps, and now need stronger and stronger chemicals to kill them. Then there are others that scientists are not able to conquer at all.

Because of this and other factors, epidemiologists and infectious disease experts report that the threat from infectious diseases is increasing: "Infectious disease clearly represents a threat to human security in that it has the potential to affect both the person and his or her ability to pursue life, liberty, and happiness," a Rand Corporation study stated. It added, "In addition to threatening the health of an individual, the spread of disease can weaken public confidence in government's ability to respond, have an adverse economic impact, undermine a state's social order, catalyze regional instability, and pose a strategic threat through bioterrorism and/or biowarfare."

This prominent research company went on to outline the enormity of the problem facing the world. Consider this: "...The magnitude and nature of the threat is growing because of the emergence of new illnesses such as Acquired Immune Deficiency Syndrome (AIDS), Ebola, and hepatitis C; the increasing inability of modern medicine to respond to resistant and emerging pathogens; and the growing threat of bioterrorism and biowarfare. In addition, human actions amplify these trends by putting us in ever-greater contact with deadly microbes. Globalization, modern medical practices, urbanization, climatic change, and changing social and behavioral patterns all serve to increase the chance that individuals will come in contact with diseases, which they may not be able to survive.

"The AIDS crisis in South Africa provides a disturbing example of how a pathogen can affect security at all levels, from individual to regional and even to global. Approximately one-quarter of the adult population in South Africa is Human Immunodeficiency Virus (HIV) positive, with the disproportionate burden of illness traditionally falling on the most economically and personally productive segment of society. The true impact of the AIDS epidemic is yet to be felt. Deaths from full-blown AIDS are not projected to peak until the period between 2009 and 2012, and the number of HIV infections is still increasing."

Significantly worsening *pestilence*—disease *epidemics*—are yet another confirmation that the "end of the age" is upon us.

H1N1

For the first time in nearly a century, widespread disease epidemics are once again knocking at the doors of America and Europe, as was evidenced by the 2009 swine flu outbreak.

According to one epidemiologist, influenza is the biggest infectious disease threat in the world at this time.

An August 2009 report for the United States President affirmed the expert's predictions. According to statistics, just this disease alone could infect 30 to 50 percent of the U.S. population—about 90 to 150 million. Authorities reported the H1N1 strain could also:

• Cause 1.8 million U.S. hospital admissions during an epidemic, with up to 300,000 patients requiring treatment from intensive care units.

• Kill 30,000 to 90,000 in the United States in a typical winter flu season, concentrated among children and young adults.

• "Pose especially high risks for individuals with certain pre-existing conditions, including pregnant women and patients with neurological disorders or respiratory impairment, diabetes, or severe obesity and possibly for certain populations, such as Native Americans."

Reports from the first wave of the H1N1 pandemic revealed that a number of hospitals were swamped with patients in need of emergency care.

On average, swine flu victims required "12 days of mechanical ventilation and frequent use of rescue therapies such as high-frequency oscillatory ventilation, prone positioning, neuromuscular blockade, and inhaled nitric oxide" (*Journal of the American Medical Association*).

Think! What would happen if 90,000 Americans required the same treatments—just for this type of influenza—living their last days in hospitals? U.S. hospitals would be unable to keep up with the long lines of patients that would be knocking on their doors.

Cases in Britain doubled to 100,000 in *one week* in July 2009! The virus has had such a significant impact on the country that within minutes of opening, the National Pandemic Flu service website crashed.

Yet the initial estimated figures failed to come to pass. Due to this, many people have already forgotten about the potential death toll.

Still, H1N1 continued to spread. A map of infected areas shows that cases have stricken almost all corners of the world. So far, the only places where H1N1 has not been confirmed are Greenland, Uzbekistan and Turkmenistan, and several smaller African nations.

"Dr Alan Hay, director of the London-based World Influenza Centre, said the extensive summer outbreak in Britain had not followed expected patterns and warned the Department of Health needed to be prepared for a more deadly form of the disease" (*Guardian*).

Public health professor Dr. John Powell added, "There are enormous parallels with 1918 and our current pandemic. They are spreading at a similar rate, but we don't know if the virus will mutate. If it does, this is when it could become very dangerous" (*Daily Mail*).

To many, these numbers seem impossible—*up to 90,000 Americans dead in under a year*? Those below age 50 have never experienced even the *possibility* of a pandemic so devastating. Typically, about 40,000 die of *all forms* of the flu in the U.S. for a *whole year*.

Without firsthand experience of a nationwide disease pandemic, many can only look to history to understand the type of disease prophesied to come upon the world—and especially the modern nations of Israel—in their lifetime.

For perspective, we turn to the worst recorded flu pandemic of all time: the 1918 Spanish flu outbreak. Up to 675,000 in the U.S. were killed—along with between 40 and 100 million worldwide.

What Past Pandemics Reveal

Past pandemics demonstrated an ability to strike quickly—almost literally overnight—overwhelming medical services. Such was the 1918 Spanish Influenza.

This early twentieth-century pandemic started much the same as the one in 2009. Three years before the 1918 virus took its worst toll, it first surfaced in birds, according to the CDC.

From 1915 to 1916, the United States suffered a catastrophic respiratory disease epidemic, which significantly increased the death toll resulting from pneumonia and influenza complications. Although mortality rates decreased by 1917, the populace's weakened immune systems paved the way for the pandemic's first wave in March 1918.

The pandemic continued in three stages over a 12-month period: the first wave reached Europe, the U.S. and Asia in late spring and summer; a second—and more deadly—strain appeared approximately six months later, wiping out *entire families* from September to November 1918; and a third wave struck in the early spring of 1919.

Unlike most viruses, which normally affect the very young, the weak and the elderly, the 1918 influenza targeted *healthy* adults between the ages of 20 and 40. Victims suffocated as their immune systems broke down, filling their lungs with a reddish liquid, which often bubbled out of them as they died.

In 1918, many churches in America closed, schools also closed, the government banned public meetings, businesses collapsed from lack of customers, state institutions became overrun with orphaned children, and infected postal carriers were unable to deliver mail. Heaps of rancid garbage lined city streets. Decomposing bodies overflowed from morgues and had to be stored in nearby elementary schools. Wherever people ventured, the smell of rotting flesh haunted them.

Imagine this and the following horrific scenarios playing out *today*— unfolding on the very streets of your hometown. Imagine the disease taking someone close to you—an acquaintance, co-worker, friend or family member.

A letter written by a military doctor on September 29, 1918, described the dreadful conditions at Fort Devens, near Boston: "These men start with what appears to be an attack of la grippe or influenza, and when brought to the hospital they very rapidly develop the most viscous type of pneumonia that has ever been seen. Two hours after admission they have the mahogany spots over the cheek bones, and a few hours later you can begin to see the cyanosis extending from their ears and spreading all over the face, until it is hard to distinguish the coloured men from the white. It is only a matter of a few hours then until death comes, and it is simply a struggle for air until they suffocate."

Later he wrote, "It takes special trains to carry away the dead. For several days there were no coffins and the bodies piled up something fierce, we used to go down to the morgue...and look at the boys laid out in long rows. It beats any sight they ever had in France after a battle. An extra long barracks has been vacated for the use of the morgue, and it would make any man sit up and take notice to walk down the long lines of dead soldiers all dressed up and laid out in double rows" (*PBS*).

One pandemic survivor recounted the bodies that stacked up in Vancouver, Canada: "The undertaking parlours couldn't handle the bodies as people died...they were having to use school auditoriums and places like that to store bodies temporarily" (*The Canadian Press*).

In the book *Flu: The Story of the Great Influenza Pandemic of 1918 and the Search for the Virus That Caused It*, Gina Kolata, a reporter for *The New York Times*, stated that if the Spanish Influenza were to strike the U.S. now, it would have devastating results: "If such a plague came today, killing a similar fraction of the U.S. population, 1.5 million Americans would die, which is more than the number felled in a single year by heart disease, cancers, strokes, chronic pulmonary disease, AIDS, and Alzheimer's disease combined."

Most experts put this estimate much higher. Remember, these numbers are specific to a highly stable, First World nation. Imagine the multiple hundreds of millions who could die worldwide.

This pandemic—and the virus that caused it—is just one of many that have left their mark on society. Here is another.

The Black Death

You have probably heard that "The past is prologue." Pandemics of massive proportions can—and will—happen again.

One of the deadliest diseases in history was the Black Death—which reached virtually all parts of the world from AD 1347 to 1350. This pandemic was thought to be brought by the same bacteria that caused the bubonic plague! In Mediterranean Europe—including large countries such as Italy, France and Spain—between one-third and three-quarters of the population died. In China, one-third perished, as was also the case in the Middle East. Many, many nations were affected. The death toll worldwide was estimated at up to a staggering 200 million, or possibly half the world's population at the time. (This math will be revisited two chapters from now in a larger setting.) Europe's population alone took a century and a half—*150 years*!—to recover. Tremendous religious, social and economic upheavals were triggered, which had a profound impact on the course of world history.

Most are unaware that famine afflicted many areas of the world prior to the plague, and thus set it up. Also, extreme violence and truly bizarre behavior accompanied a general pandemonium in society that always surrounds widespread disease outbreaks. And scapegoats were needed. Jews and others were attacked. Thousands of Jews were burned at the stake—20,000 in just one city. It became every man for himself, including authority figures who almost all bailed out into isolation in the countryside. This included noblemen, generals, civil officials and even the pope.

All this from just *one* pandemic!

Although a number of theories exist regarding the Black Death, many medical historians believe it was the result of a combination of two deadly diseases: bubonic plague (spread by rats) and possibly anthrax (spread by cattle).

In his book, *In the Wake of the Plague: The Black Death and the World It Made*, author Norman F. Cantor explains in graphic detail how the plague affected individuals as it spread in three waves across the continent, similar to the Spanish Influenza: "All over Western Europe commoners were buried in mass graves with bodies stacked horizontally five layers deep. Archeologists have discovered such layered mass graves in many places, including central London. Since the earth covering the mass graves was thin, the stench rising from the cemeteries was initially unbearable."

Do not be lulled into thinking that such pestilence could not happen today. Jesus Christ said it will!

Graham Mooney of Johns Hopkins University told *The History Channel*, "There's absolutely no way that organized health systems could cope with an epidemic of the proportions of the black plague." Another disease expert stated that there is no medical "surge capacity" in society if something on this scale happens again.

Get this! This form of the plague is still alive and well in India and China—and in rodents throughout the American southwest now.

Another threat exists—as reported by *MSNBC*:

"American laboratories handling the world's deadliest germs and toxins have experienced more than 100 accidents and missing shipments since 2003, and the number is increasing steadily as more labs across the country are approved to do the work.

"No one died, and regulators said the public was never at risk during these incidents. But the documented cases reflect poorly on procedures and oversight at high-security labs, some of which work with organisms and poisons so dangerous that illnesses they cause have no cure."

Later, the article mentions several incidents in which scientists were either bitten by infected animals or exposed to deadly bacteria, including "an employee at the Lovelace Respiratory Research Institute [who] was bitten on the left hand by an infected monkey in September 2006. The animal was ill from an infection of bacteria that causes plague. 'When the gloves were removed, the skin appeared to be broken in 2 or 3 places,' the report said. The worker was referred to a doctor, but nothing more was disclosed."

Imagine what would happen if just one worker caught this deadly plague *unknowingly* and returned to his home. An entire neighborhood could quickly become infected—and wiped out!

Silent Carriers

One of the reasons certain diseases became so deadly in the past was their transmission by animals. Animal and insect-borne diseases have had a great impact on history. According to prominent Harvard bacteriologist Hans Zizsser, "Swords and lances, arrows, machine guns, and even high explosives have had far less power over the fates of the nations than the typhus louse, the plague flea, and the yellow-fever mosquito."

In the case of the Black Death, the main carriers were rats. In some cases fleas that came into contact with the rats also transferred it to human beings. In other cases, dogs began to eat infected people who could not be buried fast enough. They then passed the disease on to other human beings, continuing the fatal cycle. And house cats that became infected spread it to their owners by simple coughing when being held.

The idea of disease moving from animals to humans is not new. According to a joint United Nations-World Bank study, "an estimated 75 per cent of new human diseases originate in animals and an average of two new animal diseases with cross-over capabilities emerge every year."

The 1918 Spanish influenza originated in birds and then was transferred to pigs, as was the case with the swine flu, which killed 17,700 people in 2009.

In fact, dozens of diseases once only found in animals have infected humans during the past 20 years, with more soon expected to cross over. Examples (that are emerging or re-emerging) include HIV, hantavirus (from rodents), bird flu, rabies, malaria, West Nile virus (from mosquitoes), H1N1, SARS, and Lyme disease (from ticks).

United States Environmental Protection Agency (EPA) experts warn that a growing spread of diseases could result from environmental changes and more people moving into rural areas.

"We appear to be undergoing a distinct change in global disease ecology," Montira Pongsiri, an environmental health scientist at the EPA in Washington, told *The Independent*. "The recent emergence of infectious diseases [such as swine flu and SARS] appears to be driven by globalisation and ecological disruption."

David Murrell, lecturer in ecology at University College London, said scientists have identified a shocking pattern: "Since 1940, over 300 new diseases have been identified, 60 per cent of which crossed to humans from animals and 70 per cent of these came from contact with wildlife," he said. "I would expect the emergence of new diseases from contact with animals to continue in this century" (ibid.).

Think about the potential consequences, especially in cities where certain disease-carrying animals outnumber people! In Paris, for example, the population is over two million—yet the number of rats in its sewers is estimated at 8 million. How easy would it be for those living on the streets to contract any type of illness and then spread it?

The situation is much the same in New York City, where *The New York Times* reported that subway officials have been unable to control the pest population: "In the first study of its kind, officials scoured the city's subway system to discover what accounts for the perennial presence of rodents, a scourge since the system opened more than a century ago... Rodents, it turns out, reside inside station walls, emerging occasionally from cracks in the tile to rummage for food."

"Of 18 stations examined in Lower Manhattan, about half of the subway lines got a fair or poor rating for infestation, meaning they exhibited the telltale culprits—overflowing trash cans, too much track litter—that can lead to a rodent jamboree."

"[Rodentologist Robert M.] Corrigan told health officials that while rats were a problem in the subways, the rodents inhabited many other public spaces, particularly parks. 'Virtually all of New York,' he said, 'is vulnerable to this uncanny mammal.'"

Rats are of special concern to health officials, as they carry *40 different diseases*, some of which are fatal to humans!

The potential for disease is not only in rats, but also in birds, cows, pigs—and even in household pets! As the world grows more and more amoral, there has also been a resurgence in bestiality. Human diseases such as brucellosis have been thought to have originated this way. A 1948 study showed a stunning 8 percent of all males—almost one in 12!—reportedly engaged in sexual intercourse with an animal. In the over 60 years that have elapsed since, how much has this likely increased, especially when all mankind is now awash in every conceivable kind of sexual pleasure, fantasy, perversion and pursuit?

Best-selling author Jared Diamond summarizes the correlation effect between diseases and animals in his book *Guns, Germs, and Steel*: "The major killers of humanity throughout our recent history—smallpox, flu, tuberculosis, malaria, plague, measles, and cholera—are infectious diseases that evolved from diseases of animals, even though most of the microbes responsible for our own epidemic illnesses are paradoxically now almost confined to humans. Because diseases have been the biggest killers of people, they have also been decisive shapers of history. Until World War II, more victims of war died of war-borne microbes than of battle wounds...the winners of past wars were not always the armies with the best generals and weapons, but were often merely those bearing the nastiest germs to transmit to their enemies."

In fact, in perhaps the earliest use of bio-terrorism, invading Mongols catapulted the infected corpses of their dead fellow soldiers over city walls during sieges of European cities in order to spread the plague into the city.

Are Antibiotics the Answer?

In the modern age, people place great faith in the power of antibiotics to protect them from disease. However, many diseases are proving to be antibiotic-resistant. Antibiotics (any drug that either kills bacteria or hampers their growth) are no longer solving the problem as they once did.

Staph super germ MRSA successfully resisted the first new type of antibiotic in 35 years—a little more than just one year after it was introduced.

Penicillin and the more powerful drug vancomycin once easily controlled the staphylococcus bacteria. But staph has now transformed into a superbug, which in many instances now has the capability to resist penicillin and vancomycin. Thousands die each year in America from incurable hospital-acquired staph infections. Many now are those who have friends or family who have battled this scourge—some losing and some winning the battle.

A September 2010 *Associated Press* article reported, "An infectious-disease nightmare is unfolding: Bacteria that have been made resistant to nearly all antibiotics by an alarming new gene [in the bacteria] have sickened people in three states and are popping up all over the world, health officials reported...How many deaths the gene may have caused is unknown; there is no central tracking of such cases. So far, the gene has mostly been found in bacteria that cause gut or urinary infections. Scientists have long feared this—a very adaptable gene that hitches onto many types of common germs and confers broad drug resistance, creating dangerous 'superbugs.'

"'It's a great concern,' because drug resistance has been rising and few new antibiotics are in development, said Dr. M. Lindsay Grayson, director of infectious diseases at the University of Melbourne in Australia. 'It's just a matter of time' until the gene spreads more widely person-to-person..."

The article quoted microbiology professor Dr. Patrice Nordmann at South-Paris Medical School: "'The ingredients are there' for widespread transmission, he said. 'It's going to spread by plane all over the world.'"

Do you doubt this? Think. *500 million* people fly internationally every year. *70* million work outside their country.

What Went Wrong?

How did these near unstoppable bacteria grow to such formidable strength? Sadly, mankind invited them—by overusing antibiotics. Doctors, threatened with lawsuits if they cannot demonstrate that they did everything possible to protect a patient from possible disease, have now been overprescribing antibiotics for years.

For each decade following the invention of penicillin, physicians prescribed antibiotics as a "cure-all": Have an earache? Take some *Amoxicillin*. Have bronchitis? Try *Zithromax*. Sinusitis? *Trimethoprim-sulfamethoxazole*. Still won't go away? Take *moxifloxacin*. It's stronger.

Entire generations have grown up with this thinking. Nearly every trip to the doctor ends with a stop at the local drugstore—antibiotic prescription in hand.

Over time, bacteria "learn" to resist antibiotics. After an unwanted bacterium is introduced to the body, the immune system fights back. Physicians will typically then prescribe antibiotics to aid the immune system. But, with each use, bacteria can begin and then continue to "resist" the drugs, using certain "tricks." Some make themselves less permeable and the antibiotic cannot be absorbed. Others change their structure so antibiotics no longer recognize it and cannot find it to destroy it.

In the worst case, researchers now document bacteria that produce an enzyme to *dissolve* the antibiotic, rendering it useless. In effect, the *hunter* antibiotic has become the *hunted*!

Two Superbugs

The result is antibiotic-resistant hospital super-bacteria like Clostridium difficile (C. difficile) and MRSA.

Spores from MRSA can be entombed in a body during surgery, which if not treated soon after infection can result in the loss of a limb, or even death. This hard-to-cure superbug, which is an extreme staph infection, usually manifests itself as sores on the skin, but can also lead to fatal necrotizing pneumonia. Worse, MRSA can be carried unknowingly on hands, clothes, paper or even a "get well" card tied to a bouquet of flowers.

Doctors can take it into exam rooms, family members can infect a patient they are visiting—surgeons can even carry it into the operating room. Again, the bacterium can sneak in on a nose or hand, and can infect a person through a wound the size of a mosquito bite.

300 The Bible's Greatest Prophecies Unlocked!

According to the CDC, "MRSA occurs most frequently among patients who undergo invasive medical procedures or who have weakened immune systems and are being treated in hospitals and healthcare facilities such as nursing homes and dialysis centers." The organization also stated, "MRSA in healthcare settings commonly causes serious and potentially life threatening infections, such as bloodstream infections, surgical site infections, or pneumonia."

As resistance to antibiotics has worsened, hospitals have had to resort to "the drug of last resort"—*vancomycin*—to combat MRSA.

Consider again the super bacteria C. difficile. The CDC describes it as "a bacterium that causes diarrhea and more serious intestinal conditions such as colitis." Symptoms include diarrhea for two or more days, fever, loss of appetite, nausea, and abdominal pain or tenderness.

An estimated 28,000 people die of "C. diff" infections per year in America, which primarily occur in hospitals, and tens of thousands more in nursing homes also become infected.

The United Kingdom Department of Health recorded 36,674 deaths between 1997 and 2007 for the two infections (C. difficile claimed 26,208 and MRSA 10,466).

Researchers from the University of Nottingham reported, "Official figures show that 5,000 people die from a healthcare-associated infection every year in the UK and tackling the superbugs costs the NHS £1bn a year [approximately US$1.5 billion]. One in 12 of us will pick up an infection during a stay in hospital. There's a one in 77 chance of contracting MRSA and a one in 50 chance of developing C. diff."

An April 2008 CDC report showed that U.S. hospital patient infections doubled from 2001 to 2005. *The New York Times* reported, "Several years ago, the mortality rate from a C. difficile infection was around one to two percent. But today, various studies estimate that the death rate is six percent. The reason is that a hypervirulent strain has emerged that emits higher levels of toxins than earlier strains."

Scientists fear community-acquired MRSA could team up with the swine flu virus to produce absolutely horrific results. Those whose immune systems are weakened by H1N1 virus then are highly susceptible to contracting MRSA-induced necrotizing pneumonia.

An infections expert at the University of Nottingham, Professor Richard James, told the *Telegraph*, "The threat from [community-acquired MRSA] in the US is a very serious concern, especially if there is an epidemic. It could trigger a large number of cases of necrotizing pneumonia, which has a mortality rate of 50 per cent in 72 hours."

Each time man attempts to fix a problem, it generally ends up worse in the end. The case of antibiotics is no different. The solution has come back to bite humanity. The superbugs grow consistently more resistant with the passing of time, and many older diseases like tuberculosis, gonorrhea, yellow fever and cholera—once considered eradicated—are now re-emerging and, worse, are more difficult to cure than before they disappeared.

If just one looming disease pandemic runs through the now global "village," weakened immune systems—and a dwindling arsenal of powerful drugs—will leave wide-open a door to other little-known diseases waiting in the wings.

Disease and the Modern World

The threat of disease is widespread. Dirty water, pollution, warfare, livestock, pets, wild animals, a lack of proper nutrition, and overall degeneration of the body (including weakened immune systems) are paving the way for a perfect storm of pandemics to come.

"Just because we've just had a pandemic does not mean we've decreased our chances of having another," said Dr. Carolyn B. Bridges, an epidemiologist in the flu division of the CDC. "We have to stay vigilant" (*The New York Times*).

Consider how easy it is to spread disease in our modern society. A person going to another country on business or leisure contracts a disease, returns to his home country showing no symptoms, and infects those he comes in contact with. It is that easy.

An example of how disease can be spread in this modern age is West Nile Virus. It is believed that this disease was transported to the United States through mosquitoes that crossed the ocean in airplane wheel wells. They arrived in New York City in 1999.

Another was the rapid rise of Severe Acute Respiratory Syndrome (SARS) in 2003. When this disease suddenly spread from China to infect people in 37 countries, it showed the glaring vulnerability of the world to disease epidemics.

In his book *The Life of Reason*, famed historian George Santayana wrote, "Those who cannot remember the past are condemned to repeat it."

Judging from history, humanity is setting itself up for the "Mother of All Pandemics"—and maybe several, or even many. Most will choose to ignore the clear pattern of history—that history *always* repeats itself.

Take this out of the realm of sterile statistics. Make it real. Take heed and understand. These things will come to pass in *your* lifetime!

The entire world will soon learn that God is the only One who can truly cure or heal all forms of sickness and disease (Ex. 15:26; Psa. 103:3). God alone has the ability to forgive sin, which is directly related to why people get sick (Matt. 9:1-6; Psa. 41:3-4).

How will this come about?

What Is Prophesied to Come

From the time of Adam and Eve, mankind has lived in rebellion against God, breaking His laws with impunity. As a result, He has used pestilences to punish disobedience so that man could eventually learn the path to happiness and prosperity.

More than 3,000 years ago, God used a series of plagues to force the pharaoh in Egypt to release Israel from slavery (Exodus 7 to 12). Later, He brought a pestilence against Israel to punish King David (II Sam. 24:15).

God will yet again use pestilence to punish the nations. Notice this warning in Deuteronomy 28: "But it shall come to pass, if you will not hearken unto the voice of the LORD your God, to observe to do all His commandments and His statutes which I command you this day; that all these curses shall come upon you, and overtake you: cursed shall you be in the city, and cursed shall you be in the field. Cursed shall be your basket and your store. Cursed shall be the fruit of your body, and the fruit of your land, the increase of your kine, and the flocks of your sheep. Cursed shall you be when you come in, and cursed shall you be when you go out.

"The LORD shall make the *pestilence* cleave unto you, until He have consumed you from off the land, whither you go to possess it. The LORD shall smite you with a *consumption*, and with *a fever*, and with an *inflammation*, and with an *extreme burning*, and with the sword, and with blasting [again, hot, dry winds and drought], and with mildew [too much rain]; and they shall *pursue you until you perish.*

"And your carcass shall be meat unto all fowls of the air, and unto the beasts of the earth, and no man shall fray them away. The LORD will smite you with the *botch* of Egypt, and with the *emerods*, and with the *scab*, and with the *itch*, whereof you cannot be healed. The LORD shall smite you with madness, and blindness, and astonishment of heart" (vs. 15-19, 21-22, 26-28).

In Revelation 6:8, God again specifically mentions using "beasts of the earth" to punish. Hungry animals desperate for food will *attack* vastly more people in the future. Others carrying every kind of disease will *infect* people. This is coming. It is SURE!

Understand that even in the prosperous nations of the West, millions upon millions of vermin (including rats, but also bats, skunks, raccoons, chipmunks, squirrels, foxes and pigs) live side by side with human beings. In some of the biggest cities, they actually (greatly) outnumber people.

In the coming scramble for food, these creatures will compete with mankind for dwindling supplies, causing disease of every kind to spread like wildfire across many nations.

I take no pleasure in reporting the awful things of just this chapter. But they must be said. And you must be willing to heed.

When the terrible worsening of disease comes from just over the horizon panic will become the greatest pandemic. Sheer terror will keep people from buses, planes, trains, restaurants, schools, malls, homes, places of work, and virtually all indoor public places. Nothing will reassure them. Nothing will quiet their fear. (Remember that they will also be hungry.) Pause at least for a moment to ask where you expect to be.

Final Warning

The citizens of the countries privileged to be part of the Western world understand little about most of the diseases described. Usually it is only through newspaper headlines or news reports that they come to their attention. Even then, pandemic threats and health organizations' gloomy statistics seem unreal.

Make no mistake! It is no longer a matter of *if* pestilence will strike these nations, but *when*. Millions upon millions will die. Recall that 82,000 people now die of disease every day, and that this translates to 30 million a year. Again, this would be the equivalent of the entire nation of Canada. But these people are dying the world over, not just in one place. If any whole city of 82,000 disappeared in one day, with all of its citizens dying in a host of terrible ways—and this always followed by a slightly bigger city wiped out the next day—the world would understand what is *already happening*.

Long ago, God foretold that disease would come on the peoples of the world if they did not obey Him. This is now happening—and is prophesied to grow FAR worse. Diseases now primarily found in the

"Third World" are foretold to soon enter the West. Many scientists and doctors tell us these diseases are poised to "make the leap."

Some scientists think they can control the spread of illness. How wrong they are! Modern medicine's efforts to eradicate disease can be compared to a man attempting to plug the gash in the Titanic's hull with caulking compound. The ship is going down!

The threat of global epidemics looms large over the earth. They *are* coming, they WILL happen, and they WILL threaten the very existence of civilization! Yet we have seen that disease is just another of the means God will use to punish a stubborn mankind. He will use others to *shake* the world...

Earthquakes and Volcanoes

Earthquakes and volcanic activity have become *regular* in the news—and there is a reason. While most take Earth's surface for granted, danger lies within its thin and fragile crust.

Throughout history, God has used earthquakes to serve His purpose. The Bible foretells that the *greatest* period of earthquake activity in history lies just ahead. In fact, earthquakes and volcanoes will soon affect the security and stability of the whole world—including *your life*.

God's Word is plain. Yet most "prophecy watchers" speak little about this subject beyond the warning that "earthquakes are increasing" or "will increase." You are about to learn things *no one else* is telling you about earthquakes and volcanoes!

Earthquakes in Recent History

In the past 500 years, earthquakes of every size have claimed many *millions* of lives. The danger is now greater than ever—since the population has dramatically increased during the last two centuries, and some of the world's most earthquake-prone regions have become the most densely populated.

Before thoroughly examining what God reveals about earthquakes—and volcanoes!—past and present—here are some facts.

The Pacific Rim has long been the most volatile region in the world. It accounts for 90 percent of all earthquakes. Several thousand small to moderate quakes occur annually around the west coasts of North and South America to the eastern Pacific Rim. Southeast Asian countries and many island nations are also experiencing heightened activity. Each year, Japan alone is shaken by over 1,500 tremors—over four every day.

Earthquakes occur when tension in the tectonic plates of Earth's crust exceeds the strength of resistant rock at the edge of the affected plates. Some plates may move only an inch in a given year. But periods of no movement mean danger because energy is being stored and increased.

A worldwide network of seismographs detects about a million small earthquakes annually. According to records since 1900, the U.S. Geological Survey expects about 18 major earthquakes (7.0-7.9-magnitude) and one great earthquake (8.0 or higher) every year.

Some examples of recent devastating earthquakes: May 2008—a 7.9-magnitude quake struck China, killing 69,000 people. Then came the January 2010 Haitian earthquake that destroyed much of the capital city and killed about 230,000, occurring on a fault line never before detected. There was also the immense and destructive 8.8-magnitude Chilean quake in February 2010—the fifth largest since 1900. In February also came a 7.0 Japanese quake. Others regularly followed.

History is filled with the stories of very destructive earthquakes, having killed millions of people in virtually *all parts* of the world. The same is true of volcanoes.

Beyond death and destruction, bigger earthquakes invite famine and disease, with displaced populations forced to go without food and sanitation. And this says nothing about the incredible *economic* hardship caused by earthquakes, costing from millions to billions of dollars in damage overall, but also including widespread loss of employment due to destroyed businesses and transportation.

Conflicting Experts

Are earthquakes and volcanic activity on the rise—and if so, *why?* This is a subject of debate among scientists. Some assert that earthquakes are *not* increasing. J. Ramón Arrowsmith, a geologist, stated, "From our human perspective with our relatively short and incomplete memories and better and better communications around the world, we hear about more earthquakes and it seems like they are more frequent...But this is probably not any indication of a global change in earthquake rate of significance" (*LiveScience*).

Bob Holdsworth, an expert in tectonics, said that nothing strange is happening, declaring, "I can definitely tell you the world is not coming to an end" (*The Associated Press*).

Other scientists say earthquakes *are* increasing. Stephen S. Gao, a geophysicist, stated, "Relative to the 20-year period from the mid-1970s to the mid-1990s, the Earth has been more active over the past 15 or so years...We still do not know the reason for this..." (*LiveScience*).

Which side is right? Since the experts do not agree, how can you *know*—and what does *God* say?

Natural Disasters Foretold

It should by now be evident to every reader that God will soon involve Himself in the affairs of this world in a way He has never done before. Earthquakes will play a major role in what is coming.

Immediately following His warning about false Christianity, war, famine and disease, Jesus also warned of another pivotal sign that would precede His Return. He listed a *fifth* condition: "There shall be...earthquakes, in divers [various] places" (Matt. 24:7). This says that earthquakes would be scattered here and there—but must also mean they would increase in both *frequency* and *intensity* as His Second Coming drew near. (Mark 13:8 and Luke 21:11 also reference them.)

Think. Since earthquakes have existed throughout history, their mere *ongoing presence* could not indicate the time of the end. By all honest accounts, earthquakes are coming more often, and are more severe—and this will greatly worsen. As we proceed, you will be left to believe scientists or God.

Jesus Himself clears up the question of intensity—the *severity* of earthquakes at the end. Soon scientists will no longer be able to doubt. Slightly different from Matthew's and Mark's accounts, Jesus' statement in Luke adds a very important element about these earthquakes—how *powerful* they will be. Notice: "And *great* earthquakes shall be in [various] places, and famines, and pestilences..." (21:11). First, notice that the word translated "great" is *megas* in the Greek and means "big, great, high, large, loud, mighty, strong."

Take this word for exactly what it means—and what Christ intended. Think of these as MEGA-EARTHQUAKES! These are quakes of tremendous magnitude that would result in terrible, widespread destruction. This differentiates the final period of earthquakes—when they come more often and are more destructive—from relatively "average" quakes coming also farther apart in all previous periods of history. It will become evident that the same would be true of volcanic activity.

But a *second* point is seen by comparing Luke and Mark to Matthew's account. The latter lists earthquakes at the end of war, famine and disease. Luke and Mark list them before these things. The point is obvious. They will occur throughout the final years when false Christianity, war, famine and disease will have also grown much worse.

Volcanoes—in Nature and Prophecy

Volcanoes are *related* to earthquakes—both geologically and in Scripture. Their forces are shared and their effects are similar, with the devastation of both beyond comparison to anything in nature. When earthquakes are mentioned in prophecy, volcanoes are sometimes referenced.

A volcano is a crack, or vent, in the surface of the earth—its crust. Beneath the crack is a cavity. Over time, melted rock—magma—fills this area, called a magma chamber or reservoir, and causes pressure to build. The volcano, which may form over thousands of years or very suddenly, then becomes a path for magma to push its way to the surface. An eruption is the releasing of pressure.

Scientists state that over 3,000 volcanoes have erupted in just the last 50 years. Around 50 to 70 are active each year. Some are slowly spewing lava, while others are quietly building, or rebuilding, pressure. Actually, if a volcano is leaking slowly, it is considered "safe." The danger arises when pressure builds enough to erupt violently. Depending on internal construction, eruptions vary from slow flows to massive explosions.

Massive Devastation

The 1980 eruption of Mount St. Helens in the western U.S. was one of the largest in modern times. The first explosion had the force of 24 megatons of thermal energy and flattened 230 square miles. Six-foot-thick trees 15 miles away were mowed like grass!

Sometimes following the initial explosion, which can consist of steam, gas or magma, volcanoes spew what are called *pyroclastic flows*. Larger volcanoes, like St. Helens, also experience pyroclastic surges. Both consist of hot ash, rock fragments and gas that can reach temperatures of 1,500 degrees Fahrenheit, and travel at an astonishing 150 miles per hour! Surges carry more energy and are mostly rock fragments and super-heated gas. They move faster than flows, but both bring similar devastation. St. Helens generated a *series* of pyroclastic flows that completely sterilized the soil for six square miles.

Flows are generally followed by what are called *lahars*. These combine water, rock, sand and mud, which rush down valleys away from volcanoes. They move like rivers, and sometimes have enough force to uproot trees, rip houses from foundations and bridges from their supports. The lahar from St. Helens destroyed 27 bridges, 200 homes, 185 miles of roadway and 15 miles of railway.

Earthquakes also cause landslides. The one that followed the St. Helens eruption was the largest ever recorded. Some areas were buried in up to 600 feet of mud and debris!

The final fallout from an eruption is the ash cloud. A volcano can spew ash over 12 miles above the opening in just 10 minutes. The ash from St. Helens landed over an area of 20,000 square miles. If the volcano is near a city, the weight of the particles can collapse buildings.

The danger and colossal destruction of volcanoes become evident.

Detection is done by checking the "heaving" of the land. This shows how much pressure is building in the magma chamber. An additional method is to record the earthquakes around a volcano. As their frequency and intensity increase, the volcano is destabilized, making conditions ripe for eruption.

This explains why earthquakes and volcanic eruptions are so connected. While the most powerful earthquakes are not caused by volcanoes, all eruptions cause a series of smaller quakes.

Mounting Forces

With St. Helens, a large earthquake triggered an already sensitive volcano to erupt. This is the danger in many volcano-sensitive areas throughout the world. Volcanoes sit silently building pressure until a nearby earthquake becomes the catalyst for eruption. Everything that follows is random—entirely unpredictable.

Another common type of volcano is underwater. The floor of the ocean is littered with them. The entire Hawaiian Islands are a direct result of underwater eruptions. Tsunamis pose the greatest danger with these, and can move at speeds of up to *500 miles per hour*. Both earthquakes and volcanoes can create these devastating waves. They usually result from underwater mudslides that follow the eruption. One of the most devastating tsunamis in history was in 2004 in Indonesia. Caused by an earthquake, almost 300,000 people perished.

Following the eruption of the Indonesian volcano Tambora in 1815, normally temperate areas experienced snow every month for a year, resulting in poor crop yields in places as far away as New England. Many believe Tambora was a factor in bringing about the Irish Potato Famine.

The 1883 explosion of Krakatoa, also in Indonesia, was heard over 2,000 miles away! The eruption spewed ash 50 miles high, with the dust cloud repeatedly circling the earth. The surrounding region experienced darkness for over two days. Nothing in nature compares to such an event.

In the Philippines, Mt. Pinatubo erupted in June 1991, displacing millions of people and destroying much farmland. Pinatubo's ash cloud lowered the *average world temperature* by almost two degrees Fahrenheit!

An awesome volcanic eruption in Iceland occurred in March 2010. It caused tremendous floods, but also brought fears that it would trigger a *second* much larger volcano nearby to erupt. Catastrophic global climate changes—were this to occur—enter the picture.

Soon we will see more powerful earthquakes. They will awaken giant volcanoes. These will be the largest eruptions of all time. But earthquakes and volcanoes will not just alter the face of single mountains. They will alter the face of the WHOLE EARTH!

Earthquakes in the Old Testament

It is critical to understand *why* God has used earthquakes and volcanoes through history. It is also important to take extra time to set up God's repeated use of these most powerful of disasters to serve His purpose.

The Bible shows earthquakes reveal God's presence, His deliverance, His wrath and His power. God will also use them to announce Christ's Return—to accompany prophetic events, we have already seen this—and to reshape the earth's surface.

The Bible reveals that just God's presence can cause Earth to shake. Notice: "Tremble, you earth, at the presence of the Lord, at the presence of the God of Jacob" (Psa. 114:7). Volcanoes can be triggered: "The mountains quake at Him, and the *hills melt* [lava-producing volcanoes]" (Nah. 1:5), and "He looks on the earth, and it trembles: He touches the hills, and they *smoke*" (Psa. 104:32).

There was thunderous trembling when God gave the Ten Commandments: "And all the people saw the thunderings, and the lightnings, and the noise of the trumpet, and the mountain *smoking*: and when the people saw it, they removed, and stood afar off" (Ex. 20:18). Now this: "And Mount Sinai was altogether on a *smoke*, because the LORD descended upon it in *fire*: and the smoke thereof ascended as the smoke of a furnace, *and the whole mount quaked greatly*" (Ex. 19:18).

God's presence generated an earthquake, and likely volcanic activity, to get Israel's attention.

On another occasion, the faith and courage of King David's friend Jonathan, and his armor-bearer, moved God. Here is what happened: "And there was trembling in the host, in the field, and among all the people: the garrison, and the spoilers, they also trembled, and the *earth quaked*: so it was a *very great trembling*" (I Sam. 14:15). The confused, terrified Philistines then turned on each other. The result was thousands died.

Another earthquake, in Numbers 16, involved 250 Israelite leaders under Korah who rebelled against Moses. The result? "The earth opened her mouth and swallowed them up" (vs. 32)—with their wives and children. Again, thousands died.

New Testament Earthquakes

Other earthquakes occurred just after the New Testament Church began. Here is one, with Peter and John both speaking and praying: "And now, Lord, behold their threatenings: and grant unto Your servants, that with all boldness they may speak Your word, by stretching forth Your hand to heal; and that signs and wonders may be done by the name of...Jesus. And when they had prayed, the place was *shaken* where they were assembled together; and they were all filled with the Holy [Spirit], and they spoke the word of God with boldness" (Acts 4:29-31). The quake became part of the proof God had heard.

Another earthquake occurred involving the apostle Paul and Silas in Philippi. They had been illegally beaten and imprisoned. But God delivered them: "And suddenly there was a *great earthquake*, so that the foundations of the prison were *shaken*: and immediately all the doors were opened, and every one's bands were loosed" (Acts 16:26).

While skeptics, and even many theologians, generally dismiss such miracles in Scripture, earthquakes have also accompanied great events, such as Jesus' crucifixion: "And, behold, the veil of the temple was rent in twain from the top to the bottom; *and the earth did quake*, and the *rocks rent*" (Matt. 27:51). What happened next? "Now when the centurion, and they that were with him, watching Jesus, *saw the earthquake*, and those things that were done, *they feared greatly*, saying, Truly this was the Son of God" (vs. 54).

Another great earthquake accompanied Christ's Resurrection: "And, behold, there was a *great earthquake*: for the angel of the Lord descended from heaven, and came and rolled back the stone from the door, and sat upon it" (Matt. 28:2).

Again, earthquakes can also reflect God's wrath. Let's read: "Then the earth *shook* and *trembled*; the foundations also of the hills *moved* and were *shaken*, because He was *wroth*" (Psa. 18:7) Also, read Jeremiah 10:10, "But the LORD is the true God, He is the living God, and an everlasting King: at *His wrath* the earth shall *tremble*, and the nations shall not be able to abide His *indignation*."

Five Great Future Earthquakes

Many prophesied end-time earthquakes will carry this message. These primarily involve great quakes listed in the book of Revelation. They will convey God's wrath to a world that refuses to heed His warnings and correction. While some are referenced elsewhere in this volume, consider them in the context of this chapter for impact.

First, a probably smaller earthquake is referenced in Revelation 12, and involves the miraculous escape of God's Church to a place of safety as the Great Tribulation begins. An army pursuing the Church is completely swallowed and destroyed (vs. 15-16). Notice similar wording to Numbers 16: "And the earth helped the woman [God's Church], and... *opened her mouth*, and *swallowed* up the flood [obviously an army—like the Egyptian army pursuing Israel until the Red Sea swallowed it] which the dragon [the devil] cast out of his mouth" (Rev. 12:16).

The book of Revelation foretells *five* specific powerful earthquakes preceding and surrounding Christ's Return. Each is unique, and occurs at a particular juncture of God's *final prophetic timeline*.

The Tribulation Ends

The *first* earthquake is in Revelation 6:12: "I beheld [John is writing] when He had opened the sixth seal, and, lo, there was a *great earthquake*; and the sun became black as sackcloth of hair, and the moon became as blood."

This earthquake occurs after the fifth seal, as the sixth is opened. Recall that the cataclysmic fifth seal involves the military invasion and the captivity of the modern-day descendants of Israel. This involves two and a half years of unparalleled suffering—the worst in all history—to be brought upon this generation. This earthquake's timing proclaims the *end* of the Great Tribulation and beginning of powerful signs that appear in the heavens.

Jesus also spoke of this in Matthew: "Immediately *after the tribulation* of those days shall the sun be darkened, and the moon shall not give her light, and the stars shall fall from heaven, and the powers of the *heavens shall be shaken*" (24:29). And in Luke: "And there shall be signs in the sun, and in the moon, and in the stars; and upon the earth distress of nations, with perplexity; the *sea and the waves roaring* [obviously including tsunamis]; men's hearts failing them for fear, and for looking after those things which are coming on the earth: for the powers of heaven shall be *shaken*" (21:25-26).

We saw earlier the context of Revelation 6 reveals more: "and every mountain and island were *moved out of their places*" (vs. 14).

Now read Isaiah's description of this time: "In that day a man shall cast his idols of silver, and his idols of gold, which they made each one for himself to worship, to the moles and to the bats; to go into the clefts of the rocks, and into the tops of the ragged rocks, for fear of the LORD, and for the glory of His majesty, *when He arises to shake terribly the earth*" (2:20-21).

This powerful description parallels Rev. 6:15-16. Physical possessions will be of no use to anyone not truly serving God.

The Seventh Seal Opens

The *second* earthquake is found in Revelation 8:5. As the seventh seal is opened, seven angels stand before God and receive seven trumpets. Another angel took a censer "and filled it with fire of the altar, and cast it into the earth: and there were voices, and thunderings, and lightnings, and *an earthquake*."

This earthquake marks the beginning of the *seven trumpet plagues* and begins fulfillment of the seventh seal and *Day of the Lord*.

Certain scriptures speak of the solemn gravity and horror of this time. Consider Joel: "Alas for the day! For the day of the LORD is at hand, and as a *destruction* from the Almighty shall it come" (1:15).

The prophet Joel also shows the precise timing of this event: "The sun shall be turned into darkness, and the moon into blood, *before* the great and the terrible Day of the LORD come" (2:31). This matches the sequence in Revelation, as the heavenly signs immediately precede the Day of the Lord—the Day of God's wrath.

Jesus Christ's Return Announced

The *third* earthquake is in Revelation 11:12-13: "They heard a great voice from heaven saying unto them [the Two Witnesses], Come up hither. And they ascended up to heaven in a cloud; and their enemies beheld them. And the same hour was there a *great earthquake*, and the tenth part of the city [Jerusalem] fell, and in the *earthquake* were slain of men seven thousand: and the remnant were *affrighted*, and gave glory to the God of heaven"!

This earthquake occurs after the final *two special prophets* are resurrected—before the seventh trumpet and the First Resurrection of I Corinthians 15:51 and I Thessalonians 4:16. It appears to be *mainly* in Jerusalem, but could still be worldwide in scope. It cannot be the same one described in Zechariah 14:4, because all nations will not yet have gathered at Armageddon.

This earthquake precedes and announces the most pivotal event in human history—Jesus Christ's Return!

Christ Is Present

The *fourth* earthquake is in Revelation 11:19: "And the temple of God was opened in heaven, and there was seen in His temple the ark of His testament: and there were lightnings, and voices, and thunderings, *and an earthquake*, and *great hail*."

This earthquake occurs immediately *after* Christ's Return and the First Resurrection, and marks the fulfillment of these events: "...and there were great voices in heaven, saying, The kingdoms of this world are become the kingdoms of our Lord, and of His Christ; and He shall reign forever and ever" (vs. 15).

Jesus' Return makes every following event within God's Plan possible. Earthquakes before and after it underscore its momentous importance in His Plan. No other event bears such distinction. This earthquake directly results from the *presence* of God. Jesus Christ is now *present* as King—assuming rulership in glory over all nations!

The Greatest Earthquake of All Time

The *final* earthquake is in Revelation 16:17-18: "And the seventh angel poured out his vial into the air; and there came a great voice out of the temple of heaven, from the throne, saying, It is done. And there were voices, and thunders, and lightnings; and there was a *great earthquake, such as was not since men were upon the earth*, so *mighty* an earthquake, and so *great*."

This last earthquake will be the most powerful to occur since Creation. The remainder of Earth's topography changes. Notice: "And every island *fled away*, and the mountains *were not found*" (vs. 20).

This earthquake appears to complete the process begun by the one in Revelation 6:14, in which "every mountain and island were *moved out of their places*." This is the earthquake mentioned in Zechariah 14 that follows all nations gathering at Armageddon, and it coincides with the sixth vial of God's wrath.

We earlier read Zechariah 14, which states, "And [Christ's] feet shall stand in that day upon the mount of Olives, which is before Jerusalem on the east, and the mount of Olives shall *cleave in the midst thereof* toward the east and toward the west, and there shall be a very great valley; and half of the mountain shall remove toward the north, and half...toward the south" (vs. 4) and "the LORD shall be King over all the earth..." (vs. 9).

Words fail in describing the impact of such an awesome, immense river, made possible because God used an earthquake to cleave a mountain!

Foretold Long Ago

Other prophets of the Old Testament also spoke about the enormous earthquakes of Revelation, especially the final, greatest one preceding Christ's Return.

Isaiah 13:13: "I will shake the heavens, and the earth shall remove *out of her place*, in the wrath of the LORD of hosts, and in the day of His *fierce anger*."

Isaiah 24:19-20: "The earth is utterly broken down, the earth is clean dissolved, the earth is *moved exceedingly*. The earth shall reel to and fro like a drunkard, and shall be removed like a cottage..."

Ezekiel 38:20: "...all the men that are upon the face of the earth, shall shake *at My presence*, and the mountains shall be *thrown down*, and the steep places shall fall, and every wall shall fall to the ground."

Joel 3:16: "The LORD also shall *roar* out of Zion, and utter His voice from Jerusalem; and the heavens and the *earth shall shake*..."

Haggai 2:6-7: "For thus says the LORD of hosts; Yet once, it is a little while, and I will *shake* the heavens, *and the earth*, and the sea, and the dry land; and *I will shake all nations*, and the desire of all nations [Jesus Christ] shall come…"

Earth's Topography Changed

Beyond the immediate purpose of the five Revelation earthquakes, these will also serve to reshape Earth's surface. The same God who formed the hills and mountains will *reform* them and *reshape* the planet. (Take time to read Amos 4:13 and Psalm 90:2.)

Notice this: "Every valley shall be exalted, and every mountain and hill shall be made low: and the crooked shall be made straight, and the rough places plain: and the glory of the LORD shall be revealed" (Isa. 40:4-5).

This speaks of truly dramatic—monumental—changes! Vast mountain ranges will *disappear*. A few remaining mountains and hills will be used for God's specially appointed purpose. Other verses show this. (Of course, while the Mount of Olives in Jerusalem cleaves in two, it does obviously remain. And huge, jagged mountains will be "made low," they will not completely disappear.)

The renewal of Earth's surface will accommodate the vast number of human beings who will exist by the later stages of Christ's millennial rule, but also the many billions (all those who have lived since Creation) who will come up later in the general resurrection at the end of the Millennium—the White Throne Judgment of Revelation 20:11. A much larger population is possible—and made comfortable—once more usable land becomes available for farming and living.

More land will be reclaimed from the deserts and oceans, with the oceans scheduled to be *purified* (Ezek. 47:8-10). All of this will bring favorable weather, replacing the harsh destructive weather patterns felt throughout history. Without droughts and floods, and the terrible extremes of temperature, precipitation and destruction from other elements in nature, farming will be more productive.

There is a PURPOSE for every aspect of God's Creation. We have seen that earthquakes, sometimes accompanied by volcanoes, have long served God's Plan, and in numerous ways. While ultimately the means by which God will reshape Earth's topography for the good of all, these natural disasters will in the short term contribute to a level of destruction the world has never seen—and a mounting death toll…

A Fourth of Men!

M any are intrigued by the "idea" of prophecy, but not the *truth* of prophecy. These are unable to translate mere knowledge on paper of what is to come to the awesome REALITY of what these prophecies actually *mean* for planet Earth—that they will strike all nations with absolute SLEDGEHAMMER FORCE!

To many, prophecy is a puzzle to work out—a game to play—one in which they can "figure out" what happens next. It is *exciting*! But prophecy is neither a game nor mere *futuristic puzzle* for the intellectually curious. Far—FAR—from it! It is a deadly serious matter, and in all of its component parts. All *recreational* prophecy readers will soon wish they had looked elsewhere for "stimulation," and brought much more serious interest to God's Word.

No Exceptions

Many years ago, a popular television commercial illustrated how most people were not inclined then to wear a seatbelt when riding in a car. Of course, laws have changed and this is now generally required everywhere in the United States, as well as in many other countries. The message sought to convince travelers of the danger of "not buckling up."

The commercial worked off a familiar cliché—"accidents only happen to others." It went something like this: "Of course, we all know that accidents only happen to others, but, just in case *you* are one of the 'others,' please wear your seatbelt." The commercial took a left-handed approach to get people's attention. I never heard statistics demonstrating whether it worked before laws changed, but it was catchy and it certainly came from a correct premise in the thinking of the majority of human beings.

Most people *do* live their lives believing that bad things generally only happen to others—*other* people get cancer—*other* people's houses burn down or are struck by tornadoes—*other* people's children die of drug overdoses—and so forth. The truth is that for everyone who is forced to suffer one of these tragic events there is someone who probably believed such awful things could only happen to someone else.

But *all mankind* is on a collision course with cataclysmic events so stunning—*so staggering*—they defy imagination. *Horrific* prophecies will soon affect every human being on Earth—*every* human being—no exceptions! They do not describe a mere few hit by "accidents" of "time and chance."

While the vast majority remain ignorant of the precise *sequence* of key prophetic fulfillments, even fewer understand the correct *timing* and true IMPACT of these events—with *both* of these of paramount importance in assembling the final prophetic picture.

The reader—*any* reader—*every* reader—is unprepared for what this chapter will cover. Millions may *think* they understand the MAGNITUDE of what will happen when certain Bible prophecies occur, but all popular assumptions will soon pale against the awful crush of reality in just the FIRST GREAT WAVE of punishment foretold by God.

Sadly, most are *blissfully* unaware of impending calamity.

By now the reader understands that the four horsemen's impact will increase, and in a big and growing way. But God has actually given a *precise measurement* of just how many they will affect.

"The Fourth Part" of Men

Recall two earlier verses in Revelation 6 describing the opening of the fourth seal—pestilence. Together they become one of the Bible's most powerful single passages—or what might be called *summary statements*—on the entire subject of prophecy.

Read again, this time very carefully: "And when He had opened the *fourth seal*, I heard the voice of the fourth beast say, Come and see. And I looked, and behold a pale horse: and his name that sat on him was Death—and Hell followed with him. And POWER was given unto *them*"—all four horses and riders (false Christianity, war, famine and disease) in the context—"over *the fourth part of the earth* [one in every four people!], to KILL with *sword*, and with *hunger*, and with *death*, and with the *beasts of the earth*" (vs. 7-8).

Grasp the sheer awesome magnitude of what you have read. One out of every four people on Earth is foretold to perish—and all or almost all of this will happen *before* the Tribulation, which is the *fifth* seal! All four horsemen, riding together, with certain paralleling factors accompanying them, will have the power to kill one full quarter of all human beings on Earth!

Walk outside and look across and down the street. Then picture one of every four people you see gone and dying faster than graveyards can even begin to receive them! This is not mere speculation—it is CERTAIN.

This worldwide calamity starts with religious deception, which results in war, followed by famine and disease. Factor in both intensifying—"great"—earthquakes (and volcanoes) and an overlooked reference to "with the beasts of the earth," and the result is mass death—one in four people alive today, plus many not yet alive.

So says God!

A Graphic Picture Unfolds

We are about to learn—and in the most raw detail—the awesome scope of how and in what way these *nearly incomprehensible* NIGHTMARISH prophecies will soon strike all nations of the world. The Bible is PLAIN on this subject—with scriptures that are *impossible* to misunderstand.

The way to fully *comprehend* and *personalize* the horror brought by the four horsemen, the beasts of the earth, and different kinds of natural disasters is not to examine the entire world as a whole, but to first look at what will happen to modern Israel at the *end* of this first wave of punishment—after the "*beginning* of sorrows"—just into the period of the Great Tribulation.

Why examine the future of only the modern descendants of ancient Israel?

Just before the opening of the fifth seal of the Great Tribulation—at the conclusion of the time of the first four seals (the four horsemen)—God also describes the chilling next phase of events—the punishment of the *nations of Israel*—in explicit terms—in *most graphic* detail. By studying what happens to these peoples, and what is a second wave of death that will ensue, we can comprehend what will later befall the ENTIRE WORLD! Israel's death toll is but a *fraction* of "the fourth" to perish the world over. (In fact, Israel's suffering is actually on top of the "one fourth," but similar in kind.) Through them God paints a representative picture of *all nations of the world* in bone-splintering language!

A later chapter will give the reader much more background about who are the people of Israel today, and why their identity, including America and Britain, with certain other nations, opens up giant areas of prophetic understanding now completely lost to almost all. The reader will better appreciate that chapter in light of what is now discussed.

Horror Like None Other

Most people do not recognize the power of language used by the God of the Bible when He wants to drive points home. He pulls absolutely NO PUNCHES. He often uses especially descriptive language so that those who read are left *without excuse* regarding what they have just learned. Such is the prophecy in Ezekiel 5.

Related to this point about language is that God also wants people to have *no excuse* when pondering the specific details of what will occur when world conditions will have collapsed as they are foretold to do. Since we cannot read every passage, *my* task is to make clear to you, in the most graphic language I can summon, what *God* says will happen.

One can only try to imagine the worldwide chaos of the coming conditions brought by the four horsemen, worsening earthquakes and other natural disasters, as well as what God is referring to when He mentions the "beasts of the earth." Understand again that when people are hungry, they grow desperate—and desperate people do desperate things. Of course, it is important to meditate on every message given to us from God in His Word. But some passages require a kind of special thoughtfulness and repetition (which God brings) to appreciate them.

We first repeat a verse from Ezekiel 5 that hearkens to a subject already covered. It is in the fuller context of what *God* is going to do to His people: "Therefore the fathers *shall eat the sons* in the midst of you, and the sons *shall eat their fathers*; and I WILL EXECUTE JUDGMENTS IN YOU, and the whole remnant of you will I scatter into all the winds" (vs. 10).

How bad will world conditions get? Make yourself come to terms with the fact that food will become so scarce in nations accustomed to unbounded abundance that parents will resort to *cannibalism*! Again, so says God! While hard to comprehend, understand that this *will* happen—just as it happened when ancient Israel was under siege thousands of years ago (Lam. 4:10). Solomon said there is "no new thing under the sun" (Ecc. 1:9). This is another way in which the past is prologue.

The rest of Ezekiel 5:11 indicates that God's wrath is so great, He will show no pity: "...neither shall My eye *spare*, neither will I have *any pity*." What could be more frightening!

Pursued Relentlessly

Ezekiel 5:12 continues: "A third part of you shall die with the *pestilence*, and with *famine* shall they be consumed in the midst of you: and a third part shall fall by the *sword* [war] round about you [these countries become surrounded by enemies]; and I will scatter a third part into all the winds, and I will draw out a *sword* [war] after them."

Notice the similarity here to Matthew 24 and Revelation 6. We again read regarding *war*, *famine* and *pestilence*. As we have seen, to truly understand prophecy, one must allow the Bible to interpret itself. When this is done, a clear picture emerges every time.

Allow God's Word to paint again a sobering image in your mind as we next read the portion of Scripture just *after* God describes breaking the staff of bread in Israel: "And *pestilence* and *blood* shall pass through you; and I will bring the *sword* upon you" (Ezek. 5:17).

Blood and death will blanket the earth! God has appointed punishment to be everywhere, and He means it! Ministers of this world are not talking about these things. They *will not* talk about them! They know that if they do, they will lose their following—and almost certainly their jobs. This information is not pretty or popular. But *God's* ministers *never* worry about what men will say in response to God's Word.

We learn more in Ezekiel, chapter 6: "Alas for all the evil abominations of the house of Israel! for they shall fall by the *sword*, by the *famine*, and by the *pestilence*. He that is far off shall die of the *pestilence*; and he that is near shall fall by the *sword*; and he that remains and is besieged shall die by the *famine*: thus will I accomplish My fury upon them" (vs. 11-12).

Here are more shocking passages from Ezekiel: "The *sword* is without, and the *pestilence* and the *famine* within: he that is in the field shall die with the sword; and he that is in the city, *famine* and *pestilence* shall devour him" (7:15), and repeated and expanded by God for emphasis is also, "Thus says the Lord GOD; As I live, surely they that are in the wastes shall fall by the *sword*, and him that is in the open field will I give to the *beasts* to be devoured, and they that be in the forts and in the caves shall die of the *pestilence*" (33:27). The picture just within these three passages is almost too horrifying to contemplate.

There is seen in these descriptions to be *no way out*! God permits *no escape* for those who will not turn to Him! Many will try to flee, but will be unable. Death will literally pursue them like a posse or trained tracker would an outlaw.

Great numbers will wish they had heeded *the very message* explained in these many chapters before it was too late!

Wild Animals Unleashed

But there is more. Now note another element within the prophetic framework of what lies ahead. God also speaks in Jeremiah of sending wild animals through the land as punishment. He is again graphic: "Wherefore a *lion* out of the forest shall slay them, and a *wolf* of the evenings shall spoil them, a *leopard* shall watch over their cities: every one that goes out thence shall be *torn in pieces*: because their transgressions are many, and their backslidings are increased" (5:6).

Ezekiel sheds light on the immense *scope* of this punishment: "If I cause noisome [bad, evil] beasts to pass through the land, and they spoil it, so that it be desolate, that *no man may pass through* because of the beasts..." (14:15).

Think about this scene! Predatory animals will *literally* have free reign on Earth—controlling the land. Understand that, while man was created to "have dominion over...every creeping thing that creeps on the earth" (Gen. 1:26)—the roles will soon reverse. *Wild animals* will dominate the landscape—"that no man may pass through"!

Now read this from Leviticus 26: "I [God] will also send *wild beasts* among you, which shall *rob you of your children*, and destroy your cattle, and make you *few in number*; and your high ways shall be desolate" (vs. 22). Children disappear. Livestock are killed. The human population dwindles.

And this from Deuteronomy: "...I will also send the *teeth of beasts* upon them, with the *poison of serpents* of the dust" (32:24).

Finally, notice what God also states through Jeremiah: "And I [God] will appoint over them FOUR KINDS, says the LORD: the sword to slay, and the *dogs to tear*, and the *fowls of the heaven*, and the *beasts of the earth*, to *devour* and destroy" (15:3).

Statistics show that the populations of rats, rabbits, chipmunks, mice, deer, coyotes, squirrels, possums and skunks are multiplying. So are bears, wolves and mountain lions. And so also are now wild bands of roving domestic dogs in certain communities, which when released or escaped find each other and naturally revert to their hunter's *pack instinct*—and become extremely dangerous.

The Bible reveals God will unleash all these on a sinful mankind!

Adding this element to the devastation trailing natural disasters seen in the last chapter is all the more sobering to contemplate. Even though I have been aware of and studied these prophecies for almost 45 years, they are always just as nightmarish to consider. Their weight and force upon the thinking mind never lessens with time.

One is left with whether he believes God.

Individual Responsibility

Understand that God is no respecter of persons. In the New Testament, Christians are commanded to "work out your own salvation with fear and trembling" (Phil. 2:12). Ezekiel echoes this: "When the land sins against Me by trespassing grievously, then will I stretch out My hand upon it, and will break the staff of the bread thereof [there it is again], and will send *famine upon it* [here is this again], and will cut off man and beast from it: [Now notice this.] Though these three men, *Noah, Daniel*, and *Job*, were in it, they should deliver but *their own souls* [lives] by their righteousness, says the Lord GOD" (14:13-14).

The sentence beginning "Though" is repeated in verse 20. There it is followed by "...how much more when I send my FOUR SORE JUDG-MENTS upon Jerusalem, the *sword*, and the *famine*, and the *noisome beast*, and the *pestilence*, to cut off from it man and beast?"

This is one of the most chilling single passages in the entire Bible. These are things God says HE will do—"when I [God] send..." These are not things that *men* are causing—the case with many of the terrible things occurring on Earth today, and regarding others to occur during the coming time. Recall from Chapter One that prophecy is something *God* brings to pass. It does not turn—none of it—on whether men agree with it. God has said that He will do certain things—and He will. These are God's "judgments" on sinful nations.

Do not forget this!

An important distinction must be made. Notice that the *four sore judgments* do not *exactly* correspond to the *four horsemen*. False Christianity is left out, while attacks from wild animals are included (but these *are* found in Revelation 6). *Prior to* the Tribulation into which Israel will be sent, false Christianity—the white horse rider—does not *yet* play a very large role in the death of great numbers. We have seen, of course, that with the coming mark of the Beast, administered by the false Christian system centered in Europe, this will change.

Another Message

Also grasp *what else* God is explaining here! Even if three of the most righteous men who ever lived were present during this coming time of calamity, they would save only themselves as a result of their righteousness—*no one else*! Their godly conduct would not shield wives, children, parents or friends from the terror ahead.

These men were considered righteous because they *obeyed God.* Your future hinges on *your actions alone*! Most people just will not believe that obedience is important to God! They certainly want God's blessings, but they do not want Him sticking His nose into their business in regard to any requirements He may have.

Realize that themes of obedience and consequences are not specific to the prophets, but are woven throughout the Bible. More detailed description can be found in Leviticus and Deuteronomy—books recorded by Moses in the Old Testament that most dismiss.

Notice now the THEME of *obedience/disobedience* and *consequences* from Leviticus 26: "But if you will not *hearken unto Me*, and will not DO all these *commandments*; and if you shall despise My *statutes*, or if your soul abhor My *judgments*, so that you will not DO all My *commandments*, but that you *break* My covenant: I also will do this unto you; I will even appoint over you terror, consumption, and the burning ague, that shall consume the eyes, and cause sorrow of heart: and you shall sow your seed in vain, for your enemies shall eat it. And I will set My face *against you*, and you shall be *slain* before your enemies: they that hate you shall reign over you..." (vs. 14-17).

Take time to read the remaining verses in the long chapter of Leviticus 26, with its 46 verses. Then read the even longer parallel chapter of Deuteronomy 28, with its 68 verses. These chapters are very detailed about God's intention, and are specific in regard to obedience and consequences. They add to the grim picture of what lies ahead for the nations of modern Israel if they do not repent of their sins. Allow them to jar you out of complacency—and into *action*!

Many other Old Testament prophecies describe the scope and severity of national punishment that God has in store for ALL NATIONS. As we have only begun to see, many hundreds of millions will die from *war, famine, disease, wild beasts, earthquakes* and *volcanoes*—and vast millions of others will be taken into *captivity*—enslavement—in foreign lands.

It is crucial to stress one more time that the four horsemen wreak most or all of their devastation prior to the Great Tribulation. All nations taste their fury. When understood in light of the verses above, they are seen to *continue into* the lands of Israel at the Tribulation's outset, as things *temporarily* get better for the rest of the world.

The Towering Question

At this most critical turning point in prophecy—as the world explodes toward the brink of the FIFTH SEAL of Great Tribulation—we ask a sobering question that *should* be on every reader's mind: How far— to *what degree*—have the seals of false Christianity, war, famine, and pestilence come to bear?

You have already seen that the first four seals *are* NOW open! The previous five chapters thunder this undeniable fact. Just as evident is that we have not *yet* entered the time of "*great* tribulation, such as was not since the beginning of the world to this time, no, nor ever shall be" (Matt. 24:21). The world now rests on the fulcrum of these great prophecies—the tipping point!

How critical is the question of the timeline surrounding the fulfillment of the first four seals?

Understand! The arrival of the Great Tribulation hinges *entirely* on the complete unlocking of the four seals preceding it! Until the horrors that these seals bring claim a quarter of all men, the Tribulation will not come. The *depth* to which the first four seals have been opened is therefore the KEY INDICATOR of our proximity to the Tribulation—to discerning the correct "milemarker" on God's prophetic timeline!

What could be more important for you to comprehend in regard to time?

A Caution to Readers

Before examining the facts surrounding this question of the precise transition between the first four and the fifth seals, a critical *warning* specific to this juncture in prophecy must be made. As the age draws to a close, self-deception and pursuit of materialism has grown so great that mankind cannot comprehend what is *presently* occurring the world over—what is happening RIGHT NOW!

Most *cannot* fathom a human death toll approaching two billion—it is beyond their scope of comprehension and acceptance. And despite the *undeniable fact* that SCORES OF MILLIONS are perishing *every year* due to the first four seals, they ignore—knowingly or unknowingly—these horrifying numbers. They simply are not looking for the carnage and are not recognizing it when they see it. So great is this self-deception that, at the tail end of the "fourth part of the earth" fulfillment—when the rising body count is greatest!—Earth's inhabitants will be lulled into believing the soothing lies of the devil's agents, soon to declare, "Peace, peace; when there is no peace" (Jer. 6:14).

Will you be among the undiscerning and gullible—or deny the *undeniable*? Or will you wake up to the Bible's clear warnings and to the cold, hard—CONCRETE!—statistics screaming from newspapers, magazines, journals, television stations and websites the world over?

Understand though. Conditions will to a degree *seem* normal or no thinking mind would take any such "peace, peace" declaration seriously, no matter who was saying it. When comparing our time with the days of Noah and Sodom and Gomorrah, Jesus, in Matthew 24:37-39 and Luke 17:26-29, added to His warning that a semblance of normal routine continued in society even *immediately* prior to the Flood and *immediately* prior to the destruction of Sodom and Gomorrah.

A 20th-century Example

We must again now "reason together." Follow carefully the next several all-important paragraphs. It has become time for some basic math.

For perspective, we return to the worst recorded flu pandemic of all time: the 1918 Spanish flu outbreak. Recall that about 675,000 in the United States were killed—along with between 40 and 100 million others worldwide. To understand the effect at the time, consider some comparisons. With a 1918 U.S. population of 103 million—almost exactly one-third of today's 310 million in the U.S.—675,000 equals over two million dying in America if this flu came *today*. Now, with *world* population at about 1.9 billion in 1918, and if we use the midrange-estimate of 70 million dying worldwide then, the current 6.8 billion world population would yield *251 million* dying *today* by this pandemic!

Therefore, do not say such extreme horrific disaster could not strike the world. The 1.9 billion people alive in 1918—were they still alive—

would say you were wrong! And remember the Black Death. This *single plague* killed from *one-third* to *one-half* the world's population in the mid-1300s. No one doubts this occurred because it is a fact of history. So why would they doubt when Jesus Christ said that just *one-fourth* will die from the horsemen?

Here is why: The Black Death is *past*—the stuff of history books. The horsemen are still largely *future*. No one wants to imagine such an awful FUTURE—even if GOD foretells it will come!

See the contradiction in thinking and acceptance here!

Next, remember that war is worse than ever today, as is famine, and that there are many more deadly diseases on Earth now than ever in history—far more than in the 1300s, or even in 1918.

In Review

An encapsulation of what we have learned becomes necessary to understand the extent to which the first four seals are open. Some computation is required.

The specter of the white horse of false Christianity—while not yet taking victims by the scores of millions—is ratcheting up in readiness! There is seemingly no end to the increase of churches and deceivers.

The horror of war—while not presently claiming lives in the double and triple-digit millions—will soon grip the world as never before. Consider that we saw about 250 million died during the 20th century alone due to wars and related genocides—and this estimate may be conservative! Then remember the "commotions" Luke referenced. The newer phenomenon of terrorism, worsening in the 21st century, including bombings, riots and mass shootings, as well as serial killings, are occurring with greater frequency the world over. Civil wars now plague underdeveloped nations as never before. Politico-military power plays edge nations closer to war, now almost daily! Worldwide tension—extreme volatility!—coupled with spectacular weapons advancements, have made the "rumors" Jesus spoke of about war more common than Hollywood gossip.

So then, millions are *currently* dying annually due to one or another form of war. Next, recall that about 24,000 people now starve daily. This is almost *9 million* annually! And remember that disease now claims 82,000 victims a day—or the *30 million* each year referenced earlier. Factor in natural disasters—*great* earthquakes (300,000 died in total in Haiti, which also suffered a Cholera outbreak in its wake), plus volcanoes, and many kinds of storms and tsunamis—and the annual death toll rises. But there are also such things as *unprovoked* animal attacks that are on the rise.

We might also ask: What of the 46 million unborn babies who are MURDERED in a very real war by abortionists each year? This would have to be included in the "death" referenced in Revelation 6:8. Almost certainly a *direct* component of the horsemen, this ongoing worldwide atrocity commands inclusion within this math.

Now recognize that Mark's account of the Olivet Prophecy adds a word not found in either Matthew's or Luke's account. Instead of mentioning pestilences—which both Matthew and Luke do, as well as does Revelation 6 in regard to the *pale* (or sickly) horse—Mark says this: "For nation shall rise against nation, and kingdom against kingdom: and there shall be earthquakes in [various] places, and there shall be famines and *troubles...*" (13:8). The rest of the passage continues paralleling Matthew and Luke.

The Greek word translated "troubles" means "disturbance, that is, (of water) roiling, or (of a mob) sedition: trouble." This word brings to mind riots, civil uprisings, protests, violent crime and gang war, as well as a range of difficulties, some severe, that would come from floods (just think Pakistan in the summer of 2010), and probably tremendous hurricanes, cyclones and typhoons, and other severe storms—all forms of "roiling water." Mark's gospel indicates that these things will also grow worse. And each will bring its own additional death toll toward the one-fourth of all humanity that is losing their lives.

Stepping Back

Given a current world population of 6.8 billion, "the fourth part of the earth" is on its face 1.7 BILLION human beings! But this number is only at our present population. So it is no more than a snapshot of a world population growing ever larger.

Understand! As the population grows, a quarter of a larger base number yields a larger death count. And recognize that with so many already dying, world population is *still rising* by 77 million annually. Therefore, in the midst of a population explosion, 1.7 billion becomes the *smallest* possible death toll. Read and reread this paragraph if necessary until it is completely clear in your mind.

But there is also the difficulty, if not *impossibility*, of determining the exact number of people on Earth. Birth and death rates are in many places estimated. The world's best statisticians cannot precisely determine either of these figures. Neither can they perfectly track *causes* of death such as the number that war, famine and disease might include.

What *can* be known is that scores of millions now die each year because of the four horsemen—perhaps nearing a total of 100 million annually counting 46 million abortions—and many, *many* more hundreds of millions are yet to perish as a result of these conditions as we approach whatever is the population in God's mind at which the fourth is calculated.

Now think of *this*. If just those who have already died in the last ten years, for instance, were added back on top of the 6.8 billion to get a *correct* larger base number, Earth's total population would be many hundreds of millions bigger—or perhaps a billion or more bigger—than it is. (Consider if we went back 25 years to add even more.) What if the true base number were just a conservative eight billion?

This would translate to around *two billion* people who would perish—and we are speaking of the next *handful* of years! But recognize again that even this number perishing could be somewhat low.

Grasp what you have here learned! Fix it in the center of your mind. Then recognize that *everything* is in place for the *worst wave* of death ever to storm the earth to occur. The seals are open and the horses, as though being whipped by their riders, are running faster every day! Their effects are not a switch that flips off suddenly, taking a room to darkness, but rather are like a gradual turning down of a dimmer switch until a room—in this case, the world—is dark (John 9:4).

So then, prior to even the *start* of the Tribulation—the opening of the dreaded FIFTH SEAL—an entire quarter of man's population will perish! May God help you to comprehend just this one sentence.

No *mystery*, no *symbolism*, no *cryptic coded language* is involved in Revelation 6:8. God is PLAIN!

And yet the death of so many—coupled with the economic upheaval and chaos this will bring—will drive the world to a thought-to-be political/religious solution that is INFINITELY WORSE than this mere *opening salvo* of all that will happen!

The Greatest Proof

This book has already mentioned several times how most do not take God's words seriously. Of course, while He knew it would happen, this was never what Jesus intended when He uttered the prophecies described in this and the previous five chapters. In fact, so no one could possibly miss the *certainty* of all these horrific fulfillments to come just before His Return, He concluded all three accounts of the Olivet Prophecy—Matthew, Mark and Luke!—with a similar statement. Since Jesus' words are repeated in *three* of the gospel accounts for emphasis, they are all included here for the same reason.

After listing all that we have been discussing, Jesus said in Matthew, "Verily [truly] I say unto you, THIS GENERATION shall not pass, till all these things be fulfilled. *Heaven and earth shall pass away, but My words shall not pass away*" (24:34-35).

Now Mark: "Verily I say unto you, that THIS GENERATION shall not pass, till all these things be done. HEAVEN AND EARTH SHALL PASS AWAY: BUT MY WORDS SHALL NOT PASS AWAY" (13:30-31).

And Luke records, "Verily I say unto you, THIS GENERATION shall not pass away, till all be fulfilled. HEAVEN AND EARTH SHALL PASS AWAY: BUT MY WORDS SHALL NOT PASS AWAY" (21:32-33)!

Now ask if Jesus took seriously His own words. He literally elevated the fulfillment of all the prophetic horrors described through this book above the certainty of the continued existence of the entire universe, including Earth. And, again, this is repeated *three times* so no one could doubt what would happen—so there would be no room for dismissive thinking or minimizing what would occur.

How could anyone find a way to believe the prophecies described by Christ will not come to pass?

On only one other occasion did Christ call the existence of heaven and earth into the equation to demonstrate the certainty of His words. It is instructive: "Think not that I am come to destroy THE LAW, or *the prophets* [the Old Testament]: I am not come to destroy, but to fulfill. For verily I say unto you, *Till heaven and earth pass*, one jot or one tittle shall in no wise pass from THE LAW, till all be fulfilled" (Matt. 5:17-18).

Impossible to misunderstand, right? And also impossible to ignore or dismiss, right?

Wrong! The vast majority of ministers in the world of professing Christianity, with their millions of parishioners happily agreeing, have rejected the Ten Commandments (The Law) as "only for the Jews"—having convinced themselves they were "done away"—"nailed to the cross"—supposedly by the very Jesus Christ who spoke of their certain continuance.

NEVER underestimate the power of human beings to delude themselves through human reasoning into rejecting the plain words of God—words that are IMPOSSIBLE TO MISUNDERSTAND! If you doubt this, just hand this book to one of your friends and then, assuming they will read it, see if they share your conviction about it.

Let's summarize. The greatest proof that the four horsemen of the Apocalypse have *not* been riding for the last 2,000 years—but rather represent conditions that only come to pass at the end of the age—is that their entire fulfillment would be contained within A SINGLE GENERATION! The evidence is in. We are now *deep* into that generation.

The room will soon go black!

If you still find it difficult to believe that all of this could really happen so fast in the modern age, remember that up to one-half of a much less interconnected world died due to a single plague in a period of just three years—AD 1347 to 1350—in regard to the Black Death. Christ declares one-quarter will die in a "generation"—much more than three years.

Take Heed

Again, the God of the Bible is a *loving* God. He always sounds an alarm to those in harm's way. He wants no one to have an excuse!

The Church of God has the responsibility to "CRY ALOUD, *spare not*, lift up [our] voice LIKE A TRUMPET, and show My people their *transgression*, and the house of Jacob [Israel] their *sins*" (Isa. 58:1). The modern nations of Israel—and the world—need to be warned that punishment is coming. *You* are now learning about this punishment—and *you* are being warned! There will soon be no time remaining to do this (John 9:4; Amos 8:11).

Make yourself think about what is being reported in your newspaper and on your television *every day*. People are dying here and there, and here and there, in increasing numbers, and in a broadening array of sometimes new and different ways, more and more of them terrible. For these, we can say in a sense that the Great Tribulation or Day of the Lord already came. Sometimes what took these victims can be small events—other times they can be large.

Consider. For the thousands of people killed in the terrorist attack of September 11, 2001, the "tribulation," in a sense, came and went in an instant. For them it is over. There is nothing that can any longer be done for them. They are asleep, awaiting the time when they will be resurrected and given an opportunity to learn the truth of God's awesome Plan for mankind. Only then will they understand why they died—or (because the dead are asleep, waiting to be resurrected) even in many cases *that* they died!

Here is the point. While the worst is over for them, it is not yet over for America, the rest of the world—or *you*! Do not say that we have years to go and "I can take my time" with matters involving eternal life, or even protection through the years ahead. And do not say, "All the things of this chapter (and others) just cannot be." Scripture says they can. And the thousands of victims who died without notice in two tall buildings testify to the truth of how *suddenly* calamity can come. (Take time to read what amounts to an extraordinary parallel account from Jesus found in Luke 13:4-5 regarding a "tower in Siloam," and how death can be immediate, random and entirely unexpected for those who are not under God's protection.)

Even greater numbers—vastly greater—will perish *beyond* the horsemen. Take seriously the *meaning* behind world-shaking events and calamities. The prophecies of this chapter are certain—they WILL come to pass. Any who believe God—and Jesus Christ—will accept His inspired Word. This same Word also reveals the way to avoid the false hope of *how* a final escape will come...

A Secret Rapture?

Tens of millions believe in a coming "secret rapture," when Jesus will "unexpectedly take Christians to heaven." After the last six chapters, it is easy to see *why* many hope for protection. (And those chapters did not describe the most destructive prophecies.)

Is a rapture what the *Bible* teaches? God *does* promise protection. But where? Is it a place on Earth—or in heaven? And can we *know*? All who care had better know.

There is a group who do not much concern themselves with the *details* of prophecy. They are only barely looking for what lies ahead, if at all. They are busy trusting in a RAPTURE. They expect to be "snatched away"—so why worry? Many others, also believing in a rapture, *unnecessarily* fear that they will be "left behind"—that they will be left out when the time comes.

By now, if you are even a somewhat serious reader, YOU are thinking about how to escape all that has been described!

Is a Secret Rapture Coming?

According to fundamentalist Christians, all "believers"—those who have "accepted Jesus"—are scheduled to be whisked away to heaven without notice—no matter where they are or what they are doing. All "unbelievers" will be "left behind," as rapturist thinking declares, to suffer under the antichrist, and through the popularly believed to be *seven*-year

Tribulation—when war, disease, famine and religious deception explode worldwide. These missed being "vacuumed" to the safety of heaven at Christ's supposed *secret* coming.

We saw the theory continues further that the antichrist will permit the Jews to build another temple in Jerusalem, which he will attack and destroy three and a half years later.

Recognize there are two major competing positions among rapturists. It occurs *before* or in the *middle of* the thought-to-be seven years of Tribulation. But, either way, the sudden disappearance of millions, it is said, will "shock the world." After the Tribulation, Christ returns—this being His *visible* and, in effect, *third* coming—and defeats the antichrist and his army.

Theory Run Wild!

Try to imagine these headlines after the widescale confusion caused by Christ's initial supposed "rapturing" away of His saints: "Driverless bus crashes—hundreds killed"—"Schools in chaos: Where are the teachers?"—"Hundreds killed when pilot-less airplanes collide"—"200-car traffic jam: 'Where did all the drivers go?'"—"Factory employees gone, management wondering 'Why?'"—"Baseball game canceled: Some players missing." The possibilities are endless.

Many have become so consumed by this doctrine that there has developed a series of movies and bestselling books, as well as board games, about the aftermath of such a worldwide vanishing act!

One group created a "Rapture Index" that it terms a "Dow Jones Industrial Average of end time activity" and a "prophetic speedometer." Supposedly, by calculating world conditions, this index can closely forecast when the Return of Christ will take place. "The higher the number," the group's website states, "the faster we're moving towards the occurrence of pre-tribulation rapture."

Another group has even gone so far as to program a "post-rapture" email chain letter, which would automatically be sent to family and friends after the rapture. The letter states in part, "Dear Friend, This message has been sent to you by a friend or a relative who has recently disappeared along with millions and millions of people around the world. The reason they chose to send you this letter is because they cared about you and would like you to know the truth about where they went. This may come as a shock to you, but the one who sent you this has been taken up to heaven…"

The email continues, "I am sure that there will be a lot of speculation as to what happened to all these people. The theories of some scientists and world leaders will have so much credibility that most of the world will believe them. It will sound like the truth!"

Have *you* accepted the rapture, because it also "sounds like the truth"? Great numbers of sincere people have been captured by this idea! Have *you* placed *your* hope in this belief without *Bible proof*?

We could ask: Will Christ come one or two more times—with the first of these being a secret coming for His saints, and the second one to the world as a whole?

History of the Rapture Theory

While many believe a rapture has always been the Bible teaching, the idea was *unknown* before the sixteenth century.

Some important history. During the fifteenth and sixteenth centuries, reformers John Calvin, Ulrich Zwingli, Martin Luther and John Huss campaigned against the dominance of the Catholic Church. These men shook Catholic theology to its core—even calling that church the antichrist! Previously, Rome would have forced its beliefs and traditions on those who disagreed. However, support for the reformers quickly mounted. This publicly undermined Catholic authority.

Rome called for reconciliation, and convened the Council of Trent in 1545 to assess events. From this council sprang the "counter-reformation" teachings of three Jesuit priests—Francisco Ribera, Luis de Alcazar and Cardinal Bellarmine.

Ribera followed later with a commentary on the book of Revelation. To dispel the church's label of antichrist, he created the belief of *futurism*. This declared that all the prophecies of Revelation *only* applied to the last seven years preceding Christ's Return!

Recognize again that the Catholic church *openly* admits it creates beliefs—as well as traditions—entirely apart from the Bible. This is why Ribera could get away with inventing a *completely non-biblical* theory. Read this again: "A rule of Faith, or a competent guide to heaven, must be able to instruct in all the truths necessary for salvation. Now the Scriptures alone do not contain all the truths which a Christian is bound to believe, nor do they explicitly enjoin all the duties which he is obliged to practise..." (*Faith of Our Fathers*, James Gibbons, pp. 111-112).

Catholic leadership makes no attempt to hide their belief that tradition outweighs Scripture. In fact, this has become its own tradition. Yet most are unaware of this. The Council of Trent gave *tradition*—in this case, the humanly invented *futurism*—equal authority to the Bible.

It was Ribera's idea that opened the door to the rapture theory.

Here comes the irony. Almost 300 years later, Protestants adopted Ribera's "futurism" invention. Thanks to the Catholics, John Nelson Darby, the Anglican preacher who is called the "father of the rapture," could pick up where Ribera left off with his own invention—*dispensationalism.* Unlike any need the Catholics felt, Protestants—in this case, Darby— needed a way to get the Bible to say what they wanted to believe about a rapture. His way of interpreting the Bible taught that Christ would first *secretly* collect His followers, and later return to defeat the antichrist. This teaching continued through Darby's disciple, Cyrus Scofield, who assembled the Scofield Bible.

In *Heralds of the Dawn*, John A. Anderson records more history of what was originally "counter-Protestantism": "The Catholic Apostolic Church had its beginning in 1830. It was founded in Britain by...men and women who claimed divine inspiration. They said the Holy Spirit revealed to them that the last days had come [this proved false], that the Lord was about to return [also false], that first He would rapture the believers...at a secret coming...after which Christ would come in manifested power."

Since the early nineteenth century, countless millions have blindly accepted the rapture theory—fearing what would happen if they did not. But grasp this. The doctrine began in the minds of Catholic priests, then continued its development in the minds of the *reformers*—not *God's* mind, as revealed in the Bible! The Protestants simply bought in and picked up later.

Now think. Disagreeing theologians—remember rapture theorists do not agree—found different ways of interpreting the Bible to present the rapture. Which should one listen to? The answer? None! Again, this is because the belief is not in the Bible. Inventing theologies such as *futurism* or *dispensationalism* will not unlock God's Word! By merely letting the Bible unlock itself one can understand all the events surrounding the Tribulation and Christ's Second Coming.

What Will Really Happen?

Some review provides necessary foundation. Jesus describes a period when society becomes "as the days of Noah were" (Matt. 24:37). That time was "filled with violence" (Gen. 6:11), yet people were going about their daily business, pursuing pleasure and gain. This is when disaster fell on them.

People are again foretold to be so immersed in their lives that the Tribulation will take the world by surprise. Recall yet again Jesus' warning: "For *as a snare* shall it come on all them that dwell on the face of the whole earth" (Luke 21:35). Solomon added, "For man also knows not his time: as the fishes that are taken in an evil net, and as the birds that are *caught in the snare*; so are the sons of men snared in an evil time [certainly true of the end time], when it falls suddenly upon them" (Ecc. 9:12).

In an upcoming chapter we will see that before Christ returns, armies will again surround Jerusalem. Just before the Great Tribulation begins, God's people are warned to flee to safety (Matt. 24:16-22; Luke 21:20-27).

Matthew 24:16 states, "Then let them which be in Judea *flee* into the mountains." At the third and final fulfillment of the "Abomination of Desolation," immediately before the Tribulation, God states in Revelation 12:14 that His people will literally *flee*.

God's promise to protect His people is as real as the Great Tribulation. But, unlike the rapture theory, the Bible reveals there is a designated place on Earth—not heaven—where His Church will be safe during the three and a half (not seven) years of Tribulation. Luke 21 and Matthew 24 together revealed that the surrounding of Jerusalem by foreign forces and the abomination standing in the holy place are the events that signal when God's people should *flee* to safety—not be *raptured* away to heaven! (The next chapter necessarily covers separately, and in detail, the biblical place of safety.)

Jesus was concerned for His people. He warned of what was coming, and of the need to escape invading armies and escalating war. He knew *three problems* would be apparent. First, those with small children, and especially nursing babies, would have particular difficulty escaping (Matt. 24:19). Second, God's people should pray that the time of flight not be "in winter"—meaning *wintry conditions*, because a related prophecy points directly to a wintertime flight. The third had to do with the Sabbath (vs. 20).

Obedience to the sanctity of God's seventh-day Sabbath—which God's Church has always observed, and would therefore still be faithfully observing right to the end—could make flight more difficult.

Consider: Why would Jesus instruct to pray concerning the time of flight if His servants were going to be supernaturally sucked away? Rapturists ignore this by incorrectly focusing on, "Let him which is on the housetop not come down to take anything out of his house" (Matt. 24:17; Mark 13:15). Such misrepresentation bypasses any need for *personal responsibility*! In the first century, homes were largely joined and people could remove themselves more quickly by traveling from roof to roof. Jesus was merely using a term His disciples could understand. So must we understand.

Jesus wants His people prayerfully involved in their escape (Luke 21:36)—not self-assured, lazing back, expecting a heavenly vacuum cleaner to do it all for them! See through not only the false—but also *irresponsible*—rapture theory. But the theory does bring with it a carefully crafted theology used to sell it.

Supporters cite five verses as "proof" of the rapture. The first two are repeated here with much the same explanation from other chapters. This is so the reader will see their role within the overall rapture error.

Daniel 9:27

(1) Daniel 9:27: "And He shall confirm the covenant with many for one week: and in the *midst of the week* He shall cause the sacrifice and the oblation to cease, and for the overspreading of *abominations* he shall make it *desolate*, even until the consummation, and that determined shall be poured upon the desolate."

Again, due to the muddled prophetic understanding of rapture theorists, they claim the phrase "one week" refers to the last seven *years*, or seven "prophetic days," of mankind's society. This is false!

This verse *actually* references the abomination of desolation when occupying forces stop the Jews' daily sacrifice in Jerusalem. It also addresses the final week of what is called the *70 weeks prophecy* (of Daniel 9:24-27) about the Messiah and that *Jesus* Christ would be cut off in the middle of the week, after three and a half prophetic "days"—three and a half *years*—of His earthly mission. Daniel 9:27 is simply *not* a prophecy about how the *anti*christ will turn on the Jews halfway through the Tribulation.

Matthew 24:36, 40-42

(2) Matthew 24:36 and 24:40-42: "But of that day and hour knows no man, no, not the angels of heaven, but My Father only...Then shall two be in the field; the one shall be taken, and the other left. Two women shall be grinding at the mill; the one shall be taken, and the other left. Watch therefore: for you know not what hour your Lord does come."

Comprehending any difficult scripture begins with knowing its context. Beginning in verse 40, Jesus explains the condition of society in the last days. People will be "in the field" and "at the mill," carrying on daily activities. They will also be "eating and drinking" and "marrying and giving in marriage." In other words, life will *seem* normal *just before destruction—just before the snare takes them.* Verse 42 confirms that this will come *unexpectedly.* This is just before famine, pestilence and military invasion claim two-thirds of the population of the modern nations of Israel.

John 14:2-3

(3) John 14:2-3: "In My Father's house are many mansions: if it were not so, I would have told you. I go to prepare a place for you. And if I go and prepare a place for you, *I will come again,* and receive you unto Myself; that where I am, there you may be also."

The question becomes: Where will Christ be?

One of the greatest problems with the rapture is that heaven is not, and has never been, the reward of the saved. Jesus said, "The meek shall inherit *the earth*" (Matt. 5:5). He was quoting Psalm 37:11, which says the same thing. Now add this passage: "And has made us unto our God kings and priests: and we [Christians] shall *reign on the earth*" (Rev. 5:10). These verses explain why He also said, "No man has ascended into heaven" (John 3:13). So then, not only are God's people not raptured to heaven before Christ returns, they are not going there later. Further, no one is in heaven *now.* God has a salvation infinitely greater in store for His people, and this book has only begun to hint at it.

Jesus' coming again in John 14 will be to *Earth.* Remember, His kingdom is coming *here!* He will be *here.* The word translated "mansions" means "rooms, abode or residence." The Temple held rooms for various priests who administered there. Different rooms signify differing *positions of authority.* Jesus' parable of the pounds, in Luke 19:11-27, makes these positions over cities easy to understand. "Mansions" simply refers to offices—or positions of authority.

I repeat, true salvation is infinitely greater than going to heaven. John 14 reveals that, after His Return, Jesus' faithful servants will work under Him as kings and priests. Just the truth of salvation—rulership over cities beside Jesus Christ *on Earth*—reduces the rapture to a pile of scrap. (To understand the much bigger picture here, read another of my books, *The Awesome Potential of Man.* The millions who worry about being "left behind"—due to the popular *fiction* book series—never hear the truth about salvation. This inspiring book brings it.)

I Corinthians 15:50-52

(4) I Corinthians 15:50-52: "Now this I say, brethren, that flesh and blood cannot inherit the kingdom of God; neither does corruption inherit incorruption. Behold, I show you a mystery; we shall not all sleep, but we shall all be *changed*, in a moment, in the twinkling of an eye, at the last trump: for the trumpet shall sound, and the dead shall be raised incorruptible, and we shall be changed..."

There is no proof—or even *hint*—of a rapture here! Notice the phrase "last trump." Recall that this refers to the *seventh* trumpet, which announces Christ's Return to *the whole world*. This last trumpet is also referred to in Revelation 11:15 and I Thessalonians 4:15-16. It sends an immense—piercing—and reverberating—sound that *all* inhabitants of Earth will hear.

Notice this in Matthew: "And then shall appear the sign of the Son of man in heaven: and then shall *all the tribes of the earth mourn*, and they shall *see* the Son of man [nothing secret here] coming in the clouds of heaven with power and *great glory*. And He shall send His angels with a *great sound of a trumpet* [this has to be the last one], and they shall gather together His elect from the four winds, from one end of heaven to the other" (24:30-31). This references the saints wherever they are, either buried or alive on Earth. This becomes more clear.

Nothing "secret" is being described! This trumpet blast announces Christ's Return, and it is *then* when He gathers His people. At this point, His true followers will be changed into perfect, immortal beings. This is the time of the Resurrection, when the "dead in Christ" are raised to spirit-born immortal life. They first meet Him in the clouds, not as a rapture—not so that they can U-turn with Him for a return trip to heaven—but so they can return *with* Him to begin rule of Earth.

I Thessalonians 4:15-17

(5) I Thessalonians 4:15-17: "For this we say unto you by the word of the Lord, that we which are alive and remain unto the coming of the Lord shall not prevent them which are asleep. For the Lord Himself shall descend from heaven with a shout, with the voice of the archangel, and with the trump of God: and the dead in Christ shall rise first: then we

which are alive and remain shall be *caught up* together with them in the clouds to meet the Lord in the air: and so shall we ever be with the Lord."

But *where* will the saints "be with the Lord"? We read earlier Zechariah's answer: "And [Christ's] feet shall stand *in that day* [not three and a half or seven years later] upon the mount of Olives, which is before Jerusalem on the east...and the LORD my God *shall come* [recall John 14], and all the saints with [Him]" (14:4-5).

What could possibly be *plainer*?

These verses obviously describe Christ's *only* additional coming, which is announced by the *seventh* and *last* trumpet blast. There can only be *one* last trumpet—*one* seventh trumpet! To state Christ will return a secret additional time suggests He misrepresented His Second Coming to Earth! If Christ returns to Earth a third time, there must be another trumpet blast, which would make it the "eighth trumpet," and the seventh and last trumpet really the "second-to-last trumpet." This is of course ridiculous! The rapture idea makes Jesus a *liar*—and the perpetrator of *confusion*!

After examining the plain words of the Bible, the above supposed "proof texts" actually prove the *falsehood* and *deceptiveness* of this doctrine!

The Bible states, "God is not the author of *confusion*, but of *peace*, as in all churches of the saints" (I Cor. 14:33), and adds a little later, "Let all things be done *decently and in order*" (vs. 40). There is nothing *orderly* or *peaceful* about millions of human beings suddenly vanishing from beds, buses, workstations, automobiles, airplanes, etc. This is a picture of *chaos* and *confusion*! If the rapture were true, this disorder would not be the work of men, but of God.

Let's state this plainly for effect! The rapture is a doctrine of chaos, and makes God and Christ the *authors* of this confusion.

"Astrape" and "Parousia"

Revelation 1:16 describes Christ's appearance as "the sun [that] shines in his strength." That is bright! Jesus Himself describes His Coming this way: "For as the *lightning* comes out of the east, and shines even unto the west; so shall also the *coming* of the Son of man be" (Matt. 24:27).

Two Greek words should be noted here. These are altered and misapplied by rapturists to change Jesus' intended meaning.

"Lightning" comes from *astrape*, meaning "lightning, glare, bright shining." Would any suggest that people could not see lightning occurring *worldwide*? Some *do* suggest this about Christ's Return, even though it is foretold to be as a *glare* and *bright shining* that "comes out of the east, and shines even unto the west."

The word translated "coming" is *parousia*, meaning "being near, coming, presence." Rapture supporters claim this does not really mean "coming," but instead, a *"secret* nearness" or *"invisible* presence." Ridiculous! This is plain dishonesty with Scripture. Jesus said what He meant. Had He meant "secret nearness," He would have said this to His disciples—and to all who would read ever after.

Parousia is used in many other scriptures (Matt. 24:3, 27, 37, 39; I Cor. 15:23; 16:17; II Cor. 7:6-7; 10:10; Phil. 1:26; 2:12; I Thes. 2:19; 3:13; 4:15). In all of them it refers to the same meaning—not some mysterious "secret nearness." Remember, rapture theorists speak of Jesus' *secret* coming and His *visible* coming. The secret one is fiction, fantasy, invention—pure imagination. It may be real in its authors' minds, but it is not in the Bible.

Christ's Second—Final—Coming

As we have seen, the rapture theory has *some* truth mixed with *much* error. But the difference between this teaching and what God's Word really says about Christ's Return is astounding.

God's Word reveals a future last fulfillment of the "abomination of desolation," when a religious-military force stops the daily sacrifices at the Temple in Jerusalem. This destruction will be one of the two aspects of the sign for God's people to flee, as you are about to learn, to a physical place of protection. Soon after, the Tribulation will strike the world—to the complete surprise of all its inhabitants.

We saw this explained by the apostle Paul in I Thessalonians 5:2: "For yourselves know perfectly that the day of the Lord so comes as a *thief in the night* [to the world, not the Church]." The apostle Peter underscored this: "But the day of the Lord will come as a *thief in the night*; in the which the heavens shall pass away with a great noise, and the elements shall melt with fervent heat, the earth also and the works that are therein shall be burned up" (II Pet. 3:10).

While no one knows when a thief is going to come, homeowners certainly do know when he has broken and entered their house. No one will—or *could*—miss such an event, or Christ's Return!

Revelation 1:7 declares, "Behold, He *comes with clouds*; and *every eye shall see Him* [again, nothing secret here]...and *all kindreds* of the earth shall *wail* because of Him." Also, how could anyone miss *such a verse*? It practically screams off the page! Jesus further confirmed in Acts 1:9-11 that He will return in the clouds.

Sadly, most just do not read their Bibles, choosing to trust deceived ministers instead.

Let's repeat from Matthew 24: "And then shall appear the *sign* of the Son of man in heaven: and then shall all the tribes of the earth *mourn* [this would be closely connected to wailing], and they shall see the Son of man coming in the clouds of heaven with power and great glory. And He shall send His angels with a great sound of a trumpet, and they shall *gather* together His elect *from the four winds* [the "dead in Christ" will be resurrected—not raptured—from their graves], from one end of heaven [the first heaven—our atmosphere—the only place winds blow] to the other" (vs. 30-31).

This should be literally *impossible* to misunderstand. Jesus and His saints will then rule for 1,000 years in the established kingdom of God. This is the obvious truth of what will occur at Christ's Second Coming.

Do not be fooled by teachings claiming that Jesus Christ has *already* returned a second time, or that He is returning in secret. As seen in a previous chapter, but here bringing out more of the context, Christ strongly warned in Matthew 24:23-27: "Then if any man shall say unto you, Lo, here is Christ, or there; *believe it not.* For there shall arise false christs, and false prophets [what follows should sober you], and shall show great signs and wonders; insomuch that, if it were possible, they shall deceive the very elect. Behold, I have told you before [this is then a repeated warning from Jesus]. Wherefore if they shall say unto you, Behold, He is in the desert; go not forth: behold, He is in the *secret* chambers; believe it not. For as the *lightning* comes *out of the east,* and shines even *unto the west*; *so shall also the coming of the Son of man be.*"

Why the Rapture Theory

The events preceding Christ's Return are certainly terrible to contemplate. How to get through them naturally engenders more than worry—rather it begets *tremendous fear*! So, it is also natural to want to *escape* what is coming. The rapture is merely a humanly devised path for escaping the horror of the Tribulation. The problem has always been that it is *not* what GOD says!

Jesus warned that many false teachers would arise. Deception about His Second Coming would not—and could never—be an exception. Peter warned: "For we have not followed *cunningly devised fables* [Greek: a tale, fiction, myth], when we made known unto you the power and *coming* of our Lord Jesus Christ..." (II Pet. 1:16).

While this verse refers to accurately representing Christ's *First* Coming, the principle applies to His Second. The rapture is a tale—a myth!—a fable!—aimed at giving false hope to the unwitting and unsuspecting!

The Bible records the unmistakably LOUD and BRIGHT Coming of Christ. His Second—final—Coming will inaugurate the 1,000-year reign of Christ and His saints *on the earth.*

Jesus Christ built His Church—the *true* Church—the only one He built—2,000 years ago. This Church believes and teaches the truths of the Bible—*all* of them—not human ideas—*any* of them! The people of *this* Church have always stood in the plain certainty of what God *does* promise for those alive at the end—not the unscriptural false hope of human invention.

Reject the fiction of the rapture theory—and accept the truth of what God *really* promises in your Bible...

The Place of Safety

If the rapture is unbiblical, and God will not unexpectedly "vacuum" the saints to heaven, how *does* He plan to protect His faithful servants? While the rapture is fiction, the horrific plagues and earth-shaking events of the Day of the Lord and the Great Tribulation are not! This includes all that happens before these periods.

The Bible reveals that those who take heed *can* escape! *How* is another story. And this time, unlike the rapture, there is plenty of proof.

A Way of Escape

Even Jesus' disciples, who heard His Matthew 24 prophecy, did not *at first* grasp the timing of events preceding His Return. Similarly, we saw Daniel did not understand what he recorded: "I heard, but I understood not..." (12:8).

The only place to start this subject is by re-examining a plain statement that the reader either believes or does not believe: "Watch you therefore, and pray always, that you may be accounted worthy to ESCAPE all these things that shall come to pass, and to stand before the Son of man" (Luke 21:36). The phrase "all these things" means *all* end-time events—those just before Christ's Return. The previous verse was the one warning that all others would be taken unexpectedly by the "snare" of global calamity.

It *is* God's purpose that some be spared—that they *escape*.

The coming cataclysm will be so unprecedented in severity that without God's intervention "...*there should no flesh be saved* [alive]: but for the *elect's sake* those days shall be shortened" (Matt. 24:22). The elect, God's people, are to be protected. This is but one reason God will not permit the entire world population to be destroyed—His people are counted in that number.

Since Daniel adds, "There shall be a *time of trouble*, such as never was since there was a nation even to that same time..." (12:1), and Jeremiah states, "Alas! For that day is *great*, so that none is like it: it is even the *time of Jacob's trouble*, but he shall be saved out of it" (30:7), we might use the vernacular and ask, "Just how in the world *does* God protect His people from all of this?"

Understanding Church Eras

One of God's most explicit promises of safety is found in Revelation 3:10, addressing what is the Philadelphian era of His Church: "Because you have kept the word of My patience, *I also will keep you from the hour of temptation* [or trial, meaning the Tribulation], which shall come upon *all the world*, to try them that dwell upon the earth." This has to be the same as the "snare" of Luke 21:35. Yet, rapturists actually cite Revelation 3:10 as proof of a secret rapture. You will soon see it to be proof of ignorance.

The promise of safety is directly tied to the biblical understanding of Church eras, outlined in Revelation 2 and 3. The *sixth* era—*Philadelphia*—is promised special protection at the end. This is *only* understood when one recognizes the earlier explanation that the Church of God has existed through seven eras. Protection is connected to the very closing history of the true Church. Those who reject one unified true Church, and its eras, are destined to never understand a literal place of safety—or be included.

Overview of the True Church

Those who will be protected, as well as how this will happen, cannot be understood without at least a brief overview of the true Church of the New Testament.

Jesus Christ built one Church (Matt. 16:18), which does His Work of announcing the true gospel around the world and warning the greatest nations of impending punishment. It also holds to and declares *all* of the

Overview of Church Eras

Below is a listing of the seven successive eras along with the approximate dates and key events of each era. (The term "RC" in the chart is an abbreviation for Roman Catholic.)

CHURCH ERA	DATES (approx.)	EVENTS
Ephesus (Rev. 2:1-7)	AD 31-100	Apostolic era (AD 31-98). Persecution begins at Rome (AD 64). Church flees to Pella; Jerusalem falls (AD 69-70).
Smyrna (Rev. 2:8-11)	AD 100-325	Church leaders attempt to combat heresy (AD 150s-190s). Ten years of severe persecution (Rev 2:10; AD 303-313). Nicene Council outlaws true religion; Church flees (AD 325).
Pergamos (Rev. 2:12-17)	AD 325-1000	Constantine of Mananali leads Church (about AD 675). Sergius leads Church (about AD 800). Paulicians relocate to Balkans (about AD 800-900).
Thyatira (Rev. 2:18-29)	AD 1000-1600	Peter DeBruys and Henry of Lausanne lead Church (1104-1135). Peter Waldo leads Church (1161-1217). RC Inquisition begins against Church (1229). Gutenberg Bibles printed (1450). RC persecution for the 1,260 years restrained after 1585. Destruction of Spanish Armada (1588).
Sardis (Rev. 3:1-6)	1600-1934	Church revives in England as persecution abates (1600s). Bampfields and Stennetts lead Church (about 1650-1750). Stephen Mumford establishes Church in America; 1668. Arriving immigrants set up churches in Pennsylvania and New Jersey (1700s). Many depart Church to align with Adventists (1840s-1860s). Church of God Seventh Day established in Stanberry, Mo. (early 1900s).
Philadelphia (Rev. 3:7-13)	1934-1980s	Herbert W. Armstrong begins first radio broadcast (1934). Radio broadcast begins in Europe (1953). Literature, TV and radio reach over 100 million (1970-1980s). Mr. Armstrong dies (1986).
Laodicea (Rev. 3:14-22)	1980s-present	Remnants fragment after apostasy into many disagreeing, doctrinally compromised groups and organizations.

many truths of the Bible. This Church exists and functions under God's government, which in part enables it to be as wonderfully efficient and productive as it is. Of course, it has the guidance and backing of the all-powerful living Jesus Christ in all that it does (Matt. 28:19-20).

Revelation 12:1-4 reveals that Satan attempted to destroy Christ when He was born of the "woman" depicted there. This woman symbolizes the Old Testament Church that was ancient Israel—called "the church in the wilderness" (Acts 7:38).

We saw verse 6 adds, "And the woman [now *spiritual* Israel, the New Testament Church] fled into the wilderness, where she has *a place* prepared of God, that they should feed her there a thousand two hundred and threescore [1,260] *days*." We will see that, on several occasions—this is one—history demonstrates that God has sent His people into *hiding* in a SPECIAL PLACE to protect them.

The day-for-a-year principle of Bible prophecy appears again here. With the Nicene Council in AD 325, the Roman Empire forbade the true Church from functioning within its domain, forcing God's people to flee into northwestern Europe. Ultimately, this allowed God's Church somewhat greater religious freedom. Catholic domination ended in Britain and Holland in about 1585. Thus, 1,260 *years* of suppression and martyrdom came to an end.

Revelation 12 continues, "And the great dragon was cast out, that old serpent, called the Devil, and Satan, which deceives the whole world: he was cast out into the earth, and his angels were cast out with him" (vs. 9). This leads to the event described in verse 13: "When the dragon saw that he was cast unto the earth, he persecuted the woman [the true Church] which brought forth the man child." The timing of this persecution is now in the *near future*.

Notice how the woman is to be protected: "To the woman were given *two wings* of a great eagle, that she might fly into the wilderness, into HER PLACE, where she is nourished for a *time*, and *times*, and *half a time*, from the face of the serpent" (vs. 14).

A biblical "time" is equal to a prophetic year of 360 days. Revelation 12:14 refers to the same period, that of three and a half times (Revelation 11:2 says "42 months") or 1,260 days (3½ x 360 days). In this case, the context of time is in units of literal days. This will be important when we revisit Daniel 12:11-12 because the 1,260 days correspond with verses and *two* key time periods revealed there. The Revelation 12 woman was taken into "her place" in the wilderness for three and a half years—the length of the Tribulation.

Some have misunderstood the phrase "she might *fly* into the wilderness." This does not indicate the mode of transportation, but rather that the woman escapes, or flees—"flies"—from Satan's persecution. Notice how Exodus 19:4 uses this same term: "You have seen what I did unto the Egyptians, and how *I* bore you *on eagles' wings*, and brought you unto Myself." The Israelites did not literally *fly* out of Egypt—they walked! Yet *God* (obviously the "eagle") still carried them on "eagles' wings"— He *provided for* and *protected* them in their journey.

The providing of a place for the Church (Rev. 12:14) directly corresponds to the promise given to Philadelphians (Rev. 3:10).

Miraculous Intervention

Revelation 12:15-16 continues this prophetic account: "And the serpent cast out of his mouth water as a *flood* after the woman [the Church], that he might cause her to be carried away of the flood. And the earth helped the woman, and the earth opened her mouth, and *swallowed* up the flood which the dragon cast out of his mouth."

This paints a dramatic picture. Incredible, absolutely miraculous delivery is here seen to be necessary for God's people to survive. The term "flood" represents an army sent to destroy the Church. A number of scriptures use this analogy.

For example, notice Isaiah 59:19: "When the enemy shall come in like a *flood*, the Spirit of the Lord shall lift up a standard against him."

Speaking of Korah's rebellion against Moses' authority—and we saw this in the earthquake chapter—Numbers 16:32 gives the following account: "And the earth opened her mouth, and *swallowed* them up, and their houses, and all the men that appertained unto Korah, and all their goods."

The account of the earth swallowing up the "flood" is also analogous to the Red Sea closing in and drowning the Egyptian army pursuing the Israelites. The parallels are clear. Revelation 12:15-16 points to God's deliverance of His Church during the time of protection when the woman is "in *her place*, where she is nourished" (vs. 14). The timeframe indicates Satan's attempt to destroy the woman.

Here is the devil's next move: "And the dragon was wroth with the woman, and went to make war with the remnant of her seed [children—brethren], which *keep the commandments of God*, and have the testimony of Jesus Christ" (vs. 17).

This obviously occurs very early during the Tribulation—the time of Satan's wrath against the modern nations of Israel and the true

Church. The Greek word *loipoi* translated "remnant" also means "remaining ones," "residue," or "the rest." These are those of the lukewarm Laodicean seventh era—who have neither held to pure biblical truth nor stressed personal growth and overcoming in their lives as they should. But they *do* still keep God's Law—His Commandments.

The "remnant of her seed" are brethren who will *not* be protected. Scripture shows that none of the seventh era of the Church, Laodicea, survive the Tribulation. Those who purchased "gold tried in the fire" (Rev. 3:18) will die *physically*, but survive *spiritually*—they do enter God's kingdom. Those who yield under pressure and take the mark of the Beast (13:15-17) to save their physical lives will lose out on eternal life for failing to hold to all of God's truth, including aiding in His final Work before the age concludes.

Thus, within the Revelation 12 overview of the true Church are the first clues to *how* God will protect His people.

Sobering Prophecy

An earlier prophecy in Ezekiel 5 concerning the modern nations of Israel reveals more about God's promised protection of His faithful servants. Some review sets it up.

Verse 1 states, "And you, son of man, take you a sharp knife, take you a barber's razor, and cause it to pass upon your head and upon your beard: then take you balances to weigh, and divide the hair."

Verse 2 shows what Ezekiel was to do next: "You shall burn with fire a *third part* in the midst of the city, when the days of the siege are fulfilled: and you shall take a *third part*, and smite about it with a knife: and a *third part* you shall scatter in the wind; and I will draw out a sword after them."

Verse 3 introduces a fascinating detail: "You shall also take thereof *a few* in number, and bind them *in your skirts*." Verse 4 expounds on this: "Then take of them again, and cast them into the midst of the fire, and burn them in the fire; for thereof shall a fire come forth into all the house of Israel."

To understand this passage, we must yet again allow the Bible to interpret itself. Verse 1 is thoroughly explained in verse 12, referenced earlier: "A *third part* of you shall die with the PESTILENCE, and with FAMINE shall they be consumed in the midst of you: and a *third part* shall fall by the SWORD round about you; and I will SCATTER a *third part* into all the winds, and I will draw out a sword after them."

A third of the populations of all modern Israelitish nations are foretold to perish from disease and famine. Another third will die from military invasion. Then, the remaining third attempt to escape—unsuccessfully. The surviving third is taken into captivity—modern enslavement.

Notice the clarity with which Jeremiah records their fate: "And it shall come to pass, if they say unto you, Where shall we go forth? Then you shall tell them, Thus says the LORD; such as are for death, to death; and such as are for the sword, to the sword; and such as are for the famine, to the famine; and such as are for the captivity, to the captivity" (15:2).

The term "skirts" in Ezekiel 5:3 is from the Hebrew word *kanaph*, better translated "wings" (as noted in most Bible margins). This is the same Hebrew word translated "wings" in Exodus 19:4, where God bore Israel on "eagles' wings"! This parallels Revelation 12:14, in which the Church is taken to "her place" by the wings of an eagle. Ezekiel 5:4 shows that some (the lukewarm remnant) who initially survive are cast back into the fire—the Tribulation.

Three Overlapping Time Periods

An earlier passage in Daniel 12 reveals God's Plan for His people, here presented with more context: "Many shall be *purified*, and *made white* [righteous], and *tried*; but the wicked shall do wickedly: and none of the wicked shall understand; but the wise shall understand" (vs. 10).

There are two times of trial to understand. One is already taking place and the other is future. The first involves God's people, who are being *spiritually* "purified, made white, and tried." Their *conversion* is being purified. This process continues into the *second* trial—the Tribulation—which, recall, "shall come upon all the world, to try them that dwell upon the earth" (Rev. 3:10), and modern Israel in particular—"the time of Jacob's trouble" (Jer. 30:7). Also recall the Revelation 12:13 persecution of God's Church by the devil.

Let's look at three critical time periods. The Great Tribulation and Day of the Lord together last 1,260 days, or three and a half years before Christ's Return. The others are "1,290 days" and "1,335 days."

The 1,290 appears in Daniel 12:11: "And from the time that the daily sacrifice shall be taken away, and the abomination that makes desolate set up, there shall be *a thousand two hundred and ninety days*." These are obviously also *literal* days, beginning with the setting up of the abomination of desolation. So then, with the Church to be protected for only *1,260* days, there are 30 days before it arrives at its designated place of protection.

The 1,335-day period is introduced one verse later in Daniel: "Blessed is he that *waits*, and comes to the *thousand three hundred and five and thirty days*" (vs. 12). What is this?

Starting 45 days before the 1,290-day "mile-marker," the 1,335 date also counts down to the Return of Christ. This moment signals the end of God's Work of preaching the true gospel and warning the world's greatest nations. The 1,335 is when the "call" goes out to God's people to assemble for flight to safety. Then, when the abomination is set up—45 days later—events culminate in Jerusalem and the Church flees. The 45-day period permits the Church time to gather from around the world in what we will see to be Judea. (In a longer scriptural exercise, beyond the natural bounds of this book, the 45-day period can be fully proven.)

These periods begin with *different* events, but end with the *same* event—Christ's Return! The graph on the facing page illustrates how these three durations of time overlap.

1,335 Days—1,290 Days—1,260 Days

Since Daniel prefixes the event beginning the 1,335 days with "blessed is he that waits," this is designated as the *signal*, with a possible accompanying event—at this *specific* time—for which the Church has patiently waited (Matt. 24:13; 10:22; Luke 21:19; Rev. 14:12).

The arrival of the critical 1,335 days moment is something that will only be known to those *in God's one, undivided Church*. An internal warning will be inspired by the Church's true Head, Jesus Christ (Col. 1:18-19; Eph. 1:22-23). Of course, no *man* could be the source of such a signal. Real faith will be required. Probably prepared beforehand, God's people will plainly understand.

Miracles, almost certainly many, will have to be involved. Merely recall how God supernaturally eliminates Satan's army (the flood) right before the Church arrives at her place. How many *other* miracles will be needed just for God's servants from all over the world to gather, let alone escape?

You will soon learn how the abomination of desolation involves the Jew's sacrifices being stopped, a religious figure entering the holy place and, the most obvious aspect of it, the city of Jerusalem being surrounded by armies (Luke 21:20).

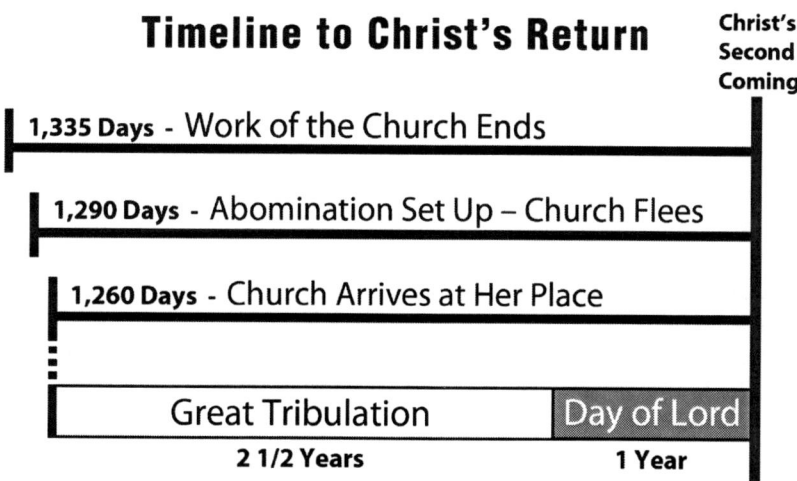

Grasp this. All who believe in the rapture—all of them!—are being set up to enter the Tribulation. They have literally been *set up* to patiently wait until the Tribulation falls on them like a snare. And they have been *set up* for what will be the indescribable shock, anger and disappointment from betrayal by trusted religious leaders.

Consider. They have been told the worst of the Tribulation begins three and a half years *after* they will have supposedly already been sucked into heaven. They have been lulled into believing therefore that it would not be something that really concerns them. In truth, the Tribulation will *blindside* millions of rapturists with the force of a *100-car runaway freight train!* They are oblivious to what is coming—and you cannot convince them otherwise. But the Tribulation also awaits *other* vast millions of professing Christians because virtually all of *their* beliefs can just as easily be proven to be *unbiblical* human inventions and traditions.

Great Haste!

Directly contradicting rapturists, notice what Christ instructed regarding the abomination's appearance: "Then let them which are in Judea *flee* to the mountains; and let them which are in the midst of it *depart out*; and let not them that are in the countries enter thereinto" (Luke 21:21). The message is clear: *leave quickly!* This warning is so urgent, the need to get out fast so great, that those who flee are told not to return home for *anything* (Matt. 24:17-18).

The prophet Hosea describes the same 30-day period before the destruction of Judah, America, Britain and certain other nations: "They [Judah and Israel] shall go with their flocks and with their herds to seek the LORD; but they shall not find Him [Why? They waited too long!]; He has withdrawn Himself from them…Now shall A MONTH devour them with their portions" (5:6-7).

No wonder the Church must flee in great haste. During that short interval—from 1,290 to 1,260 days—God holds back events, just as He did when Noah prepared the ark and when Lot had to leave Sodom. Imminent destruction was delayed until these men and their families had reached safety.

Let's look again at how Jesus described Noah's time: "As it was in the days of Noah, so shall it be also in the days of the Son of man. They did eat, they drank, they married wives, they were given in marriage, *until the day* that Noah entered into the ark, and the flood came, and *destroyed them all*" (Luke 17:26-27). Once Noah's family was safe, the Flood slammed into a disbelieving world!

Let's now re-examine Lot's situation: "*Likewise* also as it was in the days of Lot; they did eat, they drank, they bought, they sold, they planted, they builded; but *the same day* that Lot went out of Sodom it rained fire and brimstone from heaven, and *destroyed them all*" (vs. 28-29). As with *Noah's* time, destruction came "the same day"—immediately *after* Lot had escaped!

First God protected Lot's family in the little city of Zoar, but they later also took refuge in nearby mountains. Here is God's directive to Lot: "Haste you, escape there [Zoar]; *for I cannot do anything till you be come there…*" (Gen. 19:22).

Understand! God held back events until *certain individuals* were taken from harm's way! Events will *again* be held back until the true saints have left their gathering place in Judea.

More in Isaiah

Two incredible passages in Isaiah speak of those whom God will protect: "Let My *outcasts* [God's people] dwell with you, Moab; be you a covert [a cover] to them from the face of the spoiler [the devil and his pursuing army]" (16:4). (The *location* of Moab introduces a fascinating key to identifying the place of safety. The Bible does offer certain real clues—

but exactly *where* God may choose to protect His people is not the subject of this book.) An interesting clue is contained in the word "outcasts." Paralleling Israel being cast from Egypt, God's people will be "cast out" of their host countries all over the world.

Now God's direct promise, also in Isaiah, to these outcasts: "Come, *My* people, enter you into *your chambers*, and shut your doors about you: *hide yourself* as it were for a little moment [three and a half years], until the indignation [God's wrath during the Day of the Lord] be overpast. For, behold, the LORD comes out of His place *to punish the inhabitants of the earth* for their iniquity [lawlessness]: the earth also shall disclose her blood, and shall no more cover her slain" (26:20-21).

These passages are most plain!

Historical Parallel

Now let's examine the extraordinary—and truly *fascinating*—parallel event in the first century when God protected the Jerusalem congregation. This was just before another time of great trial for that city and for Judea. It is instructive.

Provocations by Roman officials against the Jewish priesthood, starting in AD 60, finally led to a revolt by Jewish separatists. This brought escalating Jewish military reprisals. The end result was *miraculous delivery* of God's people from the Romans. Let's learn how.

In AD 66, intending to crush the rebellion, the Roman army under General Cestius approached the walls of Jerusalem to capture the city. For unknown reasons, Cestius turned away from the city prior to the planned assault. Later, a second Roman advance, this time under General Vespasian, also suddenly halted so he could race back to Rome to become emperor.

These delays were not random. God's people were *still in Jerusalem,* and Christ was guiding events to allow them to flee!

The historian Josephus gave a detailed account of what occurred three years later. Many had witnessed, just before Pentecost AD 69, formations in the clouds of troops and chariots surrounding cities. Josephus recorded: "Moreover, at that feast which we call Pentecost, as the priests were going by night into the inner [court of the] temple...they said, that in the first place they felt a quaking, and heard a great noise, and after that they heard a sound as of a multitude, saying, 'LET US REMOVE HENCE'" (*Wars of the Jews*, bk. VI, ch. V, sec. 3, emphasis mine).

God's people did flee Jerusalem at that time. But without God's intervention, they would have never been able to leave. While the Roman army was readying for siege, the congregation exited in *full view* of the soldiers, before crossing the Jordan River. The brethren also had

Fanatical Belief?

Some may find it embarrassing to believe in a literal place of safety. They associate it with religious fanaticism, such as the Jim Jones cult, who retreated to Guyana in the late 1970s, and the crisis at Waco, Texas in the 1990s under David Koresh, and other religious groups with fanatical or bizarre conduct.

The actions of such leaders, and the groups following them, distort and taint the Bible's teachings, repelling many from the truth. Such fanatics personify this prophetic scripture: "But there were *false prophets* also among the people, even as there shall be *false teachers* among you...And *many* shall follow their pernicious ways; *by reason of whom the way of truth shall be evil spoken of* " (II Pet. 2:1-2).

Some who have been called, and who became aware of growing world trouble, have expressed that they do not want their relatives, friends, neighbors or associates to look upon them as religious fanatics. They seem to prefer to suffer the greatest time of trouble the world has ever known, rather than obey God and risk suffering ridicule and scorn.

What about those who fled Jerusalem in AD 69, who may have been considered traitors, fanatics or cowards? Then, what about those who stayed behind, concerned about what friends and associates would think? In the end, these were victims of starvation, crucifixion and other horrors of war. Those who *obeyed* and *trusted* God—following His instructions to flee—survived. Certainly many around them would have thought them fanatical.

Obedience and faith in God will again be crucial in the prophesied flight to come!

to contend with patrolling Jewish fighters who considered them traitors. With God's protection, the new exiles went northeast to *another little town*—Pella. Within months, after horrible suffering and starvation, Jerusalem fell.

God of Unlimited Power

God is unlimited in His ability to choose *any* form of *miraculous* intervention—whether earthquake, cloud formations or the noise of a multitude. Without His intervention, the Jerusalem congregation would have perished. Those in tune with God both heard and heeded. Others may not have heard the warning. But the Temple priests *did*.

Some ridicule the promise of a flight to a place of protection on the premise that "there is no way to know the time to flee" or "one cannot know that the signal is valid," among others. These are but *shallow excuses* to those who serve and believe the true God!

God's servants must steadfastly look to Him to know *what* to do, and *when* to do it. Timing is vital to God's protection. Suppose some in the Jerusalem congregation learned beforehand that Pella would be their place of protection. Suppose they fled there even just a little in advance. The result? They would have been killed by the Roman armies that had devastated Pella just months previously. God sent His people there only *after* Pella had been overrun!

Also, critics might have insisted at the time that Pella was the worst possible choice because it was within territory easily accessible to the Romans. And Jewish patriots also patrolled the region around Pella. But God protected the Jerusalem congregation exactly where *He* led them. They survived, and even thrived there for decades. This is connected to why—of all places—God's people are foretold by Jesus in three gospels to gather in Judea.

God can reveal all necessary events to His people. The first-century leadership of His Church eventually would have known their destination, as well as other necessary details. The Bible does not reveal what the sign will be for the Church's flight in the years just ahead. But there will be no doubt among those willing to trust God's instructions.

Do You Believe God?

Those who reject a place of safety deny clear promises of God. Scripture emphatically *proves* there will be a specific, designated place preselected by God! And the previous chapter proved that there will be no secret rapture.

Remember Jesus' admonition: "But pray you that your *flight* be not in the winter [again, meaning *in wintry conditions*], neither on the Sabbath day" (Matt. 24:20). He listed a series of events to occur *sequentially* through the time of flight, and continuing until His Return, adding, we saw earlier, "whoso reads, let him *understand*" (vs. 15).

Tragically, most today do not—and *will not!*—understand the shocking crush of events soon to smash into civilization. This is because they are not willing to obey God, which, as we learned, is the prerequisite to achieving proper understanding (Acts 5:32; Psa. 111:10; Prov. 2:5-6).

All who yield themselves to obey God, and strive to serve Him in all points, *will* understand these great events, and *will* be found worthy to escape this worst time of trouble ever (Luke 21:36)!

God *will* supernaturally hide and protect His people in a specific location. Will *you* believe His promises? Will *you* qualify for deliverance and protection?—or await a rapture that will never come?—or be among the greatest number at the end who remain skeptics—scoffers—disbelieving all things prophetic.

Do not stand in doubt. You *can* be among those whom God protects—and you can *escape*...

Those Who Escape

Faithful Christians will be taken to a specially prepared place of safe protection, and kept from the "hour of trial" to come on the "whole earth." Their flight will occur *just before* earth-jarring punishment from God strikes all nations in two more waves.

Many of God's people will *not* be protected. Also, like the vast numbers caught unprepared when atomic bombs struck two Japanese cities at the end of World War II, and when millions of Jews lost their lives because they could not believe the Nazis capable of the Holocaust, many today will be unnecessarily swept away into suffering punishment and death when they could have been *protected*—could have SURVIVED!

One central question looms: *What is it* that God requires of those who *escape*?

Misreading Events—and Times

One of the most critical warnings Jesus directed to those living at the end of the age was that many would have slipped into the belief that more time remained than God had planned. He summarized this attitude as "My Lord delays His coming" (Matt. 24:3, 48). Jesus knew that circumstances in the world would mesmerize many into assuming they could enjoy their lives a little longer before "things blow up."

The problem?

When calamity strikes without warning, many will be shocked, thinking, "I thought we had more time."

A review of Jeremiah and Ezekiel reveals that this thinking reflects how people would *incorrectly perceive* the speed and seriousness of end-time events between nations. They would not be able to recognize prophecy, and the *rate* of its advancing fulfillment, playing out before them. Follow closely, because critical understanding is about to unfold.

Recognize that both Jeremiah and Ezekiel foretold a *strange interval* in world events when, just before the end—even after the death of up to two billion people—religious (and probably some political) leaders, among others, in the nations of Israel and elsewhere, would offer public reassurance to the masses who would be concerned about what they were observing on the domestic and international scene.

We saw the prophet Jeremiah wrote this about the efforts of leaders in latter-day Israel. Let's read more closely: "They have *healed* also the *hurt* of the daughter of My people *slightly*, saying, Peace, peace; when there is no peace" (6:14). For emphasis, God inspired Jeremiah to repeat this statement verbatim in chapter 8, verse 11.

Here is how the prophet Ezekiel describes the fruitless efforts of leaders who apply patchwork solutions to huge, impossible problems towering over the world: "Because, even because they [the leaders] have seduced My people, saying, Peace; and there was no peace; and one built up a wall, and, lo, others daubed it with *untempered mortar*" (13:10).

Understand the terms being used here—grasp God's meaning. "Untempered mortar" allows bricks to come loose under pressure where "walls" were thought to be stronger than they were. These ineffective "solutions" (the untempered political mortar used by world leaders) will involve military, political, economic, social and religious solutions—and will almost surely include the spreading of the counterfeit "Jesus" and his band-aid "kingdom-building" social-improvement "gospel."

Because the One who became Jesus Christ inspired both the Old and New Testaments, it is not surprising that the problem of misreading events at the end would be a theme referenced by numerous Bible writers. In fact, Jesus Himself spoke more than once of how His Return would arrive without notice, as would a "thief" entering your home late at night when you would be asleep. We saw Peter and Paul were also inspired to speak of events at the end coming "as a thief in the night" (II Pet. 3:10; I Thes. 5:2).

Thieves do not telephone in advance of their coming. They "break and enter" homes or businesses without notice. Truly, the Great Tribulation and Day of the Lord will suddenly "break" into world peace and "enter" the course of every nation and every life on Earth!

Not All True Christians Protected

As we have seen, Revelation 6:9-11 symbolically paints a revealing but grim picture of martyred Christians from previous ages awaiting a final time when "their fellow servants also and their brethren, that should be killed as they were, should be fulfilled." Revelation 12:17 identifies who these "fellow servants" are. We have seen that they are described as "the remnant of her [the Church's] seed"—those that "keep the commandments of God, and have the testimony of Jesus Christ." This remnant is directly persecuted by Satan, as he "makes war" with them, eventually causing their death.

Understand! As stated, even some *true* Christians will not escape the devil's wrath in the Tribulation! This is serious, and should make the question of how to receive God's protection much more sobering!

Consider. If even certain genuine servants of God will not be spared from coming martyrdom, because their conduct and beliefs are deficient in various ways from what God expects, then He must have very high standards for those He *does* select for protection. Recognize that your life hangs in the balance. Quite literally, if you miscalculate or falsely assume, the personal price you pay will be catastrophic.

It is time to WAKE UP to what is at stake!

Grasp this! You have a personal responsibility, and the remainder of this chapter covers basic, vital points that you must know—if you hope to escape what others will not!

Also recognize that, however important, just "keeping the commandments of God" (Rev. 12:17) is not enough to be protected from—to escape—the devil's angry attack. Although the world rejects this marvelous SPIRITUAL LAW, God requires far more than just basic obedience to escape the coming time of world trial.

You Have a Responsibility

Consider for a moment what may be the worst part of the fictional rapture theory. Merely waiting to be whisked away—mysteriously *vacuumed* into heaven—produces a largely carefree and careless attitude in those awaiting Christ's Return. This thinking subtly defeats the need for any *personal responsibility*—for taking action in a host of vital areas of Christian conduct and behavior. Tragically, millions *are* in fact now being conditioned to simply "Believe in Christ, and He will take care of everything else."

This is short-sighted, dangerous thinking! It is also very irresponsible.

Numerous verses demonstrate that TRUE Christianity involves *active effort*. TRUE conversion does not allow for *passive bystanding*. Of course, just the act of escaping implies effort. But Luke records that one must do at least two other specific things for escape to be possible: "*watch…*and *pray always*" (Luke 21:36)!

Certainly not the whole picture, this does further introduce the need for taking action and accepting personal responsibility!

Watch and Pray

Take Jesus' instruction at face value. There is no room in Luke 21:36 for disinterest, or even passive semi-interest, in the exact sequence of crucial events, as they lead up to the fulfillment of the greatest single prophecy in the Bible—Jesus Christ's Return. All who wish to truly be God's servants—and to stand before Christ in His kingdom—will be found carefully watching for *many* specific trends and events, either occurring now or lying just over the horizon.

The Restored Church of God has prepared many tools to help look ahead to—and carefully watch—BIG EVENTS, soon to EXPLODE on the world scene! Force yourself to develop a burning interest in what will happen and to learn while there is still time. If necessary, read this book again until the weight—the THUNDERING REALITY!—of future events becomes clear. Determine to grasp, with full understanding, how and in what order they will occur. Nothing less will do.

Luke also said to "pray always." Obviously, prayer—"effectual [poured out], fervent [intense] prayer" (Jms. 5:16)—requires real effort. Such prayer is not done automatically or easily, and you must set your hand to learn *how* to do it and to *work* at it.

Most people have no idea how to pray, or even that they should *regularly* talk to God. That is what prayer *is*—talking to God. Most offer empty, canned, self-righteous platitudes, repeating the same thing over and over, contrary to Jesus' plain teaching in Matthew 6:7. Others merely pray selfish prayers, reflecting the "gimmes." Still others seem to confuse thinking "happy thoughts" or "positive thinking" with prayer. Of course, these *are* good, if correctly based. But they are not PRAYER!

Understanding the keys to prayer, which come from a simple study of the New Testament on this subject, will forever change the way you view the powerful, personal tool of prayer. This means taking the time to learn how to *study* God's Word, and to *meditate* on what you are reading, sometimes accompanied with *fasting*. You can understand and master these tools. Done effectively, they will change—and SAVE—your life!

Real Faith Is Vital!

Paul wrote that, "Without faith it is *impossible* to please [God]" (Heb. 11:6). Do not complicate this passage. Take it for *exactly* what it says. Then recognize that the Bible teaches in both the Old Testament and New that "The just shall *live* by his faith" (Hab. 2:4; Rom. 1:17).

While God's establishing of His kingdom will be the most wonderful event the world has ever seen, what precedes it will be something very different. Humanity now hurtles toward untold catastrophe. Tumultuous events will soon engulf *every* society, *every* nation—affecting the lives of *every* human being of *every* race, culture and religion. Even for the strong, with events simultaneously overlapping *and* crescendoing, it will take immense trust—real FAITH!—in God's POWER to avoid panic, and to hold steady, simply believing His promises. Surely, there is no time in human history when the need for *true* faith would be greater than when the worst prophecies begin to unfold.

Therefore, Jesus asks this all-important and *wide open* question about faith, directed to each person who will consider it in the time just prior to His Return: "When the Son of man comes, shall He find *faith* on the earth?" (Luke 18:8).

God wants you to rely on Him—to *trust* Him completely in everything. Remember. You really have no choice if you hope to please Him. In the near future, when others are gripped by fear, uncertainty and confusion, their whole world collapsing around them and having no idea where to turn for answers, God does not want *His* people to fret, worry or agonize over what will happen next—or to themselves.

Think of it this way. One of the greatest things you *should* worry about is if you do *not overcome worry*. God promises to provide your every need *if* you believe Him, obey Him, trust Him and wait on Him without doubting (Matt. 6:33-34). Having done this, you should *expect Him* to continually deliver you, no matter how impossible your personal circumstances may become—as long as you are truly one of His servants and part of the only Church Jesus Christ built!

The Crucial Role of Patience

In the context of closing events swirling around God's people, Jesus instructs, "In your *patience* possess you your [lives]" (Luke 21:19). He knew that having and *exercising* great patience, in the face of swirling, confusing events, is an inseparable companion to real, believing faith.

In the middle of Revelation 13, which describes cataclysmic events happening in Europe and impacting the whole world, verse 10 states, "Here is the PATIENCE *and* the FAITH of the saints." The rise of the false system described there certainly requires enormous patience and faith to endure, because of the almost nonstop persecution it has brought to God's people.

Further, in Revelation 3:10, recall how Christ commends His faithful people in the end time: "Because you have kept *the word of My patience,* I also will keep you from the hour of temptation…"

The New King James Version renders the italicized passage as "My command to persevere." This helps to better convey Christ's meaning. Scripture shows in numerous places how patience, endurance and perseverance are *vital* in a Christian's life, especially in the end time, when the severity of world conditions will be without parallel in history.

Other scriptures stress the importance of having patience at the end of the age.

In Matthew 10:22, Jesus states, "And you shall be *hated* of all men for My name's sake: but he that *endures to the end* shall be saved." Now notice Matthew 24:13. When outlining all that will occur prior to His Return, Jesus repeats, "But he that shall *endure* unto the end, the same shall be saved."

If Christianity were compared to a track meet, it would be more like running a marathon than a sprint. It involves endurance, yet it also means running to win (I Cor. 9:24). But do not be fooled, with time now running out—with few years left in the 6,000 years allotted to man's rule—we might say it is more *today* like a short middle-distance race or even closer to a long sprint.

Next, read Acts 14:22. It recounts part of Paul's ministry: "Confirming the souls of the disciples, and exhorting them to continue in the faith, and that we [all Christians] must through *much tribulation* [trial] enter into the kingdom of God."

Now recall Revelation 14:12: "Here is the *patience* of the saints: here are they that *keep the commandments* of God, and the *faith* of Jesus."

We have already seen that Daniel 12:12 states, "Blessed is he that *waits…*" Ask: Why would there be a *defined waiting period*—until the 1,335 days begin—if extraordinary patience—and real patient *endurance*—were not necessary? As trends and conditions decline and become ever more serious, some, unresolved to hold steady in advance, will be unable to defeat panic.

Galatians 5:22 includes *longsuffering* as one of the nine fruits of God's Holy Spirit to be evident in every Christian's life. "Suffering long," enduring through trials, requires a great degree of patience to always remember that God has promised a way of escape (I Cor. 10:13) for those *praying* and seeking His will, and *watching* world conditions.

A Life of Growing and Overcoming

Most people feel trapped, unable to *overcome*—unable to grow in areas of weakness, fault and sin. Instead of overcoming their problems, most are overcome *by* their problems. This should not be—this *need* not be! You CAN overcome in your life.

Through the years, I have pastored thousands who have been called to God's Way. All people struggle against the pulls of the flesh and the temptations of Satan and his world. Some overcome. Others do not.

Jesus said, "Enter you in at the *strait* [difficult] gate: for wide is the gate, and broad [easy] is the way, that leads to destruction, and many there be which go in thereat: because strait [again, *difficult*] is the gate, and narrow is the way, which leads unto life, and few there be that find it" (Matt. 7:13-14). Most seek the easy, "broad" path in life.

Overcoming is hard—DIFFICULT!—and it is a continuous struggle. But it *is* possible (Matt. 19:26). You *can* overcome (Phil. 4:13). And if one desires to be a Christian, you *must*!

Yet this world is drifting along, completely unaware of God's great purpose for man, which is to build holy, righteous CHARACTER in this life. God is preparing a team of those who will qualify to be part of restoring His government to Earth at Christ's Return (Acts 3:19-21).

God's Purpose for Christians

Throughout His ministry, Jesus' message about the *kingdom of God* carried more than is seen upon first examination. Hidden within this message is the understanding of the awesome, INCREDIBLE HUMAN POTENTIAL for the one who truly yields to God. Wherever Jesus went,

He spoke about the coming *kingdom*—or GOVERNMENT—of God. While most of His parables were centered on this message, few that heard them understood their meaning. And when He spoke them, He always included how true Christians were *qualifying* to become part of that government!

Matthew 13 contains a half dozen "kingdom" parables. This chapter begins with the parable of the "Sower and the Seed," depicting one throwing seed into various locations and kinds of soil. The parable described how, in some cases, the seed grew and flourished in the person who received it. In others, it either died quickly after starting to grow, or took no root at all. Some who received the seed grew in character "thirty, sixty or one hundred fold" on the way to the kingdom.

This is followed by the parable of the "Wheat and Tares." This parable discusses "fruit" that appears in Christians' lives prior to the time God gathers them into His "barn." The fruit, good or bad, represents Christian growth, or lack of growth. The barn is a type of the kingdom.

The third parable depicts the kingdom beginning as a tiny "grain of mustard seed" that grows into a great tree. This is followed by the parable of leaven, depicting God's kingdom as leaven spreading until it has permeated the dough (the earth, all nations) that contains it. The fifth compares the kingdom to "hidden treasure" found in a field. The finder sells all that he has to buy this field.

The sixth parable describes God's kingdom as the "pearl of great price," which a person buys after selling all that he has to raise sufficient money for the purchase. The seventh and final parable of this one chapter describes the kingdom as a "net" gathering all kinds of fish. The "good" fish are kept—the "bad" are thrown away. Jesus explains that the good fish are those who enter the kingdom. The bad represent those burned (vs. 50) and destroyed in a "furnace of fire" (the lake of fire).

In each of these parables, the message is the same. A few (not most) are willing to pay the price to be a Christian. They are willing to spiritually grow and develop real Christian character so they may later inherit the eternal reward of becoming *born* (no longer merely *begotten*) sons of God—in the God Family—ruling with Him in the kingdom of God.

There are many other New Testament parables. Much of Christ's teaching was through the use of these stories about common, well-known things. They were intended to carry deep lessons about a Christian's calling, for those whose *minds have been opened* by God to understand them.

Jesus said, "No man can come to Me, except the Father which has sent Me draw him" (John 6:44, 65). *You* cannot understand God's truth unless God has drawn you—called you—to it through the power of His Spirit. So, the process of coming to true Christian conversion begins with a calling or drawing directly by the Father.

The parables of the talents, penny, marriage supper, 10 virgins, sheep and goats, unjust judge, fig tree, lost sheep, lost coin, prodigal son, unjust steward, Lazarus and the rich man, the good Samaritan and others, all involve or depict a Christian entering the coming kingdom, or governing Family, of God at Christ's Second Coming. Space could be taken to more closely examine each parable and demonstrate this. Though some are very short, and others quite long, the purpose of most of Christ's parables is essentially the same. For those who follow Peter's instruction to "grow in grace, and in the knowledge of...Jesus Christ" (II Pet. 3:18) on a daily basis, rulership in the government of God under Christ is attainable.

In addition to entering God's kingdom, all of these parables carry the additional element of having everything to do with whether one will *escape* all that lies ahead.

Great Reward

We now ask *how* does one qualify? In Revelation, Jesus stated, "And he that *overcomes*, and keeps My works unto the end, to him will I give *power over the nations*: and he shall *rule* them with a rod of iron..." (2:26-27). A chapter later, He adds, "To him that *overcomes* will I grant to sit with Me in My throne..." (3:21).

These verses picture Christ re-establishing God's government over all nations on Earth. Christians will receive *real power* to rule. But first, they must overcome sin—defeating, with God's help, their flesh, this world and the devil!

Overcoming is rarely easy, nor does it happen overnight. It is a life-long battle against well-established attitudes and a former way of life that the Christian has now rejected and turned from. The one who is walking God's path is striving to *curb* and withhold himself wherever God's Word instructs him. He strives to *exercise* himself in matters where God says to do so. When God gives instruction to *do* something, the Christian strives to *do* it! When God instructs *not* to do something, he strives *not* to do it.

Christians are those who follow—who COPY!—Jesus Christ (I Pet. 2:21). What then is the pattern Jesus established for us to follow? Did *He* overcome? We saw in an earlier chapter that He did.

In reference to His own struggle to remain free of sin and perfect in character, Jesus said, "In the world you shall have tribulation [how true today!]: but be of good cheer; *I have overcome the world*" (John 16:33). Jesus had overcome both the world and its god—Satan (II Cor. 4:4). He also said, "*even as* I also overcame, and am set down with My Father in His throne" (Rev. 3:21). Jesus' overcoming qualified Him to rule. As He *qualified* to replace Satan, so must we!

Such enormous power to rule—to guide and affect millions of lives during Christ's millennial rule—could never be given to people who are *unprepared*—who have not *qualified* to properly use it. God will not hand this unprecedented authority to people who might rebel and revert to Satan's ways. God's servants must diligently use *this life* to build His very holy character, so necessary for those who will one day hold offices of great authority!

True Conversion Understood

At this point, the specific role of God's Holy Spirit must be addressed. This is the powerful *force* sent by God that helps a person grow and overcome. Literally, this *power* is Christ living His life in the Christian. Without His help, the new convert gets nowhere—fast! When Christ said, "bring forth much fruit" (John 15:5), He followed it with "For without Me you can do *nothing*." Human power—human energy—only helps a person overcome in physical areas. *Spiritual* problems cannot be conquered through *physical, mental* or *emotional* effort.

Jesus said that He is the "Vine" and His true followers are the "branches" (John 15:5). Branches must be *connected* to the Vine, and this happens through God's Spirit working in a mind.

When speaking of this, Christ said, "out of his belly shall *flow rivers of living water*. (But this spoke He of the *Spirit*, which they that believe on Him shall receive...)" (John 7:38). As it performs good works, God's Spirit flows "out of" the Christian. Therefore, it *must* be replenished, or it will be depleted and disappear completely. This is why Jesus said, "If you...know how to give good gifts unto your children: how much more shall your heavenly Father *give the Holy Spirit* to *them that ask Him?*" (Luke 11:13). The *true* Christian *regularly* asks, in prayer, for *more* of the Holy Spirit.

Paul wrote, "I can do all things through *Christ* which *strengthens me*" (Phil. 4:13), and, "My brethren, be *strong* in the Lord, and in the *power of His might*" (Eph. 6:10). Jesus also said, "with God all things are possible" (Matt. 19:26). With God's Spirit actively working and growing in you, this can be true of you!

But truly deep conversion does not occur overnight. The Corinthians had to be told that they were "babes [babies] in Christ" (I Cor. 3:1). Paul described how they required "milk," instead of "meat," for food. The brand new Christian is much like an infant. By analogy, he first learns to roll over, then crawl, before walking (and even then at first in an unsteady, toddling fashion). Only later does he finally learn to run (spiritually).

Paul understood this. He compared conversion to running a race (I Cor. 9:24). Of course, though not right away, the runner must, at some point, develop more speed, because he wrote, "run, that you may obtain [win]."

Such is the Christian way. Slow, steady growth, through daily practice, produces progress in the person who is copying Jesus Christ. The new Christian sincerely strives, from the heart, to be different—to turn around and go the other way—the way of God—for the rest of his life!

But most who know certain or even many of these things do not truly apply them.

Zeal Lacking

The final era of Christ's Church—Laodicea (Rev. 3:14-22)—lacks sufficient *zeal* to receive God's blessings and promise of protection. We have seen that Jesus describes those of this era as "lukewarm," stating that because they are "neither cold nor hot, I [Christ] will spew you out of My mouth" (Rev. 3:16). Verse 17 continues with Jesus describing a smugness that has taken hold of even many of His people.

In the world at large, most people do not get excited about much of anything, preferring to "relax"—"be cool"—"take it easy"—not get "worked up." But this is not a picture of the true Christian. He is one who is on fire—for *all* things of God! His whole heart, mind and being is committed to living God's Way. He continually seeks to fully submit to God, yielding to God's direction in all matters. He recognizes and practices this instruction: "I beseech you...brethren, by the mercies of God, that you present your bodies a *living sacrifice*, holy, acceptable unto God, which is your *reasonable service*" (Rom. 12:1).

Most in the world do not want to sacrifice for any but themselves, feeling this to be very *unreasonable*. They are committed to "getting while the getting is good"—unconsciously seeming to follow the unstated goal of "seeing who can die with the most toys." The vast majority of people lead lives reflecting little more than seeing how much they can accumulate in this life. And dynamite cannot separate them from possessions or money.

But the Christian recognizes that his life belongs entirely to God. He is then committed to using it entirely for God's purpose. He is interested in serving others—in giving rather than getting (Acts 20:35). His heart is in preaching (giving!) the gospel to the world (Matt. 24:14) and God's warning message (Ezek. 33:1-9) to the modern nations descended from ancient Israel. He wants to help fulfill Christ's command, incumbent on His servants for 2,000 years: "Go you therefore, and *teach all nations*, baptizing them [into] the name of the Father, and of the Son, and of the Holy Spirit: teaching them to *observe all things* WHATSOEVER I have commanded you" (Matt. 28:19-20).

In a covetous, pleasure-driven world, few any longer understand *sacrificing* and going without *wants* they previously thought were *needs*, as the 1930s generation came to understand by suffering through over 10 years of the Great Depresssion, before going straight into World War II.

In a sense, it could be said that those who escape all that will come will have paid a certain "price" so that this could happen. There is no free lunch for *anyone*. These will have given of themselves beyond all measure. They will have truly comprehended Jesus' words, "For whosoever will save his life shall lose it: and whosoever will lose his life *for My sake* shall find it" (Matt. 16:25).

The Church of God is truly an exception in the modern world. Each member understands that bearing an historic "much is given, much is required" burden is *individually* required (Luke 12:48)—and according to ability—to complete the Work set before the Church. But all *willingly* and *cheerfully* (II Cor. 9:6-7) shoulder the burden of this *necessary* duty—involving time, prayers, service and FINANCIAL SACRIFICE!—so others can learn—be given!—what they were privileged to receive.

The Church and God's Work

Jesus understood and taught His disciples that of Himself He could "do nothing" (John 5:30). The Spirit of God enabled Him to accomplish all that He did. Prior to His ascension to heaven, Jesus told His disciples He would soon send *them* God's Holy Spirit.

This event, the beginning of the Church of God, occurred in AD 31. Jesus described the significance of what happened at that time: "But you shall receive *power*, after that the Holy Spirit is come upon you: and you shall be *witnesses* unto Me both in Jerusalem, and in all Judea, and in Samaria, and unto the *uttermost part of the earth*" (Acts 1:8). Ten days later, God gave His Spirit, initially to just 120 disciples.

Infused with His Spirit, God's people were now empowered to fulfill His mission. Like the first-century Church, this same *twenty-first-century* Church has neither millions of members nor political power or clout.

Only One Church

Jesus said, "I will build *My Church*" (Matt. 16:18). No matter how men interpret this verse, it speaks of a single Church! Jesus continued, "and the gates of hell [the grave] shall not prevail against it." He promised that *His* Church could never be destroyed. At this point in the book, it should be obvious that Jesus kept His word.

In a previous chapter we read, "But in vain they do worship Me [Christ], teaching for doctrines the *commandments of men*" (Matt. 15:9). In Mark's parallel account, Christ continued, "Full well you *reject the commandment of God*, that you may keep your *own tradition*" (7:9).

The world's Christianity is filled with traditions, assumed by most to be biblical—when the Bible often teaches the *exact opposite*. One of the largest is the traditional view of what *is* the New Testament Church. Most ministers, theologians and religionists typically define the church in this way: "All those who sincerely believe in Jesus as their Savior constitute the church." This is often followed with the also familiar cliché, "There are many routes to heaven." Though the Bible nowhere teaches that heaven is the reward of the saved, the clear implication of this statement is that people can largely believe what they want, or be part of any group they choose, and still be Christians. While people may sincerely believe these traditional ideas—they are sincerely WRONG!

Since "God is *not* the author of confusion, but of peace" (I Cor. 14:33), *His* Church would reflect peace—not confusion! You need not be confused about the identity of the true Church. Recall God inspired Paul to write, "*Prove* all things; hold fast that which is good" (I Thes. 5:21). Surely God would not exclude something of such magnitude—such supreme importance!—as the matter of what and where His true Church is. And He would never tell people to prove what cannot be proven!

God's Church walks in complete unity—agreement—with all of the Bible's doctrines. God's servants *live* Christianity, practicing all the truths and ways of the Bible *without compromise*. While persecuted in a world that rejects God's authority, they press forward, determined to fulfill their incredible human potential!

When speaking to His disciples about the importance of seeking the kingdom of God, we saw Jesus said, "Fear not, *little flock*; for it is your

Father's good pleasure to give *you* the kingdom" (Luke 12:32). By no stretch of the imagination can churches comprised of over *two billion* professing Christians be considered a "little flock." However, somewhere on Earth today is that same little flock faithfully yielding to and obeying God, and fulfilling His supreme plan in this age.

You must set out to prove the location of God's true Church! Time is running out to do this—and it is running out both to HEAR the *Word* of God and to help DO the *Work* of God!

Under God's Shadow

One of the most remarkable passages in the Bible is Psalm 91. It speaks of those who "abide under the shadow of the Almighty" (vs. 1) during times of great difficulty and distress. It speaks of those whom God protects.

These "say of the LORD, He is my refuge and my fortress: my God; in Him will I trust" (vs. 2). God in turn delivers them "from the snare of the fowler, and from the noisome pestilence [disease]. He shall cover you [each faithful Christian] with His feathers, and under *His wings* shall you trust: His TRUTH [what only one Church teaches!] shall be your shield and buckler" (vs. 3-4).

Verse 5 reveals how *completely* those whom God protects are to rely on Him. Notice: "You shall not be afraid for the terror by night; nor for the arrow that flies by day." Understand! An atmosphere of terror, even missiles flying over—"arrows that fly by day"—will not shake God's people! Verse 6 states that those God protects will not fear "the *pestilence* that walks in darkness; nor...the *destruction* that wastes at noonday."

How all-encompassing is God's promised protection? "There shall *no evil* befall you..." (vs. 10), and "A thousand shall fall at your side, and ten thousand at your right hand; but it *shall not come near you*. Only with your *eyes* shall you behold and *see* the reward of the wicked" (7-8).

For the relative few who seek and obey God, protection is certain! Amidst thousands—millions—even billions!—*only these* faithful individuals avoid punishment! They are THOSE WHO ESCAPE.

Once time has run out for God's Work to be done, certain specific events—absolutely critical to understand—will come to pass. They represent matters of extraordinary importance in God's timeline of "what will happen next"—and what to watch for. At a point, all eyes will be on Jerusalem. But most will not know what to look for.

One specific event towers above all others...

The Abomination of Desolation

The book has used the term "prophetic milemarker." No milemarker may be bigger than the subject of this chapter. What it is—all that turns on its fulfillment—the all-important *signal* it sends to God's people—and what it heralds is soon to follow when it appears—make understanding this subject of SUPREME IMPORTANCE.

You must comprehend!

Many know the term "Abomination of Desolation," but almost *none* know what it means. Complicating the problem, misguided, deceived—and deceiving—"prophecy watchers" the world over have remained *ignorant* of the TRUTH of what the prophet Daniel called "the abomination that makes desolate." They neither understand what this is nor the prophetic implications it carries.

What is this "abomination"? Has it already come?—or is it yet to appear? How will we know it when we see it?

The confusion surrounding this prophecy will soon be stripped away—but only if you follow God's *clues* with an open mind. When fully understood, this prophecy is not only fascinating, but CHILLING! Brace for shocking facts.

Key Scriptures

The first important clue that Jesus gave about the abomination of desolation is found in Luke: "And when you shall see Jerusalem compassed with armies, then know that the *desolation* thereof is nigh [or near]" (21:20). This verse often causes confusion, with some mistakenly assuming the surrounding of Jerusalem by armies *is* the abomination.

When the verse describes the city being surrounded, it does not say the desolation "has happened," but that it "is near." If something *is near*, it *has not happened yet.* So, the abomination of desolation is NOT Jerusalem being surrounded by armies. These are separate events that occur at different times. Get this clear before continuing!

Matthew's account reveals more about what to look for: "When you therefore shall *see* the abomination of desolation, spoken of by Daniel the prophet, *stand* in the holy place, (whoso reads let him *understand*:)..." (24:15).

This verse approaches the subject from a different and slightly *later* point in time than Luke 21, which describes the abomination just *before* its fulfillment. Therefore, Luke 21:20 and Matthew 24:15 are slightly *offset*, as the latter speaks of the period in which God's people, who are watching for this, "see" it fulfilled.

We have clarified two points: (1) armies around Jerusalem precede the abomination, and (2) this prophecy involves something "stand[ing] in the holy place." Keep this simple. Do not allow mixed up theories, suppositions and assumptions you might have heard to cloud the plain understanding of what God reveals.

Before reading further, recognize another aspect of the prophecy. In both *Matthew and Mark*, the instruction "...whoso reads, let him *understand*..." is found (Matt. 24:15; Mark 13:14). God inspires this to be recorded *twice* for special emphasis.

Will you accept this instruction for what it so obviously means? God wants you to *understand*. Ignore the ridiculous claims of those who suggest prophecy is sealed—and that, while God would inspire many prophecies, He does not want them understood. God *does* want His servants to comprehend—to grasp—them! Hence, *my* emphasis so many times in this book on the very point ("let him understand") that God states three times (including Daniel's original statement) for His own special emphasis.

Mark Reveals More

Mark 13 removes all doubt about the abomination "standing in the holy place"—and whether it is supposed to be there: "But when you shall see the *abomination of desolation*...standing where it *ought not* [meaning, in the "holy place"]..." (vs. 14). Clearly, the abomination is something that does *not* belong in the holy place.

But what exactly *is* this "holy place"? The context in which the term is used makes plain that it is not figurative, but refers to a literal place—a religious site. Recognize, however, that this place cannot be a *pagan* religious site. It must be a location *God* considers or once considered holy, with something foreign and blasphemous placed there. History and other scriptures outside the gospels reveal that this must be an at least partially rebuilt Jewish Temple in Jerusalem.

A significant event for all of God's people who are watching *follows* the abomination of desolation being set up. This reference is brought from Mark's account: "...*then* let them that be in Judea flee to the mountains" (vs. 14).

The appearance of the abomination is the signal for God's people to flee. This makes understanding the prophecy much more crucial.

Another reference to this fleeing is found in Luke's account. We read some of this passage earlier in the book, but it returns for its new importance in a fuller context. First, notice once again: "And *when* you shall see Jerusalem compassed with armies, *then* know that the desolation thereof is *near. Then* [what happens next] let them which are in Judea *flee* to the mountains; and let them which are in the midst of it depart out; and let not them that are in the countries enter thereinto. For these be the days of vengeance, that all things which are written [by the prophets] may be fulfilled. But woe unto them that are with child, and to them that give suck, in those days! For there shall be *great distress* in the land, and *wrath* upon this people [the modern nations of Israel]. And they shall fall by the edge of the sword, and shall be led away captive into all nations: and Jerusalem shall be trodden down of the Gentiles, until the times of the Gentiles be fulfilled" (21:20-24).

The book of Revelation offers a parallel description brought by Christ through John of what happens to Jerusalem. The context is coming directly off of chapter 10, and how the "little book" described there is the book of Ezekiel, as well as a reference in chapter 11, verses 1 and 2, about the "Temple of God" being "measured."

What follows this "measuring"? Let's read: "...the Gentiles: and the holy city shall they [the Gentiles] tread under foot *forty and two months*" (11:2). The very next verse continues by introducing the work of the Two Witnesses for this same 42 months (three and a half years)—or "1,260 days," the term used in Revelation to describe the length of their commission.

It should be obvious that this "treading" by the "Gentiles" in Revelation 11:2 has to be referring to the length of time that Jerusalem is being "trodden down of the Gentiles," as Luke so similarly put it.

An inset: The faithful people of God's Church (not those who have grown lukewarm and confused) know that there is more very special (and truly sobering) understanding tied to additional details about what *is* the holy place, what—and also *who*, because it includes a human figure (Dan. 11:45)—it is that stands in this place, as well as the spiritual implications tied to being on the wrong side of events in Jerusalem when the Temple is measured. (It is not the purpose of this volume to cover those details. They are for another place.)

It does need to be at least briefly stated, however, that the "temple" being measured in Revelation 11 is *not* the physical one that the Jews will rebuild. It is speaking of the New Testament Church (or Body of Christ), which is referred to in numerous places by the apostle Paul as the "Temple of the Lord" (I Cor. 3:17; Eph. 2:20-22). The more-than-curious reader will want to at least read these verses for proof of understanding how the *true Church* and the (spiritual) *Temple of the Lord* are synonymous terms in the New Testament.

The seriousness of the events and time periods that follow the setting up of the abomination of desolation should bring a new level of gravity to understanding this prophecy. All who care to escape what is coming—to "flee" at the right moment with the rest of God's people—must know exactly *what* to watch for.

We have still not answered the question of what the abomination *is*.

An Earlier Type

Now for *another* clue about the abomination. Recall the biblical principle of DUALITY—a former and latter fulfillment—in prophecy. God usually gives a *former* TYPE to help us understand the *latter* fulfillment. The former is not the *primary* fulfillment of a prophecy. It only points to the latter fulfillment, which *is* the main focus and purpose of the prophecy itself.

This duality is seen with the "abomination of desolation" prophecy. And what it reveals is fascinating! Let's examine the historical TYPE of what has already occurred. First, recall the lengthy Daniel 11 prophecy. A crucial part of that prophecy comes up for review and expansion at this juncture.

In about 176 BC, Antiochus IV (king of the north, and TYPE of the future final civil ruler who embodies the Beast system) acquired the kingdom from his older brother. After this, Antiochus Epiphanes removed the high priest in Jerusalem and installed someone loyal to himself. Upon a triumphant return from Egypt, in 168 BC, Antiochus sacked the Temple at Jerusalem and took its golden vessels.

Recall that Antiochus also sent troops to Judea in 167 BC. They destroyed the Temple and its sanctuary. This act stopped the commanded twice daily sacrifices at the Temple (Ex. 29:39-42; Num. 28:4-6). This was an overt attempt to wipe out the Jewish religion with all of its doctrines.

This military leader also stationed a garrison atop the Jewish Temple Mount, desecrating it. Also recall that Daniel wrote, "Yes, he magnified himself even to the prince of the host, and by him [Antiochus] the daily sacrifice was taken away, and the place of [the] sanctuary was cast down" (8:11).

Daniel added this in chapter 11: "And arms shall stand on his [Antiochus'] part, and they shall pollute the sanctuary of strength [the Jewish Temple], and shall take away the daily sacrifice, and they shall place the *abomination that makes desolate*" (vs. 31).

Now then, *what exactly* is this coming "abomination" that will be "set up" again? The truth—born of history—is beyond eye-opening in regard to prophecy.

The first fulfillment was not just Antiochus' armies coming into Jerusalem—an early "treading it down" for three years until 165 BC—but the fact that those armies set up an IMAGE—a specific IDOL—on the Temple's altar, which *defiled* and made it *desolate*. Antiochus further polluted the Temple by offering swine's blood upon the altar.

These historical events of Daniel 8 are an unmistakable fulfillment of the prophecy in Daniel 11:31, and a FORERUNNER of the end-time fulfillment of the "abomination of desolation" spoken of by Christ in Matthew, Mark and Luke.

We are left to ask: *What* was this statue and *where* is it now?

Incredible History Unveiled

Now comes fascinating knowledge. You have almost certainly never heard it. History reveals that the idol Antiochus placed in the Temple—or "holy place"—was a statue of Zeus or Jupiter Olympus, the chief deity of pagan Hellenists of Greece and Macedonia.

Volume Four of *A Dictionary of Christian Biography, Literature, Sects and Doctrines* makes this clear. The context has to do with Simon (Magus) the sorcerer, described in Acts 8: "When Justin Martyr wrote

[AD 152] his *Apology* [his book] the sect of the Simonians [from Simon Magus] appears to have been formidable, for he speaks four times of their founder, Simon [Magus]…and we need not doubt that he identified him with the Simon of the [book of] Acts. He states that he was a Samaritan [Acts 8 makes that clear], adding that his birthplace was a village called Gitta; he describes him as a formidable magician, and tells that he came to Rome in the days of Claudius Caesar [which is AD 45], and made such an impression by his magical powers, that he was honoured as a god, a statue being erected to him on the Tiber [River], between the two bridges, bearing the inscription 'Simoni deo Sancto'" (p. 682). This inscription means "Holy God Simon." Also note that Simon's followers generally called him Jupiter.

We can ask: Is this the very same statue placed by Antiochus?

Following the journey of this statue is vital. Do not miss the flow of events. Remember, God expects they be understood!

Statue Reappears

It has been well reported that many centuries ago a statue of the pagan god Jupiter was found in Rome. The large bronze statue was altered and renamed St. Peter. One strong indication of this comes from John Parker: "…by some writers it is affirmed to be no other than the statue of Jupiter, with a new head and hands; others stating that this famous statue was melted down by order of Pope Leo I. in the middle of the fifth century, and recast into this figure of S. Peter, holding the keys of heaven with one hand, whilst the other is raised in the act of benediction in the Roman manner, with the first and second fingers extended" (*The Archaeology of Rome*, p. 38).

Ralph Woodrow, author of *Babylon Mystery Religion*, goes further: "This statue is looked upon with most profound veneration and its foot has been *kissed* so many times [by devotees] that the toes are nearly worn away!" (It is more than interesting to note that the Catholic religion has a long tradition of kissing idols—feet, rings and crosses—yet the *pagan origin* of this practice can clearly be found in I Kings 19:18 and Hosea 13:1-2.)

Incredible! Yet these are the facts from history. This same statue—directly related to the abomination of desolation—is now prominently displayed in Rome!

Remember, Jesus said His servants—those who understand God's prophecies and know what to watch for—shall "see" the abomination of desolation. This must be referring to something that is physically set up and visible in the holy place.

Will this statue be brought back, full-circle, to Jerusalem to fulfill this end-time prophecy? God, through the initial fulfillment, has almost certainly provided the answer for those willing to believe His Word and plain accounts of history regarding the role of this image and its connection to the end-time civil ruler (Beast), and the religious leader (False Prophet) who will direct that it be placed—with himself—in Jerusalem.

In Place of God

Ezekiel 28 provides a fuller picture of the *audaciousness* of the False Prophet when he enters Jerusalem: "The word of the LORD came again unto me, saying, 'Son of man, say unto the *prince of Tyrus* [a man, not to be confused with the *king* of Tyrus referenced in verse 12, who is clearly Satan]...Thus says the Lord GOD; because your heart is lifted up, and you have said, 'I AM A GOD, I sit in the seat of God, *in the midst of the seas*" (vs. 1-2).

Daniel 11:45 explains that the king of the north will "plant the tabernacles of his palace *between the seas* in the glorious holy mountain..." Of course, the Mediterranean Sea and the Dead Sea are about equidistant on either side of Jerusalem, east and west. Any map of the Middle East shows this. The False Prophet will obviously participate in this move and join him.

Continuing in Ezekiel 28 about the False Prophet: "Yet you are a man, and *not* God, though you *set your heart as the heart of God*: behold, you are wiser than Daniel [this man will think he is]; there is no secret that they can hide from you [describing his proud thinking]. With your wisdom and with your understanding you have gotten you riches, and have gotten gold and silver into your treasures" (vs. 2-4).

Let's pause to summarize. A United Europe will transform the crashing global economy and usher in a time of world prosperity unlike any previous time. The False Prophet will proclaim himself to be God. Amazingly, *hundreds of millions* will believe him, having been seduced by accompanying miracles. The world will rejoice and also worship the Beast because he will bring peace and prosperity back to the world.

Verses 5-8 describe more of this religious leader's pride in the context of what his end will be: "By your great wisdom and traffick have you increased your riches, and your heart is lifted up because of your riches: therefore thus says the Lord GOD; *because you have set your heart as the heart of God*; behold, therefore I will bring strangers upon you...they shall bring you down to the pit."

Antiochus Epiphanes was a forerunning TYPE of the False Prophet (but also of the Beast because he too is worshipped).

Future Fulfillment

The ULTIMATE fulfillment of the abomination of desolation is not only the statue, it is the final leader of the religious system—the human personification of the Babylonish whore herself—who enters into Jerusalem and says, "I am God."

In fact, the entire *Babylonish system* that this False Prophet—supported by the Beast—represents is *twice* referenced regarding "abominations." A previously referenced passage is important to revisit in this context: "So he [an angel] carried me [the apostle John] away in the spirit into the wilderness: and I saw a woman sit upon a scarlet colored beast full of names of blasphemy, having seven heads and ten horns. And the woman was arrayed in purple and scarlet color, and decked with gold and precious stones and pearls, having a golden cup in her hand full of *abominations* and filthiness of her fornication: and upon her forehead was a name written, MYSTERY, BABYLON THE GREAT, THE MOTHER OF HARLOTS AND *ABOMINATIONS* OF THE EARTH" (Rev. 17:3-5).

God does not just describe this false religious system as abominable, but refers to it as "the *mother* of...abominations."

This religious leader is described in II Thessalonians and there referred to as the "man of sin." Quoted previously, this passage reappears because of the broader application it brings to this chapter. "Let no man deceive you by any means: for that day [Christ's Return] shall not come, except there come a *falling away* first [a prophecy fulfilled in the twentieth century] and that *man of sin* be revealed, the *son of perdition*... Who opposes and exalts himself *above all that is called God*, or that is worshipped; so that he *as God* sits in the temple of God, *showing himself that he* IS GOD" (2:3-4).

Verses 9 and 10 explain how this deceiver will sway great numbers to worship him and the civil leader: "Even him, whose coming is after the working of *Satan* with *all power and signs and lying wonders*, and with *all deceivableness* of unrighteousness in them that perish; because they received not the love of the *truth*..." The allure of miracles will seduce the masses into supporting and even worshipping the Beast. (See also Revelation 13:11-14 and 19:20.)

This is clearly the False Prophet of Revelation 16:13, *not* the Beast. But do not be confused. They *both* are seen as divine. Remember, Antiochus Epiphanes—the *civil* ruler—as well as the statue—representing the *religious* system of Babylon in Jerusalem—was a TYPE of the coming Beast and False Prophet.

True Motivation

What is the *motivation* behind the setting up of the abomination of desolation? Examining a passage in Psalm 83 reveals *why* the Beast power will come against Jerusalem to destroy it and desecrate the Jewish state and religion:

"Come…let us [certain nations acting in alliance] cut them off from being a nation; that the name of Israel may be no more in remembrance. For they have *consulted together* with one consent: they are *confederate* against you [this describes an association of nations in the Middle East who decide to ally with the 10 European nations under the Beast]… Who said, Let us take to ourselves the *houses of God* in possession" (vs. 4-5, 12).

First, it is certainly no secret that forces exist today in the Middle East who want to "cut off" the modern nation of Israel—the Jews. We also read from Luke that this was a time of (Gentile) "wrath" against the "people" of "this land." However, in the next chapter we will learn that many *other* countries within the "nation" identified here as Israel are also to be included in this destruction that is being planned.

Now focus on the term "houses of God." We saw that the final powerful religious leader will "plant the tabernacles of his palace *between the seas* [Mediterranean Sea and Dead Sea] in the glorious holy mountain" (Dan. 11:45). Comparing this passage with Psalm 83 makes clear they describe the same holy places in Jerusalem where the Jews' daily sacrifices must already by then have been restarted.

So then, the *religious* motive behind the confederation is to wipe out the nations of Israel—and to seize the holy places in Jerusalem, the "houses of God." And just as Antiochus entered Jerusalem centuries ago, destroyed the city and desecrated the Temple, a final fulfillment of the abomination of desolation is drawing nearer.

Understand. The Vatican has long said they want to proclaim Jerusalem an "international city." But this seemingly peaceful desire will only be a pretense for taking possession of the city's holy sites. Realize that this false system will declare, "They are safe with us! You can trust us! We will be the guarantor of Jerusalem—and its three 'great religions.' And we are prepared to bring armies *to ensure it.*"

Longing for "Peace in our time"—reminiscent of British Prime Minister Neville Chamberlain's report upon returning from Berlin just before World War II—this will please and reassure the ears of the majority—and the decision makers!

Understand. For the daily sacrifices to *stop* they must first be *restarted*. There must come at least a temporary *restoration* of these Old Covenant sacrifices in Jerusalem at the Temple Mount under the direction of a re-established priesthood. While a full temple is not needed, *something* must be rebuilt.

When the False Prophet directs the Beast to erect this statue at the site of the reconstituted daily sacrifices, the abomination will officially "stand in the holy place"!

Next come events foretold for the greatest nations in history...

America and Britain

Imagine knowing in detail exactly what is in store for the United States and Britain—the greatest nations ever. The governments and leaders of the West do not know the shocking, world-shattering changes just over the horizon for the United States, Britain, Canada, Australia, New Zealand, South Africa and certain Western European nations—with the Middle East at the center of the coming explosion of events.

But you can know—and, if you read carefully, you will!

Against the backdrop of growing fear, mixed with ignorance, many wonder—and are openly asking—about America and Britain's role in the prophecies foretold to occur in the "last days." Recognizing their rise to extraordinary prominence, having become so big and dominant that their impact on the world at large is without parallel, people naturally wonder, "What about the United States and Britain?" Surely, among the Bible's great prophecies, God would not *ignore* them. Are they mentioned? If so, *where*? And will these nations be exceptions to the collapse of all the great civilizations that preceded them?

Not knowing who or what to believe, some ask their ministers—and find that they *do not know*!

Master Key

We now turn our attention to specific nations—in fact, the greatest nations on Earth.

No book on the Bible's greatest prophecies would be even close to complete without examining the identity of the modern descendants of ancient Israel, and what is foretold to happen to them in the last days. This knowledge is paramount to understanding so much of Bible prophecy and the many topics covered in this volume.

What follows are certain basic sections, and most of two chapters, taken from my book *America and Britain in Prophecy*. This summary will suffice for this book. Since there is much context that cannot be included here, the serious reader will see the whole of *America and Britain* as a must-read.

A master lock has padlocked the source revealing where civilization is going. Until the twentieth century, the KEY to this lock had been lost. Have you ever lost your keys? The world, like you, has been literally "lost without them." Unlike you, the world had not known where to look. But this MASTER KEY has been found.

This GREATEST KEY to correctly recognize major end-time events has only recently been discovered.

The identity of America and Britain—and what is foretold to happen to *these countries* just prior to Christ's Return—is the most important *single* key, unlocking the over 80 percent of prophecy yet to be fulfilled.

Some Background

Here is basic understanding completely unknown to most: The original nation of Israel split into TWO *separate* nations. Literally hundreds of prophecies talk about ancient Israel, often using both the terms "House of Israel" and "House of Judah." Each of these was taken into captivity by foreign invaders, Israel being taken about 125 years before Judah.

Over a space of three years, 721-718 BC, the House of Israel was invaded, defeated and taken captive by Assyria to the headquarters of their empire located in the Caucasus region (II Kings 17:18, 23-24). By the time Daniel recorded his prophecy, he was a Jewish slave with the conquered House of Judah in Babylon—and about 125 years had passed. Judah (with the tribe of Benjamin) had been attacked, slowly conquered over the period from 604-585 BC, and then finally transported as slaves from their homeland. Therefore, Daniel's prophecies could not have had anything to do with what had *already happened* to Israel and Judah well before he wrote his book.

The ancient Assyrians—modern Germany—eventually migrated to northwestern Europe, taking with them many of their Israelite captives.

The world has lost sight of these people—the "Lost Ten Tribes"—because they were taken captive and transported, in two stages—far from their homeland. These tribes themselves lost track of certain basic revealed knowledge, which would have kept them in remembrance of their identity. Instead, because the Jews have ostensibly retained certain knowledge that Israel lost—the weekly Sabbath and annual Feast days are big examples— the world *correctly* identifies the Jews (and they identify themselves). As a result, the world has generally believed that the Jews *are Israel*, instead of merely *one* of TWELVE tribes, which descended from Israel.

The world does not know how to identify America, Britain, Germany, Russia and other great nations—by their *Bible* names. Again, they have not known how or where to look—or they would know exactly what lies ahead, for themselves and the other prominent, indeed most dominant, nations of the world!

Deceived by wrong education, consisting of false knowledge and values, the best minds and "thinkers" are biased against the revealed Word of God's *Instruction Manual* to mankind. Thus, incredible truths remain locked away from access to the world's leaders and other "intellectuals" who disdain the Source that reveals them.

Why National Decline?

Longstanding but now open outright hatred for America and Britain is at unprecedented intensity. This will grow worse—*much* worse. The truth of the Bible is that the American and British peoples will eventually lose all national wealth, power, influence and greatness. They are going to sink into such complete ignominy that the whole world will hold them in utter contempt.

You are watching this decline—and it will continue, picking up speed. Britain was reduced in world stature before and faster than America, which is rapidly following on the heels of her decline. This is happening faster than any could imagine—but it is only the *beginning* of what God has in store for our peoples. They will be stripped naked before the world, left in wonderment at how they could not see what led up to their monumental collapse. Their leaders are now groping in the dark for answers they cannot find to the colossal problems confronting them.

But God shall finally reveal to them the CAUSE of untold suffering and punishment, lying just beyond view. They will be forced to learn that "*Righteousness* exalts a nation: but *sin* is a reproach to any people" (Prov. 14:34).

Our nations are choking and drowning in sin!

Sir Winston Churchill, the famous Prime Minister of formerly *Great* Britain, proclaimed, "Some great purpose and design is being worked out here below." He knew that in some fashion, a Supreme Being was working out a little-understood (and virtually unseen) plan on Earth.

But what is it? Churchill never explained because he did not know.

Why Israel's Prophesied Greatness Never Came to Judah

God's Master Plan directly collides with the plans of modern America and Britain, as well as Canada, Australia, New Zealand and certain other countries of northwestern Europe.

But some brief history is necessary in order to introduce the prophecies about these nations.

Like every *human* project, God's Plan—*His* project—to save mankind, has a starting point. God had to select one nation with which He would initially work. In essence, the entire Bible, Genesis to Revelation, is primarily the history of one single people—the nation of Israel!

Virtually all prophecy revolves around God's purpose with this lone nation. Other nations are generally mentioned only as they come in contact with Israel. Think of it this way: The central theme of the entire Bible is the story of the Israelite nation and their relationship with the true God.

The story is not complicated, unless men choose to make it so. Once properly addressed, the ancestry of our modern peoples becomes plain. Our national origin comes clear.

Many have mistakenly thought, "The *Jews* are God's chosen people." This is only partially true, and it denies the tremendous truth about why the United States and Britain rose to such unprecedented prominence and power.

God's Holy Word clearly reveals that His entire plan of salvation is inseparable from, and relates to, the nation of Israel. Notice this New Testament passage about her: "Who are Israelites; to whom pertains the adoption, and the glory, and the covenants, and the giving of the law, and the service of God, and the *promises...*" (Rom. 9:4).

The Jews never fulfilled the national greatness prophesied—and PROMISED—to come on the modern descendants of ancient Israel. Have you wondered why?

Now ask yourself: Why is it then that the English-speaking peoples most profess to believe in the Bible and the God it describes? Why is it that all peoples of the world who also profess worship of this God were at one time taught by these English-speaking, Anglo-Saxon people? Why is it that these same people have done more to *preserve* the Bible than any other? Is it not also strange that *these* nations, and not the Jews, have *proliferated* the Bible around the world far more than all other nations put together?

The Jews were prophesied to become scattered, and were *never* foretold to achieve national greatness. It is a far different story for the United States and British Commonwealth! It has been said that "Never in history has any country or commonwealth been so blessed," and that because of this blessing, "Never have so few produced so much to feed so many for so little." How true of these nations—but this has never been true of the Jews!

Yet, this in no way espouses the racist concept of *British Israelism*, which teaches that Britain is the kingdom of God on Earth. This is impossible, because Britain is declining not increasing. The Bible teaches no such silliness, but rather that the kingdom of God is vastly greater than the British Empire ever was. God's promises of eternal salvation were never, and never will be, achieved through the horribly decadent and now shattered British Empire.

Before Israel Appeared

Prior to Moses leading the emerging nation of Israel from Egypt, God did not work with any single nation or people. Also, before this time, there was no Bible—no recorded Scripture. This spans the first 2,500 years of human history. Yet, again, this period of early history reflects no dealings by God with any specific nation. In fact the Bible records very little—just 11 chapters of Genesis—of the first two millennia, taking us to about 400 years after the Noachian Flood.

The Creation account shows how God began His work with humans on the smallest possible scale—*one* man and *one* woman. God introduced Himself to this first couple, explaining the basics of His Plan, offering RE-

VEALED KNOWLEDGE to life's great purpose. He showed the way to peace, happiness, abundance and health—through the building of holy, righteous character, chosen by free moral agency. God explained how mankind, through eating of the Tree of Life, could achieve eternal life in the kingdom of God. This included revealing His binding, eternal, spiritual law.

Of course, Adam rejected God's revealed way and rebelled. His sons followed the way of greed and vanity, trusting in themselves to solve problems through human reason apart from God. Humanity multiplied, and followed the same way—and has reaped uncounted misery, troubles, evils and woes as a result.

Throughout early history, only a very few individuals chose to obey God. Abel was referred to as "righteous"—and a few generations later, "Enoch walked with God" (Gen. 5:24), as did Noah. We saw these men were called "preacher[s] of righteousness" (II Pet. 2:5), which means obedience to God's Commandments (Psa. 119:172). Shem, Noah's son, may have been the only other person to serve God in the period up to and immediately following the Flood.

God Calls Abraham

After Shem came Abraham, about four centuries after the Noachian Flood. By this time, all knowledge of the true God and His revealed purpose had disappeared. Once again, as in the period just prior to the Flood, men had completely turned from God's Way. It was in this circumstance that God began His Work with one man, Abraham, the one through whom He would build the nation of Israel.

As with the one man Adam, God purposed to initially reveal Himself to just one man—Abraham. This single extraordinary, determined, obedient man was all God needed to start His nation. Notice God's simple command to him, and what was at stake if he obeyed it: "Now the LORD had said unto Abram, Get you out of your country, and from your kindred, and from your father's house, unto a land that I will show you: and I WILL MAKE OF YOU A GREAT NATION…I will bless you, and make your name great" (Gen. 12:1-2).

Faced with a clear decision, what did Abraham do? Did he drag his feet, make excuses or complain? It says, "…So Abram departed" (vs. 4). Abraham accepted the condition and obeyed without excuse, question or human reasoning. He did not rebel, following Adam's way, and the world's course for 6,000 years. Abraham obeyed God without question, setting an example for every person—ever after—who will serve God. Obedience qualified him to inherit the promises—and it can qualify you, too.

Do not lose sight of what really happened in this remarkable account. How many today would react as Abraham did? Most would argue with God's logic by suggesting a variety of ways God could fulfill His promise to Abraham *where he was*. Other scriptures show that Abraham was a very prominent, successful man. This meant he had much more to leave behind than would the average person.

He still obeyed without delay!

Much more is contained in this account than meets the eye—or than meets the shallow understanding of almost every Bible student who, at best, only partially understands what was at stake here. We shall see that incredible consequences flowed from this decision.

"A Great Nation"—But Far More!

Recognize that Abraham's obedience was attached to—"I will make of you A GREAT NATION." Virtually no one grasps the significance of this huge statement, carrying implications almost beyond comprehension. Fascinating knowledge and understanding will soon open before your eyes.

Sometime later, God changed Abraham's name (originally Abram) because Abraham was to be the father of God's nation, Israel, established for a great purpose. Notice: "This people [Israel] have I formed for Myself; they shall show forth My praise" (Isa. 43:21).

Isaiah's prophecy is still future, not yet fulfilled. God never forgets His purpose—and it will be fulfilled just beyond events of the next few years.

Most Bible students do not recognize that God's Plan also carries *duality* throughout. The first Adam was made physical and material. The second Adam, Christ, was made divine and spiritual. The Old Covenant is material and temporal, the New Covenant is spiritual and eternal. Man was made physical, from the dust—mortal and of the human kingdom. Yet, through Christ, man may receive God's Spirit, become spiritual—and then be made of spirit, immortal and of the kingdom of God.

This sets up what almost everyone has missed: The promises to Abraham, in like manner, carry *two separate phases*. Most who know anything of the Bible are aware that salvation, through the promised Messiah, was promised through Abraham—that God gave the promise that Christ would appear as Abraham's descendant. In other words, we receive salvation through Christ, who was born of Abraham generations later.

I must at least add that most have no idea what salvation really is. They simply have never heard the truth of exactly what is the Christian's inheritance. But this extraordinary understanding is covered in detail in my other books. The focus here is on the second promise to Abraham, not just misunderstood, but entirely overlooked by Christianity and the world at large.

Let's return to Genesis 12 for a moment and notice the awesome DUAL promise to Abraham, with the first part having to do entirely with promised physical, material greatness: "Now the LORD had said unto Abram, Get you out of your country, and from your kindred, and from your father's house, unto a land that I will show you: and I WILL MAKE OF YOU A GREAT NATION… I will bless you, and make your name great…and in you shall *all families of the earth be blessed*" (vs. 1-3).

The last part of verse 3, pointing to salvation, though largely misunderstood, has been the world's focus. But, plainly, there is *duality* here. This promise has TWO separate aspects: (1) An *unrecognized* promise with physical, material, national implications—"I will make of you a GREAT NATION"—which is a reference to the RACE foretold to descend from Abraham, and (2) the generally recognized (but not truly understood) spiritual promise of *grace* through Christ, Abraham's "Seed."

Next notice Genesis 22:18, which is nearly identical to this promise of Genesis 12:3, stating, "And in *your Seed* shall all the nations ["families"] of the earth be blessed." Galatians 3:8, 16 confirms that this particular "one Seed" is a specific reference to Christ.

Some have tried to say that *both* promises are fulfilled in the New Testament Church, asserting that the Bible calls the Church a nation. It is true that God describes His New Testament Church as a nation: "But you are a chosen generation, a royal priesthood, *a holy nation*, a peculiar people; that you should show forth the praises of Him who has called you" (I Pet. 2:9).

Certainly, the New Testament Church IS *spiritual* Israel today. But we will see that it is *impossible* for the Church to fulfill God's reference to become "a great nation," promised to Abraham.

Salvation Through Christ

It is at this point that most Bible students and professing Christians go astray. We must briefly examine *how* Abraham is tied to spiritual salvation for all human beings. It is critical to understand that salvation *and* material promises of national greatness to Abraham's physical descendants are part of what God promised him.

While some wish to "spiritualize away" the *physical* promise to the *physical* race descending from Abraham, you will find this impossible to do when certain verses are clearly understood—and in some cases merely just read for what they say. As these verses are examined here, it will also become clear that they point directly to the United States, Britain and other Western countries.

First, you may not have understood that *every* Christian is a child of Abraham. Yet this is what Paul told the *Gentile* Galatians: "Know you therefore that they which are *of faith*, the same are the *children of Abraham*" (3:7).

The book of Galatians calls Abraham "the father of the faithful." This is because those "of faith" are his "children." Understanding the phrase "children of Abraham" is *key* to understanding WHAT Christians will inherit.

The New Testament also speaks of this PROMISE TO ABRAHAM. Notice: "Now to Abraham and his seed [children] were the *promises* made..." (Gal. 3:16). This speaks of specific promises made to Abraham and "his seed"—his children. Here is how this is tied to Christians: "And if *you* be Christ's, then are *you* Abraham's seed, and *heirs* according to the *promise*" (vs. 29). While millions sing "Standing on the Promises," they do not know what the promises *are*!

This verse is a fascinating statement. All faithful Christians are *heirs*—not yet *inheritors*—to whatever was promised to Abraham.

Grasp this. *Your* salvation is tied to this promise!

Therefore, *you* need to know WHAT was promised to Abraham. The answer is all-important since it explains how you will spend eternity!

Surely God would not expect anyone to blindly accept what was promised without investigation. (No agreement, contract or covenant works this way.) The Bible does reveal the nature of this promise. Once you discover what God said, His entire purpose for mankind can be understood. It is revealed in a *series* of verses, because it is an *unfolding* promise, not all revealed in any one passage. God's extraordinary promise slowly expands to enormous proportions.

Prepare to be astonished! You are about to read things no one understands—or even can—without God revealing them. Paul wrote, "Eye has not seen, nor ear heard, neither have entered into the heart of man, the things which God has prepared [His promises] for them that love Him. But God has revealed them unto us *by His Spirit*" (I Cor. 2:9-10).

May God open your mind to see. What He promised Abraham—and has promised you—is beyond the wildest dreams of your imagination!

Confirming the Promise

Jesus' role, at His First Coming, had a direct bearing on the promises to Abraham: "Now I say that Jesus Christ was a minister of the circumcision for the truth of God, to *confirm the promises* made unto the FATHERS" (Rom. 15:8).

We will see how Jesus' sacrifice did this. But first we must identify who the "fathers" are. Acts 3:13 holds the answer: "The God of Abraham, and of Isaac, and of Jacob, the God of our *fathers*, has glorified His Son Jesus."

So, the fathers referred to are Abraham, Isaac and Jacob. Christians will inherit whatever was promised to *them*!

The Land of Promise

Abraham was obedient—faithful. Whatever God told him to do, he DID! Because true Christians also faithfully obey God, this is another way in which Abraham is a father, in *type*, to them. He obeyed God without question, setting an example for every Christian. I repeat: Obedience qualified Abraham to inherit the promises—and it can qualify *you*.

The promises become more specific in the next verses of Genesis 12 as Abraham begins his journey: "And Abram passed through the land unto the place of Sichem, unto the plain of Moreh. And the Canaanite was then in the land. And the LORD appeared unto Abram, and said, Unto your seed [children] will I give *this land*" (vs. 6-7).

The land he went to is the modern-day nation known as Israel. This is the first indication of *what* God promised him. It is now evident that the promise involves LAND with unspecified boundaries—"this land."

But how much land?

The answer to this question develops in stages. We will examine each. Notice: "And the LORD said unto Abram, after that Lot was separated from him, Lift up now your eyes, and look from the place where you are northward, and southward, and eastward, and westward: *for all the land which you see*, to you will I give it, and *to your seed* FOREVER" (Gen. 13:14-15).

At this point, what Abraham could "see," looking in four directions, was the immediate region around where he stood. Yet, it was to go to his children *forever*. Notice that. Forever means eternally!

Verse 16 adds this about his descendants: "And I will make your seed as the dust of the earth: so that if a man can number the dust of the earth, then shall your seed also be numbered."

This means that an immense and uncountable number of people would eventually descend from Abraham. It also introduces two related points: (1) A number of this magnitude—"as the [grains of] dust of the earth"—has to be far more than just the Jews, and (2) a passage suggesting *other* nations must be included.

Genesis 15 adds further to the promise, and begins to show the magnitude of what "to your seed" means. Let's read what God showed Abraham in a vision: "And He brought him forth abroad, and said, Look now toward heaven, and tell the stars, if you be able to number them: and He said unto him, *So shall your seed be*" (vs. 5).

But the scope of the promise, and the land involved, is about to increase *beyond* the boundaries of Canaan. As with a deed, when one inherits land, specific boundaries must spell out exactly *how much* land is involved. Obviously, God understands this. Notice: "In the same day the LORD made a covenant with Abram, saying, Unto your seed have I given this land, from the *river of Egypt* [the Nile] unto the great river, the *river Euphrates* [in present-day Iraq]" (Gen. 15:18).

This is specific! The Nile River bisects Egypt—and the Euphrates River divides present-day Iraq almost directly down the middle, from northwest to southeast. So this is land *on Earth*, not heaven, as some suggest. And any map will show you that it is *much* land. It is also much more than Abraham could see. But the final amount God described is actually far greater than *this*.

Several scriptures explain that, ultimately, the entire earth was the land to be given to Abraham. Here is one: "Our father Abraham…for the *promise*, that he [Abraham] should be the HEIR OF THE WORLD…" (Rom. 4:12-13).

Recall Jesus taught, "The meek…shall inherit *the earth*" (Matt. 5:5). Christians will be "heirs" of the *whole world* because God keeps His promises!

But let's return to the immediate development of what the promise to Abraham encompassed.

"Father of Many Nations"

The following expansion of the promise shows that blessings were promised regarding more than just the "one Seed," Christ of Galatians 3:16. This is crucial to grasp because many miss this point entirely.

Let's read the next stage, expanding God's intent of both RACE and GRACE: "And when Abram was ninety years old and nine, the LORD appeared to Abram, and said unto him, I am the Almighty God; walk before Me, and be you perfect. And I will make My covenant between Me and you, and will *multiply you exceedingly*. And Abram fell on his face: and God talked with him, saying, As for Me, behold, My covenant is with you, and you shall be a father of MANY NATIONS. Neither shall your name any more be called Abram, but your name shall be Abraham; for a father of MANY NATIONS have I made you" (Gen. 17:1-5).

If Abraham obeyed God—so the promises were still *conditional* at this point—this passage reveals that Abraham would father more than one nation—"many"—and his descendants would be multiplied.

Understand what this verse is saying. It cannot be solely referring to the Jews, because they have never been more than one nation. (They *have* always been *scattered* into *many* nations.)

In addition, there is no possible way that this could refer solely to Christ. Verse 6 makes this even plainer: "And I will make you *exceeding fruitful,* and I will make NATIONS [plural] of you, and KINGS [plural] shall come out of you." This last phrase adds something new—and extremely important!

Consider. How could a reference to "nations" and "kings" possibly refer to Abraham's spiritual children (Gal. 3:29) and *scattered individuals* in the Church, forming one "holy nation" (I Pet. 2:9)? The answer is, *it cannot*—and it must be referring to ethnic descendants of Abraham, the promise of race.

Now notice the next verse in Genesis 17: "And I will establish My covenant between Me and you and *your seed* after you in *their* generations for an *everlasting* [forever] covenant..." (vs. 7). The reference here to *"their* generations" confirms that this is more than one seed—more than Christ alone.

Verse 8 strengthens the promise: "And I will give unto you, and to your seed after you, the land wherein you are a stranger, all the land of Canaan, for an everlasting possession; and I will be their God," with verse 9 repeating this for emphasis: "You shall keep My covenant therefore, you, and your seed after you in *their* generations."

These are astonishing words! The very course of history is reflected in them. For many "generations," God promised to bless Abraham's physical descendants. Of course, the fact that salvation comes by following Abraham's pattern of obedience and unquestioning belief in God's instructions is of enormous importance spiritually, because it defines the path to salvation for every human being (Rom. 15:8)!

Abraham Qualified Through Obedience

Remember, God's original promise to Abraham was *conditional.* Abraham had to prove that he was obedient to *whatever* he was instructed to do. In chapter 22, God took the test to a new level, commanding him to sacrifice his only son according to promise, Isaac (Rom. 9:7-8). Without hesitation, he did exactly what God said.

Notice: "And the angel of the LORD called unto Abraham out of heaven the second time, and said, By Myself have I sworn, says the LORD, for because you have done this thing, and have not withheld your son, your only son: that in blessing I will bless you, and in multiplying I will multiply your seed *as the stars* of the heaven, and *as the sand* which is upon the sea shore; and *your seed shall possess the gate of his enemies*; and in your seed shall all the nations of the earth be blessed; BECAUSE YOU HAVE OBEYED MY VOICE" (Gen. 22:15-18).

At this point, the promise became *unconditional.* How many people would be willing to sacrifice their child, if God required it? Abraham *was* willing, and obeyed God in every point, no matter the personal cost. This is how God described his obedience: "Because that Abraham OBEYED [past tense] My *voice*, and kept [past tense] My *charge*, My *commandments*, My *statutes*, and My *laws*" (Gen. 26:5).

The Bible plainly says, "Sin is the transgression of the law" (I John 3:4). Abraham kept *this* law, and so must you to inherit what was promised to him.

One other crucial point must be understood here. God told Abraham that his descendants would "possess the gate of his enemies." This has to be a reference to real nations on Earth, not salvation through Christ. You must grasp this!

Genesis 24:60 makes even plainer the material, physical aspect of this promise concerning the number of descendants occupying actual nations *and* strategic positions *on Earth.* Notice: "Be you [Rebekah] the mother of thousands of millions [billions], and let your seed *possess the gate of those which hate them.*"

The Jews have never held such strategic "gates." They have always lived among or been surrounded by their enemies. Do not let deluded people, ignorant in the Bible, assert that this means the Jews, or convince you to "spiritualize away" or ignore such plain texts. For the Bible to be true, we must look for, and be able to find, in history, one people who occupy more than one nation. Remember, they must be *one* people and they must possess the gates of their enemies—or the Bible stands disproved!

Isaac Included

In the next account, God included Abraham's son, Isaac, in the promise. Notice that God repeated much of what He had said to Abraham: "And the LORD appeared unto him [Isaac], and said, Go not down into Egypt; dwell in the land which I shall tell you of: sojourn in this land, and I will be with you, and will bless you; for unto you, and unto *your seed* [now Isaac's], I will give ALL THESE COUNTRIES, and I will perform the oath which I swore unto Abraham your father; and I will make your seed *to multiply as the stars of heaven*, and will give unto your seed ALL THESE COUNTRIES; and in your seed shall ALL THE NATIONS OF THE EARTH BE BLESSED" (Gen. 26:2-4). Isaac's son, Jacob, also similarly qualified to receive God's promise, and we will come to this account.

The obedience of one man, Abraham, was sufficient to pass on astonishing blessings that would eventually encompass "all the nations of the earth." This then must include *Gentile* nations as well.

Abraham Has Not Yet Inherited

An important inset is added here, explaining the *eternal* implications of the promise to Abraham. It involves all who obey God: When do Christians become inheritors, no longer merely *heirs*? Abraham is also a key to properly understanding this. Where is he now? Is he in heaven? Has he already inherited the promises made to him? When put together, three verses answer these questions, forming a complete picture.

Here is what Paul said about Abraham's obedience: "By faith Abraham, when he was called to go out into a place which he should *after receive for an inheritance*, obeyed; and he went out, not knowing where he went. By faith *he sojourned in the* LAND OF PROMISE, as in a strange country, dwelling in tabernacles *with Isaac and Jacob*, the HEIRS with him of the same PROMISE: for he *looked for* a city which has foundations, whose builder and maker is God" (Heb. 11:8-10).

There are several important elements here. Abraham was to "*after* receive" his inheritance. In faith, he "looked for" what God was building, but understood that he was in a "strange country." He and his son (Isaac) and grandson (Jacob) remained "heirs" all during their lifetimes—and they still are!

Next comes a remarkable statement. Every Christian must grasp and live by it: "These all died in faith, NOT *having received the promises*, but having seen them afar off, and were persuaded of them, and embraced them, and confessed that they were *strangers* and *pilgrims* on the earth" (vs. 13).

The land that Abraham, Isaac and Jacob sojourned in never became theirs during their lifetimes. They died "in faith," but they did see God's promises "afar off."

Many do not want the truth of God's words explained to them. They prefer the empty platitudes and traditions of men to the awesome truth of God—and *this* is AWESOME UNDERSTANDING!

Some have even paid with their lives for telling others what I have just told you.

The deacon Stephen was stoned to death—*martyred*—just moments after telling his listeners the following: "Men, brethren, and fathers, hearken; the God of glory appeared unto our father *Abraham*, when he was in Mesopotamia, before he dwelt in Charran, and said unto him, Get you out of your country, and from your kindred, and come into the land which I shall show you. Then came he out of the land of the Chaldeans, and dwelt in Charran: and from there, when his father was dead, he removed him into this land, wherein you now dwell. And He [God] gave him *none inheritance in it*, no, not so much as to set his foot on: *yet He promised that He would give it to him* for a possession…" (Acts 7:2-5).

This confirms Hebrews 11. Abraham received "none inheritance" during his lifetime—"not so much as to set his foot on [the land]."

How much plainer can God be?

So then, where *is* Abraham? The Bible answers through Christ who said, "Abraham is dead" and "the prophets are dead" (John 8:52-53). This means that Christians are merely HEIRS in this lifetime. Like Abraham, they see God's promises "afar off." Also like Abraham, when they die, they are dead. They wait in the grave to become inheritors upon Christ's Return. Verse after verse confirms this.

A "Nation" and a "Company of Nations"

Isaac's son Jacob was also included in the promise, with the following verses adding that Gentile, heathen nations were also to be ruled by the nations of Israel who received the birthright: "Therefore God give you of the *dew* of heaven, and the *fatness* of the earth, and *plenty* of corn and wine: let people serve you, and nations bow down to you: be lord over your brethren, and let your mother's sons bow down to you: cursed be every one that curses you, and blessed be he that blesses you" (Gen. 27:28-29).

This passage is plain! It is a direct statement that physical peoples on Earth will serve certain Israelite countries. This prophecy expands the promise to include the types of blessings that flow out of or from under the ground.

The next passage in the unfolding and amplifying of the promises made to Abraham demonstrates that Israelitish nations would eventually spread around the world. Their geographic distribution would literally circle the globe.

God is speaking to Jacob: "And, behold, the LORD stood above it, and said, I am the LORD God of Abraham your father, and the God of Isaac: the land whereon you lie, to you will I give it, and to your seed; and your seed shall be as the dust of the earth, and you shall *spread abroad* to the WEST, and to the EAST, and to the NORTH, and to the SOUTH: and in you and in your seed shall all the families of the earth be blessed" (Gen. 28:13-14).

Notice the phrase "spread abroad." The Hebrew means literally "to break forth," implying there would come a point when this spreading would happen suddenly. Recall from Romans 4:13 that Abraham was to become "heir of the world." But Genesis 28 does not state that physical Israelite nations would control the entire world *prior* to the time when Abraham, in the Resurrection to occur at Christ's Return, would inherit the promises made to him. Also recall that all true Christians—Jew or Gentile—are Abraham's children.

Yet, *physical* descendants of Abraham *have* spread to the four directions of the compass, to locations around the world. After their captivity of 721-718 BC, their captors allowed them to migrate with them, and eventually beyond, to their own lands. This sets up verse 15: "And, behold, I am with you, and will keep you *in all places where you go*, and will bring you again into this land; for I will not leave you, until I have done that which I have spoken to you of."

This is a truly astonishing prophecy. God promised to remain with Israel "in all places" where their migrations took them. But it will not be fulfilled in the greatest sense until the Return of Christ. Take time to read Jeremiah 23:7-8; 50:4-6, 19-20. These and other passages clarify when and how this will happen.

We now come to the all-important passage where God repeats His promise to Jacob. In this account, Jacob's name was changed: "And God said unto him, Your name is Jacob: your name shall not be called any more Jacob, but *Israel*...And God said...I am God Almighty: be fruitful and multiply; *a nation* and *a company of nations* shall be of you, and kings shall come out of your loins; and the *land* which I gave Abraham and Isaac, to you I will give it, and to *your seed* after you will I give the *land*" (Gen. 35:10-12).

This is translated by Ferrar Fenton as "A Nation and an *Assembly* of Nations." Moffatt's translation states, "a nation, [and] a *group* of nations." Thus, the earlier reference to "many nations" is now revealed to mean, when put with Genesis 27:28-29, one powerful, wealthy nation—and another wealthy group, assembly or company of nations—or commonwealth of nations.

How plain can God be? You do not need to believe some private interpretation by me or anyone else. Believe God's Word!

The Jews Have Not Fulfilled This

Many scholars have studied this promise. Any grade-schooler can recognize what the terminology means. Yet, where and how it was fulfilled has perplexed, indeed baffled, these same scholars, theologians and Bible students. Such men as Robert Ingersoll and Thomas Paine completely lost faith in the God of the Bible, rejecting Him and it, because they could not prove the fulfillment of these explicit promises.

Make no mistake! If these promises were not fulfilled, you cannot have confidence in a single promise or passage in the Bible. The very authority of the Bible stands at stake on the fulfillment of these ancient promises.

No reasonable mind can think that the Jews fulfilled them. Nor has the true Church of God fulfilled them—because it has always been described as the "few," a "little flock," never prophesied to grow great in this age—let alone into a nation and company of nations! The people of God are scattered throughout the nations of the world (Matt. 28:19-20, and other verses). Certainly it cannot be explained away as having occurred through Christ.

Ask any minister for the literal explanation of what these crucial passages mean, and—if he is honest—he will tell you that they remain a mystery, that he does not know the answer.

But God *does* know the answer and you can read it for yourself. Though unrecognized by even the greatest historians, this enormous promise has been fulfilled!

Birthright and Scepter—Different Promises

Most have not understood God made a distinction between the promises of prosperity, power and great material and national wealth, relating to "many nations," which He calls "the birthright"—and the promise of salvation through Christ, which the Bible identifies as "the scepter."

But the Bible is absolutely clear on this two-fold distinction. Let's read: "The *scepter* shall not depart from *Judah*..." (Gen. 49:10)—"...but the *birthright* was *Joseph's*" (I Chron. 5:2).

Before discussing these terms, we must define them.

Scepter: "Ornamented rod or staff born by rulers…as an emblem of authority and sovereignty"—*Encyclopaedia Britannica*; "kingly office," "royal power," "badge of command or sovereignty"—*The Comprehensive Standard Dictionary of the English Language*.

Birthright: "Native right or privilege"—ibid.; "A privilege granted a person by virtue of his or her birth"—*Webster's II New College Dictionary*.

A kingly line was prophesied to descend from Judah through David. Christ was born of Judah and was to eventually become a King bringing salvation—*grace*—to all people. On the other hand, a *birthright* has nothing to do with grace—unmerited pardon of sin—but rather comes as one's right *by birth*. Fathers generally pass birthright possessions to firstborn sons.

Vital Distinction

Most scholars have recognized that the *scepter* did indeed go to Judah, where it was passed down from Jewish king to king. King David was of the tribe of Judah, with David's dynasty having all succeeding kings also born to the House of David and tribe of Judah. Of course, Christ was born of both Judah and the House of David.

However, almost none have understood that the Jews were only a fraction of the nation of Israel. Of the *twelve* tribes of Israel, only Benjamin and Levi remained with the Jews. Again, almost everyone has erroneously associated *all* Israel with the Jews. This error totally blocks understanding of the birthright—and the distinction of tribes.

This absolutely vital distinction must be made clear. Both promises made to Abraham—the *gift of grace* and *right of birth*—were made unconditional by God, and were repromised to Isaac and to Jacob.

The promise of grace—the scepter promise of David's kingly line culminating in Christ—was foretold to be exclusively of Judah, one of Jacob's sons. But the independent, separate, distinct promises of birthright *never* pertained to the Jews. The promise of grace through Christ is summarized in John 4:22, where Christ said, "Salvation is of the Jews." Paul reiterated, "For it [the gospel of Christ] is the power of God unto salvation to everyone that believes; to the *Jew* first, and also to the Greek [Gentiles]" (Rom. 1:16).

I repeat: This promise, fulfilled in Christ, has nothing whatsoever to do with the *birthright*.

How sad that so few understand this crucial knowledge, made so *clear* by God to those who will just believe His plain words. It is sadder still that so few are even willing to explore God's Word for the facts!

The Bible states that the "birthright was Joseph's." Joseph was Jacob's (Israel's) second youngest son. While Joseph was Judah's younger brother—he was not Judah, or *of* Judah. He was the father of two sons—Ephraim and Manasseh—whose role must be understood to unlock both the fulfillment of the birthright—and the entirety of crucial end-time prophetic events.

All rights of birth are separate from the gift of eternal life, which God, through Jesus Christ, freely offers to all who yield to and obey Him. If salvation came by birth, it would not be of grace—God would *owe* it to people. Jesus' sacrifice, death and Resurrection become unnecessary if salvation is by *race*, by birthright. However, material blessings—possessions of wealth, prosperity and national abundance—can be passed through any number of generations by right of one's birth. But this much has to be understood: The birthright has nothing to do with *spiritual* blessings. It is entirely physical and material in nature, of *race* not grace. The reader must get this straight before proceeding.

Unlike salvation, requiring the believer to meet certain conditions in order to receive it, there are no preconditions to receiving blessings of birthright. Sons do nothing other than pass from the womb to receive this. Of course, a son could certainly disqualify himself from either receiving or keeping his birthright.

The gift of salvation means eternal life in the very Family of God. But God would never give such awesome power to one who has not developed righteous character, and is hostile, rebellious, and defiant to God's Law. Imagine if God owed, by right, immortality in the kingdom of God (salvation) to an atheist or criminal. Such would bring division and misery—for all eternity—to God's entire Family.

Qualifying to Receive Grace—and Salvation

When a young rich man approached Jesus, inquiring how he might receive eternal life, we saw Jesus said, "If you will enter into [eternal] life, *keep the commandments*" (Matt. 19:17). While this would not *earn* the young man salvation, it was a *qualifier*—a *precondition*—to receiving it. Millions today ignore this requirement, set forth so plainly by Christ. They listen to twisted arguments from law-hating, rebellious ministers and theologians falsely telling them that obedience to God *earns* salvation, making it no longer of grace, God's gift.

But if there are no *preconditions* to salvation, all could demand it of God! The rich young ruler might have told God, "I *demand* you give me salvation—it is my *right*!" Speaking of the Holy Spirit, Peter said, "God has given to them that *obey Him*" (Acts 5:32). Indeed, God's Spirit is a gift ("God has *given*"), but only those who obey Him can receive it. Only Christ's sacrifice makes this gift possible!

Make no mistake. Salvation cannot be earned—it is a free gift!

Now get this point straight! We must remove all doubt about what brings salvation. It is a free gift from God. There is absolutely nothing that a Christian can do to *merit* or *earn* it. The only wage that human beings can earn is *death* (Rom. 6:23). Recognize that no one can earn eternal life through *works*.

Salvation is by God's grace. But what *is grace*? It is completely unmerited pardon of one's sin. Salvation means that one is *saved* from death. Unless God intervenes to apply the blood of Jesus Christ to cover the repentant sinner's past, there can be no salvation.

What scriptures directly state this? Ephesians 1:5, 7 says, "Jesus Christ...In whom we have redemption through His blood, the forgiveness of sins." Colossians 1:14 states the same thing, verbatim. God gives grace—forgiveness—through Christ's blood.

But also think of salvation in the following way: A wealthy father approaches his 18-year-old son, heading off to college, with this offer. He states, "Son, upon graduation in four years, I will give you one million dollars if you (1) maintain a B average, (2) abstain from drunkenness, (3) impregnate no girls, and (4) never cut classes."

Ask these questions: If the young man meets these conditions, will he *receive* the million dollars? Yes! Has his conduct *earned* him the million dollars? No! Of course not. He merely did what *all* young men should do when they go to college. Yet, he would *not* receive the million dollars if he did *not* meet the preconditions—the *qualifiers*!

It is the same with salvation. Of course, God offers far more than a million dollars, but only those who obey Him may receive what He offers. Why cannot millions of Christians understand such basic logic, applicable in every contract and agreement entered into by men?

We saw the Bible so plainly says that Satan has "deceived the whole world" (Rev. 12:9), and this matter of how salvation is achieved may be his greatest deception. Do not fall for it!

Salvation is through Christ's free gift of grace. Yes, it is a *gift*—but it is one that God only gives to those who meet His biblically prescribed *standards*. In this way, God ensures that no future member of His Family will misuse and abuse such enormous power, conferred on him at the time of salvation.

Take a moment to reflect on this basic knowledge of *how* the *scepter* promise of salvation is achieved "of the Jews" (John 4:22) through Christ. While the world has understood that the promises to Abraham involve salvation through Christ, almost complete ignorance reigns within modern, orthodox Christianity regarding when, where and how this happens. These are subjects for other books.

We now fast-forward thousands of years…

The Birthright Blessing—at Its Peak and After

The blessings of birthright, prophesied millennia ago to arrive, have been most obvious in the modern nations descended from ancient Israel!

For two centuries, America and Britain have led the world in agriculture, manufacturing, production, technology, trade, and acquiring key sea gates and strategic defensive strongholds. Also, the United States, Britain and Israel (Judah) still have the three most elite armies, with the most sophisticated weaponry, that the world has ever seen! Even in decline, the Royal Navy still today evokes a certain awe.

Jumping from virtual obscurity to great prominence, and dominance, the rise of Great Britain and the United States to global supremacy came suddenly—and relatively recently. Up until 1800, America and Britain were small in strength, resources and power. This marked the end of the 2,520 years of the withholding of their birthright blessings (carefully explained in my book).

Certain events, meticulously timed (particularly Napoleon's need of additional funds for his war with England, leading to the American purchase of key French territories), added to their surge in power. Just the Louisiana Purchase propelled America toward becoming the world's single richest nation.

The well-known journalist John O'Sullivan was the first to enunciate the concept of *Manifest Destiny*. This is what he wrote in promotion of this idea: "the right…to overspread and to possess the whole of the continent which Providence has given us for the development of the great experiment of liberty and federated self-government entrusted to us" (*Encyclopedia of American Foreign Policy*, vol. 2, p. 68).

Within 50 years of the Louisiana Purchase, additions from the British Cession, acquisition of Florida, Texas Annexation, Oregon Territory, Mexican Cession and the Gadsden Purchase provided this budding nation with the world's richest, most fertile lands.

Meanwhile, Great Britain's population was exploding, jumping from 7.7 million to 20.7 million, from the 1750s to the 1850s. In addition, London became the financial capital of the world. These factors set the stage for the Industrial Revolution.

With these changes, these nations also acquired most of the world's wealth. After World War II, the United States emerged as the world's top economic and military power, taking the role of "leader of the free world." In September 1949, they were in possession of nearly two-thirds of all gold under governmental control—nearly 24 billion dollars in reserve!

This quick rise to national dominance is unmatched in history. No other nation has experienced such advancements in so short a time. In fact, outside these lands, the incredible prosperity taken for granted by so many here is non-existent. Devastating famine, crippling disease, raging war, disastrous natural calamities, outright ignorance and oppressive governments are a reality to almost all but the modern children of Jacob. Yet so few seem to truly recognize this.

But the people of America, Britain and the other descendants of Israel have ignored the Provider of these great blessings. They have disregarded biblical accounts as "myths," "fables" or "fairy tales," and have credited their dominance to their own ingenuity and cleverness, ignoring clear prophecies recorded in the Bible!

"And Your Seed Shall Possess the Gates of His Enemies"

The birthright nations would own the gates of their enemies. Historians have been able to observe the extraordinary acquisition and developing control of crucial trade routes and military strongholds: "By tracing the rise and decline of past maritime powers," acclaimed historian David McCullough explains, "national greatness and commercial supremacy were directly related to supremacy at sea" (*The Path Between the Seas, The Creation of the Panama Canal: 1870-1914*).

For over 200 years, Great Britain—and later America—dominated the seas by possessing vital points of passage. By controlling most of the world's strategic sea gates, their economic expanse and military capability flourished. These ports of passage directly affected British and U.S. victories in the First and Second World Wars.

These included the Suez Canal, the Strait of Gibraltar, Cape of Good Hope, Cape Horn, the Straits of Hormuz and Singapore, the Panama Canal, Malta and Hong Kong. Although these sea gates fell under the control of the children of Abraham through conquest or purchase, they were *destined* to be in their control long ago!

Remember God's promise to Abraham: "In blessing *I will bless you…* in multiplying *I will multiply your seed* as the stars of the heaven, and as the sand which is upon the sea shore…your seed shall possess the *gate* of his enemies…in *your seed shall all the nations of the earth be blessed*; because you have obeyed My voice" (Gen. 22:17-18). The Fenton translation reads, "I will *increase your race as the stars of the skies*, and like the sand upon the sea-shore; and *your race* shall possess the *gates* [plural] of its enemies; and I will *benefit all the nations of the earth through your heir*, because you have listened to My voice."

Abraham's heirs were to be: (1) A great people, in tremendous strength and numbers—"as the stars of the skies"; (2) they were to be a source of help to other nations—they would "benefit all the nations of the earth"; and (3) they were to possess the "gates of their enemies"—key strategic sea "gates," which would help establish and fortify world dominance! Through identifying the *people* receiving *these* blessings—the descendants of Abraham are discovered!

We saw God's promise was then also passed to Abraham's daughter-in-law Rebekah. Let's read again with a different emphasis on the same verse: "…and [Rebekah's relatives] said unto her, You are our sister, be you *the mother of thousands of millions*, and let your seed possess the *gate* of those which hate them" (Gen. 24:60). This is billions!

How ironic that, beginning in the 1800s, these key "gates" began to fall into the hands of Great Britain and America while, soon after, the first steam engine came into existence, allowing great ships to reach them quickly, thus accelerating and expanding world trade!

Which nations have fulfilled these prophecies? Which have claimed these promises? Certainly not the Jewish people!

The following scripture further reveals the identity of the recipients of these blessings: "And of *Joseph* he said, Blessed of the LORD be his land, for the precious things of heaven, for the dew, and for the deep that couches beneath, and for the precious fruits brought forth by the sun, and for the precious things put forth by the moon, and for the chief things of the ancient mountains, and for the precious things of the lasting hills, and for the precious things of the earth and fullness thereof…let the blessing come upon the head of Joseph [Ephraim—Britain and other countries; Manasseh—America]…His glory is like the firstling [the birthright holder] of his bullock, and his horns are like the horns of *unicorns* [the national seal of Britain]: with them he shall push the people together to the ends of the earth: and they are the ten thousands of Ephraim, and they are the thousands of Manasseh" (Deut. 33:13-17).

These scriptures, with history, *confirm* who claimed these promises, and fulfilled great prophecies.

The Rise of Ephraim and Manasseh

These passages can be proven. Since the 1800s, two nations stand out in growth unlike any in history!

In the second half of the nineteenth century, the rapid advancement of technology and economics, beginning in Britain, changed the lives of most of the population. Technical achievements, such as the invention of the steamboat, assured Great Britain total and complete authority over the sea. It allowed her to colonize new lands, to the point that the "sun never set" on her holdings. The British Empire covered almost a quarter of the earth's land mass—14 million square miles—and became the largest empire the world had ever seen!

America has a greater concentration of natural resources than any other geographic location. Utilization of new, rich resources kept raw material costs down and allowed for unprecedented growth.

From 1800 to 1950, both nations came to control nearly every important resource on the planet!

Oil, still civilization's primary source of fuel, has been called "the lubricant of the world economy." The control of this *vital* resource has been the cause of many geopolitical and military struggles. In 1950, America produced 52 percent of the world's oil supply. (Together, America and Britain produced over 60 percent.)

The 1950 snapshot also shows that these two great nations produced over 75 percent of the world's steel—over 60 percent from America alone!

They also controlled the world's production of coal—a more critical fuel in the 1950s—producing 50 percent more than all other nations on Earth *combined*! Imagine the stability of the world today if just these three products were still under the control of either of these nations.

Virtually every precious metal was mined from the United States and Britain. More tin, iron, lead, copper and chromite were also produced by these nations than the rest of the world *combined*!

Our nations produced 80 percent of the aluminum, 75 percent of the zinc and nearly 95 percent of the world's nickel. Such important metals were almost completely under the control of just *two* truly blessed nations.

Another metal vital to construction is pig iron. These nations once produced 33 percent more pig iron than the rest of the world *combined*!

But America and Britain dominated many *other* raw minerals, producing 100 percent of the world's chromite supply in 1950. That same year, they produced one-fourth of the world's copper and nearly 6.5 percent of the world's bauxite.

Over 66 percent of the world's electricity was produced and used by these two nations in 1950. This almost doubled the rest of the world.

They produced far more ships, cars, planes and trains than any other nation—with over 50 percent of the world's railway mileage!

Nearly any index of wealth—from gold to silver to precious stones—would have shown these nations to be the world leaders.

How did such power—such wealth—fall to such new and unknown nations? The skeptic will say that it came by the sweat and effort of our peoples—that *our* workmanship and *our* effort brought our peoples to this pinnacle of power.

But God's promises were made thousands of years before either nation appeared. *He* foretold their growth—and He is the Source of such prosperity, strength and worldwide influence!

What I Saw and Learned

As a grade-schooler starting in the mid-1950s, I learned of America's unmatched greatness in ways far too numerous to recount here. Classes were filled with stories about America's unique place in the world.

I also witnessed firsthand, in my own hometown of Lima, Ohio, America's unsurpassed industrial might at work. Superior Coach Corporation led the world in school bus production. This massive factory had earlier produced tanks for the American war machine in World War II, having a direct impact on the Allies' ability to literally outmass the weaponry of the Axis powers, and save the U.S. and Britain's birthright!

Lima Locomotive was the world's largest manufacturer of the powerful steam-driven locomotives that once pulled some of the longest trains the world had ever seen—with just one engine.

My hometown was also home to the Baldwin-Hamilton Corporation, which produced some of the largest steam shovels (and other heavy equipment) in the world. I grew up right around the corner from "Mr. Hamilton," and often heard the story of his large corporation and the influence that it had.

Standard Oil Corporation had a giant refinery and storage capability in Lima that was so big, it practically dwarfed the imagination. I recall regularly driving past the vast areas that it encompassed. The father of one of my childhood friends became its president in the 1960s.

I can remember how I felt about these things as though it were yesterday. Every American student or citizen who was paying attention recognized that we were far and away the most dominant nation on Earth. We were simply unrivaled—in either the world of that time, or in *history*!

The Source of Wealth and Blessings

America's forefathers could *never* have envisioned this nation as the global superpower it became. The United States has continually been at the forefront of economic prosperity, medical science, technology, food production, sanitation, architecture, space exploration, etc. Its citizens enjoy freedoms completely unattainable to so many. The income and standard of living for most Americans, Britons, Australians and Canadians is still higher than even most other industrialized nations.

But we have forgotten where these blessings came from! Only God's promises to Abraham kept these nations from joining the Third World's "brotherhood of poverty." We have not had to face the grim reality of famine or pestilence continually sweeping our cities and countryside.

From rolling green pastures to oil-rich lands, it is evident that our wealth and countless resources are God-given blessings. Nevertheless, this same national power, prestige and wealth has caused many to become blind to where this awesome bounty came from. The general national attitudes of arrogance and pride demonstrate a gross lack of gratitude toward God—the Provider!

Another famous Abraham, Abraham Lincoln, the 16th American President, said in a January 27, 1838 address, "We find ourselves in the peaceful possession of the fairest portion of the earth, as regards extent of territory, fertility of soil, and salubrity of climate. We…found ourselves the legal inheritors of these fundamental blessings. We toiled not in the acquirement or the establishment of them."

In proclaiming a "National Day of Fasting and Prayer" (March 30, 1863), Lincoln also said, "It is the duty of nations as well as of men, to own their dependence upon the overruling power of God…and to recognize the sublime truth, announced in the Holy Scriptures and proven by all history, that those nations only are blessed whose God is the Lord… We have been the recipients of the choicest bounties of Heaven. We have been preserved, these many years, in peace and prosperity. We have grown in numbers, wealth, and power as no other nation has ever grown; but we have *forgotten* God!

"We have *forgotten* the gracious hand which preserved us in peace, and multiplied and enriched and strengthened us; and we have *vainly imagined*, in the deceitfulness of our hearts, that all these blessings were produced by some superior wisdom and virtue of our own. Intoxicated with unbroken success, we have become too self-sufficient to feel the necessity of redeeming and preserving grace, too proud to pray to the God that made us!

"It behooves us then, to humble ourselves before the offended Power, to confess our *national sins*, and to pray for clemency and forgiveness."

But there are also statements from other leaders in American history demonstrating how they recognized where this national wealth and greatness came from:

First, "It is the duty of all nations to acknowledge the Providence of Almighty God, to obey His will, to be grateful for benefits, and humbly to implore His protection, aid, and favor" (George Washington, 1732-1799, first president of the United States).

And, "...The divine Author of our blessed religion; without an humble imitation of whose example...we can never hope to be a happy Nation" (George Washington).

And also, "How little do my countrymen know what precious blessings they are in possession of, and which no other people on earth enjoy" (Thomas Jefferson, 1743-1826, third president of the United States).

And then, "And can the liberties of a nation be thought secure when we have removed their only firm basis, a conviction in the minds of the people that these liberties are a gift of God? That they are not to be violated but with His wrath? Indeed I tremble for my country when I reflect that God is just; that His justice cannot sleep forever" (Thomas Jefferson).

And finally, "The rights of man come not from the generosity of the state, but from the hand of God" (John F. Kennedy, 1917-1963, 35th president of the United States).

These men recognized God as the Source of this sudden rise to power—and warned of the need to be grateful for His provisions and blessings.

Now think of the attitude in today's American Congress, courts and schools, where references to the Ten Commandments in public buildings elicit lawsuits and court injunctions. The God that these presidents spoke of is now almost *persona non grata* in the same government from which they spoke of him with such authority.

Moses warned Israel long ago: "Then beware lest you *forget* the
LORD, which brought you forth out of the land of Egypt, from the house of
bondage" (Deut. 6:12). Moses understood—and recognized—that when
people receive much, it is in their nature to become ungrateful and arro-
gant, and to forget the Source of their blessings—God!

But how long will America and Britain's prosperity last? Indefinitely?
Although Abraham's modern descendants are seemingly "on top of the
world," they are not destined to stay there.

The Fall

Revealing seeds of the inherent weakness of Americans, the renowned
American President Theodore Roosevelt said this of America's expansion
to greatness: "It means nothing. There is not an imperialist in the country
that I have yet met. Expansion? Yes; playing the part of a great nation…
Expansion has been the law of our national growth. Our fathers worked,
we rest; our fathers toiled, endured, dared, and we stay at home to avoid
trouble; our fathers conquered the West, but we are a feeble folk and we
cannot hold the Philippines."

We are *now* witnessing the sudden evaporation of the national wealth
and greatness given to these nations. Just as fast as Britain, no longer
"Great" Britain, and America became global superpowers, their greatness and power is coming to an end. All our allies—our biblically described "lovers"—are turning against us, despising us. The once-powerful
economic engine of America and Britain is quickly coming to a sudden,
screeching halt—and it is futile to try to stop it!

Why? We have ignored our Creator and turned from His laws and
commands. As Lincoln exclaimed, "We have forgotten God"!

Now, God is turning Himself from us. And He is *removing* the wonderful blessings bestowed to us through Abraham's obedience. The skeptic, who thinks that the power and influence our nations had in the world
was our own doing, cannot explain why our seemingly unlimited wealth
and prestige is slipping from our grasp. (Politicians are usually blamed.)

Just as history proves the power and blessing poured upon our nations, recent world developments evidence our decline.

The loss of most of our strategic sea gates should be a shrill trumpet
blast of alarm, announcing the downfall of our nations. The national security, military accessibility and economic stability, provided by these gates,
are all but gone. One by one, they are being returned to "those which hate"
us (Gen. 24:60).

GEORGE WASHINGTON

THOMAS JEFFERSON

ABRAHAM LINCOLN

THEODORE ROOSEVELT

In 1942, Japan seized Singapore. Later, the Suez Canal was turned over to Egypt. In 1977, the U.S. president signed an agreement to relinquish control of the Panama Canal at the end of 1999. Hong Kong was given to the Chinese. Time will tell which sea gate is to be surrendered next by the people no longer destined to control them!

More than their sea gates have been lost by our once mighty nations. Many vital resources are no longer produced on our soil.

We no longer dominate coal production—or supply the world with it. America *now* produces only 17 percent of the world's coal. Together, Britain, Canada, Australia and New Zealand produce just another 8 percent. While *using* more coal than any other nation except China, America now only *produces* about one-sixth of the world's supply.

In 2005, America, Britain, Canada, Australia and New Zealand also only produced a dismal 12.7 million barrels of crude oil per day— a mere 15.4 percent of the world's production! From 1997 to 2001, oil exports from these nations dropped 72 percent! Today, we rely heavily on allies—and enemies—to supply us with the fuels that run our economy!

Pig iron and steel remain vital indicators of a nation's power and economic success. Machinery, ships, cars, etc., all need iron and steel. We now produce less than 4 percent of the world's pig iron and less than 8 percent of its steel. As with oil and coal, we must rely on the nations around us to build and supply us with cars, trains, ships and machinery.

No longer is our economy self-sufficient!

But there is more. Similar comparisons can be made with *many* basic resources: While once literally controlling the world's nickel supply, there are no longer *any* active nickel mines in the U.S. Aluminum has also seen striking drops—from 80 percent to 8 percent.

In the 1950s, we produced over half of the world's zinc, but that number has now dropped to less than 8 percent. From completely controlling the world's supply of chromite, we now produce *none*. Bauxite is also now *entirely* produced in *other* countries.

Copper has seen similar reductions—from 23.4 percent to below 8 percent today. The production of so many goods and services that were once the "bread and butter" of our powerful economic engines has dwindled, many now having to be purchased from abroad.

After World War II, America loaned hundreds of millions of dollars to nations in Europe to help rebuild their war-torn cities. Nations literally lined up to receive aid in this rebuilding process, and to fortify themselves against the sweeping expansion of Communism. As the leader of the free world, America increased its spending to combat this.

No longer is this once great nation a lender—it is now a debtor!

Once possessing much of the world's wealth—including large reserves of gold and precious metals—America is declining from her status of richest single nation ever. (Chapter Five reviewed more of this.)

American gold reserves, used to fortify the dollar, have all but disappeared. The same is true of silver, which is disappearing from American coinage. America's reserves are now far below her *debt* to foreign nations. If all her creditors demanded payment in full, the United States would go bankrupt!

As statistics have shown, this nation *was* a powerhouse in the world. In 1950, we were a nation *exporting* goods and services. Today, we see a very different picture. Most products are made in *other* countries. Many resources and services are also imported from foreign nations. This has changed the leading *production* country to one with a massive and growing trade deficit, now *importing* scores of billions of dollars of goods more than it exports. While we no longer *produce* more, we continue to *use* more, *spend* more and *waste* more than any other nation!

We are now beholden to the nations around us—because we have chosen to *forsake* allegiance to God!

Israel Must Turn Back to God

Our nations only have one remaining hope. They must cease from their evil ways, and turn back to God. They must give Him the praise and honor He deserves!

In 1974, a Senate member proposed a resolution to declare April 30 as a "National Day of Humiliation, Fasting and Prayer." Modeled after President Lincoln's 1863 "Proclamation Appointing a National Fast Day," the purpose of this day was to repent for "national sins."

However, the resolution was overturned. Members of the House, and some of the Senate, did not approve use of the word "humiliation." Cynics equated "repent of our national sins" to Americans feeling sorry or ashamed for the wealth and prosperity of the nation. The purpose of the resolution, as originally introduced by President Lincoln, was dismissed—even ridiculed!

Atheists and cynics actually concluded that there was no *need* to repent of anything! (Ironically, today, some in America's leadership are *apologizing* across the world for ever having been great.)

That was the world of 1974. How much worse this nation has become in the intervening decades!

America has forgotten God. So has Britain. They have dealt falsely with Him—no longer recognizing that He is the great Provider. Due to this national rebellion and ingratitude, He is withdrawing His hand of blessing from us. Soon He will cause our peoples (America, Britain, Israel, Canada, Australia, New Zealand and certain Western European nations) to suffer horrible national punishment, through war, famine and disease—to be followed by invasion, capture and slavery!

The very blessings now taken for granted by these people will be completely stripped away. We are already witnessing this!

The only way to stop this prophesied fall is to turn to God, repent and follow His WAY!

Final Prophecies for America and Britain Today!

Most people will not seek God unless forced to—unless severe trials or other circumstances *drive* them to God. During good times, most are happy to trust in their own strength, crediting themselves for their successes and achievements, when they may have had little to do with blessings that came to them. On the other hand, these same people generally *blame* God when things go wrong in their life.

But understand this. God does not and has never *owed* blessings to anyone. He may *choose* to bless individuals or nations, for His own purposes, but no one automatically *deserves* prosperity, wealth, abundance and a generous portion of God's bounty.

The Bible says that all have sinned (Rom. 3:23), which means all have qualified themselves for *death* (Rom. 6:23)—and nothing more!

So it is with the peoples of America and Britain. God has bestowed to them astonishing, unparalleled blessings beyond what any nation has ever enjoyed. He has kept His promise to Abraham to make many nations from him and to give the sons of Joseph the promised awesome birthright blessings after two and one-half millennia.

But our peoples have neither been grateful for these birthright blessings, nor sought God, repenting of our *national sins*!

No Further Obligation

Our peoples have not known that they are Israelites, thinking themselves Gentiles and that the Jews constitute all of modern Israel.

How tragically wrong we have been. Yet, we have acted in the same stubborn, rebellious and stiff-necked fashion as ancient Israel. We have been unthankful for what we have received, though it came to us when we had done *absolutely nothing* to merit it. Instead of ingratitude, we should have sought God and yielded to Him so that such unrivaled blessings could have continued.

But we did not do this, *and will not*—though we still could!

Since God, after building to it for thousands of years, has now kept His promise, He has no further obligation to continue His birthright blessings—and this He will not do! Leviticus 26:1-18 is explicit regarding how God said that if ancient Israel would *not* yield to Him after numerous punishments, He would punish them for a full 2,520 years. (*America and Britain in Prophecy* explains this in detail.)

After this long withholding of the birthright, it would come time to be fulfilled—and it was—and then would come the following, first, if there were no repentance. Recall: "And I will break the pride of your power; and I will make your heaven as iron, and your earth as brass" (Lev. 26:19).

Our national pride is being broken. The decline of Britain is nearly complete, with America following on her heels. Both these countries have lost their sense of national honor and pride in the extraordinary political, economic and military might they once enjoyed in such splendid grandeur. Now, we are hated, vilified, held in contempt by even the nations we once helped so generously. No matter our true intent or purpose, our motives are constantly impugned. The tiniest of nations no longer fear to spit on or burn the American flag. Insignificant nations now freely ridicule us.

When we are castigated and excoriated abroad, or when our ambassadors and citizens are assassinated, or our embassies bombed, we merely issue anemic protests, crying "foul." Why? Because God has also kept His promise to "break the pride of [our] power" in front of the nations who once trembled before our mighty greatness.

Already mentioned, when the heavens turn to iron (no rain), the earth turns as hard as brass. No rain means few crops and little food. Thus, God foretold that unprecedented famine and disease will soon follow with such intensity that countless millions will die.

What will happen next? Notice: "And your strength shall be spent in vain: for your land shall not yield her increase, neither shall the trees of the land yield their fruits" (vs. 20). But this will no more cause national repentance within America and Britain than have any of God's previous punishments of His people, anciently. We will see that only one kind of national calamity will bring repentance to Israel.

Next will come this: "And if you walk contrary unto Me, and will not hearken unto Me; I will bring *seven times more plagues* upon you according to your sins" (vs. 21). The Revised Standard Version better renders this verse, "I will bring more plagues upon you, *sevenfold* as many as your sins."

As Never Before

Modern Ephraim and Manasseh are rushing headlong into a punishment so awful, so staggering—so *intense*—as to nearly defy description. What lies ahead for our peoples is truly as *terrible* as the birthright blessings were *wonderful*. The cesspool of rottenness and perversity— of every heinous sin—of every evil imaginable, has risen as a stench to God's throne. Degeneration, followed by rampant immorality, and now amorality, has become the social norm. The scourge of pornography is literally everywhere. Same-sex marriage is here. And routine mass murder, politely called "abortion" and "a woman's right," is an abomination for the ages.

Truly, a punishment *sevenfold* as severe as the level of *national sins*, now routinely committed by countless millions of our people, is a chastisement poured out—*unleashed by* God—beyond belief!

All the punishments of the 2,520-year "times" of Leviticus 26:1-18 also *reapply*. For instance, recall God said He would "appoint terror" over His people if they did not obey Him. Who can doubt this is now happening in a way never seen in our nation's history?—just think of "9/11"—and no man or government can stop what God has appointed!

Again, be careful you do not say, "But this could *never* happen to America and Britain." Do not assume we earned such marvelous blessings by our own ingenuity, forgetting that they were simply the fulfillment of a unique promise made 4,000 years ago. This assumption stands on the supposition that we will always be able to *rescue ourselves* from any national dilemma because we were able to bring these blessings on ourselves. We were not—they were given to us!

The same God who once sent Israel and Judah into captivity can do it again. The facts are in! The handwriting is on the wall—and you need to *wake up* to the reality of what has *already* happened to Britain's greatness, with America now following her decline headlong! And yet, the steepest decline—and *complete crash*—has yet to occur even to Britain. What lies ahead is so horrible, so awful—so truly terrible!—that you *must* shake yourself to understand!

Punishment Certain

God's warnings through His prophets are still recorded in His Word for us today. They show the absolute *certainty* of God's purpose to punish His chosen people. He called and chose them for a wonderful purpose (Ex. 19:5; Deut. 4:5-8; Isa. 43:21) more glorious than they were willing to understand, and they rejected Him—and still do today!

Isaiah, Jeremiah, Ezekiel, Daniel, Joel, Hosea and others prophesied *great* punishments to come upon our peoples. What Moses foretold, Christ also foretold. But all of this has remained locked up from all who do not understand or will not accept the identity of our peoples throughout these awesome, apocalyptic prophecies.

But within this understanding, it must be recognized that God is *chastening* people He *loves*. He has always wanted human beings to enjoy spiritual values and principles, having His Holy Spirit guiding and directing their lives, after having come to deep repentance—both as individuals and nations.

Again, some *few* individuals will yet repent, and will be *spared* the horrible prophecies we are examining.

Already Worsening Conditions

The pride of American and British power continues to be broken, with our leaders in fear of what our critics and enemies—and the ever-relentless press—will say. Authoritative leadership and decision making is now systematically undercut and checkmated by this endless chorus of professional naysayers. Also, any leader daring to even hint that *God* might be involved in the affairs of men is virtually *lampooned*—and *accused* of crossing boundaries between church and state. God never intended such an unnatural division.

As both manmade and natural disasters increase in number and intensity, it is evident God's protection around His people is even now being withdrawn. Headlines daily blare warnings of budget shortfalls, job losses, lack of growth, rising fuel and food prices, economic problems, growing social problems, war, difficulties and uncertainties, divided government, enormous problems in our schools and families, and so much more!

All of this will soon grow infinitely *worse* as God also turns our foreign political "lovers" against us (Ezek. 23:22; Jer. 4:30).

Astonishing, Specific Prophecy

What we have read above is only the *beginning* of what God says is yet to happen. The book of Micah, carrying special insight into our pride being broken, our loss of possessions and sea gates around the world, and worsening weather conditions, serves as its own tremendous *proof* of *who* and *where* are the peoples of Israel today. Simply reading this prophecy identifies America and Britain as the only nations that have fulfilled what is described in Micah 5.

Notice the enormous wealth, and ensuing downfall, of the people described, beginning in verse 7, as the "remnant of Jacob." Note that references to "dew" and "showers" have a direct bearing on agricultural productivity and reflect the direct blessings of God: "And the *remnant of Jacob* shall be in the midst of many people [nations] as a dew from the LORD, as the showers upon the grass, that tarried not for man, nor waited for the sons of men."

Recall that, anciently, Joseph himself stored food in Egypt and helped other peoples and nations as a result. When God's blessings were still being poured out upon *our* peoples without measure, over and over, *our* blessings became blessings to *other* nations of the world. This same spirit in *modern* Joseph—Ephraim and Manasseh—gave birth to the Alliance for Progress, Marshall Plan, Hoover Program, Four Point Program and so many others that saved millions from starvation after World War I and World War II. No other nations ever did *any* of these things, let alone all of them.

The next verse in Micah depicts Israel as a lion among all other nations on Earth. It *was* as a lion that America entered these two terrible wars and pulled the world back to temporary peace—until God's final time had come. Notice: "And the *remnant of Jacob* shall be among the Gentiles in the midst of many people *as a lion* among the beasts of the forest, as a young lion among the flocks of sheep: who, if he go through, both treads down, and tears in pieces, and none can deliver" (5:8).

Who can doubt that this describes what have been the roles of America and Britain?

The next scripture pictures what these two countries did throughout the nineteenth century and into the twentieth century, until they could no longer win wars in countries as small as Korea and Vietnam: "Your hand shall be lifted up upon your adversaries, and all your enemies *shall be cut off*" (vs. 9).

Invariably, in wars and skirmishes, this is exactly what America and Britain did to their adversaries and enemies. Our enemies were *always* cut off!

Shocking Devastation

At this point in the prophecy, God's description of His people takes a sharp turn: "And it shall come to pass in that day, says the LORD, that I will cut off *your horses* [Moffatt: "war horses"] out of the midst of you, and I will destroy *your chariots* [tanks, ships, aircraft, missiles]: and I will cut off the cities of *your land*, and throw down all *your strongholds* [military bases]" (vs. 10-11). Since God says He controls the outcome of war (Psa. 33:10-19), have no doubt that He will fulfill this prophecy.

Men now often speak of "disarming" terrorists, rogue dictators and their nations. This passage is God's promise to literally disarm *His own people*. Micah explains *why*: "And I will cut off *witchcrafts* out of your hand; and you shall have no more *soothsayers*: your graven images [idols] also will I cut off, and your standing images [idols] out of the midst of you; and you shall no more worship the work of your hands. And I will pluck up your groves [places of false worship in ancient Israel and today] out of the midst of you: *so will I destroy your cities*" (5:12-14).

God is tired of looking at modern "churchianity," which condones rank idolatry, spawns soothsayers (false ministers), condones sexual perversion and tolerates now widespread abominable witchcraft. These *modern* soothsayers should have thundered from their pulpits that if God's Law continues to be broken, the penalty is that the country doing this will also be "broken" as a natural consequence.

These deceitful false teachers defaulted in their responsibility, choosing to protect themselves instead.

"Behind the Scenes"

We saw that a European power bloc—the "Holy Roman Empire," a political system ruled by religion—is taking shape in Europe today away from the world's focus. A European constitution is being drawn up and its new currency is already in circulation. It is evolving a system of courts and laws, to be governed by a parliament guided by an elected president. Having endorsed its birth, the Vatican has appealed to this developing system for the inclusion of "Christian roots" in its future constitution. Germany is already leading the push for such "Christian inclusion." Shortly, a charismatic super-dictator will come to power over 10 other kings (leaders) within this union.

This religious-political combine will have its own army—and this army will eventually unleash World War III. At the heart of the military machinery of the forming European Union will be modern Germany—which we saw history reveals to be none other than the ancient Assyrian people. We also learned that these people migrated to central Europe, transporting with them many of the ancient Israelitish people they had taken into slavery starting in 721 BC. Space does not permit detailed evidence of the record of Germany's identity, but history emphatically proves it. The details are many. History also demonstrates that the modern Italians are the ancient Babylonians, often called the Chaldeans, who themselves migrated west to that peninsula. The proofs are many.

The world will one day stand shocked to learn that these two peoples, more than any other, have directly promoted the Babylonian (and Assyrian) Mystery Religion, which has merely appropriated the name of Christ. It was *this* system that turned "grace into lasciviousness [license]" (Jude 4) and deceived the whole world into believing it to be the true Church of God, the "woman" of Revelation 12, instead of the one of chapter 17.

The world will stand in stark wonderment and absolute astonishment at how this great Gentile "woman" church has bamboozled the people of national Israel—America and Britain—into believing that they also are Gentile nations!

God's Controversy with Israel

Let's carefully read this long and revealing passage in Hosea. It opens describing God talking to Israel while she is in slavery, but then at a point she is ready to hear His instruction: "Therefore, behold, I will allure her, and bring her into the wilderness, and speak comfortably unto her. And I will give her her vineyards from there, and the valley of Achor for a door of hope: and she shall sing there, as in the days of her youth, and as in the day when she came up out of the land of Egypt. And it shall be at that day, says the LORD, that you shall call Me *Ishi* [my Husband]; and shall call Me no more Baali. For I will take away the names of *Baalim* out of her mouth, and they shall no more be remembered by their name. And in that day will I make a *covenant* [the New Covenant] for them…And I will betroth you unto Me forever…in righteousness, and in judgment, and in loving kindness, and in mercies. I will even betroth you unto Me in faithfulness:

and you shall know the LORD. And it shall come to pass in that day, I will hear, says the LORD…and I will have mercy upon her that had not obtained mercy; and I will say to them which were not My people, *you are my people*; and they shall say, *You are my God*" (2:14-23).

The context of God's *present* statement and final message to Israel picks up at the outset of chapter 4: "Hear the word of the LORD, you children of Israel: for *the* LORD *has a controversy with the inhabitants of the land*, because there is no truth, nor mercy, nor knowledge of God in the land. By swearing, and lying, and killing, and stealing, and committing adultery, they break out, and blood touches blood. Therefore shall *the land mourn, and every one* that dwells therein shall *languish*, with the beasts of the field, and with the fowls of heaven; yes, the fishes of the sea also shall be taken away" (vs. 1-3). This passage speaks of Britain, America and other Western nations, as well as their lands and the awful conditions of all inhabitants, human and animal.

The next few verses are directed specifically to the *ministers* of churches throughout America and Britain. Here was God's blunt message to them about the *cause* of the appalling conditions and lack of character described above: "My people are destroyed for *lack of knowledge*: because you have *rejected knowledge*, I will also reject you, that you shall be no priest to Me: seeing you have forgotten the law of your God, I will also forget your children. As they were increased, so they sinned against Me: *therefore will I change their glory into shame*" (4:6-7).

These nations have rejected God. Therefore, all attempts to solve America's problems through politics by restoring "constitutional-based government" or "taking back Washington" or "changing the party in charge" or "getting out the vote" will fail. And all attempts to rid the nation of its evils by returning to "sound fiscal policy" or "cutting taxes" or "restoring capitalism" or "reducing the debt" or "creating jobs" or "redistributing the wealth" or "changing laws" will also fail in the end—and abysmally! Addressing a host of bad *effects,* while ignoring the true CAUSE of America's and Britain's troubles, could *never* yield real and permanent success.

Israel's Punishment Executed

Grim passages in the Old Testament describing what is to come on the modern-day house of Israel give shape and depth to the events (the first six seals) foretold throughout Revelation 6.

Ezekiel prophesied the *forms* of punishment on modern Israel. God pulls no punches: "Thus says the Lord GOD; This is Jerusalem: I have set it in the midst of the nations and countries that are round about her. And she has *changed My judgments into wickedness* more than the [Gentile] nations, and My statutes more than the countries that are round about her: for they have refused My judgments and My statutes, they have not walked in them" (5:5-6).

Continue reading: "Therefore thus says the Lord GOD; Because you *multiplied more than the nations that are round about you*, and have not walked in My statutes, neither have kept My judgments, neither have done according to the judgments of the nations that are round about you...Behold, I, even I, am against you, and will execute judgments in the midst of you in the sight of the nations" (vs. 7-8).

It will be due to disobedience that these peoples in particular will suffer from war, famine and disease. We saw God's Word was most specific: "A *third part of you shall die* with the PESTILENCE, and with FAMINE shall they be consumed in the midst of you: and a *third part* shall fall by THE SWORD round about you" (vs. 12).

Get this picture in mind a final time. One third dead from war in the West! Another third from famine and pestilence! (Occurring at the outset of the Tribulation, these would *possibly* be counted among the "fourth part" of humanity who perish *before* the Tribulation—the fifth seal. But they could be 400 million deaths on top of the fourth.)

Do not think these events are already past. This account is not describing *ancient* Israel! Neither Israel then nor the tiny Mediterranean nation of Israel today have been "multiplied more than the nations that are round about" them. Its citizens have always been relatively few in number! Therefore, this passage cannot apply to them. It represents a people much, much bigger.

Verse 9 continues with how God plans to "do in you that which I *have not done*, and whereunto I *will not do any more the like*, because of all your abominations."

Think. If Jerusalem had gone through any punishment unto which God had "not done" before and "will not do any more the like," would not it be well-known in history? Imagine the worst period of war, famine and disease of ALL TIME! These events would certainly be detailed in history books. Yet they are not.

So what nations fit this profile? They must be "multiplied more than the nations that are [a]round" them. Indeed, if a country is speeding toward the worst period of war, famine and disease *ever*, it is vitally important that its inhabitants know the words of Ezekiel apply to *them*. It is *crucial* they know what is coming!

Through examination of Israel's fate, and why punishment will come, we are setting up the thinking in God's mind—which in turn sets the table for powerful understanding. This means briefly looking backward before looking forward at what is coming on Israel—and then the world.

From Abundance to Crisis

Return to the shelves of modern supermarkets in America, Britain, Australia and other Western nations. These are lands of abundance and plenty. In fact, most citizens of these countries cannot imagine life any other way. Additionally, *these* nations have long produced and exported a large percentage of the world's grain supply. *These* are the only nations that fit this description. *These* are peoples "multiplied more than the nations that are round about" them! *These* are the nations who have descended from the twelve tribes of Israel.

Ungrateful for so many blessings daily at the hand of God, many will scoff: *"What?* America and Britain descended from ancient Israel? Two-thirds of these prominent, powerful Western nations killed by war, famine and disease—and the rest go into enslavement? Impossible!" Since most *lesser* nations would hold a similar view regarding any such terrible calamities that could end their existence, it would be difficult to penetrate Israel's smugness and sense of permanent security. Such denial in Israel is reflected in Jeremiah: "They have belied [denied] the LORD, and said, It is not He; neither shall *evil* come upon us; *neither shall we see sword nor famine"* (5:12).

God's warning in these passages will also be rejected outright by religious leaders, theologians and pastors. Instead, they will declare that there will be peace. They will counter God's warnings, and here is how: "Behold, the prophets say unto them, You shall *not* see the *sword*, neither shall you have *famine*; but I will give you assured *peace* in this place" (Jer. 14:13). The United Nations will say similar things to *all* nations of the world after hundreds of millions have already died, declaring, "the worst is now behind us."

Most will ignore the warning here from a loving God. The great majority will not heed until it is too late. The peoples descended from ancient Israel will today continue their lives in blissful ignorance. God's response to those who refuse to listen?: "Thus says the LORD of hosts, the God of Israel; Behold, I will *cause to cease* out of this place in your eyes, and in your days, the voice of *mirth*, and the voice of *gladness*, the voice of the *bridegroom*, and the voice of the *bride"* (Jer. 16:9).

Only after war turns to devastating famine and widespread pestilence will these nations cry out: "And it shall come to pass, when you shall show this people all these words, and they shall say unto you, Wherefore [why] has the LORD pronounced all this great evil against us? Or what is our iniquity? Or what is our sin that we have committed against the LORD our God?" (vs. 10). God replies, "Because your fathers have forsaken Me, says the LORD, and have walked after other gods, and have served them, and have worshipped them, and have forsaken Me [Chapter Thirty-two brings this home], and have not kept My law; and you have done *worse than your fathers*; for, behold, you walk every one after the imagination of his evil heart, that they may not hearken unto Me" (vs. 11-12).

Punishment is due to DISOBEDIENCE!

And to the pastors and priests who contradict God's warning, as well as those who deny His words, God declares, "Therefore thus says the LORD concerning the prophets that prophesy in My name, and *I sent them not*, yet they say, Sword and famine shall not be in this land; by SWORD and FAMINE shall *those prophets be consumed*" (14:15).

Deceit and gross dereliction of duty by the self-appointed spiritual leaders of our nations will bring consequences no one can imagine—or is worrying about. But Israel's punishment is far from the end of consequences. The plainness of God's words and purpose with Israel carry a *second* purpose because all *other* nations have also practiced sin...

Why World Punishment!

We have seen in previous chapters *what* will occur during these two distinct time periods, the Great Tribulation (described as *Satan's* wrath on modern Israel) and the Day of the Lord (*God's* wrath poured out on the whole of rebellious mankind).

The Bible reveals that only a tenth of Israel will survive into the Millennium. But Isaiah 6:11-13, Amos 5:3 and Ezekiel 5:12 and 6:8 are also representative as a parallel of the other nations of the earth. Most of Israel will perish in the Tribulation while the remaining nations will fall during the plagues, wars and calamities of the Day of the Lord.

The first four seals, coupled with the second woe, mentioned in Revelation, take over one half of all humanity, and this does not include the other trumpet plagues, earthquakes or the seven last plagues.

As the Millennium begins, it is truly only a remnant of *all* humanity that will have survived the unspeakable horrors at the end of the age.

We now formally ask the most central question in this volume: *Why* world punishment? *Why* is God angry? *What* has mankind done that incurs so much divine wrath and such incredible chastisement?

Not Popular

Realize the scriptures you are about to read are neither popular, nor pleasant. Ministers of this "present evil world" (Gal. 1:4) *will not* address them because they do not lend themselves to fuller offering plates. In fact, saying too much of them—and in most cases anything at all—will get a minister fired! But I will not be fired—and on God's authority, I show you the TRUTH of these enormous future events soon to crash into the world!

I hold no illusion: This book will be fiercely attacked by some. It steps on toes because bluntness must be brought from God's Word to prophecies so central to the lives of all peoples at the end of the age.

When Harry Truman fired the popular General Douglas MacArthur in 1951, he was attacked unmercifully for over a solid year by the press. While Truman suffered miserably in the polls, his response was to say that neither Moses nor Christ took polls to mean anything. Otherwise, he continued, Moses would not have led Israel from Egypt and Christ would never have died on the stake. He knew courageous leaders do not do and say what is *popular*, but what is *right*!

All with ears to hear, now is the time to *truly* heed!

Israel's Punishment—Warning to the World

Comprehending what happens to Israel becomes an important prelude to understanding *why* God will then punish the rest of the world—*again*, on top of the four horsemen. We read that God declares He "will make you [the American and British peoples] waste, and a reproach among the nations that are round about you, *in the sight of all that pass by*" (Ezek. 5:14).

Let's see what this means for the *rest of the world*. What God does with Israel occurs on the world stage, not in a corner. There is a reason.

Ezekiel 5 continues: "So it shall be a *reproach* and a *taunt*, an IN-STRUCTION and an *astonishment unto the nations that are round about you*, when I shall execute judgments in you in anger and in fury and in furious rebukes. I the LORD have spoken it" (vs. 15).

All other nations of Earth are to learn from this terrible punishment!

When these events occur, the rest of Earth's inhabitants are to consider—be *instructed*—by the war, famine, disease and other distresses upon Israel. They are to see that after centuries of disobedience the Israelitish peoples will receive the severest chastisement.

Dark days are prophesied to *first* slam into the descendants of Israel's twelve tribes, with this followed by punishment on the whole world. To avoid these terrible times, Israel—and the world at large!—must listen to God's warnings *before* the four horsemen ride with full force, and *before* the Tribulation, heavenly signs and Day of the Lord arrive.

Today's nations of Israel have *forsaken* God and His ways. They have altogether *rejected* His rule over them. In response to their rebellion, we saw God declares He will move "against" (Ezek. 5:7-8) these peoples. Nations the world over will behold as God executes mind-wrenching judgments on His people—judgments culminating in the Tribulation that are so terrible they will be unlike *anything* the world has seen, or will see again.

Notice God brings this punishment because His people have committed *abominations*—they have SINNED. They have disregarded, and BROKEN His holy Law—and have done this without shame! These are the very nations that most *profess* to know the God of the Bible.

Rather than embracing sin, Christians are to *hate* it! But how many who profess to know God actually *despise* sin? Yet we saw Jesus declared, "*If* you will enter into life, KEEP THE COMMANDMENTS" (Matt. 19:17). And, "Whosoever commits sin transgresses also the *law*: for sin is the *transgression* of the *law*" (I John 3:4).

Ask: If the Law of God has been "nailed to the cross," why is God going to *punish* Israel—and then the whole world—for disobeying it? For those who say the reason is people have not "accepted Jesus as their Savior, thus being freed from the law and judgment," God says, "Let no man deceive you: he that DOES *righteousness* is righteous, even as *He* [Jesus Christ] *is* righteous. He that commits sin [on the other hand] is *of the devil*; for the devil sinned from the beginning" (I John 3:7-8).

This is *most* plain! One must DO righteousness—in other words, OBEY GOD—to be righteous. Just "believing on Jesus" will not suffice.

Now Romans 4:15: "Where no law is, there is no transgression [sin]." If God's Law were no longer in effect, there can be no sin. And God could not punish mankind for sin it was not committing.

The Purpose of the Law

A God-hating world rejects the path set forth in the Bible. Proverbs 6:23 states, "For the commandment is a LAMP; and the law is LIGHT." The Hebrew word for "law" is *torah*, which literally means "to cause to see the light." All are familiar with the phrase "see the light," but probably few know that it springs directly from the word "law."

The Psalms expand this statement in 119:105: "*Your word* is a LAMP unto my *feet*, and a LIGHT unto my *path*." A New Testament passage expands this equation. But it uses a different way of stating what God's Word is: "*Your word* is TRUTH" (John 17:17). When placed together, God's Word—the Bible—is revealed to be a LAMP OF LIGHT, identically defined as TRUTH.

The one thing blind people do not see is any *light*. Their world is pitch BLACK! We read from II Corinthians 4:4 that the devil has blinded the world.

The apostle John records additional insight into the natural tendency of human nature in every person to actually *choose darkness* over light, as well as why they do this. Read—and *believe*—these verses: "This is the condemnation, that LIGHT is come into the world, and *men loved darkness* rather than LIGHT, because their *deeds were evil*. For everyone that *does* evil hates the LIGHT, *neither comes to the* LIGHT, lest his deeds should be reproved. But he that *does truth* comes to the LIGHT, that his deeds may be made manifest [obvious for what they are, good or bad], that they are wrought in God" (3:19-21). John

At the outset, it was explained how prophecy is a light shining in a dark world. Upon completion of the book you carry the authority to flip the switch back to darkness. After all, extreme punishment is not yet visible on the horizon for the majority. And most are too lazy and comfortable to exercise their mind's eye.

The Role of Ministers

This volume could scarcely say enough about the role of the ministers of this world and their effect on listeners. These millions of ministers have *openly defied God* and taught that it is permissible to break His Law. Rather than feeding people *true* understanding, ministers today feed their congregants *falsehoods* and fatten themselves with offerings that result from "feel good" sermons. They do not tell people to repent of evil ways, but rather, in net effect, to *continue* in them and "all will be well."

Notice more of their message: "They say 'still' unto them that despise Me [by being disobedient], the LORD has said, You shall have peace; and they say unto every one that walks after the imagination of his own heart [lives a life of sin], No evil shall come upon you" (Jer. 23:17).

God does not take sin, or deception about it, lightly. He abhors both. Notice Ezekiel 34, verses 2 and 3: "Thus says the Lord GOD unto the shepherds; *Woe* be to the shepherds of Israel that do feed *themselves*! Should not the shepherds feed the *flocks*?" And Ezekiel 13:22: "Because with *lies* you have made the heart of the righteous sad, whom I have not made sad; and strengthened the hands of the wicked, *that he should not return from his wicked way*, by promising him life."

Ministers of professing Christianity promise those *practicing sin* that they can expect to receive eternal life! This is contrary to God's Word, and He *will* require they answer for it. "Therefore thus says the LORD God of Israel *against the pastors* that feed My people; you have scattered My flock, and driven them away, and have not visited [cared for] them [by teaching them to obey God]: behold, I will visit upon YOU [false ministers] the evil of your doings, says the LORD" (Jer. 23:2).

Any sampling of sermons given by the professing Christian ministers of this world's false Christianity include a liberal mentioning of "God's mercy" and "kindness" and especially "love" for "mankind" or for "you." They are never truly *corrective*, nor do they contain *rebukes* for wrong conduct. Why, for instance, do they largely ignore passages such as "Behold therefore the goodness *and severity* of God" (Rom. 11:22).

Why do they never speak about how God's love requires Him to punish for disobedience? But disobedience to what?—the very law that these same ministers refuse to tell people is binding upon all peoples today! The ministers of this world have been derelict in their duty of warning that sin brings *consequences*—none of them good!

Understand. If there were no transgression of God's Law—there could come no punishment! Widespread and ever-worsening SIN directly causes the death of 9 out of 10 human beings alive today! Only *one tenth* of humanity will survive the Tribulation and Day of the Lord. Make yourself focus on this until your head pounds! The culmination of end-time events will result in the loss of 90 percent of humanity!

Again, *why* the coming horror?—*why* the fulfillment of dreadful prophecies?: "Wherefore, as I live, says the Lord GOD; surely, because you have defiled My sanctuary with all your *detestable* things, and with *all your* abominations, therefore will I also diminish you..." (Ezek. 5:11).

Sin is the reason! God reveals SIN is the cause of the horrific chastisement to come. We now leave Israel for the subject of *world* punishment.

"A Controversy with All Flesh"

The prophet Micah shows that God's punishment, after dealing with America and Britain, moves to inclusion of *all* nations: "And I will execute vengeance in *anger* and *fury* [the Day of the Lord] *upon the heathen*, such as they have not heard" (5:15).

Mind-numbing terror, springing from international chaos, lies just beyond the view of leaders, nations and billions of people hurtling toward disaster. *Every* continent, nation and tribe of Earth will be sucked into the vortex of what must occur because of the wretchedness, violence, corruption, degeneration, war, strife and oppression practiced worldwide.

God cares about *all* human beings—and the *entirety* of humanity has ignored Him and rejected His ways and laws. While Israel was taught and understood these laws more personally, all nations, starting at Creation with Adam and Eve in the Garden, have also disobeyed the true God. But it has been God's intention from Creation to fashion *every* human being in His own character and likeness (Gen. 1:26). This is why Paul was commissioned to preach the gospel to *Gentile* nations.

Jeremiah expands on what Micah prophesied. Few verses are more sobering: "A noise shall come even to the ends of the earth; for the LORD has a *controversy with the nations*, He will PLEAD with *all flesh...*" (25:31). Since all Gentile peoples—"the heathen"—are also God's children, His love for them requires He also punish non-Israelite countries.

Ultimately, *every* nation must learn to submit to the wonderful GOV-ERNMENT OF GOD. *Every* nation must come to recognize that God's Way brings supreme happiness and joy! *Every* person on Earth must see personal application of that Way.

Verse 31 shows that God first "pleads" with those He is about to punish. This pleading to "all flesh" includes a warning of exactly what will follow if they do not listen. Our books and other publications, reaching every country on Earth, are God's patient pleading with humanity before time runs out and this occurs: "...He will give them that are wicked to the sword...Thus says the LORD of hosts, Behold, evil shall go forth *from nation to nation*, and a great whirlwind shall be raised up from the *coasts of the earth*" (vs. 31-32).

Why God Sends Punishment

God *loves* His children. He is not suddenly going to change and *hate* mankind. But He does hate *sin*—because of the misery, pain and unnecessary suffering it brings to His children. Like any wise human parent, we saw God uses physical punishment to discipline His children. Proverbs 3:11-12 states, "...despise not the *chastening* of the LORD; neither be weary of His *correction*: for whom the LORD *loves* He corrects; even as a father the son in whom he delights." Quoting this proverb, the apostle Paul in the New Testament adds that God "chastens, and scourges [to afflict with severe punishment and pain] *every* son whom He receives" (Heb. 12:6).

A fair and just God must *punish* all nations for longstanding DISOBE-DIENCE—first modern Israel, and then the rest of the world. Mankind has bitter lessons to learn, and it is *our* generation—the *last* generation—who must bear the brunt of God's anger.

When Christ came announcing God's kingdom, He was tortured and crucified. Every one of the apostles, except John, was put to death by awful means, often after imprisonment, sometimes including torture. And the prophets of old who warned nations, kings and peoples to repent and acknowledge God as sovereign over their lives were placed in dungeons, forced to flee for their lives, stoned, sawn in two, or otherwise killed in most cruel fashion. Invariably, they were rejected and ignored. Noah preached for perhaps 100 years and only a few of his own family heeded.

The stiff-necked, rebellious, pleasure-seeking, self-willed, God-hating nations of the world have *never* heeded the *true* servants of God. Except for a few, my words here—in fact, *God's* words—will not change many. I *fully* recognize they will make some people *very* angry!

Punishment is coming for a reason. Six thousand years of ignoring God's commands have come to the *full*—and God is filled with *fury*!

Human beings, having human nature, will not enjoy the correction, possibly initially thinking it is unfair—that the masses do not really *deserve* it. This is because people want to be thought of as good, but do not want to *do* good—*do* what is right! Most will deceive themselves about what have been their ways. But *powerful* correction will soon soften stubbornness.

This correction will get people's attention in the only way left for God to do this. The world will come to recognize what sin brought—that they did these things to themselves. Their spirit of rebellion and disobedience will be shattered. They will learn that *spiritual* happiness greatly exceeds the value of physical, material prosperity.

God sees everything: "For the eyes of the LORD run to and fro throughout the whole earth" (II Chron. 16:9). God has seen every act of violence and cold-blooded murder, every vile rape, every calculated theft, every act of self-serving adultery, every covetous thought, every lie and deception—EVERY SIN!

Imagine witnessing *every* lawless act of mankind all over the world for just *one day*. What human being could cope with this? Yet God has witnessed 6,000 YEARS OF SIN!

No wonder Psalm 7 records, "...God is angry with the wicked every day" (vs. 11).

But Proverbs states, "He that *is soon angry* deals foolishly" (14:17). God has not been *soon* angry. He allotted six millennia for men and nations to heed Him and cease from sin. Man has refused, and his time of self-rule has almost expired.

Wrong Foundation from the Beginning

The world has always been devoid of *right* values—TRUE values—which would have brought it to enjoy every wonderful and good thing that a loving God could give to His Creation. Like human parents with their children, God has wanted His children to enjoy all the good things that He could provide for them.

The problem is that God's children have ingested false values, having wandered out of the "house" and into the "neighborhood," where they absorbed the thinking of different "parents." For generations, humanity has sought the wrong goals, it has had the wrong purposes in mind. Even though it has reaped a host of wrong results, and pain of every imaginable sort, it has not sought to examine the *faulty foundation* upon which it stands—wrong values!

This comes at a price.

Children of Disobedience

Here is *exactly* what brings God's wrath. Let's read His words. This first passage was quoted in a previous chapter, but bears repeating here in context: "…fornication, uncleanness, inordinate affection, evil concupiscence, and covetousness, which is idolatry: for which things' sake the WRATH OF GOD comes on the *children of disobedience*" (Col. 3:5-6).

DISOBEDIENCE draws God's anger.

Now another passage, from Ephesians: "But fornication, and all uncleanness, or covetousness…filthiness…For this you know, that no whoremonger, nor unclean person, nor covetous man, who is an idolater, has an inheritance in the kingdom…Let no man deceive you with vain words [false ministers today]: for because of *these things* comes the WRATH OF GOD upon the *children of disobedience*" (5:3-6). The next verse in Ephesians shows what Christians are instructed *not* to do with those who practice what Paul describes: "Be not you therefore partakers with them" (vs. 7).

Those who "partake" of this conduct, or who fraternize "with them" (the world and its ways), will *partake* of God's plagues on a whole world of rebellious nations.

The prophet Zephaniah we saw speaks most bluntly of this terrible day when God's wrath is poured out. Notice again: "The great day of the LORD is near, it is near, and hastens greatly [once it begins], even the voice of the day of the LORD: the mighty man shall cry there bitterly. That day is a day of wrath, a day of trouble and distress, a day of wasteness and desolation, a day of darkness and gloominess, a day of clouds and thick darkness, a day of the trumpet and alarm against the fenced cities, and against the high towers. And I will bring distress upon men, that they shall walk like blind men, *because they have sinned against the LORD*: and their blood shall be poured out as dust, and their flesh as the dung" (1:14-17). The *cause* of God's wrath—*why* world punishment—is here made plain—"they have sinned against the LORD."

It becomes "Behold...the...severity of God" (Rom. 11:22). Humanity will behold, during the Day of the Lord, God's GREATEST SEVERITY!

Human Nature "Desperately Wicked"

Writers, philosophers and scientists cannot agree on what is human nature. To understand the truth of human nature (also called carnal nature), we must again permit God's Word to answer.

God declares, "The heart [the seat of man's thoughts, motives and feelings] is *deceitful above all things*, and *desperately wicked*: who can know it?" (Jer. 17:9). The latter phrase is equivalent to "who could believe this?" And of course most cannot. Nor can they believe this inspired statement. Recall: "...the carnal mind is *enmity* against God: for it is not subject to the law of God, neither indeed can be" (Rom. 8:7).

The carnal mind naturally hates God, the Supreme Lawgiver, and therefore abhors His laws, as well as the laws of men. No wonder riots and rampant lawlessness abound when law and order collapse!

Romans 3:23 states, "For *all* have sinned, and come short of the glory of God." Every human being has sinned on his own account! All are responsible for and guilty of their *own* sins!

Let's examine more of what is occurring today for which God is angry, and why He will punish all mankind. The picture is not pretty.

The *worldwide panorama of sin* is WHY WORLD PUNISHMENT!

Sex-Drenched World

The world is now drenched—actually drowning—in a deluge of sex, with much or most of it having no connection to any real meaning or right purpose. More than ever in history, all mankind is awash in every conceivable kind of sexual pleasure, fantasy, perversion and pursuit—in or out of marriage, and with fewer and fewer people any longer making a distinction between the two. There has come to be no end to—and virtually no limits on—advertisements, television programs, movies, books, magazines, articles, photographs and websites for every kind of pornography and sex-related activity that the misguided creative genius of human beings could devise.

Barriers everywhere have dropped—and are still dropping as they near complete collapse on all fronts. Seemingly, every day establishes new lows in immorality, perversion, debauchery and "anything goes" when it comes to sexual habits and appetites. Experimentation and indulgence have become the norm. Most today have come to believe that free sex of every conceivable kind, with the same or opposite sex—or both—is a simple matter of personal preference. Vast millions have come to believe that achieving sexual pleasure in any setting, for any purpose, and involving any kind of experimentation or activity is perfectly acceptable—and is now, at least unconsciously, even seen to be a kind of human "right" of sorts.

You have seen how God foretold that in the "last days...men shall be...lovers of pleasures more than lovers of God" and "without natural affection" (II Tim. 3:1-4). In the age of gross materialism, mixed with rank hedonism, the three "Ls" of *leisure, luxury* and *license* have come to dominate the thinking of whole societies and nations.

God declares of our wanton, lascivious age, through Jeremiah, that "Every one neighed after his neighbor's wife" (5:8). His now almost completely forgotten Seventh Commandment—"Thou shall not commit adultery"—is routinely ignored by vast numbers.

Also in Jeremiah is this passage describing all peoples of the earth: "For they be *all* adulterers, an assembly of *treacherous men*. And they bend their tongues like their bow for *lies*: but they are not valiant for the TRUTH upon the earth; for they proceed from *evil to evil*, and they know not Me, says the LORD. Take you heed *every one* of his neighbor, and trust you not in any brother: for *every brother* will utterly supplant, and *every* neighbor will walk with slanders. And they will deceive *every one* his neighbor, and will not speak the TRUTH: they have taught their tongue to speak lies, and weary themselves to commit *iniquity* [lawlessness]. Your habitation is in the midst of deceit; *through deceit they refuse to know Me*, says the LORD" (9:2-6). All so telling of modern nations.

Do not permit yourself to reduce this description to "God is given to hyperbole"—to "the overuse of superlatives." The living God chooses His words carefully. He means *exactly* what He says. Read Psalm 12:6!

Rampant Adultery and Fornication

Return to adultery—just one sin in this long list. It is now rampant in all nations, with four out of five American households experiencing—and afflicted by—adultery, being committed by either one or both mates. Then consider South Korea, where 79 percent of men and 15.5 percent of women *admitted* to committing adultery in their 30s and 40s. The suffering of all kinds connected to just illicit sex by married people is staggering to consider. At what point will we find 90 percent—95 percent—or even 100 percent!—of couples no longer faithful in marriage (never mind chaste beforehand)?

The widespread practice of adulterous "pleasure marriages" has grown stronger in the Middle East. This is the custom of men marrying *several* so-called "widows" for the sole purpose of sex outside marriage, but done under the guise of taking care of women in need. In addition, because of China's explosion of economic prosperity, adultery in that country has grown so widespread that there are now tens of thousands of private investigators whose sole task is to track and report the marital infidelity of wealthy executives whose wives doubt their faithfulness. Incredibly, only one in 100 is found to be faithful! Then there are the various cultures of Europe, where having a mistress has long been considered a badge of honor—and many wives willingly accept the status quo.

With the idea that any kind of commitment is unnecessary, or even a nuisance, a truly horrific new practice emerged that now sweeps society—*hooking up*. Also called "no-strings sex," this no-limits-of-*any*-kind mindset is best described as "I had a beer last night, I hooked up last night," as one psychologist described it. Today's college campuses are fueled by alcohol, which serves to create a sexually charged atmosphere in which up to 80 percent of students on many campuses engage in sex with complete strangers, with the prevailing practice being to not even ask the name of their "partner." The feeling has come to be, "It's just sex. What's the big deal?" The countless thousands who now do this several nights a week have come to believe there is only a problem if they "catch feelings" for the person with whom they are having sex.

The awful culture of hooking up pictures a generation of morally bankrupt young adults in which the pursuit of sexual conquests—"trophy nights"—could be compared to big game fishermen out on the open ocean, with the engine idling on low power and the boat moving at low speed, as these "fishermen" troll for "big game" sex. Vast numbers of college students and others now seem to exist for the purpose of moving from one sexual encounter to another.

Prostitution, legal for a long time in Nevada, was in 2002 legalized in Germany. Incredibly, because of technicalities in German unemployment law, women have been told that they may have to be prepared to "take a job as a prostitute" to prevent the government from "stop[ping] your benefits." One wonders how far governments could go.

Related to the sex that is everywhere, the plague of pornography has also come to be a booming industry raking in billions of dollars across the world. The sexual appetite of people for this pursuit seems to be without limit, as are the magazines, movies, and hundreds of thousands of websites that make it available. Studies show 70 percent of hotel television revenue generated "in-room" is from pornographic films, meaning all other categories *combined* represent the other 30 percent.

Pornography is a powerful addiction for millions. Like alcohol, nicotine and drugs, it clutches ever-growing numbers who cannot find a way—the strength—to stop. Heartrending letters come to us describing marriages and families torn apart by this destructive social plague.

Homosexual *marriage* has become an explosive topic in the United States and Europe. Yet, it has been legal in the Netherlands since 2001. The process began in Europe in 1989, when Denmark was the first country to officially sanction such "partnerships," opening up a host of different related issues that eventually found their way to courtrooms. Whatever the moral issue, it is the misuse of man's adversarial legal system that invariably leads to the collapse of existing barriers. In December 2009, Mexico was the first Latin American country to legalize same-sex marriage, with the high court upholding it seven months later. Argentina followed soon after Mexico.

Of course, the entertainment industry today thinks nothing of homosexual conduct and routinely depicts it in movies, comedies and a host of television serials and sitcoms.

Also, lesbians and homosexual men have sought and received the legal right to adopt children in various countries, while other lesbians are willing to have a homosexual man impregnate them so they can "enjoy children" with the rest of society.

As this issue takes its place in the "cultural war," governments are being forced to address it. Politicians are being forced to choose between the most basic Judeo-Christian values and "giving the people what they want" in the name of "human rights" or "equal rights." The result has been nation after nation, particularly in the West, legalizing homosexual marriage. Some individual states are following suit in America.

Related to this issue are politicians who are even being pressured to create legislation regarding cross-dressing and transgender restrooms in high schools so that "gender neutral" children and teens can enjoy a "gender neutral" restroom. Truly astonishing!

Mass Murder

Next revisit abortion—the continual outright *mass murder* by doctors and people who function as legal serial killers—occurring around the globe. First, an important inset thought. To understand what God thinks of abortion, one must understand the difference between crime and sin. They are not the same, nor are they defined by the same set of laws.

According to most of man's governments, abortion is a "legal procedure." In countries where it is illegal, it is a crime to have an abortion, often resulting in a prison sentence. Another simple example is if someone holds up a bank and steals money, it is a crime. Crime is the breaking of *man's* laws.

Sin is similar, and we saw I John 3:4 defines it. Sin is the breaking of *God's* laws. Depending on where you live, it may not necessarily be a crime to have an abortion, but it *is* a SIN—and is a clear *breaking* of the Sixth Commandment, *"Thou shall not kill"* (Ex. 20:13).

Living contrary to God's Law, man has resorted to killing millions of innocent babies by simply creating his *own* laws. Here are sobering statistics:

The estimated number of *legal* abortions performed in America alone since 1973 is over 50 million—and this number is said to be even greater, since it only represents abortions *reported by licensed agencies.*

According to the Department of Defense, the American casualties for the Revolutionary War, War of 1812, Mexican War, Civil War, Spanish-American War, World Wars I and II, Korean War, Vietnam War, Gulf War and the Iraq War, in addition to deaths attributed to September 11—combined—are estimated at 1.27 million. In *2000 alone*, 1.31 million pregnancies in the *U.S. alone* ended in abortion—*down* from the all-time high of 1.61 million in 1990.

According to the World Health Organization, an estimated 46 million babies are aborted *each year* worldwide! This equates to over 126,000 MURDERS each day—87 per minute—or one and a half per second!

Stop and think. God considers every life to be precious. Yet humanity has taken upon itself to end millions of lives every year! The ongoing holocaust against completely innocent and defenseless babies is one more BIG reason God's wrath—His fury—is coming! And weak-kneed, cowardly, immoral, broken-headed leaders, educators, doctors, politicians, sociologists, parents and "churchmen" are squarely in God's focus!

The Ravages of Drug Abuse

Drug abuse has long been a global phenomenon. It is found in uptown penthouses, neighborhood slums, and everywhere in between. The *United Nations World Drug Report 2005* estimated that as many as 200 million people worldwide are drug users—some now report that up to one half of all professional people in America use drugs, with some being recreational and others quietly hardcore.

Drugs such as methamphetamines are ravaging the world. Just one example is "crystal meth," which is so powerful that it can *immediately* transform casual users into out-of-control junkies. Once a person is seduced by this drug, the end result is a life destroyed. Innocent family members can be included.

Even prescription drugs are being routinely abused. For example, a 2005 study by the Partnership for a Drug-Free America places teen abuse of cold medications on par or higher than the abuse of illegal drugs such as ecstasy, cocaine, methamphetamines and heroin. Prescription and over-the-counter drug abuse is not limited to America. A United Nations group recently reported this problem is quickly passing the abuse of all illegal drugs worldwide.

Look at the world around you. Drug abuse, alcoholism, gambling, lying, cheating, stealing, promiscuous sex, prostitution, pornography, sexually transmitted diseases and increasing violence are now commonly found in the lives of most teenagers. They have grown up in a society that looks for every possible pleasing, stimulating sensation. They seek to appeal to the senses—touch, sight, feeling, hearing and smell—in any way possible. All that they do must be "approved" by their senses. And this does not speak to their wildly foul mouths and disrespect for all authority, starting with parents.

Modern Entertainment

Now consider the modern generation's music of choice. In past decades, rock and roll became the spearpoint in music, influencing virtually every segment of society. Yet even the worst of yesterday's music is tame in comparison to today's mainstream monstrosity masquerading as music!

The most common themes glorified by today's recording artists are illicit sex, anger, extreme violence of every sort and drug use. But because it is only "music," it is legal.

Rebellion against authority has been a widespread message for decades. Many songs promote the thinking that work, school, parents and the law are enemies to be disrespected, disregarded and disobeyed.

Some groups and genres are directly connected to outright Satanism. Some bands literally pray to the devil before going on stage. Others hold séances before performing, seeking "higher powers" to enter them, using performances as an avenue to supernatural contact.

Look at the "Hollywood-ization" of the occult: countless films and television programs desensitize the viewer to demonism, witchcraft and magic, many times with blood and gore. These feature witches, vampires, voodoo and black magic, attracting millions of dedicated viewers. Harry Potter is tame compared to the routine vileness of so many books, movies, television programs and video games today.

This "entertainment" has real consequences: Across college campuses in the U.S., paganism and witchcraft are thriving and spreading. An ever-growing number of teens and young adults are delving openly into ancient pagan rituals. Ironically, more students than ever are studying world religion, with many universities reporting these classes are "maxed out."

Destroying the Earth

Pollution is also rampant across the globe. In an effort to live the good life, mankind is constantly improving and replacing products in society. But something has changed in today's consumer-driven way of life. Industry has produced many products that people do not *consume*, but simply *use*. Newspapers, magazines, clothing, packaging, electronics of all sorts, etc., are never consumed! People simply purchase products, only to later throw them away, replacing them with the newer, better version. This describes *user-driven* societies.

The end result? Vast amounts of pollutants—and new and ever bigger—giant!—landfills.

Every day, earth becomes more and more polluted. Air pollution fills our lungs with deadly substances. Water pollution is rapidly destroying what little freshwater we have left. Land pollution is causing once-fertile lands to become little more than deserts. Mankind is poisoning this planet on such a scale that the earth would never recover without God's intervention!

Developing countries dump 90-95 percent of their untreated sewage and 70 percent of their untreated industrial waste into surface waters. Population growth ensures that this problem always gets worse. In addition, acid rain and chemical runoff from fertilizers and pesticides sufficiently ruin water quality, making it largely unusable.

Fully 60 percent of all disease on Earth is sanitation-related. Each year, air pollution kills nearly 3 million people in developing countries alone, with poor sanitation killing another 12 million. Various forms of indoor air pollution (soot, dung, coal for cooking and heating, etc.) affect 2.5 billion people a year and kill 2.2 million.

God commanded Adam to *protect* and *preserve* the world that was created for him—not rape and destroy the beauty and blessings around him. Imagine how different this world would be if Adam—and everyone who followed—had simply listened to God's very first directive to man. But this is not the *only* warning God has given to man about pollution—the destruction that man would visit upon God's Earth. Here is what Isaiah said about our age: "The earth is drooping, withering...and the sky wanes with the earth; *for earth has been polluted by the dwellers on its face...*Therefore a curse is *crushing the earth*, alighting on its guilty folk; mortals are dying off, till few are left" (24:4-6, Moffatt translation).

The people of Earth *are* under a "curse." But why? Hosea expands this: "Israel, hear the word of the Eternal, for the Eternal has a charge to bring against the dwellers in the land: no fidelity, no kindness, no knowledge of God in the land, nothing but perjury, lying, and murder, stealing, debauchery, burglary" (4:1-2, Moffatt).

Not knowing God, men walk blindly in their societies, unaware of how to take care of the planet put in their charge. Because of their ignorance, "even the *beasts* and *birds* and the very *fish* within the sea *are perishing*" (4:3, Moffatt). Just look at oil spills!

Greed and the desire for self-titillation have put everything—including God—second in the eyes of men. The fruits of human nature are the destruction of the earth. The result? As we saw earlier, "Your wrath is come...and should *destroy them which destroy the earth*" (Rev. 11:18).

Pleasure and Greed

Over the last several decades, the shift toward materialism has been undeniable. Across all nations, the accumulation of goods has become an obsession. This obsession has led directly to the emergence of a modern mix of humanism and hedonism—the belief that happiness and enjoyment of the "here and now" is the central purpose of life.

For increasing numbers, this is taking a newer form—the sin of *gluttony* (Prov. 23:21). Almost one-third—73 million—of all adults in the United States are obese, the Centers for Disease Control and Prevention (CDC) reported. According to the CDC, from 2007 to 2009, the number of obese adults aged 18 and over rose by 2.4 million—a 1.1 percent increase. These statistics are double the national numbers of 30 years ago.

For extreme examples of carnal pleasures, look no further than the average modern city. Strip clubs are essentially a "dime a dozen." Many cities across the globe are no less than a modern day Sodom and Gomorrah, where "pleasure" is seemingly the main impetus for each day. So many now "work for their weekends," which are often filled with parties, drinking and sexual exploits.

The spirit of "tolerance" becomes necessarily a main theme, and many are taking it to an extreme. All forms of "pleasure" are not only tolerated, but actually encouraged. With all of this pleasure-seeking, one might think there would be increased joy and happiness. Yet people's lives are now filled with worse problems of every shape and form.

Hoping pleasure will bring happiness, people live "in *pleasure* on the earth, and [have] been *wanton*" (Jms. 5:5). Millions have *no idea* what brings true happiness. So many are "...foolish, *disobedient*, deceived, serving [various] *lusts* and *pleasures*..." (Titus 3:3).

We saw that the main motivating factors behind the recent global financial crisis were *greed* and *covetousness*. Banks were greedy for ever-higher profits. So were investors who took foolish risks for higher return on investment. And greedy individuals sought loans they could not repay to purchase material goods they coveted.

God sees—and hates—all of these things!

Violence, Crime and Corruption

Consider how often acts of *mass* violence now occur in schools, restaurants or other places in ways that were virtually unheard of until recently! Who ever heard of "serial snipers" in previous decades? The relatively modern phenomenon of terrorism is now worldwide! Gang violence and warfare have never been greater—or spreading faster. Truly, violence is now a global epidemic, just as in Noah's time.

According to the World Health Organization, violence is responsible for the deaths of more than 1.6 million people worldwide every year. It is "among the leading causes of death for people aged 15-44 years of age, accounting for 14% of deaths among males and 7% of deaths among females. On an average day, 1,424 people are killed in acts of homicide, almost one person every minute."

Looking at just a few newspapers today provides a reader with accounts that are but a brief snapshot of an ever spiraling trend in today's society. News presents a picture of a world truly "full of bloody crimes." Many cases (as evidenced in high-profile cases of recent years) are so often left unsolved.

Gone are the days when parents did not have to worry if their children left the front yard without them. Today, trust and confidence have been replaced by *suspicion* and *fear*! People no longer consider the effects their actions will have on others. Human life has been increasingly devalued, as evidenced by some who kill merely because they have been "disrespected" or to enter a gang, or even just for the sake of killing. Many thousands are murdered every year on just the streets of America. Millions more are slaughtered worldwide each year.

More and more, when things do not go their way, people simply "lose it." They go on killing sprees and, in some cases, end it by taking their own lives. They seem to believe the solution to their own problems must necessarily involve wreaking misery, unhappiness, suffering and death on others. The rationale seems to be, "I'm going down, and I'm going to take as many with me as I can."

Studies also show that "Over two-thirds of the world's countries are rife with corruption" (*Reuters*).

Turn on your television or radio, or go to the Internet. Pick up a newspaper or news magazine. Watch local, national or world newscasts. No matter your source for news, one of the regular, big headlines is CRIME—and on personal, corporate and governmental levels.

What has been covered is but the briefest glimpse of what God sees when "the eyes of the LORD…run to and fro through the whole earth" (Zech. 4:10). A sin-sick world!

But when these things are brought to people's attention, most blame others, rather than taking responsibility.

The Blame Game

Many today specialize in playing the "blame game." Large numbers of people feel little or no personal responsibility for what happens to them. Many now see themselves largely as blameless, innocent *victims* of any number of possible *perpetrators*.

People who get lung cancer from cigarettes blame and sometimes sue the tobacco manufacturers. People who kill in a rage blame temporary insanity. Other killers blame society or their bad childhood. The victims' relatives also blame the gun manufacturers. People who drive drunk blame the bartenders for letting them get behind the wheel. Addicts blame the easy access to drugs for their substance abuse. The increase in youth violence is generally attributed to Hollywood and video game manufacturers (partly true), instead of parents taking their fair share of the blame. Overweight people who cannot control their appetites blame the fast-food industry for their "addiction," and often seek huge "damage" awards through the courts.

Realize that you have been conditioned to blame others for what is *your* fault—and *your* responsibility to change. You must recognize that you live in the age when there are no longer *perpetrators*—unless it is someone else—but rather only "innocent VICTIMS."

Who is to blame for all of the wrong conduct described above?

Some blame religion. Others blame Hollywood, or the decadent West. Still others point the finger at educators. Yet others claim politicians are at fault. And more and more now blame capitalism or other forms of the free market.

There *is* certainly plenty of blame to go around. Every institution of man *has* played a role in the awful and sin-filled condition of society. Terrible evils *have* been committed by leaders of every facet of society, and all people *will* answer for their part in them. God's vengeance is real (Rom. 12:19; Deut. 32:35). Many verses reveal that His justice—described as His "judgment and fiery indignation, which shall devour the adversaries" (Heb. 10:27)—*will* strike great numbers of unsuspecting people suddenly—severely—and soon.

But stop blaming *others* for wrong conduct in *your* life!

Without Excuse!

Some will ask: What about those who never knew God's Law? Why will *they* be held accountable? This is a natural question. While not the larger purpose here, it is important to understand that all who will perish before and during the Day of the Lord will get an opportunity for salvation after the Second Resurrection. The question remains—why will those who are *ignorant* of God's Law be punished?

Two chapters in Romans reveal in a series of eye-opening verses why all mankind is without excuse—why *all* will be held accountable for breaking God's Law, including those who never knew of it.

Start with three of the Commandments: "You shall not kill," "You shall not steal" and "You shall not bear false witness" (Ex. 20:13, 15-16). Even those who do not know God understand it is wrong to lie, kill, steal, cheat people or commit adultery. Every society has instituted laws to uphold these things. Many once were willing to outlaw adultery, knowing it to be intrinsically wrong. Of course, such countries or states are fewer today.

Now a critical verse: "For when the Gentiles [or unbelievers], which *have not the law* [they do not have it explained to them, and could claim ignorance], do *by nature* the things contained in the law..." (Rom. 2:14). Men naturally recognize some things are evil!

The point expands in the next verse, "Which shows the work of the law written in their hearts, their *conscience also bearing witness*, and their thoughts the mean while *accusing* or else *excusing* one another" (vs. 15).

Man's conscience bears witness to his every action! Everything one does is either "excused" or "accused" by his own mind. Most people have at least a rudimentary sense of right and wrong. Of course, some do lose this in time, but this would have been by choice. Anyone claiming he never knew "You shall not kill" is without excuse because "by nature" he knew it is wrong to kill. His "*conscience*" bore witness. The same with lying, stealing, adultery and cheating people.

Let's make the point clear: Human beings will protest, "I never knew God's Law"—but God exclaims, "Your conscience told you many things were wrong and you violated them anyway. Your mind 'accused' you at these moments. You are without excuse!"

Within the same context in Romans it says: "TRIBULATION and ANGUISH, upon *every* soul of man that does evil, of the Jew first, and also of the Gentile [unbeliever]" (2:9).

(Great) Tribulation and (equally great) anguish are coming! Mankind is without excuse. World punishment is necessary. But first another prophecy now being fulfilled is giving all people and all nations space to repent...

Awesome Announcement!

One of the most dramatic prophecies in the Bible relates to a *unique commission*—a responsibility to issue A SPECIAL ANNOUNCEMENT—given to God's Church at the end of the age. The *good news* of *this* prophecy is overlooked within the bad news of so many other future events. It involves the central, final Work of the true people of God.

Read again Christ's *last* reference to the gospel of the kingdom of God during the Olivet Prophecy: "And this *gospel of the kingdom* shall be preached in *all the world* for a witness *unto all nations*; and then shall the *end* come" (Matt. 24:14). This obviously describes a major effort, global in nature. Anything reaching all nations cannot be small.

It is crucial to comprehend the importance of this prophecy. Its fulfillment must occur before the "end" can come. Jesus brought only *one* gospel message—with all others FALSE! What does this fulfillment involve?

You are about to learn more incredible knowledge!

Hidden—and Revealed!

Now note again Jesus' very *first* reference to the gospel, recorded in Mark 1:15, where He commanded, "Repent you, and believe the gospel." But exactly what is it that we—YOU!—must come to believe?

Modern Christendom does not know the vital—all-important—answer to this most basic question, and many others *related to* the true gospel of the Bible! This is because knowledge of what the gospel is has remained hidden from the world for centuries!

At Jesus' First Coming, He came as a first-century NEWSCASTER, bringing advance GOOD NEWS of staggering events to occur beyond the horizon, and the *bad news* occurring throughout today's world. This climactic news involves you—and every human being!

Six books on religion are published every day in America. And there are over 2,000 forms of Christianity in the U.S., with a new one appearing about every three days! Yet there has never been more confusion and disagreement about the answers to humanity's problems.

Why is there so much knowledge available to mankind, yet so much ignorance of the truth of the answers to life's BIG questions? All of this has *everything* to do with the gospel!

We saw that "Satan...deceives the whole world" (Rev. 12:9). This deception would certainly apply to a matter so crucial as the meaning and correct understanding of the only gospel message Jesus brought!

Before examining the Matthew 24:14 prophecy, we must learn what the true gospel *is*, and the importance God places on THIS MESSAGE!

Many False Gospels

The world has believed a false gospel for 2,000 years. It has generally supposed that Jesus Christ *is* the gospel rather than the Messenger *of* it. This is false. The Message—the centerpiece—of the gospel is *not* Christ. By focusing on Him—His *Person*—the *Messenger*—religious deceivers have been able to successfully suppress and cover up His *Message*!

Some proclaim a "gospel of salvation," others a "gospel of grace." Still others believe a "gospel of miracles" or a "social gospel." Yet others think of the "gospel of foods" or of "healing" or of "faith." And there are some who merely think of "gospel music" when they hear this word. These manmade ideas all ignore the TRUTH of the Bible!

Notice more of Mark's account: "Now after that John was put in prison, Jesus came into Galilee, preaching the gospel of the *kingdom of God*" (1:14). *This* is the gospel that Jesus preached. It was in *this* context that He said, "Repent you, and *believe the gospel*." Which gospel? "...of the kingdom of God."

Verse 1 in Mark refers to *this* message, when it states, "The beginning of the gospel of Jesus Christ." The gospel of Jesus Christ was about the KINGDOM OF GOD—not something else! One must believe *that* gospel—not a humanly devised counterfeit or substitute. So says Christ!

Notice more proof that Jesus' gospel message was not about Himself and His sacrifice. He declared, "For I have *not spoken of Myself*; but the Father which sent Me, He gave Me a commandment, *what I should say*, and what I should speak. And I know that His commandment is life everlasting: whatsoever I speak therefore, even as the Father said unto Me, *so I speak*" (John 12:49-50).

Plainly, Jesus functioned as a messenger of—a *representative* of—a SPOKESMAN for—the coming kingdom of God. He stated, "The word which you hear is not Mine, but the Father's which sent Me" (John 14:24). Jesus brought the Father's message. This *must* be clear!

Strong Warning Not to Pervert It

We saw that this subject is so important that God inspired the apostle Paul to pronounce a DOUBLE CURSE on anyone who preached "another gospel," or "*any* other gospel." The fuller quote was seen earlier.

This is a very blunt statement! Repeated here for emphasis, it is seen to be a strong warning to all who will heed!

A little later, Paul stressed his hope that the "*truth* of the gospel might continue with you" (Gal. 2:5). So there is ONE true gospel—with all others FALSE! I didn't say that! God did, through Jesus and Paul.

Although some assert Paul taught a different or *additional* gospel, this is ridiculous. In fact, God used Paul to pronounce a *curse* on anyone—man or angel—who violates this command (1:8-9).

Paul also explained that the apostles were entrusted by God to *preserve* the true gospel. Notice I Thessalonians 2:4: "We [apostles] were allowed of God to be put in trust with the gospel, even so we speak; not as pleasing men, but God, which tries our hearts."

This is a responsibility not to be taken lightly. *True* ministers must always teach what *God* commands—not what pleases *men*. So any claim that Paul taught a different or second gospel is impossible. Had he done this, he would literally have been pronouncing a curse on himself!

Jesus Was Foretold to Bring the Gospel

The Old Testament reveals that Jesus was to come as a MESSENGER. Malachi 3:1 declares, "Behold, I [Christ] will send My messenger [John the Baptist], and he shall prepare the way before Me [Christ]: and the Lord, whom you seek, shall suddenly come to His temple, even the Messenger [Jesus Christ] of the covenant, whom you delight in."

As we have seen, Jesus was the MESSENGER of the gospel, not the message. And His message is the core—the very *centerpiece*!—of the Bible.

Now compare the passage in Malachi with another in Luke: "The law and the prophets were until John [only Old Testament scriptures had been preached previously]: *since that time* the KINGDOM OF GOD is preached, and every man presses into it" (16:16). Remember, in Mark Jesus preached the "kingdom of God" and called it the gospel.

Meaning of "Gospel"

The word *gospel* is an old English word meaning "god spell" or *good news*. The word *kingdom* is also an old English term, simply meaning "government." Therefore, it is accurate to say that Jesus preached "the good news of the government of God." We will come to learn the *who*, *what*, *where*, *when*, *why* and *how* of this "news," and its relation to the very greatest prophecy in the Bible.

The kingdom of God is the dominant theme of not only the New Testament, but of the whole Bible. Yet, incredibly, most know little or nothing of it. This world's ministers are oblivious to this gospel, and never preach about it. Instead, claiming God's kingdom is here *now*, and is spread by "kingdom building," they stress "preaching Jesus" (not the kingdom) to the masses. Therefore, virtually the whole world stands in complete ignorance of the single greatest truth in God's Word!

When Jesus Christ began preaching the message of God's kingdom from the beginning of His ministry, He set the standard for His Church of the most awesome announcement the world would ever hear. Incredibly, uncounted millions cannot even get the meaning of the *word* "gospel" clear. They have no idea what Jesus talked about, even though He said the same thing over and over and over, everywhere He went!

How Many Times Mentioned?

The word *gospel* is found over 100 times in the Bible. Sometimes it is found alone, and sometimes the phrase "of the kingdom" follows it. Other times, it includes "of the kingdom *of God*," or the equivalent phrase "of the kingdom *of heaven*."

Note that this phrase says, "*of* heaven," not "*in* heaven." It is heaven's kingdom and there is a big difference between the two. Just as kingdom *of* God means God's kingdom—not the kingdom *in* God—the same is true of the kingdom *of* heaven or *heaven's kingdom*. Unlike all the kingdoms of men, this kingdom belongs to heaven, meaning to *God*. Grasp this crucial point, lost on almost everyone!

Throughout the New Testament, the word "kingdom" is found 27 times, "kingdom of God" 75 times, and "kingdom of heaven" 34 times. All are one and the same.

What Paul Preached

While the apostle Paul preached the kingdom of God, notice two verses in the book of Acts showing that he did not neglect the subject of Christ's role in the salvation process.

First, Acts 19:8 establishes which gospel he preached: "And he went into the synagogue, and spoke boldly for the space of three months, disputing and persuading the things concerning the *kingdom of God*." In many of his epistles, he taught the kingdom to Gentile congregations. His message was always the same. He continually preached, taught and referred to the *kingdom of God*.

Next, Paul states in Acts 20:25, 21, "I have gone preaching *the kingdom of God*...repentance toward God, AND *faith toward* our Lord *Jesus Christ*." He preached the same gospel to both Jew and Gentile.

Now notice Acts 28:30-31: "Paul dwelt two whole years in his own hired house, and received all that came in unto him, preaching the *kingdom of God*, AND teaching those things which concern the Lord *Jesus Christ*."

Luke, the one who recorded Acts, differentiates between preaching the *kingdom of God* and preaching *Jesus Christ*! While both are vitally important, they are clearly separate subjects!

In Acts 8:12, we saw the deacon Philip also preached both of these same teachings: "But when *they believed* Philip...concerning the *kingdom of God*, AND the name of *Jesus Christ*, they were baptized, both men and women." We see that Philip not only preached God's kingdom, but he also differentiated it from the teaching *about* Christ. Remember, the *messenger* is not the MESSAGE.

Notice that these in Samaria were baptized only after "they believed" the right message—not some human substitute for it. Jesus' name and role were taught as an important, but *additional*, understanding.

Finally, recall the powerful warning in II Corinthians 11:4. Paul makes the distinction between the *gospel* and the *Person* of Christ: "For if he that comes preaches *another Jesus*, whom we have not preached...OR *another gospel* which you have not accepted, you might well bear with *him*" (most Bible margins correctly render "him" as "me"). Paul wanted the Corinthians to reject false teachers and hold to what *he* had taught them. The point here is that Paul distinguishes between the teaching of a *false Jesus* and that of a *false gospel*. These are—and always have been—two separate things!

Ask: If Jesus *is* the gospel—*is* the kingdom of God—why did Paul (four times) and Philip speak of them *as separate matters*?

Jesus Christ is NOT the gospel—and He is certainly NOT God's kingdom!

All the Apostles Preached This Same Gospel

What evidence is there that other New Testament writers preached this same message? A great deal!

The apostle Peter also preached the kingdom of God: "For so an entrance shall be ministered unto you abundantly into the *everlasting kingdom* of our Lord and Savior Jesus Christ" (II Pet. 1:11).

So did the apostle James: "Hearken, my beloved brethren, has not God chosen the poor of this world rich in faith, and HEIRS of the *kingdom* which He has *promised* to them that love Him?" (2:5).

The apostle Matthew's account mentions "gospel of the kingdom" three times. Here is one: "Jesus went about all the cities and villages, teaching in their synagogues, and preaching the *gospel of the kingdom*, and healing every sickness and every disease among the people" (9:35). In most of His parables, Jesus taught the basics of God's kingdom. Matthew alone makes over 50 references to it.

Luke records that Jesus commissioned His disciples to preach this message: "He called His twelve disciples together...and He sent them to preach the *kingdom of God*" (9:1-2). Soon after, He sent 70 others to preach, and they also carried the message of the "kingdom of God" (10:1, 9).

All God's Prophets Preached the Kingdom

The book of Acts contains an extraordinary passage for our examination: "Repent you therefore, and be converted, that your sins may be blotted out, when the times of refreshing shall come from the *presence of the Lord*; and He *shall send Jesus Christ*, which before was preached unto you: Whom the heaven must receive until the times of *restitution* [or restoring] *of all things*, which God has spoken by the mouth of *all His holy prophets since the world began*" (3:19-21).

Notice Peter, the one speaking, refers to the Coming of Christ (vs. 19) as "the presence of the Lord," meaning in context He is now back on

Earth. Verse 20 states God "shall send Jesus Christ." Verse 21 describes God's kingdom as the "restitution of all things." Peter declares this "restitution" (Christ establishing His kingdom) is something "God has spoken by the mouth of *all* His holy prophets *since the world began*."

This is a truly eye-opening statement! Did God actually use *all* of His prophets to announce His kingdom? Bible scholars and religionists ignore this passage—and reject it without examination.

Let's review just a few examples. In fact, we start in the period before the flood. The apostle Jude, Jesus' brother, recorded that "Enoch [Noah's great-grandfather]...prophesied...saying, Behold, *the Lord comes* with ten thousands of His saints, to *execute judgment upon all*" (vs. 14-15). These verses clearly refer to Jesus Christ coming to establish a world-ruling *government* under Himself and the saints.

The Bible calls Enoch a "preacher of righteousness" (Jude 14; II Pet. 2:5). Including Abel, there were *seven other men* who held this role, with their lives spanning the entire period between Adam and the Flood. All of them spoke the same message. Remember, Peter said, "...since the world began" (vs. 21).

Is there evidence the gospel was preached in the period *following* the Flood?

In Genesis 12:3, we saw God said to Abraham, "...in you shall *all families* of the earth be blessed." This verse is also referenced in Galatians 3:8, but is phrased a little differently: "...in you shall *all nations* be blessed." This verse adds that "the *gospel* was preached before *unto Abraham*." This is fascinating understanding! Considering what you have learned about Abraham, not only would he have had the gospel preached to him (probably by Melchizedek), but it was then preached in *Genesis*, through *Moses*! *All nations* will ultimately be blessed when Christ establishes His government *on Earth*—where "the nations" are.

Moses was the first man God raised up to lead ancient Israel. As both a prophet and judge, he preached the gospel to Israel in the wilderness. Also read Numbers 24:17-19.

Acts 3:24 references Samuel as a prophet, and as having preached the gospel. Notice: "Yes, and *all the prophets from Samuel* and those that follow after, *as many as have spoken*, have likewise foretold *of these days*."

These are powerful statements that cannot be glossed over. This verse says *all* God's prophets—"as many as have spoken"!—foretold of these days!

The book of Psalms records the kingdom of God coming. Notice: "...for You [God] shall *judge* the people righteously, and *govern the na-*

tions upon earth" (67:4). This obviously refers to the *divine government* of God.

Here is what Isaiah wrote: "For unto us a Child is born, unto us a Son is given: and the *government* shall be upon His shoulder: and His name shall be called Wonderful, Counselor, The Mighty God, The Everlasting Father, The Prince of Peace. Of the increase of His *government* and peace there shall be no end, upon the throne of David, and upon *His kingdom*, to order it, and to establish it with *judgment* and with *justice* from henceforth even *forever*" (9:6-7).

This is so obvious it needs no explanation!

Now Jeremiah: "Behold, the days come, says the LORD, that I will raise unto David a righteous Branch, and *a King shall reign* and prosper, and shall execute *judgment* and *justice* in the earth. In His days Judah shall be saved, and Israel shall dwell safely [neither of these are happening now]: and this is His name whereby He shall be called, THE LORD OUR RIGHTEOUSNESS" (23:5-6). This passage also needs no explanation.

We saw Daniel preached God's kingdom: "And in the days of these kings shall the God of heaven set up a *kingdom*, which shall never be destroyed: and the *kingdom* shall not be left to other people, but it shall break in pieces and consume all these kingdoms, and it shall stand forever" (2:44).

All the so-called *minor* prophets also spoke of the kingdom of God in one way or another. Remember, the phrase "gospel of the kingdom of God" is not the only proper way of describing this coming government!

Peter was right. "God *has* spoken by the mouth of *all* His holy prophets since the world began...[of] the restitution of all things" (Acts 3:21).

An important final point from this verse. It says, "GOD has spoken..." The gospel of the kingdom of God is a message *from God*. It should be clear that *God speaks* through whatever kind of servant He is using—apostle, prophet, patriarch, judge, deacon, preacher of righteousness or pastor! His servants *always* spoke the *same message*!

Has anyone told you about *any* of these verses? Almost certainly not. Yet, so basic, the Bible has held them for thousands of years!

What Is the Kingdom of God?

This chapter would not be complete without at least a brief description of what it was Jesus meant when He spoke of the *kingdom of God*.

Matthew 6:33 states, "But seek you *first* the kingdom of God, and His righteousness..." If you are to seek something as your *first* goal in life, all would agree you should know what it is!

Matthew 6 also contains what many call "The Lord's Prayer" (vs. 9-13). Jesus instructs Christians to pray "after this manner," and then continues by adding the phrase, "Thy kingdom come." One must know *what* he is praying for or prayers have no meaning! It is not this chapter's purpose to explain *everything* there is to know about God's kingdom, but understanding some basics is essential.

We should at least ask: What *is* the kingdom of God? Again, the word *kingdom* simply means "government." Of course, you cannot have a government without a nation to govern. Therefore, a kingdom is at least one nation with a government.

There are FOUR necessary components of *any* kingdom: (1) Land, property or territory—however large or small. In other words, one must have a specific and definite set of boundaries establishing the size of the kingdom, (2) people or subjects living within the territory governed, (3) a system of laws and rules, and a basic structure of government, and (4) a ruler, king, monarch or governor leading the government.

No kingdom is complete without all of these basic elements.

But how does this apply to *God's* kingdom? Is this to be a literal, physical place on Earth, with people and laws, presided over by a ruler?

Most do not understand even these most rudimentary things of the kingdom of God. Some believe this kingdom is in the hearts of men. Others believe it is wherever you find a particular church. And others think it is the British Empire. Still others we saw believe it is Jesus Christ Himself. Some believe that it is on Earth *now*, with others believing it is yet to come, but not understanding how or when this will occur.

Such confusion!

It has been the duty of *this Church* to answer all of these questions, and so many other, related questions—through various publications and books such as this one, as well as in *World to Come* broadcasts—about the coming kingdom of God, and how this divine government will solve ALL problems on Earth!

The True Gospel—A Coming Utopia!

Billions today live with no hope. Yet all wish for better lives, a better tomorrow for themselves and their families. More and more are those who recognize that the collective future of all nations seems equally hopeless. If one considers history, the course of the past 6,000 years, it is difficult to avoid pessimism. When the full picture is brought into view—when all facts are considered—*this* world *is* hopeless. Modern civilization is beset—overwhelmed!—with every conceivable problem, evil, and ill that competing, grasping, self-promoting human beings could devise. Having always been sick, it is now deep in *terminal* illness, wheezing out its final desperate gasps before breathing its last.

The present world is a condemned building. It is like an old, empty row house—abandoned, overgrown, burned out, littered with trash, marred by broken windows, and covered in graffiti. Built on a *wrong foundation* from the beginning, its already weak underpinnings have now eroded to the point of collapse under its own weight. Like all condemned structures, dangerous if left standing, this "building" *must* come down. With "explosive charges" in place, it is soon to be imploded and the rubble scraped away in advance of a new and magnificent "world architecture" foretold long ago to replace it.

The plight of all nations today stands in stark contrast to the world that is coming—to what the governing kingdom of God will mean to all peoples. An artistic masterpiece soon to be unveiled, a fantastic future—truly incredible!—lies ahead for every nation of the world! But it will not, and could never, occur under the hand of men.

Everything on Earth begins with government. The governments of men do not, and have never, worked. Themselves one of the biggest problems, these ineffective human inventions will not—and in fact are unable to—"snatch victory from the jaws of defeat" at the last moment before disaster!

But a better, PERFECT GOVERNMENT—one not left to the devices, machinations, and confusion of men—is coming. It will usher in peace, happiness, unity, abundance, and prosperity for every human being and every country on Earth. While such a vision may seem impossible, it *will* happen—and in your lifetime!

It was always the Creator's Plan that a whole new and infinitely better world would come—one built from the beginning on the *right* foundation. Large sections of the one-third of the Bible that is prophecy describe the establishment of another world, one completely different from anything ever before seen on planet Earth. The coming utopian age that God planned long ago will be absolutely marvelous—breathtaking to behold!—and it appears scripturally in vivid colors, with sharp outlines, and in exquisite detail, as a stunning, beautiful, panoramic, and previously unimagined future worldscape.

A wonderful new world *is* on the way, and this offers but the smallest *advance preview*!

I repeat: It has been the task—and truly inspiring responsibility—that the awesome announcement Jesus Christ began 2,000 years ago be continued and completed through His little, but faithful, flock. There has never been a *more* awesome announcement heard on Earth.

The Beginning of the Fulfillment

The chapter's introduction stated that in Matthew 24:14 Jesus foretold that a worldwide effort to spread the gospel would come onto the scene at some point *before* the end! This means *someone* will be preaching it NOW, in our present age, because the end—close as it now is—has not *yet* come!

Preaching the truth of the gospel to the world was restored by Herbert W. Armstrong beginning in 1934. From the time of the apostles, until the beginning of the 52-year ministry of this one man, the true gospel did not go out in any real power to the world as a whole. It was primarily preached locally by resident faithful pastors here and there as they could. There were always a few conversions in every age, but the means simply were not available for a *great*—globe-girdling—Work to *all nations* prior to the twentieth century.

Mr. Armstrong reached an unprecedented hundreds of millions during his long ministry. This included a readership of approximately 25 million people (in seven languages) of *The Plain Truth* magazine just at the time of his death in 1986. Mr. Armstrong personally visited over one-third of all heads of state during the last two decades of his life. He always brought the message of God's coming kingdom. There were *few* places on Earth where it was not heard on either radio or television.

An immense administrative superstructure—much of which was in Pasadena, California—produced an incredible number of quality media programs. Beginning for over 40 years with *The World Tomorrow* radio program, Mr. Armstrong later permanently moved into television under the same name, and this program grew in viewership until it was number one in the Arbitron ratings for all religious programs in America. (These programs served double duty as radio broadcasts in some areas of the world.)

As a student, I was in awe of the television production department and, looking back, at how advanced it was for that time.

Then there was the colossal publishing operation that distributed three monthly, four-color magazines (*The Plain Truth, The Good News, Youth 81, 82, 83...*) and a tabloid, biweekly newspaper called *The Worldwide News* for church members.

But there was *much more* that the Church published in the form of many books, booklets, brochures, reprint articles, Bible story books, youth Bible lessons in seven levels, an extensive Bible correspondence course and hundreds of form letters, all sent from headquarters and the regional offices by the millions annually.

The production of these quality magazines was itself truly something to behold. The sheer magnitude of what took place with just *The Plain Truth*—published month after month—was staggering! I could never forget regularly binding and sacking them for mailing in 1969, during the summer between my sophomore and junior years of college.

Inseparable from the publishing operation, and directed from the Church's headquarters, was the *Plain Truth Newsstand Distribution Program*. Under the umbrella of this highly structured program and regular close communication regarding it, local churches around the world achieved what could only be called spectacular success in distributing countless millions of magazines in multiple languages so that God's truth could be accessed everywhere on Earth. Stories of how this program was blessed by God and what it achieved are legion.

The true gospel went out in POWER—like no other time in history!

Christ's prophecy is still true! Today, His commission *continues* in POWER, but for only a few more years.

A Church—and a Commission!

Delivering Christ's *real* gospel to the world—the *good news* of the coming KINGDOM OF GOD!—is and always has been the true Work of God's Church! While the commission began with the original apostles, The Restored Church of God continues it today. The message and goal are the same—only the methods differ.

When Jesus stated, "I will build My Church" (Matt. 16:18), it went far beyond beginning, increasing and protecting that Church—beyond just ensuring its survival. There is a great TRANSCENDENT PURPOSE for the Church that Jesus built—the only true Church of God!

Preaching the gospel of a coming, world-ruling *supergovernment* over all nations is the MISSION of God's Church, and every member in it is called to become part of this exciting Work. Those assisting realize the need to spread the truth of God's real message—to *announce* a new world order coming to a struggling, suffering civilization, incapable of even addressing, let alone fixing, its mounting troubles and difficulties.

This commission is TWO-FOLD. First is to "Go you into all the world, and preach the gospel to every creature" (Mark 16:15). Second is to "feed the flock of God"—to supply each member of God's Church with strong spiritual food (I Pet. 5:2; John 21:15-17). As God's members are fed, they grow spiritually, allowing them to serve and dedicate themselves more to the Church's great First Commission.

Today, large numbers of people can learn God's full truth as *never* before. Many thousands around the world are learning sound, proven principles, straight from their Bibles, helping them to live happier lives and become better citizens.

The Restored Church of God is a fountain of true knowledge in a parched world with ever-increasing evils!

We offer *more literature*—more TRUTH in writing (in number of pages *and* publications)—than at any other time in the history of God working with mankind. (You may wish to carefully check this for yourself.) We also offer all of it on our websites (*thercg.org, realtruth. org, worldtocome.org*), thus making it more *readily available* around the world than at any other time in history. In fact, we are the largest (most extensive) religious *publishing operation* in the world today.

Also, our three websites, collectively, are now the largest (and most extensive) *religious websites* of any kind in the world!

God's people are on a CRUSADE to take Christ's announcement of the kingdom of God—the most important message in existence—to a sick, dying world. They are passionate about—consumed with—and know that they need to *complete* Christ's Great Commission while there is still time (John 9:4). *You* are now reading God's FINAL ANNOUNCEMENT—and WARNING—offered to all who will take heed!

It has been average people toiling quietly in the background who believe and *live* Jesus' words, "It is more blessed to *give* than to receive" (Acts 20:35) that have made possible the fulfillment of Matthew 24:14 and Matthew 28:19-20. It is their unselfishness and sacrifice that have allowed for the many offers of free books and booklets—not cheap tracts that are easy to produce and distribute—referenced throughout this volume. (There are scores more that have not been mentioned.) Dependent on God to empower them, they have almost completed this historic "heavy lifting"— their "bearing the heat of the day" while others pursued pleasure—of warning great nations and announcing the coming kingdom of God.

There is still time to lessen their burden—to "give" help!

"Authority and Power"

Here is more proof that this gospel message was foretold to be preached across the world. We saw Jesus told His disciples just before His ascension, "All *power* is given unto Me in heaven and in earth. Go you therefore, and teach *all nations*…to observe *all things* WHATSOEVER I have commanded you: and, lo, I am with you alway, even unto the end of the world [or age]" (Matt. 28:18-20).

Much inspiring knowledge springs from this passage.

First, the reference to "going" and teaching "all nations" could only be accomplished with today's technological advancements. The entire world *is* being taught "all things"—"whatsoever"—Jesus commanded His servants to teach. This of course includes the true gospel.

Second, Jesus promises that He will be "with" His servants "unto the end of the [age]" and that "the gates of hell shall not prevail against [the Church]" (Matt. 16:18), meaning it would never die out.

For this Church to endure centuries of persecution, opposition and trials, much more than human determination or even great zeal would be required. Let's understand. In Luke 4:36, it states that the Scribes and Pharisees "were all amazed" at Jesus' ability to cast out demons, remarking, "What a word is this! For with *authority* and *power* He commands the unclean spirits, and they come out." Notice "power" and "authority," and that those observing recognized both at work.

Five chapters later, in 9:1, Jesus transferred this capability to His disciples. Notice what they received: "Then He called His twelve disciples together, and gave them *power* and *authority* over all devils [demons], and to cure diseases." Again, both terms together.

Shortly after, in Acts 1:8, ten days before Pentecost, as Jesus was about to ascend to heaven, He told the disciples, about to formally receive office as apostles, "But you shall receive *power*, after that the Holy Spirit is come upon you: and you shall be witnesses unto Me both in Jerusalem, and in all Judea, and in Samaria, and unto the uttermost part of the earth." Note this crucial passage!

Later, in Acts 4:33, Jesus' promise is confirmed: "And with great *power* gave the apostles witness of the resurrection of the Lord…" In fact, the apostle Paul wrote regarding *all* spirit-led minds, "For God has not given us the spirit of fear; but of *power*, and of love, and of a sound mind" (II Tim. 1:7).

That Jesus gave His disciples special supernatural power to carry on through everything that they would endure is evident from just these passages. But what about *authority*? Did He follow through later and give this also? Let's ask: Would Christ unleash the greatest power in the universe—vastly beyond what human governments possess—without putting it under strict control—AUTHORITY?

God *has* given *authority* to His Church today. This means that He has also given His Church real *power behind it*! Conversely, the same is true. Since God has given His Church POWER today, it is evident that this Church carries His AUTHORITY!

"All Authority in Heaven"

The end of Jesus' statement explaining that authority would come to the disciples—He had "all authority," and thus could give it—carries the real promise that He would be with them *always*. Not only would His authority reside with them, but there is clear evidence that *His* VERY REAL POWER would accompany it. The Greek word translated "authority" in this passage is *exousia*, and it means BOTH power and authority. In fact, the *King James Version* we saw stated, "All POWER is given unto Me…"

It is consistent then that in more of the Matthew 28 conversation, found in Acts 1, Jesus explained that "power" would be given to the apostles. He was simply reiterating the equation of POWER accompanying AUTHORITY, and vice-versa, referenced in Luke 4:36 and 9:1.

Both of these crucial elements in the apostles' ministry were to be given them on Pentecost. This was the Holy Day in which the Holy Spirit was to be first given to large numbers. Of course, this meant that there would be an immediate need for *responsible authority with power* to be in place within the governance of the Church, as well as in the preaching of the gospel to every nation. The day of Pentecost symbolized this remarkable beginning, as Jesus built His New Testament Church. He had to *simultaneously* give it the *two* most important *keys* to its survival through the ages—POWER and AUTHORITY! Just imagine the administrative challenge of managing 3,000 converts (plus mates and children) arriving on the Church's *first* day in existence!

At Christ's Return

God's people know that when the kingdom of God arrives, and the saints begin their rule with Christ, the government of God will be established over all nations. Truly, *this* government will have ALL power and ALL authority under it. The Feast of Trumpets (Rosh Hashanah to the Jews) pictures this event, with the three other annual fall Feast days picturing other events from this point forward that occur through the rest of God's Plan over the next 1,000 years, and beyond.

God's people also realize that the governments of men will soon be replaced by the governing Family of God, called the kingdom of God. But Paul describes this in a way that puts what we have just examined in a very different light. And it has everything to do with *how* the government of God works—both from the outset of the Millennium forward, and within the Church that Jesus built 2,000 years ago!

Here is what was written to those in Corinth in what is often thought of as the "resurrection chapter" about the first order of business with the arrival of the kingdom of God. Note well this extraordinary passage: "Then comes the end, when He [Jesus Christ] shall have delivered up the kingdom to God, even the Father; when He shall have put down all *rule* and all *authority* and *power*" (I Cor. 15:24).

This is a fascinating verse. It reveals that Christ, with the newly resurrected saints, must dispel or "put down"—Daniel 2:44 states, "break in pieces"—all the ruling governments of men, wherein rests power and authority derived solely from *human* origin, backed by Satan.

We focus on "rule," "authority" and "power." The word "rule" comes from the Greek *arche*, from which comes our word ARCH. Of course, an arch is a bridge *above* something. The word translated "authority" is *exousia*—and the word translated "power" is *dunamis*. This is the same word translated "power" in II Timothy 1:7, describing what *each Christian receives at baptism*. It is also the same word that is translated "strength" within the description of the Philadelphian era of the Church (Rev. 3:7-13). It is certainly true that the overall rule of men, with their governments, does "arch" above every form of human authority and power held today. But not for much longer.

All of men's governments, whether over nations (including the United Nations) or religions, the returning Jesus Christ and the glorified saints will "put down," meaning to "abolish, cease, destroy, do away, make of no effect, bring to naught, vanish away and make void." From that time forward, there will be no more authority ever again in the universe other than GOD'S GOVERNMENT!

Signs, Wonders and Miracles

A final point must yet be introduced. Jesus understood there had to be an *additional* special means that distinguished His servants from all imposters, counterfeits and deceivers. The Bible reveals there *is* such special evidence. This forms *some* of the evidence of where God's government is found—and at work today.

Paul's ministry demonstrated "*signs* and *wonders* and *mighty deeds*" (II Cor. 12:12). The Greek words in this text are again fascinating to understand—and deeply sobering—when we tie them in a moment to the greatest time of deception the world will ever see!

The word translated "sign" comes from *semeion* and means "an indication, especially ceremonially or supernaturally: miracle, sign, token, wonder." The word translated "wonders" is *teras*, and it simply means "a prodigy, omen—wonder." (A prodigy is a phenomenon.) The phrase "mighty deeds" is also translated from *dunamis*, with this longer definition than that given earlier: "force...specifically miraculous power (usually...a miracle itself): mighty deed, (worker of) miracle(s), power, strength."

Mark's account of what was said to the apostles in Matthew 28:19-20 clarifies and strengthens Matthew: "And He [Jesus] said unto them, Go you into all the world, and preach the gospel to every creature...and these *signs* shall follow them that believe; in My name shall they cast out devils; they shall speak with new tongues; they shall take up serpents; and if they drink any deadly thing, it shall not hurt them; they shall lay hands on the sick, and they shall recover" (Mark 16:15, 17-18).

All of this is critically important to comprehend for all who would be true followers of Christ. Remember, the Bible warns of imposters—false teachers, false prophets, false apostles and even false christs—coming as "angels of light," who will deceive those who "received not the LOVE OF THE TRUTH, that they might be saved" (II Thes. 2:10). This will then result in countless millions—tragically, some of God's people among them—being sent "strong delusion, that they should believe a lie." The subject becomes more serious.

All of this is connected to falling under the seduction of the final False Prophet who works miracles and influences the masses in the presence of the Beast "after the working of Satan with all *power* and *signs* and *lying wonders*" (vs. 9). The words "power," "signs" and "lying wonders" here tell a chilling story. All derive from the very same words—*dunamis*, *semeion* and *teras*—used to describe the power, signs and wonders performed by God's true servants.

How is one to distinguish a counterfeiter who is performing *false* signs, and *lying* wonders and miracles, from true servants of God doing the *exact same things*?

Healings, miracles, tongues, interpretation of tongues, discerning of spirits (for the purpose of casting out demons), among others, are all listed as gifts given by Christ *exclusively* within His "Body"—the true

Church—the *only* place where He is infusing power and authority! Take time to read I Corinthians 12.

The point? There will be TWO kinds of supernatural events occurring through the end of the age. They will both involve signs, wonders and miracles, and they will often look alike to the untrained observer. In fact, *false* miracles will likely be far more dramatic in size and scope to the world than *true* ones largely happening relatively quietly within the true Church.

How then is one to know if they are *true* or *false*? Certainly not through the Greek definitions, which show that these things are the same, whether true or false! Obviously, Satan cannot perform healings, which are the forgiveness of sins (he *can* certainly counterfeit them with gimmicks—"lying" healings), but he is capable of many *other* "miracles." The False Prophet will soon prove this, and close every doubter's mouth.

There is only *one way*—ONE THING that will protect you from the final strong delusion that will soon strike the whole world (II Thes. 2:11). You must know where is the Church of God, where Jesus Christ is Head.

Open Door, Then Slammed Shut

We now combine all of this knowledge with Revelation 3, where Jesus makes a special promise: "And to the angel of the church in Philadelphia write; these things says He [Christ] that is holy…He that opens, and no man shuts; and shuts, and no man opens…behold, I have set before you *an open door*, and *no man can shut it…*" (vs. 7-8).

Grasp this! This open door refers to the Work that God's Church must carry out. It is by God's power that this special effort is being carried out.

Satan can read the Bible. He knows the last chapter of God's Work is prophesied to be the most powerful in history, and he will stop at nothing to impede, cripple, hamper, oppose and obstruct it. The devil hates the message being announced because it describes the day he will be bound and replaced as the god of this world.

Once the open door God has given His Work is shut, the *famine of the Word*, described in Amos 8:11 and covered in greater detail later, will suddenly settle over the nations of Israel. This will come because the Church's *duty*—its God-ordained RESPONSIBILITY—has been completed. The fulfillment of Matthew 24:14 and 28:19-20 will be finished! God's kingdom will be imminent.

The announcement and warning will pass to two special servants…

The Two Witnesses

Mystery is a word used often in regard to prophecy. Few subjects elicit more curiosity and interest due to mystery than the next one—the Two Witnesses.

We have seen that Christ and other New Testament writers spoke and warned often of *false* prophets infecting the Church and corrupting the truth of understanding. But there are also two final *true* prophets described in the Bible. This chapter strips away the mystery and confusion about who and what they are—and what they do—what is their *commission*—what it is they "witness."

Two Men

The Bible specifically foretells the arrival of two special servants just before the outset of the Tribulation, who wield tremendous—*unprecedented*—POWER. Guided by and imbued in a special way with God's Spirit, they will contend with the Beast, the False Prophet, and all under their sway. Surrounded by hostile forces, but in direct contact with Jesus Christ (Zech. 4:14), these final prophets will issue GOD's FINAL WARNING to a deceived world.

The subject of the Two Witnesses is one of great speculation. These little-understood figures have brought almost unending commentary from people who have no idea what they are talking about. With the passing of time, this interest will only increase as their arrival becomes more imminent. Very few, however, understand what they *do* and where they will *come from.*

When all relevant verses are combined, the picture is clear. But before examining the also unprecedented *commission* given to the Two Witnesses, questions about their origin must be answered.

Where Will the Two Witnesses Come From?

Many seem to have the idea that the Two Witnesses will appear "out of nowhere" without warning. It is as though they will suddenly—and *dramatically*—emerge, perhaps overnight. Or that they will have been hiding somewhere, waiting to be revealed! Popular prophecy writers have simply been unable to unravel the puzzle of their origin.

The first indication of where these men will come from can be found in the office they hold. First notice Revelation 11:3: "And I will give power unto My *two witnesses,* and they shall *prophesy* a thousand two hundred and threescore [1,260] days, clothed in sackcloth." In verse 10, they are referred to as "these two *prophets.*" Clearly then, these men hold the office of prophet. But "witness" in the Greek comes from the word "martoos," meaning "to witness, literally, judicially, and figuratively, to be a martyr."

This is important. Everyone knows what a witness is in a courtroom. He is one who testifies to the truth about past events, generally involving a crime, civil transgression or a disputed contract. The Two Witnesses are no different, except that *martyrdom* is tied to the meaning of "witness" in the Greek. There is a reason for this.

The form of *government* that Jesus Christ installed into His Church—that we learned is also called the Body of Christ in I Corinthians 12 and Ephesians 4, among other places—consists of various ordained offices. The unified, organized, uncompromising Church that Jesus Christ built is the *only place* where His government can be found. It is the only place where Christ gives offices. And Christ's Body is *not divided* (I Cor. 1:10, 13). Now notice: "And He [Christ] *gave* some, apostles; and some, *prophets*; and some, evangelists; and some, pastors and teachers" (Eph. 4:11). Why? "For the perfecting of the saints, for the work of the ministry, for the edifying of the *Body of Christ*" (vs. 12).

The rank of prophet—seen to be the second-highest New Testament office—is occasionally given within the Body of Christ, the Church (Eph. 1:22-23; Col. 1:18-19). This means the Two Witnesses will be given their office by Jesus Christ from *within His one Church*! Jesus would not—

and does not ever—work any other way—in any *other place!*—else He would work against Himself. I Corinthians 12:27-28 makes clear that such men will not—actually *cannot!*—be given their offices from *outside* the Body of Christ! This would be contrary to Scripture.

These men will have to appear *well before* the Tribulation, and everyone *within* Christ's Body will have no doubt about their arrival. If this point is not understood, the reader will never be able to correctly discern the *only possible origin* of the Two Witnesses. Recognition of what *is* Christ's Church and Body makes understanding their identity easy. No discernment will be involved—or needed. It becomes vital then to identify where is the true Church. (The book *Where Is the True Church? – and Its Incredible History!* becomes even more important.)

Defining "Prophet"

Some general background would be helpful in regard to what is a prophet.

First, let's understand the Greek word translated "prophet." Interestingly, much like its English equivalent, it is *prophetace*—pronounced pro-fay'-tace. It means "a foreteller [prophet], by analogy an inspired preacher." The Hebrew equivalent is virtually identical—"a prophet or (generally) inspired man."

The word "prophet" is found 160 times in the *New* Testament. This is largely because New Testament Scripture quotes the Old Testament prophets so often. The apostles wrote in a fashion that could be described as intermingled with the office and writings of (the early) prophets.

The mission of prophets in the first century was to receive messages or prophecies directly from God and to convey these to the apostles.

Now remember II Peter 1: "For the prophecy came not in old time by the will of man: but holy men of God [Old Testament prophets] spoke as they were *moved by the Holy Spirit*" (vs. 21). And remember, prophecy comes from *God. He* inspires His servants to record *His* words.

So then a prophet is an "inspired man"—one who is a tool of God and not acting on his own—but he is also one who "foretells," meaning one who reveals things yet to come. Plainly, prophets foretell events *before* they happen. This summarizes both the chief duties of prophets.

Ministry Begins

The last chapter explained when the final Work of God will come to an end—the "night...when no man can work" (John 9:4). World conditions will become so bad that God "shuts the door" of His Work (Rev. 3:7-8), ending it. The Church will have come to be so persecuted and hindered by this time that miracles—perhaps many—may be needed just for God's Work to be completed. The Church must *at this point* be taken to a place of safety for its own survival and protection.

This is where the Two Witnesses enter. The "baton" of the Work must also *at this point* be handed to them. They are imbued with SPECIAL, MIRACULOUS POWER not seen in any other servants of God except perhaps the prophet Elijah. Themselves under terrible persecution, this will be the only way they will be able to carry out their task.

Consider. As they appear on the world scene, just before the Great Tribulation, they will no doubt deliver a final warning to the government *leaders* of the world, but also to all *nations* of the world, whose eyes will no doubt be riveted upon them.

Revelation 11:6 describes "the days of their *prophecy*," while verse 7 references "when they shall have finished *their testimony*." Again, witnesses *testify* to matters that are in doubt. Realize that everything that you have read so far in this book, plus succeeding chapters are ALL matters that the Two Witnesses must clarify with finality. Based in Jerusalem, they will represent God by addressing and warning nations—for a period of 42 months (Rev. 11:2)—of the coming Day of the Lord.

Incredible Power!

It is crucial to recognize that these men will possess tremendously great "power"! Verses 5-6 in Revelation 11 leave no doubt of this: "...if any man will hurt them, *fire proceeds out of their mouth*, and devours their enemies: and if any man will hurt them, he must in *this manner be killed*. These have POWER to shut heaven, that it rain not in the days of their prophecy: and have POWER over waters to turn them to blood, and to smite the earth with all plagues, as often as they will."

Grasp this! If anyone tries to harm these men and interfere with their commission, fire will devour him! Then, to get the attention of the world, to highlight the terrifying coming Day of the Lord, to bring certain punishment and perhaps to hold enemies temporarily at bay, they will be able to stop the rain, turn rivers and lakes to blood and unleash horrific plagues—and all of these as often and for however long they choose!

The power that Jesus Christ gives them is so great they cannot be killed by anyone or anything for their three-and-a-half-year ministry. This makes them unique among all previous prophets.

Again, this is comparable to the power given to Elijah, as demonstrated in II Kings 1:9-15. These prophets will be empowered to bring drought and famine upon the earth, just as Elijah did (I Kings 17:1-7; Luke 4:25).

"Two Olive Trees"

Revelation 11 reveals more: "These are the *two olive trees*, and the *two candlesticks* standing before the God of the earth" (vs. 4).

But what do the olive trees and the candlesticks symbolize? And how does it relate to the commission that the Two Witnesses possess? We must again allow the Bible to interpret itself.

Note that the Two Witnesses are referred to by the prophet Zechariah as "two olive branches," which "empty...golden oil out of themselves" (4:12). Two verses later he states that "these are the two *anointed ones*..." (vs. 14).

What is this "golden oil" and what is its connection to the two "anointed ones"? The answer ties directly to their AWESOME POWER.

Jesus' parable of the foolish and wise virgins brings understanding. The foolish virgins are seen to lack *oil* for their lamps. Having lost God's Holy Spirit—*symbolized by oil*—they are "shut out" of the kingdom of God (Matt. 25:10)! Other verses show that all Christians are "anointed" with God's Spirit (I John 2:27), as would normally occur with oil. We saw II Timothy 1:7 refers to the Holy Spirit as the spirit of "*power*, and of love, and of a sound mind." And we saw Paul wrote this admonition to all Christians: "Be *strong* in the Lord, and in the *power* of His MIGHT" (Eph. 6:10), as well as, "I can do all things through Christ which *strengthens* me" (Phil. 4:13).

These deeply converted men obviously must be anointed with a much-larger-than-usual measure of God's Spirit—the source of their extraordinary power.

Men of Strength and Character

Now realize this crucial point. With such enormous control over world conditions, the Two Witnesses must be men of great spiritual depth and understanding. The living Jesus Christ would NEVER select one to be used as His instrument to receive such power and authority *if* he were not humble, obedient to God, faithful in all matters and *doctrinally sound*—strong in the truth!

When understood, this alone means that these men must come from the only Church on the face of the earth that understands all the doctrines of God. The Two Witnesses then will be men who speak the *truth* of God—and the TRUTH alone!—and who will have built the *courage* to do this under tremendous pressure during previous training. They will be men of great strength and conviction, able to stand *completely alone* in a hostile world that wishes them DEAD!

Politicians, weaklings and menpleasers will not suffice!

The Two Witnesses will be men of judgment, wisdom and understanding—who know exactly when and when *not* to use their extraordinary power. They must be able to issue the *right message* in different situations to both the nations and leaders whom they confront.

Of course, these men will have to fully understand the *scope* and *magnitude* of their own office.

A point of emphasis. All of this is another central reason the Two Witnesses must arise from *within* the Body of Christ. They will be men who understand where Christ is the "Head" (Eph. 1:22-23; Col. 1:18)—where He is leading, because they will need to constantly tap Christ's own awesome power on a daily basis. They will be men who have *submitted* to His government, and who will have been doing this for a considerable time!

Offices in Christ's ministry are never given to untrained or inexperienced men. God has *never* worked this way, particularly with the highest offices in the Church. He does not hand out great authority and power willy-nilly. The Two Witnesses will have been faithfully serving in God's Church, almost certainly first in one or more lower offices, before they are ready to be given the higher office of prophet—one that history records has not been assigned by Christ for almost 2,000 years. And understand that these men would not receive their office *immediately* before their ministry begins. There will be prior evidence that they have been *given* the office of prophet, probably including their obvious ability to perform great miracles.

Christ Works with Them Directly

Notice again Revelation 11. Christ calls these prophets "MY two witnesses" (vs. 3). Zechariah 4:14 also mentions that these men "*stand by* the Lord of the whole earth."

This passage reveals a special, *direct* relationship and proximity to Christ Himself. All three *stand together*. It is obvious the Two Witnesses report *directly* to Christ in carrying out their duty.

God *always* worked directly with prophets throughout the Old Testament. Jesus Christ, the God of the Old Testament (I Cor. 10:4), always spoke face-to-face—communicated *directly*—with those whom He was using.

With few exceptions, you will notice a pattern throughout the major and minor prophets. Each starts with phrases such as, "The Word of the Lord came expressly unto Ezekiel…" or "The words of Jeremiah…To whom the Word of the Lord came…" or "The Word of the Lord that came to Micah…," and so forth. Christ worked directly with these prophets. Sometimes He also appeared as Melchizedek when He spoke to the patriarchs, and others, face-to-face.

When considering the role these men play, it should be even clearer *why* they work so closely with Christ. Again, just recognize that fire must at times come out of their mouths to devour their adversaries.

Martyred

The city of Jerusalem, where the Two Witnesses complete their commission, is the most fought over, and coveted, piece of land on Earth—and in history. It becomes obvious that this is one of the biggest reasons the Beast and False Prophet will want to rule from there. (They would certainly know that the Bible foretells Christ will rule from this city for 1,000 years.)

The False Prophet and the Beast will want the competition eliminated—their message stopped. This will eventually lead to a final supernatural showdown, one in which God will evidence the greatness of His power over Satan and his servants once and for all. But God will protect His witnesses until "they shall have finished their testimony" (Rev. 11:7).

After three and a half years, the Beast system will finally be permitted by God to kill these men. Let's read the rest of the account: "And when they shall have finished their testimony, the beast that ascends out of the bottomless pit shall make war against them, and shall overcome them, and kill them" (Rev. 11:7).

The world enjoys the Two Witnesses' death, and "their dead bodies shall lie in the street of the great city, which spiritually is called Sodom and Egypt, where also our Lord was crucified" (vs. 8). Now notice: "And they of the people and kindreds and tongues and nations [the whole world] shall see their dead bodies three days and an half, and shall not suffer their dead bodies to be put in graves" (vs. 9).

Global Event

In the modern age of globalization, this event will certainly be televised, with people also no doubt able to witness it via cellphones and computers.

Many will feel vindicated at what they perceive to be just punishment due to the drought, fire and terrible plagues these "evil men have brought." The whole world will eagerly seek proof they are dead, excited that these "intolerant" men who spoke against their way of life—their SIN—are finally gone. Life can now return to normal.

Instead of worldwide repentance at their testimony, verse 10 records: "And they that dwell upon the earth shall *rejoice* over them, and *make merry*, and shall send gifts one to another; because these two prophets tormented them that dwelt on the earth."

The next three verses in context show that the Two Witnesses are resurrected, and this is accompanied by an earthquake that kills 7,000 people in Jerusalem.

Signal to the World

The Two Witnesses have not yet appeared. Neither will they arrive in the way that popular opinion suggests. Most professing Christians sincerely believe they will embrace these men. How wrong is this view!

The Bible indicates that most will likely believe *the Two Witnesses* to be the Beast and miracle-working False Prophet, whom the world will be worshipping. And the Beast and False Prophet *may* in fact be received by some as the Two Witnesses! Such will be the power of the devil's final deceit. II Thessalonians 2:10-11 shows the Christian world—and the whole world—is being set up for such MASS DELUSION sent by God!

But Bible prophecy reveals there will be a special, large number that *ultimately* rejects this deception. Independent of the Church, this group today hears—but does not yet *heed*—God's warning…

An Israelite Remnant

The Bible contains another colossal, but little recognized, prophecy having to do with the nations of Israel today. Most have never heard of this prophecy, never mind understood it. Yet it carries implications almost beyond imagination. For those who can comprehend what they will now learn, this chapter will be incredibly exciting. In fact, it will leave you stunned at knowledge that almost no one knows.

The significant majority of those of Israel alive today have *never been told* of what the last chapters of prophecy have in store for the descendants of the twelve tribes of Israel! These many millions simply have no idea what is coming on our lands, and on our peoples!

Since no human parent would ever punish a child for something that the child had not been told (warned) was wrong, I repeat, neither would God do this with His children. The patient and all-wise God of the Bible is literally obligated to explain to all today *why* "the sword" is coming on 600 million people in 22 Israelite nations and territories around the world. Only a parental monster would neglect such a responsibility to so many "children" (of Israel) who hang in the balance. And recognize again that the generation alive today is the most rotten in the history of the world, and we saw is one that Jesus likens to both the universal corruption of Noah's day (Matt. 24:37; Luke 17:26-27) and the awful perversion of Sodom and Gomorrah (Luke 17:28-30).

Take a moment to glimpse a tiny snapshot of this final generation reflected in Proverbs 30:11 through 14. The God of the Bible would never shirk His duty to trumpet a warning to such an abominable "filthy" generation—just one of several descriptive terms Solomon recorded.

This chapter will examine a great many passages from the Old Testament, some of them extensive, all of them graphic. These verses form a picture, at the same time both beautiful and ugly—wonderful and horrible. Together, they present a reality more astonishing than one could believe—almost beyond comprehension for those who try as hard as they can to grasp it. Yet, these sobering and cataclysmic prophecies *must* be comprehended!

You are about to take a truly extraordinary journey into and through the immediate future of modern nations.

"For Our Admonition"

One of the greatest principles of the Bible is found in I Corinthians 10:11, and references the Old Testament: "Now all these things happened unto them [Israel] for *ensamples* [types]: and they are *written for our admonition*, upon whom the *ends of the world* are come."

This passage speaks to God's people alive at the "ends of the world," and how they are to *learn* from Old Testament "ensamples"—not *examples*, but rather *types* applicable for us today. This volume has already covered numerous "types" from history.

I Corinthians 10 itself opens with a remarkable statement about a past event. Notice verse 1: "Moreover, brethren, I would not that you should be ignorant, how that all our fathers were under the cloud, and all passed through the sea." You will soon see ancient Israel's exodus from Egypt as but a *tiny* TYPE (ensample) of what will be *repeated*—and in the very *near future*!

What I Corinthians 10:1 states is one of the greatest applications of this principle in the Bible. The succeeding chapter will bring one more enormous application of such *duality*.

Romans 9 and Isaiah 10

The story begins by examining Romans 9:27-29. Paul recorded, "Isaiah also cried concerning Israel, Though the number of the children of Israel be as the sand of the sea, a REMNANT [take note how often this word appears] shall be SAVED: for He [God] will finish THE WORK and cut it short in righteousness: because A SHORT WORK will the Lord make upon the earth. And as Isaiah said before, Except the Lord of Sabaoth

[Hosts] had left us a seed, we had been as Sodom, and been made like unto Gomorrah."

Notice Paul was quoting Isaiah here. Let's take a broader look at the full passage in Isaiah, found in chapter 10, for context. This chapter begins with a description of how God will punish Assyria (modern Germany) at the beginning of the Day of the Lord (vs. 3), after Assyria has carried out the punishment of His people, Israel.

Let's notice: "And it shall come to pass in that day, that the REMNANT [note again the term] of Israel, and such as are *escaped* of the house of Jacob, shall no more again stay upon him [Assyria in context] that smote them [the Israelites]; but shall stay upon the LORD, the Holy One of Israel, *in truth*. The REMNANT shall return, even the REMNANT of Jacob, unto the mighty God. For though your people Israel be as the sand of the sea, yet a REMNANT of them shall return: the consumption decreed [on Israel] shall overflow [in] righteousness" (vs. 20-22).

This first passage sets the stage to understand all that will follow. A surviving "remnant" of Israel (referenced four times in just this passage) is foretold to "escape" and "return" from captivity at the end of the Great Tribulation to serve God "in truth."

Isaiah also said this about the time when Israel will be freed from coming enslavement: "Shake yourself from the dust; arise, and sit down [only possible if lying prostrate], O Jerusalem: loose yourself from the *bands* of your neck, O CAPTIVE daughter of Zion" (52:2).

There will come a dramatic moment in Israel's future captivity when she will be told by God to get up and move, that the enslavement is over and a very different future lies ahead. Let's watch this develop in other passages.

Jeremiah Adds More

We saw that Israel escapes the "bands" of Assyria. We also saw that during World War II the tribe of Judah was enslaved in death camps and murdered on a grand scale by this same Assyria, utilizing places in Germany and Poland such as Auschwitz, Dachau, Treblinka, Sobibór, Bergen-Belsen and Buchenwald. Put another way, enslavement then involved just one tribe (and only part of it) sent into two nations. The picture continues to grow.

Jeremiah adds to what Isaiah recorded. Notice this about the escaping remnant: "And I will gather the REMNANT of My flock out of *all countries* where I have driven them, and will bring them again to their folds;

and they shall be fruitful and increase" (23:3). This pictures God's chosen "flock" returning from "all countries" where He had "driven them." Let this and other passages speak to you in the plain language presented.

Later in Jeremiah more is added to this expanding picture of Israel being brought by God out of captivity and back to her homelands. The next passage describes Israel's attitude—that of a people who have been shattered by nuclear war, famine, disease, and the final capstone of abject enslavement under the brutal hand of her enemies. She is seen at this point to view herself very differently than the attitudes evident in these same nations today. Let's read: "In those days, and in that time, says the LORD, the *children of Israel* shall come, they and the *children of Judah* TOGETHER, going and *weeping*: they shall go, and seek the LORD their God. They shall ask the way to Zion [the general location of the modern nation of Israel in the Mid-East] with their faces toward it, saying, Come, and let us join ourselves to the LORD in a perpetual covenant that shall not be forgotten" (50:4-5). —Jeremiah

First, notice that more than Judah is involved in this captivity. As with the original escape from Egypt, all twelve tribes, here called the children of Israel and Judah, leave enslavement. Then notice the attitude of "weeping," with a readiness to "join [to] the LORD their God" as they "ask" directions back to their homeland, Zion.

While an incredible canvas should already begin to be unfolding in your mind, there is a great deal more to understand.

Let's continue with one more fascinating passage in Jeremiah about this coming second and future great exodus.

Chapter 16, verses 10 to 12, describe a pre-Tribulation, self-righteous Israel unable and unwilling to see *why* God has "pronounced all this great evil against us." She asks, "What is our iniquity?" and "What is our sin that we have committed against the LORD?" Jeremiah is instructed in verses 11 and 12 to be sure he tells Israel WHY the captivity—that they would not listen to God's warning to repent!

The result is "Therefore will I cast you out of this land into a land that you know not, neither you nor your fathers; and there shall you serve other gods day and night; where I will not show you favor" (vs. 13). This is a description of enslavement but also the loss of all religious freedom. The context continues with God's promise that He will regather Israel to her own land: "Therefore, behold, the days come, says the LORD, that it shall no more be said, The LORD lives, that brought up the children of Israel out of the land of Egypt; but, The LORD lives, that brought up the children of Israel from the land of the north [Assyria], and from *all the lands* [we will see that these are nations all over the world] whither He had *driven them* [there this is again]: and I will bring them again into their land that I gave unto their fathers" (vs. 14-15).

Verse 16 offers an absolutely fascinating vision of *how* God will regather His people. Let's read it before comment: "Behold, I will send for many *fishers*, says the LORD, and they shall fish them; and after will I send for many *hunters*, and they shall hunt them from every mountain, and from every hill, and out of the holes of the rocks."

At the end of the Tribulation, the remnant of Israel is left literally scattered all through the nations of Earth. Collecting her involves the work of "fishers" and "hunters"—no doubt angelic recovery workers—locating surviving individuals, finally ready to seek God. It becomes evident these "workers" leave none behind.

More Detail from Ezekiel

When God desires a truth to be understood, and wants no room for misunderstanding to be possible by the honest Bible student, He repeats His message for emphasis in different ways in multiple passages, usually adding more details and facts to the tapestry He is weaving toward the full picture.

You have learned the book of Ezekiel describes a "watchman" (3:17; 33:1-9) to the nations of Israel who takes a warning message to these countries. It should be obvious that Ezekiel would have to speak to Israel's return from a captivity she brought on herself because she would not listen to the words of God through the "watchman" sent to warn of the consequences of disobedience to God.

Here is a more detailed description of parts of the punishment leading up to the captivity, and the resultant escape of a remnant: "In all your dwelling places the cities shall be laid waste [by nuclear attack], and the high places [false churches] shall be desolate; that your altars may be laid waste and made desolate, and your idols [the false gods who could not save Israel] may be broken and cease, and your images may be cut down, and your works may be abolished. And the slain shall fall in the midst of you, and you shall know that I am the LORD" (Ezek. 6:6-7).

This describes national calamity and widespread destruction, and death on a staggering scale. Of the initial 600 million people who go into the Great Tribulation, only 200 million will survive the initial effects. We already saw that 200 million, one-third, will be victims of a surprise nuclear attack on the nations of the West. Another 200 million, another third, will die of resultant famine and disease epidemics. (Ezekiel 5:10-12, among other places, we saw referenced and explained these "thirds.") The first two-thirds are, in effect, the "lucky" ones—because the remaining, surviving third goes into ENSLAVEMENT!

We will return to discuss a specific number *within* this final 200 million when it is time to see how many God says comprise the survivors.

Ezekiel continues: "Yet will I leave a REMNANT [yet again this term], that you may have some that shall *escape* the sword among the nations, when you shall be scattered through the countries. And they that *escape* of you shall remember Me among the nations wherever they shall be carried *captives*, because I am broken [God's attitude toward what He sees] with their whorish heart, which has departed from Me, and with their eyes, which go a whoring after their idols: and they shall *loathe themselves* for the evils which they have committed in *all their abominations*" (6:8-9).

The reason Israel will come weeping from captivity is because the survivors have come to "loathe themselves for the evils which they have committed." This is because they have come to grips with how God saw their conduct. But what made them able to know His perspective?

Consider for a moment that *someone* will have to have told these millions what these evils were—WHAT were the abominations—and WHY the captivity came. How else could they, *at this point*—at the moment of escape and liberation—know what brought their punishment? Recall that Isaiah said Israel would know how to serve God "in truth."

Ask: Who would have told them what "truth" was? How would they have come to understand this? The Work of this Church and the succeeding work of the Two Witnesses are seen to be evident.

Ezekiel 20

The next passage is the longest one quoted, and it all comes from Ezekiel 20. There was no way to lessen the verses included, but they are broken into segments to better grasp what God wants the reader to comprehend. The setting is how Israel continually chose to pollute God's Sabbaths. This disobedience is cited by God multiple times through the chapter. The reader would gain from a slow read of this long Bible description.

The passage opens with God's fury being poured out on a sinful world at the outset of the Day of the Lord: "As I live, says the Lord GOD, surely with a mighty hand, and with a stretched out arm, and with FURY POURED OUT [on the heathen around them as the Day of the Lord begins], will I rule over you: and I will *bring you out* from the people, and will *gather you out* of the countries wherein you are *scattered*, with a mighty hand, and with a stretched out arm, and with FURY POURED OUT" (vs. 33-34). Sobering words!

The next section looks ahead through the remainder of the time up to the Return of Christ, and after, when God will offer Israel a new covenant: "And I will bring you *into the wilderness* of the people, and there will I plead with you face to face. Like as I pleaded with your fathers in the wilderness of the land of Egypt, so will I plead with you, says the Lord GOD" (vs. 35-36).

Verses 37 to 40 are a kind of inset to God's thinking. They look past the Day of the Lord to Christ's Return, about a year after liberation from captivity, to when He will *convert* the remnant of Israel: "And I will cause you to pass under the rod [under the scepter of God's authority], and I will bring you into the bond of the covenant: and I will purge out from among you the rebels, and them that transgress against Me: I will bring them forth out of the country where they sojourn, and they shall not enter into the land of Israel: and you shall know that I am the LORD. As for you, O house of Israel, thus says the Lord GOD; Go you [for the time being], serve you every one his idols [God's anger is especially against all forms of religious pollution], and hereafter also, if you will not hearken unto Me: but pollute you My holy name no more with your gifts, and with your idols. For in Mine holy mountain, in the mountain of the height of Israel, says the Lord GOD, there shall all the house of Israel, all of them in the land, serve Me: *there will I accept them*, and there will I require your offerings, and the firstfruits of your oblations, with all your holy things."

Verses 41 and 42 reset the timing of WHEN the earlier verses are to be fulfilled: "I will accept you with your sweet savor, WHEN I bring you out from the people, and gather you *out of the countries* wherein you have been *scattered*; and I will be sanctified in you *before the heathen* [they will all see what is happening]. And you shall know that I am the LORD, when I shall *bring you into the land of Israel*, into the country for the which I lifted up Mine hand to give it to your fathers."

It is unmistakably plain from this passage that God will bring His people back *to their ancient homeland of Israel* after they have been literally scattered across the world. This remnant will be mindful of everything in their past—thousands of years of it—that brought this most horrific punishment upon them, and are seen again to "loathe" themselves (next passage below).

Notice that God could have wiped them out entirely but chose not to, leaving the promised remnant: "And there shall you *remember your ways*, and all your doings, wherein you have been defiled; and you shall *loathe yourselves* [there this is again] in your own sight for all your evils that you have committed. And you shall know that I am the LORD, when I have wrought with you for My name's sake, not according to your wicked ways, nor according to your corrupt doings [or all would be destroyed], O you house of Israel, says the Lord GOD" (vs. 43-44).

Notice that Israel comes to "remember her ways" and "all her doings." Ask again: How does she do this? *What* did she once hear that is now *remembered*—and *where* did she hear it? The only possibility is a warning coming back to mind that went unheeded.

Hosea Paints the Picture!

The fifth chapter of Hosea paints a graphic and painful picture of what lies ahead for those to be punished. It includes the *reason* for the punishment and exactly what God is looking for before He will intervene on Israel's behalf. It also offers hope. Let's read more fully what was quoted in part in a previous chapter: "And the pride of Israel does testify to his face: therefore shall Israel and Ephraim [America, Britain, Canada, Australia, New Zealand, South Africa, etc.] fall in their iniquity; Judah also shall fall with them. They shall go with their flocks and with their herds to seek the LORD; but they shall *not* find Him [why is this the case?]; *He has withdrawn Himself from them.* They have dealt treacherously against the LORD: for they have begotten strange children [today's rotten, "filthy," Proverbs 30:11-14 generation]: now shall *a month* devour them with their portions" (vs. 5-7).

Notice that after a certain point God will not be found of those who seek Him because "He has withdrawn Himself from them." This presents an irony. Today, Israel *can* still seek God—as can YOU!—because He *can* still be found. But she will not. The time is coming when Israel will seek God, but He cannot be found—and this is because the punishment has begun and NOTHING can stop it until God's purpose is completed!

The above passage ends with a curious reference to how "a month" shall "devour them." Here is what this means, and it is touched upon earlier in the book: At the 1,290 days before Christ's Return, when the Church flees to the place of safety, the Great Tribulation is only 30 days away. This is the *same month* that will at its end "devour" Israel after the Work of God's Church is over and the Church is protected.

Recall what Christ said in Matthew 24 *right after* His instruction to flee at the abomination's arrival: "For THEN [30 days later] shall be great tribulation, such as was not since the beginning of the world to this time, no, nor ever shall be. And except those days should be shortened, there should no flesh be saved [alive]: but for the elect's sake those days shall be shortened" (vs. 21-22).

If God did not intervene, Earth's entire population would be wiped out. Of course, this would include Israel. The only reason there is a *remnant* of her saved is God "cuts short" events, including her punishment.

Famine of Hearing God's Word

Let's momentarily move backward in time to the point just before the beginning of the Tribulation. Recall that there is to be a prophesied "famine" of hearing God's Word that comes suddenly as the final Work is "cut short" (Rom. 9:28). At this point, the John 9:4 "night" will have come when "no man can work," including the Work of God's Church warning those who had better heed NOW!

First, let's read what God inspired Amos to record. Then let's understand the prophecy: "Behold, the days come, says the Lord GOD, that I will send a famine in the land, not a famine of bread, nor a thirst for water, but of *hearing the words of the LORD*" (8:11).

Next, Amos describes what happens at the time of this famine. How do people react? "And they shall wander from sea to sea, and from the north even to the east, they shall run to and fro to seek the word of the LORD, and shall not find it" (vs. 12).

This is a shocking moment for frantic scores of millions who can no longer hear (find) what God has been declaring through His Church. Another prophecy implied here is that people will have been *accustomed to* "hearing the Word of the Lord." Do not miss this.

This takes us back to Ezekiel 33 and an attitude that will become dominant through Israelite lands, because of what *this Church* will have been announcing. Notice how this chapter about the "watchman," referenced earlier, *concludes*: "Also, you son of man [a modern Ezekiel], the children of your people still are talking against [Hebrew: "about"] you by the walls and in the doors of the houses, and speak one to another, every one to his brother, saying, Come, I pray you, and *hear* what is the word that comes forth from the LORD" (vs. 30).

The unceasing and intensifying message from *His Work*—the *only place* that word *from the LORD* could come—will eventually be a subject on many millions of lips. These will be regularly coming to hear what

God's Church and Work has to say on the most salient and important matters of the time. Great numbers—an audience of vast proportion—will be talking about and debating the meaning of powerful prophecies. This very book will be part of—in fact the center of—the debate. However, most, even of those who understand, will remain unwilling to *act* on what they are learning. Let's see why: "They come unto you as the people comes, and they sit before you *as* My people [in appearance only], and they *hear* your words, but they will *not* DO them: for with their mouth they show much love, but *their heart goes after their covetousness*" (vs. 31).

The last phrase in the passage introduces the problem.

The "Music" Suddenly Stops

Tragically, the pull of materialism will overpower people's desire to ACT on ominous, impending prophecies made plain in Scripture by God's Work. Covetousness will continue to rule the thinking of most. But people will *remain interested* because the message will be so compelling: "And, lo, you are unto them as *a very lovely song* of one that has *a pleasant voice*, and *can play well* on an instrument: for they HEAR your words, but they DO them not" (vs. 32).

But abruptly, as though in the middle of the "song," the "music" and "lyrics" stop. God suddenly concludes the warning. Space to take action is gone. Those who would not heed will realize they have made a horrible miscalculation about how much time remained. Desperate millions will be searching the airwaves, newspapers, the Internet and every other outlet used for what can no longer be found—because the greatest "famine" of all time has struck! And it has become too late to escape!

This brings us back to Hosea 5 where the context continues with God speaking about *Himself* at the moment of famine: "I will go and *return to My place*, till they [Israel] *acknowledge their offense*, and seek My face: in their *affliction* [brutal enslavement] they will seek Me early" (vs. 15). When God "withdraws Himself," He describes it as a "return to His place" in the third heaven (II Cor. 12:2).

He will remain ready to intervene—but this will not happen until His CHASTISEMENT is complete!

Moment of Intervention

Let's continue in Hosea and see what triggers God's intervention on Israel's behalf. Recognize that the message about Israel's condition overlaps into the next chapter. (Remember, men added chapter divisions in the Bible.) Let's read what happens to her as the Day of the Lord arrives. Notice Israel's attitude at the point where "they acknowledge their offense" before God: "Come, and let us return unto the LORD: for He has *torn*, and He will *heal* us; He has *smitten*, and He will *bind* us up. After two days will He revive us: *in the third day* He will raise us up, and *we shall live in His sight*" (6:1-2).

This presents a fascinating point of prophetic understanding about the nature and timing of the Great Tribulation and Day of the Lord. It reveals what God will do for Israel and how He will "raise...up" the surviving remnant in the "third day," meaning third *year* (each day for a year), of the Tribulation. Israel recognizes what is happening and declares, "We shall live in His sight."

Get these crucial time periods straight in your mind. Remember that the Day of the Lord is also called the *Year* of the Lord in other places.

An inset: Note a passage previously referenced—that Ezekiel 20:35 stated how God *pleads* with the regathered tribes of Israel "in the wilderness"—and that God also reveals He will take *spiritual* Israel, the Church, "into the wilderness, into her place" (Rev. 12:14).

We might speculate: Is it possible that the remnant of Israel is brought back to a large area near, but outside, the place of safety?

Back to Isaiah—God "Tithes" on His People

Recall that 200 million Israelites—the final third—go into captivity. Also recognize that these do not all survive the *new* World War III version of what will function like death camps.

It is Isaiah who reveals *how many* in Israel will survive the coming catastrophe. Here is the verse that, in effect, reveals A NUMBER of survivors! This is an astonishing passage, so read carefully. An earlier chapter of the book actually offered a clue when it was speaking of the whole world: "Then said I, Lord, *how long*? And He answered, Until the cities be wasted without inhabitant, and the houses without man, and the land be utterly desolate, and the LORD have removed men far away, and there be a *great forsaking* [the total breakdown of all law and order and character, triggering punishment] in the midst of the land. But yet in it shall be a TENTH, and it shall return, and shall be eaten: as a teil tree [these can regrow quickly even if cut down at ground level], and as an oak, whose substance is in them, when they cast their leaves: so the holy seed shall be the substance thereof" (6:11-13).

The prophet Amos is even more explicit regarding the number—the overall *percentage* of survivors—among the people of Israel and Judah who return from captivity, and one critical passage becomes a corroboration of what Isaiah is saying. Some background first.

Amos has much to say in the early chapters of his book about God's view of Israel, and what lies in store for her. For instance, chapter 3, verse 1, begins, "Hear this word that the LORD has spoken against you, O children of Israel…" Then verse 2 declares, "I will punish you for all your iniquities [lawlessness]" before God then asks this in regard to His relationship with Israel: "Can two walk together, except they be agreed?" (vs. 3). Few who read this passage check the all-important context of what this rhetorical question in Amos is actually talking about. God is stating the obvious through means of a question—that *He* cannot any longer walk with His people, Israel. All semblance of birthright blessings from Him cease.

Chapter 5 then opens with another lamentation against Israel and how she was "fallen" and "forsaken" with "none to raise her up" (vs. 2). Then verse 3 records, "For thus says the Lord GOD; the city that went out by *a thousand* shall leave *an hundred*, and that which went forth by *an hundred* shall *leave ten*, to the HOUSE OF ISRAEL."

This presents a mind-boggling reality!

No more than 60 million Israelites—just ONE TENTH of 600 million today!—will survive the soon-coming Great Tribulation to participate in the greatest exodus of all time. Yet, compared to perhaps 3 or 4 million leaving Egypt, this is a vastly bigger number for the angelic "fishers" and "hunters" to regather and bring back to Israel's land of nativity.

Still, over a half-billion human beings just in Israel will not have survived by this point, having through procrastination and inaction terribly miscalculated the seriousness of what would come, and when.

Assembled and Recovered a "Second Time"

Before discussing the surviving number further, let's move to Isaiah 11:11, as we continue to make ever more clear the picture of what will occur. This passage offers more about the many places where God's people have come to be scattered across the globe: "And it shall come to pass in that day, that the Lord shall set His hand again the *second time* [the first time was when Israel was delivered and brought out of captivity in Egypt] to recover the REMNANT of His people, which shall be left, from

Assyria, and from Egypt, and from Pathros, and from Cush, and from Elam, and from Shinar [modern Iraq], and from Hamath, and from the islands of the sea." These locations indicate East and West Africa and Europe—also notice Assyria and Egypt again—plus perhaps certain other African nations, and suggest South America along with various "islands of the sea."

Truly, this will have been a *worldwide* scattering and enslavement. Take time to mull—to ponder deeply—what lies ahead for whole populations who still—today!—have absolutely no idea—not a hint, inkling or clue—what is coming or why, and ask again whether God would, in effect, "ambush" His people with such awful punishment without having given powerful prior notice of its arrival.

Verse 12 then describes how God will "ASSEMBLE the *outcasts* of Israel, and gather together the dispersed of Judah from the four corners of the earth." (Also see Ezekiel 12:14-16, Jeremiah 30:11 and 49:32.) Verses 15 and 16 describe how God will dry up the multiple mouths of the Nile River delta so that escaping Israelites can come back again from Egypt, but also from other places in Africa ("Cush").

A Trumpet Blast!

It is also in Isaiah that we are given the method of just how God will notify the entire world that Israel is being brought from captivity: "And it shall come to pass in that day, that the *great trumpet* shall be blown, and they shall come which were ready to perish in the land of Assyria, and the *outcasts* in the land of Egypt, and shall worship the LORD in the holy mount at Jerusalem" (27:13).

Words cannot describe the poignancy of this most special moment to God. It is interesting to notice how Numbers 10:2 explains that trumpets were always blown whenever God wanted to *assemble* the tribes of Israel. This pattern is seen to reappear one final time at the end of the age, except that the awesome volume of the blast will exceed human comprehension. More of God's mind in a moment.

Realize first that something else accompanies the trumpet blast in this moment like none other.

Also a Mighty Earthquake

At the time of the heavenly signs, introducing the Day of the Lord, and as the trumpet blast occurs, the Bible records that Israel's moment of liberation is also accompanied by a mighty earthquake. This earthquake was covered earlier in the book.

The description of the sixth seal of Revelation 6—the heavenly signs—we saw begins with this: "And I beheld when he had opened the sixth seal, and, lo, there was a *great earthquake*; and the sun became black as sackcloth of hair, and the moon became as blood; and the stars of heaven fell unto the earth, even as a fig tree casts her untimely figs, when she is shaken of a mighty wind. And the heaven departed as a scroll when it is rolled together; and *every mountain and island were moved out of their places*" (vs. 12-14).

Compare this description to what Jesus said about the heavenly signs and it becomes clear *why* the earthquake is so great: "*Immediately* after the tribulation of those days shall the sun be darkened, and the moon shall not give her light, and the *stars shall fall* from heaven, and the powers of the heavens shall be *shaken*" (Matt. 24:29).

How great is an earthquake that moves *every* mountain and *every* island—"out of their places"? The answer is one that involves even the heavens shaking, rocking the earth's orbit as stars fall. The world has never seen such a powerful earthquake. But it is no accident that an earthquake accompanies Israel's escape from enslavement. It is, in fact, another TYPE of ancient Israel's escape from Egypt.

Let's read most of the short Psalm 114: "When Israel went out of Egypt...The sea saw it, and fled: Jordan was driven back. The mountains skipped like rams, and the little hills like lambs. What ailed you, O you sea, that you fled? You Jordan, that you were driven back? You mountains, that you skipped like rams; and you little hills, like lambs? Tremble, you earth, at the presence of the Lord, at the presence of the God of Jacob" (vs. 1, 3-7).

Just the earthquake described in Psalm 114 would probably shatter every seismograph on Earth. The one described by Christ and John in Revelation is obviously *much greater*!

Back to Isaiah

We return to Isaiah 27, verse 12: "And it shall come to pass in that day, that the LORD shall beat off from the channel of the river unto the stream of Egypt [the Nile], and you shall be gathered *one by one*, O you children of Israel."

What an absolutely astonishing picture presents itself as millions of broken, shattered, terrified human beings are brought together "one by one" out of enslavement. This regathering process begins with a trumpet blast unlike anything ever heard before—an ear-splitting sound no doubt heard in every corner of the world. This will be accompanied simultaneously with a planet-rattling earthquake, also greater than anything ever experienced. When these occur, they will also be heard and felt by God's people, then protected in the place of safety, and will send a special signal of this awesome moment for Israel.

Try to imagine 60 MILLION HUMAN BEINGS being brought literally from all over the world—every part of the earth!—weeping, loathing themselves, seeking God as never before, as they ask the way back to Zion. Beginning with the heavenly signs, plagues of every sort will be occurring all around these deeply humbled and sorrowful people during their incredible journey back to the homeland in which God always intended they reside.

One is left scarcely able to imagine the combination of pathos, repentance and, at the same time, electrifying excitement, all amidst continuing miraculous intervention, that this scene brings to mind. In fact, a very *different* kind of miracles than those allowing Israel's escape will also be occurring all around the world. But none will want to experience them...

The Year of the Lord

The Day of the Lord has now *begun*—the time we saw of GOD'S WRATH on the rebellious, sinning nations of Earth! (Recall this one-year period begins with the heavenly signs.) While God's faithful are being protected in the place of safety, this entire year is *witnessed* by these same millions who are promised by God that they will "live in His sight."

To get a better picture of what is occurring during this period all around the escaping and protected Israelite remnant, a number of final passages, all but one from Isaiah, must be examined. The "world setting" tells its own most amazing story.

The Day of the Lord is not merely a reckless God's mindless BIG BLAST against the world. The true God's carefully crafted purpose is at work. Besides the need for their own punishment due to sin, the Gentile nations receive special attention from God. Remember again this basic difference: The Great Tribulation is *Satan's* wrath on the people of Israel, allowed by God because it serves His purpose in punishing His rebellious people, but the Day of the Lord is *God's* wrath on the also sinning nations who enjoyed carrying out the punishment. This comes mostly in the form of powerful plagues.

Vengeance and Recompense!

Here is Isaiah's brief but potent summary of the Day of the Lord repeated. The passage introduces a big reason God is angry with the nations, but it also introduces something else: "For it is the day of the LORD'S VENGEANCE, and the *year* of RECOMPENSES [repayment] for the *controversy* of Zion" (34:8).

Did you notice that "vengeance" is involved in God's thinking, and that it has to do with "the controversy of Zion"? Truly today, the peoples of Israel, especially Judah, the Israelis, are given no end of trouble by the Gentile nations around them. No matter how *humanly* reasonable and generous in times of need that all the Israelite nations have striven to be (despite national immorality and corruption, and all that God said Israel has become), the peoples around them are never truly grateful, and never satisfied, and have "plagued" them for millennia. The result has been never-ending "controversy" in Jerusalem and Israel.

Next, Isaiah also records God speaking this: "For the day of *vengeance* is in My heart, *and* the year of My redeemed is come" (63:4).

This passage describes two entirely different aspects to God's mind, both occurring at the *same time*. Notice that He also calls this time of vengeance "the year of His *redeemed*." This passage introduces fascinating understanding. God literally buys back (redeems) His people from bondage. In effect, the nations are "paid" in plagues, literally plagued by God as they plagued Israel. On the one hand, God feels tenderly toward His broken and redeemed people—but toward the heathen He feels very REAL VENGEANCE!

"Ransom" Payment Like No Other

This introduces a longer and very graphic passage from Isaiah 43. It summarizes all of what we have just described. Read it carefully for the expansive picture presented: "But now thus says the LORD that created you, O Jacob, and He that formed you, O Israel, Fear not: for I have *redeemed* you, I have called you by your name; you are Mine. When you pass through the *waters*, I will be with you; and through the *rivers*, they shall not overflow you: when you walk through the *fire*, you shall not be burned; neither shall the *flame* kindle upon you" (vs. 1-2).

This describes an unbelievable scene—the horrors of nuclear war and fiery plagues occurring all around Israel during her return, crossing "waters" and "rivers" to reach her destination!

Now notice how God says that Israel must be "ransomed"—redeemed—bought back: "For I am the Lord your God, the Holy One of Israel, your Savior: I gave Egypt for your *ransom*, Ethiopia and Seba for you. Since you were precious in My sight, you have been honorable, and I have loved you: therefore will I *give men for you*, and *people for your life*. Fear not: for I am with you..." (vs. 3-5).

This latter passage describes an incredible exchange of lives that is part of God's plan to redeem His people on the way back from scattering and bondage. Quite literally, God says that certain peoples (nations) will have to die for Israel (by plagues)—and this is part of God's "ransom" plan—so that she can safely return "home." This is very different from the usual form of ransom in which the *kidnappers* receive financial payment to secure release of the hostages. In this case, with the hostages freed, the hostage *takers* are "paid" by God with *their own blood*. At this point, Israel has been released from all further debt of slavery to her enemies. Her captors have received payment (their own blood and lives) for the slaves they lost.

Now continue: "I will bring your seed from the *east*, and gather you from the *west*; I will say to the *north*, Give up; and to the *south*, Keep not back: bring My sons from far, and My daughters from the ends of the earth; even every one that is called by My name: for I have *created him* [Israel] *for My glory*, I have formed him; yes, I have made him" (vs. 5-7).

God fulfills at last what was always His purpose for the once little ancient slave nation, Israel!

Finally, National Conversion

The 31st chapter of Jeremiah is one long prophecy that speaks of Israel's return from captivity, her coming to deep repentance, with many details offered, and her coming to conversion later in the chapter. The chapter offers insets about her past abominations, but focuses on conversion from verse 31.

Here is what verses 33 and 34 state: "But this shall be the covenant that I will make with the house of Israel; *after those days* [after the Great Tribulation, the Day of the Lord, Israel's return to Zion and the kingdom of God has been established at Christ's Return], says the Lord, I will put My law in their inward parts, and write it in their hearts; and will be their God, and they shall be My people. And they shall teach no more every man his neighbor, and every man his brother, saying, Know the Lord: for *they shall all know Me*, from the least of them unto the greatest of them, says the LORD: for I will forgive their iniquity, and I will remember their sin no more."

Because of the final Work done by God's Church in the few years that remain, there will be a *remnant tenth* of Israelitish peoples with whom God can work, to whom He can give His Law and into whom He can put His Holy Spirit at the outset of the Millennium. And these nations will play a role in leading the entire world to the same condition and blessings. In fact, the remnant does not return alone from captivity.

Large numbers will join them in the journey...

The Great Multitude

The subject of the Israelite remnant introduces another large number of people that suddenly appear on the world scene at the same time. This is the little-understood "Great Multitude," often referred to as the "Innumerable Multitude." This group is described in Revelation 7:9-17 (just after the mysterious 144,000 is introduced). You will learn that this enormous mass of people are linked in a fascinating way to the survivors among Israel.

A variety of questions arise about this unidentified "Great Multitude" of Revelation: *Who* are they? *Where* could so many people come from? *How* does such a large number arise so suddenly? Could they be the same as the Israelite remnant? If not, how are they different? Or, since the Great Multitude is seen to come out of "tribulation" right as the Great Tribulation ends, is this large group in any way *related* to the returning remnant of Israel? Recall that the remnant appears at the exact same juncture in God's carefully prophesied timeline, which is just before the Day of the Lord begins. Is this an accident? And would two such similar big groups be different?

The answers to these questions must be understood! You will find that the identity of this huge throng of people is vastly more important than most could realize. None of the supposed prophecy experts can discern this group's identity. (Of course, many attempt this.) But you *can* understand! Prepare to learn the truth of this vital—and truly *inspiring*—prophecy.

A Look at the Prophecy

The Great Multitude is actually referenced in several Bible passages. But this has been unrealized. It becomes one of the surprising things you will learn in this chapter. You will see that most have simply not known how to find these verses. We will later examine several.

The prophecy is best introduced by just reading Revelation 7:9-17. While we will also later examine the specifics of this longer passage in more detail, first take the time again to read all that John recorded:

"After this I beheld, and, lo, a great multitude, which no man could number, of all nations, and kindreds, and people, and tongues, stood before the throne, and before the Lamb, clothed with white robes, and palms in their hands; and cried with a loud voice, saying, Salvation to our God which sits upon the throne, and unto the Lamb.

"And all the angels stood round about the throne, and about the elders and the four beasts, and fell before the throne on their faces, and worshipped God, saying, Amen: Blessing, and glory, and wisdom, and thanksgiving, and honor, and power, and might, be unto our God forever and ever. Amen. And one of the elders answered, saying unto me, What are these which are arrayed in white robes? And whence came they? And I said unto him, Sir, you know. And he said to me, These are they which came out of great tribulation, and have washed their robes, and made them white in the blood of the Lamb.

"Therefore are they before the throne of God, and serve Him day and night in His temple: and He that sits on the throne shall dwell among them. They shall hunger no more, neither thirst any more; neither shall the sun light on them, nor any heat. For the Lamb which is in the midst of the throne shall feed them, and shall lead them unto living fountains of waters: and God shall wipe away all tears from their eyes."

Understand that there are many points to examine within what is an extensive prophecy. There is much more here than meets the eye. But, this discussion can be simplified if we first look at an overview.

Examining the Description

Recognize that the prophecy is infinitely more important than is first evident. Also, many have misunderstood it, reducing it to a relatively small number of people linked to the 144,000 because they do not understand the Greek words translated "Great Multitude" *or* who the 144,000 are.

The term *Great Multitude* derives from the Greek *polus ochlos*, and translators have given the most accurate rendering for these words. But this same phrase is found in a number of *other* New Testament passages, in which the size of the group being referenced can be anywhere from a small gathering or mob to great numbers. Therefore, it is important to look at the key verses within the prophecy, beginning with God's own description of the group's size.

Let's start with verse 9, which begins the prophecy and records what John next observed after seeing the 144,000 sealed: "*After this* I beheld, and, lo, a great multitude, which no man could number, of *all nations*, and *kindreds*, and *people*, and *tongues*, stood before the throne, and before the Lamb, clothed with white robes, and palms in their hands."

This describes what will be seen later to be a vast and diverse wave of human beings literally from every corner of the world. Careful reading reveals that *five* key words can be examined to help demonstrate this.

Let's examine the italicized words in the verse. The word "all" is translated from the Greek word *pas*, and this word means what it says: "all...every...thoroughly." Obviously, people from *every* nation of the world are involved in this event. This means that the Great Multitude is anything but a small number, as some have suggested.

Next is the word "nations." The Greek word here is *ethnos*, pronounced eth'-nos, and the modern word *ethnic* derives from it. It means "a *race*...that is, a *tribe*, specifically a *foreign* (non-Jewish) one (usually by implication *pagan*)." It is interesting that *ethnos* also means "Gentile, heathen or nation." This is then obviously talking about the non-Israelite nations of the world—the other over 6 billion people of the earth's population. So this is referencing a people quite different from the Israelite remnant.

Then comes the word "kindreds," and this comes from the Greek word *phule*, which carries this meaning: "offshoot...race or clan...tribe." This is a key word in the prophecy. When understood, it is the term that God uses to be sure the reader does not miss the fact that *every* kind of ethnic group within the nations of the world is included in—has representation within—the Great Multitude.

The word "people" in the Greek is *laos*, and is pronounced lah-os'. First, realize the meaning here must be at least somewhat different from nations and kindreds. In fact, it carries a more narrow definition and usually means "a people...all those who are of the same stock and language."

Finally is the word "tongues." This comes from the Greek *glossa*, pronounced gloce'-sah. The English word *glossary* derives from it, and it simply means "the *tongue*; by implication a *language*." This is almost certainly another way of saying that virtually every possible kind of racial, ethnic and cultural background that a human being could possess, defined to some degree by the world's many different languages and dialects, will be included among those who repent at the end of the Tribulation.

Why Innumerable?

In light of what we have seen, it should by now be clear that the number of people within the Great Multitude is almost certainly gigantic—probably hundreds of thousands at least. In all likelihood, the number may well be *much* bigger than this, maybe millions, or even tens of millions.

On a side note, no matter its size, no matter how big the multitude might be, there is no number that cannot be counted by the mathematical systems of men. Men are able to count the now estimated 10 billion trillion stars in the universe, as well as numbers much, much larger. Thus, the only reason that the Great Multitude would be *innumerable* is because it is a number *not yet established*—a number that will only be known once it can be determined how many people around the world have chosen to repent as a result of what they have witnessed and experienced.

Every person possesses the same free moral agency. Each human being must decide what he will do when cataclysmic prophesied events about which he has been forewarned actually come to pass. People choose—numbers change.

"Came Out of Tribulation"

Verses 10 to 12 are not difficult to understand. But verses 13 and 14 offer the biggest clue to *when* the Great Multitude appear: "And one of the elders answered, saying unto me, What are these which are arrayed in white robes? and whence came they? And I said unto him, Sir, you know. And he said to me, These are they which *came out of great tribulation*, and have washed their robes, and made them white in the blood of the Lamb."

Obviously, this conversation involves a *vision* wherein John, on Earth, is talking with one of the twenty-four elders, in heaven. However, the verse plainly reveals that these people have repented—and that they "came out of great tribulation," exactly as do the remnant—as well as that they come at the same time. (Yet they are not described as having been "sealed," as were the 144,000, meaning they do not yet have God's Spirit. Also, there is not yet mention of *when* they will be saved.)

The next several verses offer the biggest clue to how the process of conversion fits the multitude. As you read the final three verses of the prophecy, five times referencing "shall," it becomes evident the multitude complete their conversion at Christ's Return.

Now notice again: "Therefore are they before the throne of God, and serve Him day and night in His temple: and He that sits on the throne *shall* dwell among them. They *shall* hunger no more, neither thirst anymore; neither *shall* the sun light on them, nor any heat. For the Lamb which is in the midst of the throne *shall* feed them, and *shall* lead them unto living fountains of waters [the Holy Spirit—see John 7:37-39]: and God *shall* wipe away all tears from their eyes" (vs. 15-17).

It is obvious from the future tense used throughout that the Great Multitude are only fully converted upon Christ's Return.

Now we begin to examine a fascinating parallel.

When Israel Left Egypt

Recall once more the principle of *duality*—and again in the context of Israel coming out of Egypt. Exodus 12 tells the story of Israel's departure from Egyptian slavery and of the first Passover, instituted annually from that point. Verse 37 describes how the "children of Israel journeyed" from Egypt with "about six hundred thousand on foot that were men, beside children." When wives and the size of families at that time are included, the 600,000 number likely grows to several million.

The *size* of the escaping Israelite nation of that earlier time becomes significant in a way that most have not recognized. This number was so large—this event so enormous, and with many powerful miracles surrounding God's intervention on behalf of His people—that the local inhabitants of Egypt saw what God was doing and wanted to follow their escaping "employees" (slaves) to wherever God was leading.

The First "Great Multitude"

Many more than those of Israel chose to depart when Pharaoh gave permission to leave. Here is what the Exodus account records about the number of Gentiles, or what the Old Testament often refers to as "strangers," who departed with Israel: "And a *mixed multitude* went up also with them; and flocks, and herds, even very much cattle" (12:38).

This is a fascinating statement, and carries within it a dramatic *duality* foretold to play out again in regard to the future Israelite remnant's coming escape from the "Egypt" that, in this age, has become *all the nations of the world*. (Of course, while scattered worldwide, we did learn that some of the remnant are enslaved in literal Egypt once again.)

The Hebrew words translated "mixed multitude" offer a vital clue in regard to this very exciting prophecy of what lies ahead for people of all nations. The word *mixed* comes from the Hebrew *ereb*, which has this definition: "mixture...mongrel race...mingled people." The word *multitude* is *rab* in the Hebrew, and means, "abundant...great...many... plenteous, populous."

The picture here is that peoples of every kind—a diverse, mongrelized mixture or mingling of humanity, probably in many cases peoples who were also slaves in bondage beside their Israelite counterparts—came in large numbers. In other words, the size of the multitude was *great*, *plenteous*, *populous* or *abundant* in number. In fact, Exodus 12:38 could just as correctly have stated that a "Great Multitude" came with Israel from Egypt!

Remember that I Corinthians 10:1 and 11 tell us that Israel's original exodus was an "ensample" or "type" for us today. Do not forget this! Of course, this would have no meaning if we could not know that God has *specifically foretold* a second, future, and much, MUCH greater exodus than happened 3,500 years ago.

Now we ask: Did God foretell, possibly in some kind of coded form, the appearance of the Revelation 7 Great Multitude in an *Old Testament* passage, one that is linked to Israel's coming exodus from captivity? Can we find further corroboration of this co-mingled "escape" event beyond the parallel of the original Exodus account?

The answer to the first question is that *God did*, and thus to the second is *we can*!

Powerful Prophecy

We have seen that Isaiah recorded more than any other prophet about the circumstances surrounding the escaping Israelite remnant. It is not surprising that his prophecy introduces the subject of "strangers" (Gentiles or foreigners) who come with Israel.

An extensive passage in chapter 56 reveals what God has known all along would occur. The chapter opens with God describing the arrival of salvation and the revealing of His righteousness to all mankind. We will momentarily learn the time setting of this prophecy. Verse 2 introduces the Sabbath connection to righteousness. Immediately, and in this context, God invites *all Gentiles* to be included in what is now to be a plan for ALL nations. Sabbath obedience plays an immediate role.

First read carefully verses 3-7 leading up to how the "stranger" can also have access to the true God: "Neither let the *son of the stranger*, that has joined himself to the LORD, speak, saying, The LORD has utterly separated me from His people: neither let the eunuch say, Behold, *I am a dry tree*. For thus says the LORD [even] unto the eunuchs that keep My sabbaths, and choose the things that please Me, and take hold of My covenant; even unto them will I give in Mine house and within My walls a place and a name better than of sons and of daughters: I will give them an everlasting name, that shall not be cut off. Also the *sons of the stranger*, that join themselves to the LORD, to serve Him, and to love the name of the LORD, to be His servants, *every one* [Gentiles, too] that keeps the sabbath from polluting it, and takes hold of My covenant; even them will I bring to My holy mountain, and make them joyful in My house of prayer: their burnt offerings and their sacrifices shall be accepted upon Mine altar; for Mine house shall be called an house of prayer for *all people*."

The context of the stranger being able to know and serve the true God is at this point brought in. Notice the context of how and where this happens. Now read carefully the next verse: "The Lord GOD which gathers the OUTCASTS OF ISRAEL [the remnant] says, Yet will I gather *others* to Him, beside those that are gathered unto Him" (vs. 8). It is evident that the "others" gathered here (the King James translators added this word because the phrase following commands it) appear at the same time when God gathers Israel. It is the only possible conclusion.

Do not miss a key point that God looks for immediately. Will these strangers keep His Sabbath?

The Big Picture

Let's now take a moment to bring some more important conclusions, some by way of questions.

By now it should be clear that the Israelite remnant and the Great Multitude of Revelation are not synonymous—are *not* the same group. But we are forced to ask: Would God introduce such an incredibly important event as is the appearance of the Great Multitude as late as the book of Revelation, and offer the reader no *other* clues about their identity—or how and why it was that hundreds of thousands, or more likely many millions, would suddenly repent and turn to God? And is it mere coincidence that this repentance comes at exactly the same time the remnant of Israel comes to repentance?

This alone should tell us that these events have to be in some way connected.

Some have thought the Great Multitude receive salvation upon Christ's Return. Why would this occur when it is evident that even the remnant is not scheduled for salvation at the end of what would just be one year of conversion for these scores of millions? The entire process of character-building would certainly not be possible in one year, and for such vast numbers besides. This is certainly not God's pattern through the Bible. The Great White Throne Judgment for billions (described in Revelation 20:11-12) lasts 100 years—a long time! So it makes no sense this would happen here for *great numbers* all at once.

In this same vein, some would naturally note that the Great Multitude are "clothed with white robes" (Rev. 7:9) and that they have "washed their robes...in the blood of the Lamb" (vs. 14). This certainly describes part of the conversion process. But the prophecy offers no evidence that, as happens with the 144,000 (discussed in the next chapter), the *spiritual* "sealing" that comes with the receiving of God's Spirit has taken place. (See John 6:27, Ephesians 1:13, 4:30 and II Corinthians 1:22.) If it had, why would God mention this all-important sealing in regard to the 144,000, but not in regard to the Great Multitude?

Some extra space is taken in this chapter to explain certain things about the Great Multitude that make understanding the 144,000 easier.

Recall that Christ promises to "lead" the Great Multitude *to* the "living waters," which we saw is the Holy Spirit (John 7:37-39). This happens *later*, because it is something we also saw "shall" occur, along with the other things that Christ declares He "shall" do for this vast throng of strangers coming with Israel. The arrival of God's Spirit to the Gentiles means that they are no longer "a dry tree." Recall Isaiah 56:3.

The Great Multitude (as well as of course the remnant) is shown to have access to God's throne—they are "before the throne of God and serve Him day and night in His temple" (Rev. 7:15). Christians realize they can come before God's throne anytime they wish.

Here is a description of what is actually happening every time a Christian prays: "Let us therefore come boldly *unto the throne* of grace, that we may obtain mercy, and find grace to help in time of need" (Heb. 4:16). This passage alone demonstrates the Great Multitude "before God's throne" is not a picture of people who have achieved salvation or gone to heaven. It is merely a picture of peoples around the world who now realize they can come in prayer to the throne room of Almighty God—a God they never knew, having always served false gods—any time they wish. This marvelous gift of access has been officially granted.

It is critical to understand that the one-year gap between the appearance of the Great Multitude and the Return of Christ is not a statement of *when* the multitude will be saved. The same is true of the remnant. Although the reason is obvious, this is now made plain. However, it is also plain that—and this is the important point—both the Israelite remnant and the Great Multitude are *protected* from the plagues coming during the Day of the Lord.

But here is what is *vitally* important to realize will occur at the outset of the Millennium—Jesus' 1,000-year reign on Earth. It becomes apparent that all nations of the world will have a kind of early representation—an "advance guard"—who will almost certainly be part of the human structure of government in each nation, who serve under the God Family—those of the ruling kingdom of God. (It should be noted here that prophecy shows *most* of Earth's remaining population will be temporary "holdouts" who will not quickly repent without more "stimulus" from God. See Zechariah 14:16-19.)

Foundation Laid!

Let's pull back for a moment and look at this from a grander perspective. While all of what you have seen is certainly an exciting prophecy, the true picture is even much bigger than we have yet seen.

A repentant Great Multitude from all nations (of course with the Israelite remnant) will bring a foundation—a starting point—from which the Law of God will spread throughout the world. (Isaiah 2:1-4 and Micah 4:1-4 show how this will happen from Jerusalem.) So, from the outset of the Millennium people in every nation—the "holdouts"—will be able to observe that some once around them reflect changed lives. They will see dramatically different attitudes and conduct—and that a new and different God is being worshipped by small enclaves of people under His protection in every corner of the globe!

How This Will Happen

You can know with certainty that millions around the world *will* be able to *know* what it means to repent and turn to the true God at the outset of His year of wrath. Here is why:

(1) The Two Witnesses will already have been at work for the two and a half years of the Tribulation, explaining God's Plan, as well as the timing of the Day of the Lord soon to occur, and they will have certainly called the nations to repent before time has expired and it is too late to avoid punishment. Of course, many will see the power and magnitude of the miracles that these two prophets will perform and *will* recognize they are *true* servants of God. Not everyone should be expected to blaspheme God and be unwilling to repent in the face of punishment, as many are foretold to do (Rev. 16:9, 11, 21).

(2) Realize that the many millions constituting the remnant will have had extended *daily contact* with the Gentile "strangers" among whom they live. These Israelite slaves will surely have talked about what it was—the national sins and abominations—that brought the last two and a half years of punishment upon their lands and themselves. They will certainly also speak of the very Work of God that warned them of what lay ahead, and that they did not heed!

Similar to the "locals" of ancient Egypt, many will learn that they can escape the incredible one-year destruction about to come upon the rest of the nations of the world. Again, the Israelites will surely tell them of the prophecies described in the Bible—the things in this book. And they may have earlier heard them independently.

Recall that the word "peoples" within the Great Multitude description is one that can also refer to the Israelite tribes. Here is the point. Certainly a multitude involving ALL nations would necessarily have to include the *Israelite* nations coming as part of, and probably the largest percentage of, the *overall* migration! But generally think of these groups as *alongside* each other.

After experiencing the Great Tribulation, the Great Multitude will come to recognize everything that God foretold would happen has come to pass. While presently consumed with "the cares of the world" (Mark 4:19), this segment of the world will remember what they learned and turn to God in full obedience!

But those who choose to listen and repent *now* will be part of a different, *much smaller* group…

The 144,000

The Bible makes mention of certain numbers that are a mystery to nearly *all* who read them. We have seen several—the number of the Beast, as well as the periods of 1,335, 1,290 and 1,260 days, among others. As with the distinct 666 number of the Beast, when God lists a number, it is no accident: "The words of the LORD are pure words: as silver tried in a furnace of earth, purified *seven times*" (Psa. 12:6). God means what He says. Now, regarding the 144,000, add to this that we saw God spells out His teachings "here a little" and "there a little" (Isa. 28:10-13).

The prophecy to be explained in this chapter can be likened to a large puzzle. The box cover features a picture as the only guide to assembling it. God has revealed to His Church how to *assemble* the individual scriptural pieces necessary for understanding.

Only in Revelation

The identity of the 144,000—a group described only in the book of Revelation—is a subject of interest, fascination, excitement, confusion and *real mystery!* Some have offered ideas on who these are—either as speculation, or Church dogma—but have missed the mark.

Two cautions must be kept in mind when approaching any prophecy: (1) The temptation to set dates, and (2) the danger of counting—more specifically, *miscounting*. But of course for certain verses counting is essential.

Incredibly, most of the world's churches think the prophecy of the 144,000 is not to be known, and thus cannot be important. However, recall God's bold statement about *all* of His prophecies—that they are important *to Him*: "Remember the former things of old: for I am God, and there is none else; I am God, and there is none like Me, declaring the end from the beginning, and from ancient times the things that are not yet done, saying, My counsel shall stand, and I will *do all My pleasure...* yea, *I have spoken it*, I will also bring it to pass; I have purposed it, *I will also do it*" (Isa. 46:9-11).

The understanding of the 144,000 will forever change your outlook on *how*—with *whom*—and with *how many* people—God has been working for the past 6,000 years.

Confusion Abounds!

Of the ministers and groups that have offered theories on the identity of the 144,000 of Revelation, a well-known, non-mainstream American Christian sect has been most dogmatic. And their ideas are completely false! Among them are the following:

• According to the sect's founder, 144,000 members of the group, whom he called Spiritual Israel, would "go to heaven."

• These would all be born before 1935, the year that (according to this leader) the "doors of heaven" would be "shut." The author of this thinking died in 1916, with the membership of his sect at that time numbering somewhere in the low four-digit range.

• The successor to the group's founder could project that its total membership would eventually *surpass* 144,000. So an urgent doctrinal correction was necessary! It was announced in May 1935: Those who missed this cut-off point would be in a *different class*—they would spend eternity in the "paradise" of a *restored Earth*, rather than heaven. This group is called the "Great Crowd."

• The "Heavenly Kingdom" supposedly took effect in 1914 with the also supposed invisible enthronement of Christ as King on Earth. An "anointed class" of about 135,300 people currently occupies this "kingdom." All of these were selected *after* Christ's ascension to heaven (Pentecost, AD 31), and in subsequent centuries. The selection of the full complement of 144,000 was "completed" in 1935. (About 8,700 of these are still alive.) This group would rule over the remaining "Christians."

• Jesus, who in this group's view is actually the archangel Michael, is not one's mediator unless that person is among the 144,000.

This entire stream of convoluted thinking can be refuted with a single verse: "But when the first came, they supposed that they should have received more; and they likewise received *every man a penny*" (Matt. 20:10). In context, this verse explains the fact that all who achieve salvation are given the same *basic* reward of eternal life, regardless of when they were called—right up to Christ's Return. *Many* other verses could be cited proving this. (The amount of authority conferred, however, is based on works in this life—Luke 19:11-27.)

But let's see what *God* teaches. To those who simply read and understand the relevant passages in the right sequence—assembling the puzzle pieces properly—the truth about this subject should be plain.

First, necessary background.

Israel's Unique Role

Even a superficial reading of the Bible makes obvious that the entire Book revolves around the nation of Israel, first an ancient, *physical* nation, then later *spiritual* Israel (the New Testament Church). You have seen this.

The forefathers of this nation—Abraham, Isaac and Jacob (renamed Israel)—begin to appear in the 11th chapter of Genesis, and "the twelve tribes of the children of Israel" are still being described in Revelation 21—the next-to-last chapter of the last book of the Bible. Other nations are almost invariably mentioned in Scripture *as they come in contact with Israel*. We saw these other nations flow later into God's Plan.

God's relationship with this extended family grown large is described in Isaiah: "I am the LORD, your Holy One, the creator of Israel, your King...I give waters in the wilderness, and rivers in the desert, to give drink to My people, My chosen. *This people have I formed for Myself*; they shall show forth My praise" (43:15, 20-21). (This earlier-quoted passage will be seen to today parallel I Peter 2:9.)

Remember that *modern* Israel is found in the largely English-speaking nations of the West. This has a direct bearing on the 144,000, who *also* pertain to "Israel."

When Do the 144,000 Appear?

Before the 144,000 are first mentioned, the time sequence of Revelation has set the stage with the fifth and sixth seals. Reading several verses in review begins the discussion: "And when He had opened the fifth seal, I saw under the altar the souls of them that were slain for the word of God, and for the testimony which they held" (Rev. 6:9).

For our purposes here, suffice to repeat that there are no "immortal souls" in heaven. Revelation 6 continues: "And they cried with a loud voice, saying, How long, O Lord, holy and true, do You not judge and avenge our blood on them that dwell on the earth? And white robes were given unto every one of them; and it was said unto them, that they should rest yet for a little season, until their fellowservants also and their brethren, that should be killed as they were, should be fulfilled" (vs. 10-11).

We saw this happens *before* the Great Tribulation, with the martyrs from 2,000 years of New Testament Church history *symbolically* waiting for the last martyrs to pay the ultimate price: "I beheld when He had opened the sixth seal, and, lo, there was a great earthquake; and the sun became black as sackcloth of hair, and the moon became as blood; and the stars of heaven fell unto the earth, even as a fig tree casts her untimely figs, when she is shaken of a mighty wind. And the heaven departed as a scroll when it is rolled together; and every mountain and island were moved out of their places. And the kings of the earth, and the great men, and the rich men, and the chief captains, and the mighty men, and every bondman, and every free man, hid themselves in the dens and in the rocks of the mountains; and said to the mountains and rocks, Fall on us, and hide us from the face of Him that sits on the throne, and from the wrath of the Lamb: for *the great day of His wrath is come*; and who shall be able to stand?" (6:12-17).

The context here again is the Day of the Lord. This one-year period immediately follows the fifth seal, the two-and-a-half-year Tribulation, when the Israelite remnant and Great Multitude are established.

But at this point, there is an important pause—the flow of catastrophic events is temporarily suspended! "After these things I saw four angels standing on the four corners of the earth, holding the four winds of the earth, that the wind should not blow on the earth, nor on the sea, nor on any tree. And I saw another angel ascending from the east, having the seal of the living God: and he cried with a loud voice to the four angels, to whom it was given to hurt the earth and the sea" (7:1-2).

144,000 Sealed

Before this "hurting" of the planet takes place, one thing must occur: "Saying, Hurt not the earth, neither the sea, nor the trees, till we have SEALED the servants of our God in their *foreheads*" (vs. 3).

A very specific, pre-determined, finite number of these servants must be included in this sealing process: "And I heard the number of them which were sealed: and there were sealed *an hundred and forty and four thousand* of all the tribes of the children of Israel. Of the tribe of Juda were sealed twelve thousand. Of the tribe of Reuben were sealed twelve thousand. Of the tribe of Gad were sealed twelve thousand. Of the tribe of Aser were sealed twelve thousand. Of the tribe of Nepthalim were sealed twelve thousand. Of the tribe of Manasses were sealed twelve thousand. Of the tribe of Simeon were sealed twelve thousand. Of the tribe of Levi were sealed twelve thousand. Of the tribe of Issachar were sealed twelve thousand. Of the tribe of Zabulon were sealed twelve thousand. Of the tribe of Joseph were sealed twelve thousand. Of the tribe of Benjamin were sealed twelve thousand" (vs. 4-8).

Shortly after this, the seventh seal is opened, containing the seven trumpet plagues and culminating in Christ's Second Coming: "And when He had opened the seventh seal, there was silence in heaven about the space of half an hour...And the seven angels which had the seven trumpets prepared themselves to sound" (8:1, 6).

One Tribe Absent

Remember that there were *twelve* tribes in Israel, but Joseph's birthright blessing was passed on to both of his sons, Ephraim and Manasseh. This would total 13—so who is missing?

A comparison with Genesis reveals the answer—the tribe of Dan is left out. The obvious question is why?

Other verses show this tribe had a long history of falling into Gentile, pagan practices and rank idolatry well ahead of the other tribes, leading the way to the other tribes' later decline.

The Danites are singled out as worshipping idols even while the Temple was present in Jerusalem! "And the children of Dan set up the graven image: and Jonathan, the son of Gershom, the son of Manasseh, he and his sons were priests to the tribe of Dan until the day of the captivity of the land" (Judges 18:30).

This tribe also took advantage of the absence of a king during the period of the Judges, attempting to pick their own heritage. However, they ended up getting "leftovers": "In those days there was no king in Israel: and in those days the tribe of the Danites sought them an inheritance to dwell in; for unto that day all their inheritance had not fallen unto them among the tribes of Israel" (Judges 18:1).

Much of this tribe did not enter the Promised Land. While Israel was in the wilderness, the Danites struck out on their own, embarking on a journey that would take them to the northwest, where they eventually settled in the British Isles and certain other spots in northern Europe. (*America and Britain in Prophecy* has an entire chapter on this.)

Time and again, the Danites went it alone in stubborn independence, not wanting to accept the path that God had set before Israel. Looking back on a key battle, the judge Deborah asked, "Gilead abode beyond Jordan: and why did Dan remain in ships?" (Judges 5:17). The Danites, though they were effective warriors, were "absent without leave" during this skirmish! They took the difficult path of disobedience, and faced many hard times as a group.

The patriarch Israel, foretelling the destinies of the twelve tribes, was inspired to say, "Dan shall judge his people, as one of the tribes of Israel. Dan shall be a serpent by the way, an adder in the path, that bites the horse heels, so that his rider shall fall backward" (Gen. 49:16-17).

This tribe left markings like a snake's path—including variations in their own name, left in various locations as they made their way across Europe. Examples are the Don, Danube and Dniester Rivers, as well as the nation of Denmark. (The Irish, who form the bulk of Dan's descendents, were among the earlier groups to migrate to the United States.)

The name Dan means "judge." Danites tended to "judge" and look down on other tribes, although they never properly judged themselves!

Israel's (Jacob's) prophetic description of Dan concludes with, "I have waited for Your salvation, O LORD" (Gen. 49:18). This tribe must wait for a later time in God's Plan, which will take effect after the initial 144,000 are assigned to the *other tribes*!

Connecting Old Testament and New Testament Israel

Some review. We first return to the "inset" chapter of Revelation 12, which outlines 2,000 years of true Church history: "And there appeared a great wonder in heaven; a woman clothed with the sun, and the moon under her feet, and upon her head a crown of twelve stars" (vs. 1).

This represents the Old Testament, *physical* nation of Israel—with verse 5 making clear that Jesus Christ arose from this "woman."

Now notice: "And to the woman were given two wings of a great eagle, that she might fly into the wilderness, into her place, where she is nourished for a time, and times, and half a time, from the face of the serpent" (vs. 14).

As we saw, this is the three and a half years during which a portion of God's people are protected from the horrors of the last three seals.

Next notice that this woman wears a crown of *twelve stars*—from Old Testament times all the way to the end of the age. The reason becomes all too obvious.

Other References to Sealing

Recall that the 144,000 are "sealed." Jesus Christ Himself, the first of the firstfruits, sets the example His people would follow. Notice: "Labor not for the meat which perishes, but for that meat which endures unto everlasting life, which the Son of man shall give unto you: for Him has God the Father SEALED" (John 6:27).

All Christians who endure to the end—either by dying in the faith or enduring until Christ's Return—are sealed. Notice: "Whom you also trusted, after that you heard the word of truth, the gospel of your salvation: in whom also after that you believed, you were SEALED *with that Holy Spirit* of promise" (Eph. 1:13), and also, "Grieve not *the Holy Spirit* of God, whereby you are SEALED unto the day of redemption" (4:30), and finally, "Who has also SEALED us, and given the *earnest of the Spirit* in our hearts" (II Cor. 1:22).

Here, "hearts" represent "minds." Sealing then plainly means receiving God's Spirit.

An Old Testament passage is helpful in showing a certain type, or forerunner, of this sealing. Let's read: "The LORD said...Go through... Jerusalem, and *set a mark upon the foreheads* of the men that sigh and that cry for all the abominations that be done in the midst thereof. And to the others He said in mine hearing, Go you after him through the city, and smite: let not your eye spare, neither have you pity" (Ezek. 9:4-5).

This setting of a mark is much like the 144,000 being sealed in their foreheads—again, the frontal lobes of the brain, the seat of the mind and decision-making capacity that allows human beings to be set apart from animals. Recall explanation in the chapter about the mark of the Beast.

The Identity Revealed!

Now to another key passage regarding the 144,000, from the only other chapter in which this number is stated: "I looked, and, lo, a Lamb stood on the mount Sion, and with Him *an hundred forty and four thousand*, having His Father's name written in their foreheads" (Rev. 14:1).

This was foreshadowed by Jesus' prayer on the last night of His earthly ministry: "And now I am no more in the world, but these are in the world, and I come to You. Holy Father, keep through *Your own name* those whom You have given Me, that they may be one, as We are" (John 17:11). Paul adds, "Of whom the whole family in heaven and earth *is named*" (Eph. 3:15).

Continue in Revelation 14, "I heard a voice from heaven, as the voice of many waters, and as the voice of a great thunder: and I heard the voice of harpers harping with their harps: and they sung as it were a new song before the throne, and before the four beasts, and the elders: and no man could learn that song but the *hundred and forty and four thousand,* which were redeemed from the earth" (vs. 2-3). "Redeemed" means these men and women were called out of this world, and had lived God's way of life. (The word literally means "bought back." Read in I Corinthians 6:20 and 7:23 how *all Christians* are bought with the price of Christ's blood.)

We might ask if some who receive salvation would learn a song others receiving salvation could not know. Of course not.

Next, "These are they which were not defiled with women; for they are virgins. These are they which follow the Lamb whithersoever He goes" (vs. 4). "Women" here symbolizes false churches. It is obviously not stating that no Christian in history ever committed adultery, or King David will not be saved. The warning is about "women" churches. Think of the great whore and her daughters.

Verses 4 and 5 continue with the crucial statement: "These were redeemed from among men, being THE FIRSTFRUITS unto God and to the Lamb. And in their mouth was found no guile: for they are without fault before the throne of God." Reread these verses before continuing.

How plain! It is an equation—the 144,000 ARE the firstfruits! They are those who have qualified to be in God's kingdom during the 6,000 years of man's rule on Earth. The first harvest of those whom God has called and chosen has a definite total—"an hundred forty and four thousand"!

This prompts an entirely different look at Church history, and gives *powerful new meaning* to Jesus' description of His Church as a "little flock" (Luke 12:32)!

Very few in the Old Testament period had God's Spirit. Again, perhaps only three (and no more than eight) people appear to have served God by Noah's time (II Pet. 2:5)—Abel, Enoch and Noah.

In the New Testament period, Jesus taught "many are called, but *few* are chosen" (Matt. 22:14). Many who have been associated with the

Church, and outwardly have been considered members, did not truly *live* the Bible (Matt. 4:4; Luke 4:4). Consider how history in fact records that Linus and Clement, trained directly by the apostle Paul, fell away and became the second and fourth popes, respectively!

The record of history shows that many, if not most, give up and choose various "women"—false churches—when persecution or other trials set in. This background helps explain why, when false leaders become associated with the Church, the "many" are deceived into following them. This is the pattern of Church history and the very reason Christ guides His Church through seven phases or eras. New leaders must invariably be raised up to rekindle what was lost.

In any event, human weakness and free moral agency notwithstanding, 144,000 is a most crucial number to God—He will make it work out!

When Is the Sealing?

The sealing of the saints is completed at a specific time, as revealed in the Revelation sequence: "And the seventh angel sounded; and there were great voices in heaven, saying, The kingdoms of this world are become the kingdoms of our Lord, and of His Christ; and He shall reign forever and ever" (11:15).

This is the last trump, heralding the Second Coming. Continuing, "Saying, We give You thanks, O Lord God Almighty, which are, and was, and are to come; because You have taken to You Your great power, and have reigned. And the nations were angry, and Your wrath is come, and the time of the dead, that they should be judged, and that You should GIVE REWARD unto Your servants the prophets, and to the saints, and them that fear Your name, small and great; and should destroy them which destroy the earth" (vs. 17-18).

Note that God's wrath is not over at this time—it is paused, suspended.

Now compare Revelation 7: "And after these things I saw four angels standing on the four corners of the earth, holding the four winds of the earth, that the wind should not blow on the earth, nor on the sea, nor on any tree. And I saw another angel ascending from the east, having the seal of the living God: and he cried with a loud voice to the four angels, to whom it was given to hurt the earth and the sea, saying, Hurt not the earth, neither the sea, nor the trees, till we have sealed the servants of our God in their foreheads" (vs. 1-3).

This passage does not say *all* are sealed *right then*, since likely the great majority were sealed long before this (recall the "souls under the altar" in Revelation 6:9). But it is clear that a full 144,000 have—at this point—*now been sealed.* The number is complete. This includes both Philadelphian and Laodicean Christians, the final two eras of God's people. Many in Laodicea—the "wise virgins"—will by then have returned to faithfulness and died in martyrdom, helping complete the number.

A Key Word!

But does this suggest that all of God's chosen firstfruits have been *physical* Israelites? Far from it.

Recall that there are twelve groups of 12,000 each. And each group is "of" one of the Israelite tribes. Can this mean God will only choose His advance guard to rule beside Christ at His Return from those of *Israelite* stock?

How could this be, when many of Paul's epistles were written to Gentile Christians? All of the congregations that he oversaw were primarily Gentile. Titus, the recipient of one of Paul's letters, was Greek (Gal. 2:3), and Timothy, to whom two canonized epistles are directed, was half Greek (Acts 16:3). Also, Cornelius and his family (of Acts 10-11) were Italian. And what about the Ethiopian eunuch of Acts 8, among others?

Add to this the important fact that very few who are called into God's Church can be considered "pure" Israelites. For example, my last name, "Pack," appears to be Jewish, but I am not a Jew in the ethnic, physical sense, as far as I know. Finally, I know a great many non-Israelite brethren and they are some of the most deeply converted people one could meet.

This becomes the second key point in the correct understanding of how the 144,000 are assigned to each tribe. The Greek word translated "of" is *ek*, which means "in accordance with" or "according to."

These are *not* 12,000 who were of Judah *physically*, 12,000 of Reubenite descent, 12,000 coming from Gad, 12,000 of Asherite descent, and so on. These are 144,000 *Christians*—who had been both Israelites and Gentiles, with many being mixtures of both. These became part of spiritual Israel—the Church—past and present—who are assigned to rule the physical twelve tribes in the Millennium!

So there are evidently 12,000 Spirit Being saints *assigned* to—in accordance with or according to—rule Judah, 12,000 designated to lead Reuben, and so forth. Some who had been Gentiles in the flesh will help lead the physical nations of Israel in the Millennium, beginning immediately with the very Israelite remnant itself.

How marvelous, just, and wonderfully *inclusive* is God's Plan! Because He started with a single nation, some have actually accused God of being *racist*. Incredible—and far from the truth! Israelite and Gentile receive the same reward in every regard!

Strangers in Old Testament Israel

This offer to both Israelites and Gentiles should not come as a surprise. Even in the Old Testament, strangers (foreigners) could always join themselves to Israel if they accepted the nation's laws. Let's read six passages:

First, "But the *stranger* that dwells with you shall be unto you as one born among you, and you shall love him as yourself; for you were strangers in the land of Egypt: I am the LORD your God. You shall do no unrighteousness in judgment, in meteyard, in weight, or in measure" (Lev. 19:34-35).

Next, "And the Levite, (because he has no part nor inheritance with you,) and the *stranger*, and the fatherless, and the widow, which are within your gates, shall come, and shall eat and be satisfied; that the LORD your God may bless you in all the work of your hand which you do" (Deut. 14:29).

And, "Seven days shall there be no leaven found in your houses: for whosoever eats that which is leavened, even that soul shall be cut off from the congregation of Israel, whether he be a *stranger*, or born in the land" (Ex. 12:19).

As well as, "You shall have one manner of law, as well for the *stranger*, as for one of your own country: for I am the LORD..." (Lev. 24:22).

And again, "And when a *stranger* shall sojourn with you, and will keep the Passover to the LORD, let all his males be circumcised, and then let him come near and keep it; and he shall be as one that is born in the land: for no uncircumcised person shall eat thereof" (Ex. 12:48).

And finally, "One law shall be to him that is homeborn, and unto the *stranger* that sojourns among you" (Ex. 12:49).

The Firstborn

Consider another parallel between Old and New Testament Israel: "And you shall say unto Pharaoh, Thus says the LORD, Israel is My son, even My firstborn" (Ex. 4:22).

Firstborn here means God's choice (Jacob's brother Esau was born first), as described in different terms in a later chapter of Exodus: "You have seen what I did unto the Egyptians, and how I bare you on eagles' wings, and brought you unto Myself. Now therefore, if you will obey My voice indeed, and keep My covenant, then you shall be a *peculiar treasure* unto Me above all people: for all the earth is Mine. And you shall be unto Me a *kingdom of priests*, and an *holy nation*" (19:4-6). These terms will reappear almost verbatim in the New Testament describing the Church.

However, meant to be an entire nation of priests, Israel did *not* keep God's covenant, backsliding and tempting Him repeatedly. So He narrowed this priesthood to one tribe: "Behold, I have taken the Levites from among the children of Israel instead of all the firstborn that opens the matrix among the children of Israel: therefore the Levites shall be Mine; because all the firstborn are Mine; for on the day that I smote all the firstborn in the land of Egypt I hallowed unto Me all the firstborn in Israel, both man and beast: Mine shall they be: I am the LORD" (Num. 3:12-13). By this time, only the Levites are designated as firstborn, rather than all twelve tribes.

Moving forward many centuries, Jesus spoke of a new "nation" that would pick up the mantle that had been cast aside even by the Levites: "Therefore say I unto you, The kingdom of God shall be taken from you, and given to *a nation bringing forth the fruits* thereof…And when the chief priests and Pharisees had heard His parables, they perceived that He spoke of them" (Matt. 21:43, 45). Of course, the Jews and the other tribes of Israel largely rejected Christ at His First Coming. His plan was to find other peoples who would respond to His direction.

So then the Levites would be supplanted by a *new group* who would bring the right fruits: "But that on the good ground are *they*, which in an honest and good heart [anyone, Jew or Gentile, man or woman], having heard the word, keep it, and bring forth fruit with patience" (Luke 8:15).

A New Nation

The decline and failure of the civil nation of Israel caused Paul to lament their state during his lifetime. Notice this: "I have great heaviness and continual sorrow in my heart. For I could wish that myself were accursed from Christ for my brethren, my kinsmen according to the flesh: [now notice from earlier] who are Israelites; to whom pertains the adoption, and the glory, and the covenants, and the giving of the law, and the service of God, and the promises; whose are the fathers, and of whom as concerning the flesh Christ came, who is over all, God blessed forever. Amen. Not as though the word of God has taken none effect. For [Get this!] they are *not* all Israel, which are OF Israel" (Rom. 9:2-6). Here Paul summarizes the shift from a physical nation to a spiritual nation, which includes Gentiles! Non-Israelites can become *of* Israel.

This group of firstfruits will be changed to spirit at the First Resurrection: "Blessed and holy is he that has part in the first resurrection: on such the second death has no power, but they shall be priests of God and of Christ, and shall reign with Him a thousand years" (Rev. 20:6).

The apostle Peter adds additional understanding, mirroring Exodus 19:4-6. Recall from earlier: "But you are a chosen generation, a *royal priesthood*, an *holy nation*, a *peculiar people*; that you should *show forth the praises of Him* who has called you out of darkness into His marvelous light: which in time past were not a people, but are now the people of God" (I Pet. 2:9-10). Now recall Isaiah 43:21.

God tells His Church that He has made them—coming from all kinds of ethnic backgrounds—into "*a* people," a single "nation," etc. Now back to Revelation: "And they sung a new song, saying, You are worthy to take the book, and to open the seals thereof: for You were slain, and have redeemed us to God by Your blood out of *every kindred*, and *tongue*, and *people*, and *nation*; and have made us unto our God kings and priests: and we shall reign on the earth" (5:9-10).

Paul concisely defines who Israel is. Writing to a *Gentile* congregation, the power and clarity of his words make it impossible to misunderstand: "As many as walk according to this rule, peace be on them, and mercy, and upon the *Israel of God*" (Gal. 6:16).

God is still working with Israel—but Paul clarified that this group is the "Israel of God." By Paul's time, physical Israel was no longer "of God"—they had strayed far from Him centuries before.

"Twelve Tribes"—in the New Testament

But what about individual tribes? Is the Israel of God now just given this broad label, without any further distinction? A number of verses fairly shout the answer. Here is one from the book of Acts, no less impossible to misunderstand than Galatians 6:16: "Unto which promise *our twelve tribes*, instantly serving God day and night, hope to come. For which hope's sake, king Agrippa, I am accused of the Jews" (26:7).

This is a stunning verse. The *physical* twelve tribes were by this time mostly scattered and lost, and were not serving God *at all*!

Here is another: "James, a servant of God and of the Lord Jesus Christ, to *the twelve tribes* which are scattered abroad, greeting. My *brethren*, count it all joy when you fall into divers [various] temptations..." (Jms. 1:1-2).

The apostle James, Jesus' brother, was not writing to the physical twelve tribes! Any doubt is removed by just reading his epistle. It is obviously intended for Christians. Its message does not fit regarding carnally minded tribes or nations. For confirmation, just notice he was writing to "brethren." Who are these "brethren"? Jesus Christ defined them as His disciples (Matt. 12:47-50). Paul, in the book of Hebrews, equates brethren with "the Church" (2:12)!

"The Number"!

Returning to Revelation 6: "And white robes were given unto every one of them; and it was said unto them, that they should rest yet for a little season, until their fellowservants also and their brethren, that should be killed as they were, should be fulfilled" (vs. 11).

The King James translation leaves out a crucial word that makes the meaning here most clear. Let's look at a series of additional translations.

New King James Version: "...until both *the number* of their fellow servants and their brethren, who would be killed as they were, was completed."

Moffatt: "...until *their number was completed* by their fellow servants and their brothers who were to be killed as they themselves had been."

Phillips: "...until *the number* of their fellow-servants..."

Revised Standard: "...until *the number* of their fellow servants..."

New English Bible: "...until *the tally* should be complete..."

Amplified: "...until *the number* should be complete..."

20th Century New Testament: "...till *the number* of their fellow-servants..."

So this verse references a specific NUMBER. "Fulfilled" comes from the Greek *pleroo*—"to satisfy, finish, accomplish, complete, fill up, make full." There is so obviously a NUMBER that must be *completed*!

The dead "souls," God's people who died in the faith over the last 6,000 years, are *part* of this number, with a final martyrdom to add to and complete the tally—144,000.

Let's now return to Revelation 15: "I saw another sign in heaven, great and marvelous, seven angels having the seven last plagues; for in them is filled up the wrath of God. And I saw as it were a sea of glass mingled with fire: and them that had gotten the victory over the beast, and over his image, and over his mark, and over the number of his name, stand on the sea of glass, having the harps of God. And they sing the song of Moses the servant of God, and the song of the Lamb, saying, Great and marvelous are Your works, Lord God Almighty; just and true are Your ways, You King of saints" (vs. 1-3).

This closely parallels the scene in Revelation 6:9: "And when He had opened the fifth seal, I saw under the altar the souls of them that were slain for the word of God, and for the testimony which they held."

This is the group that we saw was required to face the woman of Revelation 17 in previous ages, and who endured martyrdom, thus gaining eternal victory over this ancient, false system.

No Difference in the Church

In this light, consider more passages explaining there is no difference, after conversion, between Gentile and Israelite Christians:

First, "And have put on the new man, which is renewed in knowledge after the image of Him that created him: where there is neither Greek nor Jew, circumcision nor uncircumcision, Barbarian, Scythian, bond nor free: but Christ is all, and in all" (Col. 3:10-11).

Next, "There is neither Jew nor Greek, there is neither bond nor free, there is neither male nor female: for you are *all one* in Christ Jesus. And if you be Christ's, then are you Abraham's seed, and heirs according to the promise" (Gal. 3:28-29).

And, "Remember, that you being *in time past Gentiles* in the flesh, who are called Uncircumcision by that which is called the Circumcision in the flesh made by hands; that at that time you were without Christ, being aliens from the commonwealth of Israel, and strangers from the covenants of promise, having no hope, and without God in the world" (Eph. 2:11-12).

At one time these Ephesians were considered Gentiles, but then became part of the "commonwealth of Israel"! Paul continues, "Now therefore you are no more strangers and foreigners, but fellowcitizens with the saints, and of the household of God" (vs. 19).

The same holds true of the term "Jew." Paul again: "And shall not uncircumcision which is by nature, if it fulfill the law, judge you, who by the letter and circumcision do transgress the law? For he is not a Jew, which is one outwardly; neither is that circumcision, which is outward in the flesh: but *he is a Jew, which is one inwardly*; and circumcision is that of the heart, in the spirit, and not in the letter; whose praise is not of men, but of God" (Rom. 2:27-29).

In this age, *true* Christians are the *true* Jews. The sign of this is a circumcised heart, regardless of ethnic background.

"The Fullness of the Gentiles"

Another scripture makes clear that a *set number* of Gentiles must be added to the Church to complete the 144,000. We remain in Romans: "For I would not, brethren, that you should be ignorant of this mystery, lest you should be wise in your own conceits; that blindness in part is happened to Israel, until the *fullness* of the Gentiles *be come in*" (11:25).

Turning to other translations again strengthens and clarifies the meaning of "fullness" assigned to the Gentiles.

New King James Version: "…until *the fullness of the Gentiles* has come in."

Moffatt: "…until *the full number of the Gentiles* come in."

Phillips: "…until *the full number of the Gentiles* has been called in."

Revised Standard: "…until *the full number of the Gentiles* come in."

"Fullness" is translated from *pleroma*, meaning "*repletion* or *completion*," "that which fills or with which a thing is filled…fulfilling." This indicates a certain quota, proportional share or allotment of Gentiles is to be fulfilled, instead of (or in place of) an equivalent number of Israelites.

But there has been an order to the process. Remember this, still in Romans: "Tribulation and anguish, upon every soul of man that does evil, *of the Jew first*, and *also of the Gentile*; but glory, honor, and peace, to every man that works good, *to the Jew first*, and *also to the Gentile*: for there is no respect of persons with God" (2:9-11).

Remember, the New Testament Church was initially comprised solely of Jews—until God made clear that salvation was also being offered to the Gentiles (Acts 10).

"Ten Thousands of His Saints"

An unusual passage in the New Testament confirms the relatively small number of those who will be resurrected to eternal life at the Return of Jesus Christ, while also providing a glimpse of one of the earliest examples of the true gospel being preached.

Notice this again in Jude, here quoted in a different context for a different purpose from before: "And Enoch also, the seventh from Adam, prophesied of these, saying, Behold, *the Lord comes with* TEN THOUSANDS *of His saints*, to execute judgment upon all, and to convince all that are ungodly among them of all their ungodly deeds which they have ungodly committed, and of all their hard speeches which ungodly sinners have spoken against Him" (vs. 14-15).

"Ten thousands" in Greek is *murias*. The word's primary and secondary meanings are this: "ten thousand, also by extension (more unlikely, but a possible translation) a myriad or indefinite number."

"Ten thousands" means the number is at least 20,000, but determining the upper limit requires only a little more thought. Here are a series of passages from the Old and New Testaments that paint the full picture of one of the Bible's very greatest truths.

First is a passage from Daniel: "A fiery stream issued and came forth from before Him: thousand thousands ministered unto Him, and ten thousand times ten thousand stood before Him: the judgment was set, and the books were opened" (7:10). The Hebrew for "ten thousand" here is *alaph*, which is either "thousand" or "thousands" depending on the context.

Now another, this time back in Revelation, "And...I heard the voice of many angels round about the throne and the beasts and the elders: and the number of them was ten thousand [*murias*] times ten thousand [*murias*], and thousands of thousands" (5:11). Here, "thousands" at the end of the verse is *chilias*, which means either thousand or thousands.

If Jude 14 were referencing a number greatly exceeding "ten thousands" (in the range of millions for instance, as most would suppose the number of true Christians through the ages would be at a very *minimum*), we might expect to see the expression "ten thousand *times* ten thousand," as used in Daniel 7:10 and Revelation 5:11.

While these verses are not conclusive of themselves, they give further evidence that the total number of saints is in the range of "ten thousands" rather than "ten thousand times ten thousand"—in the range of 100 million or so.

Looking at the entire picture, Jude 14 must be taken literally. So in determining the upper limit of this number, *murias* could describe a number up to 190,000. If the number of saints reached 200,000, it would more accurately be described as "hundreds of thousands."

The sum of 144,000 fits within the range of 20,000 to 190,000.

Saints in Heaven?

A final question must be resolved: If the saints will reign "on Earth," how is it that the 144,000 are before the throne of God?

John 3:13 certainly cannot be set aside by the 144,000. Remember: "No man has ascended up to heaven, but He that came down from heaven, even the Son of man which is in heaven."

The special event that Paul experienced (in II Corinthians 12), wherein he was taken into the third heaven (in vision), was to receive a glimpse of his future as a member of the God Family, to be encouraged and to receive strength to endure the course of his incredibly difficult ministry. While Paul's reward, like every other Christian, is to rule the nations of Earth (Matt. 5:5), there is nothing in Scripture to suggest God's children will be *prohibited* from God's heavenly throne room. The book of Job makes plain that even Satan has occasional access there. Would members of God's Family have less?

Thus John's visions in Revelation harmonize with Paul's, and are consistent with the correct understanding of the reward of the saved.

The Firstfruits Are the Church

Recall that Revelation 14 plainly labels the 144,000 as "the firstfruits." That there be no misunderstanding, yet another list of passages should be reviewed. These make the firstfruits' identity unmistakable:

First, "For we know that the whole creation groans and travails in pain together until now. And not only they, but *ourselves also*, which have *the firstfruits* of the Spirit, even we ourselves groan within ourselves, waiting for the adoption, to wit, the redemption of our body. For we are saved by hope: but hope that is seen is not hope: for what a man sees, why does he yet hope for?" (Rom. 8:22-24).

Next, "Every good gift and every perfect gift is from above, and comes down from the Father of lights, with whom is no variableness, neither shadow of turning. Of His own will begat He us with the word of truth, that WE should be a kind of *firstfruits* of His creatures" (Jms. 1:17-18).

And, "But now is Christ risen from the dead, and become the *firstfruits* of them that slept. For since by man came death, by man came also the resurrection of the dead. For as in Adam all die, even so in Christ shall all be made alive. But every man in his own order: Christ the firstfruits; *afterward they that are Christ's* at His coming" (I Cor. 15:20, 21-23).

"They that are Christ's," of which Paul and James considered them-selves a part, God calls *firstfruits*. These are symbolized by the early grain harvest collected at the time of Pentecost.

"Jerusalem…Above"

Now the final piece of the puzzle. God gives His Church—already established as "Israel" and the "twelve tribes" and "spiritual Jews"—the name "Jerusalem." This is important because this city was *Israel's capital*. Still one more list presents itself.

First, "But Jerusalem which is above is free, which is the mother of us all" (Gal. 4:26).

Next, "I saw a new heaven and a new earth: for the first heaven and the first earth were passed away; and there was no more sea. And I John saw the holy city, *new Jerusalem*, coming down from God out of heaven, prepared as a bride adorned for her husband. And I heard a great voice out of heaven saying, Behold, the tabernacle of God is with men, and He will dwell with them, and they shall be His people, and God Himself shall be with them, and be their God" (Rev. 21:1-3).

And, "He carried me away in the spirit to a great and high mountain, and showed me that great city, the *holy Jerusalem*, descending out of heaven from God, having the glory of God: and her light was like unto a stone most precious, even like a jasper stone, clear as crystal; and had a wall great and high, and had twelve gates, and at the gates twelve angels, and names written thereon, which are [notice carefully] the *names of the twelve tribes of the children of Israel*: on the east three gates; on the north three gates; on the south three gates; and on the west three gates. And the wall of the city had *twelve foundations*, and in them the names of the twelve apostles of the Lamb" (vs. 10-14).

It could not be mere coincidence that the capital of physical Israel is the very designated name for New Testament *spiritual* Israel.

High Calling for a Select Group

Jesus declared that during the Millennium each of the twelve apostles will oversee one of the twelve tribes, assisted by thousands of other God Beings under Him: "Then answered Peter and said unto Him, Behold, we have forsaken all, and followed You; what shall we have therefore? And Jesus said unto them, Verily I say unto you, that you which have followed Me, in the regeneration when the Son of man shall sit in the throne of His glory, you also shall sit upon twelve thrones, judging the twelve tribes of Israel" (Matt. 19:27-28).

Out of the billions of human beings that have lived since Adam, a mere (initial number of) 144,000 will rule with Jesus Christ at His Return. This makes the Christian calling today a truly mind-boggling opportunity and privilege not to be squandered.

Is it any wonder that Jesus admonishes the Philadelphian Christians of Revelation 3, "Behold, I come quickly: hold that fast which you have, that no man take your *crown*" (vs. 11)? If one of God's selected number lets go of—gives up!—his crown, it will be "taken" by another "man."

God's purpose will be carried out—His number *will be fulfilled*!

144,000—12 times 12,000—is the number of foundations and organizational beginnings in perfect form. The twelve apostles, including twelve groups of 12,000 spirit-born saints, ruling the twelve physical tribes, will finally perfect Israel, allowing the nation to achieve God's original purpose for it as a model nation! And through Israel's salvation, just a year away from when the 144,000 are sealed, God will govern and set the example for *all* nations who will follow later in salvation.

But first comes unspeakable horror…

Armageddon!

Nearly everyone has heard of *Armageddon*! Hundreds of authors have written books on the subject, and dozens of movies have been produced depicting the "final battle between good and evil." Generals, scientists and world leaders also use the term, generally to reference the possible annihilation of mankind through nuclear, chemical or biological means.

Some thought Armageddon would be the final battle of World War I. They were *wrong*! Others thought World War II would end with this battle. They were also *wrong*! More recently, during the Gulf War, thought-to-be Bible experts were announcing, "Armageddon is here!" Again, they were wrong!—as have been *many* other scenarios.

What exactly *is* Armageddon? Is it a place or an event? Who will take part in it? What does the Bible *really* say?

Over 1,900 years ago, while exiled on an island off the Greek coast, the apostle John recorded what would happen—culminating in *our time*! We saw he was thrust forward in time into the "Lord's Day" or "Day of the Lord" (1:10) and was given messages regarding "...things which are, and things which shall be hereafter" (1:19).

Most of what John saw in vision was foreign to him. He had to record things in a way that could be understood. For instance, how would someone from the first century describe a helicopter gunship? What about a jet—or nuclear explosion? Jesus would have inspired him to use symbols or items familiar to him.

Important History

A certain amount of historical background to the subject of Armageddon must precede proper understanding of this improperly understood subject.

Surprisingly, the Bible mentions Armageddon in only *one* verse: "And He [God] gathered them together into a place called in the Hebrew tongue Armageddon" (Rev. 16:16). Though the New Testament was written in Greek, Armageddon is not a Greek word. It comes from two *Hebrew* words—"har" and "megiddo." *Har* means hill—or sometimes figuratively hill country.

Megiddo, or Megiddon, was a royal city of the Canaanites until Joshua captured it (Josh. 17:11). Located on the southern edge of the great plain of Issachar (also known as the Plain of Esdraelon and Valley of Jezreel) (Josh. 17:16), it was given to the Israelite tribe of Manasseh (I Chron. 7:29). Megiddo was a fortified city that guarded the strategic passes around Mt. Carmel.

Now for two of several vital points. Grasp them. (1) God brings certain people (armies) to Megiddo, and (2) the Bible says Armageddon is a *gathering place*, not an EVENT—and not a BATTLE (Rev. 16:16). When the Bible speaks of Armageddon, it is *not* referring to either the end of the world *or* the final battle between "good and evil," as so many believe. This is critical to understand—and it will soon be obvious.

The site of Megiddo is within the borders of the modern state of Israel, about 60 miles north of Jerusalem and about 20 miles east of the port city of Haifa. The location of up to 30 different cities over thousands of years, Megiddo is today little more than a 15-acre pile of rubble on a hilltop.

In ancient times, this area included a main highway between Africa and Asia. It provided a natural gathering place due to the flatness of the surrounding topography. Archaeology shows evidence of frequent, extremely heavy defense facilities there through the centuries, and involving many periods of development. I have carefully walked the area, and seen this.

Megiddo is a famous setting for several great slaughters through history. The first was when Joshua overthrew it in the 1400s BC. Later, when Deborah was judging Israel, she ordered Barak into battle there against the Canaanites, led by Sisera. Every soldier in Sisera's army was killed. (This story is in Judges 4 and 5.)

The well-known defeat and slaughter of 120,000 Midianite soldiers by the army of Gideon *may* have also taken place near Armageddon. Judges 7 describes how God first reduced Gideon's army from 32,000 to 300 prior to this battle.

I Kings 9 describes how King Solomon turned Megiddo into a fortified stronghold that housed hundreds of horses for his fleet of chariots. The foundation of his enormous stable is still visible today. I have also walked through and studied these.

When Jehu, king of Israel, wounded Judah's King Ahaziah in battle, Ahaziah fled to Megiddo, where he died.

The Egyptian king Pharaohnechoh came to the aid of the Assyrians and defeated the Israelites led by Josiah at Megiddo—where Josiah died (II Kings 23:29-30).

This valley has also seen military conflict in *modern* times. On September 19, 1918, British General Edmund Allenby won a decisive battle there in World War I, defeating the Ottoman Turks. This led directly to the birth in 1948 of today's nation of Israel.

Because Megiddo is identified as a place of historic conflicts, and because more battles have been fought there than at any other place in the world, it has become emblematic—like Waterloo, Gettysburg or Normandy.

More Background

More background and review is now important to establish the setting surrounding the biblical Armageddon. Without this necessary review, the truth about Armageddon—what God wants understood about it—simply cannot be seen.

We saw the Bible foretells a period of seven trumpets blown, each heralding its own terrible event. We saw that throughout history, trumpet blasts have been used as warnings of imminent danger, such as war or another calamity (Zeph. 1:16; Jer. 4:19; Ezek. 33:2-6).

However, the seventh (or last) trumpet will announce to the world that Jesus Christ is coming to establish God's rule on Earth. Man's way of governance is ending. Also heralded by this final trumpet are the seven *last plagues* (bowls or vials of wrath) God will use to punish a *rebellious* mankind. Revelation describes seven angels who "pour out the vials of the wrath of God upon the earth" (Rev. 16:1).

Let's also review these, because Armageddon *and* the mark of the Beast are involved. When the first vial is poured out, "there fell a noisome and grievous sore upon the men which had the mark of the beast" (16:2). Of course, by now you understand these belong to the great, false church-state system. (More on this in a moment.)

The *second* plague mirrors what the Egyptians suffered before the Exodus: "The second angel poured out his vial upon the sea; and it became as the blood of a dead man: and *every living soul* died in the sea" (16:3).

The next three plagues involve the rivers and fountains turning to *blood*, the sun becoming so hot it *scorches* people, and darkness and pain becoming unbearable. After all these plagues, men will continue to "blaspheme the God of heaven because of their pains and their sores, and *repent not* of their deeds" (16:11).

We saw the last generation before Jesus' Return is so vile, corrupt and contemptuous that God will subject them to the *worst punishment possible*—and they still will not repent.

The Important Sixth Plague

The sixth of the *last* plagues sets the stage for the final battle to resist Christ at His Return. Forces of spiritual wickedness—demons—are released to gather armies to bring about destruction and devastation on the inhabitants of Earth. Notice how these armies are able to gather: "The sixth angel poured out his vial upon the great river Euphrates; and the water thereof was dried up, that the way of the *kings of the east* might be prepared" (Rev. 16:12).

The Euphrates River originates in Turkey and flows southeast through Syria and Iraq, finally reaching the Persian Gulf. God will cause this river to dry up, enabling, it says, the "kings of the east" to easily cross into the Holy Land. But this is just a prelude—the setting of the stage for even *more* significant events to come.

Verse 13 continues, "I saw three *unclean spirits* like frogs come out of the mouth of the dragon [Rev. 12:9—the devil], and out of the mouth of the beast [the civil end-time ruler possessed by the devil], and out of the mouth of the false prophet [the also possessed religious leader with the Beast]." We saw Revelation 17:5 calls this Babylon the Great.

Whose Battle Is It?

Revelation 16:14 states, "For they are the spirits of devils [demons], working miracles, which go forth unto the kings of the earth and of the whole world, to *gather* them to *The Battle of that Great Day of God Almighty.*" So then this is GOD'S battle! These "spirits of devils" are fallen angels who followed Lucifer (now Satan) in rebellion against the Creator long ago (Isa. 14:12-14; Ezek. 28:12-17; Rev. 12:4).

Now let's read Revelation 9:11 as we continue to understand events building toward Armageddon: "And they [the final revival of the Holy Roman Empire] had a *king* [a supreme ruler] over them, which is the *angel* of the bottomless pit, whose name in the Hebrew tongue is Abaddon, but in the Greek tongue has his name Apollyon."

Some review leads directly to what *actually* happens regarding God's battle. The aforementioned leader will be accompanied by a *religious* leader who, with the power and influence of the devil, will perform mesmerizing, *counterfeit* miracles. When peoples of the earth witness these, they will be deceived into thinking that this false system is of God—and will fight what we saw they will think to be *invaders from outer space!* The Beast and False Prophet will drive their religious-political-economic-military system toward final confrontation.

The World Scene

Let's understand what will then be the world scene. By that time, the revived Holy Roman Empire—the Beast of Revelation—will have already conquered some parts of the Middle East. It will have established a foothold in Jerusalem. This "king of the north" (Dan. 11:40)—the same as the fourth beast of Daniel 7—will invade the Middle East under the *pretense* of bringing peace. *Oil* will also likely be a factor in prompting the Beast system into seeking control of the region.

Notice what Daniel says: "But tidings out of the *east* and out of the *north* shall trouble him [the Beast]..." (11:44). Remember that the Bible reckons these directions from Jerusalem. While the Beast's army is in the holy land—*other* military giants will move in to oppose it.

What big countries today are *east* and *north* of Jerusalem? Russia, China, India and Japan! It is likely that these, with possibly other nations in the region, will compose the massive *200-million-man* army mentioned in Revelation 9:16. Read this verse. Again, all indications are that oil will be a key factor for this war machine from the East. Ezekiel 25:4 and 10 call this army the "men of the east."

The world will have come to the point in world events that Jesus referred to: "And except those days should be *shortened*, there should no flesh be saved [left *alive*]..." (Matt. 24:22).

Thought-to-be Enemy

As these armies position for war, an unlikely "enemy" arrives on the scene—Christ. Mankind will see Christ this way! And here is why: "The seventh angel sounded; and there were great voices in heaven, saying, The kingdoms of this world are become the kingdoms of our Lord, and of His Christ; and He shall reign forever and ever" (Rev. 11:15).

Christ appropriates for God the nations' governments and lands without asking permission!

Now realize this! There is no battle foretold at Armageddon! What happens is called THE BATTLE OF THE GREAT DAY OF GOD AL-MIGHTY! Again, this is GOD'S battle! This last great clash will be fought by armies that will have *already gathered* at Armageddon. These two major forces will obviously see Christ coming out of the clouds. Considering *Him* a threat, they will join forces, forming an alliance to fight their common adversary. These men will be angry. They will not submit to God's government. Repeating for crucial emphasis, these will think JESUS Christ is in fact the "ANTI-christ." The result? They will "make war with the Lamb" (17:14).

Christ's feet will rest on the Mount of Olives just outside Jerusalem. Notice Zechariah: "Behold, the day of the LORD comes...For *I will gather all nations against Jerusalem to battle* [not Megiddo]; and the city shall be taken, and the houses rifled, and the women ravished; and half the city shall go forth into captivity, and the residue of the people shall not be cut off from the city. Then shall the LORD go forth, and *fight against those nations*, as when He fought in the day of battle. And His feet shall stand *in that day* upon the Mount of Olives, which is before Jerusalem on the east, and the Mount shall cleave in the midst thereof..." (14:1-4).

Again, where will this battle of the Lord take place? Let's read from Joel: "Proclaim you this *among the Gentiles*; prepare war, wake up the mighty men, let all the men of war draw near; let them come up: beat your *plowshares into swords*, and your *pruninghooks into spears* [the opposite of the famous Millennial prophecy in Micah and Isaiah]: let the weak say, I am strong. *Assemble* yourselves, and *come* [from Megiddo], all you heathen, and *gather* yourselves together round about: there [outside Jerusalem] cause Your mighty ones to come down, O LORD. Let the heathen be wakened, and come up [again, from Megiddo] to the *Valley of Jehoshaphat*: for there [outside Jerusalem] will I sit to judge all the heathen round about. Put you in the sickle, for the harvest is ripe: come, get you down; for the press is full, the fats overflow [great slaughter is coming]; for their wickedness is great. Multitudes, multitudes in the *valley of decision*: for the Day of the LORD is near in the *valley of decision*" (3:9-14). Compare this with Revelation 14:19-20.

Valley of Decision

The Valley of Jehoshaphat is also known as the "valley of decision." This valley lies just east of Jerusalem, between the city and the Mount of Olives—not 60 miles north at Har-Megiddo. I know. I have also been there and walked *this* valley. Today, the Jews use this area, called the Kidron Valley, as a burial ground.

Jehoshaphat means "the Eternal judges" or the "valley of the judgment of the Eternal." King Jehoshaphat overthrew the people of Moab, Ammon and Mt. Seir when they came against Jerusalem. God fought without Jehoshaphat lifting a finger. Let's read: "You shall not need to fight in this battle: set yourselves, stand you still, and see the salvation of the LORD with you, O Judah and Jerusalem: fear not, nor be dismayed; tomorrow go out against them: for the LORD will be with you" (II Chron. 20:17).

When "tomorrow" came, *every one* of the enemy was *dead!* God had done the fighting and wiped them all out!

What about this last battle? What will be the final outcome? Let's continue in Zechariah 14: "And this shall be the plague wherewith the LORD will smite all the people that have fought against Jerusalem; their flesh shall consume away while they stand upon their feet, and their eyes shall consume away in their holes, and their tongue shall consume away in their mouth" (vs. 12).

The God of the Bible pulls no punches in choice of language!

Graphic Picture

Revelation 19 says much more—and it is graphic: "And I saw heaven opened, and behold a white horse; and He that sat upon him was called Faithful and True [Jesus Christ], and in righteousness He does judge and *make war*...And out of His mouth goes a sharp sword, that with it He should *smite* the nations: and He shall rule them with a rod of iron...And I saw an angel standing in the sun; and he cried with a loud voice, saying to *all the fowls that fly* in the midst of heaven, Come and gather yourselves together unto the *supper* of the great God...That you may *eat* the *flesh* of *kings*, and the flesh of *captains*, and the flesh of *mighty men*, and the flesh of *horses*, and of them that sit on them, and the flesh of all men, both free and bond, both small and great...I saw the beast, and the kings of the earth, and their armies, gathered together to make war against Him that sat on the horse [Jesus Christ], and against His army [the resurrected saints returning with Him]..." (19:11, 15, 17-19).

So then, let's understand! Vast millions will actually *fight against Jesus Christ*! They will *not* view His Return as reason to rejoice because, many of them serving a different Christ—"another Jesus"—they will not recognize the *true* Christ.

Grasp this! Puny human beings, who think they can oppose God because they have man's most advanced weapons of war, will be *utterly destroyed* by Him. What happens will be quick and decisive, with the armies left in complete destruction.

Note what happens first: "And the beast was taken, and with him the false prophet that wrought miracles before him, with which he deceived them that had received the mark of the beast, and them that worshipped his image. These both were cast alive into a lake of fire burning with brimstone...[Now what happens to the army?] And the remnant were slain with the sword of Him [Christ] that sat upon the horse, which sword proceeded out of His mouth: and all the fowls were *filled* with their flesh" (19:20-21).

This description is truly horrible. While many dismiss it as allegory or impossible-to-understand symbolism, its message is *real*—and the events it describes are real!

We have seen that the final battle to end man's rule on Earth is *not* named after Armageddon. Nor will this battle be fought there. Rather, it happens outside Jerusalem. Christ is not going to bring the battle to the individual nations—the battle will *come to Him*. The armies of the world will literally march 60 miles south to be executed by Christ as He arrives on the Mount of Olives—"in that day." Now recognize all these events will take place in *our lifetimes*—and SOONER than you think!

You have learned the TRUTH about the battle *at Jerusalem*, only *thought* to be at Armageddon. Consider. There will be two sides. On one will be the men of the east and all who took the mark of the Beast. On the other are Jesus Christ and the saints.

All who *truly* want to follow and obey God still have time to qualify to join Christ in what only *begins* with a terrible battle. Consider carefully the path before you. Your answer has everything to do with where you might fit in the picture within the next chapter...

Finally—World Peace!

The world is filled with war, terrorism, and threats of more war and terrorism. This has been a constant in every age. Yet, all nations long for peace. Leaders negotiate for it. Millions pray for it. Of course, armies fight for it. Everyone wants it. Yet it remains more elusive than ever. The second horse and rider foretold by Christ—the red horse of war—certainly makes clear that an end to war is not yet just beyond the horizon.

Universal Desire

All people long for happy, peaceful, abundant lives. But how many today actually enjoy this kind of wonderful life?

Knowledge is exploding! Mankind has produced astonishing materialistic progress. Breakthroughs in science and technology have never been greater. But have they been able to bring a rich, full, joyful life to everyone? Have education and the knowledge explosion brought this? Has religion succeeded in producing peaceful, abundant lives worldwide? Have governments found the answers to mankind's greatest questions? Are statesmen providing the example leading to the way that produces true happiness?

In every case, the clear answer is NO! Plain answers are lacking.

Vast new frontiers of expanding scientific knowledge have not brought the happiness that leaders and scientists foretold would accompany them. Neither have laborsaving devices, which were supposed to bring people more leisure time to "enjoy themselves." Instead, mental illness, loneliness, self-pity and despair, suicide, alcoholism, drug addiction, as well as other forms of escapism, and general dissatisfaction with life, are everywhere.

Thousands of wars have been fought in the name of religion. Hundreds of millions of lives have been wiped out in the name of peace! Still there is no peace! Humanly devised solutions always fail to bring lasting peace—anywhere in the world.

Efforts are being made by economists, politicians, sociologists, and other "thinkers." But it will *not* turn out all right. Religion, politics and other conservative movements, however well intentioned, will fail—abysmally.

At every turn, mankind has bungled and botched all efforts to solve its biggest problems. As a result, humanity suffers from every conceivable evil and ill. Misery, confusion, unhappiness, discontent, desperation—and military confrontation!—abound.

But there *is* a way that produces true happiness and peace.

Ugly History

War is the primary means by which nations have settled disputes throughout history. It is considered a natural state of affairs, while peace has been considered a time of recuperation from the previous conflict, and when preparation is being made for the *next war.*

Georges Clemenceau, the WWI French statesman, said this: "I don't know whether war is an interlude during peace, or peace is an interlude during war" (*Quotes for the Air Force Logistician*, United States Air Force Logistics Management Agency, p. 66).

Recall General Douglas MacArthur's famous speech, stating man's dilemma in the starkest terms: "We have had our last chance. If we will not devise some greater and more equitable system, Armageddon will be at our door" (April 19, 1951, speech to the United States Congress).

But the Bible says world peace *will come*—and SOON!

The presidential historian and columnist, Peggy Noonan, summarized the jumbled, awful course that has been man's history: "In the long ribbon of history, life has been one long stained and tangled mess, full of famine, horror, war and disease. We must have thought we had it better because man had improved. But man doesn't really 'improve,' does he? Man is man. Human nature is human nature; the impulse to destroy coexists with the desire to build and create and make better" ("His Delicious, Mansard-Roofed World," *The Wall Street Journal*, Oct. 26, 2001).

While men have created many amazing technological inventions, they cannot "create" peace. Scientists have unleashed the power of the atom, but are powerless to "unleash" peace upon Earth. Astronomers have discovered much about the size, majesty and precision of the universe, but they cannot "discover" the way to peace. They can find galaxies far away throughout the universe, but they cannot "find" peace here on Earth. Neither can leaders end famine, disease, poverty, overpopulation, religious confusion and hatred, as well as every other misery, evil and woe that unchecked human nature can produce.

I repeat: The Bible declares that peace, and solutions to all these troubles, will come—and *soon*.

One World Government?

Men today are planning a world government behind the scenes—a new world order. Discussions are well underway in certain corners of Europe toward this end. Various treaties have begun to point the way.

In 1966, as God began to reveal His truth to me, I had the opportunity to meet with my United States Congressman—William McCulloch—a highly respected man in his time. I was nominated to attend the United States Naval Academy. All nominees were required to have a personal interview with their Congressman prior to acceptance. When the interview ended, Mr. McCulloch asked if I wished to ask any questions.

I had only one.

I was learning about a world-ruling government to be established at the Return of Jesus Christ. So I asked the Congressman's opinion of one world government—if it were in the hands of men. His answer was immediate and emphatic, "I do not believe it would work, but if I did, I would shout it from the housetops." This made a lasting impression on me. I never forgot what a Congressman of over 30 years' experience in the world's most powerful government stated.

Since that time, many have suggested *one world government* IS the only way to world peace and stability. But many questions arise. Who would bring it? How would it be phased in? What laws would it administer? How would they be enforced? Would sovereign nations relinquish authority to it? Would it succeed, or would it eventually oppress and enslave all mankind? These questions always stop thinkers, planners, leaders and scientists in their tracks!

Therefore, world peace remains elusive as ever. Seemingly everyone yearns for it, but no one knows how to obtain it. Why? Why cannot the experienced leaders and intelligent thinkers of our time find the way to peace? Why do people understand the only solution that could bring peace is one world government, yet at the same time acknowledge this is utterly impossible if left to men? We might ask: If men are incapable of governing their own individual lives, how could they possibly govern the entire world?

Why No Peace?

Mankind, in his rebellion against God, likes to present his own versions of civilization in the best possible light. In this regard, we saw Ezekiel foretold that modern false religious leaders, with political leaders at their side, will deceitfully declare, "Peace; and there was [is] no peace" (13:10). God shows that peace will continue to evade those who forsake His ways.

It has been said that all nations are either *preparing* for war, *at* war or *recovering* from war. We saw that history recorded over 14,500 wars just through the mid-1960s. How many more have come since?

Men seem to invariably go to war in search of peace. Eventually, wars usually come to a truce, which always fails to yield *permanent* peace. This is because men cannot, and never will, find the way to peace *on their own*—without outside help. In reality, they have no chance to achieve world peace. *Why?*

As part of an extensive prophecy about world conditions in our time, Isaiah answers: "The *way* of peace *they know not*; and there is *no judgment* in their goings: they have made them crooked paths: whosoever goes there *shall not know peace*" (59:8). The solutions of men always lead to more wars, ruin, misery, death and destruction. Paul quoted Isaiah in the New Testament: "And the way of peace have they *not known*" (Rom. 3:17).

While men may talk about, call for and pretend to seek peace, world leaders always seem to fall back on the tool of war to achieve it—and suffering, misery and unhappiness *increase* in its wake. Even Napoleon warned, "You have got to be very careful with war, because, with all the excitement, you may grow to love it." Nations *have* grown to love war—indeed, they are addicted to it. For 6,000 years, man has proven himself unable to break the cycle of war.

I have stood at the very lectern in the United Nations General Assembly where so many presidents, prime ministers, dictators, kings and popes have called for world peace. I could not help but think of which had ever made a difference—from 1946 in San Francisco, when that institution was founded in the wake of World War II, to today.

The institutions of men are woefully uninformed—and ultimately *toothless*—concerning the *causes* of peace, leading to the right *effects* all peoples long for—*world peace*. In the end, neither diplomacy nor war has worked, while knowledge of the right *causes* that lead to peace remains unseen, eliminating any hope of success.

The Failed Governments of Men

The governments of men—all of them—simply do not work. They have *never* succeeded in finding permanent solutions to what are, for them, *insoluble* problems.

You have probably supposed that the governments of modern nations generally reflect God's Way. This is almost everyone's assumption. Yet, while God does, in fact, establish and remove nations—and leaders—this is not *His world*! This is why the Bible foretells the arrival of a *divine* government to *replace* the confused, competing, inefficient and *ineffective* governments of men that are so powerless to solve the world's biggest problems.

Look at the governments of this world. Generally, there are three types—*monarchies, dictatorships* and *democracies.*

Monarchies involve nobility—royalty—where bloodline is the key to succession of power. When a king or queen dies, a prince or princess ascends the throne. This cycle can last for centuries. History records that monarchies are almost always replaced, either violently or peacefully, with the king or queen often allowed to retain minimal power.

Dictatorships and totalitarian governments are usually created through violence—by coup or revolution. They are often short-lived, with something similar replacing them.

Democracies and republics are collaborative or representative. Leaders are elected, and represent "the will of the people." This involves a voting or balloting process to select one candidate in preference to others. This form is generally considered the best of men's governments. Yet the great twentieth-century British Prime Minister, Winston Churchill, called democracy "the *worst* form of government except [for] all...other[s]..." This is a startling admission from an insider.

Fruits of Democracy

In one of the most profound statements in the Bible, Jesus instructed, "You shall know them *by their fruits*," and, "Wherefore by their *fruits* you shall *know* them" (Matt. 7:16, 20). He also taught, "For the tree is known *by [its] fruit*" (Matt. 12:33). These verses are primarily speaking about leaders, but the principle has broad application.

Let's examine, for instance, the fruits of the "tree" called "*politics, voting and democracy.*" This system is based on *competition* between political parties. Each party seeks to gain an advantage over the other and will even undercut good ideas if it will cast a bad light on the opponent. During the period preceding an election (called "election year politics"), the challenger opposes the incumbent at *every* turn, and on virtually *every* issue, to present himself as different, and in the best light, solely to get elected. Over time, this has a devastating effect on the unity of a country that is supposed to stand behind its government. This openly—and often bitterly—divides the citizenry of any nation.

Democracy is the form of government in three-fourths of the world's nations. Think of just some of its fruits: favoritism, endless debates and arguments, bribes, lust for power, corruption, lying and deceit, scandals and cover-ups, greed, exploitation, maneuvering and manipulation, relentless accusation, inefficiency, vanity, decisions based on polls, voter apathy, strife and backstabbing. Democratic politics are shot full of division and disagreement, over nearly every issue that arises.

The fruit of democracy is *chaos*!

But, as bad as democracies are, they are *far better* than any *other* form of government—when it is in the hands of men. Democracy at least attempts to ensure more individual "freedoms" than other kinds of humanly devised government.

In the end, however, *none* of man's governments work either very well or for very long.

Men's governments do not have *any* of the answers to mankind's biggest questions. It has not been given to men to understand the path to peace—or, for that matter, the way to abundance, happiness, health and prosperity. No wonder the greatest thinkers, leaders, educators and scientists have failed miserably in their quest for peace on Earth!

They lack the essential knowledge necessary to solve them.

Is it also any wonder God inspired Hosea to record, "My people are destroyed for *lack of knowledge*: because you have *rejected knowledge*, I will also *reject you*" (4:6)? Mankind could have known, understood and had access to far more important, vital knowledge about how to live, but chose to reject it. As a result, God rejected—cut off—man from access to Him. And this cuts men off from the very solutions to the terrible, worsening problems they now have.

God has not yet revealed to mankind collectively the only SOLUTION to its unending wars, and world troubles.

Not God's World

Why can the governments of men not get along, avoid war—and find peace and agreement? *Why* such constant instability, scandal and division among leaders everywhere? *Why* so much favoritism, antagonism between parties, ethics violations, political arm-twisting and lobbying, infighting, poor judgment, corruption, bribery, misrepresentation—and outright lying—in virtually all national governments? *Why* are there seemingly endless revolutions and military coups? *Why* no shortage of demagogues, dictators and revolutionaries, always promising to make things better, yet invariably bringing *worse* problems and conditions?

Where did the governments of men come from? *Who* is behind them?—*Who* guides them? What is the *source* of the strife and competition in today's world? We must ask again in this light: Is this *God's* world—reflecting His Way, and His direction and guidance?

Most religionists and churchmen blindly assume it is. Thus, they conclude that if, as they usually put it, "All Christians work together, in love and unity, to make this world and its governments a safer and better place for everyone"—or for democracy and freedom, as some emphasize—"we can bring peace, happiness and prosperity to all." Many *naïvely* believe that if they can "fix the world"—or even just *improve* it—they can usher in God's kingdom on Earth. Also, and even *more* naïve, is that many believe they can influence governments to become more godly.

This is fantasy!—a completely wrong view, and it is *not* what God expects—or wants! Nowhere did Jesus say, "Go into the world and strive to make it a better place by becoming part of it." He said, "Go you into all the world and preach the gospel"—about *His* coming government—as well as teach "*all things* whatsoever I have commanded you" (Mark 16:15; Matt. 28:20). And the Bible also commands, "Come out *from among them* [the world], and *be you* SEPARATE" (II Cor. 6:17), and further, speaking of society's Babylonish ways, "Come *out* of her, My people, that you be not partakers *of her sins*, and receive not of her *plagues*" (Rev. 18:4).

Why did Jesus instruct His disciples to come out of the world's systems and governments?

The Bible speaks of Satan who "deceives the *whole* world" (Rev. 12:9). Remember, it says, "the *whole* world." Recognize that this staggering statement is in *your Bible*—the one in *your house!*

For now, let's focus on one aspect of the enormous understanding within this passage. If Satan has deceived the entire world, how can it be *God's* world? Since the *whole* world is deceived—and the apostle John also recorded that "the *whole* world lies in wickedness" (I John 5:19)—modern civilization cannot be of God. It is cut off from Him (Isa. 59:1-2; Jer. 5:25).

Now, if you do not accept Revelation 12:9 as revealed knowledge from God, any hope of *personally* breaking free of this deception is lost! If you *do*, think! Worldwide deception would certainly include influence upon, and control over, the human governments of *all* nations.

Message About Government

Prior to Jesus' birth, an angel appeared to His mother, Mary. Here is what she was told: "...the angel Gabriel was sent from God unto...Nazareth, to a virgin...and the virgin's name was Mary. And the angel came in unto her, and said, Hail, you that are highly favored...you shall conceive in your womb, and bring forth a Son, and shall call His name JESUS. He shall be great, and shall be called the Son of the Highest: and the Lord God shall give unto Him the *throne of His father David*: and He shall *reign* over the house of Jacob *forever*; and of His *kingdom* there shall be *no end*" (Luke 1:26-28; 31-33).

Jesus told Pilate, "My *kingdom* [His government] is not of this world" (John 18:36). Pilate asked, "Are you a king then?" Jesus responded, "You say that I am a king. *To this end was I born*, and for this cause came I into the world" (18:37). Jesus Christ was born to be a *King*!

Here is what was foretold in Isaiah about Christ. It begs to be repeated at this point: "For unto us a Child is born, unto us a Son is given: and the GOVERNMENT shall be upon His shoulder: and His Name shall be called Wonderful, Counsellor, The mighty God, The everlasting Father, *the Prince of Peace*. Of the increase of His GOVERNMENT and PEACE there shall be no end, upon the *throne of David*, and upon His KINGDOM, to order it, and to establish it with *judgment* and with *justice* from henceforth even *forever*" (9:6-7).

When Christ establishes God's government on Earth, it will usher in peace for all nations!

Literal Nations and Peoples

Soon the whole world will see that "the kingdoms *of this world* are become the kingdoms *of our Lord*, and of His Christ; and He shall reign forever and ever" (Rev. 11:15). Just as there is no doubt that countries today represent real, literal, physical governments (kingdoms), this passage leaves no doubt that God's coming government is also real and literal.

Jesus Christ was born to rule all nations of the earth forever. This is the central theme of the entire Bible: "And out of [Christ's] mouth goes a sharp sword, that with it He should smite the nations: and He shall *rule them* with a rod of iron...and on His thigh a name written, KING OF KINGS, AND LORD OF LORDS" (Rev. 19:15-16).

Have you ever been told about these passages? Any of them? I never learned or even *heard* of them in the church of my youth—yet here they are, available with unmistakable clarity.

The City of Peace, Finally!

The capital city of the modern Jewish nation of Israel is Jerusalem. Though this city has known nothing but war, strife and bitter division throughout its history, its name means *"city of peace."* This is because Christ will return there to establish His kingdom. The *Prince of Peace* will rule from the *City of Peace*. Beginning in this single city, peace will spread around the world (Isa. 2:1-4; Micah 4:1-4). Eventually, it will "break out" everywhere!

Final, true—permanent—world peace and prosperity will come in your lifetime. It is as certain as the Word of God! In the end, the world will *not* be disappointed! Awesome news lies ahead.

Most assume that God is trying to save the world now—that *today* is the only opportunity for salvation for all mankind. The whole world has been deceived about salvation and the most important questions and answers of life. Most people have no idea *why* they were born—*why* they were put on Earth. No wonder they do not understand why man cannot find peace, happiness, health and abundance on his own.

We must ask: When Jesus establishes His world-ruling government, who else might be part of the structure He establishes? If the governments of men require the efforts of many, who assist a supreme leader, is God's government different? No!

Daniel Is Plain

Let's examine some of what the prophet Daniel recorded about God's kingdom.

Just before Jesus' Return, God officially grants Him the authority to rule the world to which He is returning. Notice: "There was *given* Him dominion, and glory, and a kingdom, that all people, nations, and languages, should serve Him: His dominion is an everlasting dominion, which shall not pass away, and His kingdom that which shall not be destroyed" (7:14).

Again we ask whether Christ rules alone, or are others to rule with Him? Exactly *how* does God intend to manage all the peoples and nations of Earth?

More verses in Daniel 7 are critical to understand: "But *the saints* of the Most High shall *take the kingdom*, and *possess the kingdom* forever, even forever and ever" (vs. 18).

BELIEVE THIS VERSE FOR WHAT IT SAYS! The ultimate calling of Christians is to join with Christ to share rulership in the kingdom of God over ALL nations and ALL peoples. Truly, Christ will be "King *of kings* and Lord *of lords*" (Rev. 19:16).

These other kings and lords can be you or anyone willing to accept God's terms for entering His kingdom.

What could be plainer? No wonder Jesus stated, "And he that *overcomes*, and keeps My works unto the end, to him will I give *power over the nations*: and he shall *rule them* with a rod of iron; as the vessels of a potter shall they be broken to shivers: even as I received of My Father," (Rev. 2:26-27), and, "To him that *overcomes* will I grant to sit with Me *in My throne...*" (3:21).

Luke 1:32 revealed Christ will sit in Jerusalem on the Throne of David. When Christ Returns, the saints will rule *with* Him—*on Earth!*—as spirit-composed beings in the kingdom of God.

How Much Longer?

All want to know *when* Christ will return. This is why the disciples asked Him, "What shall be the sign of Your coming?" (Matt. 24:3).

Just a few weeks later, in Acts 1, prior to Jesus' final ascension back into heaven, the disciples proved they still did not either understand or really accept His previous explanation. So they probed further. Notice: "...they asked of Him, saying, Lord, will You *at this time* restore again the kingdom to Israel? And He said unto them, *It is not for you to know the times or the seasons*, which the Father has put in His own power" (1:6-7).

But this book has removed all doubt of whether time is *very* short!

Think. The New Testament Church was to be established just *10 days* after this encounter (read Acts 2:1). Why would Jesus answer, "it is not for you to know the times or the seasons" if God's kingdom was to be the Church—as so many millions believe!—which was to be almost immediately established on Pentecost just *10 days later*?

The same is true for us today. We cannot know *exactly* when Christ's kingdom will come, but we can now know a very close approximation. At the end of Luke's long prophecy that parallels Matthew 24, Jesus stated, "*When* you see these things come to pass, know you that the kingdom of God is [near] at hand" (Luke 21:31).

Jesus *did* want His disciples to know that "you shall receive *power*, after that the Holy Spirit is come upon you" (Acts 1:8)—but *not* to know *precisely* when the kingdom would arrive. The same is true for all who are converted today. They *can* know that they will receive POWER now to grow and overcome—and to preach the gospel of the kingdom of God, until He does return.

False teachers almost universally proclaim that the kingdom of God is *now* on Earth. They contradict the Christ they profess to follow.

Not Activists

True Christians are not activists seeking to "make *this* world a better place"—thereby bringing God's kingdom to Earth. They have their "*feet shod* with the preparation of the *gospel of peace*" (Eph. 6:15). They walk through life having their "feet" covered with the knowledge of how the true gospel spells the *only way* to final world peace. They understand with certainty that the kingdom of God—bringing "government *and peace*" (Isa. 9:7)—*is* coming. They know what lies ahead for this world. They do not go off to serve and kill in the endless, futile wars of men and nations—or participate in the affairs of failing, doomed governments.

They do not take matters into their own hands, and try to supposedly "spread the kingdom"—or, the more popular term, get involved in "kingdom-building"—thereby attempting to neutralize God's purpose, which is to show man that he is not capable of governing himself!

How can one spread what is not yet here?

All who understand the truths of this book are no longer in the dark about God's Plan—or their awesome potential role within it. A new world order *is* coming—but it is far from what *men* are planning.

Citing Isaiah 52:7, Paul also recorded, "How beautiful are *the feet* of them that preach the *gospel of peace*, and bring glad tidings [good news] of good things." He further cited Isaiah: "But they have not all *obeyed* the gospel. For Isaiah said, Lord, *who has believed our report?*" (Rom. 10:15-16).

Sadly, most people will *not* believe "God's report" of what lies ahead for civilization. They will *not* believe that they are unable to bring world peace through human effort. Many will shout "Peace, peace"—and most will eagerly continue believing their false predictions, even in the face of abject failure.

The professing Christians of this world will continue desperately striving to bring about the kingdom of God and world peace through organizations and efforts of men. Deceived religious leaders will tell them that this is their "Christian duty." Vast numbers will see this as the sole mission of their church.

I repeat, this is not God's world! The devil governs a vast realm of fallen spirits. Together, they deceive, confuse and exert far-reaching influence over *all* the governments and activities on Earth, including the many religions of men. Get this! These governments cannot be fixed or improved. They must be REmoved!—by God!

But understand. True Christians never disobey—or resist—civil authority—unless that authority directly instructs them to disobey the higher authority of God (Acts 5:29). Christians *never* participate in protests or demonstrations, even non-violent ones, never mind violent ones—or participate in *any* form of war, which is of course always much more violent. Not ever! Remember Jesus said, "My kingdom is *not of this world*: if My kingdom *were* of this world, *then* would My servants fight, that I should not be delivered to the Jews: but now is My kingdom *not from hence* [meaning, from *here*—this world]" (John 18:36). But understand. Participating in the governments of men and obeying or submitting to them are entirely different matters. Christians do not confuse the two! They yield to—as very *models* of obedience—men's governments at *every level*. Romans 13:1-7, among other scriptures, explain what God expects.

Millions are looking for peace and security around every corner— but they will be bitterly disappointed—in the *short term*. This is because world conditions, leading into a final devastating period of worldwide calamity, will get *infinitely worse* before they ultimately get better.

Greatest Phrase Ignored

Most people know of what is called "The Lord's Prayer." Many can recite it from memory, having practiced this without understanding that it is simply a *model* or *guideline* for how to pray. I learned it at age four. It begins, "Our Father which art in heaven, Hallowed be Thy Name. *Thy kingdom come*. Thy will be done in earth..." (Matt. 6:9-10). Of the masses who recite it, how many actually think about the phrase "Thy kingdom come"—or, for that matter, God's "*will* [His Master Plan] being done on Earth"?

For 2,000 years, countless millions have sought to follow Jesus' instruction, praying, "Thy kingdom come" without ever really pondering the staggering *meaning* behind this small phrase. Almost none know what you saw earlier, that Jesus stated just 23 verses later, "But seek you *first* the kingdom of God, and His righteousness" (Matt. 6:33).

The Ultimate Good News

Beyond all the *bad* news is wonderful GOOD NEWS—and it is just as detailed! Sadly, few speak of it! Most talk only about the end of the world and the supposed *annihilation* of humanity. This is because they are ignorant of the most important parts of Bible prophecy. We teach more on Bible prophecy by far—and most importantly the *truth* of it!—than anyone else. You do not need to be ignorant. But you must study diligently.

Soon after Christ's Return and the establishment of God's kingdom on Earth—not in *heaven*—suffering will disappear. War will be a thing of the past. So will terrorism. Crime will vanish. Children will play safely everywhere. Drugs and alcohol will no longer enslave people. Poverty will be gone. As will illiteracy. Mass healings will occur. A pure language will help re-educate the population (Zeph. 3:9). Earth's polluted environment will finally be restored. Air will be clean. Pure drinking water will be abundant. Even the nature of animals will be changed.

As "King of kings," Christ will rule all nations as they have *never* been ruled. He will be compassionate, perfect in character, truthful and full of wisdom—as well as have love for those He governs. He will *never* compromise God's Law, which is summarized as the way of *outgoing concern for others*. While firm, He will administer the commandments in every nation with patience and understanding, and grant forgiveness to all who seek it, sincerely desiring to change.

The world will become a perfect environment for all to finally be able to live God's Way according to His perfect Law—which is the WAY of peace, prosperity and joy. Religious deception and confusion will no longer exist. Humanity will finally be humble, and thus teachable. *Every-*

one will learn God's truth: "For the earth shall be *full* of the knowledge of the Lord, as the waters cover the sea" (Isa. 11:9). What a marvelous time is coming. You will want to read my inspiring book *Tomorrow's Wonderful World – An Inside View!* It offers a picture from God's Word truly beyond the grandest plans of men.

Only one God could bring such powerful intervention in the affairs of men…

The True God

Chapter One opened with words of challenge from the Author of the Bible. The book would be incomplete without emphasis—special focus upon—*this* God. Correctly identifying the *true* God from all others has absolutely *everything* to do with whether one will come to understand prophecy. Thus, a closing chapter of a book about biblical prophecy must address the great questions about the God of the Bible.

The subject of God is mysterious, confusing to almost all. Yet, the single most important knowledge in the universe would be that of the true God. What could be more important than which god one worships? Millions, indeed billions, have asked WHO and WHAT is God? This all-important question has confounded man for millennia.

He has still not found the answer.

With the explosion of new and different brands of Christianity, this confusion about God has grown worse in the modern age. And the so-called "great religions" of the world have only *added* to this confusion. Yet, correctly identifying the true God is the central issue and question towering over EVERYTHING that is important in life. The answer to this question lies at the very core of all that is true religion. And, for those who believe the God of Creation authored the Bible—Christians!—the question comes into sharper focus.

Who and What is the God *of the Bible*?

Millions of professing Christians believe in, speak of and weekly sing about God as a "trinity"—"Father, Son and Holy Spirit." Acceptance of *this god* has become perhaps the greatest litmus test of orthodox or traditional Christianity. But is the Bible's God a trinity—*three persons* in ONE BEING? Can this be proven? Or is God something else—and can *this* be proven? If the "trinity god" is false—if this is *not* the God of the Bible—it must be rejected.

In its place must come an understanding of the *true* God.

Fraud

Most people are, and certainly every student of law is, familiar with the crime known as *fraud*. In short, this is an act in which some form of deception is deliberately perpetrated on an unsuspecting victim (or victims) for the purpose of embezzling or stealing money. In the world, fraud involves a high stakes game of confidence. Often incredibly audacious scam artists—"con"(fidence) men—devise a scheme usually involving some complexity. This crime takes much forethought and can involve very intricate sophistication. The jury hearing such cases must pay strict attention. There can be no daydreaming, or the value of evidence will be missed.

In the case described here, the fraud—and you can learn the *methods* in which it is being carried out—is being committed in the name of God and Truth. In the world, those convicted of this crime usually go to prison. Of course, this does not occur when it happens in the world's churches.

Hold no illusions. What is being offered—what is being *packaged* as "god"—the trinity—to millions of unsuspecting "Christians" constitutes *spiritual fraud*. And the fraud is PLAIN!

Which Is Better?

Consider this question. Which would be better: Having correct understanding of every single doctrine in the Bible, including all knowledge of prophecy, but having neither true knowledge of, nor contact with, the God who inspired it?—*or*, having absolutely no knowledge of even one Bible truth except the nature and identity of the true God, and access to Him?

Let's examine this further. The Bible is filled with a great many distinct, separate doctrinal truths: the gospel, salvation, baptism, identity and location of the true Church, the name of that Church, whether one should observe and keep holy Saturday or Sunday, whether one should observe the annual festivals of Leviticus 23 or various humanly devised holidays, financial laws, the purpose of marriage, principles of proper childrearing, divine punishment, the nature of repentance, conversion and proper baptism, the unpardonable sin, dietary laws and health, healing, the Law of God, the role of Christ, and of course scores of prophetic truths, plus many, many more. I ask again: Would it be more important (assuming this could be possible) to know the truth of *all* of these Bible teachings while at the same time lacking the knowledge of who is the true God—or to know *nothing* of them, but to have direct contact with the God who recorded them?

Think! If one knew and were worshipping the TRUE GOD, he would automatically be led into all the *right knowledge* offered by that God, revealed only to those who have a *relationship* with HIM. We could even speculate this might happen relatively quickly after entering into such contact. The *true* God would not leave such a one in ignorance about exactly *how* He was to be worshipped—in other words, the knowledge of all the many truths contained in His Word enabling one to do this correctly. The knowledge of the true Plan of God, the location of the true Church and Work of God—and every other divinely revealed point of understanding—flows from being in direct contact with the *right God*. On the other hand, possessing all of the knowledge about every Bible doctrine would be *utterly useless* if one were worshipping the WRONG GOD! Mere knowledge of true doctrine would not automatically lead such a person to the God who authored it, and thus his religion would likely be in vain.

God has to *reveal Himself* to any who come to know Him! (Read John 6:44 and 65.) He must distinguish Himself from all other supposed gods or deities. Set aside all personal bias and see if the true God is revealing Himself to you, possibly starting with this book. Be ready to pursue at all costs the right understanding of eight words from the God of the Bible— "You shall have *no other gods* before Me."

Founded on False Knowledge

A concluding section of the white horse chapter returns, this time as a question: Have you ever examined why people believe as they do? *Why* have so many come to accept the doctrines that they hold—and for that matter their view of prophecy—as having come from the Bible? Why have YOU believed and accepted the things that YOU do? Almost all who consider themselves Christians have carelessly *assumed* from childhood the answer to the most important question that they could address—do they have and are they worshipping the RIGHT GOD?

Many come into adulthood having accepted without question what they repeatedly heard, read or were taught in Sunday school. They have been unwilling to *challenge* what their peers have also accepted without question. Strangely, these same people will often vigorously defend their beliefs, while feeling absolutely no need to examine PROOF of *why* they believe what they do—or to consider *how* they came to such beliefs. Human nature wants to follow the crowd. And we have at least briefly seen this has been the case with virtually every one of the popular teachings, traditions and practices found in orthodox Christianity—which have been taken almost entirely from paganism, false customs and human reasoning. *This* is why the masses have followed a triune god that was conceived and developed entirely outside the pages of the Bible.

Incredibly, I have even seen those who knew the true God become willing to carelessly exchange Him for another god as easily as taking trash to the dumpster. Yes, throughout history, many who have *known* the God of the Bible have been willing to slowly blur and then lose altogether the knowledge of who and what He is. An "arrow" of lies and deceit (read Jeremiah 9:3) from the one riding the white horse was able to pierce their understanding.

Source of Deception, Confusion

We saw the apostle John described Satan the devil as having "deceived the whole world" (Rev. 12:9). And we saw that his greatest goal has been to keep man from a relationship with his Creator. The apostle Paul described Satan as "the *god* of this world" who we also saw "has blinded...them which believe not" (II Cor. 4:4). Is it strange to think of Satan as this world's GOD? Does this seem impossible to believe? Yet, there it is in your Bible. After all, as arch-deceiver, on what point would the devil most want to deceive—blind—mankind, other than the identity of the true God? Satan is the *author* of the trinity—a false, counterfeit, substitute deity—designed sixteen centuries ago to deceive millions into unwittingly worshipping *him*, while thinking they serve the God of Christianity and the Bible.

The highly educated of this world ought to know WHO God is! But they do not, because this is *spiritual* knowledge, DIVINELY REVEALED by the very God these scholars and educators have been unable to discover on their own—and Whom they could *never* discover on their own.

These modern educators have been steeped in the false under-standing of the theory of evolution. Because they have believed this fable, they have taught it to unsuspecting minds, and conditioned them to reject God's revelation of Himself at the very beginning of Gen-esis. Then, having rejected the Creation account of this same Genesis, inspired by the God of the Bible, these have become blinded to the identity of the true God—leaving them utterly unable to find their way out of the maze of confusion in which they have *placed themselves.* Evolution has taught them self-reliance, and ultimately cut them off from the knowledge that would have freed them from ignorance in all the most important matters of life. There they sit, left without the answers to life's greatest questions. Because intellectual vanity—plain PRIDE!—would not let them seek a higher power greater than their own minds, these have literally *trapped* themselves in confusion, with no idea where to turn for light.

The Unknown Book

If the Bible is as it has been called—"The *Book* that nobody knows"—then the One who authored it is truly the *God* nobody knows! While this was *not* what He intended, this God has remained a mystery, concealed from a humanity willing to follow a "mystery god" that *cannot* be understood.

Some years ago, a world-famous evangelist declared of the trinity, "When I first began to study the Bible years ago, the doctrine of the Trinity was one of the most complex problems I had to encounter. I have never fully resolved it, for it contains an aspect of mystery. Though I do not totally understand it to this day, I accept it as a revelation of God...To explain and illustrate the Trinity is one of the most difficult assignments to a Christian."

How true! With at least 10 recognized versions or descriptions—definitions—of the trinity, no wonder it cannot be understood.

In the world, mystery books are often the bestsellers. The same with movies. Everyone seems to like the proverbial "Whodunit?" Any mys-tery in which a crime was committed involves several critical elements that must eventually come to light—perpetrator, victim, crime scene, weapon, witnesses, motive and other evidence. When this happens, there is tremendous satisfaction and excitement. No one would read a mystery book or watch a mystery movie if he knew in advance that the writer or producer was not going to solve the mystery in the end.

The mysteries of men's religions are different, however. They always *remain* mysteries. In the end, they are never explained—never SOLVED—and followers of these religions are told that they must accept this. This is never more true than when it comes to the concept of a triune god. Why would vast numbers be willing to accept, for a lifetime, a mystery *about God*, when they would not accept this of a mere *book* or *movie*?

Yet, they do—and this has cut them off from understanding the truth about prophecy!

If the trinity represents the true God, we could ask: *Why* is there such widespread confusion and division—such disagreement—about Him? Why is not the subject of God *clear—plain*—to the common man? Remember, "God is not the author of confusion" (I Cor. 14:33). He never wants His servants to be in confusion. Why then have so many been willing to accept without question this disagreement and confusion on the nature of God? So many of these same people readily admit, "God just doesn't seem real to me." Yet they seem willing to let Him *remain* this way.

Not only do the masses on Earth today stand in ignorance of life's most important knowledge, including both the identity of the true God and correct understanding of the many biblical truths that this God teaches, most do not appear to *care* about any of this. Billions do not even seem to *want* to know—to *want* to solve the mysteries of God and His Word, as well as of prophecy. Strangely, in this case, they seem willing to read a mystery book or see a mystery movie, knowing in advance the mystery will not be solved.

Counterfeit Church

The teaching of the triune, "three-in-one" god comes from the great false, universal religion. This "woman" has used the trinity to infiltrate and deceive all of traditional Christianity. Originally introduced with much controversy, she has been able to successfully use this doctrine to limit her "god" to a supposed three persons.

Part of her seduction has been then to necessarily introduce "another Jesus" (II Cor. 11:3-4), who becomes the centerpiece of "another gospel" (same passage), taught as a replacement of the *true* gospel of Jesus Christ you now know to be about the KINGDOM OF GOD. All of this deception in turn is derived from and has been impelled by "another spirit" (same passage)—that of the god of this world—active throughout this world's "churchianity" in the form of the counterfeit trinity god.

Most assume the word *trinity* is surely found in the Bible. But this is not true—the word itself is nowhere in Scripture. The term and its meaning—as are the words *triune, three-in-one,* etc.—are complete inventions of deceived men. With this cobbled-together god, the universal church has, in fact and effect, been responsible for literally *disfellowshipping*—EXCOMMUNICATING!—the *true* God from the world of supposed Christianity!

WHO and WHAT then is God? Can He be understood? You can pull back the veil concealing the true God from mankind and watch Him be introduced to you. My book *The Trinity – Is God Three-In-One?* explains the origin and history of the trinity doctrine—and covers the principal scriptures often cited to supposedly "prove" it. The book exposes the silly logic—actually the *illogic*—of trinitarian theology. It explains the true nature and role of the Holy Spirit. It also answers the question, "Who and what was Jesus Christ?"—and is the Christ of the Bible the same as the one worshipped in popular Christendom? And it brings irrefutable *proof*—the TRUTH—from God's Word about the *real* nature of the *true* God of the Bible and Creation. It opens the door to understanding the truth of God's awesome Plan for mankind.

You will be stunned at what you will learn. The subject of God is compelling reading and unlike what you might expect on a topic that *appears* to be esoteric or only able to be understood by scholars and intellectuals. In fact, you may also find yourself wondering how anyone could possibly believe a "trinity" teaching so easily seen to be wrong, and of pagan origin.

The Hardest Thing

The most difficult thing for any person to do is to admit being wrong. Unlearning false knowledge and learning true knowledge in its place is not easy, and it can sometimes be a painful, shattering experience. But you must put aside all bias. If you come with an open mind, once the evidence is laid out, you will be able to make a clear choice. This means that you must be willing to confess mistakes about beliefs and convictions, which in this case may have been held for a lifetime. This is true of *many* doctrines taught by the God of the Bible.

The book of Acts describes those of the Greek city of Berea as "… more noble than those in Thessalonica, in that they received the word with all *readiness of mind*, and *searched the scriptures daily*, whether those things *were so*" (17:11). These new converts were open-minded—but they wanted PROOF. In all points, they turned to God's Word as their sole source of truth on matters of teaching.

This is why Paul wrote the following instruction to *every* Bible student regarding *every* doctrine of the Bible: "PROVE all things; *hold fast that which is good*" (I Thes. 5:21). Nowhere did Paul ever state, "Trust me, and just believe." God wants people to stand on the firm rock of Scripture on all matters. Further, Paul told the Romans, "PROVE what is that good, and acceptable, and perfect, will of God" (12:1-2).

Surely all such proof of doctrine would include proving who and what is GOD!

Four Commands

Moses recorded God's words in Exodus 20: "You shall have no other gods before Me" (vs. 3).

Surely, if the Bible is the inspired INSTRUCTION BOOK of an all-wise and all-powerful Creator God, who was also the *only true God* in the universe, His *First* Commandment could not have been otherwise. Under no circumstances would that God want *other gods* worshipped in His place. In fact, in the very next commandment, the Author of these laws describes Himself as "a jealous God."

Notice this second, longer command: "You shall not make unto you *any* graven image, or *any* likeness of *anything* that is in heaven above, or that is in the earth beneath, or that is in the water under the earth: you shall not bow down yourself to them, nor serve them: for I the LORD your God am A JEALOUS GOD" (vs. 4-5). This commandment is a broad, sweeping, explicit prohibition intended to cover *every* form of false worship involving *every* other kind of supposed "god," and *representation* of such, that human beings with creative human reasoning could devise. Like any parent whose children chose to come home to a different house and to different parents after school, the Parent who made all human beings—*His* children—*would* certainly be jealous if they went off after idols and false gods.

How is it that the entire world is literally brim full and running over with all manner of idols? How did this happen? More specifically, how did all of Christendom become so shot full of statues, baby "Jesuses," "Christ" on crosses, stained-glass windows with icons, Mary on millions of lawns, as well as patron saints and so much more, when the Second Commandment so directly *prohibits all of this*? Yes, how?

The Third Commandment is tied directly to the first two. It describes the special reverence with which God wants His name to be used at all times. Here is that command: "You shall not take the NAME of the LORD your God in vain; for the LORD will not hold him guiltless that takes His NAME in vain" (vs. 7). The intent of this command is that when people even *reference* the true God, they should be very careful—reverential—in how they do it (Psa. 111:9). They should each time think about the purpose—the reason—for which they mention His most holy name.

The fourth and final commandment to examine for our purposes here is also tied to the identity of the God of the Bible. Let's first read this considerably longer command before examining it more closely: "Remember the SABBATH day, to keep it holy. Six days shall you labor, and do all your work: but the SEVENTH DAY is the SABBATH of the LORD your God: in it you shall not do any work, you, nor your son, nor your daughter, your manservant, nor your maidservant, nor your cattle, nor your stranger that is within your gates: for in six days the LORD made heaven and earth, the sea, and all that in them is, and rested the SEVENTH DAY: wherefore the LORD blessed the SABBATH day, and hallowed it" (Ex. 20:8-11).

This is an extraordinary command, given for a vital purpose. It also creates a special problem for the evolutionist—even one who professes to believe in God, including the God of the Bible.

Here is how: God expects all of His servants to observe the seventh-day Sabbath. But why? So that they would never forget *which God* it was who "in six days" created (actually when properly understood *recreated*) "heaven and earth," and who sealed this by resting on "the seventh day." In this way, the God who authored the Bible directly ties *all* of the Ten Commandments to the Creation account, which, in turn, leaves no room for His servants to drift into following and worshipping *other gods*. While one may not otherwise be correctly worshipping God, at least by observing the Sabbath every seven days, the adherent is forced to be at least somewhat cognizant of the sole God of Creation.

The God of the Bible leaves no room for doubt in the first four commandments. He expects to be worshipped for *who He is* and *as He is*, including on the day that He, not man, has selected for this worship. He allows no room for confusion and does not want human opinion added— He accepts no substitution of the false for the true.

God Most Plain

These commandments are not difficult to understand. The God of the Bible speaks plainly—He says what He means and means what He says! (Note that God repeats for emphasis in Deuteronomy 5 the same Ten Commandments, verbatim.)

We might pause at this point and ask: Do these four commands, when understood collectively, sound like the laws of a God who takes lightly those who worship any other but Himself? Do they seem like mere wishful instruction on the part of this God—things that He only *hopes* His followers will remember to do? Do they sound like the words of a God who is willing to let people worship idols, false gods or even any other wrong *form* of supposedly who and what He is, as long as the proponent proclaims such to represent the true God? Can you connect all the knowledge throughout this volume to the God who challenges those who read His Book through the additional proof of His existence—that of fulfilled prophecy?

It has been said that the first four commandments reveal how to love God and the last six how to love one's fellow man. Put another way, the first four commandments reveal and explain how to establish a *relationship* with the Creator God and the last six how to build *relationships* with all those He has created.

A relationship with the Bible's God begins with a recognition, understanding and acceptance of the first four commandments. All other approaches will preclude contact with Him. Obedience to them opens the door to all of God's truth, prophecy being but one-third.

The Record of Israel

The nation of Israel never lived up to her promises to God made in the book of Exodus. What follows next could all have been part of Chapter Twenty-three, "America and Britain."

God intended that ancient Israel be a MODEL NATION that all other nations would copy. This was always His purpose. He expected His people to set an example for surrounding nations of how happiness, peace, abundance, blessings and protection from enemies would result from obedience to Him. Sadly, despite an early willingness and determination to obey God, starting when the commandments were first given at Sinai, Israel repeatedly found herself *copying* the nations around her and worshipping their gods, thus achieving the very opposite of God's purpose! (Israel almost immediately fell into worship of the "golden calf" after the Ten Commandments were given—in fact before Moses could even get down the mountain to them.) This worship of false gods has had repercussions lasting thousands of years.

The long, broken history of Israel is that she turned from the true God and fell into the seductive trap of idolatry and the worship of foreign gods, doing this over and over again. Each time this pattern repeated itself, God sent her back into captivity and slavery. After a time, she would cry out in bondage, offering repentance, and God would raise up a judge and deliver her. But His people would quickly fall right back into the worship of false gods and idols, leading back to captivity, then to later repentance, again followed by God's merciful deliverance—I repeat, all of this happening time and again.

This centuries-long cycle, described in the book of Judges and elsewhere, was never broken until ancient Israel and Judah finally went into captivity, with ten tribes becoming lost to history as a result. Only the Jews have retained their national identity, and this is almost entirely attributed to their having continued observing God's Sabbath.

Jeremiah and Isaiah Summarize

Here is how God, through the prophet Jeremiah, describes and laments the continual actions of His people—His "nation": "Has a nation *changed their gods*, which are yet no gods? But My people have changed their glory for that which does not profit. Be astonished, O you heavens, at this, and be horribly afraid, be you very desolate, says the LORD. For My people have committed two evils; *they have forsaken Me* the fountain of living waters, and hewed them out cisterns, broken cisterns, that can hold no water" (2:11-13).

The last phrase in this passage accurately describes *all* the false gods devised by men and nations over the last 6,000 years. These man-made "gods"—made of wood, stone, metal and *false thinking—are* truly "broken cisterns, that can hold no water." Yet, nations (and religions) cleave to these fictional gods with a faithfulness Israel never showed to the true God.

Jeremiah continues, describing Israel's approach to gods she had copied and created: "Saying to a stock [of wood—a mere carved idol], You are my father; and to a stone, You have brought me forth: for they have turned their back unto Me, and not their face." Speaking for God, Jeremiah then says of these gods, "but in the time of their trouble they will say, Arise, and save us. But where are your gods that you have made you? Let them arise, if they can save you in the time of your trouble: for according to the number of your *cities* are your gods, O Judah" (vs. 27-28).

This is a classic description of what is seen throughout the world in all the modern nations that consider themselves to be based upon Judeo-Christian roots. Again, idols, carvings, religious statues and stained-glass windows abound on and in every church in every city, with no one thinking anything of it.

Continuing with Jeremiah's account. God had always made Himself available to Israel, easy to find if she sought Him: "O generation, see you the word of the LORD. Have I been a wilderness unto Israel? A land of darkness? Wherefore [Why] say My people, We are lords; we will come no more unto You? Can a maid forget her ornaments, or a bride her attire? Yet My people have *forgotten* Me days without number" (2:31-32). God has never been "a wilderness" to those who seek Him. The question for Israel was always *whether* she would seek and obey Him.

How many young women would permit themselves to dress up for a special occasion, but forget to put on jewelry—her "ornaments"? Surely few. More, what *bride* at her *wedding* could possibly forget to put on her wedding dress—her "attire"? Surely none.

Yet, incredibly, Israel had forgotten THEIR GOD! And she still does.

Of course, this was only able to happen because she disregarded God's basic instruction—and Commandments!—and got involved with the gods of surrounding nations.

The prophet Isaiah records this from God about the woeful—and ignorant—state of His people, then and today: "Hear, O heavens, and give ear, O earth: for the LORD has spoken, I have nourished and brought up children, and they have *rebelled against Me*. The ox knows his owner, and the ass his master's crib: but Israel does not know, My people do not consider. Ah sinful nation, a people laden with iniquity, a seed of evildoers, children that are corrupters: they have *forsaken the LORD*, they have provoked the Holy One of Israel unto anger, they are *gone away backward*" (1:2-4).

Isaiah is describing a nation that had fallen into every conceivable kind of corruption, evil and sin, all of which could be attributed to having forsaken the *true God*!

Worldwide Confusion—Gods and More Gods

What follows in the next two sections could as easily have been in Chapter Twenty-four, "Why World Punishment!"

The world is filled with gods of every sort. It is as though mankind has reserved the very best of its creative powers for the invention of every conceivable type of god and goddess—whether composed of physical matter or defined by ethereal concepts in the mind. The world's billions worship literally millions of gods.

The apostle Paul expresses it best as he introduces the true God of the Bible: "For though there be that are called gods, whether in heaven or in earth (as there be gods many, and lords many), but to us there is but one God, the Father, of whom are all things, and we in Him; and one Lord Jesus Christ, by whom are all things, and we by Him. Howbeit there is not in every man that knowledge..." (I Cor. 8:5-7). (How interesting that Paul references "the Father" and "Jesus Christ," differentiating them from all other "gods" and "lords," but, missing the perfect opportunity, fails to mention the Holy Spirit, the supposed third member of the trinity.)

The Romans worshipped and built temples to an endless array of gods and goddesses. But history reports that the ancient Greeks worshipped as many as 30,000 gods. Not to be outdone, the Hindus of today are said to have *5 million* gods, including their own trinity consisting of Shiva, Brahma and Vishnu! Of course, the Egyptians, with Osiris, Horus and Isis, also had their brand of the trinity, as did other civilizations. Then there is Tao, Confucius, Buddha, Allah and a host of other gods, goddesses and idols worshipped today, including totem poles, nature, snakes, other animals and fish in the sea, volcanoes and mountains, fire, wind, rocks, the sun, moon, planets, stars and even certain human beings who are considered divine. And there are all the different kinds of *metaphysical concepts* of gods that are adored and worshipped *in the mind*—some of which have been depicted by physical symbols and representations rendered by artists. This describes the trinity.

Yet, and most are probably not aware of this, vastly more people believe in the three-in-one god of modern Christianity than any other form of god.

"The Unknown God"

At this point, we must read a fascinating but longer passage that illustrates how superstitious mankind will worship almost anything, including many gods at the same time to avoid possible offense to whatever god they may have overlooked. This account paints an astounding picture. Note carefully the last sentence. The story from Acts involves Paul in Athens:

"Then Paul stood in the midst of Mars' hill, and said, You men of Athens, I perceive that in all things you are too superstitious. For as I passed by, and beheld your devotions [gods], I found an altar with this inscription, TO THE UNKNOWN GOD. Whom therefore you ignorantly worship, Him declare I unto you. God that made the world and all things therein, seeing that He is Lord of heaven and earth, dwells not in temples made with hands; neither is worshipped with men's hands, as though He needed any thing, seeing He gives to all life, and breath, and all things; and has made of one blood all nations of men for to dwell on all the face of the earth, and has determined the times before appointed, and the bounds of their habitation; that they should *seek* the Lord, if haply they might *feel after Him*, and *find Him*, though he be *not far* from every one of us: for in Him we live, and move, and have our being; as certain also of your own poets have said, For we are also his offspring. Forasmuch then as we are the offspring of God, we ought not to think that the Godhead is like unto gold, or silver, or stone, *graven by art and man's device*. And the times of this ignorance God winked at; *but now commands all men everywhere to repent*" (17:22-30)!

Focus on Paul's reference "TO THE UNKNOWN GOD" (emphasized in capital letters in the King James Bible). God had to reveal Himself to the superstitious Greeks through Paul. They had devised a "catch-all" inscription intended to include any other god missed in their "devotions." Paul took note of how they had covered themselves in their determination to leave no stone unturned in the worship of every deity. But they had not tried to "seek," "feel after" and "find" the true God.

King Solomon recorded that there is "no new thing under the sun" (Ecc. 1:9). Truly, the God of the Bible *has been unknown* since the Garden to countless millions who have been content to worship a triune god *selected for them* by men. Theologians and religionists sought the opinions of philosophers, scholars and supposed experts about God instead of the only important opinion—that of God, found in His Word. Over sixteen centuries ago, these religious leaders began reporting their "findings" to the masses who were only too willing to swallow what was presented to them without proof.

The God Who Is Alive

Ultimately, we ask, What is the difference between the God of the Bible and all other gods? How does God Himself differentiate who and what He is from all others?

Throughout Scripture, God describes Himself over and over as "the living God"—the "Eternal"—"I AM THAT I AM" (the name in Exodus 3:14 that Moses was instructed by God to use when representing Him to Pharaoh). In other words, the God of the Bible establishes who He is and separates Himself from all other gods by declaring Himself to be ALIVE!—LIVING!—meaning ALL other gods are non-existent or, in a sense, "dead." In effect, put another way, the true God states, "I AM," meaning other gods "ARE NOT"—period.

It is vital that the reader ask himself whether he or she is worshipping the ONE TRUE GOD—the God who is ALIVE—or something non-existent, inert and "dead," a god who *is not*.

This question towers over all others presented in this volume!

The Heart of the Problem

Let's return to both ancient Israel and today's theologians, educators and evolutionists. We saw the prophet Hosea summarized Israel's problem then and that of religionists and supposed "rationalists" of the modern age: "My people are destroyed for LACK OF KNOWLEDGE: because you have REJECTED KNOWLEDGE, I will also reject you, that you shall be no priest to Me: seeing you have FORGOTTEN the law of your God, I will also forget your children" (4:6).

This is *the* problem every reader must squarely face. Will you reject vital *knowledge* offered here? Or will you "seek" and "feel after" the true God?

The New Testament further records God's view of those who have consciously, willingly rejected THE TRUTH of Who and What He is, so plainly visible throughout His Creation: "For the *wrath of God* is revealed from heaven against all ungodliness and unrighteousness of men who *suppress* [Greek: *hold back*] the truth in unrighteousness, because that which is *known about God* [Get this!] is *evident within them*; for God made it *evident to them*. For since the creation of the world His *invisible attributes*, His *eternal power* and *divine nature*, have been *clearly seen*, being understood through what has been made, so that they are *without excuse*. For even though *they knew God*, they did not HONOR Him as God or give thanks, but they became futile in their speculations, and their foolish heart was darkened. Professing to be wise, they became *fools*" (Rom. 1:18-22, NASB).

This passage so fittingly describes the intellectually vain, but foolish, originators of the evolutionary theory, who found the existence of God, as presented by the Bible and theologians, to be so much superstition they could neither understand nor accept. It also describes modern prophecy "experts" who are so eager to bring nothing more than *human imagination* to their view of a Book written by an Author they do not know. It further describes those who would even "hold back"—deliberately *suppress*—the truth about Who and What is the God of the universe!

This God thunders that the facts—the evidence seen throughout His Creation, on Earth and in the heavens—leave them "without excuse." The ancients knowingly rejected CLEARLY EVIDENT KNOWLEDGE that unmistakably pointed to the existence of a God, that He was the God of Creation—and was *never* a trinity. The same is true today. Why? Because so many will not "honor"—they refuse to OBEY—Him, when His existence and identity can be known!

A little later in context, verse 28 of Romans 1 describes how God dealt with mankind collectively because it would not admit the Creation proved His existence. Notice: "And even as they did not like to retain God in their knowledge, God gave them over to a reprobate mind." The word "reprobate" in part means "void of judgment."

Humanity *has* been void of judgment on virtually all important matters. This is why the problems and troubles of all nations have only multiplied. But has all this led humanity to search out the true God from the false? Paul answers the question later in Romans, and adds much to the picture of basic human nature when it comes to whether human beings will seek God: "There is *none* that understands, there is *none that seeks after God*. They are *all* gone out of THE WAY" (3:11-12). These verses reveal that there have been no exceptions in who chooses to seek God and stay in "the way"—His Way. But again God does call some few (John 6:44, 65).

In his letter to Timothy, the inspired Paul described mankind collectively as "ever learning, and never able to come to the knowledge of THE TRUTH" (II Tim. 3:7). This has certainly included the knowledge—the truth—of God Himself. God must REVEAL Himself to individuals or they *cannot* know Him (also John 6:44, 65).

What is written here is SPIRITUAL KNOWLEDGE, unknown to all but a tiny few, and knowledge that you could not discover on your own. Ask yourself these questions: "Is the true God revealing Himself to me?"—and "Will I treasure this special, all-important knowledge?"

Basic Honesty Required

So many ministers and theologians have *professed* themselves to be Christians, meaning they have wanted to *appear* to be followers of the God of Creation. Again, in the end, these have not been willing to face the facts about their fictional triune "god." They have not been willing to come to understanding of the TRUE God—the LIVING GOD!

Then, in succession, millions of professing Christians, unwilling to explore the facts for themselves, follow such men. They remain duped by dishonest, seductive arguments designed by the god of this world to lead them to worship of himself. This is because, in their vanity (Rom. 1:22), they have foolishly rejected vital knowledge. The result has been that so many have unnecessarily become "darkened"—blinded—to the plain understanding of the true God.

For God to require strict obedience to His first four commandments without explaining who and what He is would be tantamount to cruel and inhuman punishment. If God had given this instruction without carefully *equipping* His worshippers to be *able* to distinguish Him from all other gods, He would have been grossly unfair.

Which God?

The world of Christendom is wrought with division, confusion and disagreement. Instead of getting better, instead of churches coming to, or at least toward, agreement and unity in truth, things only grow worse.

Yet none seem to ask WHY? *Why* all the fighting, competing and multiplying denominations, sects and cults associated with the world's brand of Christianity?

There is *cause* and *effect* in virtually all aspects of life, and this book has at least touched on this great principle. With all these BAD EFFECTS plaguing the world of traditional, orthodox Christianity, why does no one ask the CAUSE? (When one includes all the religions *outside* "Christianity," which encompass two-thirds of the world's population, the picture is even worse, the bad effects greater.)

Remember, the trinity is acknowledged to be a mystery that people are supposed to accept—a god that followers are told they cannot comprehend, and that they should not even *attempt* to comprehend. Yet, blind worship of this god has produced a "Christianity" that is a tangled mess of utter confusion—truly the blind following the blind.

Why does no one ask: Do we have the RIGHT GOD? Could it be we are not serving the *correct* God—the TRUE GOD? Why are people not approaching their ministers and demanding answers? Why do so few seem to care? Why are so few able to, or even interested in, "connecting the dots"?

We saw Jesus taught, "You shall *know them* by their fruits," and "By their fruits you shall *know them*" (Matt. 7:16, 20). Like the fruits of men's governments, the fruits of what is labeled "Christianity" are deplorable. If we are to believe Jesus' warning, the "god" behind all of this is exposed as one with AWFUL FRUITS. On the basis of fruits alone, none should want to serve the trinity!

Yet billions do!

Many of these will oppose this book, and especially this chapter, to the point of vehemently attacking it. Your friends will almost surely resist its contents. This is because truth, when it disagrees with central tenets of accepted Christianity, is invariably relegated to cult status.

Knowledge Brings Responsibility

It has been said that knowledge is of no purpose unless it is used. This book is no exception. You have been given much knowledge in what is the most comprehensive volume you will *ever* read on prophecy—never mind on the *truth* of it!

Almost certainly, most or all of what you have learned from God's Word through this book is entirely new to you—truly EXTRAORDINARY KNOWLEDGE, completely unknown to you before now. You have received knowledge that only a relative few have understood throughout history, and then only in part because so much of prophecy was sealed until our time. Your mind has been opened to understand precious information.

With such a privilege comes responsibility.

You no longer "lack knowledge" (Hos. 4:6), but are now left with the question of whether you will accept or, like Israel, REJECT this knowledge. Jesus declared, "For unto whomsoever much is *given*, of him shall be much REQUIRED" (Luke 12:48).

I repeat: With knowledge comes responsibility. It usually means that CHOICES must be made.

Colossal Decision

Here are examples of how God REQUIRED Israel to make a decision with the knowledge He had given them.

Just before Moses died, and before giving the reins of leadership over to Joshua, he spoke this on God's behalf—seen earlier in a different context—to all Israel: "I call heaven and earth to record this day against you, that I have set before you life and death, blessing and cursing: therefore CHOOSE life, that both you and your seed may live: that you may love the LORD your God, and that you may OBEY *His voice*..." (Deut. 30:19-20).

Similarly, a generation later, just before Joshua died, he spoke these words to all of Israel, assembled before him: "Now therefore fear the

LORD, and serve Him in *sincerity* and in *truth*: and *put away the gods* which your fathers served on the other side of the flood, and in Egypt; and serve you the LORD. And if it seem evil unto you to serve the LORD, CHOOSE you this day whom you will serve; whether the gods which your fathers served that were on the other side of the flood, or the gods of the Amorites, in whose land you dwell: but as for me and my house, *we will serve the LORD*" (Josh. 24:14-15).

Much later, the prophet Elijah presented a stark choice to Israel, shortly before putting to death in the people's presence 450 prophets of the false god Baal, which Israel could never leave alone: "And Elijah came unto all the people, and said, How long halt you between *two opinions*? If the LORD be God, follow Him: but if Baal, then follow him. And the people *answered him not a word*" (I Kings 18:21).

Also, in the New Testament, Jesus declared, "No servant can serve *two masters*: for either he will hate the one, and love the other; or else he will hold to the one, and despise the other" (Luke 16:13).

Decide!

The decision facing you is the same one Israel faced time and again, and that many thousands before you have faced since Jesus Christ built His Church.

God tells you that He does not accept indecisiveness—that you cannot serve two masters—that you cannot halt between two opinions as Israel did. And God does not permit you to "answer Him not a word." To make *no choice* is to make the WRONG CHOICE! One must decide whether he will implement knowledge—he must decide which master he will serve—and he must decide WHICH GOD HE WILL SERVE!

We saw in Acts reference to the "unknown god" on Mars' Hill: "And the times of this IGNORANCE God winked at; but now COMMANDS all men everywhere to repent" (17:30). Ignorance is the state of being without knowledge. Once knowledge is given—and is received—ignorance is no longer an excuse. God commands the one who has received knowledge to decide what he will do. This begins with the decision to serve "no other gods before" the true God!

What Counts!

When the greatest prophecies in the Bible come to bear full force your personal wealth will not count. Who you know will not count. Your level of education will not count. Your last name—who you are related to—descended from—will not count. Number of years "in a church" will not count. Reputation for character and service among peers will not count. Being beautiful, handsome, young, old, white, black or yellow will not count.

Here is what counts: taking *personal* responsibility for your life, knowing that if "Noah, Daniel and Job" were facing your decision, they "would only save *themselves* by *their* [personal] righteousness" (Ezek. 14:14).

This also counts: carefully "work[ing] out *your own* salvation with fear and trembling" (Phil. 2:12-13), because no one else can do this for you!

This towering question looms: What will you DO with almost 600 pages of such awesome knowledge? Will you disregard it—reject it—and merely move on with your life? Will you think about it at some more "convenient time"? Or will you *act* on—put to *use*—what you have learned and go on to serve the true God—and fulfill your INCREDIBLE HUMAN POTENTIAL?

The perfect, brilliant, all-powerful, all-wise, and now *unveiled* eternal God who made the heavens and the earth awaits your decision. Square your shoulders and address your future—that of ruling membership in God's coming WORLD GOVERNMENT!

At the same time, do not forget that the master counterfeiter, Satan the devil, now works feverishly toward a world government of *his* approval and making...

Europe and the Vatican

Events will *soon* unfold in Europe that will shake the world. An unmatched superpower will arise. Wielding enormous *political, economic* and *military* power, it will challenge the world's greatest nations for global supremacy.

Ten countries or ten groups of nations will combine to impose their will on a sleeping, unsuspecting world. These will work in tandem with a *religious* power. Where will this union *come from*? How will it operate? How will it work with the religious power? Is there European precedent? The answers will affect *you*. In fact, *everything* around you will change.

The world is a dangerous place. And never more so than now. The threats of global terrorism, rogue nations, economic collapse, and nuclear proliferation are ever present. There are many more than these. There also exists a lack of leadership in the world. The United Nations is at best ineffective. America is in steep decline. Russia is rebuilding. China is emerging. So is India. The Middle East continues boiling over. The European Union is striving to integrate. No clear leader is evident.

Seeing the void, Pope Benedict in June 2009 formally called for a "world political authority" with "real teeth"—with *power* to enforce its rules upon all nations.

All who think this way will get their wish.

Pope John Paul II called for Europe to return to its "roots"—to recapture what made it great. Benedict repeated this. Many others have called on Europe to take the mantle of global leadership.

Who Will Lead?

For 500 years, Europe has played the leading role in shaping the world. The continent has produced matchless advances in art, music, science, business, education, agriculture, technology and architecture.

Think. Monumental historical developments began in Europe before impacting other continents—the Renaissance, the French Revolution, the Industrial Revolution and two World Wars. The richest and most powerful nations in history have been European or those founded by their descendants. In short, Europe has been the axis around which the world has revolved.

However, at this time the continent is troubled, beset by problems of *every* kind: economic stagnation, terrorism, illegal immigration, low birthrates, widespread crime, clashes of culture and difficulties with integration, among others.

The result? Europeans have become disenchanted with their leaders. Increasingly, in European Union elections, citizens show their displeasure by voting out center-left incumbents, often now preferring right-wing extremists that they would *never* have previously considered.

Feeling their concerns have been ignored too long, many millions have become very unhappy.

Both the current and previous popes identified Europe's problems as "spiritual." For one and a half millennia, religion has played the biggest role in shaping the continent. It has been the only glue capable—albeit always temporary—of galvanizing diverse cultures and competing national agendas.

As problems multiply, Europeans are looking for direction—for someone with a "map and compass" to lead them out of their troubles, and to provide real solutions. At the same time, the Vatican is concerned about the state of Europe, and of the world. A strong leader is VITAL.

Will one arise? What role will *religion* play?

History's Pattern Begins—Justinian

To answer these questions, it is crucial to first understand the 1,500-year relationship between Europe and the Vatican.

Recall that in AD 324, the Roman Emperor Constantine, after seeing a vision, established "Christianity" as the official religion of the Roman Empire. Until that time, professing Christians lived under constant threat of persecution. We saw that countless numbers were put to death, often in horrible fashion.

In 325, Constantine convened the Council of Nicea to settle doctrinal disputes. Most accepted its decrees. Those who did not were forced to flee for their lives, especially after the Council of Laodicea in 363 decreed Sunday the official day of "Christian" worship—replacing God's Seventh-day Sabbath.

The church at Rome was now a *key player* in Europe's affairs. Over the next 300 years its influence grew. In AD 476 the unthinkable happened. The powerful Roman Empire fell to barbaric German tribes. This colossal event rocked both Europe and the Vatican.

After Rome fell, the papacy worked behind the scenes to eliminate the invaders. In 554, Justinian restored the empire as the "*Holy* Roman Empire." This was significant. "Holy" was added to signify God's kingdom on Earth. This began the Vatican's role as the most influential factor in selecting the emperor.

From this time forward, the relationship of church and state would be the primary driver of European affairs. The emperor ensured the state carried out the church's wishes. In return, the church's support gave him credibility with the people. The Vatican was now the dominant player in Europe.

The empire declined after Justinian's death in 565. Over the next 200 years, it would ebb and flow with successive rulers, never returning to its former glory. How would events turn?

Charlemagne

During the eighth century, a powerful Germanic Frankish kingdom emerged in France and Germany. In AD 732, the Franks rescued Europe from invasion by defeating the Muslim Saracens in a momentous victory at Tours, France. A grateful Vatican recognized the Franks as the "defenders of Christianity."

After the Frankish Emperor Pepin died in 768, his son Charles took the throne. He would become known as Charlemagne or Charles the Great—or to the Germans, Karl der Grosse. Charles immediately undertook several military campaigns—successfully uniting Western Europe. Responding to a desperate plea for help from Pope Adrian I, Charles defeated the Lombards, and in the process united Italy.

After several victorious campaigns—and a generous donation of land to the church!—Charles was hailed as "defender and guardian of the Christian faith." The alliance between the church and the Franks was strengthened.

Charles' defining moment came in 800. Pope Leo III crowned him "Imperator Romanorum"—Emperor of the Romans. The crowning cemented the marriage between church and state, and restored the Holy Roman Empire.

Most significantly, it elevated the church *above* the secular power and showed the crown to be the pope's to give and to take away. Pope Leo XIII would later declare, "There must, accordingly, exist between these two powers [church and state] a certain orderly connection, which may be compared to the union of the soul and body in man." So very telling.

Europe fell into disarray after Charlemagne's death, as foreigners continually invaded the continent. Time and again, the church and various governments were at loggerheads. Disunity reigned. Weakness in the church proved to be tied to weakness in Europe—and vice versa.

Both awaited a leader to point the way forward.

Otto the Great

In AD 936, Otto the Great, son of a Saxon duke, came to power, having been elected by participants who raised their right hand and shouted, "Sieg und Heil!"—victory and salvation—eerily similar to the Nazis of the twentieth century. Otto then went about expanding his kingdom.

The continent drifted into another period of decline. Pope John XII in 961 asked Otto to restore order and defend the church. Otto soon swept into Italy and defeated all enemies. The grateful pontiff crowned him "*Holy* Roman Emperor." Once again, church and state moved together. Otto's kingdom was the beginning of what would be called "The Holy Roman Empire of the German Nation." This was the *First Reich* (or empire).

The Holy Roman Empire and Germany were now forever linked, with German leaders assuming the mantle of kingship with the imperial crown—the symbol of European unity—on their heads. Germany became Europe's power center.

However, a struggle for power between church and state developed throughout the Middle Ages. Again Europe declined. In the 1100s and 1200s, Europeans launched unsuccessful Crusades to take Jerusalem from the Muslims.

In AD 1453, disaster struck. Constantinople, capital of the eastern Roman Empire (known as the Byzantine Empire), fell to the Muslim Turks.

A shaky Europe desperately looked for a strong leader to lead it back to its proper place.

Charles V

In the 1500s, an influential Germanic family, the Habsburgs, came to prominence, having amassed huge swaths of land across Europe. Pope Clement crowned Charles V Holy Roman Emperor in 1530, making him "defender of the faith."

The Habsburgs, through a series of marriages, were so connected with Spanish, Dutch and other European royalty that Charles' empire stretched from Europe to South America. Through Charles' efforts, the Habsburgs controlled a vast global empire—the first of modern times. He proudly declared, "In my realm the sun never sets."

The emperor's goal was all Europe under one religion. This idea endured, with the march toward a united Europe and religious ecumenism moving forward. With the ascent of the Habsburg Empire, many dreamed of a world-ruling "Christian" European empire. But with Charles' death, decline once more set in.

The 1600s and 1700s would see the church struggle against threats to its power. These included the rise of Protestantism, the decline of the Spanish and Portuguese empires, conflict between France and Germany, and the emergence of the Ottoman Turks and Protestant Britain as formidable powers.

So the church *again* awaited a leader to champion its cause.

Napoleon

A dashing superstar suddenly emerged in the late 1700s. Napoleon Bonaparte, a young, brash but brilliant military leader from the French island of Corsica, burst onto the scene. By age 26, he was already commanding the French army in Italy, and by 30 he had seized power in France.

Ambitious, this student of Roman history dreamed of a resurrected Roman Empire, with himself as emperor. He declared himself such in 1804 after snatching the imperial crown from the pope's hand to crown himself! This goal accomplished, he set about unifying Europe.

Napoleon saw many early successes—most notably, the defeat of Prussia in 1806. However, one disastrous campaign after another eventually led to his defeat and downfall, first in Russia and then by the

British at Waterloo. With his defeat in 1814, 1,260 years of the Holy Roman Empire came to an end.

The Vatican had lost *another* champion.

Garibaldi and Bismarck to Mussolini and Hitler

A period of rebuilding in Europe followed. By 1870, Giuseppe Garibaldi had reunited Italy. Otto von Bismarck reunited Germany the following year—calling it the *Second Reich*. Bismarck then forged an alliance with Italy, rekindling ties to the days of Charlemagne.

In the twentieth century, Benito Mussolini sought to revive the Holy Roman Empire. He reconciled a longstanding rift between church and state, and even entered into a Concordat—a secretly signed agreement—with the Vatican. But his reign was short-lived. It ended in abysmal failure with his public hanging in 1945.

Adolf Hitler's visions of glory for now a *Third* Reich also failed.

But the dream of European unity lived on. After World War II, the European Economic Community was established to improve trade between European nations. This later became the European Union, or EU. With the EU's 2009 ratification of the Lisbon Treaty, replacing the constitution that was struck down in 2005, a giant step was taken to establish the EU as an empowered and unified *government*, replacing a body of individual, sometimes squabbling, member-states. The treaty also created a stronger president. This union has expressly stated that the goal for Europe is to create a "world power."

But Europe has many problems to overcome. Strong leadership is required.

Church in Decline

Surveying the scene, the Vatican is troubled by what it sees. In his book "*Without Roots: The West, Relativism, Christianity, Islam,*" Pope Benedict—then Cardinal Joseph Ratzinger—described Europe as having denied its religious and moral foundation. He lamented a continent overtaken by secularism and materialism, a Europe that had slipped into immorality, cultural confusion and irreligiousness. He saw a Europe in danger of being overrun by outside forces.

This pope has also lamented the weakening of European churches, telling a gathering of Italian priests, "There is no longer any evidence of the need for God, let alone Christ...the so-called 'great' churches seem to be dying." Indeed, according to the Center for the Study of Global Christianity, every major religion in Western Europe is declining—*except Islam*!

The Roman leader is well aware of the dramatic and increasingly growing EU demographic shifts. Consider an article excerpt from a major British newspaper: "Britain and the rest of the European Union are ignoring a demographic time bomb: a recent rush into the EU by migrants, including millions of Muslims, will change the continent beyond recognition over the next two decades, and almost no policy-makers are talking about it.

"The numbers are startling. Only 3.2 per cent of Spain's population was foreign-born in 1998. In 2007 it was 13.4 per cent. Europe's Muslim population has more than doubled in the past 30 years and will have doubled again by 2015. In Brussels, the top seven baby boys' names recently were Mohamed, Adam, Rayan, Ayoub, Mehdi, Amine and Hamza" (*The Telegraph*).

What instability will such dramatic demographic changes cause in the years ahead? The article continues: "The study for the US Air Force...found that there were at least 15 million Muslims in the EU, and possibly as many as 23 million. They are not uniformly distributed, of course. According to the US's Migration Policy Institute, residents of Muslim faith will account for more than 20 per cent of the EU population by 2050 but already do so in a number of cities. Whites will be in a minority in Birmingham by 2026, says Christopher Caldwell, an American journalist, and even sooner in Leicester. Another forecast holds that Muslims could outnumber non-Muslims in France and perhaps in all of western Europe by mid-century. Austria was 90 per cent Catholic in the 20th century but Islam could be the majority religion among Austrians aged under 15 by 2050, says Mr Caldwell."

Think about the previous sentence! Will the Catholic church—with an extremely conservative pope in Rome—tolerate such a dramatic shift?

In 1900, almost every European professed Christianity. More recently, only three out of four even "identify" with Christianity. The number who consider themselves "non-religious" shot up from less than 1 percent to 15 percent. In 12 major European cities, 38 percent say they *never* or *rarely* attend church. France at 60 percent as a nation is the worst. But in areas of France, Sweden and the Netherlands, non-attendance is over 90 percent.

Such statistics threaten the church's very existence.

In Search of a Government

The Vatican sees a world of secular humanism—of no absolute morals—and devoid of strong leadership.

A recent article about Benedict's thinking opened this way. It ought to sober you like few things you have heard (emphasis mine): "In the past 30 years, the Vatican has moved strongly to reassert the authority of a traditional, even orthodox Roman Catholicism—to bring the notion of a 'one true church' to Europe *and then the larger world*" (*Reuters*).

The intent of this thinking is obvious—one church on Earth under the Vatican!

Next are the words of a church official from the same article regarding the connection this pope draws between the church at Rome—and its relationship to the world. The goal in the pontiff's thinking could not be clearer, and it adds to what we just read (emphasis also mine): "The world is evil and the church is pure...This is serious for Benedict. He doesn't want the church to be a joke. He's suspicious of chaos and avoidance of discipline and order, and of human efforts to adopt popular culture and create church out of the world, instead of a church that *transforms the world*. This deeply upsets him. He sees *all salvation taking place inside the Catholic Church*. He believes that."

But understand! While Benedict's efforts are undeniably *intensifying*, his beliefs are not new to him. The seeds of his vision were rooted in the thinking of decades ago. An account of this man in a late 1970s informal setting is telling. Here is a description from one who spent an evening with him during that period: "...the whole time he spoke about *restoring the old Europe*...where the *church takes precedence over the state*" (ibid.).

Now realize that Benedict was once the Archbishop of Munich (Germany). His daily place of work was Frauenkirche ("Cathedral of Our Dear Lady"). This is home to the tomb of the long-time German Holy Roman emperor, Louis IV (AD 1314-1347). The church-state connection was not missed by the Archbishop during the years he spent there—from 1977 until coming to high office in the Vatican in 1981.

In a dramatic move, Benedict released a formal statement permitting practicing Anglicans to join the Catholic Church. On the 10th anniversary of a mutual declaration between the World Lutheran Federation and the Catholic Church, the pope stated, "I sincerely hope that this important anniversary will help bring forward the path towards the *full visible unity of all the disciples of Christ."* This is a *stunning* development in Rome's call for—get this!—every professing Christian to align with Catholicism! In addition, Polish Cardinal Stanislaw Dziwisz referred to the pope in 2009 as one who "speaks like a *prophet*," when referring to the pope's call for European unity. Can the point be missed?

If any still doubt the seriousness of the Vatican, consider the following longer statement in June 2009 from Benedict. It removes all questions about *exactly* where he wishes to take Europe. His desired destination should be no surprise. Stunning on its face, and sweeping in scope, the words are from his encyclical titled "Charity in Truth" (emphasis mine):

"In the face of the unrelenting growth of global interdependence, there is a strongly felt need...for a reform of the United Nations Organization, and likewise of economic institutions and international finance, so that the concept of the *family of nations* can acquire *real teeth*...To manage the global economy; to revive economies hit by the crisis; to avoid any deterioration of the present crisis and the greater imbalances that would result; to bring about integral and timely disarmament, food security and peace; to guarantee the protection of the environment and to regulate migration: for all this, there is urgent need of a *true world political authority*, as...John XXIII indicated some years ago.

"Such an authority would need to be regulated *by law*, to observe consistently the principles of *subsidiarity* and *solidarity*, to seek to establish the *common good* [but ask: by whose definition?], and to make a commitment to securing authentic integral human development inspired by the values of charity *in truth* [also ask: would he have in mind other than Catholic doctrine for *truth*?]. Furthermore, such an authority would need to be *universally recognized* [Catholic means *universal*] and to be vested with the effective power to ensure security for all, regard for justice, and respect for *rights* [again ask: defined by whom?].

"Obviously it would have to have the authority to *ensure compliance* with its decisions from *all parties*, and also with the coordinated measures adopted in various international forums...They also require the construction of a *social order* that at last *conforms* to the *moral order* [I repeat: *defined by whom*?], to the interconnection between moral and social spheres..."

By *every definition*, this vision describes a *world government*—based in Europe—endorsed by, and in partnership with, the Vatican.

Therefore, to achieve such an alliance, Rome *must* find a powerful civil leader.

History is the guide.

Widespread Turmoil

Europe presently faces several crises. The continent is enduring its worst recession since World War II. Bank losses are projected to even exceed U.S. banks. The Irish, Spanish, Greek and Portuguese economies have been in full-blown crisis, over huge budget deficits.

Also, a staggering 20 million EU citizens are now unemployed. One in five are under age 25.

Persistently high unemployment rates are translating into widespread crime, anger, depression and feelings of hopelessness. Many are turning to extremism. The continent's social fabric is threatened.

Immigration is another contentious issue. Large enclaves of immigrants now live in Europe's cities. Due to starkly different cultures and religions, these have not been assimilated into traditional European cultures—and have *no intention* of doing so. Chancellor Angela Merkel openly declared that multiculturalism has "utterly failed" in Germany. All of this is spawning an anti-immigration backlash, worse than America. Many citizens fear losing their jobs and culture. This has led to frequent acts of violence in its capitals.

Low birthrates are another serious concern. The lack of young workers brings a host of problems: imploding tax bases, collapsing pension plans, severe industry and military recruiting shortfalls, and inadequate care for the elderly. Political and business leaders are struggling with how to address these problems. Demonstrations and riots fill the streets.

Terrorism is another concern. This is fueled by wide-open borders and large immigrant populations. Age-old contentions with Islam are flaring up, especially as the big, fast-growing Muslim population continues becoming more visibly prominent—and aggressive.

Energy is also a concern. Europe relies primarily on the Middle East and Russia for its energy needs. The Middle East is a powder keg of instability. Russia is an unpredictable partner—and historic enemy. Europe's energy supplies are by no means guaranteed. A possible energy cutoff looms large—a nightmare for Europe's leaders.

Moves toward unification have continually met roadblocks, with constant bickering between member states. Integration remains a thorny issue. A major challenge has been in integrating the newer member countries. Then there is the issue of integrating *economies*, made worse with the mix of fast- and slow-growing ones. Also the constitution. Even though it has been ratified, it has detractors.

These are just a *few* of the serious difficulties facing the continent. Both Europe and the Vatican now privately seek a strong leader to address great challenges.

A Leader Will Come!

The Bible is most clear that such a leader *will* arise. This man will galvanize and unite Europe. Endorsed by, and working with, a powerful religious leader, he will usher in a time of unmatched prosperity. Revelation 18, with parts of chapter 17, describe satisfied "merchants" trafficking in "merchandise" of every kind as perhaps never before in history. This leader will stun the world by reviving the Holy Roman Empire *one final time*. He *will* institute a "world political authority"—and it will have *very* "real teeth." The Bible in fact more correctly describes them as "great iron teeth." A pontiff willing to speak so bluntly—so plainly and with such detail—of his ultimate vision and purpose must recognize that not all ears will miss its *true* meaning.

Such plainness of speech is here acknowledged.

A revitalized Europe *will* lead the world politically, industrially, financially and militarily—and in religion. It will one more time become the world's focus—the axis around which all nations revolve.

Is this speculation? No, it is tomorrow's news written in advance—recorded in Bible prophecy.

Church and State—A Final Time

We saw that the apostle John recorded in Revelation that "I stood upon the sand of the sea, and saw a beast rise up out of the sea, having seven heads and ten horns, and upon his horns ten crowns, and upon his heads the name of blasphemy" (13:1).

Remember, "Beast" is the Bible term for a CIVIL GOVERNMENT or KINGDOM—but also for its leader. This Beast symbolically represents the Roman Empire from its inception, including six "Holy" revivals already past, to its final resurrection *in our time!*

Remember also that John spoke of a second *two-horned* beast: "And I beheld *another* beast coming up out of the earth; and he had *two horns* like a lamb, and he *spoke as a dragon.* And he exercises all the power of the *first* beast before him [the one just cited], and causes the earth and them which dwell therein to *worship* the first beast...And he does great wonders, so that he makes fire come down from heaven on the earth in the sight of men, and *deceives* them that dwell on the earth by the means of those *miracles* which he had power to do in the sight of the beast [immediately—and completely—solving the problem of declining church attendance]; saying to them that dwell on the earth, that they should make an *image* to the beast [the Imperial model of Roman government]...And he had power to give *life* [energy—vitality] unto the image of the beast, that the image of the beast should both speak [edicts will be issued], and cause that as many as would *not* worship the image of the beast *should be killed*" (13:11-15).

This other beast is also a government or kingdom, and it gives power to the first Beast—the Roman Empire. It appears as a lamb, but speaks as a dragon. In other words, it is not what it seems—it is sinister and evil.

Never lose sight of this!

Most recognize that Jesus Christ is depicted in Scripture as a lamb. But recall that Satan is always depicted as a dragon. Notice again: "And the great dragon was cast out, that old serpent, called the Devil, and Satan..." (12:9).

So this second beast *appears* to be of God, but is really of the devil. Its two horns indicate it is not only a government, but also a church. Now ask: what religious organization is both a church and a government? The chilling answer is MOST PLAIN—*if* you have eyes to see.

Notice this second beast gives power to the first—the Roman Empire. This has been happening since Justinian's crowning in AD 554. Since that time, the two entities have *when necessary* worked closely together. Roman emperors have acknowledged the supreme authority of religion throughout the empire. They understand the benefits.

This will happen again!

Growing Influence

The spreading influence of religion in the EU can be seen in Germany, where a recent high court ruling mandated that businesses close on Sunday—the first day of the week—as "a day of rest." (Liberal and conservative newspapers across Germany almost universally heralded the move.) Now recall what was decreed at the Council of Laodicea in AD 363 when Sunday-keeping was enforced *by law*. Forgotten and lost is that God commanded the *seventh* day of the week—His Sabbath—be a day of rest—*not* the first!

Watch the growing power of religion in Europe!

The *second* beast of Revelation 13 will possess such seductive power and magnetism that it will be able to induce the world to worship the *first* Beast—the Roman Empire—through extraordinary miracles. These will mesmerize the *entire* world, deceiving *vast* millions into worship of both the system and the man leading it.

History *will* repeat itself! Soon, two men, one a civil leader, the other a religious leader, will *revive* the Holy Roman Empire *in Europe*. This power *will* return the age-old union of church and state. Unmatched, it *will* tower over every nation like a colossus, dwarfing all rivals—and it *will* enforce a mark (13:16) involving direct disobedience to God. Those who fall in step with its edicts—who take its mark—will be temporarily spared, but soon after will be punished terribly by God. Most who refuse the mark will be horribly persecuted, tortured and put to death.

A few faithful, of God's people, *escape!*

Remember. British Prime Minister Neville Chamberlain, returning from his infamous meeting with Adolf Hitler in 1939, declared, "Peace in our time." Instead, World War II quickly followed. The *coming* superpower will proclaim the same thing—but will bring horrific destruction. Its attempt to institute a "world political authority" will at first succeed—but ultimately fail, meeting a bitter end described in Revelation 18.

The days of man's misrule upon the earth—and of false religions deceitfully masquerading as being of God—will finally be over. Peace, justice, happiness and abundance will come at last to a world in desperate need of them.

But these things will not come *yet*.

Time Is Almost Up!

The final Beast of Revelation, ridden by the great whore of chapter 17, will soon explode onto the world scene. No one will be expecting this truly "thief in the night" moment. The sudden joint appearance of these in union will signal without warning that *everything* will now be different. The Beast and whore's arrival and surrounding events *will* come "as a SNARE...on ALL them that dwell on the face of the WHOLE EARTH" (Luke 21:35). The message? This event will pierce world "tranquility" without notice.

The whore is already suggesting that her wayward, protesting "harlot daughter" churches stop squabbling and disagreeing. Seeking submission, she will soon *command* them to "return home NOW!" False, but *real*, miracles will reinforce her command. They *will obey!*

Only a few years remain before the False Prophet gives the chilling instruction to "saddle up" the Beast for its final ride into awesome, frightening prophecies that will leave all nations of Earth in shocked amazement—and the modern nations of Israel in captivity, their lands destroyed.

This religious-political-economic-military system will take a defeated Israel into the "bitterness," "rigor" and "affliction" of hard labor under the Beast's brutal slave masters, exactly as came upon ancient Israel under Pharaoh (Ex. 1:13-14; 2:23; 3:7).

The Beast's ride will also take the great whore directly into the lives of all who thought there was more time—who did not take seriously the truth of prophecy. These will be desperately sorry—and even *more* desperately wishing they could have another chance to make the right decision.

But it will be *too late!*—much TOO LATE!

As in centuries past, the Revelation 17 "woman" today sits poised like an attentive midwife on a stool before a pregnant mother Europe ready for delivery, waiting to "catch" a much needed civil ruler.

Evidence suggests Europe's "water" is about to "break."

So Few...

No one else is explaining the TRUTH about what lies ahead—and no one else will! This long book pulled no punches. In fact, how could it have been stronger? It has asked and answered many questions, but the greatest is the final one.

How many will *apply* its contents?

It is now time to repeat an observation from Chapter One: It has been my almost 45-year experience in the truth that most people will not listen to God's words. They cannot make themselves take seriously even His *plainest* commands, instructions and warnings.

There are exceptions...

Other Books by David C. Pack

■ The Awesome Potential of Man

■ Tomorrow's Wonderful World – An Inside View!

■ Saturday or Sunday – Which Is the Sabbath?

■ America and Britain in Prophecy

■ The True Jesus Christ – Unknown to Christianity

■ Sex – Its Unknown Dimension

110117 - GP

CPSIA information can be obtained at www.ICGtesting.com
Printed in the USA
LVOW042018270912

300540LV00001B/134/P